Oracle 11g R1/R2 Real Application Clusters Essentials

Design, implement, and support complex Oracle 11g RAC environments for real-world deployments

Ben Prusinski

Syed Jaffer Hussain

BIRMINGHAM - MUMBAI

Oracle 11g R1/R2 Real Application Clusters Essentials

First published: May 2011

Production Reference: 1170511

Published by Packt Publishing Ltd.
32 Lincoln Road
Olton
Birmingham, B27 6PA, UK.

ISBN 978-1-849682-66-4

www.packtpub.com

Cover Image by Artie Ng (artherng@yahoo.com.au)

Credits

Authors
Ben Prusinski
Syed Jaffer Hussain

Reviewers
Ann L. R. McKinnell
Ronald Rood

Acquisition Editor
Kerry George

Development Editor
Meeta Rajani

Technical Editors
Conrad Sardinha
Azharuddin Sheikh

Project Coordinator
Zainab Bagasrawala

Proofreaders
Sandra Hopper
Bernadette Watkins
Chris Smith

Indexer
Rekha Nair

Graphics
Geetanjali Sawant
Nilesh Mohite

Production Coordinator
Arvindkumar Gupta

Cover Work
Arvindkumar Gupta

About the Authors

Ben Prusinski is an Oracle Certified Professional (OCP) and database architect with more than 14 years of experience with Oracle data warehouse and Oracle E-Business applications. As a corporate database consultant, Ben has provided services to dozens of Fortune 500 clients. He is an internationally recognized expert in Oracle high availability, performance tuning, database security, and ERP implementations. As a top Oracle expert, Ben received the prestigious Oracle ACE award in 2009 in recognition of his contributions to the Oracle community. As an Oracle RAC Certified Expert (OCE), Ben is also a popular speaker at major conferences such as Oracle OpenWorld, CLOUG in Latin America, IOUG, and Oracle Collaborate OAUG (Oracle Applications User Group). Ben is also a polyglot, being fluent in several languages (Spanish, French, Korean, and English) and enjoys traveling to exotic places. In his free time, he enjoys racing in autocross events, golf, martial arts, reading, and cooking.

In addition to Oracle consulting for clients, Ben regularly updates his Oracle blog at `http://oracle-magician.blogspot.com` with the latest database technology tips and information to share with the Oracle community. He frequently contributes to answering questions from Oracle users on the Oracle OTN forums. He can be contacted via e-mail at `ben@ben-oracle.com`.

I would like to extend my thanks and appreciation, first of all to my fellow co-author Mr. Syed Jaffer Hussain who was great to work with on this book. I would also like to thank everyone at Packt who made tremendous efforts for their patience and help in the editorial process. Last but not least, my heartfelt appreciation goes out to our fantastic technical review team of Oracle experts — Fairlie Rogo, Ronald Rood, and Ann L.R. Mckinnell — who provided tons of great feedback to ensure technical accuracy and quality. I also would like to dedicate this book to all fellow Oracle DBAs and consultants who work in the trenches to solve real world Oracle issues.

I also would like to thank the many Oracle professionals who have helped me as an Oracle professional over the years to make such a book like this possible, including Julian Dyke (Oracle RAC master extraordinaire), Alex Gorbachev, Doug Hahn, Tanel Poder, Arup Nanda, Robert Freeman, Tim Hall, and all of my current and past clients who allowed me to help them with their Oracle database challenges.

Syed Jaffer Hussain is the Database Support Manager at AlInma Bank (Saudi Arabia) who has over 18 years of hands-on Information Technology (IT) experience, which also includes over 10 years as a Production Oracle DBA. Apparently he is the first person in the Middle East to be awarded the prestigious Oracle ACE award. He holds several industry recognized Oracle certifications, including Oracle 10g Certified Master (OCM), OCP DBA (v8i, 9i, 10g, and 11g), and Oracle 10g RAC Certified Expert. With broad knowledge in Oracle technologies such as RAC, DataGuard, RMAN, and Performance Tuning, he has completed several successful RAC implementations, Clusterware upgrades, and has set up disaster recovery solutions for many business-critical databases. Jaffer is a noted speaker at `BrainSurface.com`, and occasionally presents Oracle University five-day courses and one-day celebrity seminars on behalf of Oracle EMEA. He has also worked for a couple of multinational banks in Saudi Arabia.

Jaffer frequently contributes at Oracle OTN forums and many other Oracle-related forums. He regularly updates his Oracle technology-related blog, (`http://jaffardba.blogspot.com`) and he is reachable at `sjaffarhussain@gmail.com`.

First and foremost, I owe a very big thank you to my wife Ayesha and my three sons (Ashfaq, Arfan, and Aahil) for sacrificing their invaluable time and allowing me to concentrate on the book. I am also thankful to Alinma Bank management; in particular Ahmed Darwish and my immediate boss Mr. Majed Saleh AlShuaibi for their constant encouragement and continuous support. My special thanks goes to my younger brother Sabdar and my friend Khusro Mohammed Khan (who are also Oracle DBAs) for preparing required platforms, testing codes and doing initial review of the chapters. I also want to thank all my colleagues, Mohammed Farooqui, Zaheer, Khaja Mainuddin, Shaukat Ali, Naresh Kumar Markapuram, Hussain AlKalifah, Faisal Bakhashwain, Naser Ali AlEssa, Mohammed Alsalahi, Wayne Philips, Chand Basha, Rizwan Siddiqi, Sadak, Anees, Shakir, Angelo G Train, Mohammed Khidir, Asad Khan, Ibrahim Ali, Rajesh Ankuru, Sandeep, Mohammad AlHiary, Ahmed Khanj, Ahmed Bakheet, Mohammed Azar, and other friends for their encouragement and motivation.

I thank all the staff at Packt Publishing who were involved with this book and special mention to James Lumsden, Kerry George, Meeta Rajani, Zainab Bagasrawala, and Azharuddin Sheikh for being patient with me during the course of this book.

Last but not the least, I also thank other RAC Book authors (not in any particular order), Murali Vallath, K. Gopalakrishnan, Nitin Vengulkar, Julian Dyke, Sandesh Rao, Arup Nanda, Bert Scalzo, Riyaj Shamsudeen, Tariq Farooq, and other Oracle experts worldwide for being my inspiration.

About the Reviewers

Ann McKinnell has been an OCP since Oracle 7.3.4, with over eight years experience as a senior technical member of Oracle Global Support, specializing in Database Server technologies. Ann has trained Oracle Support and Consulting personnel from many countries in Database Internals and Problem Solving techniques. She has served as a technical reviewer for Oracle University course material, numerous My Oracle Support (previously Metalink) notes and whitepapers, and various Oracle Database Administration user manuals. Ann is also a co-author of Packt Publishing's *Oracle 11g Streams Implementer's Guide*. With over 16 years in the IT industry, Ann continues to specialize in practical implementation strategies and the development of distributed Oracle database systems, and database architecture, along with software and database design, integration, and engineering.

Ronald Rood is an innovative Oracle DBA with over 20 years of IT experience. He has built and managed cluster databases on about each and every platform that Oracle ever supported, from the famous OPS databases in version 7 to the latest RAC releases, currently being 11g. Ronald is constantly looking for ways to get the most out of the database to make the investment for the customers even more valuable. He has a great knowledge of how to handle the power of the rich Unix environment, which makes him a first class troubleshooter and solution architect. Next to his many spoken languages such as Dutch, English, German, and French, he also writes fluently in many scripting languages.

Currently Ronald is a principal consultant working for Ciber in The Netherlands where he cooperates in many complex projects for large companies where downtime is not an option. Ciber (CBR) is one of the few Oracle Partners on the Diamond level.

Ronald often replies on the Oracle forums, writes his own blog (`http://ronr.blogspot.com`) called 'from errors we learn', and writes for various Oracle-related magazines. He has also authored a book, *Mastering Oracle Scheduler in Oracle 11g Databases,* where he fills the gap between the Oracle Documentation and the customers' questions.

Ronald has lots of certifications, among them:

- Oracle Certified Master
- Oracle Certified Professional
- Oracle Database 11g Tuning Specialist
- Oracle Database 11g Data Warehouse Certified Implementation Specialist

Ronald fills his time with Oracle, his family, sky-diving, radio-controlled model airplane flying, running a scouting group, and having a lot of fun.

His quote is: "a problem is merely a challenge that might take a little time to solve".

www.PacktPub.com

Support files, eBooks, discount offers and more

You might want to visit www.PacktPub.com for support files and downloads related to your book.

Did you know that Packt offers eBook versions of every book published, with PDF and ePub files available? You can upgrade to the eBook version at www.PacktPub.com and as a print book customer, you are entitled to a discount on the eBook copy. Get in touch with us at service@packtpub.com for more details.

At www.PacktPub.com, you can also read a collection of free technical articles, sign up for a range of free newsletters and receive exclusive discounts and offers on Packt books and eBooks.

http://PacktLib.PacktPub.com

Do you need instant solutions to your IT questions? PacktLib is Packt's online digital book library. Here, you can access, read and search across Packt's entire library of books.

Why Subscribe?

- Fully searchable across every book published by Packt
- Copy & paste, print and bookmark content
- On demand and accessible via web browser

Free Access for Packt account holders

If you have an account with Packt at www.PacktPub.com, you can use this to access PacktLib today and view nine entirely free books. Simply use your login credentials for immediate access.

Instant Updates on New Packt Books

Get notified! Find out when new books are published by following *@PacktEnterprise* on Twitter, or the *Packt Enterprise* Facebook page.

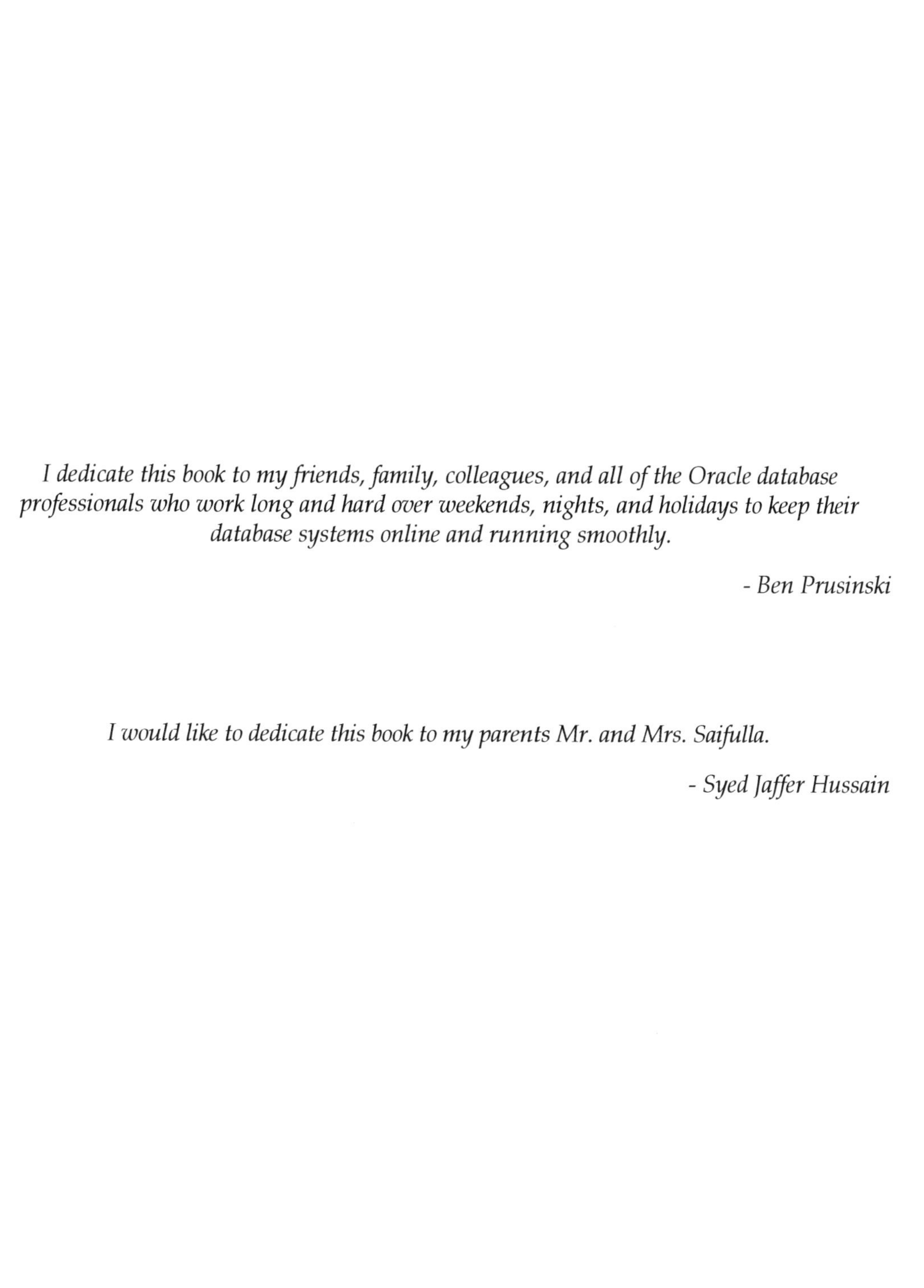

I dedicate this book to my friends, family, colleagues, and all of the Oracle database professionals who work long and hard over weekends, nights, and holidays to keep their database systems online and running smoothly.

- Ben Prusinski

I would like to dedicate this book to my parents Mr. and Mrs. Saifulla.

- Syed Jaffer Hussain

Table of Contents

Preface 1

Chapter 1: High Availability 7

High availability concepts 7
Planned versus unplanned downtime 8
Service Level Agreements for high availability 8
High availability interpretations 9
Recovery time and high availability 10
System design for high availability 11
Business Continuity and high availability 11
Disaster Recovery 12
Business Continuity and Disaster Recovery guidelines 13
Fault-tolerant systems and high availability 14
Requirements for implementing fault tolerance 15
Fault tolerance and replication 16
High availability solutions for Oracle 17
Oracle Data Guard 17
Oracle Streams 17
Oracle Application Server Clustering 18
High availability: Oracle 11g R1 Real Application Clusters (RAC) 19
High availability: Oracle 11g R2 Real Application Clusters (RAC) 19
Summary 20

Chapter 2: Oracle 11g RAC Architecture 21

Oracle 11g RAC architecture 22
Certification matrix for Oracle 11g RAC architecture 23
Hardware architecture for Oracle 11g RAC 25
Server configurations for Oracle 11g RAC 26
CPU processors 26
Choosing between 32-bit and 64-bit CPU architectures 27
Dual core and multicore processors 29

Network architecture for Oracle 11g RAC 30
The private network and the Oracle 11g RAC interconnect 30
Choices for private interconnect and 11g RAC 31
Redundancy for Ethernet interconnects with 11g RAC 33
Network bonding (NIC teaming) 39
Storage architecture for Oracle 11g RAC 39
RAID configurations for Oracle 11g RAC 40
RAID 0 (striping) 42
RAID 1 (mirroring) 42
RAID 5 (striped with parity) 42
RAID 10 (striped mirrors) 43
Third-party RAID implementations 44
IBM AIX LPAR disk volume management for RAID 44
Linux volume management for RAID configuration 45
Storage protocols for RAC 45
SCSI 46
Fibre Channel 47
Point-to-Point (FC-P2P) 47
Fibre Channel Arbitrated Loop (FC-AL) 47
Fibre Channel Switched Fabric (FC-SW) 48
Which Fibre Channel topology is best? 48
iSCSI 50
Which storage protocol is best for RAC? 50
Asynchronous I/O versus Direct I/O for Oracle 11g RAC 51
Oracle 11g RAC components 53
Voting Disk 53
Oracle Cluster Registry 53
Oracle 11g R1 RAC background processes 54
ACMS Atomic Controlfile to Memory Servicc 54
GTX0-j Global Transaction Process 54
LMON Global Enqueue Service Monitor 54
LMD Global Enqueue Service Daemon 54
LMS Global Cache Service Process 54
LCK0 Instance Enqueue Process 55
RMSn Oracle RAC Management Processes 55
RSMN Remote Slave Monitor 55
Oracle 11g R2 RAC background processes 56
Grid Plug and Play 56
Grid Interprocess Communication 56
Multicast Domain Name Service 56
Oracle Grid Naming Service 56
How RAC differs from Oracle 11g single-instance implementations 57
New ASM features and RAC 58
New SYSASM privilege for Oracle 11g R1 ASM 58
Oracle 11g R2 ASM features 59

OCR and Voting Disk stored in ASM 59
Oracle Automatic Storage Management Cluster Filesystem (Oracle ACFS) 59
New Oracle 11g ASM Disk Group compatibility features 60
Summary 61
Chapter 3: Clusterware Installation 63
Preparing for a cluster installation 63
Server (node) requirements 64
Network requirements 64
Kernel parameters 65
Operating system packages 66
OS groups and users 68
OS user settings 68
Configuring Secure Shell (SSH) 69
Verifying prerequisites with the CLUVFY utility 71
Oracle 11g R1 Clusterware installation 72
Initiating Oracle Universal Installer for Oracle 11g R1 Clusterware 73
What happens when orainstRoot.sh and root.sh is run? 82
Oracle 11g R1 Clusterware post-installation checks 86
Installing Oracle 11g R1 RAC software 88
Initiating Oracle Universal Installer for Oracle 11g R1 RAC software 88
Post-installation tasks 90
Oracle 11g R2 Clusterware installation 91
Initiating Oracle Universal Installer for 11g R2 Clusterware 92
What happens when the root.sh is run? 99
Oracle 11g R2 Clusterware post-installation checks 100
Installing Oracle 11g R2 RAC software 102
Initiating Oracle Universal Installer for Oracle 11g R2 RAC software 103
Post-installation tasks 108
Oracle 11g R2 Clusterware new features highlights 109
Removing/Reconfiguring a Grid Infrastructure configuration 110
Removing a successful Grid Infrastructure configuration 110
Reconfiguring a failed Grid Infrastructure configuration 111
Summary 112
Chapter 4: Automatic Storage Management 113
Overview of Automatic Storage Management (ASM) 114
Filesystem versus ASM storage architecture 115
ASM disk 116
ASM disk group 117
ASM instance configuration and management 118
ASM initialization parameters 119
Creating an ASM instance 120
Initializing DBCA 120
ASM background processes 122

ASM dynamic views 122
V$ASM_DISK 123
V$ASM_DISKGROUP 124
V$ASM_OPERATION 124
V$ASM_DISK_STAT 124
V$ASM_DISKGROUP_STAT 124
V$ASM_CLIENT 125
ASM instance startup/shutdown 125
ASM disk group administration 126
Creating a disk group 127
Altering a disk group 128
Dropping a disk group 129
Overview of ASMCMD 130
ASMCMD in action 131
ASM 11g R1 new features 133
ASM fast mirror resync 133
ASM preferred mirror read 134
ASM fast rebalance 135
ASM disk group compatibility attributes 135
ASM performance enhancements 136
New SYSASM role 136
ASM 11g R2 new features 137
Automatic Storage Management Configuration Assistant (ASMCA) 137
Initiating ASMCA 137
Configuring a new ASM instance 138
Managing an ASM instance 140
Managing an ASM disk group 142
Creating an ASM disk group 143
Creating an ASM disk group in silent mode 144
Automatic Storage Management Dynamic Volume Manager (ADVM) 145
ADVM volume trivia 145
Creating ASM volumes 146
Automatic Storage Management Cluster File System 152
(ACFS) 152
Using ACFS as Oracle database home 153
Oracle ACFS drivers 153
Prerequisites for creating ACFS 154
ACFS creation methods 154
ACFS mount registry 161
Managing ACFS 161
ASM new background processes to support ACFS 163
Querying V$ASM views to obtain information about ACFS 164
ACFS snapshots 164
Creating a snapshot 166
Removing a snapshot 168

ASM Intelligent Data Placement (IDP) 169
Managing IDP settings 169
Finding IDP setting information 169
ASMCMD enhancements 170
ASM backup strategies **171**
md_backup and md_restore commands 171
Summary **173**
Chapter 5: Managing and Troubleshooting Oracle 11g Clusterware **175**
Oracle 11g RAC Clusterware administration **175**
About Oracle Clusterware 176
Oracle 11g Clusterware concepts 176
Oracle Cluster Registry 177
Voting disk 177
Initialization and shutdown scripts for Clusterware 179
Oracle 11g Clusterware background processes 180
Cluster Ready Services Daemon 180
Additional background processes for Oracle 11g Clusterware 181
Fatal Clusterware processes and Oracle 11g RAC 184
Managing Oracle 11g Clusterware utilities **185**
CRSCTL 185
CRS_STAT 188
OCRCHECK 190
OCRCONFIG 192
CLSCFG 193
CLUVFY 196
Troubleshooting Oracle 11g Clusterware **197**
Failed, missing, or offline 11g Clusterware resources 198
Offline Clusterware resources for Oracle 11g RAC 199
Problems with the Voting disk and OCR 200
Vote disk issues with 11g Clusterware resources 200
Failed or corrupted Vote Disks 201
Failed or corrupted OCR 202
How to recover the OCR from backup 202
Steps to perform recovery of lost and/or corrupted OCR 203
Check status 11g RAC Clusterware 204
Root cause analysis 11g RAC 205
Oracle 11g RAC node reboot issues 206
Oracle 11g RAC Clusterware processes—node reboot issues 207
Root cause analysis for solving node reboots with 11g RAC 208
OCSSD Reboots and 11g RAC 210
OPROCD failure and node reboots 211
OCLSOMON-RAC node reboot 211

Hardware, storage, and network problems with RAC 212
Hardware, storage, and network resolutions 215
New features in Oracle 11g R2 Clusterware **215**
Oracle Real Application Clusters one node (Oracle RAC one node) 216
Improved Oracle Clusterware resource modeling 216
Policy-based cluster and capacity management 217
Cluster time synchronization service 217
Oracle Cluster Registry and voting disks within Oracle ASM 217
New features for upgrading to Oracle 11g Clusterware 218
Oracle 11g R2 Cluster Verification Utility new features 218
Zero downtime patching for Oracle Clusterware 218
Summary **219**
Chapter 6: RAC Database Administration and Workload Management **221**
RAC database configuration and creation **222**
Creating a database using DBCA 222
Choosing database storage options 231
We have created a database using DBCA—now what? 241
What's new in Oracle 11g R1 and R2 databases? **243**
Automatic Memory Management 244
New AMM dynamic performance V$ views 245
Tuning AMM 246
Database Smart Flash Cache 248
Configuring Smart Flash Cache 248
Instance caging 249
New background processes in Oracle 11g 249
Finding the alert.log file location in Oracle 11g 250
Automatic Diagnostic Repository 251
V$DIAG_INFO view 252
RAC database administration **253**
Using the Server Control Utility 253
Automatic Workload Management **255**
Overview of services 255
Creating and managing services 256
What's new in Oracle 11g services' behavior? **262**
Scalability (Load Balancing) 263
Client Side Connect Time Load Balance 263
Server Side Listener Connection Load Balance 264
Transparent Application Failover 265
Configuring Transparent Application Failover 266
Fast Connection Failover 267
Configuring Fast Connection Failover 267
Summary **268**

Chapter 7: Backup and Recovery 269
An overview of backup and recovery 270
An overview of Recovery Manager (RMAN) 270
RMAN architecture 272
RMAN performance tuning tips 273
Backup types and methods 274
Logical backup 274
Physical backup 275
ONLINE RMAN backups 275
OFFLINE RMAN backups 275
RMAN new features in 11g R1 and 11g R2 275
Database Recovery Advisor 276
Multisection backups for very large datafiles 276
Undo tablespace backup optimization 277
Faster backup compression 277
Active database duplication 278
Archivelog deletion policy enhancements 280
Automatic Block Recovery (ABR) 280
Tablespace point-in-time recovery enhancements 281
RMAN best practices for RAC 281
Configuring the Flash Recovery Area for a RAC database 282
Instance recovery versus Crash recovery in RAC 283
Parallelism for backup and recovery in RAC 287
Backing up a RAC database with RMAN 287
Configuring multiple channels 289
OCR and Voting disk backup and recovery strategies 290
Adding a Mirror location for the OCR and Voting disk 291
OCR automatic backups 291
Performing OCR manual backups 293
Voting disk manual backups 294
Restoring OCR 294
Restoring the Voting disk 297
Summary 298
Chapter 8: Performance Tuning 299
Tuning differences: single instance versus RAC 300
Oracle 11g single instance database 300
Oracle RAC 11g database 300
New Oracle 11g performance tuning features 300
Database Replay 301
SQL Performance Analyzer 302
Database Health Monitor 302

PL/SQL Native Compilation 303
Server Result Cache 304
Client Side Result Cache 305
SQL Tuning Advisor 306
New performance features in Oracle 11gR2 307
In-Memory Parallel Execution 307
Analyzing the Cache Fusion impact on RAC performance 307
Cache Fusion 308
Latency statistics 309
RAC wait events 310
Monitoring RAC cluster interconnect performance 315
Oracle cluster interconnects 315
Monitoring RAC wait events 316
Summary 321
Chapter 9: Oracle 11g Clusterware Upgrade 323
Overview of an upgrade 323
Upgrade sequence 324
Upgrading Oracle 10g R2 Clusterware to Oracle 11g R1 324
Kernel parameter values 325
Packages required on Linux 5 326
Oracle 11g R1 Clusterware upgrade steps 326
Performing preinstallation checks with cluvfy 327
Executing runInstaller.sh script 327
Post-upgrade steps for 11g R1 Clusterware 332
Upgrading to Oracle 11g R2 Clusterware 333
Overview of our environment 333
Upgrading nodes 334
11g R2 upgrade changes and restrictions 334
Kernel parameter values 335
Packages required on Linux 5 335
Performing preinstallation checks with cluvfy 336
Oracle 11g R2 Clusterware upgrade steps 336
Executing the runInstaller.sh script 337
Post-upgrade checks for 11g R2 Clusterware 349
Post-upgrade steps for 11g R2 Clusterware 351
Downgrading Oracle Clusterware after an upgrade 352
Summary 353
Chapter 10: Real-world Scenarios 355
Adding a new node to an existing cluster 356
Performing prechecks with the cluvfy utility 357
addNode.sh 360
Adding a node in silent mode in Oracle 11g R2 363

Post-installation status checks for Clusterware 364
OCR file manual backup syntax 368
Voting Disk backup syntax 368
Installing ASM and RDBMS software using addNode.sh script 368
Cloning ASM software using addNode.sh script on Oracle 11g R1 369
Post-node addition steps 370
Removing a node from the cluster 370
Adding an RAC database instance 373
Adding a new instance using DBCA 374
We have added an instance—what next? 379
Verifying new instance status 379
Using DBCA in silent mode to add an instance 380
Post-add instance steps 380
Deleting an RAC database instance 380
Using DBCA in silent mode to delete an instance 381
Converting a single-instance database to an RAC database 382
Overview of RCONFIG command-line tool 383
What you need to accomplish the conversion task 384
Sample of a modified ConvertToRAC.xml input file 384
How to test a conversion without actually performing the conversion 386
Converting a single-instance database to an RAC database 387
How to resume a failed rconfig operation 389
Checking log files 389
How to optimize rconfig to run faster 389
Post-conversion steps 390
Relocating an RAC database and instances across nodes 390
Relocating the instance 391
Adding the instance example 392
Workaround when a database and instance are configured on the same node 392
Adding the database example 393
Post-relocation steps 394
Summary 394
Chapter 11: Enabling RAC for EBS 395
EBS architecture 396
Oracle 11g RAC suitability 399
Installing EBS 12.1.1 400
EBS implementation on Oracle 11g RAC 407
RAC-enabling EBS 12.1.1 410
Configuration prerequisites 410
ASM and RAC-enabling the EBS database with the rconfig utility 412
Running AutoConfig 418

Copying AutoConfig to the new RDBMS ORACLE_HOME for Oracle 11g R1 11.1.0.7 419
Generating your database context file 422
Preparing for AutoConfig by completing the following AutoConfig steps 422
Generating and applying AutoConfig configuration files 423
Executing AutoConfig on all database nodes in the cluster 424
Performing Init file, tnsnames, and listener file activities 424
Establishing applications environment for Oracle RAC 426
Setting up load balancing 427
Configuring Parallel Concurrent Processing 428
Prerequisites for setting up Parallel Concurrent Processing 428
Cloning EBS concepts in brief 429
Preparing the source system 430
Copying the source system 430
Configuring the target system 431
Adding a new node to an existing EBS system 431
Setting up Parallel Concurrent Processing 433
Setting up Transaction Managers 434
Setting up load balancing on concurrent processing nodes 435
Summary 435
Chapter 12: Maximum Availability 437
Oracle 11g Streams for RAC 438
Oracle 11g Streams architecture for RAC 438
Capture 438
Staging 439
Propagation 439
Consumption 439
Default apply 440
User-defined function apply 440
Explicit de-queue 440
Understanding Oracle Streams rules 440
Transformations and Streams 440
Capture and Apply processes in an RAC instance 441
Streams in the RAC environment 441
New features in Oracle 11g Streams 442
Synchronous Capture 442
Splitting and merging of a Stream Destination 442
Tracking LCRs through a Stream 443
Streams Topology and Performance Advisor 443
Combined Capture and Apply 443
Best practices for Streams in an RAC environment 444
Additional configuration of RAC environments for a Source Database 444
Queue ownership 445
Propagation restart 446

Changing the GLOBAL_NAME of the source database 447
Additional configuration for RAC environments for the Apply Database 448
Changing the GLOBAL_NAME of the Target Database 448
New features for Streams in Oracle 11g R2 **448**
XStream 449
Statement DML Handlers 449
Ability to record table changes 449
SQL generation 449
Support for compressed tables 450
Support for SecureFile LOBs 450
Automatic splitting and merging 450
New Apply process parameter 450
Monitoring jobs 451
New 11g R2 Oracle Streams view 451
Oracle 11g Data Guard and RAC **451**
New features for Oracle 11g Data Guard 451
Active Data Guard 452
Snapshot Standby 452
Configuring Data Guard Physical Standby for 11g RAC 452
Configuring Oracle RAC primary database to send redo data 453
Design considerations in an Oracle RAC environment 453
Format for archived redo log filenames 453
Troubleshooting Oracle 11g Data Guard and RAC 454
Switchover fails in an Oracle 11g RAC configuration 455
How to recover from corrupt datafile on standby 455
How to recover from a corrupt block on standby 457
Automatic repairing of corrupt data blocks 457
New features for Data Guard in Oracle 11g R2 **458**
New Oracle Data Guard 11g R2 features for Redo Apply 458
New Oracle 11g R2 Data Guard features for SQL Apply 459
Summary **460**
Appendix: Additional Resources and Tools for the Oracle RAC Professional **461**
Sample configurations **461**
Reviewing and resolving manual configuration changes 464
adchkcfg utility 464
Oracle RAC commands and tips **467**
Cluster deconfig tool for Oracle RAC 468
Using the cluster deconfig tool 469
Limitations of the cluster deconfig tool 470
Problems and limitations of the cluster deconfig tool 470
Starting the cluster deconfig tool 471
Silent mode operations using cluster deconfig 471

Manual cleanup for RAC 474
Repairing the RAC environment without reinstalling 476
Reinitializing OCR and Voting Disks without reinstalling RAC 476
Using ROOTDELETE.SH in debug mode 478
Using rootdeinstall.sh 480
Reinstalling CRS on the same cluster in another CRS_HOME 480
Stopping CRS processes 480
Reinstalling CRS on same cluster in another CRS_HOME 481
Oracle 11g R2 cluster removal tools for RAC 481
Tracing RAC issues with Oradebug 482
Using Oradebug to trace Oracle 11g Clusterware 485
Server Control Utility 486
Oracle 11g R2 SRVCTL commands 486
Managing Oracle Clusterware with the CRSCTL utility 487
Differences between 11g R1 and 11g R2 syntax for CRSCTL 487
Operating system-level commands for tuning and diagnosis 492
Strace 492
Truss 495
GDB 496
Additional references and tips 499
Clusterware startup sequence for Oracle 11g R2 500
Index 503

Preface

Oracle Real Application Clusters, or Oracle RAC for short (formerly known as Oracle Parallel Server), is a clustering technology that provides the ability to scale performance and improve server availability for Oracle data center environments. Oracle RAC not only serves as a part of the Oracle Maximum Availability Architecture (MAA) for disaster recovery purposes, but it's also used for other purposes such as scaling up and out for performance by adding additional nodes to an Oracle data center environment. However, getting started with Oracle RAC can be difficult and challenging for the Oracle professional who is new to this technology and has worked only with single-instance Oracle databases. This book provides the guidance needed to overcome that difficulty, covering the key features of Oracle RAC. Each chapter introduces new features, allowing you to develop competency in the administration of this advanced technology.

By the end of the book, you will not only have experimented with numerous examples, but you will have also deployed a complete Oracle RAC environment and solution.

What this book covers

Chapter 1, High Availability, serves as the most basic introduction to concepts of high availability with regard to how Oracle RAC comes into play. The chapter includes a comprehensive review of the core areas of high availability and disaster recovery as well as how the Oracle RAC technology fits into a strategy for implementing high availability. The chapter also includes a review of key Oracle technologies that complement Oracle RAC for a disaster recovery implementation.

Chapter 2, Oracle 11g RAC Architecture, provides a blueprint from concept to finish of how to design an Oracle 11g RAC environment from the hardware and storage layers to the software and database layers.

Chapter 3, Clusterware Installation, provides step-by-step instructions on how to install Oracle 11g RAC. The chapter explains all of the steps required for the installation of the Oracle 11g R1 RAC Clusterware and Oracle 11g R1 RDBMS binaries, as well as the latest 11g R2 RAC Clusterware (grid) and RDBMS binaries.

Chapter 4, Automatic Storage Management, discusses the key concepts for Oracle 11g Automatic Storage Management (ASM) technology and provides an overview of ASM features. For this chapter, we assume that you have already worked with the ASM Oracle database 10g environment.

Chapter 5, Managing and Troubleshooting Oracle 11g Clusterware, explains how to resolve complex problems with Oracle 11g RAC clusterware failures. We show you how to identify the root cause of Oracle Clusterware issues along with timely solutions based on case study methods.

Chapter 6, RAC Database Administration and Workload Management, provides a deep dive into various methods that are available to create and manage RAC databases. The workload management segment in this chapter further explains how your application can take advantage of running on the RAC database to improve overall performance and scalability. It also discusses most of the useful new features introduced in 11g R1 and 11g R2 versions.

Chapter 7, Backup and Recovery, shows you how to back up and recover the Oracle RAC environment using different approaches. In this chapter, the emphasis will be placed on backup and recovery using RMAN. However, we also briefly discuss the various methods along with the pros and cons of each of them. In addition, new features of RMAN within Oracle 11g R1 and 11g R2 along with OCR and voting disk backup and recovery are covered in great detail.

Chapter 8, Performance Tuning, first explains how the differences between an Oracle RAC cluster and a non-RAC single-instance Oracle database pose unique challenges to the Oracle database professional. This chapter will focus on how to tune a massively parallel Oracle RAC database, consisting of many instances residing on different nodes of a cluster and accessing the same disk files residing on shared disk storage.

Chapter 9, Oracle 11g Clusterware Upgrade, explains the pros and cons of an upgrade process as well as the possibilities during upgrade scenarios. We also demonstrate how to upgrade the Oracle 10g R2 clusterware to 11g R1 and then perform a second upgrade from 11g R1 to 11g R2 versions. Furthermore, we also explain how to downgrade Oracle Clusterware to a previous version.

Chapter 10, Real-world Scenarios, teaches you how to perform many common real-world business scenarios, such as adding and removing cluster nodes, as well as how to convert non-RAC Oracle databases to Oracle RAC and how to relocate an Oracle RAC database instance, which are key skills for an Oracle RAC database administrator.

Chapter 11, Enabling RAC for EBS, discusses how to implement RAC for the Oracle R12 E-Business Suite (EBS) environment. We look at the cases for why Oracle RAC would be suitable for an Oracle R12 EBS environment to achieve a scalable and resilient architecture.

Chapter 12, Maximum Availability, discusses the complete picture of solutions for Oracle to enable high availability and disaster recovery. A detailed explanation is provided of these key technologies, including Oracle Streams and Oracle Data Guard, and how they complement the Oracle 11g RAC environment. We then move into a few case studies that show you how to enable Data Guard and Streams for Oracle RAC environments.

Appendix, Additional Resources and Tools for the Oracle RAC Professional is a handy summary of beneficial My Oracle Support notes that can provide assistance for Oracle RAC environments.

What you need for this book

Oracle 11g RAC is a complex technology that demands many resources, from logistical to hardware, to implement. This means that you will need multiple servers and technical resources to be carefully orchestrated in order to achieve a successful RAC implementation. In a sense, the Oracle RAC architect is a symphony conductor who must skillfully place all of the key chess pieces into motion to avoid failure and delays with the deployment. As many DBAs have no prior RAC exposure, we gently introduce the basic concepts first, in order to familiarize you with RAC, before jumping into the deep ocean of RAC administration. Have no fear, while RAC is a complex beast, it can be tamed. The only prerequisite is to have at least a basic understanding of Oracle database concepts and Oracle database administration before learning about RAC. It is also useful to have access to a test or sandbox environment to install and configure an RAC environment with the examples in the book. Nothing beats hands-on experience.

Having an Internet connection and Oracle database server while reading is extremely useful as well. We also recommend that if you want a virtual environment to set up and play with RAC, then you consult the many whitepapers written by Dr. Tim Hall (`http://oracle-base.com`) that provide detailed step-by-step instructions on how to download, install, and configure an Oracle 11g RAC environment in both virtual server and standalone environments.

Who this book is for

If you are an Oracle DBA who wants to administer Real Application Clusters, then this book is for you. Basic understanding of Oracle DBA is required. No experience of RAC is required.

Conventions

In this book, you will find a number of styles of text that distinguish between different kinds of information. Here are some examples of these styles, and an explanation of their meaning.

Code words in text are shown as follows: "`$CRS_HOME\log\nodename\racg` contains logfiles for the VIP and ONS resources".

A block of code will be set as follows:

```
$ clscfg -concepts
clscfg: EXISTING configuration version 3 detected.
clscfg: version 3 is 11G Release 1.
clscfg -- concepts and terminology
```

Any command-line input or output is written as follows:

```
# crsctl set css misscount 90
Configuration parameter misscount is now set to 90.
```

New terms and **important words** are shown in bold. Words that you see on the screen, in menus or dialog boxes for example, appear in our text like this: "Click on **Finish** to commence the database creation process."

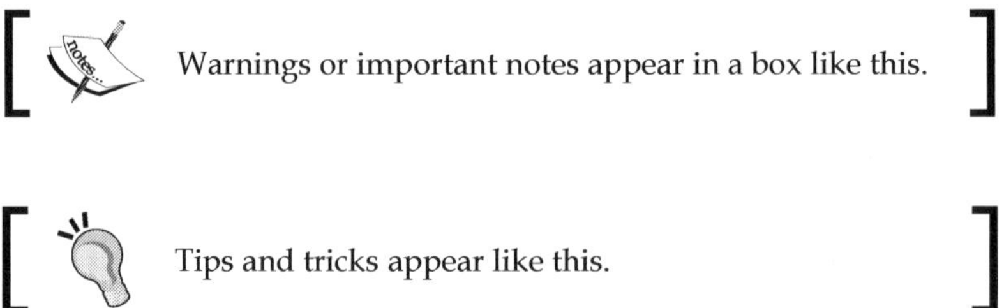

Warnings or important notes appear in a box like this.

Tips and tricks appear like this.

Reader feedback

Feedback from our readers is always welcome. Let us know what you think about this book—what you liked or may have disliked. Reader feedback is important for us to develop titles that you really get the most out of.

To send us general feedback, simply drop an e-mail to `feedback@packtpub.com`, and mention the book title in the subject of your message.

If there is a book that you need and would like to see us publish, please send us a note in the **SUGGEST A TITLE** form on `www.packtpub.com` or e-mail `suggest@packtpub.com`.

If there is a topic that you have expertise in and you are interested in either writing or contributing to a book, see our author guide on `www.packtpub.com/authors`.

Customer support

Now that you are the proud owner of a Packt book, we have a number of things to help you to get the most from your purchase.

Downloading the example code for this book

You can download the example code files for all Packt books you have purchased from your account at `http://www.PacktPub.com`. If you purchased this book elsewhere, you can visit `http://www.PacktPub.com/support` and register to have the files e-mailed directly to you.

Errata

Although we have taken every care to ensure the accuracy of our contents, mistakes do happen. If you find a mistake in one of our books—maybe a mistake in text or code—we would be grateful if you would report this to us. By doing so, you can save other readers from frustration, and help us to improve subsequent versions of this book. If you find any errata, please report them by visiting `http://www.packtpub.com/support`, selecting your book, clicking on the **let us know** link, and entering the details of your errata. Once your errata are verified, your submission will be accepted and the errata added to any list of existing errata. Any existing errata can be viewed by selecting your title from `http://www.packtpub.com/support`.

Piracy

Piracy of copyright material on the Internet is an ongoing problem across all media. At Packt, we take the protection of our copyright and licenses very seriously. If you come across any illegal copies of our works in any form on the Internet, please provide us with the location address or website name immediately so that we can pursue a remedy.

Please contact us at `copyright@packtpub.com` with a link to the suspected pirated material.

We appreciate your help in protecting our authors, and our ability to bring you valuable content.

Questions

You can contact us at `questions@packtpub.com` if you are having a problem with any aspect of the book, and we will do our best to address it.

1
High Availability

High availability is a discipline within database technology that provides a solution to protect against data loss and against downtime, which is costly to mission-critical database systems. In this chapter, we will discuss how Oracle 11g RAC provides you with mission-critical options for minimizing outages and downtime as well as how RAC fits into the overall scheme for maintenance of a comprehensive disaster recovery and business continuity policy. In this chapter, we will provide you with an introduction to the high availability concepts and solutions that are workable for Oracle 11g. As such, we will provide details on what constitutes high availability and what does not. By having the proper framework, you will understand how to leverage Oracle RAC and auxiliary technologies including **Oracle Data Guard** to maximize the **Return On Investment** (**ROI**) for your data center environment. In summary, we will discuss the following topics:

- High availability concepts
- Fault-tolerant systems and high availability
- High availability solutions for Oracle 11g R1 and 11g R2 Real Application Clusters (RAC)

High availability concepts

High availability provides data center environments that run mission-critical database applications with the resiliency to withstand failures that may occur due to natural, human, or environmental conditions. For example, if a hurricane wipes out the production data center that hosts a financial application's production database, high availability would provide the much-needed protection to avoid data loss, minimize downtime, and maximize availability of the firm's resources and database applications. Let's now move to the high availability concepts.

Planned versus unplanned downtime

The distinction needs to be made between planned downtime and unplanned downtime. In most cases, planned downtime is the result of maintenance that is disruptive to system operations and cannot be avoided with current system designs for a data center. An example of planned downtime would be a DBA maintenance activity such as database patching to an Oracle database, which would require taking an outage to take the system offline for a period of time. From the database administrator's perspective, planned downtime situations usually are the result of management-initiated events.

On the other hand, unplanned downtime issues frequently occur due to a physical event caused by a hardware, software, or environmental failure or caused by human error. A few examples of unplanned downtime events include hardware server component failures such as CPU, disk, or power outages.

Most data centers will exclude planned downtime from the high availability factor in terms of calculating the current total availability percentage. Even so, both planned and unplanned maintenance windows affect high availability. For instance, database upgrades require a few hours of downtime. Another example would be a SAN replacement. Such items make comprehensive four nine solutions nigh impossible to implement without additional considerations. The fact is that implementing a true 100% high availability is nearly impossible without exorbitant costs. To have complete high availability for all components within the data center requires an architecture for all systems and databases that eliminates any **Single Point of Failure** (**SPOF**) and allows for total online availability for all server hardware, network, operating systems, applications, and database systems.

Service Level Agreements for high availability

When it comes to determining high availability ratios, this is often expressed as the percentage of uptime in a given year. The following table shows the approximate downtime that is allowed for a specific percentage of high availability, granted that the system is required to operate continuously. **Service Level Agreements** (**SLAs**) usually refer to monthly downtime or availability in order to calculate service levels to match monthly financial cycles. The following table from the **International Organization for Standardization** (**ISO**) illustrates the correlation between a given availability percentage and the relevant amount of time a system would be unavailable per year, month, or week:

Availability %	Annual downtime	Monthly downtime*	Weekly downtime
90%	36.5 days	72 hours	16.8 hours
95%	18.25 days	36 hours	8.4 hours
98%	7.30 days	14.4 hours	3.36 hours
99%	3.65 days	7.20 hours	1.68 hours
99.5%	1.83 days	3.60 hours	50.4 minutes
99.8%	17.52 hours	86.23 minutes	20.16 minutes
99.9% ("three nines")	8.76 hours	43.2 minutes	10.1 minutes
99.95%	4.38 hours	21.56 minutes	5.04 minutes
99.99% ("four nines")	52.6 minutes	4.32 minutes	1.01 minutes
99.999% ("five nines")	5.26 minutes	25.9 seconds	6.05 seconds
99.9999% ("six nines")	31.5 seconds	2.59 seconds	0.605 seconds

For monthly calculations, a 30-day month is used.

It should be noted that availability and uptimes are not the same thing. For instance, a database system may be online but not available, as in the case of application outages such as when a user's SQL script cannot be executed.

In most cases, the number of nines is not often used by the database or system professional when measuring high availability for data center environments because it is difficult to extrapolate such hard numbers without a large test environment. For practical purposes, availability is calculated more as a probability or average downtime given per annual basis.

High availability interpretations

When it comes to discussing how availability is measured, there is a debate on the correct method of interpretation for high availability ratios. For instance, an Oracle database server that has been online for 365 days in a given non-leap year might have been eclipsed by an application failure that lasted for nine hours during a peak usage period. As a consequence, the users will see the complete system as unavailable, whereas the Oracle database administrator will claim 100% "uptime." However, given the true definition of availability, the Oracle database will be approximately 99.897% available (8751 hours of available timeout of 8760 hours per non-leap year). Furthermore, Oracle database systems experiencing performance problems are often deemed partially or entirely unavailable by users, while in the eyes of the database administrator the system is fine and available.

Another situation that presents a challenge in terms of what constitutes availability would be the scenario in which the availability of a mission-critical application might go offline yet is not viewed as unavailable by the Oracle DBA, as the database instance could still be online and thus available. However, the application in question is offline to the end user, thus presenting a status of unavailable from the perspective of the end user. This illustrates the key point that a true availability measure must be from a holistic perspective and not strictly from the database's point of view.

Availability should be measured with comprehensive monitoring tools that are themselves highly available and present the proper instrumentation. If there is a lack of instrumentation, systems supporting high-volume transaction processing frequently during the day and night, such as credit-card-processing database servers, are often inherently better monitored than systems that experience a periodic lull in demand. Currently, custom scripts can be developed in conjunction with third-party tools to provide a measure of availability. One such tool that we recommend for monitoring database, server, and application availability is that provided by **Oracle Grid Control**, which also includes **Oracle Enterprise Manager**.

Oracle Grid Control provides instrumentation via agents and plugin modules to measure availability and performance on a system-wide enterprise level, thereby greatly aiding the Oracle database professional to measure, track, and report to management and users on the status of availability with all mission-critical applications and system components. However, the current version of Oracle Enterprise Manager will not provide a true picture of availability until 11g Grid Control is released in the future.

Recovery time and high availability

Recovery time is closely related to the concept of high availability. Recovery time varies based on system design and failure experienced, in that a full recovery may well be impossible if the system design prevents such recovery options. For example, if the data center is not designed correctly with the required system and database backups and a standby disaster recovery site in place, then a major catastrophe such as a fire or earthquake will almost always result in complete unavailability until a complete MAA solution is implemented. In this case, only a partial recovery may be possible. This drives home the point that for all major data center operations, you should always have a backup plan with an offsite secondary disaster-recovery data center to protect against losing all critical systems and data.

In terms of database administration for Oracle data centers, the concept of data availability is essential when dealing with recovery time and planning for highly available options. **Data availability** references the degree to which databases such as Oracle record and report transactions. Data management professionals often focus just on data availability in order to judge what constitutes an acceptable data loss with different types of failure events. While application service interruptions are inconvenient and sometimes permitted, data loss is not to be tolerated. As one **Chief Information Officer** (**CIO**) and executive once told us while working for a large financial brokerage, you can have the system down to perform maintenance but never ever lose my data!

The next item related to high availability and recovery standards is that of Service Level Agreements or SLAs for data center operations. The purpose of the Service Level Agreement is to actualize the availability objectives and requirements for a data center environment per business requirements into a standard corporate information technology (IT) policy.

System design for high availability

Ironically, by adding further components to the overall system and database architecture design, you may actually undermine your efforts to achieve true high availability for your Oracle data center environment. The reason for this is by their very nature, complex systems inherently have more potential failure points and thus are more difficult to implement properly. The most highly available systems for Oracle adhere to a simple design pattern that makes use of a single, high quality, multipurpose physical system with comprehensive internal redundancy running all interdependent functions, paired with a second like system at a separate physical location. An example would be to have a primary Oracle RAC clustered site with a second Disaster Recovery site at another location with Oracle Data Guard and perhaps dual Oracle RAC clusters at both sites connected by stretch clusters. The best possible way to implement an active standby site with Oracle would be to have Oracle Streams and Oracle Data Guard. Large commercial banking and insurance institutions would benefit from this model for Oracle data center design to maximize system availability.

Business Continuity and high availability

Business Continuity Planning (**BCP**) refers to the creation and validation of a rehearsed operations plan for the IT organization that explains the procedures of how the data center and business unit will recover and restore, partially or completely, interrupted business functions within a predetermined time after a major disaster.

In its simplest terms, BCP is the foundation for the IT data center operations team to maintain critical systems in the event of disaster. Major incidents could include events such as fires, earthquakes, or national acts of terrorism.

BCP may also encompass corporate training efforts to help reduce operational risk factors associated with the lack of information technology (IT) management controls. These BCP processes may also be integrated with IT standards and practices to improve security and corporate risk management practices. An example would be to implement BCP controls as part of **Sarbanes-Oxley** (**SOX**) compliance requirements for publicly traded corporations.

The origins for BCP standards arose from the **British Standards Institution** (**BSI**) in 2006 when the BSI released a new independent standard for business continuity named BS 25999-1. Prior to the introduction of this standard for BCP, IT professionals had to rely on the previous BSI information security standard, BS 7799, which provided only limited standards for business continuity compliance procedures. One of the key benefits of these new standards was to extend additional practices for business continuity to a wider variety of organizations, to cover needs for public sector, government, non-profit, and private corporations.

Disaster Recovery

Disaster Recovery (**DR**) is the process, policies, and procedures related to preparing for recovery or continuation of technology infrastructure critical to an organization after either a natural or human-caused disaster.

Disaster Recovery Planning (DRP) is a subset of larger processes such as Business Continuity and should include planning for resumption of applications, databases, hardware, networking, and other IT infrastructure components. A Business Continuity Plan includes planning for non-IT-related aspects, such as staff member activities, during a major disaster as well as site facility operations, and it should reference the Disaster Recovery Plan for IT-related infrastructure recovery and business continuity procedures and guidelines.

Business Continuity and Disaster Recovery guidelines

The following recommendations will provide you with a blueprint to formulate your requirements and implementation for a robust Business Continuity and Disaster Recovery plan:

1. Identifying the scope and boundaries of your Business Continuity Plan:

   The first step enables you to define the scope of your new Business Continuity Plan. It provides you with an idea of the limitations and boundaries of the Business Continuity Plan. It also includes important audit and risk analysis reports for corporate assets.

2. Conducting a Business Impact Analysis session:

   Business Impact Analysis (BIA) is the assessment of financial losses to institutions, which usually results as the consequence of destructive events such as the loss or unavailability of mission-critical business services.

3. Obtaining support for your business continuity plans and goals from the executive management team:

   You will need to convince senior management to approve your business continuity plan, so that you can flawlessly execute your disaster recovery planning. Assign stakeholders as representatives on the project planning committee team, once approval is obtained from the corporate executive team.

4. Understanding its specific role:

   In the possible event of a major disaster, each of your departments must be prepared to take immediate action. In order to successfully recover your mission-critical database systems with minimal loss, each team must understand the BCP and DRP plans, as well as follow them correctly. Furthermore, it is also important to maintain your DRP and BCP plans, as well as conduct periodic training of your IT staff members on a regular basis to have successful response time for emergencies. Such "smoke tests" to train and keep your IT staff members up to date on the correct procedures and communications will pay major dividends in the event of an unforeseen disaster.

One useful tool for creating and managing BCP plans is available from the **National Institute of Standards and Technologies** (**NIST**). The NIST documentation can be used to generate templates that can be used as an excellent starting point for your Business Continuity and Disaster Recovery planning. We highly recommend that you download and review the following NIST publication for creating and evaluating BCP plans, *Contingency Planning Guide for Information Technology Systems*, which is available online at `http://csrc.nist.gov/publications/nistpubs/800-34/sp800-34.pdf`.

Additional NIST documents may also provide insight into how best to manage new or current BCP or DRP plans. A complete listing of NIST publications is available online at `http://csrc.nist.gov/publications/PubsSPs.html`.

Fault-tolerant systems and high availability

Fault tolerance is data center technology that enables a system to continue to function correctly in the face of a failure with one or more faults within any given key component of the system architecture or data center. If operating quality experiences major degradation, the decrease in functionality of the environment is usually in direct proportion to the severity of the failure, whereas a poorly designed system will completely fail and breakdown with a small failure. In other words, fault tolerance gives you that added layer of protection and support to avoid a total meltdown of your mission-critical data center and, in our case, Oracle servers and database systems. Fault tolerance is often associated with highly available systems such as those found with Oracle Data Guard and Oracle RAC technologies.

Data formats may also be designed to degrade gracefully. For example, in the case of Oracle RAC environments, services provide for load balancing to minimize performance issues in the event that one or more nodes in the cluster are lost due to an unforeseen event.

Recovery from errors in fault-tolerant systems provides for either rollforward or rollback operations. For instance, whenever the Oracle server detects that it has an error condition and cannot find data from a missed transaction, rollback will occur either at the instance level or application level (a transaction must be atomic in that all elements must commit or rollback). Oracle takes the system state at that time and rolls back transactional changes to be able to move forward. Whenever a rollback is required for a transaction within Oracle, Oracle reverts the system state to some earlier correct version—for example, using the database checkpoint and rollback process inherent in the Oracle database engine and moving forward from there.

Rollback recovery requires that the operations between the checkpoint (implicit checkpoints are NEVER required for transactional recovery) and the detected erroneous state can be made to be transparent. Some systems make use of both rollforward and rollback recovery for different errors or different parts of one error.

For Oracle, database recovery always rolls back failed transactions and restores the state of the rollback or undo, from which it then rolls forward using the contents of the rollback or undo segments. However, when it comes to transactional-based recovery, Oracle only rolls back. Within the scope of an individual system, fault tolerance can be achieved by anticipating exceptional conditions and building the system to cope with them, and in general, aiming for self-healing so that the system converges towards an error-free state. In any case, if the consequence of a system failure is catastrophic, the system must be able to use reversion to fall back to a safe mode. This is similar to rollback recovery but can be a human action if humans are present in the loop.

Requirements for implementing fault tolerance

The basic characteristics of fault tolerance are:

- No single point of failure
- No single point of repair
- Fault isolation to the failing component
- Fault containment to prevent propagation of the failure
- Availability of reversion modes

In addition, fault-tolerant systems are characterized in terms of both planned and unplanned service outages. These are usually measured at the application level and not just at a hardware level. The figure of merit is called availability and is expressed as a percentage. For instance, a *five nine* system would therefore statistically provide *99.999% availability*. Fault-tolerant systems are typically based on the concept of redundancy. In theory, this would be ideal; however, in reality this is an elusive impractical goal. Due to the time required to fail over, reestablish middle-tier connections, and perform application restarts, it is not realistic to have complete availability. We can obtain four nines as the best goal for high availability with Oracle systems. For Oracle RAC, you can deploy a fault-tolerant environment by using multiple network interface cards, dual **Host Bus Adapters** (**HBAs**), and multiple switches to avoid any Single Point of Failure.

Fault tolerance and replication

By using spare components, we address the first fundamental characteristic of fault tolerance in the following two ways:

- **Replication**: This provides multiple identical instances of the same system or subsystem by directing tasks or requests to all of them simultaneously. Oracle Streams and Oracle GoldenGate, as well as third-party solutions such as Quest Shareplex, are replication technologies.
- **Redundancy**: This provides you with multiple identical instances of the same system and switching to one of the remaining instances in case of a failure. This switchover and failover process is available with standby database technology with Oracle Data Guard. Oracle RAC also provides node/server failover capability with the use of services by using **Fast Connection Failover** (**FCF**) and with **Fast Application Notification** (**FAN**).

At the storage layer, the major implementations of **RAID** (**Redundant Array of Independent Disks**) with the exception of disk striping (RAID 0) provide you with fault-tolerant appliances that also use data redundancy.

Bringing the replications into synchrony requires making their internal stored states the same. They can be started from a fixed initial state such as the reset state. Alternatively, the internal state of one replica can be copied to another replica.

One variant of **Data Mirror Replication** (**DMR**) is pair-and-spare. Two replicated elements operate in lockstep as a pair, with a voting circuit that detects any mismatch between their operations and outputs a signal indicating that there is an error. Another pair operates exactly the same way. A final circuit selects the output of the pair that does not proclaim that it is in error. Pair-and-spare requires four replicas rather than the three of DMR, but has been used commercially.

If a system experiences a failure, it must continue to operate without interruption during the repair process.

When a failure occurs, the system must be able to isolate the failure to the offending component. This requires the addition of dedicated failure-detection mechanisms that exist only for the purpose of fault isolation.

Recovery from a fault condition requires classifying the fault or failing component. The **National Institute of Standards and Technology** (**NIST**) categorizes faults based on locality, cause, duration, and effect.

High availability solutions for Oracle

Oracle introduced the concept of the **Maximum Availability Architecture (MAA)** as the foundation of the high availability architecture for mission-critical applications and databases that run in large corporate data centers. Maximum Availability refers to a comprehensive end-to-end solution developed for large, mission-critical data centers that require all layers of the application, data, and system environment to be fully redundant—for example, fault tolerant, with zero data loss, and maximum uptime to protect against loss in system performance and availability. Moreover, it provides application server protection with the Oracle Application Server topology, which includes middleware services, database tier with Oracle Data Guard, and system availability with Oracle RAC.

There are four high availability solutions for Oracle:

- Oracle Data Guard
- Oracle Streams
- Oracle Application Server Clustering
- High availability—Oracle 11g R1 and 11g R2 Real Application Clusters (RAC)

Oracle Data Guard

Oracle provides a true disaster recovery solution with Oracle Data Guard. Data Guard provides a standby database environment that can be used for failover or switchover operations in the event of a database failure that may occur at the primary database site.

A complete discussion of Data Guard is beyond the scope of this book. Since Data Guard requires special care and feeding with Oracle RAC environments, we will present a later chapter on how to integrate and manage a Data Guard physical standby solution with RAC environments.

Oracle Streams

Another option for implementing the Maximum Availability Architecture (MAA) blueprint for high availability is to use Oracle Streams or Oracle GoldenGate with the Oracle RAC environments.

Oracle Streams and Oracle GoldenGate are replication technologies that allow you to replicate a copy of your database or subset of database tables to another site. Oracle Streams is not a true disaster recovery solution or high availability option, but more of a complementary solution to enhance the availability options provided by Oracle Data Guard and Oracle RAC technologies. One of the most common ways to use this technology is with large Oracle data warehouses and data marts to replicate a subset of the source data to another environment for testing and verification purposes. A better solution would be to complement the replication technologies with transportable tablespaces to enhance performance, as TTS has robust performance advantages over replication technologies. Oracle Streams uses **Advanced Queuing** (**AQ**) as the foundation of its model for propagating changes between master and target replication sites.

In addition to Data Guard and Streams, as part of the Oracle Maximum Availability Architecture (MAA) solutions, we also have failover and clustering with Oracle Application Server Fusion Middleware servers.

Oracle Application Server Clustering

Oracle Application Servers form the core web and application layer foundation for many large data center environments. In this day and age of e-commerce and intranet site operations, Oracle Application Servers are the key components in a data center environment. Furthermore, many large firms use Oracle EBS or Oracle Application environments such as Oracle 11i or Oracle 12i Financials to manage the business operations for large financial transactions and reporting. As such, Oracle Application Servers are the middle-tier or application broker component of the Oracle Applications environments.

In order to implement true Disaster Recovery (DR) for high availability and protection against costly downtime and application data loss, Oracle provides clustering and failover technology as part of the Oracle Application Server environments.

In our coverage of the Oracle Maximum Availability Architecture (MAA), we introduced Data Guard, Streams, and Application Server clustering and failover. Now we will present how Oracle RAC fits into the grand scheme of this high availability paradigm.

High availability: Oracle 11g R1 Real Application Clusters (RAC)

Oracle 11g R1 RAC provides a combination of options that could be considered to be a high availability solution. It provides server-level redundancy, as well as database instance availability by clustering hardware and database resources. However, RAC is not a true disaster-recovery solution because it does not protect against site failure or database failure.

The reason is that with an Oracle RAC configuration, the database is shared by nodes in the cluster and staged on shared storage, which is a **Single Point of Failure** (**SPOF**). If the RAC database is lost, the entire cluster will fail. Many people incorrectly assume that RAC is a true **Disaster Recovery** (**DR**) solution when, in fact, it is not. For a true disaster recovery solution with Oracle, you would need to implement Data Guard to protect against site and data failure events.

High availability: Oracle 11g R2 Real Application Clusters (RAC)

Among the numerous enhancements to the Oracle 11g RAC technology, the following new features of Oracle 11g R2 RAC improve on high availability for Oracle database technology:

- **Oracle Automatic Storage Management Cluster File System** (**Oracle ACFS**): A new scalable filesystem that extends Oracle ASM configurations and provides robust performance and availability functionality for Oracle ASM files.
- **Snapshot copy for Oracle ACFS**: Provides point-in-time copy of the Oracle ACFS filesystem to protect against data loss.
- **Oracle ASM Dynamic Volume Manager** (**Oracle ADVM**): Provides volume management services and disk driver interface to clients.
- **Oracle ASM Cluster Filesystem Snapshots**: Provides point-in-time copy of up to 63 snapshot images with Oracle single instance and RAC environments with 11g R2.

Summary

In this chapter, we discussed the concepts of High Availability Disaster Recovery and auxiliary topics. We also discussed a framework to design a **Business Continuity Plan (BCP)** that can be used to map business processes to IT infrastructure needs for mission-critical Oracle application environments. Among the core topics, we have covered:

- High availability concepts
- How Oracle 11g RAC provides high availability
- High availability solutions for Oracle 11g R1 and 11g R2 Real Application Clusters (RAC)

After explaining high availability, we discussed how each of the various Oracle technologies provide the Maximum Availability Architecture (MAA) for the large data center environment, as well as how to leverage these to best achieve maximum **Return on Investment (ROI)** within the Oracle data center. Finally, we explained why Oracle RAC is a high availability solution, as well as why it is not a disaster recovery solution.

In the next chapter, we will provide you with a detailed blueprint of how to design a solid Oracle RAC infrastructure for your data center environment and how to select and implement hardware, storage, and software for a robust Oracle 11g RAC configuration in the best possible manner.

2

Oracle 11g RAC Architecture

Oracle 11g RAC architecture differs in many respects from single-instance non-RAC Oracle database environments. In this chapter, we will provide you with a blueprint on how to apply best practices for leveraging your investment in Oracle RAC to create a highly available architecture. We will also discuss the various components of an RAC cluster.

Due to the complex nature of an Oracle 11g RAC environment, we will cover the various components that are unique to Oracle 11g RAC environments and constitute the Oracle system architecture. As such, we will provide key coverage of architectural design and implementation guidelines for successfully deploying Oracle 11g Real Application Clusters. We will also provide coverage of the most important new features that will benefit the Oracle RAC database administrator.

To summarize, we will discuss the following topics during the course of this chapter:

- Hardware and server architecture for Oracle 11g RAC
- Network architecture for Oracle 11g RAC
- Storage architecture for Oracle 11g RAC
- Storage protocols for RAC
- Oracle RAC components
- Oracle Cluster Registry and RAC
- Oracle 11g R1 and 11g R2 Automatic Storage Management (ASM) and RAC

Oracle 11g RAC architecture

We will begin our discussion of the RAC architecture for Oracle 11g at the macro level from 50,000 feet, with an example three-node Oracle 11g RAC environment as shown in the following diagram:

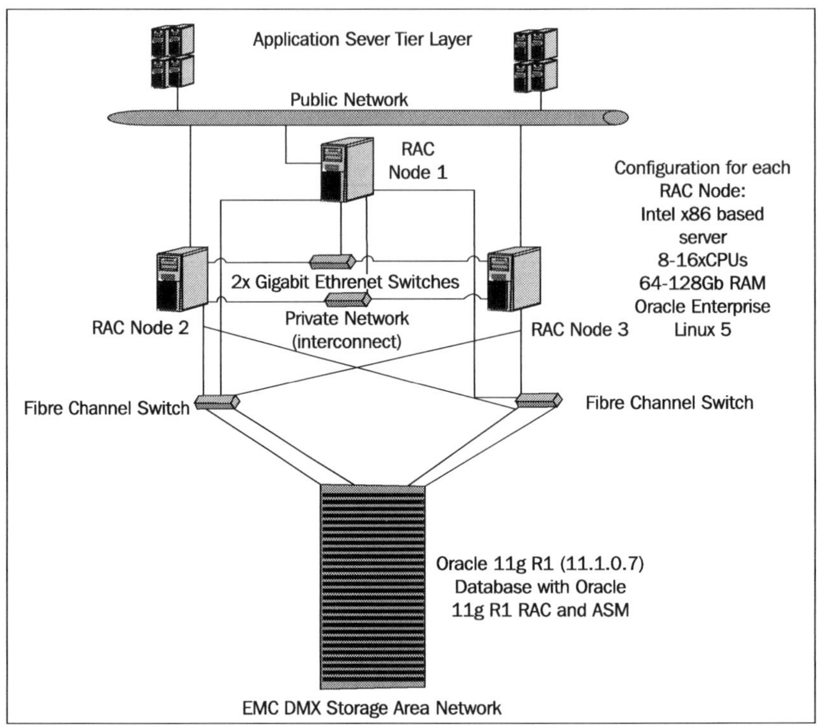

The preceding diagram illustrates a fully redundant Oracle 11g RAC architecture in terms of hardware, network, storage, and database layout and configurations. Later in the chapter, we will in turn explain each of these key components and how they function within the grand scheme of an Oracle RAC environment. We will also provide you with guidance on how to best choose the right components for your Oracle RAC environment. As you can see, Oracle RAC is a complex mix of system, network, and database technologies. This provides the ability to scale up or out for large mission-critical information systems to support either **OLTP (Online Transaction Processing)**, **DSS (Decision Support Systems)**, and **Data Warehouse**, or **ERP** environments such as Oracle 11i/R12 EBS and PeopleSoft or SAP. The robustness of RAC is also its Achilles' Heel.

As the database architect or onsite DBA, you will need to use a solid framework to best architect your Oracle RAC environments. One suitable place to begin is with the Oracle Certification Product Matrix for Oracle 11g RAC configurations.

Certification matrix for Oracle 11g RAC architecture

With powerful technology comes the added complexity of how to design and architect the best environment with RAC. So, how do we begin to architect a new Oracle RAC solution? This is a challenging question that clients have asked us time and again when proposing new solutions for a new or future data center RAC environment.

One place to begin is with the Oracle RAC support matrix. Oracle provides an excellent guide to supported and validated configurations for all of the key hardware, network, storage, and software platforms, with the help of the **My Oracle Support** (**MOS**) matrix for RAC available online at `https://support.oracle.com`.

To access the validated and supported configurations in terms of hardware and OS platform, sign in to **My Oracle Support** with your valid Oracle Metalink account and click on the **Certify** tab.

The certification matrices provide you with the option to view the supported configurations based on hardware platform or on the product.

Oracle has updated the support matrix for product configurations as a result of the recent migration from the previous Metalink Support site, which was based on an HTML format, to a new Flash-based configuration named My Oracle Support. As a result, to access the various support matrices, you need to follow a different menu path, which has changed since the legacy Metalink site was decommissioned. The My Oracle Support certification configurations can be accessed from the main screen after you log in to the site with your valid credentials. For example, after you log in to My Oracle Support, you can navigate to the certification matrix by selecting the drop-down menu item named **Certifications** under the **More...** option, as shown in the following screenshot:

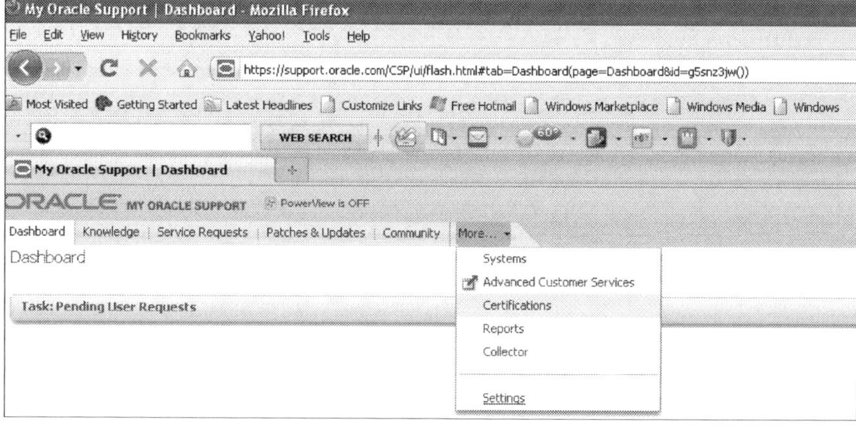

Under the **Certifications** tab, you can choose the product and system configuration to display all validated combinations for Oracle RAC and other products with your particular environment. For instance, you can choose the list of available configurations for Oracle 11g R2 RAC with Linux x86 by using the **Find Certification Information** drop-down boxes, as shown in the following screenshot:

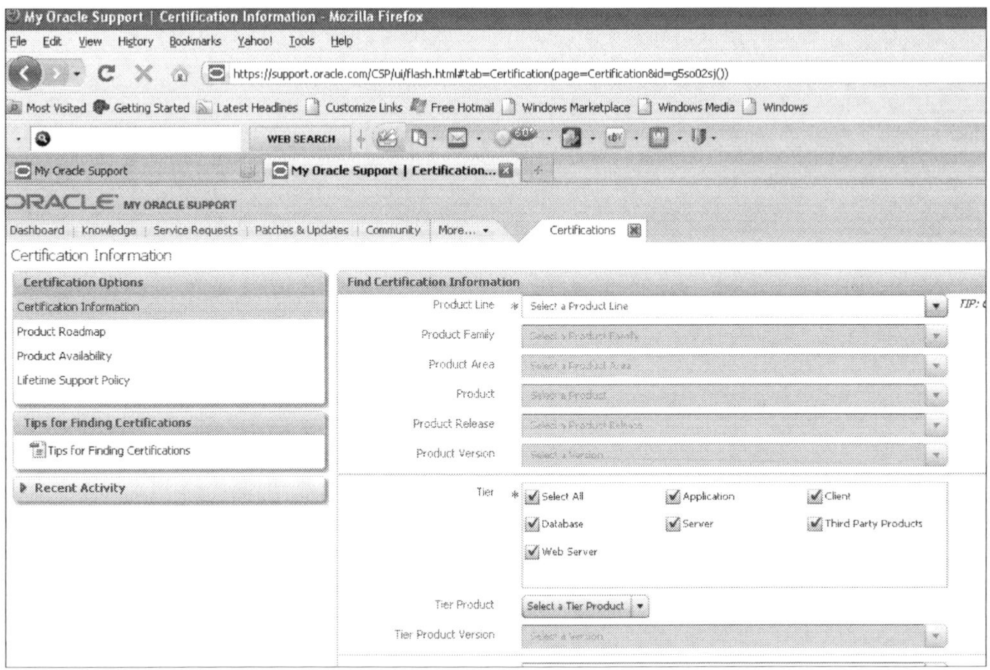

Let's illustrate how to use these features in My Oracle Support to display the complete listing of validated and supported configurations for Oracle 11g R2 RAC with the Oracle E-Business Suite. You can customize the search for validated and supported configurations for Oracle 11g RAC with different Oracle products and system architecture configurations. For instance, if you have a Linux 64-bit environment with Oracle Release 12 E-Business Suite, you can use the certification matrix to find what combinations of RAC are supported with the E-Business Suite. In the following example, we have chosen the drop-down menus as shown in the screenshot:

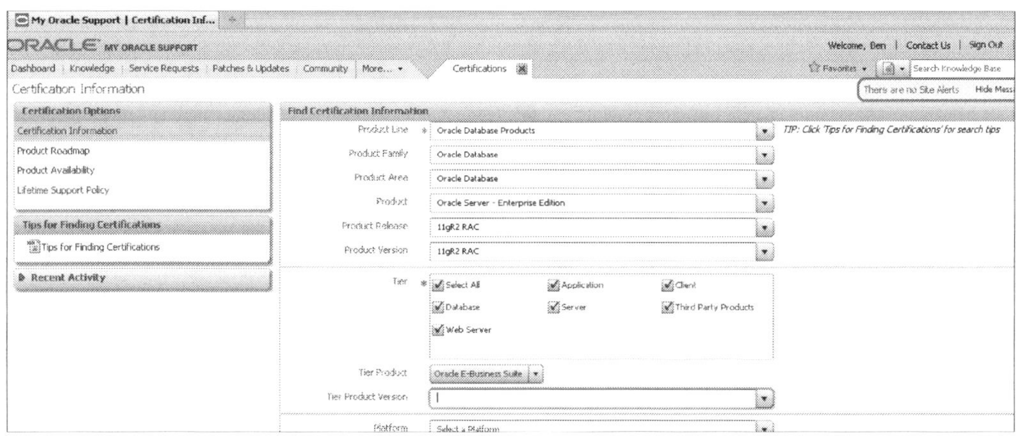

As shown in the preceding screenshot, you can display a wide range of validated configurations based on the product mix and architecture for your current and planned data center environments. By using the certified and validated configurations from Oracle, you can not only maximize your **Return on Investment (ROI)** but avoid costly issues with your RAC implementation.

Hardware architecture for Oracle 11g RAC

As database professionals, you will be tasked with finding the best hardware solution when implementing a new RAC environment for Oracle 11g. Cost, performance, and support are key factors to take into account when designing the hardware architecture for RAC. Many considerations need to be planned out for the correct hardware selection for a new or future RAC implementation. We advise that you hold meetings not only among the database team but also with the system, network, and storage administration teams to perform the initial planning of your hardware, storage, and network architecture needed for 11g RAC environments. There is no one-size-fits-all approach when it comes to laying the foundation for 11g RAC. Vendors also provide resources for sizing and validated configurations that are supported with all of the layers of the Oracle 11g RAC technology stack. The majority of long-term RAC architectural and design issues are due to a lack of using configurations supported by Oracle in addition to poor application and database design.

Server configurations for Oracle 11g RAC

Servers are the physical machines that provide the majority of power for the cluster nodes in an Oracle 11g RAC configuration. The servers provide the same function to run the operating system, yet use different technical components. Our discussion of the hardware architecture for RAC will begin with these basic items and will progress into further discussions of processors, networks, and storage components.

CPU processors

Linux servers provide you with a few different choices of CPU processors, as shown in the following table. As we mentioned earlier in the chapter, the Oracle RAC certification matrix provides a complete breakdown of validated configurations for hardware server platforms based on your particular environment.

Processor / server architecture	CPU processor details
Linux x86	Supports Intel and AMD 32-bit CPUs with the x86 architecture.
Linux x86-64	Supports Intel and AMD 64-bit x86-64 architecture.
Linux x86-64 (Continued)	Note: 32-bit version of Oracle is not supported with 64-bit operating system. However, 32-bit Oracle on this platform is supported with a 32-bit operating system.
Itanium	Support available on Intel Itanium processors that use 64-bit EPIC architecture. However, 32-bit Oracle database on Itanium is not a supported configuration.

Understanding the supported and validated combinations for processors is critical when designing the architecture for the servers with your RAC environment to avoid support and configuration issues later.

Choosing between 32-bit and 64-bit CPU architectures

Many customers are unsure of whether to choose the 32-bit or 64-bit CPU for RAC servers. To answer this query, you will first need to understand the differences between 32-bit and 64-bit CPU technologies, as well as the benefit of using a 64-bit CPU versus a 32-bit CPU. The ability to address larger memory areas with a 64-bit CPU is the chief advantage of going with a 64-bit CPU architecture for your RAC servers. Computer scientists have been able to generate the theory of memory architectures and scalability by arriving at the result that the smaller 32-bit CPU architecture can only address memory up to a maximum size of 4 GB of addressable memory for the Oracle database platform. In contrast, the larger 64-bit processor can address a much larger amount of memory for Oracle, up to a maximum of 16 exabytes (16 billion GB) of addressable memory. This larger value of memory available with 64-bit CPUs provides you with the ability to scale up for the biggest RAC environments. We recommend that you go with a 64-bit CPU server architecture if you are deploying a **Very Large Data Warehouse (VLDB)** environment or for large **Oracle E-Business (EBS)** implementations that demand heavy memory and CPU resources.

As you can imagine, with the approximate memory limit of 4 GB for a 32-bit system across the entire server, most Oracle databases will quickly run out of memory. Luckily, the Linux OS (and most Unix OSs) implement virtual and physical memory for 32-bit operating systems that can be adjusted to tweak memory requirements. The following table shows a breakdown of how 4 GB virtual memory can be split for Linux:

Configuration	Memory Allocated
Oracle Shared Libraries/Code	1.0 GB
Oracle 11g SGA (System Global Area)	1.7 GB
Stack Memory (Linux/UNIX OS)	0.3 GB
Kernel (Linux/UNIX OS)	1.0 GB

You have the potential with the 32-bit OS for Linux platforms to lower the default memory address for Oracle, by using the `genksm` command available under the `$ORACLE_HOME/rdbms/lib` directory as shown here:

```
[oracle@raclinux1 ~]$ genksms -s 0x15000000 > ksms.s
```

We can then review the output of the `genksms` command in the `ksms.s` file, which shows us that the new address for the Oracle 11g SGA has been reset.

```
[oracle@raclinux1 ~]$ more ksms.s
        .set    sgabeg,0X15000000
        .globl  ksmsgf_
        .set    ksmsgf_,sgabeg+0
        .globl  ksmvsg_
        .set    ksmvsg_,sgabeg+4
        .globl  ksmver_
        .set    ksmver_,sgabeg+8
```

Downloading the example code for this book

You can download the example code files for all Packt books you have purchased from your account at `http://www.PacktPub.com`. If you purchased this book elsewhere, you can visit `http://www.PacktPub.com/support` and register to have the files e-mailed directly to you.

We use the `genksm` utility to allocate different ranges of memory to the SGA for 11g, with the kernel for the Linux platform. To recompile and relink this new memory address to Oracle 11g RAC, you can execute the `make` command as shown here:

```
[oracle@raclinux1 ~]$ make -f ins_rdbms.mk ksms.o
[oracle@raclinux1 ~]$ make -f ins_rdbms.mk ioracle
```

This results in mapping the Oracle 11g executables for the database and libraries to use a lower memory region, which frees up to 2.7 GB for the Oracle SGA with a 32-bit server.

There is an optional workaround to this 2.7 GB memory constraint for the Oracle SGA with 32-bit processors. In a standard x86 system, you can adjust the physical memory limit up to a 36-bit limit by using the feature named **Physical Addressing Extensions (PAE)**. PAE allows you to increase the memory available for the Oracle SGA by up to 64 GB for a 32-bit architecture that translates the virtual memory allocation for this architecture. My Oracle Support (formerly Metalink) Note 260152.1 provides the complete details and test cases behind how to implement large memory with Linux. Both the Linux and Windows kernel need to implement PAE in order to overcome the 4 GB memory limitation for 32-bit processors. The way to do so for Linux is to mount a shared memory filesystem named `shmfs` for more than 4 GB of memory. The command and example to perform this task, to allocate additional memory with PAE for Linux, is as shown:

```
[root@raclinux1 ~]# mount -t shm shmfs -o size=8g /dev/shm
```

An entry is required under the `/etc/fstab` file to ensure that this filesystem is mounted by Linux at boot time. In addition, you will need to set the Oracle parameter `USE_INDIRECT_DATA_BUFFERS` to `true` for the Oracle 11g buffer cache to use this filesystem.

One item that merits further consideration when implementing PAE for Linux platforms is the memory required for page table entry mapping from virtual to physical memory allocations. As you limit the kernel memory to 1 GB based on page size, in certain cases the kernel memory could be used up before physical addressability can be used with earlier versions of the Linux operating system. This problem led to the development of the hugemem kernel to resolve such issues. The **hugemem kernel** provides a 50/50 split of 4 GB to the Linux kernel and with the 4 GB of memory allocated between the Oracle SGA memory and the Oracle database shared library code memory structures. For businesses that have a requirement to remain on 32-bit platforms with Linux, having the ability to change memory settings is a great benefit to obtain the optimum performance out of legacy hardware.

Dual core and multicore processors

Dual-core and multicore processors provide two or more individual cores on the same physical CPU, which provides you with greater processing power and efficiency within the same environment as compared to a single-core processor. Contention for resources is greatly reduced as a result, as tasks can be executed separately without saturating access to memory registers within the server. Multicore processors are ideal for Grid computing technologies including RAC. To view the configuration for your processors in Linux, you can execute the following command that provides information such as number of CPUs, memory size, and number of cores for the Linux environment.

```
[root@raclinux1 ~]# cat /proc/cpuinfo
processor       : 0
vendor_id       : GenuineIntel
cpu family      : 6
model           : 15
model name      : Intel(R) Core(TM)2 CPU          T5500  @ 1.66GHz
stepping        : 8
cpu MHz         : 0.000
cache size      : 2048 KB
fdiv_bug        : no
hlt_bug         : no
```

```
f00f_bug         : no
coma_bug         : no
fpu              : yes
fpu_exception    : yes
cpuid level      : 10
wp               : yes
flags            : fpu vme de pse tsc msr pae mce cx8 apic mtrr pge mca
cmov pat pse36 clflush dts acpi mmx fxsr sse sse2 ss pni ds_cpl
bogomips         : 2496.92
```

Each processor will display its own entry based on the output of the `/proc/cpuinfo` command for Linux. For RAC, Oracle will take the value for the physical and logical CPUs as the base of the `CPU_COUNT` parameter within Oracle 11g. By understanding the various processor architectures, you can make an informed decision about implementing the server nodes for your Oracle RAC environments at the best price and performance configuration.

Network architecture for Oracle 11g RAC

The Oracle 11g RAC technology places a lot of responsibility on the network layer within the data center; it requires a high-performing public as well as private network to deliver the optimal rate of scalability, performance, and availability. As the data within an RAC environment must pass across the interconnect network interfaces, you will need to size and tune the network interfaces accordingly or suffer from performance issues within your 11g RAC environments.

The private network and the Oracle 11g RAC interconnect

The **interconnect** functions as a network device as part of the private network between cluster nodes in an Oracle 11g RAC configuration. Its purpose is to transfer Oracle data between nodes in the cluster, over a high speed network interface, via the Cache Fusion mechanism for RAC. We will review the network hardware details in this section on how best to select and configure the right components for the private network interconnect with RAC.

Choices for private interconnect and 11g RAC

You can implement the cluster interconnect for your RAC environment with a wide choice of network technologies according to your budget and bandwidth requirements for RAC performance. Oracle allows you to select from Ethernet and **Remote Direct Memory Access (RDMA)**, technologies for the interconnection with RAC. The following table shows a complete list of supported network protocols for Oracle 11g RAC:

Operating system	Clusterware	Network hardware	Protocol
HP OpenVMS	HP OpenVMS	Gigabit Ethernet	UDP
HP Tru64	HP TruCluster	Memory Channel	RDG
HP Tru64	HP TruCluster	Memory Channel	UDP
HP Tru64	HP TruCluster	Gigabit Ethernet	RDG
HP Tru64	HP TruCluster	Gigabit Ethernet	UDP
HP-UX	Oracle Clusterware	Hyperfabric	UDP
HP-UX	Oracle Clusterware	Gigabit Ethernet	UDP
HP-UX	HP ServiceGuard	Hyperfabric	UDP
HP-UX	HP ServiceGuard	Gigabit Ethernet	UDP
HP-UX	Veritas Cluster	Gigabit Ethernet	LLT
HP-UX	Veritas Cluster	Gigabit Ethernet	UDP
IBM AIX	Oracle Clusterware	Gigabit Ethernet (FDDI)	UDP
IBM AIX	HACMP	Gigabit Ethernet (FDDI)	UDP
Linux	Oracle Clusterware	Gigabit Ethernet	UDP
Microsoft Windows	Oracle Clusterware	Gigabit Ethernet	TCP
Sun Solaris	Oracle Clusterware	Gigabit Ethernet	UDP
Sun Solaris	Fujitsu Primecluster	Gigabit Ethernet	ICF
Sun Solaris	Sun Cluster	SCI Interconnect	RSM
Sun Solaris	Sun Cluster	Gigabit Ethernet	UDP
Sun Solaris	Veritas Cluster	Gigabit Ethernet	LLT
Sun Solaris	Veritas Cluster	Gigabit Ethernet	UDP

Ethernet choices for 11g RAC interconnect

If you were to decide on the best overall choice for a low-cost standard to use for the interconnection with your 11g RAC network, *Gigabit Ethernet* would be a good basic choice. Gigabit Ethernet operates in full duplex mode along with a data communications standard switch as the minimum supported configuration for the interconnect. We do not recommend the use of crossover cables, as these are not supported with RAC on Linux platforms.

We also don't recommend the use of crossover cables because in the event that a cluster node drops the remaining node, you will have to wait for the TCP to time out before the RAC cluster discovers that the lost node is not available, at which point, the cluster will remove the lost node from the cluster. The danger is what can happen during that period in time. The surviving node has a potential to lock and freeze during the wait for the timeout, or the cluster may experience a split-brain condition, thus becoming confused if the dead node restarts and attempts to join the cluster at a point when the cluster still thinks it is there.

Instead, you really want to use a switch between the nodes to allow the signal to be sent immediately if a node fails to respond. At this instant, the surviving node will check for a timeout and, if it happens, at least the node eviction will occur to fail the dead node, allowing it to rejoin (upon reboot) into a sane and clean cluster without any problems.

Alternatives to Gigabit Ethernet for the interconnect (Infiniband)

Another option to consider instead of Gigabit Ethernet is to use Remote Direct Memory Access for your private interconnect with 11g RAC. RDMA gives you a robust platform for the interconnect with 11g RAC, as it allows parallel and direct memory transfers to occur between RAC cluster nodes. One such example of available RDMA technology is that using Infiniband. **Infiniband** is the interconnect platform used in the Oracle HP Database Machine or Exadata platform for 11g RAC. One of the main benefits of Infiniband available with RDMA network technologies is its ability to avoid the overhead costs of Ethernet networks. It can achieve this as it bypasses the context and CPU processing operations required by Ethernet, thereby boosting network performance within the RAC clustered environment. Infiniband uses **Direct Access Programming Library (DAPL)**, along with the **Sockets Direct Protocol (SDP)**, instead of the TCP/IP-based network protocols used by Gigabit Ethernet to communicate with nodes in an 11g RAC cluster.

Interconnect choices for 11g RAC—how to decide?

With the exception of a requirement to choose the most cutting-edge and high-performance network platform for your private interconnects, we recommend that you go with a Gigabit Ethernet network running under the default **UDP (User Datagram)** protocol for a default Oracle RAC cluster environment. The reason for this is the lower initial cost, as well as the simpler deployment and administration of Gigabit Ethernet. This provides a better price per performance entry point than RDBMA networks such as Infiniband for most RAC environments with Oracle. In addition, with high-performance processors and adequately sized servers, Gigabit Ethernet provides options for redundancy within the interconnect. If you know for certain that you will be deploying Oracle RAC with massive data warehouses, such as a 900 TB data warehouse that qualifies as a **VLDB** or a complex Oracle Applications R12 E-Business Financials implementation, supporting thousands of users and millions of transactions, then we advocate going with the more expensive but vastly powerful Infiniband solution for your private interconnect with Oracle 11g RAC.

Redundancy for Ethernet interconnects with 11g RAC

One common design flaw that occurs in many RAC implementations is that of a single Ethernet network interface used for the private interconnect with Oracle RAC. The following is a simple diagram to illustrate this configuration for a two-node Oracle 11g RAC cluster:

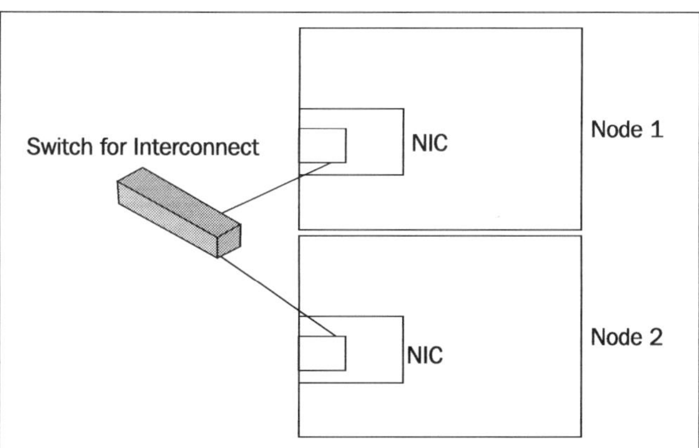

This two-node Oracle 11g RAC cluster poses a risk in that if the single interconnect Network Interface Card is ever lost due to a network or power failure, the Oracle 11g Clusterware will first try to reconnect for a short duration time of 60 seconds by default, before removing the node from the cluster. If this happens, the RAC master node will tell the Oracle 11g **Global Cache Service** (**GCS**) to perform recovery of the failed instance in the cluster.

However, if the entire private interconnect network fails for any reason such as the network switch experiencing a hardware or power failure, then every node in the RAC cluster will fail except for the master cluster node. The master cluster node will recover the failed instances in the 11g RAC cluster before attempting to provide services from a single node. As this is a *single point of failure* in the private network design caused by only having a single private network interface, we recommend that you implement multiple NICs and switches to avoid a single point of failure and loss in availability of the private interconnect with your Oracle RAC cluster. The following is an example of a fully redundant network architecture that protects against single points of failure:

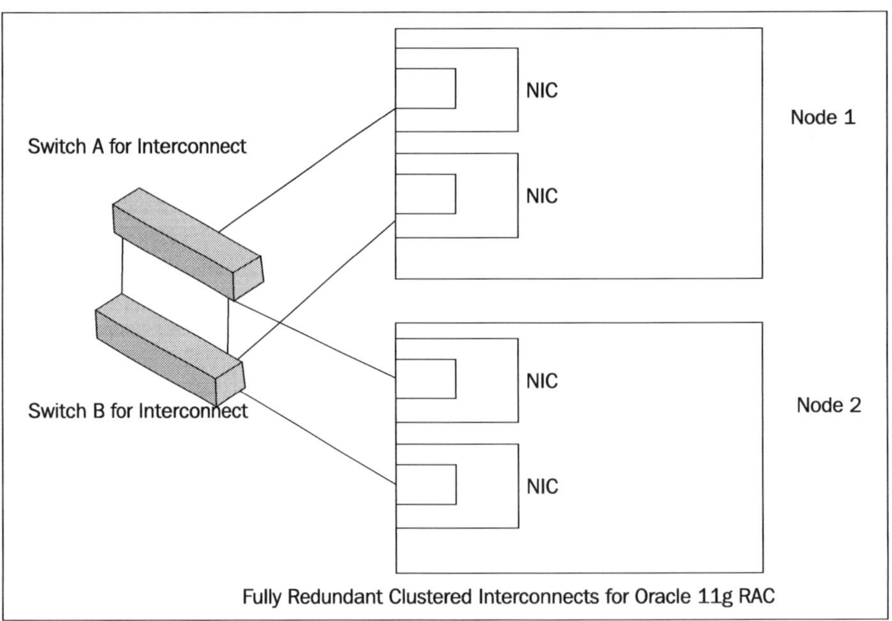

Fully Redundant Clustered Interconnects for Oracle 11g RAC

As the master node in the 11g RAC cluster must recover the failed nodes due to the loss of a single private network (interconnect), it will result in loss of services to the clustered applications. Because of this danger and risk, we recommend that you always implement redundant switches and NICs with your private interconnect design for Oracle RAC environments. The extra cost is negligible and loss of one NIC or a switch can and will happen sooner or later. Many clients have skimped on adding an extra low-cost Ethernet switch or Ethernet NIC to save a few bucks, and guess what, their single switch failed and their entire RAC cluster crashed and production outage occurred. With this in mind, you may need to set the Oracle 11g RAC database initialization parameter for `CLUSTER_INTERCONNECTS`. This parameter requires that you set details for the IP addresses that define the 11g RAC interconnect. The `CLUSTER_INTERCONNECTS` parameter distributes network traffic efficiently across one or more interfaces, which increases bandwidth available for 11g RAC interconnect traffic. However, it does not provide failover capability. As such, the failure of a single Ethernet network switch will still cause failure of the interconnect. For Oracle 11g RAC, the Oracle Cluster Registry (OCR) maintains details of the network interfaces held by the cluster. You can issue the `oifcfg` (Oracle Interface Configuration tool) command as shown next, to obtain the current details for the network interfaces:

```
[oracle@raclinux1 ~]$ oifcfg getif
eth0  192.168.203.0  global  public
eth1  10.10.10.0  global  cluster_interconnect
```

If you need to change these network interfaces for the private network (interconnect) with your 11g RAC environment, you can use the `oifcfg delif` command and then add the new IP addresses with the `oifcfg setif` command. The following is the complete listing of the `oifcfg` command with 11g RAC for your reference:

```
[oracle@raclinux1 ~]$ oifcfg

Name:
        oifcfg - Oracle Interface Configuration Tool.

Usage:  oifcfg iflist [-p [-n]]
        oifcfg setif {-node <nodename> | -global} {<if_
name>/<subnet>:<if_type>}...
        oifcfg getif [-node <nodename> | -global] [ -if <if_
name>[/<subnet>] [-type <if_type>] ]
        oifcfg delif [-node <nodename> | -global] [<if_name>[/<subnet>]]
        oifcfg [-help]
```

```
        <nodename> - name of the host, as known to a communications
network
        <if_name>  - name by which the interface is configured in the
system
        <subnet>   - subnet address of the interface
        <if_type>  - type of the interface { cluster_interconnect |
public | storage }
```

If you set the private network (interconnect) interfaces with the `CLUSTER_INTERCONNECTS` parameter, it will overwrite the value set in the OCR for 11g RAC.

If you want to find the exact value used by Oracle 11g RAC for the private network interconnect, you can query the `X$KSXPIA` table, which will display the network interface and associated address for the `NAME_KSXPIA` and `IP_KSXPIA` columns as shown in the examples listed here:

```
SQL> desc x$ksxpia
 Name                              Null?    Type
 -----------------------          --------  -------------
 ADDR                                        RAW(4)
 INDX                                        NUMBER
 INST_ID                                     NUMBER
 PUB_KSXPIA                                  VARCHAR2(10)
 PICKED_KSXPIA                               VARCHAR2(35)
 NAME_KSXPIA                                 VARCHAR2(15)
 IP_KSXPIA                                   VARCHAR2(16)

SQL> SELECT INST_ID, NAME_KSXPIA, IP_KSXPIA, PICKED_KSXPIA
  2  FROM X$KSXPIA;

   INST_ID          NAME_KSXPIA      IP_KSXPIA        PICKED_KSXPIA
 ----------       --------------- ---------------- ---------------
         1                 eth1    10.10.10.11            OCR
         1                 eth0    192.168.203.11         OCR
```

If the value for the `PICKED_KSXPIA` column from `X$KSXPIA` shows a value of OCR, this means that the setting for the network interface was configured from the OCR. On the other hand, if the value returned is CI, it indicates that the setting was derived from the `CLUSTER_INTERCONNECTS` parameter.

There is another way to verify the network settings to ensure that Oracle 11g RAC is using the correct network interfaces and UDP protocol with Gigabit Ethernet for the interconnect—simply issue the `oradebug ipc` command from within a `SQL*PLUS` session while logged into the database as a SYSDBA connection, as shown next:

```
SQL> oradebug setmypid
Statement processed.
SQL> oradebug ipc
Information written to trace file.
```

By default, `oradebug` writes the output of the session to a trace file that is defined by default via the `USER_DUMP_DEST` database initialization parameter for Oracle 11g.

You can find the network information in the resulting trace file from the `oradebug` session by opening the trace file with your favorite text editor (such as vi for Linux) and scrolling down to the heading to get information about network 0, which lists the IP address and protocol that Oracle 11g RAC uses for interconnect traffic. In the following example, you can see that Oracle is using the IP address of `10.10.10.11` with the network protocol UDP:

```
SSKGXPT 0xcc75e6c flags SSKGXPT_READPENDING     info for network 0
        socket no 7     IP 10.10.10.11  UDP 33566
        sflags SSKGXPT_UP
        info for network 1
        socket no 0     IP 0.0.0.0      UDP 0
        sflags SSKGXPT_DOWN
        active 0        actcnt 1
context timestamp 0x20
        no ports
```

What happens if the protocol is set incorrectly as reported by `oradebug`? Fortunately, you can resolve the issue by modifying the setting with the `make -f ins_rdbms` command`.mk ipc_udp ioracle` against the `$ORACLE_HOME/rdbms/lib` directory for the Oracle 11g software. For guidance on the exact steps to perform this task, you can refer to My Oracle Support (formerly Metalink) Note 278132.1 for the details.

> If you decide to change the network settings based on the steps provided by My Oracle Support Note 278132.1, be sure to first shut down all current Oracle RAC instances and relink each node one at a time.

My Oracle Support Notes 748946.1 and 787420.1 provide additional details about the interconnect for Oracle RAC. You can also query the `V$CLUSTER_INTERCONNECTS` and `V$CONFIGURED_INTERCONNECTS` dynamic performance views to correlate your settings for the interconnect.

For instance, further verifications can be provided, as shown in the following examples:

```
SQL> SELECT * FROM V$CLUSTER_INTERCONNECTS;

NAME            IP_ADDRESS       IS_ SOURCE
--------------- ---------------- --- -------------------------------
eth1            10.10.10.11      NO  Oracle Cluster Repository

SQL> SELECT * FROM V$CONFIGURED_INTERCONNECTS;

NAME            IP_ADDRESS       IS_ SOURCE
--------------- ---------------- --- -------------------------------
eth1            10.10.10.11      NO  Oracle Cluster Repository
eth0            192.168.203.11   YES Oracle Cluster Repository
```

The difference between these two views for cluster interconnects is that `V$CONFIGURED_INTERCONNECTS` shows only currently implemented cluster interconnects, whereas `V$CLUSTER_INTERCONNECTS` shows optional details for the interconnect.

Another recommendation when using Gigabit Ethernet with UDP would be to modify the value for the **Maximum Transmission Unit (MTU)** so that Jumbo Frames can be used to allow larger-sized packets of data to be able to move across the interconnect. You can set this on a temporary basis by using the `ifconfig` command for Linux or UNIX. For example:

```
[root@raclinux1 ~]# ifconfig eth1 mtu 9000 up
```

To make the setting permanent for MTU with your Linux environment and allow for Jumbo Frames, you need to make an entry of `MTU=9000` in the `/etc/sysconfig/network-scripts/ifcfg-eth1` file. We advise that you exercise caution when making these changes and that you first perform testing with the default network values for the interconnect before changing anything.

Network bonding (NIC teaming)

In order to implement fully redundant network interfaces for the private network (interconnect) for Oracle RAC, you will need to set up your network interfaces in what is called bonding or network software teaming. **Network teaming or bonding** requires you to configure the network driver software to provide dual network interfaces from a single IP address. The net result is failover capability in that one network card functions to route the network traffic while the other remains idle until the primary interface fails. Interconnect traffic is routed by the second card if the primary ever fails. At the software network driver level, this operates transparently without any input from the Oracle database layer. As such, the network driver software maps the hardware MAC address for the card and the network IP address remains the same. So, this operation behaves fluidly without any interruption to the Oracle RAC software. For network bonding to function correctly, you must configure your network switches for your RAC environment to use what is called **Switch Spanning**, in which redundancy is provided between the interconnect switches as shown in the last diagram of the previous section. Switch spanning requires you to implement the network switch protocol for **Spanning Tree Protocol** (**STP**). Furthermore, you need to make sure that your network switches support the 802.3ad dynamic mode for your network cards that are set up in a bonding configuration to be able to fail over correctly.

My Oracle Support Note 298891.1 has additional tips for Linux network teaming for RAC environments.

Make sure you specify the correct entries in your `/etc/modules.conf` file for Linux to enable network bonding for your RAC configuration. These should contain details on the network interfaces that will be used as discussed in the My Oracle Support reference note that we just saw.

Now that we have covered design considerations for network architecture, let's move on to discuss the best approach towards storage layouts for 11g RAC.

Storage architecture for Oracle 11g RAC

Oracle 11g RAC cluster nodes share the same storage array that contains the 11g RAC database. As such, the sizing and choice of the storage is of critical importance for design and implementation of your RAC configuration. By understanding disk I/O with respect to how RAC uses storage disks, you will be able to optimize your design so that performance is optimized from the ground up, rather than reacting to a poor design, which will be more difficult to resolve later.

RAID configurations for Oracle 11g RAC

Oracle RAC performance and availability is greatly affected by the storage subsystem layer of the entire system architecture. As such, your choice of **RAID** (**Redundant Array of Inexpensive Disks**) will determine a great deal of database and application performance, as well as how critical tasks such as backup, recovery, and disaster recovery processes are affected.

RAID combines multiple physical hard disks into a single logical unit by using vendor-based hardware or software.

For example, Sun Microsystems manufactures storage arrays that implement various RAID configurations such as the Sun StorageTek 9990V System (`http://www.sun.com/storage/products.jsp`), which provides enterprise-class-level storage management. In addition, vendors such as Symantec implement RAID at software level with products such as the Veritas Storage Foundation for Oracle RAC (`http://www.symantec.com/business/storage-foundation-for-oracle-rac`), which is aimed at volume management of RAID devices specifically for Oracle RAC environments.

Hardware solutions often have designs that appear to the attached system as a single hard drive that the host operating system views as a single item. For example, you might configure a 100 TB RAID 5 array using about a hundred 500 GB hard drives in hardware RAID, and the operating system would simply be presented with a single 100 TB volume. Software solutions are typically implemented at the operating-system level and present the RAID drive as a single volume to applications running upon the operating system.

There are three key concepts in RAID:

- **Mirroring**: A data copy of a disk or clone to more than one disk
- **Stripping**: A mechanism for splitting data across more than one disk
- **Error correction**: A parity configuration that maintains a copy of disk data to support problem detection and correction

Based on your specific data center requirements and application needs, your choice of RAID implementation will vary. The goal of RAID is to improve reliability and availability of data to ensure that critical data is always available with no data loss (that is a database of financial loan applications), or merely to improve the access speed to files (that is for a system that delivers real-time stock quotes to brokers and financial traders on the floor of the New York Stock Exchange).

The RAID configuration will affect reliability and performance in different ways. For instance, the problem with using more disks is that more than likely there will be one or more that will fail eventually. By using a format (listed next) that encompasses error checking, the total system can be made more reliable with the ability to recover and repair disk failures.

- RAID 1 or disk array mirroring can speed up data reads as the database system can read different data from both disks. However, it has slow performance on writes if the configuration requires both disks to acknowledge that the data has been correctly written.
- RAID 0, or striping is often the choice for disk performance since it allows sequences of data to read simultaneously from multiple disks.
- RAID 5 (parity) is efficient on reads, but slow write performance may impact your Oracle applications that require heavy write performance such as OLTP applications. However, for data warehouse environments that perform mostly data reads for Oracle, RAID 5 can be a viable choice.

As such, RAID implementation design and choice is as much an art as a science and requires understanding the requirements of the entire application and database system to make the best choice. Disk arrays today typically provide the facility to select the appropriate RAID configuration. Below are the various RAID configurations:

- RAID 0 (Striped disks)
- RAID 1 (Mirrored disks)
- RAID 2 (Hamming code parity)
- RAID 3 (Striped set with dedicated parity)
- RAID 4 (Block-level parity)
- RAID 5 (Striped disks with parity)
- RAID 6 (Striped disks with dual parity)
- RAID 10 (Or 1+0, uses both striping and mirroring)

Since RAID 2, 3, 4, and 6 are rarely if ever used in Oracle data center environments, we will not discuss these configurations.

RAID 0 (striping)

RAID 0 distributes data across several disks, which provides a high level of performance. The downside to a pure RAID 0 striped disk array configuration is that if any one disk fails then all of the data on the array will be lost because there is neither parity nor mirroring. Striped RAID 0 configurations provide improved performance and additional storage but no redundancy or fault tolerance. Any single disk failure will destroy the array thereby having greater consequences for disks in the array. A single disk failure destroys the entire array because when data is written to a RAID 0 drive, the data is broken into fragments. The number of fragments is governed by the number of disks in the array. The fragments are written to their respective disks simultaneously on the same sector. This allows smaller sections of the entire chunk of data to be read off the drive in parallel, increasing bandwidth. RAID 0 does not implement error checking, so any error is unrecoverable. More disks in the array means higher bandwidth, but greater risk of data loss.

RAID 1 (mirroring)

RAID 1 mirrors the contents of the disks that are in essence clones or carbon copies of each other. As such, the content of each disk in the array is identical to that of every other disk in the array. Mirrored RAID 1 configurations provide you with fault tolerance from disk errors and failure of all but one of the drives in the array. In addition, increased read performance is possible as well when using a multithreaded operating system such as UNIX or LINUX that supports split seeks along with a very small performance reduction when writing. Arrays that use RAID 1 configurations may continue to operate so long as one disk drive in the disk array is functional. If you decide to go with a RAID implementation for your RAC environment, then we suggest that you deploy it with a separate controller for each disk (duplexing) to avoid single point of failure issues and for redundancy benefits.

RAID 5 (striped with parity)

RAID 5 combines at least three or more disks in such a way that it protects your data against the loss of any single disk. It uses a data algorithm to stripe data across the disk array with a parity factor. This provides data protection as well as lowered cost of deployment, as storage requirements for RAID 5 require fewer disks to implement than are used with RAID 0 (Mirroring) or RAID 10 (RAID 0+1) configurations.

A striped set with distributed parity or interleaved parity requires all drives except for one to be present in order to operate. In the event of a disk drive failure, the disk will require replacement. However, the array will not be completely lost by a single drive failure. With a disk drive failure, subsequent reads will be calculated from the distributed parity so that the failure is masked from the user. If a second drive fails, the array will have data loss and will be vulnerable until the data that was on the failed drive is rebuilt onto a replacement drive. Reduced performance will result in the event of a single drive failure until the failed drive has been replaced in the array.

RAID 10 (striped mirrors)

RAID 10 (or 1+0) uses both striping and mirroring. 01 or 0+1 is sometimes distinguished from 10 or 1+0. A striped set of mirrored subsets and a mirrored set of striped subsets are both valid, but are distinct configurations.

Differences between RAID 10 and RAID 0+1

A **RAID 0+1** (also called **RAID 01**) is a RAID level used for both replicating and sharing data among disks. A **RAID 1+0**, sometimes called **RAID 1&0** or **RAID 10**, is similar to a RAID 0+1 with the exception that the RAID levels used are reversed—RAID 10 is a stripe of mirrors.

The difference between RAID 0+1 and RAID 1+0 is the location of each RAID system—RAID 0+1 is a mirror of stripes. The size of a RAID 0+1 array can be calculated as follows where n is the number of drives (which must be an even number) and c is the capacity of the smallest drive in the array:

$$Size = (n \times c) \div 2$$

The chief difference between RAID 0+1 and RAID 1+0 (RAID 10) is how the striping and mirrors are configured. With RAID 0+1, the array disks are first mirrored (RAID 0) and then striped (RAID 1) chunks are distributed across the disks. In contrast, RAID 1+0 configurations use two or more drives mirrored together. Finally, the mirrored disks in the array are striped together. So, which one is better—RAID 0+1 or RAID 10?

In either case, RAID 0+1 or RAID 10, losing a single disk drive in the array does not result in failure of the RAID system. The difference comes from whether or not the loss of a second drive from the system will result in the failure of the whole disk array system. In RAID 0+1, you would have to lose one drive from each disk set to result in the failure of the whole disk array.

Third-party RAID implementations

Many configurations other than these RAID levels are possible from third-party vendors. These hardware and software vendors have created their own non-standard configurations with the goal of resolving deficiencies in the basic RAID layouts discussed earlier. These proprietary formats have benefits that may resolve issues unique to your storage environment for Oracle RAC implementation. The following vendors provide such configurations for storage RAID design:

- EMC Corporation at one point in time provided their proprietary RAID 5 as an alternative to RAID 5 for their EMC Symmetrix SAN arrays. However, the latest generation of EMC **Symmetric storage area networks (SAN)**, the EMC DMX, no longer supports RAIDs.
- Network Appliance's NetAPP Data ONTAP uses **RAID-DP** (also known as "double", "dual", or "diagonal" parity), as a form of RAID 6. However, unlike many RAID 6 implementations, it does not use distributed parity as in RAID 5. Instead, two unique parity disks with separate parity calculations are used. This is a modification of RAID 4 with an extra parity disk.

Linux MD RAID 10 (RAID10) implements a general RAID driver that defaults to standard RAID 1+0 configuration with four disk drives, yet it can also have any number of drives in the storage array. MD RAID10 can be striped and mirrored with only two drives with the f2 layout that uses mirroring with striped reads. Normal Linux-based RAID 1 configurations do not stripe reads, but can read these in parallel.

When it comes down to performance and capacity growth, the Hewlett Packard EVA series arrays implement a form of RAID called vRAID—vRAID-0, vRAID-1, vRAID-5, and vRAID-6. This allows drives to be placed in groups—called Disk Groups—that form a pool of data blocks on top of which the RAID level is implemented. As such any of these Disk Groups may have "virtual disks" or LUNs of any vRAID type, including mixing vRAID types in the same Disk Group. These vRAID levels are more closely aligned to Nested RAID levels. Drives in an EVA array may be added on an ad hoc basis to an existing Disk Group. Existing virtual disk data is then redistributed evenly over all the drives, thus allowing for dynamic performance.

IBM AIX LPAR disk volume management for RAID

The IBM AIX platform provides volume management for RAID configurations by using a logical partitioning system called LPAR.

Advanced configuration details on the LPAR for AIX platform can be obtained from IBM Redbooks, *LPAR Configuration and Management*, available online at the following websites:

- `http://www-03.ibm.com/systems/i/os/`
- `http://www.redbooks.ibm.com/`

One nice feature of LPAR management with IBM AIX platform is the pSeries of enterprise IBM servers. The Linux operating system can be run in conjunction with the AIX operating system.

Linux volume management for RAID configuration

Linux provides you with the ability to set up RAID configurations at the operating system layer. Further details can be obtained online at `http://www.redhat.com/docs/manuals/linux/RHL-7.2-Manual/custom-guide/software-raid.html`.

In addition, if you are using Oracle Enterprise Linux instead of Red Hat Linux, there is a useful My Oracle Support Note 759260.1. It will show you, step by step, how to use the OEL (Oracle Enterprise Linux) command `mdadm`, to configure your disks and partitions for RAID 1 and other configurations. For instance, you will need to format and partition the Linux disk volumes using the `fdisk` utility.

Storage protocols for RAC

As the database architect responsible for designing the environment for Oracle RAC, you should understand that storage layout is one of the most important considerations to make for the best performance and availability factors within the system architecture. If you use the wrong storage protocol for a large RAC ecosystem, then performance issues will occur within your overall data center environment. Therefore, it is critical to have a solid understanding of storage protocols such as **Small Computer System Interface** (**SCSI**), **Fibre Channel** (**FC**), and **Internet Small Computer System Interface** (**iSCSI**) that may impact your Oracle RAC setup and configuration.

You will need to evaluate and implement these as part of your RAC configuration for Oracle 11g. The chapter will discuss the merits and weaknesses of these storage protocols for you to be able to choose the correct configuration for RAC based on your business requirements. There are additional storage protocols that exist; however, these are not viable or supported for RAC implementations. As such, the chapter will focus on the three mentioned storage protocols.

SCSI

The **SCSI** protocol for storage networks is the oldest known storage protocol and has been proven useful time and again for storage area networks. It is supported for RAC environments; however, it lacks the robust performance of the Fibre Channel or iSCSI protocols. SCSI uses a storage protocol method for data transfers across a bus interface between devices. It uses a circular process that begins and ends at the same layer. Beginning with the first layer, all of the additional layers of the SCSI protocol must be executed first, before any data transfer can take place between SCSI devices. In addition, the layers of the SCSI protocol must be completed after the data transfer is complete. For SCSI, we have multiple protocol layers that compose SCSI bus phases. These phases are the following:

- `BUS FREE` indicates point to point without bus interfaces
- `ARBITRATION` references the manner in which communication is performed
- `SELECTION` provides the algorithm for data transfers
- `MESSAGE OUT` indicates the signal transfer from source to target
- `COMMAND OUT` references the output from SCSI interface
- `DATA OUT/IN` is the indicator for I/O processing
- `STATUS IN` references that the SCSI protocol has received update
- `MESSAGE IN` references the receipt of data on target from the source
- `RESELECTION` is an indicator for new route of data transfer

The SCSI bus operates in a single phase at any given time.

Modern SCSI transport protocols use what is called an automated process of "discovery" to identify and keep track of device IDs. The SSA initiates "walk the loop", to locate existing devices and assign each identified SCSI device with a 7-bit "hop-count" value.

In contrast to SCSI, Fibre Channel FC-AL initiators use the **LIP (Loop Initialization Protocol)** to poll each device port in a Fibre Channel-based storage array for a **WWN (World Wide Name)**. The discovery processes take place during power-on initialization times and also if the bus topology changes later, such as when an extra device is added to the SCSI-based array.

For the parallel SCSI bus, a device such as a host adapter or a disk drive will be uniquely identified by an **SCSI ID**. This SCSI ID can be a number in the range of 0-7 on a narrow bus and can exist in the range of 0–15 on a wide bus SCSI configuration.

The SCSI target device (also known as a *physical unit*) is often split up into smaller logical units. For example, a typical **Storage Array Network (SAN)** may appear as a single SCSI device but contain dozens of individual disk drives. All of these drives are labeled as individual logical units, which are seen by the host and operating system as virtual disk devices.

Fibre Channel

The **Fibre Channel** is a high-performance storage protocol that provides three different topologies. It works via port layouts connected together in different configurations. The Fibre Channel uses ports in a network configuration, called fabric architecture, to communicate between storage devices and servers. In a Fibre Channel configuration, a port is often mapped to a device such as a disk, **Host Bus Adapter (HBA)**, or to a **Fibre Channel switch**.

For Fibre Channel architectures, we have the following topologies:

- Point-to-Point (FC-P2P)
- Fibre Channel Arbitrated Loop (FC-AL)
- Fibre Channel Switched Fabric (FC-SW)

Point-to-Point (FC-P2P)

Point-to-Point topology for Fibre Channel consists of two devices that are connected back-to-back. While this is the simplest topology to set up and manage, it is the least powerful and suffers from limited connectivity issues within a storage fabric architecture.

Fibre Channel Arbitrated Loop (FC-AL)

Fibre Channel Arbitrated Loop for fibre channel-based Storage Area Networks provides all devices in a loop or ring layout that appears with token ring-based networks. One weakness of this topology is that whenever devices are added to or removed from the loop, all activity on the loop will be interrupted as a result. As such, failure of any single device causes a breakdown in the topology. Fibre Channel hubs can be implemented to connect multiple devices together and may help to bypass failed ports in the event of such an issue. A loop may also be formed by cabling each port alongside each other to the next. A minimal loop contains only two ports in an FC-AL configuration. However, FC-AL differs from **Fibre Channel Point-to-Point (FC-P2P)** in terms of the protocol implementation for storage area networks. In addition, multiple pairs of ports are able to communicate simultaneously in a loop.

Fibre Channel Switched Fabric (FC-SW)

Fibre Channel Switched Fabric configurations are connected to a Fibre Channel switch with a similar layout to that used by modern Ethernet implementations.

Which Fibre Channel topology is best?

If you decide to use Fibre Channel for your storage protocol with RAC, we recommend that you use the Fibre Channel Switched Fabric for your storage topology.

- With FC-SW, the switches manage the state of the fabric, thereby providing you with optimized interconnections between the SAN or NAS and the nodes of your RAC cluster.
- With FC-SW, traffic between ports flows through the switches only, thereby reducing latency in the storage array.
- The FC-SW topology gives you added redundancy and resilience at the storage layer of your RAC configuration, in that any failure of a port can be isolated and most likely will not affect the operation of other ports.

Fibre Channel routers operate up to FC4 level and Fibre Channel switches up to FC2, with hubs only on FC0. Fibre Channel products are available at speeds between 1 Gbps and 20 Gbps.

Now let's discuss the details of how Fibre Channel ports behave in terms of network and storage configurations for Oracle RAC environments.

Fibre Channel Ports

Fibre Channel Ports categorize various FC ports into FC Node Ports and generic-based Node Ports. This means that for a Fibre Channel array or network device, we have Fibre Channel ports that interface with both Fibre Channel nodes and generic-based ports.

Fibre Channel Generic Node Ports

Fibre Channel Generic Node Ports have the following types:

- **N_port**: This is a port on the node of a server host or storage area network device. The N_port is used with either FC-P2P or FC-SW topologies and is also referred to as a Node Port.

- **NL_port**: This is a port on the node that is used with FC-AL topology configurations for Fibre Channel. The NL_port is also referred to as a Node Loop Port.
- **F_port**: This is a port on the fabric switch that connects to a node point-to-point such as connecting to an N port. The F port is also referred to as a Fabric Port. One key factor of the F port is that it is not loop capable.
- **FL_port**: This is a port on the fabric switch that connects to an FC-AL loop or NL port. The FL_port is also referred to as a Fabric Loop Port.
- **E_port**: This is a port connection between two Fibre Channel switches. The E_ports are also referred to as Expansion Ports. Whenever E_ports between two fabric switches formulate a link, the link is called an *Inter-Switch Link* (*ISL*).
- **EX_port**: This is the connection between a Fibre Channel-based router and a Fibre Channel switch.
- **TE_port**: This port is an extended Inter-Switch Link. The TE_port provides both standard E_port functions as well as routing capabilities for multiple Virtual SANs (VSANs). **TE_ports** are also referred to as **Trunking E_ports**.

In addition to FC node ports, you have a choice of generic channel-based ports with Fibre Channel as follows:

- **Auto or auto-sensing ports**: These ports are found in vendor fabric switches such as Cisco switches. Auto ports can become E_port, TE_port, F_port, or FL_port as needed on the fly.
- **Fx_ports**: These ports are generic ports that can become F_ports when linked to an N_port, or an FL_port when linked to an NL_port.
- **G_ports**: These are generic ports on a fabric switch that operate either as an E_port or an F_port. G ports are often used with Brocade and McData switches.
- **L_ports**: These ports are used for any arbitrated loop port—either NL_port or FL_port. These are also called Loop Ports.
- **U_ports**: These ports refer to arbitrated ports. They are also called Universal Ports and found only with Brocade switches.

iSCSI

The **iSCSI** storage protocol is an **Internet Protocol (IP)**-based storage networking standard for linking data storage networks together. It functions by communication of SCSI commands over IP-based networks. The beauty of this protocol is that it allows for high-speed data transfer over networks across long distances. iSCSI can also be used to send data over both **Local Area Networks** (**LANs**) and **Wide Area Networks** (**WANs**), as well as across the Internet, for data storage. The iSCSI protocol allows iSCSI clients, called *initiators*, to send SCSI commands in the form of **Command Descriptor Block** (**CDB**) transactions to SCSI storage devices called *targets*, across remote servers. It is popular as it costs less to implement and manage compared to Fibre Channel . So, it is used by multiple vendors and is a supported protocol for Oracle 11g RAC configurations. Furthermore, iSCSI does not require any special-purpose cabling, which is mandatory in case of Fibre Channel, and it can operate over long distances using the existing network infrastructure.

The iSCSI storage protocol is a promising technology for high-performance storage protocols with Oracle RAC. In a recent study, Network Appliance conducted testing for throughput between NFS, iSCSI, and FC protocols with Oracle RAC. The end result showed that iSCSI had the best overall price-to-performance value of the three storage protocols based on the test results. Details of this study can be found online at `http://media.netapp.com/documents/tr-3700.pdf`.

My Oracle Support Note 371434.1 provides a nice overview of the steps required to configure **Network-Attached Storage** (**NAS**) for usage with the OpenFiler iSCSI and Oracle 11g RAC.

Which storage protocol is best for RAC?

The best storage protocol for RAC is dependent on your business requirements and corporate IT strategy. For best-in-breed performance and value, it is advisable to use iSCSI or Fibre Channel as your storage protocol of choice with RAC deployments. The iSCSI protocol gives you a similar performance to Fibre Channel without the need for an expensive Storage Area Network.

Asynchronous I/O versus Direct I/O for Oracle 11g RAC

Asynchronous I/O gives Oracle the ability to simultaneously perform multiple I/O requests for a single system call without the need to wait for each request to complete, thereby potentially increasing the performance for the Oracle log writer (**LGWR**) and database writer (**DBWR**) processes within Oracle 11g RAC environments. LGWR is one of the key Oracle background processes that flushes out the online redo log buffers by writing to the online redo log files. DBWR is an Oracle background process that writes data from the Oracle SGA to the Oracle database file when the Oracle SGA buffer cache fills up. In most cases, asynchronous I/O will most likely benefit performance for RAC environments. However, testing is required to ensure that the payoff is matched for enabling async I/O within your RAC configuration for Oracle 11g. My Oracle Support (formerly Metalink) Note 279069.1 provides the list of Linux platforms that are compatible for async I/O with Oracle 11g RAC. Details for the configuration of asynchronous I/O with 10g and earlier versions of Oracle are given by My Oracle Support (formerly Metalink) note 225751.1.

For Oracle 11g, async I/O is enabled by default on Linux. You can use the following command to configure async I/O for releases prior to 10g R2 with RAC on Linux:

```
alter system set filesystemio_options=async scope=spfile;
```

To verify the status for async I/O with Linux, you need to look at the `/proc/slabinfo` file for Linux to ensure that async I/O has been enabled:

```
[root@raclinux1 network-scripts]# cat /proc/slabinfo|grep kio
kioctx              50     75    256    15     1 : tunables  120   60
0 : slabdata      5      5      0
kiocb                0      0    128    31     1 : tunables  120   60
0 : slabdata      0      0      0
```

In this example, for the SLAB allocator, there are three different caches involved. SLAB caches are a special type of memory pool in the Linux kernel used for adding and removing objects such as data structures of the same size. SLAB is a cache used by Oracle and Linux for commonly used objects where the kernel does not have to reallocate and initialize the object each time it is reused. The SLAB allocation scheme prevents memory fragmentation and also prevents the kernel from spending too much time on memory management. The `kioctx` and `kiocb` refer to Async I/O data structures, which are defined in the `aio.h` header file. If these show a non-zero value, this means that asynchronous I/O has been enabled. With the source code loaded, you can review it in the file for `aio.h`. This file is located under `/usr/src/linux-<version>/include/linux/aio.h` for Linux platforms. The data structures, `kioctx` and `kiocb`, are used by the operating system with Oracle to track I/O requests, and are allocated as part of the `init_aio_setup()` call in `aio.c`.

As shown in the example, these values indicate that async I/O is in use as these buffers are being allocated for Oracle 11g RAC. The default size of asynchronous I/O is set to 131072 blocks. For OLTP systems, this size is usually sufficient. However, for data warehouse systems, we recommend a larger setting for asynchronous I/O such as 1 MB or larger. The Linux kernel parameter, `fs.aio-max-size`, can be modified to adjust values of asynchronous I/O operations for Oracle 11g and Linux.

Direct I/O differs from asynchronous I/O in terms of configuration in that it is set up from Oracle and not at the filesystem operating system level. It can be used either independently from asynchronous I/O or to complement asynchronous I/O performance. The benefit of using direct I/O for Oracle RAC is that it avoids filesystem buffering issues. To enable direct I/O on Linux, you need to set the Oracle parameter `FILESYSTEMIO_OPTIONS` to `DIRECTIO`. Only by testing will you know for sure whether or not direct I/O will provide you with actual benefits for Oracle RAC performance. In some cases it will, whereas in other cases performance may actually be lower than expected. For most cases, you should first take the defaults of using asynchronous I/O and test performance without using direct I/O before worrying about using direct I/O.

Oracle 11g RAC components

In addition to the many hardware, network, and storage components that drive the foundation of Oracle 11g RAC, we have the complex software called **Clusterware** that lies at the heart of the Oracle RAC architecture. Oracle 11g RAC consists of these physical devices along with the Clusterware and **Automatic Storage Management** (**ASM**) software. ASM provides the mechanism for managing storage within RAC environments and uses both a special type of instance called an ASM instance and special disk volume management in the form of ASM disks and ASM diskgroups. Clusterware refers to the Oracle software layer that performs the operational tasks within the Oracle-clustered environment for RAC. In summary, the Clusterware consists of the following components for Oracle 11g RAC:

- Voting Disk(s)
- Oracle Clusterware Registry (OCR)
- Background processes that manage clusterwide operations and provide functionality for Oracle 11g R1 and 11g R2 RAC

In addition to the Oracle 11g Clusterware, you should understand how the Oracle 11g RAC public and private networks behave. We will touch upon these later in the chapter, but let's first discuss the components of the Oracle 11g Clusterware for RAC environments.

Voting Disk

The **Voting Disk** provides cluster quorum administration within an Oracle 11g RAC environment and is configured on shared storage for the Oracle 11g RAC environment. You may also refer to *Oracle Clusterware Installation Guide 11g Release 1 (11.1)* for Linux and *Oracle Clusterware Administration and Deployment Guide 11g Release 1 (11.1)* for additional reference materials available on the Oracle Technology Network (`http://otn.oracle.com`).

Oracle Cluster Registry

The Oracle Cluster Registry provides housekeeping tasks for maintenance of the Oracle 11g RAC Clusterware infrastructure.

Oracle 11g R1 RAC background processes

Oracle 11g RAC contains many unique background processes that perform clusterwide operational tasks and management. The majority of these background processes are integrated into the Oracle 11g Clusterware, which is special software used by Oracle to manage cluster operations for RAC environments. The Oracle 11g R1 RAC processes are listed in next sections.

ACMS Atomic Controlfile to Memory Service

In an Oracle 11g RAC environment, the **Atomic Controlfile to Memory Service** (**ACMS**) is an agent that helps to ensure that distributed SGA memory updates are either globally committed on success or globally aborted if a failure occurs.

GTX0-j Global Transaction Process

The **GTX0-j** Global Transaction Process provides transparent support for XA global transactions in Oracle 11g RAC environments. Oracle 11g RAC database autotunes the number of these processes based on workload received for these XA global transactions.

LMON Global Enqueue Service Monitor

The **LMON** Global Enqueue Service Monitor is an Oracle RAC background process that monitors the status for all global enqueues and resources across the cluster and is also responsible for global enqueue recovery operations.

LMD Global Enqueue Service Daemon

The **LMD** Global Enqueue Service Daemon manages the incoming remote resource requests within each Oracle 11g RAC instance.

LMS Global Cache Service Process

The **LMS** Global Cache Service Process maintains records for the data file status within an Oracle 11g RAC cluster and also for each cached block. It performs these tasks by recording information into the **Global Resource Directory** (**GRD**). The LMS process also controls the flow of messages to remote instances, manages global data block access, and transmits block images between the buffer caches of different instances. This processing by LMS within Oracle RAC is a key component of Oracle RAC Cache Fusion.

LCK0 Instance Enqueue Process

The **LCK0** Instance Enqueue Process manages non-cache fusion requests for resources such as library and row cache requests within Oracle 11g RAC environments.

RMSn Oracle RAC Management Processes

The **RMSn** Oracle RAC Management Processes perform auxiliary management tasks for the Oracle 11g RAC environment. These tasks include the creation of resources for Oracle RAC whenever new instances are added to the cluster.

RSMN Remote Slave Monitor

The **RSMN** Remote Slave Monitor is responsible for managing background slave process creation and communication on remote instances. These background slave processes perform tasks on behalf of a coordinating process running in another instance.

Shared storage must be accessible by all nodes in the Oracle RAC cluster or failures will cause node reboots and additional problems. Local storage per cluster node contains the Oracle 11g software binaries for each instance as well as the Cluster home directory information (`CRS_HOME`). The voting disks must be on shared accessible storage as well as the OCR files. The voting file and OCR files can either be stored on raw devices or a clustered filesystem supported by Oracle RAC such as OCFS, Sun Cluster, or Veritas Cluster Filesystem prior to Oracle 11g R2 RAC versions. As of 11g R2 RAC, you can now store the voting disk files and OCR on these configurations or, even better, these can now be stored and managed by ASM disks.

The following diagram highlights the key layout of a typical Oracle 11g RAC cluster on shared storage:

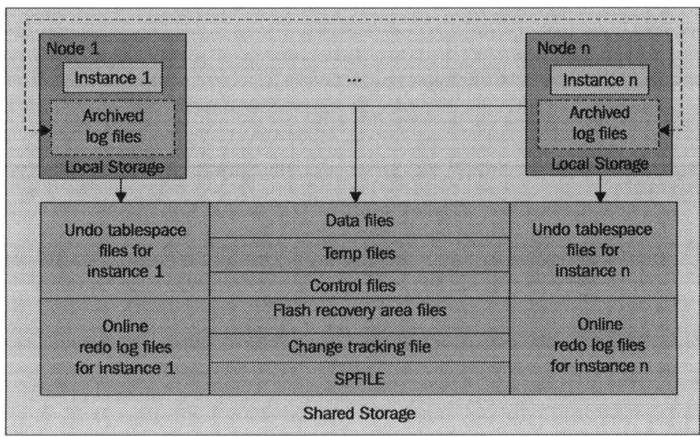

Here on the shared storage, we have the 11g RAC database files including the RAC database data files, temp files, control files, and SPfile, as along with a flash recovery area that is stored in either shared raw devices, clustered filesystem, or ASM disks. Each RAC instance has its own undo tablespace and set of online redo logs. Before Oracle 10g, archived log files presented a challenge to storing in ASM and had to be kept on a shared, cooked, and clustered filesystem. Now with 11g, the archived log files can be stored on ASM disks.

Oracle 11g R2 RAC background processes

Oracle 11g R2 RAC introduced several new clusterware background processes. Let's now take a closer look.

Grid Plug and Play

The **Grid Plug and Play** (**GPnP**) process provides access to the Grid Plug and Play profile. It coordinates updates to the profile for nodes in the cluster, to ensure all nodes have the most current profile available within the RAC configuration.

Grid Interprocess Communication

The **Grid Interprocess Communication (GIPC)** is a helper daemon process for the communications infrastructure. As of 11g R2, it has no real function; however, it will be used in later releases.

Multicast Domain Name Service

The **Multicast Domain Name Service** (**mDNS**) allows for DNS requests. The mDNS process is a background process on Linux and UNIX, and runs as a service on Windows.

Oracle Grid Naming Service

The **Oracle Grid Naming Service** (**GNS**) functions as a gateway between the cluster mDNS and external DNS servers. The GNS process performs the name resolution within Oracle Cluster Registry architecture for Oracle 11g RAC.

The Oracle Cluster Registry provides critical support for Oracle 11g Clusterware operations. The Oracle 11g Clusterware uses the OCR to store and manage information about the cluster, including details on the status and configuration of RAC databases, listeners, and services. The OCR uses a file-based repository to store configuration information in a series of key-value pairs, using a directory tree-like structure.

The following diagram illustrates the relationship between the OCR and shared storage subsystem for Oracle 11g RAC:

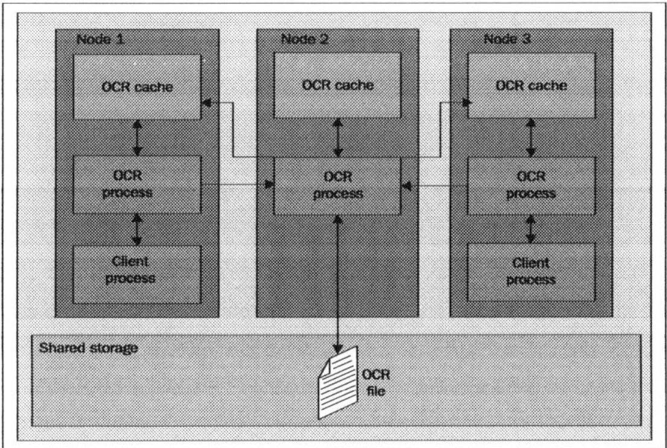

OCR stores its repository data on flat files in a tree structure on shared storage. For each node in an Oracle 11g RAC cluster, there is also an OCR cache.

In subsequent chapters, you will be provided with a detailed analysis on how to administer and maintain your Oracle 11g RAC Clusterware to take advantage of optimal performance and availability.

How RAC differs from Oracle 11g single-instance implementations

The chief difference between Oracle RAC and single-instance implementations can be explained with the help of the following diagram:

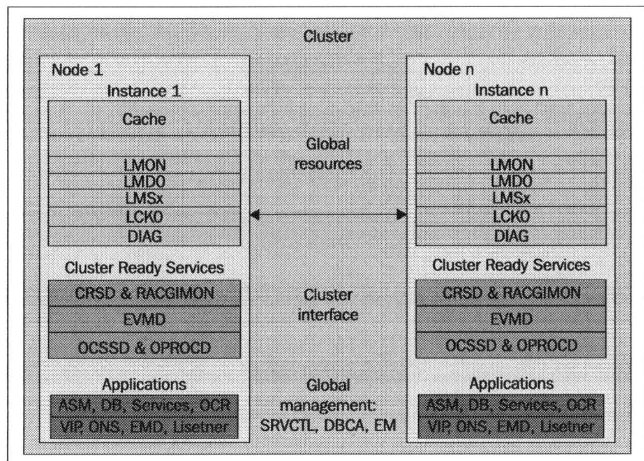

As you can see here and as per the previous discussion of the background processes and the Oracle 11g RAC Clusterware, many of these processes are unique to an RAC environment and do not exist in a single-instance Oracle 11g environment. Let's now examine a single non-RAC configuration of Oracle 11g in contrast:

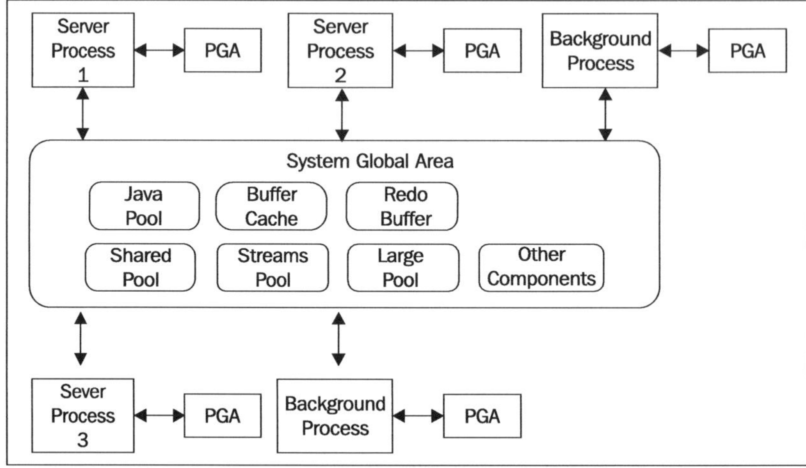

RAC has multiple instances of the Oracle 11g database software, indicative of the fact that each cluster node will have an instance of Oracle 11g with its very own SGA memory structures and background processes. RAC has its own set of background processes associated with the Clusterware that do not exist with a single-instance non-RAC Oracle 11g environment. Oracle 11g RAC has evolved over the past decade from the parallel cluster architecture that existed in Oracle 7 Parallel Server.

New ASM features and RAC

There are many new features in Oracle 11g RAC that are introduced with ASM enhancements. Many of these involve ASM configuration.

New SYSASM privilege for Oracle 11g R1 ASM

Introduced in Oracle 11g R1, the SYSASM privilege allows you to separate the database operating system credentials from ASM credentials. This can be useful in today's era of auditing controls and compliance to fulfill requirements for Sarbanes Oxley (SOX), as well as to divide storage support between system administrators and DBA staff members.

For Oracle 11g, you should now use the SYSASM privilege instead of the SYSDBA privilege to connect to and administer an ASM instance. Although before Oracle 11g R2, you were still able to manage ASM from SYSDBA, it is not recommended. In the event that you still decide to use the SYSDBA privilege to connect to an ASM instance, Oracle will send a warning to the alert log file because commands that you run using SYSDBA privileges on an ASM instance are supposed to be deprecated in future releases of Oracle.

Oracle writes these warning alert messages for Oracle 11g to the alert log files if you issue `CREATE`, `ALTER`, or `DROP DISKGROUP` statements that should now be performed by the SYSASM user. The following entry from the Oracle 11g RAC `alert.log` file displays these changes:

```
WARNING: Deprecated privilege SYSDBA for command 'STARTUP'
WARNING: Deprecated privilege SYSDBA for command 'SHUTDOWN'
SQL> create diskgroup dgex1 external redundancy disk '/dev/
raw/raw5'
WARNING: Deprecated privilege SYSDBA for command 'CREATE DISKGROUP'
```

Oracle 11g R2 ASM features

Oracle 11g R2 introduced several new ASM features; let's now take a closer look.

OCR and Voting Disk stored in ASM

Prior to Oracle 11g R2 ASM, the Oracle Cluster Registry and Voting Disks had to be stored either on raw devices or in a clustered filesystem. With 11g R2, ASM can be used to store both the OCR and Voting Disks. This simplifies management and improves performance.

Oracle Automatic Storage Management Cluster Filesystem (Oracle ACFS)

The Oracle 11g R2 Oracle Automatic Storage Management Cluster Filesystem provides a rich array of performance and availability enhancements to extend the maintenance of ASM files.

New Oracle 11g ASM Disk Group compatibility features

With Oracle 11g, there are now two new Disk Group compatibility attributes—`compatible.asm` and `compatible.rdbms`. These Disk Group compatibility attributes determine the minimum version of ASM and database instances that can connect to an Oracle 11g ASM Disk Group. By advancing these Disk Group compatibility settings, you can use the new ASM features that are available in the latest release. If you decide to advance these attributes from 10.1 to 11.1, you will enable the following key features that are new to Oracle 11g ASM:

- Preferred mirror read
- Variable size extents
- Fast mirror resync

The software version of ASM determines the default compatibility of newly created Disk Groups. You can override the Disk Group compatibility default setting when you create Disk Groups with the `CREATE DISKGROUP` SQL statement.

The `ALTER DISKGROUP` SQL statement can update the compatibility settings for existing Disk Groups.

The compatibility settings for a Disk Group can only be advanced; you cannot revert to a lower compatibility setting.

The following example shows how to create an ASM Disk Group with the compatibility attribute:

```
SQL> create diskgroup dg11gasm external redundancy disk '/dev/raw/
raw5' attribute 'compatible.asm'='11.1';
Diskgroup created.

SQL> create diskgroup dg11grdbms external redundancy disk
'/dev/raw/raw6' attribute 'compatible.rdbms'='11.1',
'compatible.asm'='11.1';

SQL> select name,compatibility,database_compatibility from
v$asm_diskgroup;

NAME        COMPATIBILITY  DATABASE_COMPATIBILITY
---------- --------------  ------ ------------
DG11GASM    11.1.0.0.0      10.1.0.0.0
DG11GRDBMS  11.1.0.0.0      11.1.0.0.0
```

Summary

This chapter has provided you with a comprehensive discussion of 11g RAC architecture, focusing on the following topics:

- Oracle 11g RAC hardware and system architecture
- Key new features for Oracle 11g R1 and 11g R2 RAC and ASM

Because understanding the initial design is important for a successful deployment of Oracle 11g RAC, the chapter focused on all aspects of the system architecture that must be accounted for to ensure success. This included an in-depth discussion of hardware server configurations, network design, and RAID configurations, as well as storage protocols for managing the disk I/O subsystem. Based on the constraints of your business operations and performance needs, you can now decide what system configurations will best suit your deployment of Oracle 11g RAC from all of these key perspectives. The chapter then moved on to discuss a summary of RAC components and new features that are important to be aware of while working with 11g R1 and 11g R2 RAC, and with ASM.

The next chapter will provide you with tips and tricks on how to install and configure the Oracle 11g RAC software.

3
Clusterware Installation

In the previous chapters, we have discussed in detail and explained to you how a cluster (HA) solution is going to help you achieve the business continuity needs to cope with 24/7 service availability challenges. In this context, you should be aware of the basic concepts, architecture, and the real advantages of an Oracle Real Applications Cluster (RAC). This chapter mainly focuses on the essential needs for building up servers and explaining Clusterware configuration. In short, the chapter deals with the following topics in particular:

- Preparing for a cluster installation
- Oracle 11g R1 Clusterware/RAC installation
- Oracle 11g R2 Clusterware/RAC installation
- Removing/Reconfiguring a Grid Infrastructure configuration

Preparing for a cluster installation

Preparing a server with the mandatory requirements of software and hardware is the key factor for any successful cluster installation. Therefore, in the following sections, we are going to explain in detail, the essential recommendations that are needed when building a server; such as hardware, software, network, storage, software groups, and users. Before you begin the actual installation process, ensure that you have prepared the servers with all the mandatory requirements that are going to be part of the cluster installation.

Server (node) requirements

During the course of the server preparations, you must ensure that each server that is going to be associated with a cluster meets the following minimum hardware-level resources and space requirements:

- A minimum of 2 GB RAM is required for the complete Grid Infrastructure and RAC software installation.
- A minimum of 1 GB free space is required in the `/tmp` directory.
- A minimum of 10 GB free space for the entire Clusterware/Grid and RAC software homes is required.
- Ensure that you have prepared shared storage in which to place Clusterware critical components: Oracle Cluster Registry (OCR) and Voting Disk.
- Also ensure that you have adequate shared storage disks for Automatic Storage Management, if you consider using ASM to host the datafiles.
- Configure the server swap size to be 1.5 time if the RAM on the server is <=2 GB. Otherwise, configure the sever swap size to be equal to the RAM size. Each server must have a minimum of two network adapters or network interface cards (NIC) configured to be able to support the public and private networks.

Network requirements

As explained earlier in this chapter, every node that is going to be part of the cluster must be configured with a minimum of two NIC interfaces (cards): one for the public communication and another for the private communication. You also need to secure three IP addresses, **Public**, **Private**, and **VIP** respectively for each individual node.

The VIP subnet must be configured on the same subnet as the public address. An optimal private network (interconnect) configuration is very important for the Clusterware to boost the interconnect performance, as well as to avoid node evictions syndrome from occurring. The interface is used for the internode communication (heartbeat mechanism) by the Clusterware and also Oracle RAC database instances to send and receive data blocks. Considering the pivotal role played by the internode communication in the Clusterware, Oracle highly advises to configure the private network on a separate dedicated network switch for this interface with high speed NICs. For example, use a 1 GB Ethernet connection and a diversified subnet address from the public access to overcome the network delays. For a better performance and high-speed network transmission, you could also use the InfiniBand technology instead of 1GB Ethernet. To avoid Single Point of Failure occurrence for interconnect connectivity, you can also implement the interconnect aggregation method by bonding multiple network interfaces together into a single logical network interface or using the redundant switches method.

These IP addresses with their fully qualified hostname and domain name either need to be configured on the Domain Name Server (DNS) or added to the `/etc/hosts` file.

Beginning with Oracle 11g R2 a maximum of three additional IP addresses in a round-robin fashion are needed for a **Single Client Access Name (SCAN)**.

Unlike the other three IP (Public, Private, and VIP) addresses and hostnames, the SCAN must be assigned a unique name across all nodes and it must remain on the same subnet as a public and VIP address.

You will need to ensure that the public network interface supports TCP/IP and that the private network adapter supports UDP.

Kernel parameters

After a successful Linux OS V5 installation over the servers, as part of the prerequisites requirements, ensure that the following Oracle recommended kernel parameters are configured or added in the `/etc/sysctl.conf` file with the values suggested for a successful installation, you need to be the root user to perform this action.

For Oracle 11g R1:

```
kernel.shmall = 2097152
kernel.shmmax = 2147483648
kernel.shmmni = 4096
kernel.sem = 250 32000 100 128
fs.aio-max-size =1048576
fs.file-max = 6815744
net.ipv4.ip_local_port_range = 1024 65000
net.core.rmem_default = 262144
net.core.rmem_max = 4194304
net.core.wmem_default = 262144
net.core.wmem_max = 1048576
```

For Oracle 11g R2:

```
kernel.shmall = 2097152
kernel.shmmax = 536870912
kernel.shmmni = 4096
kernel.sem = 250 32000 100 128
fs.aio-max-size =1048576
fs.file-max = 6815744
```

```
net.ipv4.ip_local_port_range = 9000 65500
net.core.rmem_default = 262144
net.core.rmem_max = 4194304
net.core.wmem_default = 262144
net.core.wmem_max = 1048576
```

Note: In 11g R2, when the kernel parameters fail to meet the minimum requirements, they can be dynamically fixed during the installation phase by using the `fixup` option.

Operating system packages

Apart from the basic packages (RPM) that were installed as part of the typical operating system installation, the following additional Oracle Recommended Packages (RPM) need to be configured on each server. The required packages can be found in the OS source (DVD) or you can also download them from the Internet.

For Oracle 11g R1:

```
binutils-2.17.50.0.6-2.el5
compat-libstdc++-33-3.2.3-61
elfutils-libelf-0.125.el5
elfutils-libelf-devel-0.125
glibc-2.5-12
glibc-common-2.5-12
glibc-devel-2.5-12
glibc-headers-2.3.4-2
gcc-4.1.1-52
gcc-c++-4.1.1-52
libaio-0.3.106
libaio-devel-0.3.106
libgcc-4.1.1-52
libstdc++-4.1.1
libstdc++-devel-4.1.1-52.el5
make-3.81-1.1
sysstat-7.0.0
unixODBC-2.2.11
unixODBC-devel-2.2.11
numactl-7.0.0
```

For Oracle 11g R2:

```
binutils-2.17.50.0.6
compat-libstdc++-33-3.2.3
compat-libstdc++-33-3.2.3 (32 bit)
elfutils-libelf-0.125
elfutils-libelf-devel-0.125
elfutils-libelf-devel-static-0.125
gcc-4.1.2
gcc-c++-4.1.2
glibc-2.5-24
glibc-2.5-24 (32 bit)
glibc-common-2.5
glibc-devel-2.5
glibc-devel-2.5 (32 bit)
glibc-headers-2.5
ksh-20060214
libaio-0.3.106
libaio-0.3.106 (32 bit)
libaio-devel-0.3.106
libaio-devel-0.3.106 (32 bit)
libgcc-4.1.2
libgcc-4.1.2 (32 bit)
libstdc++-4.1.2
libstdc++-4.1.2 (32 bit)
libstdc++-devel 4.1.2
make-3.81
sysstat-7.0.2
unixODBC-2.2.11
unixODBC-2.2.11 (32 bit)
unixODBC-devel-2.2.11
unixODBC-devel-2.2.11 (32 bit)
numactl-devel-0.9.8.i386
```

OS groups and users

The following mandatory OS groups and Oracle software owners (user) are required for each node. As a matter of fact, in the cluster environment, the user equivalences such as group/user name and their IDs must remain the same across all nodes of a cluster:

```
Groups : oinstall, dba, oper, asmadmin
User   : oracle
```

As the root user, use the following commands to create OS groups and a user:

```
groupadd -g 500 oinstall
groupadd -g 501 dba
groupadd -g 502 oper
groupadd -g 503 asmadmin

useradd -u 1000 -g oinstall -G dba,oper,asmadmin oracle
passwd oracle
```

As per Oracle recommendation, the `oinstall` group should be configured as the primary group and the remaining groups should be configured as secondary groups for the Oracle/Cluster software users (typically, the oracle user) on the server.

OS user settings

Once you have managed to create the necessary OS groups and users, the subsequent task is to set the limits for the user in order to improve the shell limits. You will need to add the following user limits in the `/etc/security/limits.conf` file:

```
oracle              soft    nproc   2047
oracle              hard    nproc   16384
oracle              soft    nofile  1024
oracle              hard    nofile  65536
oracle              soft    stack   10240
```

Next, add the following user session limit in the `/etc/pam.d/login` file:

```
session    required     pam_limits.so
```

The following limits and shell settings need to be added in the user profile file, `.bash_profile`. In the following example, presuming that the korn shell is being used in your environment, log in as Oracle user, edit the hidden `.bash_profile` file, and add the following lines; if another shell is being used, modify the following example accordingly:

```
if [ $USER = "oracle" ]; then
            if [ $SHELL = "/bin/ksh" ]; then
               ulimit -p 16384
               ulimit -n 65536
        else
            ulimit -u 16384 -n 65536
        fi
            umask 022
fi
```

Configuring Secure Shell (SSH)

After you have successfully completed the preceding necessary settings, the subsequent mandatory task is to configure the Secure Shell (SSH) passwordless connectivity between the nodes. Bear in mind that SSH connectivity configuration is essential between the nodes of a cluster as the OUI uses the `ssh` and `scp` commands internally during the installation phase to perform remote operations in which it copies the software from the local to other nodes.

You need to generate `RSA` or `DSA` keys on each node as part of the SSH configuration. For that, use the following set of commands to configure SSH:

1. Log in as Oracle user on the first node of the cluster (in our example, it will be on the raclinux1), and execute the following sequence of commands:

```
[oracle@raclinux1 ~]$ mkdir ~/.ssh
[oracle@raclinux1 ~]$ chmod 700 ~/.ssh
[oracle@raclinux1 ~]$ /usr/bin/ssh-keygen -t rsa
Generating public/private rsa key pair.
Enter file in which to save the key (/home/oracle/.ssh/id_rsa):
Enter passphrase (empty for no passphrase):
Enter same passphrase again:
Your identification has been saved in /home/oracle/.ssh/id_rsa.
Your public key has been saved in /home/oracle/.ssh/id_rsa.pub.
The key fingerprint is:
f0:89:ac:ba:83:31:c4:43:97:3e:9a:a5:60:c1:8e:e6 oracle@raclinux1.sjh.com
```

2. When prompted for the key location, accept the default settings by hitting the *Enter* key. Once this setup is done on the first node, repeat the same steps on the rest of the nodes (in our example, repeat the same step on the raclinux2 node).
3. Now, switch back to the first node (raclinux1) and execute the following command to add authorization keys. After adding the authorization keys, copy the `authorized_keys` file to the other nodes using the `scp` command, and enter **Yes** when prompted.

```
[oracle@raclinux1 ~]$ cd ~/.ssh
[oracle@raclinux1 .ssh]$ cat id_rsa.pub >> authorized_keys
[oracle@raclinux1 .ssh]$ scp authorized_keys raclinux2:/home/oracle/.ssh
The authenticity of host 'raclinux2 (192.168.2.202)' can't be established.
RSA key fingerprint is 52:13:31:e8:ce:ec:47:b8:06:09:4b:c9:aa:c5:35:81.
Are you sure you want to continue connecting (yes/no)? yes
Warning: Permanently added 'raclinux2,192.168.2.202' (RSA) to the list of known hosts.
oracle@raclinux2's password:
authorized_keys                                          100%  406     0.4KB/s   00:00
```

4. Now, switch back to the second node, (raclinux2) and run the following command:

```
[oracle@raclinux2 ~]$ cd ~/.ssh
[oracle@raclinux2 .ssh]$ cat id_rsa.pub >> authorized_keys
[oracle@raclinux2 .ssh]$ scp authorized_keys raclinux1:/home/oracle/.ssh/
The authenticity of host 'raclinux1 (192.168.2.201)' can't be established.
RSA key fingerprint is 52:13:31:e8:ce:ec:47:b8:06:09:4b:c9:aa:c5:35:81.
Are you sure you want to continue connecting (yes/no)? yes
Warning: Permanently added 'raclinux1,192.168.2.201' (RSA) to the list of known hosts.
oracle@raclinux1's password:
authorized_keys                                          100%  812     0.8KB/s   00:00
```

5. After adding the authorization keys on the second node, copy the file to the other nodes using the `scp` command, as demonstrated in the preceding example, and enter **Yes** when prompted.
6. After configuring the SSH setup successfully across all nodes, let's run the following test on each node, starting from the first node, to establish a passwordless connection between all the nodes to meet the Oracle recommendations:

```
ssh raclinux1 date
ssh raclinux2 date
ssh raclinux1-priv date
ssh raclinux2-priv date
ssh raclinux1-sjh.com date
ssh raclinux2-sjh.com date
```

Fortunately, with Oracle 11g R2, you are no longer required to perform the manual SSH connectivity configuration, as it can be configured automatically by the OUI during the installation phase. You will be allowed to configure SSH by the OUI interface during the installation phase. Nevertheless, it will be the same set of actions that we have manually performed earlier in this chapter, but an automated one.

The preceding configuration prerequisites are best done with the coordination of storage, system, and network teams.

Verifying prerequisites with the CLUVFY utility

Although we managed to build each node of the cluster cautiously to meet all essential recommendations for a successful cluster configuration, we can further ensure that everything is in the right place just before the installation process kicks off. With the CLUVFY utility, you can verify and validate all pre- and post-requisite checks at different levels such as hardware, software, and installation.

You will need to navigate through the Clusterware/grid software (source) location and execute `./runcluvfy.sh` to initiate the pre- and post-installation verification.

Now, let's begin with the following piece of code that verifies the node accessibility checks between the nodes in the context:

```
./runcluvfy.sh comp nodereach -n raclinux1,raclinux2 -verbose
```

Alternatively, in 11g R2, the following command could also be used to initiate checks such as node accessibility, user equivalence, network interface, and shared storage:

```
./runcluvfy.sh stage -post hwos -n raclinux1,raclinux2 -verbose
```

The following command performs the significant pre-cluster installation validations on the nodes in the context:

```
./runcluvfy.sh stage -pre crsinst -n raclinux1,raclinux2 -verbose
```

In Oracle 11g R2, when the `-fixup` flag is used with the CLUVFY utility, it creates the fixup shell script in the directory mentioned with the `fixupdir` flag, for those requirements that have failed to meet the prerequisites criteria on the servers. You can, as the root user, execute those scripts over the servers to fix the problems reported during the checks validation. The following code helps you to perform the pre-cluster installation verifications with the `-fixup` flag:

```
./runcluvfy.sh stage -pre crsinst -n raclinux1,raclinux2 -fixup -
fixupdir /tmp/fixups.sh
```

Oracle 11g R1 Clusterware installation

Presuming that the servers (referred to as nodes hereafter) are built properly and the prerequisite checks are verified thoroughly with the CLUVFY utility, it is now time to move to the Clusterware installation phase. However, let me remind you that all prerequisite validations must be met on all nodes that are going to be part of the cluster installation.

In the subsequent sections, we will be demonstrating a two-node Oracle 11g R1 Clusterware and RAC software (RDBMS/ASM) installation procedure.

The following table describes the environmental settings and sources that have been used in this book to demonstrate Oracle 11g R1 Clusterware, ASM, and RDBMS software installation and configuration:

Operating system	**Linux V5**		
Clusterware home	/u01/app/oracle/product/11.1.0/crs		
ASM home	/u01/app/oracle/product/11.1.0/asm		
Database home	/u01/app/oracle/product/11.1.0/db_1		
Shared Disks	/dev/sdb1, /dev/sdc1 for OCR disk		
	/dev/sdd1 for voting disk		
IP address, hostname, and domain names in /`etc/host` file entry	#Public IP address		
	192.168.2.201	raclinux1.sjh.com	raclinux1
	192.168.2.202	raclinux2.sjh.com	raclinux2
	#Private IP address		
	10.10.1.1	raclinux1-priv.sjh.com	raclinux1-priv
	10.10.1.2	raclinux2-priv.sjh.com	raclinux2-priv
	#Virtual IPs		
	192.168.2.211	raclinux1-vip.sjh.com	raclinux1-vip
	192.168.2.212	raclinux2-vip.sjh.com	raclinux2-vip

Initiating Oracle Universal Installer for Oracle 11g R1 Clusterware

Unlike the standalone installation process, Oracle Real Application Clusters (RAC) comes in a two-phase installation procedure; an Oracle Clusterware is configured in the first phase, followed by the Oracle RAC (RDBMS) software installation process. To begin the Clusterware configuration proceedings, in order to launch the Oracle Universal Installer (OUI), initiate the `./runInstaller` command either from the Oracle 11g R1 Clusterware staged software area or from the installation DVD/CD source.

Don't forget to set the `ORACLE_BASE` environmental variable on the OS just before you initiate the OUI, if it is not already set.

1. On the **Welcome** screen click on **Next** to proceed further.
2. Since this is the first Oracle software installation to be done on this node, OUI displays the **Specify Inventory directory and credentials** screen (shown in the following screenshot) where you need to enter the Oracle inventory location and also need to set the OS primary group. Nevertheless, if Oracle environmental parameters are set correctly, such as, `ORACLE_BASE`, OUI by default, suggest an appropriate inventory location. Unless you intend on putting the inventory files in your desired location, accept the default values and click on **Next** to continue further.

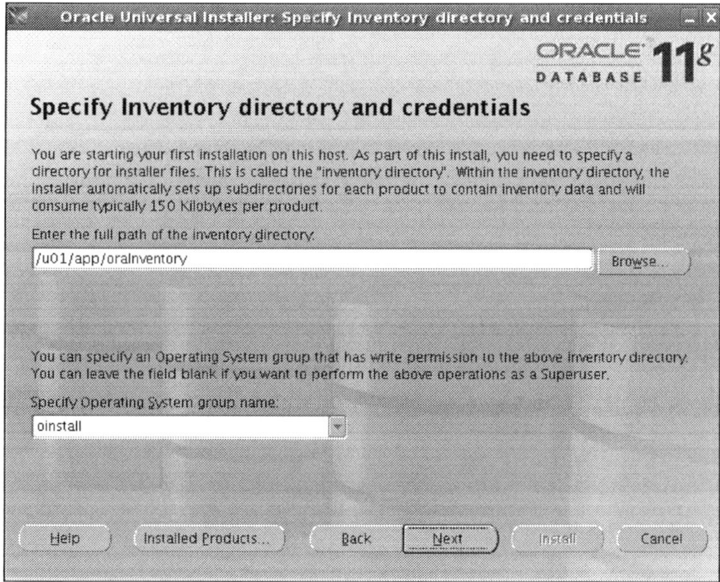

3. Enter the Clusterware Home name and specify the location details for the Oracle Clusterware software binaries on the **Specify Home Details** screen, as shown in the following screenshot:

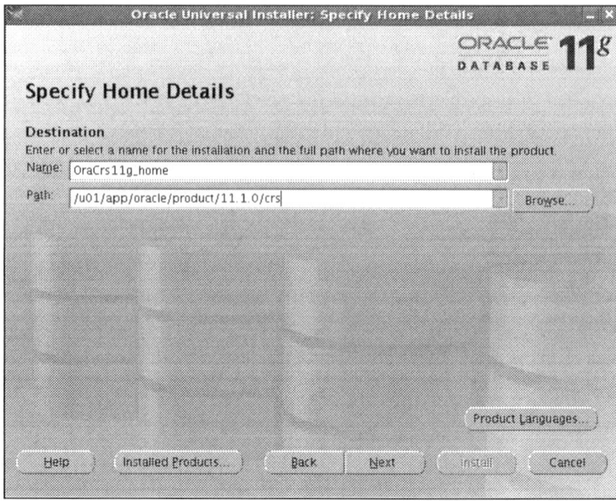

4. Click on **Next** to continue further after entering the appropriate information. OUI then performs mandatory prerequisite checks on the **Product-Specific Prerequisite Checks** screen to ensure that all essential recommendations such as kernel parameters value, physical memory, OS packages, and settings are actually met on nodes. The **Product-Specific Prerequisite Checks** screen is shown in the following screenshot:

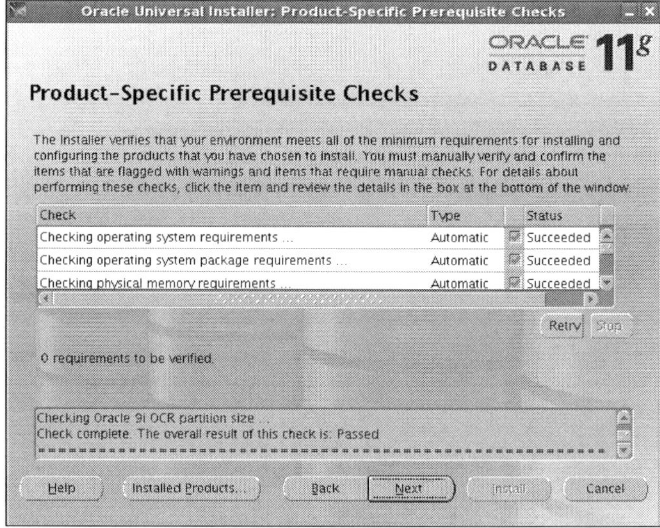

5. On the flip side, you may safely ignore the checks flagged as Warning if they won't cause any serious problems to the installation process. However, any failed status checks must be resolved before you continue further. When prerequisite checks are successfully completed, you will need to ensure that the overall checks result is passed, as shown in the preceding screenshot for a successful Clusterware installation and click on **Next** to proceed further. On the **Specify Cluster Configuration** screen, the OUI detects and displays the local node's Public, Private, and VIP name details under the **Cluster Name** section, as configured in DNS or as mentioned in the `/etc/hosts` file. In order to add more node details that are likely to be part of the Clusterware installation, click on the **Add** button and enter the Public, Private, and VIP names for each node, as shown in the following screenshot:

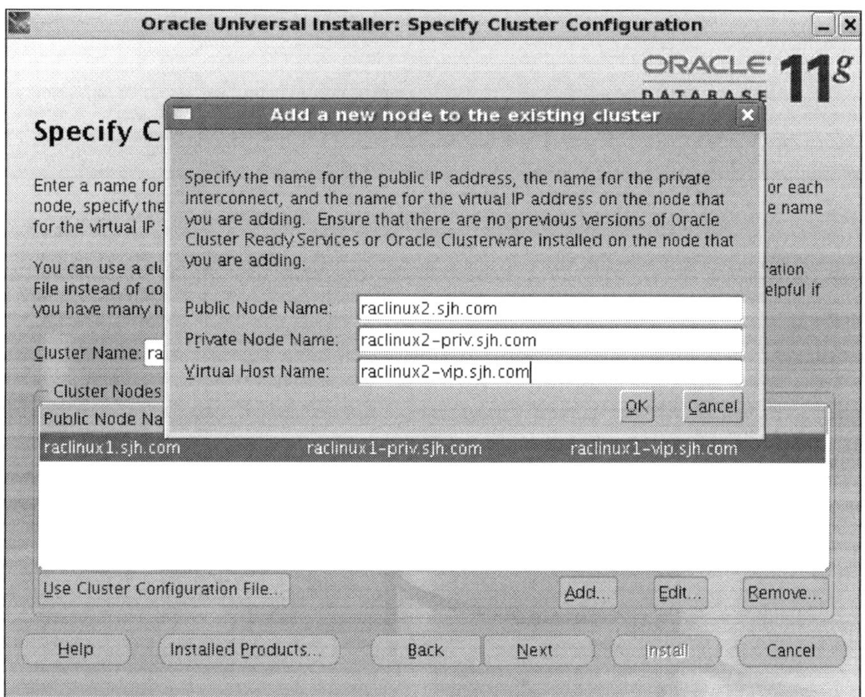

6. The **Cluster Name** field suggests a default cluster name for this cluster environment. As a best practice, ensure you set a unique cluster name if you are going to hold multiple cluster environments in your network. After successfully adding all the nodes under the **Cluster Name** section, click on **Next** to proceed further, as shown in the following screenshot:

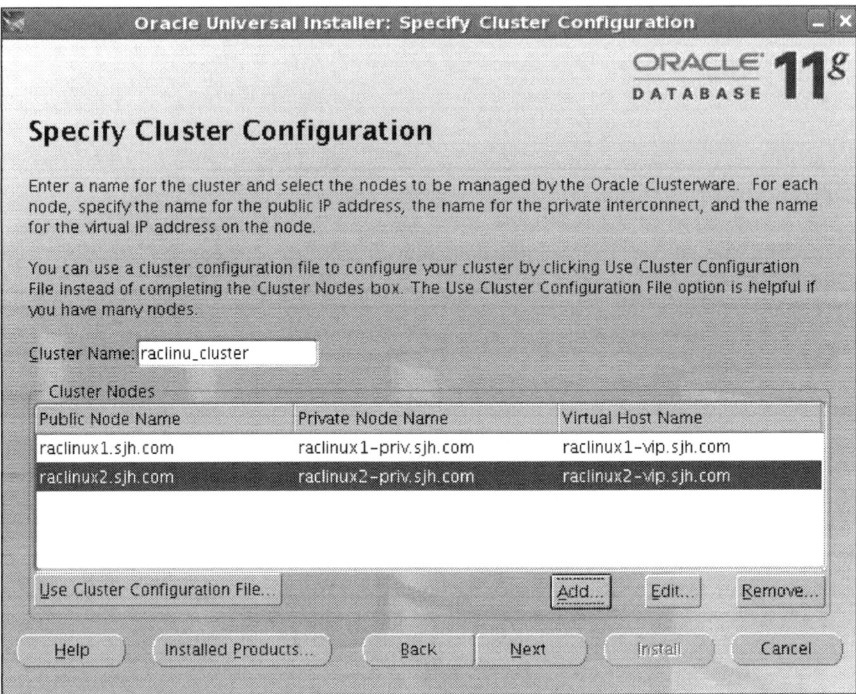

7. On the **Specify Network Interface Usage** screen, you are required to configure the network interface types for the public and the private communication. By default, the public and private interfaces are configured to private interface type. However, do not worry; select the correct interface from the list for the public interface (that is, **eth0** in our demonstration) and click on **Edit** to configure the appropriate type for this interface, as shown in the following screenshot:

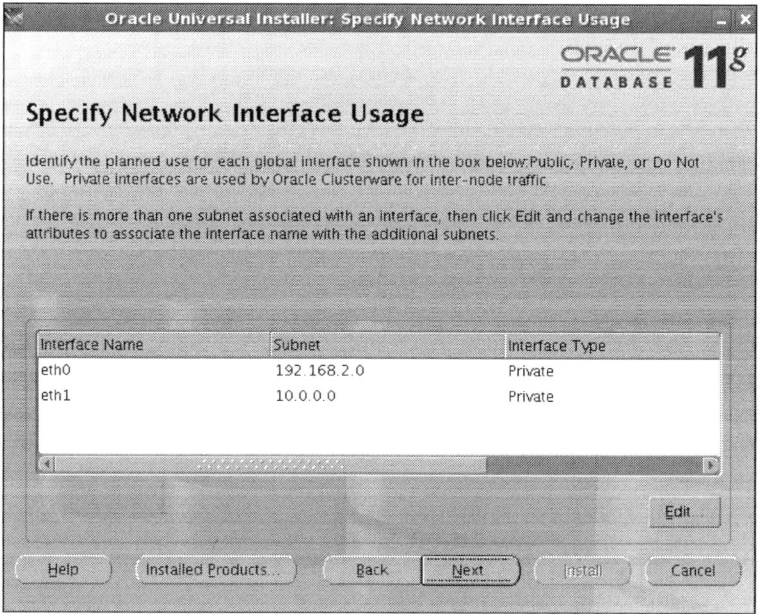

8. On the **Edit private interconnect type** dialog box, choose the **Public** option for **eth0** interface and click **OK**. You need to set the **Do Not use** option if you see additional network interface names other than eth0 and eth1. Then click on **Next** to proceed further. These options are shown in the following screenshot:

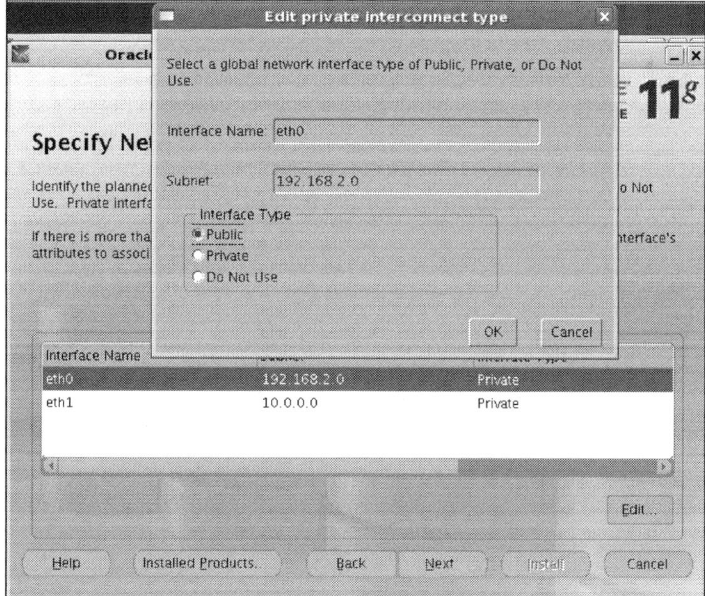

9. OCR is one of the critical components of an Oracle Clusterware, which maintains and manages essential details for the cluster sources such as RAC databases, listeners, instances, and services. As of Oracle 11g R1, OCR can be placed either on a shared block on a raw device or on a shared filesystem to which all the participating nodes must have read and write permissions.

   Considering the criticality of the OCR contents to the cluster functionality, Oracle provides an option to make (mirror) the OCR file redundant, with a maximum of two copies, to avoid a Single Point of Failure situation. To enable the Oracle redundancy option, choose the **Normal Redundancy** option and specify the mirror copy disk location accordingly.

   If you are depending on the system-provided (RAID) protection level, you can then choose the **External Redundancy** option. However, Oracle strongly recommends you to multiplex the OCR file.

10. Next, you need to enter the path for OCR on the **Specify Oracle Cluster Registry (OCR) Location** screen, as shown in the following screenshot:

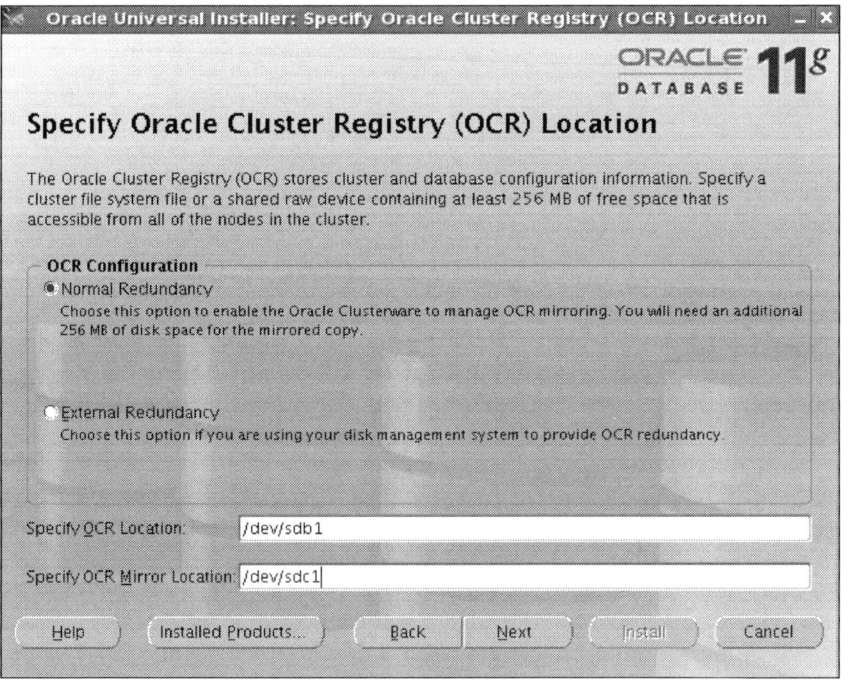

Don't configure a large disk for OCR. A small disk of around 300 MB-500 MB is a good choice.

After entering the disk and mirror path for the OCR, click on **Next** to continue further. The *voting disk* is another critical constituent of an Oracle Clusterware, which maintains and consists of important details about the cluster nodes membership, such as which node is part of the cluster, who (node) is joining the cluster, and who (node) is leaving the cluster.

Given the importance of voting disk availability, Oracle provides **Normal** and **External** redundancy options to multiplex the voting disk to maintain high availability. Similar to the OCR file, the voting disk can be placed on a raw device, on a block or a cluster file system. You will need to ensure that all the nodes participating in the cluster have read/write permissions on disks.

11. Therefore, choose the best redundant **Voting Disk Configuration** option and put the path details for the voting disks on the **Specify Voting Disk Location** screen, as shown in the following screenshot:

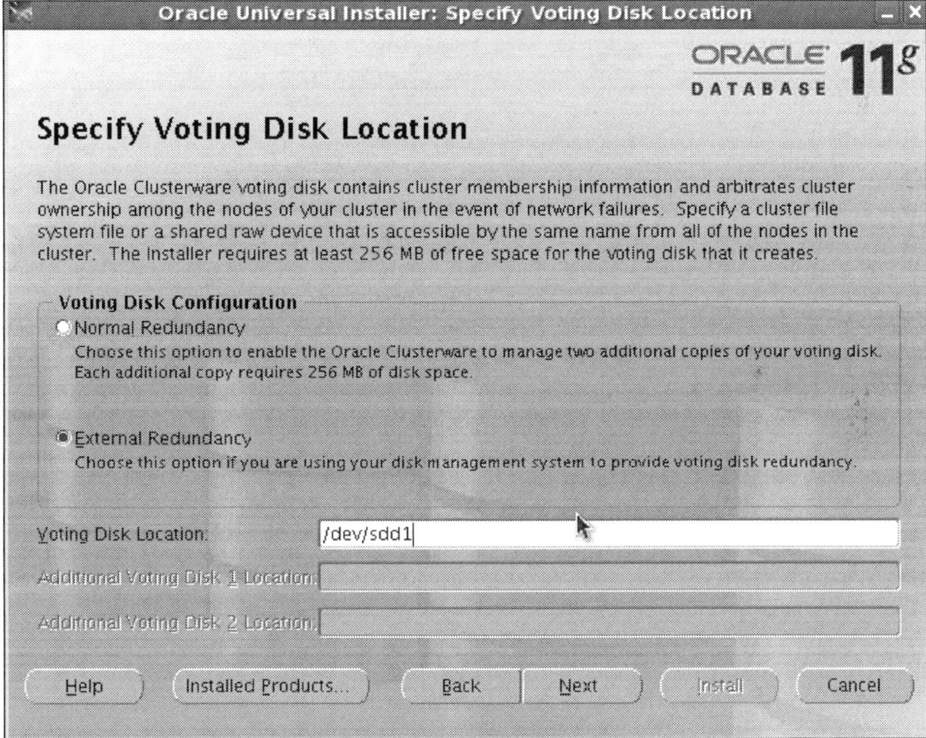

Click on **Next** to proceed further.

With Oracle 11g R1, you can configure up to 32 voting disks in your cluster.

Note: A node in the cluster must be able to access more than half of the voting disks at any time in order to be able to tolerate a failure of n voting disks. Therefore, it is strongly recommended that you configure an odd number of voting disks such as 3, 5, and so on.

12. Review the summary of the Global settings, Product Language, Space requirements, and Remote Nodes operation, and then on the **Summary** screen click on **Install** to begin the Clusterware installation process.
13. Once the installation begins on the local node, OUI displays the progress installation bar, as shown in the following screenshot:

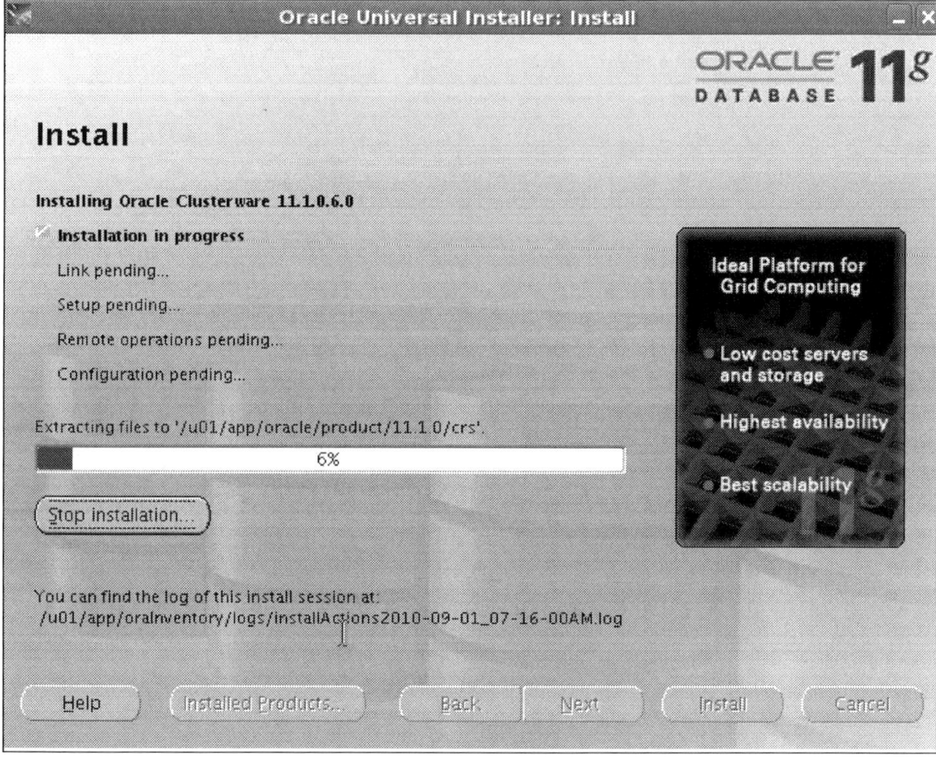

14. OUI performs remote operations towards the end of the local node installation, where it copies the software to the remote nodes that were selected during the installation.
15. When the installation progress bar reaches 100% status, OUI then brings up a pop-up **Execute Configuration scripts** window, as shown in the following screenshot:

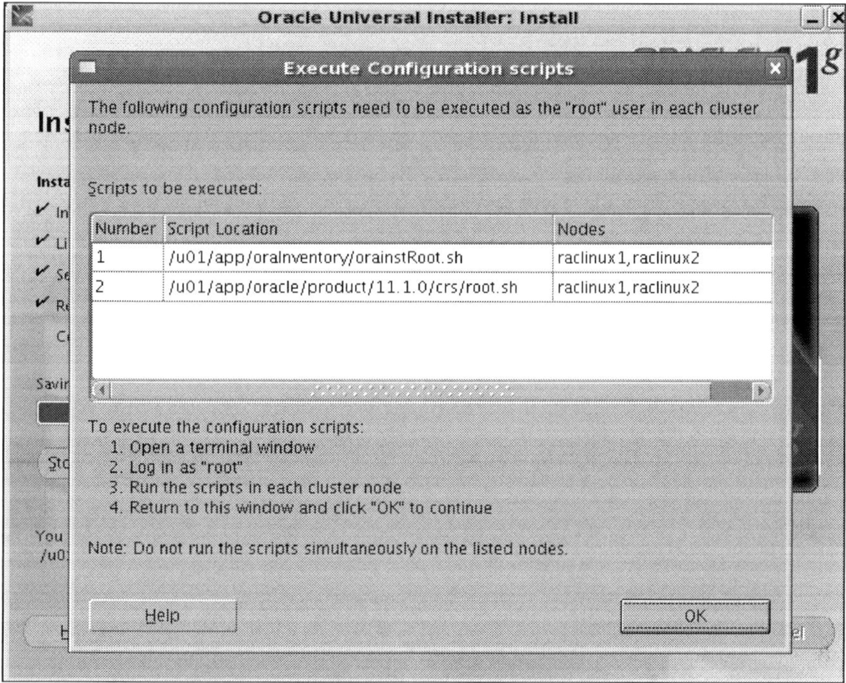

This window contains an important instruction to run a couple of mandatory scripts as root user. You will need to open a new terminal window and log in as root user, and you must run the scripts (`orainstRoot.sh` and `root.sh`) in sequence across all the nodes as instructed.

16. When the `root.sh` script is executed successfully across the nodes, click on **OK** to complete the Oracle Clusterware Installation process and proceed to the final stage.

17. OUI then moves further to configure Oracle Notification, Private Interconnect, and Cluster Verifications Utility (CLUVFY) on the **Configuration Assistants** screen, as shown in the following screenshot:

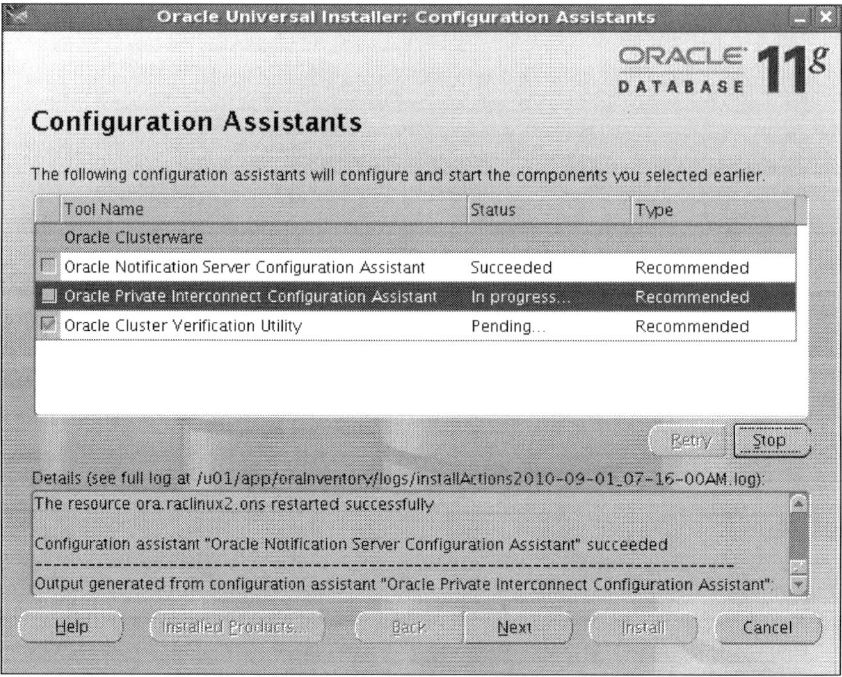

18. After the preceding configuration is completed successfully, click on **Exit** on the **End of Installation** screen to quit the installation process.

What happens when orainstRoot.sh and root.sh is run?

When the `orainstRoot.sh` script is executed as root user on the nodes in the sequence as instructed in the **Execute Configuration Scripts** pop-up window, the script changes the permissions and group ownership of the Oracle Inventory directory.

The following example demonstrates what happens when the script is run on a node:

```
[oracle@raclinux1 ~]$ su -
Password:
[root@raclinux1 ~]# /u01/app/oraInventory/orainstRoot.sh
Changing permissions of /u01/app/oraInventory to 770.
Changing groupname of /u01/app/oraInventory to oinstall.
The execution of the_script is complete
```

After executing the `orainstRoot.sh` script successfully across the nodes, you need to execute the `root.sh` script (which basically does the majority of the action of Clusterware configuration) subsequently on each node, one at a time.

The following example demonstrates the series of actions that are likely to take place when you run the script on the first node:

```
[root@raclinux1 ~]# /u01/app/oracle/product/11.1.0/crs/root.sh
WARNING: directory '/u01/app/oracle/product/11.1.0' is not owned by root
WARNING: directory '/u01/app/oracle/product' is not owned by root
WARNING: directory '/u01/app/oracle' is not owned by root
WARNING: directory '/u01/app' is not owned by root
WARNING: directory '/u01' is not owned by root
Checking to see if Oracle CRS stack is already configured
/etc/oracle does not exist. Creating it now.

Setting the permissions on OCR backup directory
Setting up Network socket directories
Oracle Cluster Registry configuration upgraded successfully
The directory '/u01/app/oracle/product/11.1.0' is not owned by root. Changing ow
ner to root
```

```
The directory '/u01/app/oracle' is not owned by root. Changing owner to root
The directory '/u01/app' is not owned by root. Changing owner to root
The directory '/u01' is not owned by root. Changing owner to root
Successfully accumulated necessary OCR keys.
Using ports: CSS=49895 CRS=49896 EVMC=49898 and EVMR=49897.
node <nodenumber>: <nodename> <private interconnect name> <hostname>
node 1: raclinux1 raclinux1-priv raclinux1
node 2: raclinux2 raclinux2-priv raclinux2
Creating OCR keys for user 'root', privgrp 'root'..
Operation successful.
Now formatting voting device: /dev/sdd1
Format of 1 voting devices complete.
Startup will be queued to init within 30 seconds.
Adding daemons to inittab
Expecting the CRS daemons to be up within 600 seconds.
Cluster Synchronization Services is active on these nodes.
        raclinux1
Cluster Synchronization Services is inactive on these nodes.
        raclinux2
Local node checking complete. Run root.sh on remaining nodes to start CRS daemon
s.
```

After you have run the `root.sh` script successfully on the local node, you then need to move on to the rest of the nodes and execute the same script, one at a time. Typically, when you run the script on the last node of a cluster, the following action is likely to take place:

```
[root@raclinux1 ~]# /u01/app/oracle/product/11.1.0/crs/root.sh
WARNING: directory '/u01/app/oracle/product/11.1.0' is not owned by root
WARNING: directory '/u01/app/oracle/product' is not owned by root
WARNING: directory '/u01/app/oracle' is not owned by root
WARNING: directory '/u01/app' is not owned by root
WARNING: directory '/u01' is not owned by root
CheckingChecking to see if Oracle CRS stack is already configured
/etc/oracle does not exist. Creating it now.

Setting the permissions on OCR backup directory
Setting up Network socket directories
Oracle Cluster Registry configuration upgraded successfully
The directory '/u01/app/oracle/product/11.1.0' is not owned by root.
Changing owner to root
The directory '/u01/app/oracle/product' is not owned by root. Changing
owner to root
The directory '/u01/app/oracle' is not owned by root. Changing owner to
root
The directory '/u01/app' is not owned by root. Changing owner to root
The directory '/u01' is not owned by root. Changing owner to root
Successfully accumulated necessary OCR keys.
Using ports: CSS=49895 CRS=49896 EVMC=49898 and EVMR=49897.
node <nodenumber>: <nodename> <private interconnect name> <hostname>
node 1: raclinux1 raclinux1-priv raclinux1
node 2: raclinux2 raclinux2-priv raclinux2
clscfg: Arguments check out successfully.

NO KEYS WERE WRITTEN. Supply -force parameter to override.
-force is destructive and will destroy any previous cluster
configuration.
Oracle Cluster Registry for cluster has already been initialized
Startup will be queued to init within 30 seconds.
Adding daemons to inittab
```

```
Expecting the CRS daemons to be up within 600 seconds.
Cluster Synchronization Services is active on these nodes.
        raclinux1
        raclinux2
Cluster Synchronization Services is active on all the nodes.
Waiting for the Oracle CRSD and EVMD to start
Waiting for the Oracle CRSD and EVMD to start
Waiting for the Oracle CRSD and EVMD to start
Oracle CRS stack installed and running under init(1M)
Running vipca(silent) for configuring nodeapps

Creating VIP application resource on (2) nodes...
Creating GSD application resource on (2) nodes...
Creating ONS application resource on (2) nodes...
Starting VIP application resource on (2) nodes...
Starting GSD application resource on (2) nodes...
Starting ONS application resource on (2) nodes...

Done.
#
```

In a nutshell, the `root.sh` script performs the following set of action on the nodes:

- Creates a `/etc/oratab` file.
- Sets an appropriate permission to the OCR base directory
- Creates the OCR backup and Network Socket directories
- Modifies the ownership to root user on the Oracle base and `/u01` (cluster home filesystem)
- Configures the OCR and voting disks (only on the first node)
- Starts the Clusterware daemons
- Adds Clusterware daemons to the `inittab` file
- Verifies whether the Clusterware is up on all nodes
- On the last node, initiates `./vipca` in silent mode to configure nodeapps, such as, GSD, VIP, and ONS for all the nodes

Oracle 11g R1 Clusterware post-installation checks

At this point in time, we have successfully managed to build a two-node Oracle 11g R1 Clusterware configuration and are now ready to move forward to perform a few post-installation checks.

Let's quickly perform the post-Clusterware-installation checks on nodes utilizing the CLUVFY utility. To achieve this, use the following example command on node1:

```
cluvfy stage -post crsinst -n raclinux1,raclinux2 -verbose
```

Now, let's move on with further checks. Verify the cluster stack health status across all the nodes using the following example:

```
[oracle@raclinux1 ~]$ crsctl check crs
Cluster Synchronization Services appears healthy
Cluster Ready Services appears healthy
Event Manager appears healthy
```

Ensure that the cluster components CRS, CSSS, and EVMD appear healthy when you query the cluster stack on the nodes.

The `olsnodes` Clusterware command is used to list the node name and their numbers configured in a cluster:

```
[oracle@raclinux1 ~]$ olsnodes -n
raclinux1       1
raclinux2       2
```

The `ocrcheck` command is used to verify the OCR integrity, size, and location. This command is very useful to find the OCR location and the synchronization between OCR files.

```
[oracle@raclinux1 ~]$ ocrcheck
Status of Oracle Cluster Registry is as follows :
         Version                  :          2
         Total space (kbytes)     :     524024
         Used space (kbytes)      :       2012
         Available space (kbytes) :     522012
         ID                       : 1437284228
         Device/File Name         :  /dev/sdb1
                                    Device/File integrity check succeeded
         Device/File Name         :  /dev/sdc1
                                    Device/File integrity check succeeded

         Cluster registry integrity check succeeded
```

Use the following set of examples to view the voting disk details (paths) and to find out the current and software versions of the cluster.

Execute the following command to list the voting-disk list:

```
[oracle@raclinux1 ~]$ crsctl query css votedisk
 0.     0    /dev/sdd1
Located 1 voting disk(s).
```

Execute the following query to view the active and software version of Clusterware:

```
[oracle@raclinux1 ~]$ crsctl query crs activeversion
Oracle Clusterware active version on the cluster is [11.1.0.6.0]
[oracle@raclinux1 ~]$ crsctl query crs softwareversion
Oracle Clusterware version on node [raclinux1] is [11.1.0.6.0]
```

Use the `crs_stat` command to verify the status and state of the cluster sources such as **gsd**, **ons**, and **vip**. Ensure all resources **Target** and **State** are flagged as **ONLINE**, as shown in the following screenshot:

```
[oracle@raclinux1 ~]$ crs_stat -t -v
Name           Type           R/RA   F/FT   Target    State     Host
----------------------------------------------------------------------
ora....ux1.gsd application    0/5    0/0    ONLINE    ONLINE    raclinux1
ora....ux1.ons application    0/3    0/0    ONLINE    ONLINE    raclinux1
ora....ux1.vip application    0/0    0/0    ONLINE    ONLINE    raclinux1
ora....ux2.gsd application    0/5    0/0    ONLINE    ONLINE    raclinux2
ora....ux2.ons application    0/3    0/0    ONLINE    ONLINE    raclinux2
ora....ux2.vip application    0/0    0/0    ONLINE    ONLINE    raclinux1
```

Before we move forward with the Oracle 11g R1 RAC software installation in the second phase, let's perform some more validations at the OS level.

The following example shows the OS-level background processes that belong to the cluster:

```
[oracle@raclinux1 ~]$ ps -ef |grep init.d
root      3634     1  0 11:23 ?        00:00:00 /bin/sh /etc/init.d/init.evmd run
root      3641     1  1 11:23 ?        00:00:03 /bin/sh /etc/init.d/init.cssd fatal
root      3642     1  0 11:23 ?        00:00:00 /bin/sh /etc/init.d/init.crsd run
root      4519  3641  0 11:23 ?        00:00:00 /bin/sh /etc/init.d/init.cssd oprocd
root      4532  3641  0 11:23 ?        00:00:00 /bin/sh /etc/init.d/init.cssd oclsomon
root      4554  3641  0 11:23 ?        00:00:00 /bin/sh /etc/init.d/init.cssd daemon
```

The following example shows the cluster stack daemon processes that are running at the OS level:

```
[oracle@raclinux1 etc]$ ps -ef |grep d.bin
oracle    4480  4477  0 11:23 ?        00:00:01 /u01/app/oracle/product/11.1.0/crs/bin/evmd.bin
root      4495  3642  0 11:23 ?        00:00:09 /u01/app/oracle/product/11.1.0/crs/bin/crsd.bin r
eboot
oracle    5009  4554  1 11:23 ?        00:00:10 /u01/app/oracle/product/11.1.0/crs/bin/ocssd.bin
```

Ensure that the following entries exist in the `/etc/inittab` OS file to facilitate the Clusterware auto startup and shutdown operations at system (node) restarts. These entries are added at the time of the `root.sh` script execution:

```
h1:35:respawn:/etc/init.d/init.evmd run >/dev/null 2>&1 </dev/null
h2:35:respawn:/etc/init.d/init.cssd fatal >/dev/null 2>&1 </dev/null
h3:35:respawn:/etc/init.d/init.crsd run >/dev/null 2>&1 </dev/null
```

Make sure you repeat the preceding set of checks across all the nodes of the cluster.

Installing Oracle 11g R1 RAC software

As part of Oracle best practices in Oracle 11g R1, you need to maintain individual Oracle homes for ASM and DB respectively. Hence, you will have to perform the RAC software installation process steps twice in this phase to comply with the recommendation. However, just before we begin the second phase of installation, let's perform the prerequisite checks verification with the CLUVFY utility in order to ensure that the nodes are ready for a smooth and successful installation.

The following example shows how to perform prerequisites for the RAC software installation checks with the CLUVFY utility:

```
cluvfy stage -pre dbinst -n raclinux1,raclinux2 -verbose
```

The `-pre dbinst` argument within the CLUVFY utility thoroughly analyzes the prerequisite verifications on the participating nodes such as network details, kernel values, daemons, packages, user, and groups. Continue with the installation phase only when the prerequisites checks are successfully completed.

Initiating Oracle Universal Installer for Oracle 11g R1 RAC software

Rather than going through a series of installation images for the RAC 11g R1 installation, we will outline the instructions required to install RAC 11g R1.

Bear in mind that we will need to perform the installation twice to have separate ASM and DB homes, as discussed earlier.

To begin the RAC software installation for the ASM home, navigate through the database software directory and initiate the `./runInstaller` command either from the Oracle 11g R1 database staged software area or from the installation DVD/ CD source. It is recommended that you always initiate any installation or other installation related to pivotal actions from Node 1 of a cluster.

The steps are as follows:

1. Click on **Next** on the **Welcome** screen.
2. On the **Select Installation Type** screen, select the type of installation that you require according to your Oracle License. After you make your choice, click on **Next** to continue further.
3. Accept the default location if OUI shows the right location and enter the name and path for the software location on the **Specify Home Details** screen. For example, enter `OraAsm11g_home` for name and the path as `/u01/app/oracle/product/11.1.0/asm` for the software location. Click on **Next** to continue further.
4. Ensure that all nodes of the cluster appear in the list on the **Specify Hardware Cluster Installation Mode** under the Cluster Installation choice (the default choice). Don't select the Local Installation option as we intend to perform cluster-level configuration. If all the nodes of the cluster do not appear in the list, hold the installation for a while and check the cluster status on nodes that are not in the list. Click the **Select All** button to select the listed nodes and click on **Next** to continue further.
5. OUI then performs the product-specific prerequisite checks on the **Product-Specific Prerequisite Checks** screen. After the prerequisites checks are performed, ensure that all the flagged status checks are passed. Press **Next** to continue further.
6. For the time being, select the **Install Software** option on the **Select Configuration Option** screen and click on **Next** to continue further.
7. Review the summary on the **Summary** screen and click on **Install t**o begin the software installation process.
8. OUI then starts the installation process on the **Install** screen where it also shows the progress bar. Once the software is installed on the local server (node), OUI carries out remote operations where it clones the software binaries to other servers (nodes).

9. Once the progress bar reaches 100%, it opens the **Execute Configuration scripts** dialog box and instructs you to execute the script (`root.sh`) as root user across the nodes. Open a new window on the local node, log in as root user and execute the script. The script sets the Oracle base and homes and prompts you to enter the full pathname of the local bin directory, (`/usr/local/bin`); simply accept the default setting and press the *Enter* key.
10. After executing the scripts across all nodes, press **OK** and click on **Exit** on the **End of Installation** screen.

At this point, we should have a successful RAC software installation of ASM home.

Now, let's perform a similar action for DB home as well. You must follow the same sequence of actions outlined earlier in this chapter. However, use a different **Name** and **Path** on the **Specify Home Details** screen. For example, you may choose `OraDB11g_home` as the Name and `/u01/app/oracle/product/11.1.0/db_1` as the path for the software.

So far, we have demonstrated how to build a two-node Oracle Clusterware and RAC (software) configuration. Before you move on to the next step, it is recommended that you complete the following housekeeping tasks (known as post-installation tasks).

Post-installation tasks

In the following section, we have outlined the post-installation tasks that you are required to complete.

- Backup the OCR file. With 11g R1 and 11g R2, you can perform a manual backup of OCR at any time using the `ocrconfig -manualbackup` command.
- Back up the voting disk. You can backup the voting disk by using the UNIX/LINUX platform OS-level `dd` command. For example, `dd if=voting_disk_name of=backup_file_name`. On Windows, you can use the ocopy utility.
- Back up the Clusterware, ASM, and Oracle DB homes respectively.
- Back up the `root.sh` script from Clusterware, ASM, and Oracle DB homes.
- Most importantly, you can download and apply the latest patches on CRS, ASM, and DB home. For example, you can download the 11.1.0.7 patch set or any Cluster bundles patches.
- Install the Grid Control agent, if you have the Grid Control server installed.

Oracle 11g R2 Clusterware installation

Presuming that the servers (referred to as nodes hereafter) are built properly and the prerequisite checks are verified thoroughly with the CLUVFY utility, it is the right time to begin the Oracle 11g R2 Clusterware installation process. However, bear in mind that for a successful installation, all prerequisite validations must be met on nodes that are going to be part of the cluster installation.

In the subsequent sections we are going to demonstrate a two-node Oracle 11g R2 Grid Infrastructure and RAC software (RDBMS) installation procedure.

The following table describes the environmental settings that have been used in this book to demonstrate Oracle 11g R2 Grid Infrastructure and RDBMS software installation and configuration:

Operating System	**Linux V5**		
Grid home	/u01/app/oracle/product/11.2.0/grid		
Database home	/u01/app/oracle/product/11.2.0/db_1		
Shared Disks	/dev/sdb1, sdc1, sdd1, sde1, sdf1		
IP address, hostname & domain names in `/etc/host` file entry	#Public IP address		
	192.168.2.201	raclinux1.sjh.com	raclinux1
	192.168.2.202	raclinux2.sjh.com	raclinux2
	#Private IP address		
	10.10.1.1	raclinux1-priv.sjh.com	raclinux1-priv
	10.10.1.2	raclinux2-priv.sjh.com	raclinux2-priv
	#Virtual IPs		
	192.168.2.211	raclinux1-vip.sjh.com	raclinux1-vip
	192.168.2.212	raclinux2-vip.sjh.com	raclinux2-vip
	#SCAN		
	192.168.2.301	raclinux-scan (not recommended)	

Note: Oracle strongly recommends that you configure the SCAN either on DNS or GNS, with a maximum of three IPs in a round-robin fashion.

Initiating Oracle Universal Installer for 11g R2 Clusterware

Unlike the standalone installation procedure, Oracle RAC requires a two-phase installation procedure. In the first phase, an Oracle Grid Infrastructure is configured, while in the second phase, the Oracle RAC (RDBMS) software is installed.

To begin with the Grid Infrastructure configuration proceedings, initiate the ./`runInstaller` command either from the Oracle 11g R2 Grid staged software area or from the installation DVD/CD source.

1. The **Setting up Grid Infrastructure** screen displays various installation types and upgrade options for a cluster. Select the **Install and Configure Grid Infrastructure for a Cluster** option and click on **Next** to proceed further, as shown in the following screenshot:

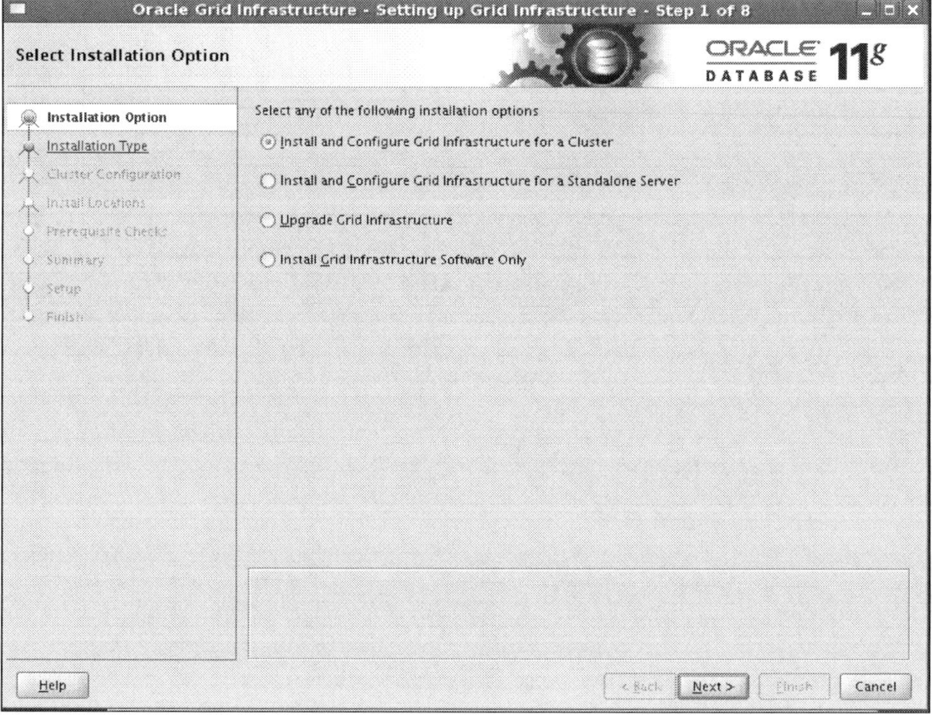

2. You can have the Grid Infrastructure installed in two ways: **Typical** or **Advanced**. The **Typical** installation is the easiest and the most recommended installation option in contrast to the **Advanced** installation option, as it comes with a handful of configuration choices. You do not require a high degree of system knowledge for this type of installation. On the contrary, the **Advanced** installation option allows you to set configuration choices for ASM, storage, and network levels. Therefore, let's choose the **Typical installation** option and click on **Next** to continue further, as shown in the following screenshot:

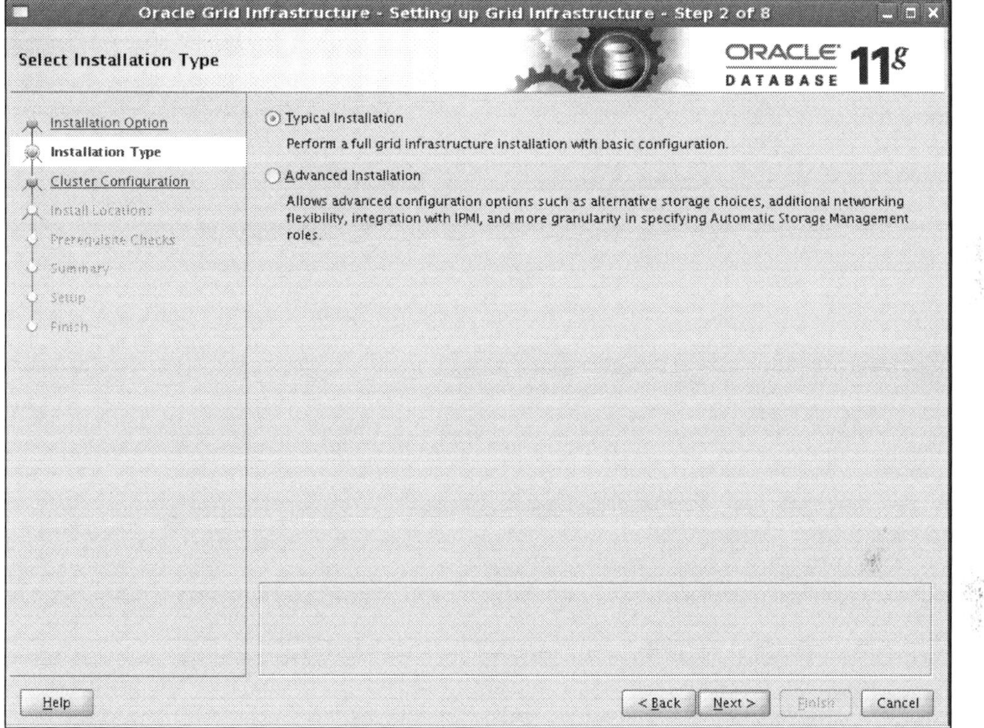

3. You have to perform a handful of important tasks on the Step 3 screen, such as adding more nodes details, naming the SCAN, testing SSH connectivity, and setting up network interfaces for public and private communication.

   As discussed previously, you will need to provide the SCAN name, which could also act as the default name for the cluster. However, the name suggested here for SCAN is based on the local name settings.

As part of the installation, local node details, such as public and VIP names, are fetched and displayed. In order to add more nodes, click on the **Add** button and enter the details of each node. Repeat the same method until you have added all the required nodes, as shown in the following screenshot:

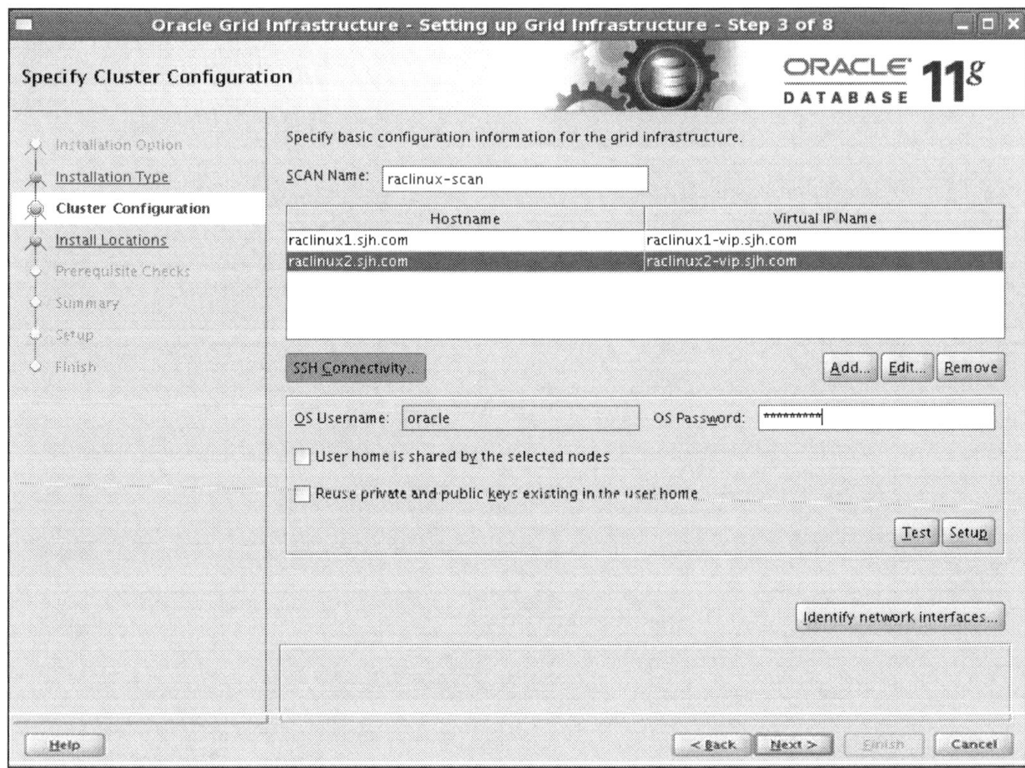

4. The **SSH Connectivity** configuration between the node members is a vital requirement for a cluster installation. Therefore, if you did not complete this step before the beginning of the installation process, you can complete this step on this screen. You will need to enter the Grid Infrastructure software owner (user) details and click the **Test** button to test and build the connectivity. To assign the right interface type for public and private interfaces, click on the **Identify Network Interfaces** button. All the network interfaces in the previous release were wrongly assigned to the Private type. However, with 11g R2, you can see that public and private interfaces have been assigned to the correct interface types. You could also choose the right type for the individual interface name using the drop-down list on the **Identify Network Interfaces** dialog box. Click on **OK** and close the **Identify Network Interfaces** window and click on **Next** to continue further, as shown in the following screenshot:

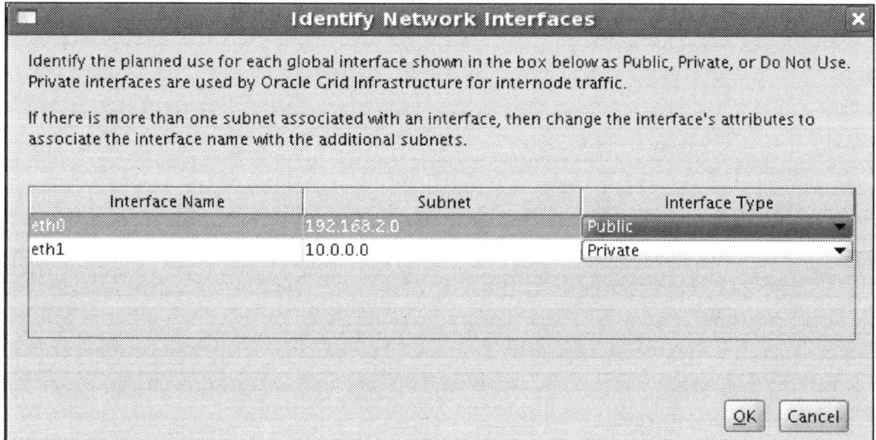

5. The next (**Install Locations**) screen requires you to make a decision about where you are going to configure the OCR and voting disks, whether it will be on a shared disk or on ASM. Unlike the previous versions, with 11g R2, you can configure the critical components of a cluster, that is, OCR and voting disk files on ASM as well. If the ASM option is being selected over the shared storage, you need to enter and confirm the **SYSASM Password** subsequently, as shown in the following screenshot:

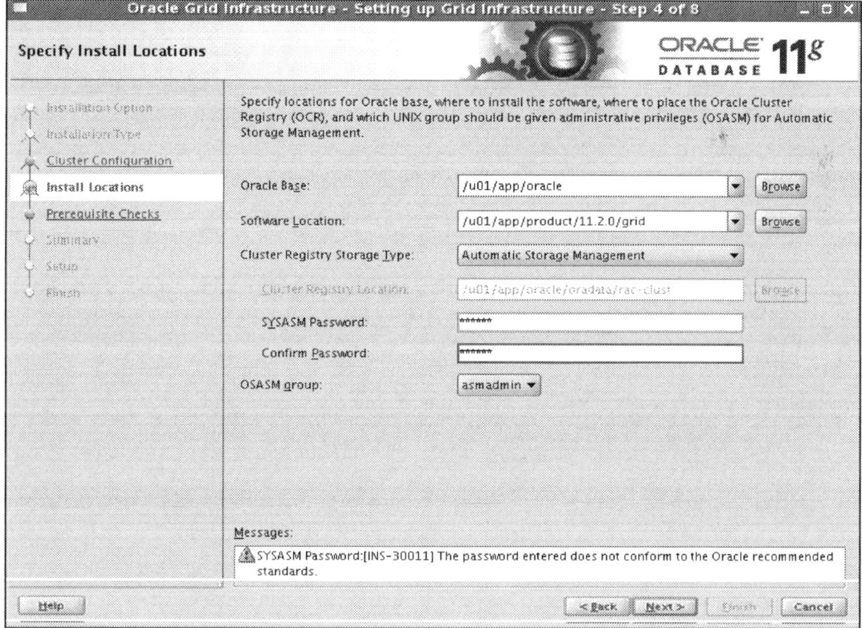

Also, on the **Install Locations** screen, enter the correct values for the Oracle base and software locations.

6. Choose one of the options from the drop-down list against **Cluster Registry Type: Filesystem** or **Automatic Storage Management**. If the ASM option is selected, then provide a password for ASM super user, that is, ASMSYS user, and assign the relevant OS group. Bypass the password warning message here, in case the password doesn't fit into the Oracle recommendation. Click on **Next** to continue. After choosing ASM as the storage option for the OCR and the voting disk, the subsequent screen requires your interaction for creating an ASM disk group in order to place the OCR and voting disks.
7. Click on the **Change Directory Path** button to define the storage path in order to discover the storage (disks) for ASM, as shown in the following screenshot:

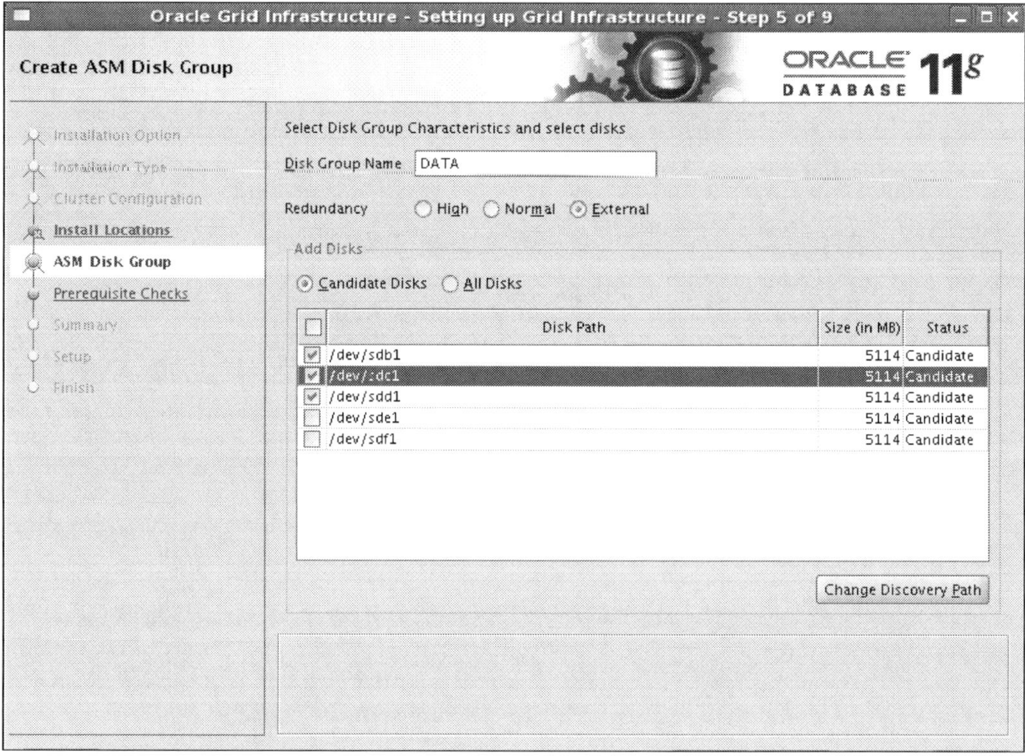

For example, enter a string value such as `/dev/sd*1` in the **Change Disk Discovery Path** dialog box and click on **OK**.

8. Upon discovering the ASM disks, select the required disks from the list and enter the disk group name and also choose **External** type for the **Redundancy** option. Click on **Next** to continue further. Accept the default inventory location, and click on **Next** to proceed further on the **Create Inventory** screen.
9. OUI then initiates the prerequisite verifications on the **Prerequisites Checks** screen. You will then need to progress towards the **Summary** screen, provided that no problems were found in the prerequisite checks. However, if any concerns are raised during the prerequisites checks, resolve them before you continue with the installation process.
10. Verify the summary details given on the **Summary** screen and click on **Next** to begin the installation process.
11. The actual Grid Infrastructure installation process will then kick off on the **Setup** screen.

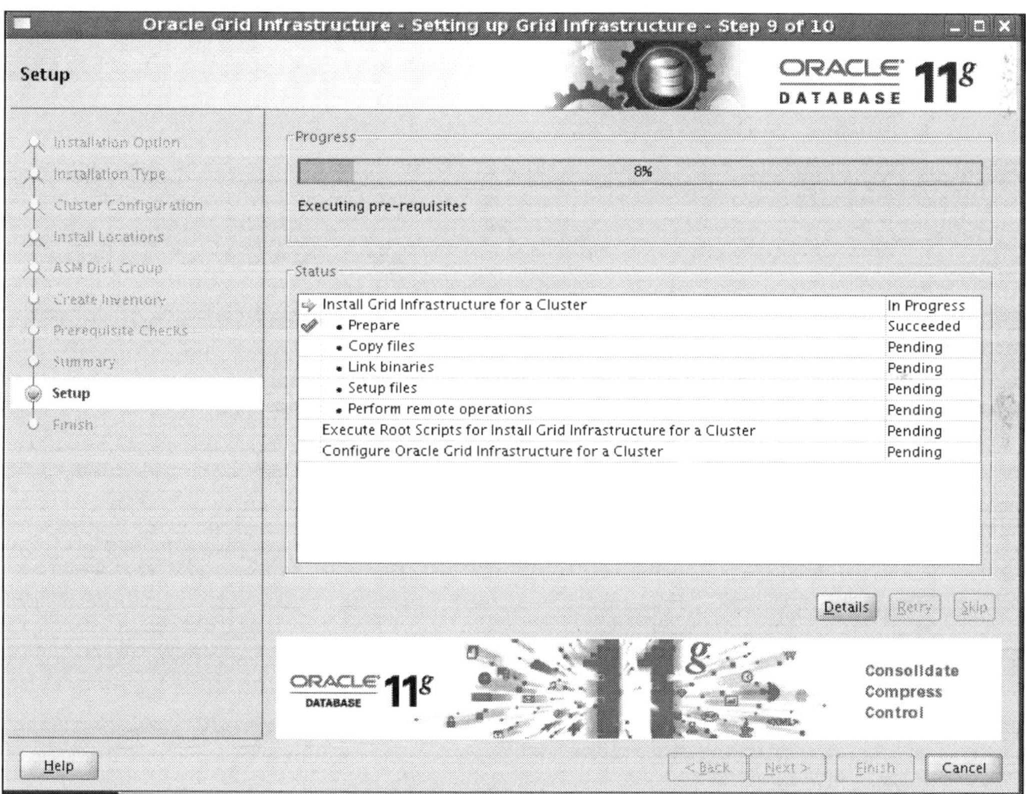

12. Towards approaching the 100% progress, a pop-up window **Execute Configuration scripts** will be displayed with instructions to run `orainstRoot.sh` and `root.sh` scripts sequentially on all cluster node members, as shown in the following screenshot:

    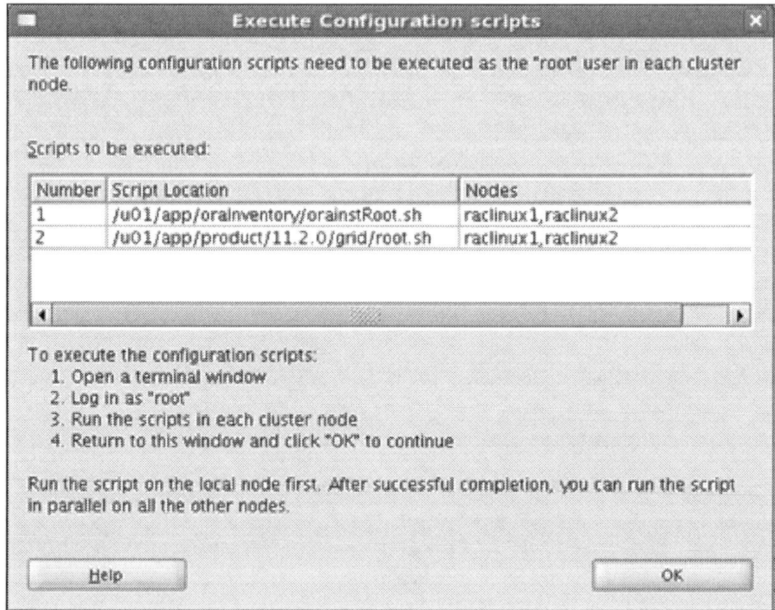

    Therefore, open a new terminal, log in as root user and run the `orainstRoot.sh` script on the local node. After the script on the local node successfully completes, move on to another node and execute the script again. You need to execute the same script on the rest of the nodes of a cluster.

13. After executing the `orainstRoot.sh` script successfully on all nodes, turn back to the first node to execute the `root.sh` script as root user. After completion, move to the second node and execute the same script. After executing the script successfully on each node of a cluster, click on the **OK** button to close the dialog box.

14. If, for any reason, the `root.sh` script is not run successfully, then refer to the deconfigure/reconfigure section at the end of the chapter to know more about how to resume from a failed installation. After the scripts are successfully run on each of the nodes of the cluster, continue further configuration of other options such as, ASM creation, Listener creation, Private interconnect, and the cluster verification utility on the **Setup** screen. Once everything is successfully completed, click on **Finish** to end the Grid Infrastructure installation process.

What happens when the root.sh is run?

It is only during the `root.sh` script execution time that the majority of Clusterware actions (configuration) are performed. Hence, the error-free completion of the script on all nodes of a cluster is the key factor for a successful cluster configuration. Typically, the script is likely to go through the following list of actions when the `root.sh` is executed on the first node:

- Sets the Oracle base and home environments
- Creates the `/etc/oratab` file
- Verifies the super user privileges
- Creates a trace directory
- Generates OCR keys for the root user
- Adds daemon information to the `inittab` file
- Starts up the Oracle High Availability Service Daemon (OHASD) process
- Creates and configures an ASM instance and starts up the instance
- Creates required ASM disk groups, if ASM is being used to put OCR and voting files
- Accumulates OCR keys for the root user
- Starts up the Cluster Ready Service Daemon (CRSD) process
- Creates the voting disk file
- Puts the voting disk on the Voting disk, if ASM type is selected
- Displays voting disk details
- Stops and restarts a cluster stack and other cluster resources on the local node
- Backs up the OCR to a default location
- Installs the `cvuqdisk-1.0.7-1` package
- Updates the Oracle inventory file
- Completes with the `UpdateNodeList` success operation

When `root.sh` is executed on the last node of the cluster, the following set of actions is likely to be performed by the script:

- Sets Oracle base and home environmental variables
- The `/etc/oratab` file will be created
- Performs the super user privileges verification
- Adds trace directories
- Generates OCR keys for the root user

- Adds a daemon to `inittab`
- Starts the Oracle High Availability Service Daemon (OHASD) process
- Stops/starts a cluster stack and other cluster resources on the local node
- Performs a backup of the `OCR` file
- Installs the `cvuqdisk-1.0.7-1` package
- Updates the Oracle inventory file
- Completes with `UpdateNodeList` success operation

Oracle 11g R2 Clusterware post-installation checks

At this point, we should have successfully built a two-node Oracle 11g R2 Grid Infrastructure and are all set to carry out a few important post-installation verifications.

To begin with, let's quickly perform a post-installation verification with the CLUVFY utility. To achieve this, use the following command on node1:

```
cluvfy stage -post crsinst -n raclinux1,raclinux2 -verbose
```

We shall now verify the cluster status (health check) on all nodes to ensure that the cluster is up and running on the nodes. Unlike previous versions, where you needed to run the command on each node individually to verify the cluster health status, beginning with 11g R2, you can verify the cluster status of all nodes from one node using the following example:

```
[oracle@raclinux1 bin]$ ./crsctl check cluster -all
**************************************************************
raclinux1:
CRS-4537: Cluster Ready Services is online
CRS-4529: Cluster Synchronization Services is online
CRS-4533: Event Manager is online
**************************************************************
raclinux2:
CRS-4537: Cluster Ready Services is online
CRS-4529: Cluster Synchronization Services is online
CRS-4533: Event Manager is online
**************************************************************
```

Ensure cluster components OHAS, CRS, CSSS, and EVMD appear healthy when the above command is run.

A `olsnodes` Clusterware command can be used to find out the number of nodes associated with a cluster:

```
[oracle@raclinux1 ~]$ olsnodes -n
raclinux1       1
raclinux2       2
```

The `ocrcheck` command is generally used to verify the integrity, size, location, and details about the OCR in the cluster, as follows:

```
      ./ocrcheck
Status of Oracle Cluster Registry is as follows :
      Version                  :          3
      Total space (kbytes)     :     262120
      Used space (kbytes)      :       2276
      Available space (kbytes) :     259844
      ID                       : 1639999098
      Device/File Name         :      +DATA
                   Device/File integrity check succeeded
                              Device/File not configured
                              Device/File not configured
                              Device/File not configured
                              Device/File not configured
         Cluster registry integrity check succeeded
   Logical corruption check bypassed due to non-privileged user
```

Let's find out the voting disk details and Clusterware active/software version using the following commands:

```
./crsctl query css votedisk
##  STATE    File Universal Id                 File Name Disk group
--  -----    -----------------                 --------- ---------
 1. ONLINE   0f5c91051bc64fb3bfd137a74b55b958 (/dev/sdb1) [DATA]
Located 1 voting disk(s).

./crsctl query crs softwareversion
Oracle Clusterware version on node [raclinux1] is [11.2.0.1.0]
./crsctl query crs activeversion
Oracle Clusterware active version on the cluster is [11.2.0.1.0]
```

We shall also do some OS-level checks as well before we move on to install the Oracle 11g R2 RAC software.

The following example shows the cluster stack daemon processes running at OS level:

```
[oracle@raclinux1 ~]$ ps -ef|grep init
root         1     0  0 09:53 ?        00:00:01 init [5]

root      3440     1  0 09:56 ?        00:00:00 /bin/sh /etc/init.d/init.ohasd run
```

The following entry must exist in the `/etc/inittab` OS file to facilitate the Clusterware auto startup and shutdown operations during the system (node) reboot. These entries were added at the time of the `root.sh` script execution:

```
h1:3:respawn:/sbin/init.d/init.ohasd run >/dev/null 2>&1 </dev/null
```

Installing Oracle 11g R2 RAC software

Unlike the previous versions, 10g R2 and 11g R1, we are not going to repeat the RAC software installation in the second phase in order to follow the recommendation to keep separate ASM and DB homes. Instead, in the second phase, we will only install RAC software once for DB home, as with Oracle 11g R2, ASM is now closely integrated with Oracle Clusterware and configured together into a single home, that is, GRID HOME.

Before we begin with the RAC software installation proceedings, let's verify the prerequisite checks using the following command, in order to ensure the nodes, readiness for a smooth and successful installation:

```
./cluvfy stage -pre dbinst -fixup -n raclinux1,raclinux2 -verbose
```

The `-pre dbinst` argument with the CLUVFY utility thoroughly analyzes the prerequisite verifications on the participating nodes. If any verification checks failed to meet the minimal requirements, do not proceed further. Fix the problems reported and then continue with the installation procedure.

Initiating Oracle Universal Installer for Oracle 11g R2 RAC software

In order to begin the 11g R2 RAC software installation, you first need to initiate the OUI utility. Carry out the following procedure:

1. Navigate through the Oracle 11g R2 database source staging location and execute `./runInstaller` to initiate OUI for the RAC installation process.
2. If you wish to receive automatic security patch updates and to install the products directly, enter your My Oracle Support (MOS) user name (typically your company e-mail ID) and the password by enabling the **I wish to receive security updates via My Oracle Support** option on the **Configure Security Updates** screen, as shown in the following screenshot:

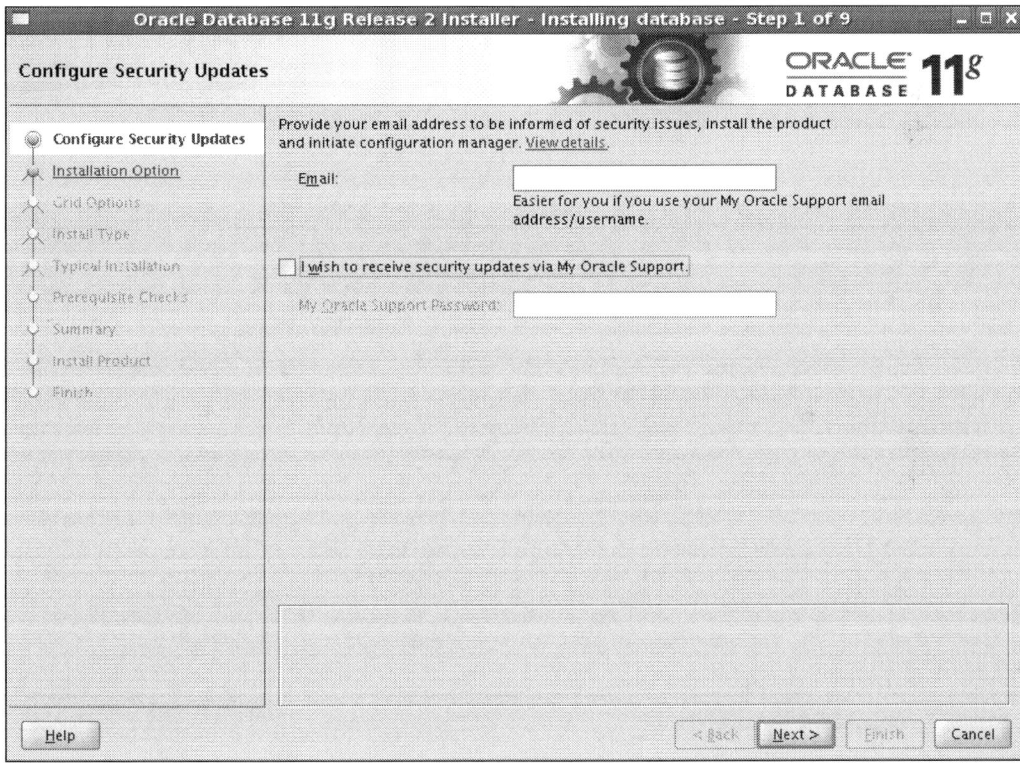

3. Pay no attention to the warning message if you uncheck this option and click on **Next** to proceed further. On the **Installing Database** screen, select the **Install Database software only**. Click **Next** to continue further, as shown in the following screenshot:

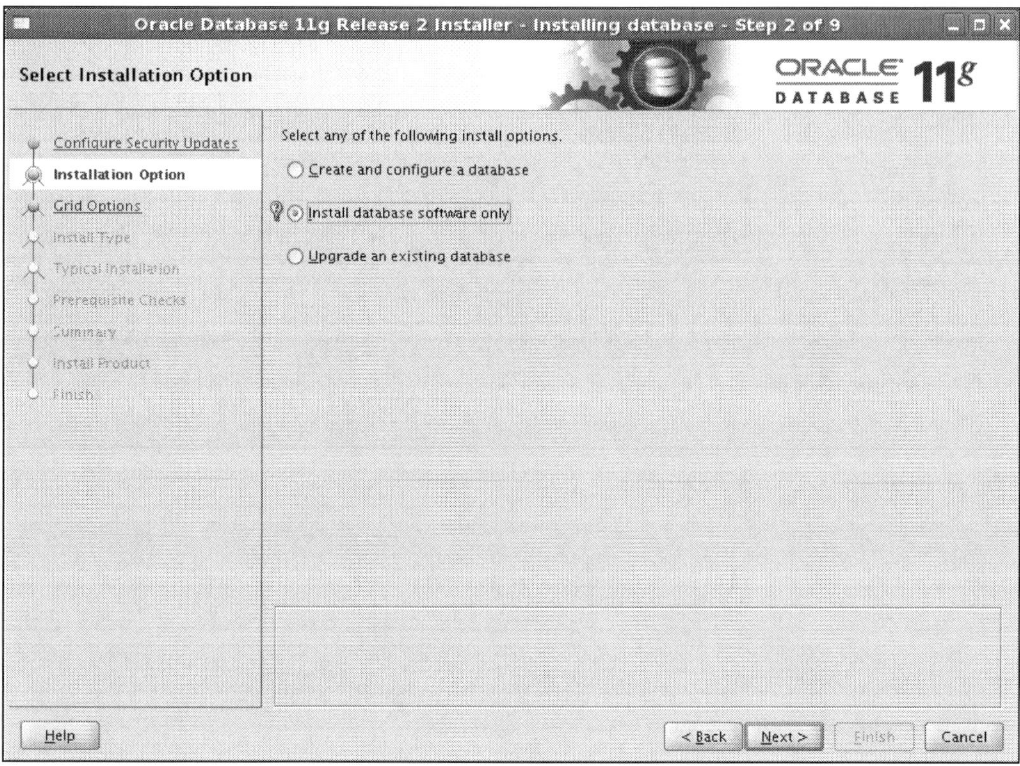

4. Select the **Real Application Clusters database installation** option on the **Grid Options** screen and ensure that you have selected all the node members listed there. Furthermore, you can also ensure the SSH connectivity between the node members by clicking on the **Test** button. Put the RAC software OS username and password details. Click on **Next** to continue, as shown in the following screenshot:

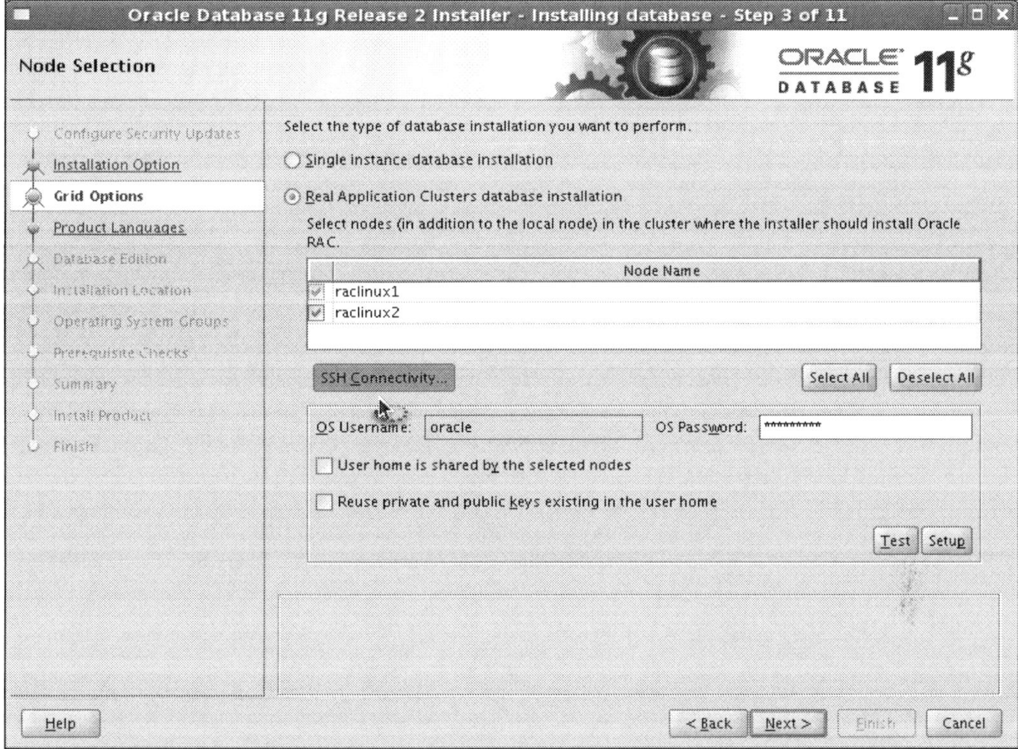

5. Select the additional language settings on the **Product Languages** screen. Click on **Next** to continue further.
6. Choose either the **Enterprise edition** or **Standard edition** option. The selection criteria must be according to the license agreement that your company holds with Oracle. Click on **Next** to continue further.

7. On the next screen, specify the **Oracle Base** and **Software Location** details. Click on **Next** to continue further, as shown in the following screenshot:

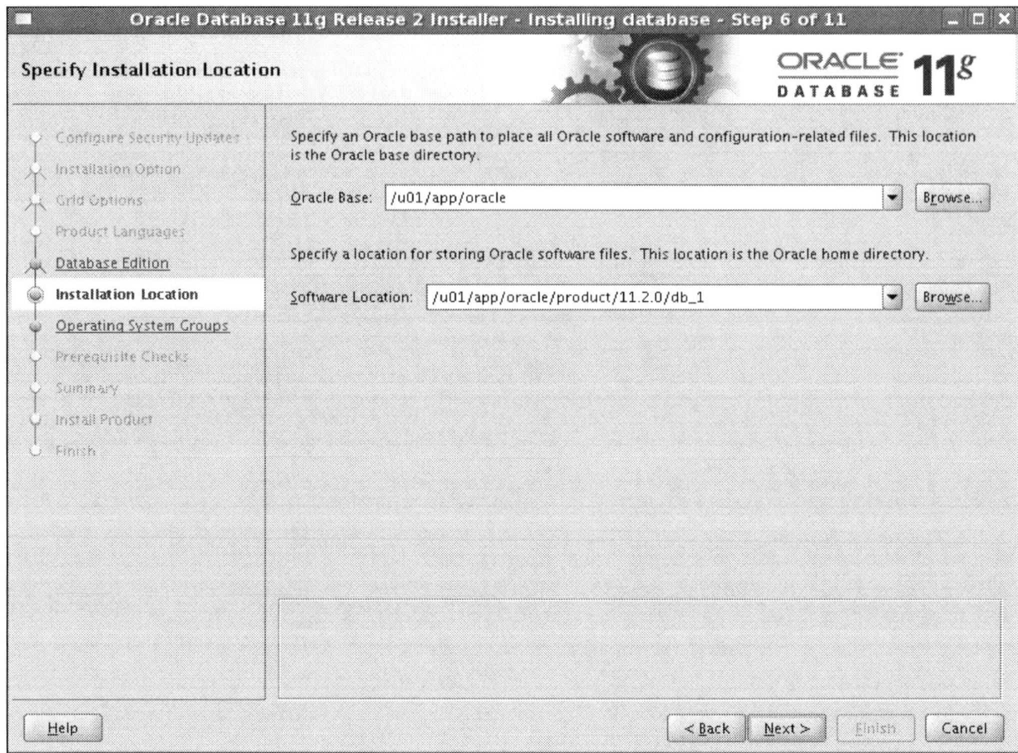

8. You are most likely to accept the default suggestion provided on the **Installation Location** screen for the Database admin and operator OS groups. Click on **Next** to proceed further.

9. OUI then subsequently performs prerequisite checks on the **Prerequisites Checks** screen to ensure that minimal configuration and installation requirements are met, on the nodes. After the verification has been done, it lists the checks that have failed to meet the requirements. Fix the problems before you continue with the installation process. If the failed checks can be ignored because they won't cause any major troubles during the installation, you can tick/check the **Ignore All** option at the top of the screen to bypass the failures and continue with the rest of the installation. Click on **Next** to proceed further, as shown in the following screenshot:

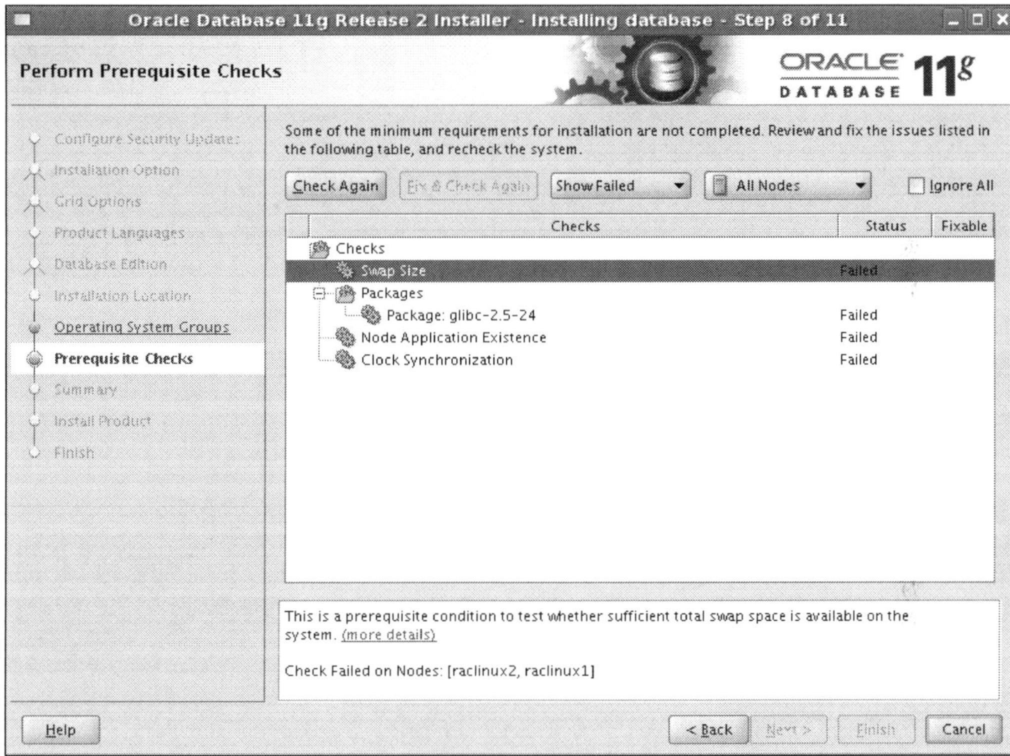

10. Review the summary information provided on the **Summary** screen and click on **Next** to commence the installation process.

11. Towards the end of the installation process, a dialog window **Execute Configuration scripts** pops up with instructions to run the `root.sh` script across all nodes. Hence, open a new window, log in as root user, and execute the script on a local node first and then repeat the same on the rest of the nodes. After you have executed the script successfully on each node, click **OK** followed by **Finish** to complete the installation, as shown in the following screenshot:

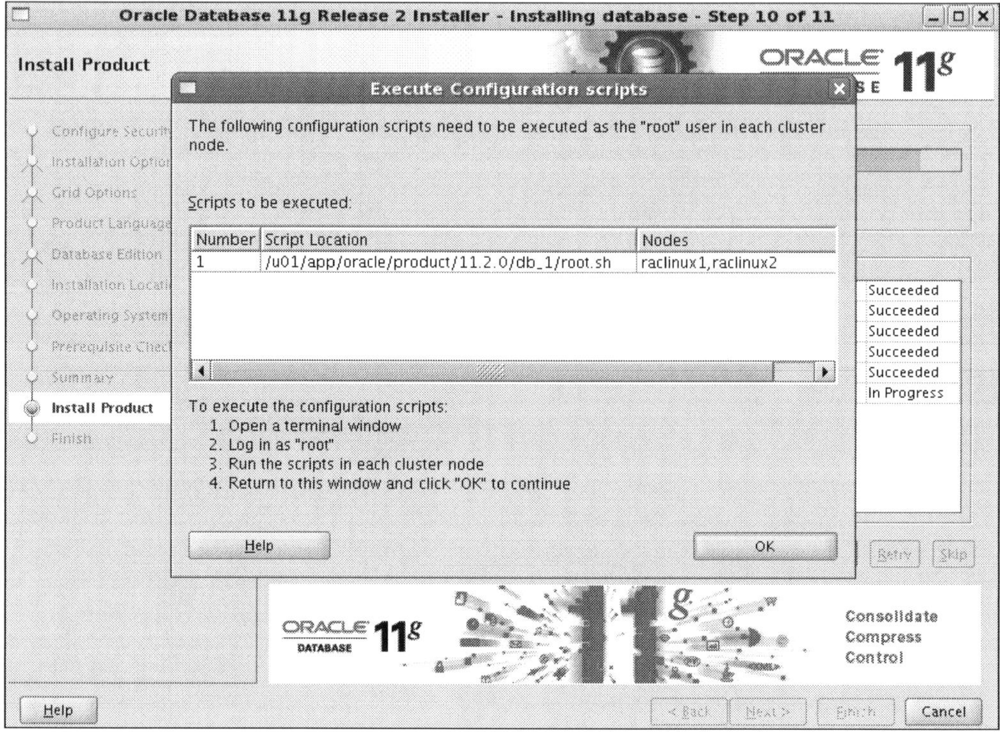

12. Click on **Close** to complete the installation and quit the OUI.

Post-installation tasks

In the following section, we outline the post-installation tasks that you are required to complete as part of a successful installation package:

- Back up the OCR file. With 11g R1 and 11g R2, you can perform the manual binary backup of the OCR file at any time using the `ocrconfig -manualbackup` command.
- Back up the Grid Infrastructure and Oracle DB home.

- Back up the `root.sh` script from both Grid Infrastructure and Oracle DB home.
- Most importantly, you can download and apply/update any of the latest patches on Grid home and DB homes, for example 11.2.0.2.
- After the installation, if for any reason you have to install the previous release of Oracle databases, you must pin the nodes first. To do so, carry out the following instructions:
  - Navigate through Grid Infrastructure bin location and execute `crsctl pin css -n node_list`.
- Install the Grid Control agent, if you have the Grid Control server installed.

Oracle 11g R2 Clusterware new features highlights

In this section, we are going to discuss some of the essential and useful new features of Oracle 11g Release 2 Clusterware:

- Grid Infrastructure: With Oracle 11g R2, Oracle Clusterware and ASM technologies are closely integrated and installed together into a single home, referred to as the GRID HOME.
- Out-of-place upgrade: With Oracle 11g R2, you can perform Oracle clusterware out-of-place upgrade methods, which allow you to install the new software of the Clusterware in a separate home. This type of upgrade would potentially reduce the planned upgrade downtime.
- OCR and voting disk on ASM: As Clusterware and ASM are closely associated with each other in 11g R2, now the OCR and voting disks can be stored on ASM. In 11g R2, you can have up to five OCR copies.
- Maximum voting disks: You can have up to a maximum of 15 voting disks. However, Oracle recommends that you do not go beyond five voting disks.
- No voting disk backup: With Oracle 11g R2, voting disk manual backup is no longer required, as voting disks content is now backed up in OCR automatically. Therefore, the traditional way of voting disk back-up with the `dd` command is no longer supported in this version.
- Single Client Access Name (SCAN): For client connections, it provides a single name access point to the RAC databases in a cluster, notwithstanding on which specific nodes the databases are actually configured. The SCAN name is configured during the installation phase and you must secure up to three IP address using a round-robin algorithm and add in the DNS.

- Redundant interconnect: With the latest patch set 1 of Oracle 11g R2 (11.2.0.2), you are no longer required to use the network bounding technique to configure interconnect redundancy. You can now define at most four interfaces for redundant interconnect (private network) usage and can be set during the installation phase.

Removing/Reconfiguring a Grid Infrastructure configuration

We are going to look at the necessary steps that are required to remove a successful Grid Infrastructure configuration or reconfigure a failed Grid Infrastructure configuration.

Removing a successful Grid Infrastructure configuration

You may find that it is necessary to remove the Grid Infrastructure configuration for technical or non-technical reasons. Keep in mind that to remove a successful configuration, you are required to perform a two-step action:

- You need to deconfigure the Clusterware services
- You need to deinstall the software binaries

Firstly, stop any active databases running on the node, followed by an ASM instance. You could use the `SRVCTL STOP DATABASE/ASM` or the SQLPLUS command `SHUTDOWN IMMEDIATE` to stop the databases and the ASM instance.

Now, log in as root user, navigate to the `$GRID_HOME/install` directory, and initiate the following command:

```
./rootcrs.pl -verbose -deconfig -force --(except on the last node)
```

Once the command has completed successfully on the node, move to the next node and repeat the command.

Once you reach the last node of the cluster, you need to run the following (slightly modified) command:

```
./rootcrs.pl -verbose -deconfig -force -lastnode --(just on the
last node)
```

When you run the command on the last node, indicated by the `-lastnode` flag, Oracle completes the deconfiguration process successfully and also zeroes out the OCR and voting disks respectively. However, the `-deconfig` option with the `.rootcrs.pl` will only deconfigure the Clusterware; it doesn't remove the software binaries from the GRID HOME. In order to remove the binaries from the home, you need to run the following command on each node of the cluster as the grid software owner, for example, as oracle user:

```
./$GRID_HOME/deinstall/deinstall
```

Reconfiguring a failed Grid Infrastructure configuration

If you would like to resume a failed configuration attempt, you first need to deconfigure the failed configuration and then proceed again with the configuration using the following actions.

Firstly, identify the failures caused during the `root.sh` script execution referring to the installation logs. For example, use the `crsconfig` log file under the `$GRID_HOME/cfgtoollogs` directory. Then, as root user, proceed with the following deconfiguration step:

```
./$GRID_HOME/install/rootcrs.pl -verbose -deconfig -force --(except
on the last node)
```

Once you run the script successfully on the first node of the cluster, proceed with subsequent nodes, repeating the same command.

However, when you reach the last node of the cluster, you need to run the following (slightly modified) command:

```
./$GRID_HOME/install/rootcrs.pl -verbose -deconfig -force -lastnode
--(just on the last node only)
```

Assuming that the problems that occurred during the `root.sh` execution time have been addressed properly and the failed configuration has been removed successfully on the node, using the preceding procedure, you need to rerun the `root.sh` script as root user to reconfigure the Grid Infrastructure installation again.

```
./$GRID_HOME/root.sh
```

Once the `root.sh` script has successfully completed on the first node, then proceed with the other nodes and repeat the same command, one node at a time.

Summary

In this chapter, we summarized the essential requirements that are necessary to build nodes with the Oracle-recommended prerequisites for a successful cluster installation. We then demonstrated a successful two-node Clusterware and Grid Infrastructures configuration (Version 11g R1 and 11g R2), followed by ASM and RDBMS software installations on the cluster. Towards the end of the chapter, we also demonstrated how to remove a successful Grid Infrastructure configuration and how to reconfigure a failed Grid Infrastructure configuration. By now, you should be able to prepare servers and perform a Cluster/Grid Infrastructure installation.

In the next chapter, we will look at Automatic Storage Management concepts, how to configure ASM instances, prepare disks and disk groups, and new features of Oracle 11g R1 and R2.

4
Automatic Storage Management

Considering the cost and other key elements associated with the currently available vendor's storage options, it is always going to be a tough and wise decision to be made by any organization to finalize on a particular storage method. However, it is for sure that a good storage method is definitely going to have its share of contribution towards improving the database and application's overall throughputs.

Fundamentally, just before the required storage is being presented to the database server to fulfill the database's need, the storage and Operating System administrators have to go through a series of actions. In this context, they have to use several available storage and OS utilities to fulfill the request, for example, a volume manager to build the volumes on the OS to create a filesystem on it. Fortunately, Oracle Automatic Storage Management technology simplifies those layers involved to prepare the volume groups and filesystem creation. Therefore, in this chapter, we will take a closer look at the **Automatic Storage Management (ASM)** and most of its key advantages. The following topics will be covered:

- Overview of Automatic Storage Management
- ASM instance configuration and management
- Overview of the ASM command-line ASMCMD utility
- ASM 11g R1 new features
- ASM 11g R2 new features
- ASM backup and restore strategies

Overview of Automatic Storage Management (ASM)

Automatic Storage Management (ASM) is an option and a new feature of Oracle 10g and onwards that simplifies the storage management for all Oracle database file types. It renders the capabilities of a volume manager and filesystem together into the Oracle database kernel. Although, it inherits the Stripe And Mirror Everything (SAME) functionality, it strips the data (extents) evenly across the ASM disks of a disk group by default and provides the mirroring functionality as an option. The management and administration of ASM is made easy through a well-known set of SQL statements, such as, `CREATE`, `ALTER`, `DROP`, and through GUI tools.

While the ASM was initially intended for managing and maintaining only the Oracle database files and other related files, its functionality has been significantly improved in 11g R1 and R2 versions to manage all types of data. The following are some of the key features and benefits of ASM:

- It simplifies the storage configuration management for Oracle datafiles and other files.
- It eliminates the need for third-party software, (for example, volume manager) to manage the storage for the databases.
- When a datafile is created, it is divided into equally sized (1, 2, 4, 8, 16, 32, or 64 MB) extents that are scattered evenly across the disks of a disk group to provide balanced I/O to improve performance and prevent hot spot symptoms.
- It is built on the Stripe and Mirror Everything (SAME) functionality.
- It supports both non-RAC and RAC databases efficiently.
- It has the ability to add and remove ASM disks online without actually disturbing the ongoing operations.
- It can be managed and administrated using a set of known SQL statements.
- It performs automatic online redistribution for the data whenever a disk is being added or dropped.
- With ASM 11g R2, in addition to all database file types, it can also be used to store non-Oracle datafile types such as binaries, images, and so on. Beginning with ASM 11g R2, it provides the ability of a preferred read functionality, when ASM mirroring features are enabled.
- It supports multiversioning of databases.
- It supports a multipathing feature to prevent outages from disk path failures.

Filesystem versus ASM storage architecture

The following image shows the comparison between a typical filesystem and ASM storage involved when a database is created:

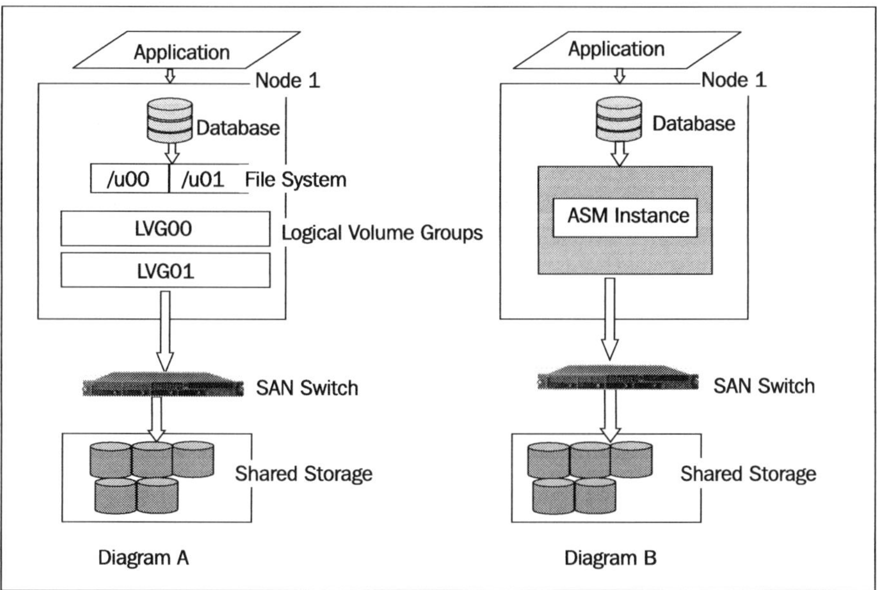

Diagram A: In this diagram, an application is being connected to a database that is running on Node 1 and the database datafiles are configured on a typical filesystem storage. As summarized earlier, the filesystem is built from a Logical Volume Group (LVG) and the LVG is prepared on the shared storage. Therefore, to prepare the storage for the database, (filesystem and volume groups), you generally need a third-party tool, such as Volume Manager.

Diagram B: In this diagram, an application is being connected to a database that is running on Node 1 and the database datafiles are configured on ASM storage. ASM storage renders the capabilities of the filesystem and volume manager and manages the storage. In contrast to a filesystem, ASM storage does not require any third-party tools to manage the storage for the database and eliminates the need of building a volume group and filesystem creation. This would bypass the layers involved between the database and storage, thus improving the read performance.

ASM disk

A disk is a primary element of an ASM instance. A disk could be built or formed either from a **Logical Unit Number (LUN)** by a storage array, a disk partition or an entire disk, or a logical volume or Network Attached File (NFS). An ASM instance discovers the disks within the paths specified with the `ASM_DISKSTRING` initialization parameter. Whenever a new disk is discovered by the ASM instance, the header status of the disk is set to the `CANDIDATE` flag and makes the disk available in the instance.

After the disks are successfully discovered by the local ASM instance, they will appear in the `V$ASM_DISK` dynamic view of the local ASM instance and the disks are ready to use to build a new ASM disk group, or can be added to any pre-existing ASM disk groups. However, when no particular paths for the disks are specified with the `ASM_DISKSTRING` initialization parameter, ASM by default look in the following OS specific paths to discover the disks:

Operating System	Path
Linux	`/dev/`
HPUX	`/dev/rdsk/*`
AIX	`/dev/*`
Solaris	`/dev/rdsk/*`
Windows	`\\.\orcldisk*`

On a cluster environment, ensure that all ASM disks are visible across all nodes and each node must have the exact set of permissions (`660`) and ownership (`oracle:dba`) to avoid running into any sorts of problems. Oracle also strongly advises to have the same size of disks in a disk group to maintain the disk group balance. On the other hand, you have the flexibility to define a different naming convention for a disk across the nodes in a cluster.

The following limits, as of 11g R2, have been imposed on ASM disks:

- A maximum of 10,000 disks
- Up to 2 TB maximum storage per ASM disk, with `EXADATA 4PB` per ASM disk

ASM disk group

A disk group is a logical container for one or more ASM disks and is the highest level of data structure in ASM. When a database is configured to employ the disk group, the disk group then becomes the default location for its datafiles. The disk group can be used to place various database file types, such as `datafiles`, `online redo`, `archivelogs`, `RMAN backupsets`, `OCR` and `Voting disks` (in 11g R2), and more. ASM also provides the flexibility of utilizing a single disk group by multiple ASM instances and databases across a cluster.

After a disk group is successfully created and mounted for the first time in the ASM instance, the name of the disk group is automatically affiliated with the `ASM_DISKGROUPS` initialization parameter to be able to mount the disk group at ASM instance restarts.

In general, when a datafile is created in a disk group, the datafile extents are striped/distributed evenly across the available disks of the disk group. Optionally, you can also set the following specified mirroring level at the disk group to protect the data integrity by storing redundant copies of data (extents) in a separate failure group to cope with the disk outage symptom:

- External redundancy: Relies on the STORAGE (RAID)-level mirroring redundancy option to protect the data
- Normal redundancy: Provides a default two-way mirroring option
- High redundancy: Provides a three-way mirroring redundancy option of ASM files

As of 11g R2, the following limits have been imposed on the ASM instance:

- A maximum of 63 disk groups in a storage system
- 1 million files per disk group

The following diagram illustrates the structure of a disk group with three disks assigned to it:

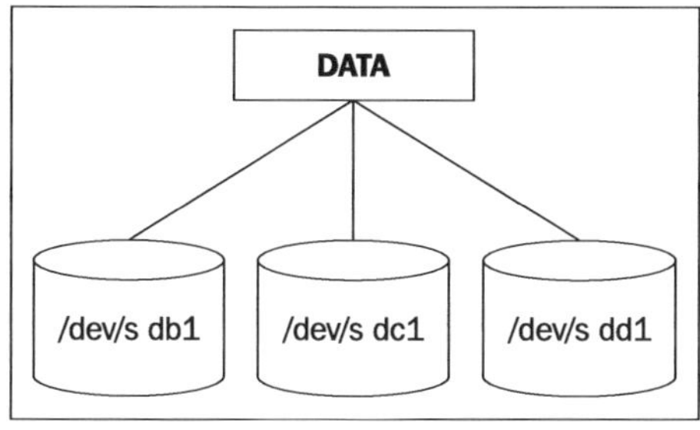

The following diagram illustrates the hierarchal structure of a disk group when multiple databases are using it:

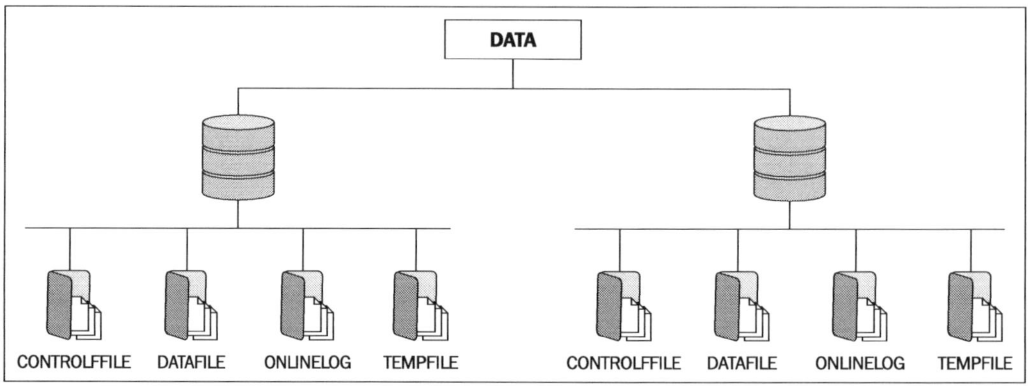

ASM instance configuration and management

Staring with 10g R1 and onwards, Oracle supports two types of instances: RDBMS and ASM. An ASM instance is a special kind of instance with only Shared Global Area (SGA) that typically consists of memory components such as Shared Pool, Large Pool, Free Memory and ASM Cache, and a set of default background process, with some additional ASM-specific background processes. The ASM instance doesn't hold any physical structure and the name of the instance typically starts with `+ASM`. The instance would be generally named as `+ASMn` (where n represents the instance number) in a cluster environment. The `INSTANCE_TYPE` initialization parameter controls the role played by these two instances. The ASM instance configuration requires only a handful of initialization parameters. These parameters are discussed in the following section.

ASM instances efficiently support both non-RAC and RAC databases. Only one ASM instance is required per node, irrespective of the number of databases/instances running on the node. In an RAC environment, you need to configure one ASM instance per node and these ASM instances across the cluster communicate with each other using an interconnected network communication. The database instances interact with the ASM instance to manage the database datafiles. ASM instances typically listen on `1521` port by default.

ASM initialization parameters

In this section, we are going to summarize the essential ASM instance initialization parameters, their usage, and recommended values:

`instance_type`	Defines the type of the instance, such as RDBMS and ASM. However, this has been made optional in an Oracle Grid Infrastructure ASM.
`asm_diskstring`	Used by the ASM instance to identify and discover the disks mentioned in the paths. Once the disks are discovered, they will appear in the `V$ASM_DISK` dynamic view. The disk discovery occurs when an ASM instance is initiated, when you issue a query against the `V$ASM_DISK/V$ASM_DISKGROUP` dynamic views, or when you `MOUNT`, `UNMOUNT`, `RESIZE`, `ADD` a disk. It is a dynamic parameter and you can specify multiple paths within this parameter.
`asm_diskgroups`	A dynamic parameter that holds the list of the disk group names that are created and mounted in an ASM instance. These disk groups are set to mount automatically at ASM instance startup. Whenever you successfully create or drop a disk group, the change will reflect to this parameter automatically and influence the subsequent instance start-up.
`asm_power_limit`	Manages the degree of parallelism to speed up the ASM disk rebalance operations, for example, whenever a disk is being dropped from an existing disk group or when the disk group rebalance is initiated manually. This is a dynamic parameter that can be set in the range from 0 to 11 (1024 in 11gR2 and above). Considering the size of a disk group, you may increase the limit of the `POWER` to speed up the rebalancing operation. Multiple ASM instances can hold the different values across a cluster. When no limit is specified, it uses the default value for the rebalancing operation.
`processes`	Apart from the SGA initialization parameter value, the `PROCESSES` initialization parameter value has some influence over the ASM instance. Therefore, you may use the following formula to tune the `PROCESSES` initialization parameter when multiple database instances are accessing the instance: Processes = 50+50*n (where *n* indicates the number of instances used to connect to the ASM instance)

Creating an ASM instance

You can create an ASM instance initially using various methods: manual, interactive GUI tools such as DBCA (in 11g R1), ASMCA (from 11g R2 onwards), and Grid Control. In the following section, we are going to exhibit the ASM instance configuration using the DBCA tool for Oracle 11g R1. Then we will cover how to configure the ASM instance using the ASMCA tool.

Initializing DBCA

The following procedure explains the steps that are involved in creating an ASM instance using the DBCA tool in 11g R1:

a. Navigate to the ASM home bin location (for example, `cd $ASM_HOME/bin`) and run `./dbca` to launch the **Database Configuration Assistance** to begin the ASM instance configuration.

b. Select the **Oracle Real Application Cluster database** option on the **Welcome** screen and click on **Next** to continue.

c. Choose the **Configure Automatic Storage Management** option on the **Operations** screen and click on **Next** to continue, as shown in the following screenshot:

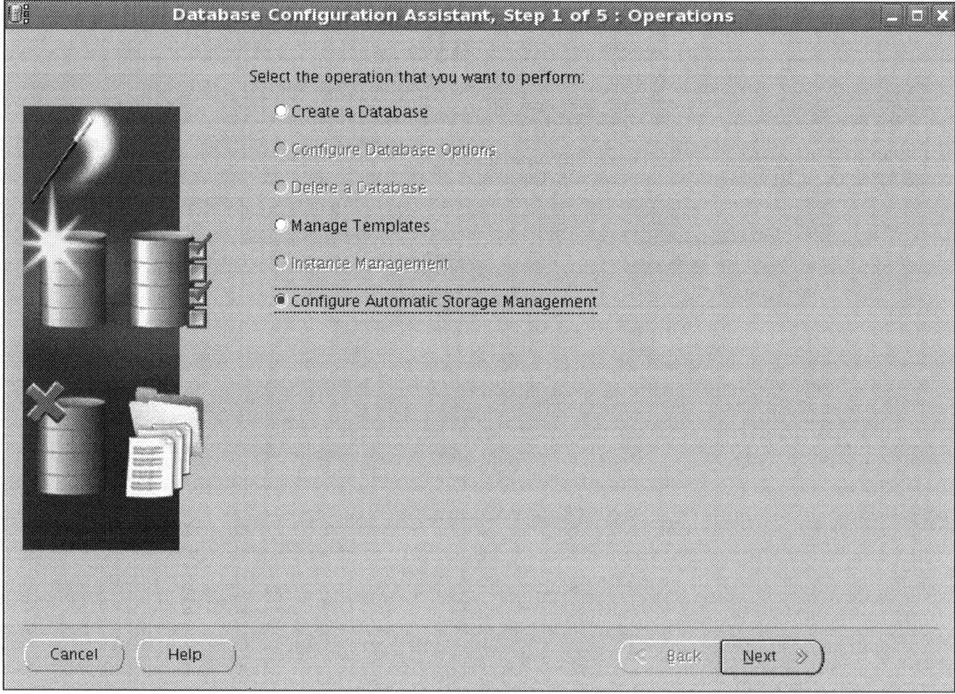

d. As this is intended for an RAC environment, select all the nodes listed in the **Node Selection** screen by clicking on the **Select All** button and click on **Next** to continue.

e. On the **Create ASM Instance** screen, enter and confirm the password for `SYS` account. Specify the location for ASM `pfile/SPFILE`.

f. Click on the **ASM Parameters** button to enter values for ASM specific initialization parameters, such as disk location and ASM, as shown in the following screenshot:

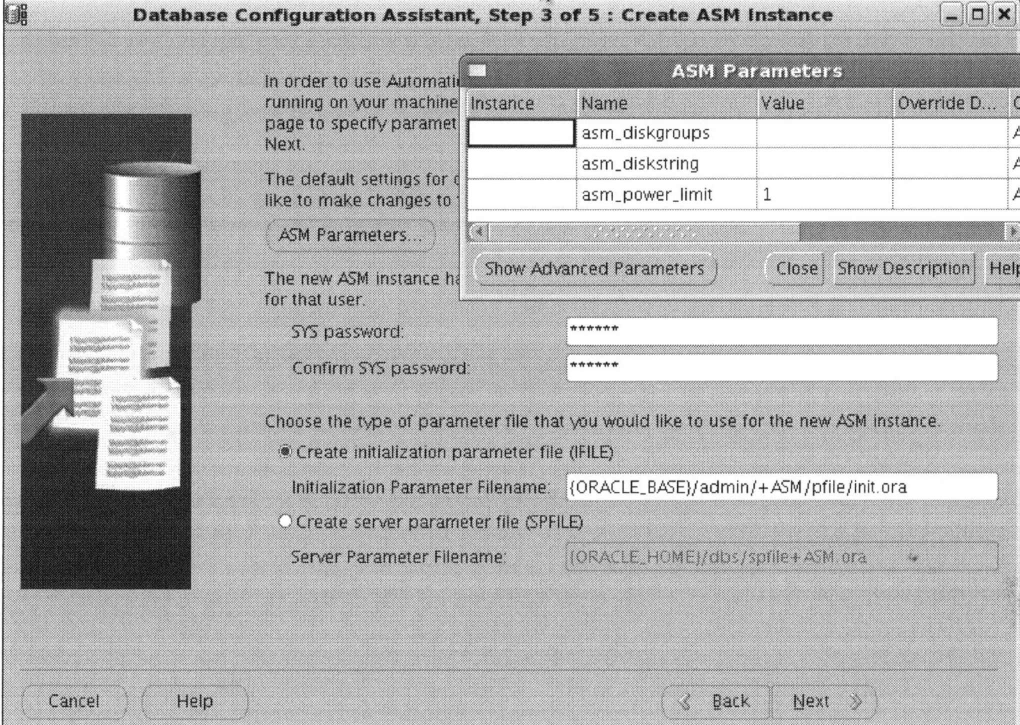

g. Subsequently, the DBCA initiates an ASM instance creation process. Upon completion, it displays the following ASM creation pop-up window:

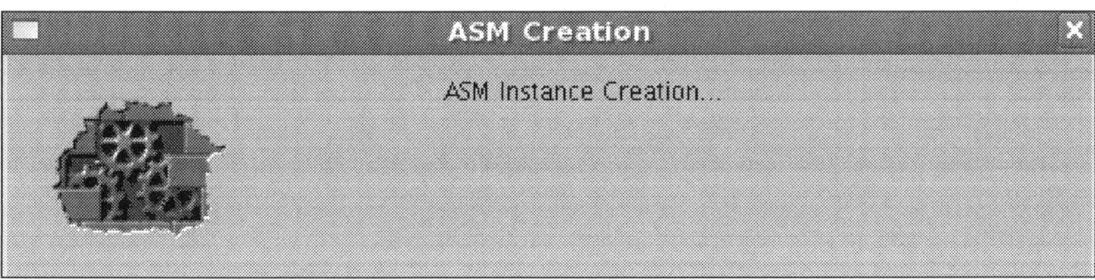

h. After successfully creating the ASM instance, the ASM disk groups screen is displayed, allowing you to build a disk group. Click on **Finish** to complete the creation and to quit from the DBCA tool.

Now we have a successful ASM instance creation across a cluster.

ASM background processes

In addition to the typical set of instance background processes, an ASM instance comes with a few additional background processes that assist the ASM instance to perform its course of action. Therefore, understanding the individual role played by these ASM-specific background processes in order to know how they help the ASM instance to manage and carry out its functionality, will be helpful to DBAs. In this section, we are going to cover the most useful ASM-specific background processes and the part played by the individual ASM-specific background processes:

ASMB	ASMB exists in both typical database instances and ASM instances and is responsible for receiving an extent map for the new file.
RBAL	Rebalance Master process exists in databases and ASM. In databases, RBAL manages ASM disk group. In an ASM instance, RBAL coordinates disk group rebalance activity. RBAL also assists in opening all device files as part of the discovery operation.
GMON	ASM Disk group Monitor Process monitors all the mounted disk groups and is responsible for maintaining consistent disk membership and status information.
PZ9n	Parallel Slave Processes are used to fetch data from GV$ dynamic view in a cluster.

ASM dynamic views

To manage and supervise the ASM instance and its primary components (disk and disk group) effectively, you really need to know the ASM specific dynamic views, and how to map them to extract useful information about disks, disk groups, and so on. This section will help you to understand the use of the ASM specific dynamic views available in ASM.

There are about 19 dynamic views available, as of 11g R2, and each dynamic view provides different helpful information. All the ASM dynamic views are predefined with `V$ASM_`. In the following section, we are going to focus on a handful of ASM dynamic views.

V$ASM_DISK

When an ASM instance completes the disk discovery operation by reading the disk header information, all disks (used and usable) will then list in the V$ASM_DISK view. Each individual disk has a row in the V$ASM_DISK dynamic view and contains very useful information. The PATH column specifies the disk's name and location. The HEADER_STATUS column, in most cases, contains the following three possible values:

- CANDIDATE: Indicates that the unused disks are ready for use.
- FORMER: Indicates that the disk was formerly part of a disk group and is now ready for use.
- MEMBER: Indicates that the disk is currently part of an active disk group.

Apart from the preceding values, the view also contains other useful information about the disks, such as total size, free size, physical reads, redundancy level, and so on. On the flipside, every time you run a query against this view, ASM initiates disk discovery operations for the new disks, where it reads all disk header information. Querying against this view could be an expensive operation at times, and could impact performance.

The following list of SQL statements demonstrates some of the useful queries against the view. However, prior to running these commands, ensure you are connected to an ASM instance through sqlplus with SYSASM privilege:

```
SELECT path,header_status,total_mb

 FROM v$asm_disk WHERE header_status ORDER BY header_status;
```

The preceding command displays information about all the disks.

```
SELECT path,header_status,total_mb,

 FROM v$asm_disk WHERE header_status in ('CANDIDATE','FORMER','PROVISIONE
D');
```

The preceding command displays information about the disks that are eligible to use.

V$ASM_DISKGROUP

After a disk group is successfully created in the local ASM instance, the disk group summary is visible in the `V$ASM_DISKGROUP` view. Each disk group maintains a row in the view along with the important information, such as disk group number and name, total disk group size, used space, free space, redundancy type, compatibility, mount state, and so on. Every time a query is run against the view, it is likely to have a similar impact to querying the `V$ASM_DISK` views. The following SQL command extracts the mounted disk group's name, total disk group size, and the free space left in the group:

```
SELECT name,state,total_mb,usable_file_mb FROM v$asm_diskgroup;
```

V$ASM_OPERATION

`V$ASM_OPERATION` is one of the useful views that displays a row for each long-running operation in the ASM instance. For example, when a disk is being dropped or attached to an existing disk group, an ASM should initiate and complete the rebalancing operations just before releasing the subject disk. Therefore, the view will present useful details, such as the amount of work that has been completed, and show the estimated time (in minutes) required to complete the operations. This should help you to understand how long the operation will take to complete. The following SQL command produces the ongoing long-running operations in the ASM instance:

```
SELECT * FROM v$asm_operation;
```

V$ASM_DISK_STAT

Although the `V$ASM_DISK` and `V$ASM_DISK_STAT` views display nearly identical information, querying the `V$ASM_DISK_STAT` view results is a less expensive operation in comparison to the `V$ASM_DISK` view. On the flip side, this view doesn't display the details about new disks on the system that the ASM instance has yet to discover. As querying the view is less expensive, it is strongly recommended that you use this view in order to display the information and statistics (read/write) about the existing disks.

V$ASM_DISKGROUP_STAT

The `V$ASM_DISKGROUP_STAT` view displays statistical information about the mounted disk groups in the ASM instance. Unlike the `V$ASM_DISKGROUP` view, a query against this view doesn't result in new disk discovery operations but is less expensive in terms of performance. Therefore, it is recommended to use this view to display existing disk group information and statistical information about the disk groups.

V$ASM_CLIENT

When the `V$ASM_CLIENT` view is queried in the ASM instance, it displays the information about the database instances that are using the disk groups mounted and managed by the ASM instance.

ASM instance startup/shutdown

Managing an ASM instance is no different from managing the typical RDBMS database instances. The ASM instance could be managed by either using a set of `SQLPLUS` commands or the cluster aware `SRVCTL` utility. Nevertheless, it is strongly recommended that you use the `SRVCTL` utility for managing the (start/stop) ASM instance in an RAC environment.

The ASM instance can be opened either in `NOMOUNT`, `MOUNT`, or `RESTRICTED` modes with the `STARTUP` command at the SQLPLUS prompt. When you have a planned maintenance on an ASM instance, you can open the ASM instance in a `RESTRICT` mode to avoid any possible connections from the database instances. When the ASM instance is opened gracefully, it first discovers the disks and then mounts all the existing disk groups on the local instance.

To shut down the local ASM instance, you can use the various options available with the `SHUTDOWN` command in the SQLPLUS prompt. The supported options are `NORMAL`, `IMMEDIATE`, `TRANSACTIONAL`, and `ABORT`. As mentioned previously, you can use the `SRVCTL` utility to bring down the ASM instance as well. The following list of examples demonstrates how to start up/shut down an ASM instance using SQLPLUS and SRVCTL utilities:

```
srvctl stop asm -n raclinux1 -o normal:immediate:transactional:abort


    export ORACLE_SID=+ASM1
    export ORACLE_HOME=$ASM_HOME (in 11gR1)
    export ORACLE_HOME=$ORA_GRID_HOME (in 11gR2)


sqlplus / as sysasm
SQL> SHUTDOWN NORMAL:IMMEDIATE:TRANSACTIONAL:ABORT
```

This example stops the ASM instance on raclinux1 node. Alternatively, you can also use either of the shutdown options.

```
srvctl start asm -n raclinux1 -o nomount:mount:restrict
    export ORACLE_SID=+ASM1
    export ORACLE_HOME=$ASM_HOME (in 11gR1)
    export ORACLE_HOME=$ORA_GRID_HOME (in 11gR2)

sqlplus / as sysasm
SQL> STARTUP NOMOUNT:MOUNT:RESTRICT
```

This startup command starts up the ASM instance on raclinux1 node. When you start the instance in `NOMOUNT` mode, an ASM instance will be started without mounting the existing disk groups. When the instance is started in `RESTRICT` mode, no database instance can attach to the ASM instance and all the disk groups are opened in restricted mode too.

Ensure that the database instances that are currently associated with the local ASM instance are stopped prior to shutting down the local ASM instance to avoid encountering an ASM instance shutdown error. In this case, the ASM instance will remain opened. Alternatively, you could use the `ABORT` option to forcefully shut down the currently connected database's instance before shutting down the ASM instance. It is also strongly recommended to dismount any existing **Oracle Cluster File System** (**ACFS**) to avoid any application I/O errors.

Note: If the voting disk and OCR files are placed in a disk group, you will not be able to stop the ASM instance. In order to stop the ASM instance, you need to stop the cluster.

ASM disk group administration

In this section, we are going to focus on the available methods to create and manage an ASM disk group. In this context, we will explain how to create an ASM disk group using the various available mirroring options, such as ASM and external mirroring options. We will also summarize how to modify existing disk group parameters and how to drop a disk group with various options.

Creating a disk group

In general, once an ASM instance completes the ASM disk's discovery operation, you can then use the ASM disks to either build a disk group or add it to a pre-existing disk group. You need at least one eligible ASM disk (with `HEADER_STATUS` either `CANDIDATE`, `FORMER`, or `PROVISIONED`) to be able to build a disk group or to add to a pre-existing disk group. There are various methods to create a disk group, such as, DBCA (in pre 11g R2), ASMCA (with 11g R2), Grid Control, and `CREATE DISKGROUP` SQL statement in the SQLPLUS prompt. Although the easiest and most convenient way to build and manage a disk group is to use the GUI tools such as DBCA, ASMCA, or Grid Control, we are going to demonstrate how to create and manage a disk group using a set of SQL statements.

In order to create a disk group on the local ASM instance, you first need to identify the eligible ASM disks discovered by the instance. The following SQL statements are useful to list the eligible ASM disks:

```
export ORACLE_SID=+ASM1
export ORACLE_HOME=$ASM_HOME (in 11gR1)
export ORACLE_HOME=$ORA_GRID_HOME (in 11gR2)


SQL> SELECT path,header_status,mode_status,total_mb
       FROM v$asm_disk
       WHERE header_status IN ('CANDIDATE','FORMER','PROVISIONED');
```

The query lists each disk's information along with the path, the header status, and size of the disk. Once you list the disks, you can use the following set of SQL statements to create a new disk group with different levels of mirroring options.

The following SQL statement creates a new disk group named `DATA` with one ASM disk, `sde1` located under the `/dev/` location. The `EXTERNAL REDUNDANCY` clause in the SQL statement indicates that you are relying on the STORAGE-level mirroring (protection) option, not using the Oracle-provided mirroring level:

```
CREATE DISKGROUP data EXTERNAL REDUNDANCY DISK '/dev/sde1';
```

The following SQL statement creates a new disk group named `DATA` that consists of two failure groups with one disk to each failure group, using the Oracle-provided `NORMAL redundancy` (a two-way mirroring) level:

```
CREATE DISKGROUP data NORMAL REDUNDANCY

 FAILGROUP fgp1 DISK '/dev/sde1',

 FAILGROUP fgp2 DISK '/dev/sdf1';
```

The following SQL statement creates a new disk group named DATA with three failure groups with one disk to each failure group, using the Oracle-provided highest level of redundancy, a three-way mirroring-level option:

```
CREATE DISKGROUP data HIGH REDUNDANCY
 FAILGROUP fgp1 DISK '/dev/sde1',
 FAILGROUP fgp2 DISK '/dev/sdf1',
FAILGROUP fgp3 DISK '/dev/sdg1';
```

Note: Failure groups are used to copy the redundant copies of every extent.

When the mirroring option is skipped, ASM applies the NORMAL REDUNDANCY (a two-way mirroring) level by default.

After a disk group is successfully built, it will then automatically mount in the local instance. If a server parameter file is being used **(SPFILE)**, the name of the disk group is successfully added to the ASM_DISKGROUP initialization parameter in order to mount the disk group automatically on ASM instance restarts. In order to make the disk group available on other ASM instances in a cluster, you simply need to mount the disk group running the ALTER DISKGROUP data MOUNT statement (ensure the same set of disks are accessible on the other nodes).

Altering a disk group

One of the prime advantages of using ASM is the ability to manage pre-existing disk groups without actually interrupting the database's ongoing operations. In other words, you can manage the disk group tasks online, where you can dynamically add and drop a disk from a pre-existing disk group at any given time without requiring any database downtime.

The following list of SQL statements (valid only in the ASM instance) demonstrates how to add an ASM disk to a pre-existing disk group:

```
ALTER DISKGROUP data ADD DISK '/dev/sdf1';
ALTER DISKGROUP data ADD DISK '/dev/sdf1','/dev/sdg2'
   REBALANCE POWER 3;
```

The first statement adds a disk to the DATA disk group and the second statement adds two disks to the DATA disk group with rebalancing power 3. The REBALANCE POWER clause helps to speed up the rebalancing operation with the degree of parallelism.

The following list of SQL statements (valid only in the ASM instance) demonstrates how to drop an ASM disk from an existing disk group.

You can get the name of the disks associated with the DATA disk group using the following SQL statement:

```
export ORACLE_SID=+ASM1 - assuming that we are logging in first ASM
 instance.

export ORACLE_HOME=$ASM_HOME (in 11gR1)

export ORACLE_HOME=$ORA_GRID_HOME (in 11gR2)


SQL> SELECT disk_number,name FROM v$asm_disk
 WHERE group_number = (SELECT group_number
 FROM v$asm_diskgroup WHERE NAME = 'DATA');
```

Once the disk names are identified, use the following SQL statements to drop a disk from an existing disk group DATA:

```
ALTER DISKGROUP data DROP DISK '/dev/sdf1';

ALTER DISKGROUP data DROP DISK 'DATA_0001'

   REBALANCE POWER 3;
```

While the disk is being dropped from a disk group, you can measure the time left to finish the task using the V$ASM_OPERATION dynamic view. The EST_MINUTES column of the view will tell you the estimated amount of time (in minutes) left to finish the ongoing operation.

Additionally, while the disk drop operation for a disk group is running, at any given time you can cancel all the pending drop operations of the disk group using the following SQL statement:

```
ALTER DISKGROUP data UNDROP DISKS;
```

However, you cannot recover an already dropped disk, or the disks that are being dropped using the FORCE clause.

Dropping a disk group

In this section, we will explore a set of SQL statements that will help you to drop a pre-existing disk group and its associated files. Ensure the disk group is mounted on the local ASM instance, from where you are going to run the DROP DISKGROUP command. The disk group shouldn't be mounted on any other ASM instance. If it is, dismount the disk group on the other ASM instances first, or use the FORCE clause to bypass the verification of the disk group being used on other ASM instances.

The following SQL statement drops a disk group `DATA`:

```
DROP DISKGROUP data;

DROP DISKGROUP data FORCE;
```

The following SQL statement drops a disk group `DATA` and all its associated files:

```
DROP DISKGROUP data INCLUDING CONTENTS;
```

After dropping a disk group successfully, ASM then rewrites the header by removing the ASM formatting information of each of the disks associated with the disk group to make the disks available for reuse. The header status of the disks will be subsequently set to the `FORMER` state.

Overview of ASMCMD

In most scenarios, when ASM is configured as a storage unit for Oracle databases, a SAN administrator prepares the required storage (LUNs) from the storage array and then presents the disks (raw disk) to the host. In turn, system administrators configure the device files for the presented disks and notify the DBAs about the availability of the disks. However, once the disks are presented to an Oracle ASM system, there is no direct method available which would allow either SAN administrators or system administrators to hold any control over the contents or on the utilization of the disks. Fortunately, the ASMCMD, a command-line utility that was first introduced in Oracle ASM version 10g R2, provides the functionality to query/navigate/view/operate an underlying filesystem inside the ASM.

Although, the ASMCMD operations were limited in the beginning to a few tasks, its functionality has been extended significantly in Version 11g R1 and 11g R2. It can now be used to repair a bad block on a disk, copy the files from an OS filesystem to an ASM disk group, and between the disk groups, backup and restore disk group metadata, and so on.

Additionally, in Version 11g R2 with ASMCMD, you can manage an ASM instance and disk group operations such as:

- Instance startup/shutdown
- Set the disk discovery paths
- Create a disk group
- Drop a disk group

- Offline/online an ASM disk group
- Mount an ASM disk group
- Rebalance a disk group

ASMCMD in action

The ASMCMD utility can be run in either interactive or non-interactive mode. However, just before you run the utility, in order to establish a connection with the local ASM instance, ensure the environmental variables `ORACLE_SID` and `ORACLE_HOME` are defined correctly. To set the environmental variables on the node, enter the following code:

```
export ORACLE_SID=+ASM1 - assuming that we are logging in first
        ASM instance.
export ORACLE_HOME=$ASM_HOME (in 11gR1)
export ORACLE_HOME=$ORA_GRID_HOME (in 11gR2)

asmcmd -p   -- connects to ASM instance in interactive mode includes
        the current directory info.
asmcmd      -- connects to ASM instance in interactive mode.
asmcmd -v   -- displays ASM version
asmcmd -a sysasm   -- connects to ASM instance with SYSASM privilege.
asmcmd <command> -- executes the command in noninteractive mode.
```

The following examples demonstrate how to view and navigate files within an ASM disk group, presuming that the `DATA` disk group and a database named `RACDB` are already configured on the node:

```
asmcmd -p

ASMCMD [+] > cd DATA

ASMCMD [+DATA] > cd RACDB

ASMCMD [+DATA/RACDB] cd DATAFILE

ASMCMD [+DATA/RACDB/DATAFILE] > ls -lt
Type      Redund  Striped  Time             Sys  Name
DATAFILE  UNPROT  COARSE   OCT 18 09:00:00  Y    SYSAUX.257.732295267
DATAFILE  UNPROT  COARSE   OCT 17 17:00:00  Y    USERS.259.732295267
DATAFILE  UNPROT  COARSE   OCT 17 17:00:00  Y    UNDOTBS2.264.732295639
DATAFILE  UNPROT  COARSE   OCT 17 17:00:00  Y    UNDOTBS1.258.732295267
DATAFILE  UNPROT  COARSE   OCT 17 17:00:00  Y    SYSTEM.256.732295265
DATAFILE  UNPROT  COARSE   OCT 17 17:00:00  Y    DATA_TS.268.732537105
```

The following command is used to identify the instances that are currently attached to the local ASM instance:

```
ASMCMD [+] > lsct
DB_Name  Status     Software_Version  Compatible_version  Instance_Name
Disk_Group
+ASM     CONNECTED        11.2.0.1.0          11.2.0.1.0  +ASM1
DATA
RACDB    CONNECTED        11.2.0.1.0          11.2.0.0.0  RACDB1
DATA
```

The following command is used to determine the disk groups statistics, which are mounted on the local ASM instance such as total size, used size, free MB, mount or unmount status, block size, and so on.

```
ASMCMD [+] > lsdg
```

The following list of commands is supported with the ASMCMD utility for performing various tasks:

```
ASMCMD [+] >
        commands:
        --------
        md_backup, md_restore
        lsattr, setattr
        cd, cp, du, find, help, ls, lsct, lsdg, lsof, mkalias
        mkdir, pwd, rm, rmalias
        chdg, chkdg, dropdg, iostat, lsdsk, lsod, mkdg, mount
        offline, online, rebal, remap, umount
        dsget, dsset, lsop, shutdown, spbackup, spcopy, spget
        spmove, spset, startup
        chtmpl, lstmpl, mktmpl, rmtmpl
        chgrp, chmod, chown, groups, grpmod, lsgrp, lspwusr, lsusr
        mkgrp, mkusr, orapwusr, passwd, rmgrp, rmusr
        volcreate, voldelete, voldisable, volenable, volinfo
        volresize, volset, volstat
```

ASM 11g R1 new features

ASM functionality has been further enhanced in Version 11g R1 with additional new features to support ASM rolling upgrades, faster ASM mirror disk resync and rebalance, preferred mirror read, new SYSASM privilege, an extended functionality in ASMCMD utility to backup and restore disk group and its metadata, disk group compatibility, and so on. In the following section, we are going to describe some of the new features:

- ASM fast mirror resync
- ASM preferred mirror read
- ASM fast rebalance
- ASM disk group compatibility attributes
- ASM performance enhancements
- New SYSASM role

ASM fast mirror resync

If a disk from a normal or high redundancy level disk group becomes unavailable (offline) for any reason, for example, due to a disk path failure caused by a cable failure, the ASM fast mirror resync feature in 11g tracks the changed extents on an offline disk to improve the time to quickly resynchronize the extents when the disk is brought back online.

To enable this feature, you must set the disk group compatibility attributes value: `COMPATIBLE.ASM` and `COMPATIBLE.RDBMS` equal to `11.1` or higher. When a disk goes offline for any reason, it will be removed automatically by the ASM after a default time. Conversely, you can extend the disk drop time by setting the disk group attribute `DISK_REPAIR_TIME` from the default `3.6h` to a higher time limit to get more time to repair the disk to prevent it from being dropped by the ASM after the default time. The default `3.6h` time limit is adequate in most environments. Fortunately, you can enable the disk group attributes during the disk group creation as well as after the creation. The following SQL statements demonstrate how to create and alter the disk group along with the attributes:

```
CREATE DISKGROUP data EXTERNAL REDUNDANCY DISK '/dev/sdb1'
   ATTRIBUTE 'compatible.rdbms' = '11.1',
   ATTRIBUTE 'compatible.asm' = '11.1',
   ATTRIBUTE 'disk_repair_time' = '6h';

ALTER DISKGROUP data SET ATTRIBUTE 'compatible.rdbms'='11.1';
ALTER DISKGROUP data SET ATTRIBUTE 'compatible.asm'='11.1';
ALTER DISKGROUP data SET ATTRIBUTE 'disk_repair_time' = '6h';
```

ASM preferred mirror read

When a disk group is created either with the NORMAL or HIGH REDUNDANCY level, ASM writes the redundant copies of the data (extents) in a failure group. These redundant copies are called the **secondary extents**. Irrespective of the number of copies of an extent present, ASM always prefers to read the data block from the primary copy of the extent, not from the secondary copy. Alas, until 11g R1, there was no option available to instruct ASM to read the data block from a particular extent copy in order to improve the read performance while an extended cluster (a multisite cluster) with separate storage at each site is being used.

In 11g R1 or higher, you can indeed configure ASM to read the data block from an extent copy, which is closer to the local node, instead of just reading from the primary extent copy. This could be more appropriate when the extended (multisite) cluster is configured and you want an ASM instance to read the data block from the extent copy that is near to the node for better performance. To enable the feature, you need to configure the failure group names with the ASM_PREFERRED_READ_FAILURE initialization parameter. The following diagram illustrates how ASM preferred mirror read could be configured in a multisite (site X and site Y) cluster setup with separate storage for each site:

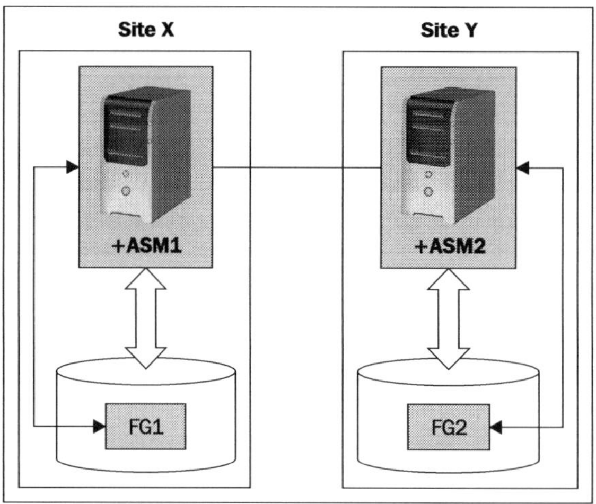

The **ASM2** instance configured on Node 2 at **Site Y** reads the mirror copy (secondary extent) from a mirrored disk group to improve the read performance. You need to configure the following in the initialization parameter (spfile) for an ASM instance:

```
+ASM1.ASM_PREFERRED_MIRROR_READ_GROUPS=DATA.FG1
+ASN2.ASM_PREFERRED_MIRROR_READ_GROUPS=DATA.FG2
```

ASM fast rebalance

When a disk group is mounted by multiple ASM instances in an RAC environment, during the course of the disk group rebalancing operation, extent map messages will be exchanged across the ASM instances using the lock and unlock mechanics. Therefore, there will be an impact on the overall rebalancing operations throughputs.

With 11g R1 or higher, ASM instances can be started in `RESTRICTED` mode to perform maintenance in an ASM instance. When an ASM instance is started in `RESTRICTED` mode, this disallows connections from the database instances and subsequently, all the disk groups are mounted in `RESTRICTED` mode as well. When the disk group is mounted in this mode, no database can access the disk group. Therefore, the disk group rebalancing operation in this mode will improve the overall throughput by eliminating the need to lock/unlock extent map messages across the ASM instance in the cluster.

ASM disk group compatibility attributes

With the disk group compatibility attributes feature in 11g R1 or higher, you are able to set the disk group compatibility to enable the minimum version level of database and ASM instances to connect to an ASM disk group and also let the database and ASM instance use the new features of ASM that are introduced in the new versions. You can set the disk group compatibility attributes while creating a disk group and these can be modified after the disk group creation.

The `COMPATIBLE.ASM` and `COMPATIBLE.RDBMS` attributes determine the minimum version of database and ASM instance that you can use for the database and ASM instance type.

This feature is mostly useful when you upgrade your ASM and databases and want to utilize the new features of the ASM version. Query the `V$ASM_DISKGROUP` dynamic view to get information about the attributes set for a disk group. The `V$ASM_ATTRIBUTE` dynamic view in the ASM instance displays one row for each defined attribute.

In 11g R2, the disk group ASM compatibility attribute is set to `11.2` and the database compatibility attribute is set to `10.1` by default.

ASM performance enhancements

Each ASM disk space in 11g R1 is allocated the same size (1 MB by default). **Allocation Units** (**AU**) are managed by the hidden initialization parameter (`_asm_ausize`). Typically, whenever a new datafile is created in a disk group, the datafile is automatically divided into equally sized extents and the extents are then striped (spread) evenly across the disks of the disk group. The pointers to the location of the extents are loaded into the ASM instance SGA memory area to assist the database instance to locate and manage data blocks. The larger the file size, the more extents are generated. The more extents there are, the more pointers will consume a significant amount of memory size.

With 11g R1 or higher, you can now reduce memory consumption by defining a variable extent size for ASM files. This will be particularly useful when you need to boost the extent management while managing very large-sized databases. To enable this feature, you need to set the `COMPATIBILITY` attribute of a disk group to `11.1` or higher. You can create a disk group with AU size between 1 MB to 64 MB. The following constraints have been imposed on the allocation behavior of the extent size:

- The first 20,000 extents (0 to 19999) are sized equal to the disk group AU size
- The next 20,000 extents (19999 to 39999) are sized 4*AU size
- Extents above 40,000 are sized 16*AU size

New SYSASM role

The `SYSDBA` role (privilege) has been deprecated from Oracle ASM 11g R1 and onwards. Although, you can continue to use the `SYSDBA` privilege to connect to the ASM instance, you cannot perform any sort of ASM administration related tasks. In fact, an error message is written to the ASM `alert.log` file when you log in as `SYSDBA` role, and you are also likely to encounter an `ORA-15032` and `ORA-15260` error when trying to perform some kind of administrative tasks on the ASM disk groups.

A new `SYSASM` system privilege has been introduced in 11g R1 and onwards to distinguish the privileges of regular database administration and ASM storage administration. Henceforth, you need to use the new role to log in to perform ASM administrative tasks. In the following example, we are going to demonstrate how to log in as a `SYSASM` user and how to create a new user with the new privilege:

```
export ORACLE_SID=+ASM1
export ORACLE_HOME=$ASM_HOME (in 11gR1)
export ORACLE_HOME=$ORA_GRID_HOME (in 11gR2)

sqlplus / as SYSASM

SQL> CREATE USER my_sysasm IDENTIFIED BY password123;
SQL> GRANT sysasm TO my_sysasm;
```

ASM 11g R2 new features

Although there are several new features and significant enhancements made with ASM 11g R2, we shall discuss and focus only on the following key new features:

- Automatic Storage Management Configuration Assistant (ASMCA)
- Automatic Storage Management Dynamic Volume Manager
- Automatic Storage Management Cluster File System (ACFS)
- ACFS snapshots
- ASM intelligent data placement
- ASMCMD enhancements

Automatic Storage Management Configuration Assistant (ASMCA)

Pre-Oracle 11g R2, DBCA (a graphical interface tool) was one of the most convenient ways to manage most of the ASM-related tasks. However, with 11g R2, the DBCA no longer supports ASM management. Instead, a new graphical interface tool, **Automatic Storage Management Configuration** (**ASMCA**) has been introduced to manage the ASM operations exclusively. ASMCA simplifies ASM instance creation and configuration, ASM disk group management, **Dynamic Volume Manager** (**ADVM**), and **ASM Cluster File Systems** (**ACFS**) operations. You can also operate the ASMCA tool in silent mode to perform all ASM-related tasks. Additionally, ASMCMD, a command-line utility which is a non-GUI tool, can also be used to manage most of the ASM operations either in an interactive or non-interactive mode.

Initiating ASMCA

As part of Oracle 11g R2 new Grid Infrastructure, ASM, and Clusterware are integrated and installed together into a new grid infrastructure home. To initiate the ASMCA tool, run `./asmca` at the command prompt from your `$GRID_HOME/bin` location.

When the `asmca` is launched from the command prompt, you are most likely to come across one of the following situations, depending on the current state of an ASM instance on the local node:

- If no ASM instance is detected, you are advised to create a new ASM instance
- When a previous version of ASM instance is found to be active, you are required to upgrade the ASM instance

- When an ASM instance is not active, you are required to start the ASM instance
- When an ASM instance is found active, you will be directly taken to the main screen of ASMCA

Configuring a new ASM instance

In the event of no ASM instance existence on the node, you can create a new ASM instance using the ASMCA tool. To create a new ASM instance, navigate through the `$GRID_HOME/bin` location and run the `./asmca` command to launch the ASM configuration assistance. Make sure your terminal supports the GUI.

1. On the **Create ASM** screen, you need to enter and confirm the passwords for **SYS** and **ASMSNMP** users of an ASM instance. The following image demonstrates the procedure to create an ASM instance:

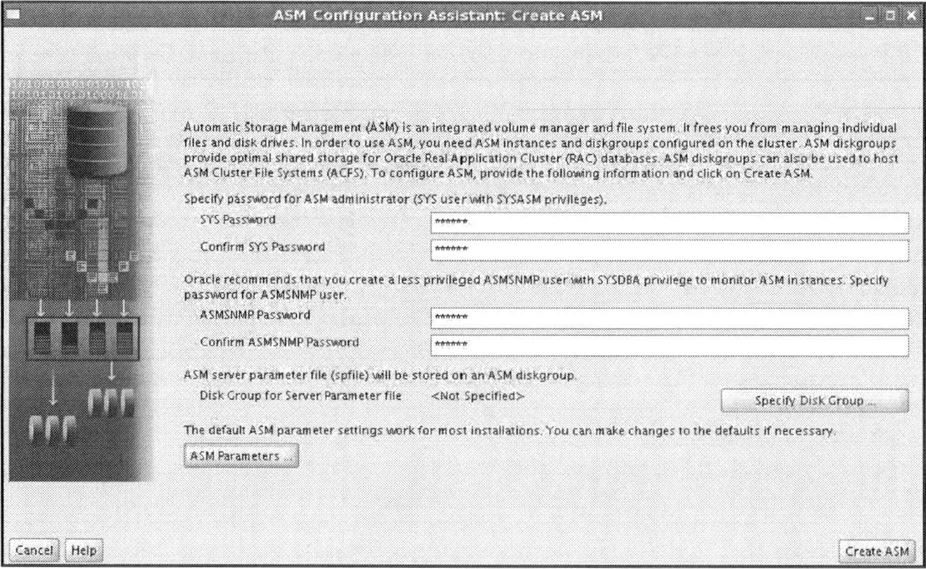

2. Click on the **ASM Parameters** button to set the ASM-specific initialization parameters, such as **asm_diskgroups**, **asm_diskstring**, and **asm_power_limit**.
3. In order to configure more initialization parameters such as SGA size and processes, click on the **Show Advanced Parameters** button and enter the values accordingly.

4. After the initialization parameters are updated, click on the **Close** button, as shown in the following screenshot:

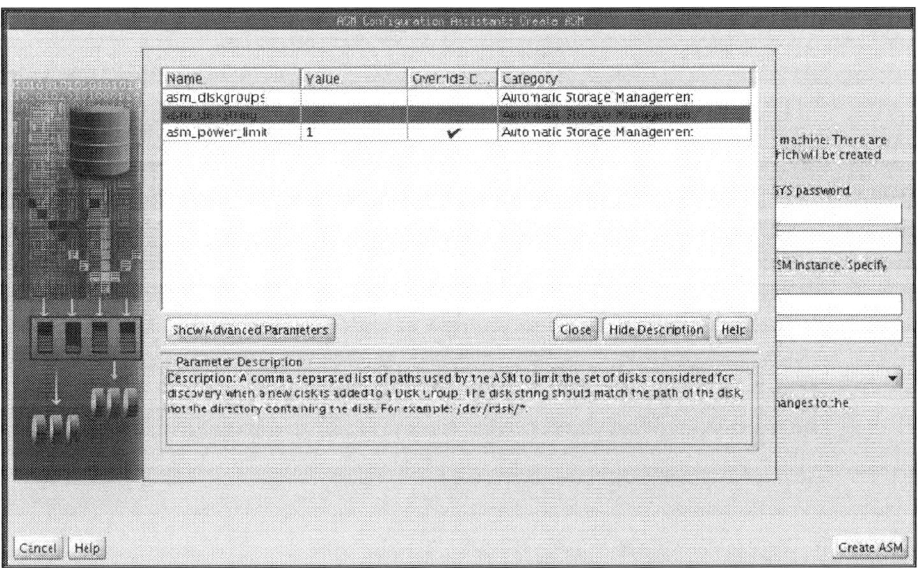

5. To put the ASM instance spfile on an ASM disk group, click on the **Specify Disk Group** button and follow the instructions shown in the following screenshot to create a new ASM disk group. As we are creating a new ASM instance and no prior disk groups exist, we need to create a new disk group here in which to put the spfile of the ASM instance:

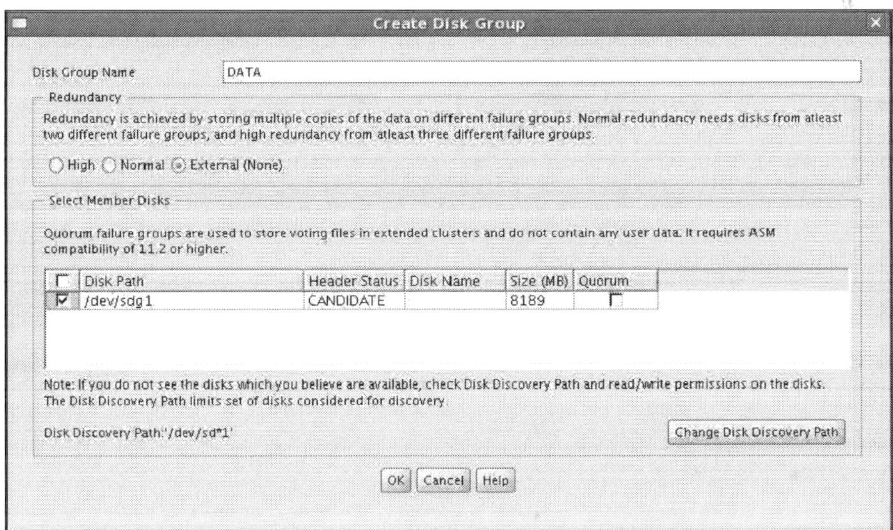

6. Once the mandatory disk group options are completed, click on the **OK** button and subsequently click on the **Create ASM** button on the **Create ASM** screen to start the ASM instance creation process.
7. You will then come across a series of screens confirming the ASM instance and the disk group has been successfully created. Click on **OK** to finish the ASM instance creation.

After a successful ASM configuration, you can use the `srvctl`, a cluster command, from `$GRID_HOME/bin` location to show all the ASM instance's configuration information. The following example demonstrates the usage of this command:

```
$GRID_HOME/bin/srvctl config asm -a
```

The preceding command produces the following output:

```
ASM home: /u01/app/11.2.0/grid1
ASM listener : LISTENER
ASM is enabled
```

Managing an ASM instance

With the existence of various methods to manage and administer the ASM instance, we are focusing on the ASMCA tool to manage the ASM instance. Run `$GRID_HOME/bin/asmca` from the command prompt to launch the tool. This should take you to the ASMCA main page.

To manage the ASM instance, click on the **ASM Instances** tab, which will list the information about the nodes on which the ASM instance is configured, along with the instance name, instance, and ASM Dynamic Volume Manager (ADVM) driver status. A **Refresh** button is also provided to refresh the contents in the list dynamically, as shown in the following screenshot:

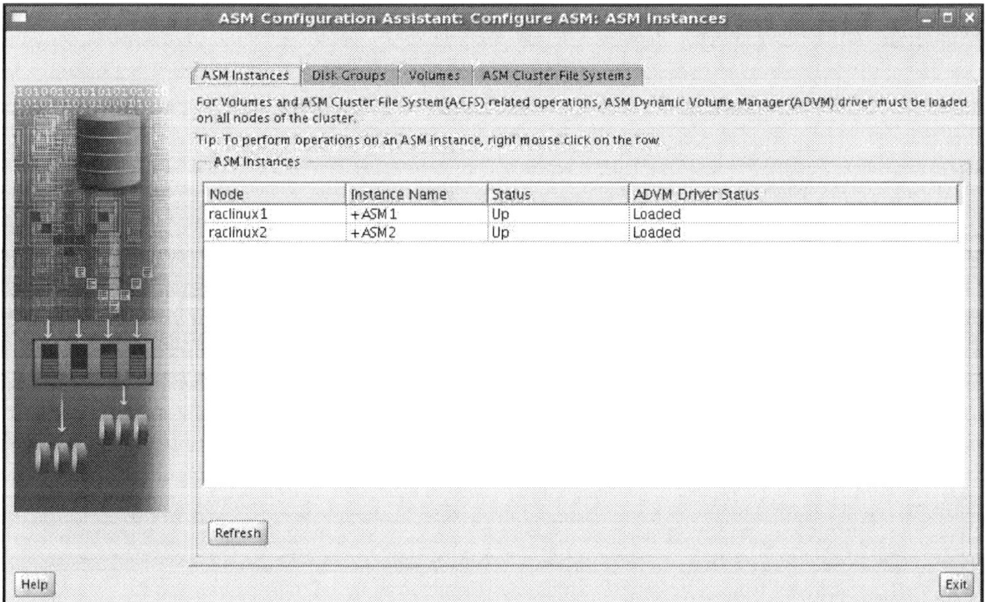

Pick a node from the given list, and right-click to view the options. The **Start Instance**, **Stop Instance**, and the **View Connected Databases** option will display the database name and version of the databases that are currently associated with the ASM instance, as shown in the following screenshot:

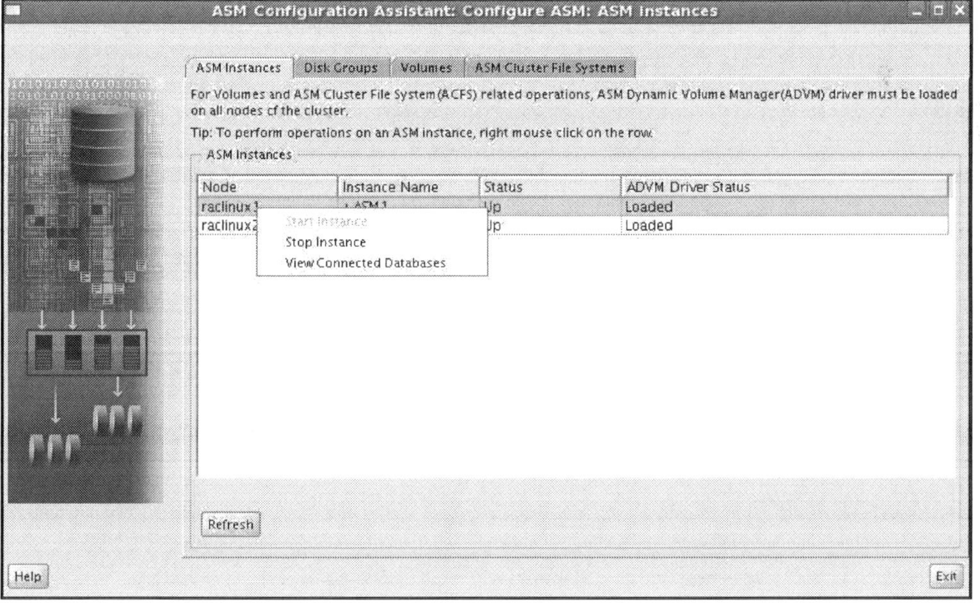

Managing an ASM disk group

Existing disk group information is fetched and listed when you go to the **Disk Groups** tab (shown in the preceding screenshot). To manage an existing ASM disk group, select the required disk group name from the list and click the right mouse button. The following options will be listed:

- **View Serviced Databases**: This lists the database names to which this disk group is associated.
- **Add Disks**: This allows you to increase the size of the disk group by adding one or more new disks.
- **Edit Attributes**: This option lets you modify the disk group compatible attributes for database and ASM and also lets you modify the disk repair time attribute.
- **Mount on Local Node**: This allows you to mount a disk group on the local node.
- **Dismount on Local Node**: This allows you to dismount a particular disk group on the local node.
- **Drop**: This allows you to remove the disk group.
- **Mount on All Nodes**: This is useful when you want to mount the disk group across all nodes of a cluster.
- **Dismount on All Nodes**: This is useful when you want to dismount the disk group across all nodes of a cluster.

Additionally, you can make use of the **Mount on All Nodes** and **Dismount on All Nodes** buttons to mount and dismount all the disk groups on the selected node in one shot.

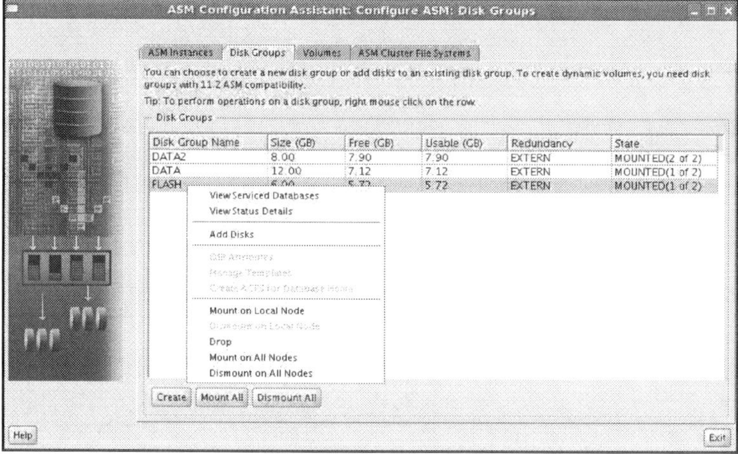

To build a new disk group, use the **Create** button and follow the instruction demonstrated in the following section.

Creating an ASM disk group

The following **Create Disk Group** screen demonstrates the procedure to create a disk group named `DG_FLASH` across all the nodes of a cluster. On the **Create Disk Group** screen, you need to provide the disk group name, choose the redundancy (mirroring) level, and select eligible disks from the given list under the **Select member disks** option.

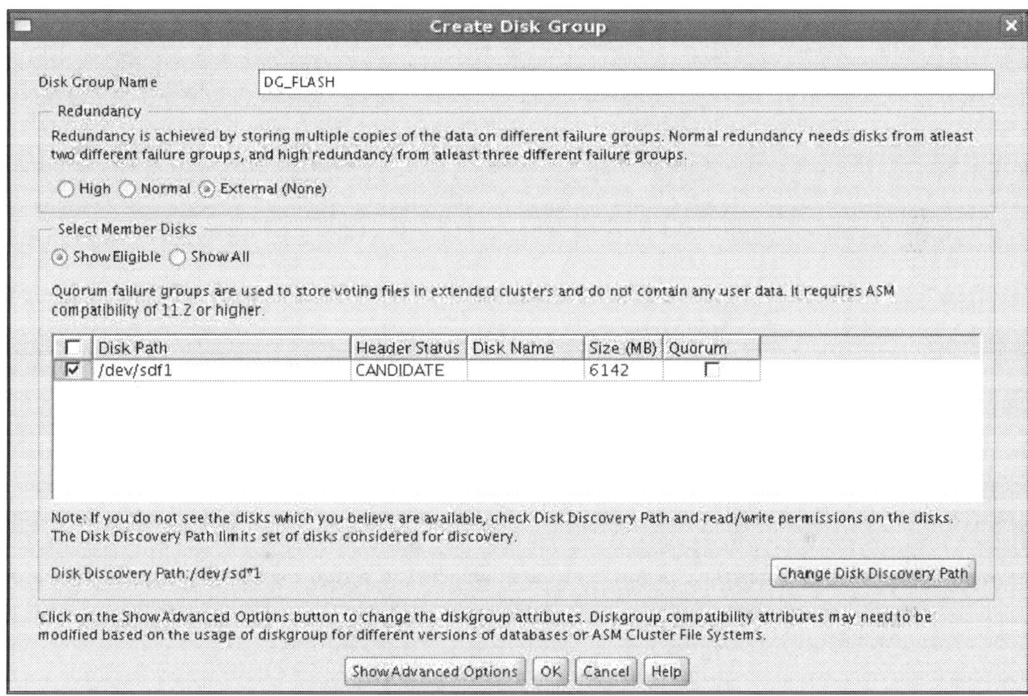

The **Show Advanced Options** button lets you set the advanced level of settings for the disk group. The options that are included are **Database Compatibility**, **ASM Compatibility**, and **Allocation Unit Size**. You can close the advanced options screen using the **Hide Advanced Options** button. Click on **OK** to start a new disk group creation. These options are shown in the following screenshot:

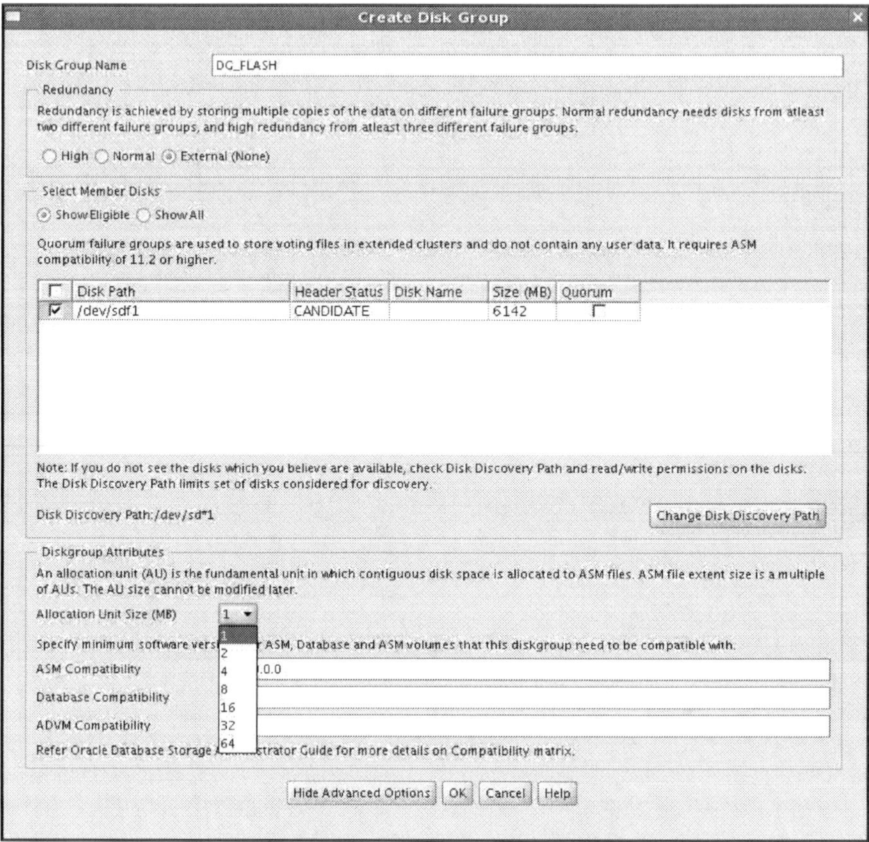

If there is any point at which you need to quit from the ASMCA, use the **CANCEL** button.

Creating an ASM disk group in silent mode

The following command creates an ASM disk group named `DT_DATA` using the ASMCA tool in silent mode; this is particularly useful when you have a terminal that doesn't support GUI:

```
export ORACLE_SID=+ASM1
export ORACLE_HOME=$ORA_GRID_HOME
```

```
asmca -silent -createDiskGroup -diskGroupName DG_DATA
      -disk '/dev/sdf1'
      -redundancy EXTERNAL
      -compatible.asm='11.2'
      -compatible.rdbms='11.2';
```

Automatic Storage Management Dynamic Volume Manager (ADVM)

Automatic Storage Management Dynamic Volume Manager (**ADVM**) is one of the new features added in Oracle ASM 11g R2, which provides volume management services and standard device driver interfaces to its clients (filesystems) such as ASM Cluster File System (ACFS), OCFS2, ext3fs, and ext4fs. An ASM dynamic volume is created within an ASM disk group using various methods such as Enterprise Manager (EM) or Database Grid Control, ASMCA, ASMCMD, or SQL statement: `ALTER DISKGROUP ADD VOLUME`.

When the ASM volume is created successfully, an ASM volume device on the operating system is automatically created under the `/dev/asm` location on Linux systems, which can subsequently be used by the ACFS or any third-party filesystem to create and manage file systems, leveraging all the power and functionality of ASM features.

ADVM volume trivia

Some of the key ADVM characteristics are outlined as follows:

- One or more ADVM volumes may be configured within a single ASM disk group.
- The ADVM volume name length is limited to 11 characters.
- An ADVM volume must be limited to only one ASM disk group. In other words, a volume cannot be part of more than one disk group.
- By default, an ADVM volume has four columns of 64 MB extents and 128 K stripe width.
- ADVM writes data in a round-robin fashion to each column before it proceeds onto the next of the four columns.
- The ADVM volumes are similar to ASM file types. Once they are created, their extents are evenly distributed across all disks of a disk group.

- An ADVM volume is not supported on NFS and Exadata Storage.
- ADVM can be resized dynamically on demand.
- ADVM is loaded at ASM startup, and functions as a standard I/O interface to filesystems.
- For extent maps, rebalancing, and I/O failure-related issues, the ADVM driver communicates with the ASM instance.
- ADVM is compatible with RAC and non-RAC systems.
- ADVM writes little information to the operating system base logs. On Linux, messages are logged at `/var/log/messages` representing the message 'Oracle ADVM' for distinct identification.
- **Dirty Region Logging (DRL)** is enabled through an ASM DRL volume file when an ASM ADVM Volume is created in the ASM redundancy disk group.
- When the ASM volume is configured and enabled in the ASM instance, the new ASM-specific background processes - the Volume Driver Background (VDBG), Volume background (VBGn) parallel processes, and Volume Membership Background (VMB)–are started to support the volume functionality.

Creating ASM volumes

Before you proceed with creating ASM volumes, ensure that the ASM instance on the local node is active, and the required ASM disk group is already created and mounted (as the ASM volumes are created within a disk group). As discussed previously, an ASM volume can be created using various methods, such as Enterprise Manager (Grid Control), ASMCA, ASMCMD, or the `ALTER DISKGROUP ADD` volume command. We will demonstrate how to create a new ASM Dynamic Volume using ASMCA, ASMCMD, and the SQL statement `ALTER DISKGROUP ADD` volume methods.

Creating an ASM volume with ASMCA

To create an ASM volume with ASMCA, you will need to complete the following steps:

1. At the command prompt, run ./`asmca` command from the `$GRID_HOME`/bin location. Click on the `Volumes` tab to create and manage existing ASM volumes.
2. To begin creating a new volume, click on the **Create** button, which will take you to the **Create Volume** screen where you need to put the specifications for the new volume.

3. Select the existing ASM disk group from the drop-down list on which you want to configure the volume and specify the volume size, as shown in the following screenshot:

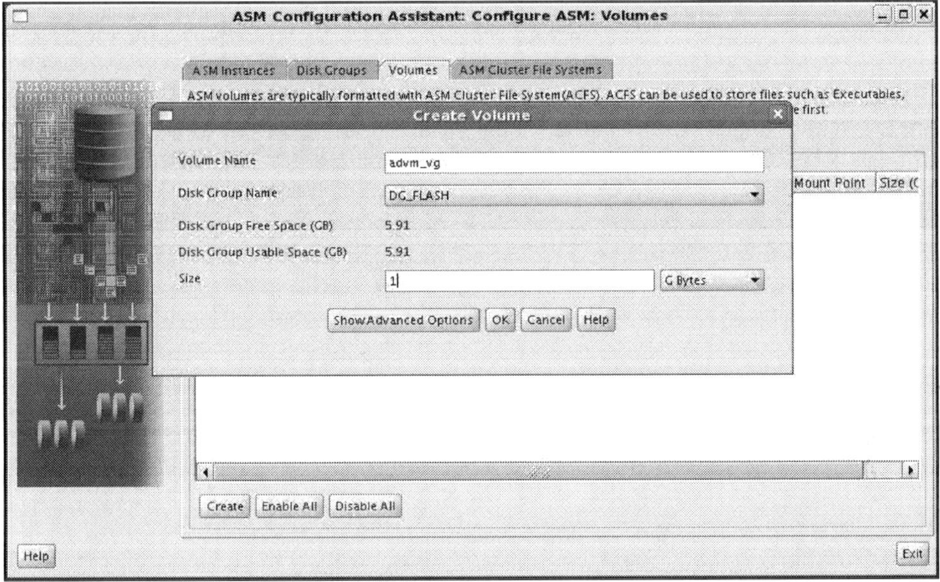

4. To set advanced options such as redundancy settings, striping width, and columns click on the **Show Advanced Options** button.
5. After you make the necessary adjustments, click on the **OK** button to proceed with the volume creation process.

[The Redundancy settings are inherited for the volume from the disk group by default. However, you have a choice to change the settings.]

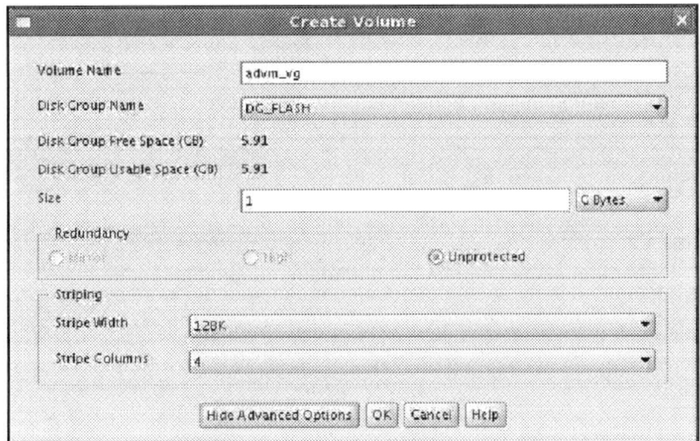

6. After a successful ASM volume creation, a pop-up window is displayed with the message: Volume <volume_name> created successfully. Click on the **OK** button to return to the ASM Volumes configuration screen.
7. At this point, the volume `advm_vg` is successfully created and a volume device on the operating system for this volume is created automatically under `/dev/asm`. To manage the newly created volume, select the volume and right-click on it. This gives you the options to enable/disable the volume on all nodes or on a local node, dynamically resizing, and removing the volume manager, as shown in the following screenshot:

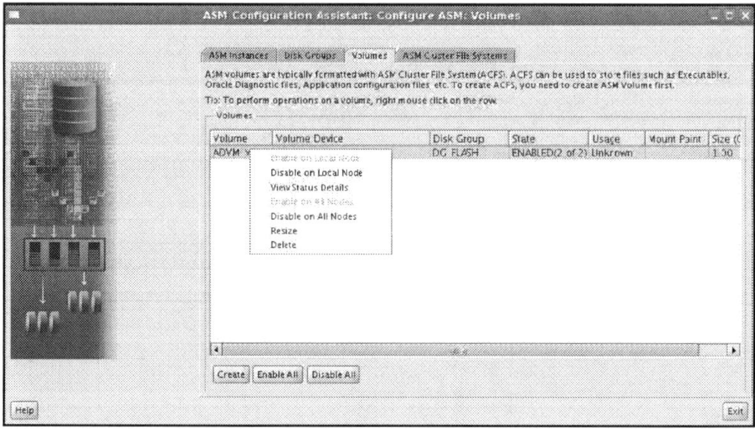

8. Click on the **EXIT** button to quit from ASMCA.
9. Now, let's verify the volume device details on the OS side. For this, you need to go to the `/dev/asm` location on the server and use the UNIX command `ls -ltr`. As you can see, a new volume device is automatically created under this location with the name `advm_vg-86` under the root ownership:
   `brwxrwx--- 1 root asmadmin 252, 44033 Nov  8 21:41 advm_vg-86`

When you create an ASM volume, a volume device name is created with a unique ADVM persistent disk group number, which is concatenated to the end of the disk group name and can be from one to three digits. On Linux, the name would be in the format of `volume_name-nnn`. The ADVM device names are persistent across all nodes.

Creating an ASM Volume with ASMCMD

ASM volumes can also be managed through a command-line utility named ASMCMD. To successfully execute ASMCMD commands, you must first set the ASM instance `SID` and `$ORACLE HOME` environmental variables (on a RAC system) correctly. The following exercise covers a few examples to manage the ASM volume using the ASMCMD command-line utility:

```
export ORACLE_SID=+ASM1
export ORACLE_HOME=$GRID_HOME
```

Once these environmental variables are set, run `$GRID_HOME/bin/asmcmd -p` at a command prompt to connect to the ASM command-line utility.

The following example demonstrates how to create a new volume group using the ASMCMD:

```
ASMCMD [+] > volcreate -G DG_FLASH -s 1G
```

- `-G` represents the name of the disk group that will hold the volume.
- `-s` represents the size of the volume to be created.

Once a volume is created, you can use the following example to obtain the details about the volume:

```
ASMCMD [+] volinfo -G DG_FLASH advm_vg

Diskgroup Name: DG_FLASH

          Volume Name: ADVM_VG
          Volume Device: /dev/asm/advm_vg-86
          State: ENABLED
          Size (MB): 1024
          Resize Unit (MB): 256
          Redundancy: UNPROT
          Stripe Columns: 4
          Stripe Width (K): 128
          Usage:
          Mountpath:
```

The following table describes the list of options that are associated with the ASMCMD to manage ASM volumes:

Option	Description	Example
`volcreate`	Creates an ASM volume within a specified disk group	volcreate -G DG_FLASH -s 1G
`voldelete`	Removes an ASM volume	voldelete -G DG_FLASH advm_vg
`volinfo`	Displays information about volume	volinfo -G DG_FLASH advm_vg
`voldisable`	Disables volume in a mounted disk group	voldisable -G DG_FLASH advm_vg
`volenable`	Enables volume in a mounted disk group	volenable -G DG_FLASH advm_vg
`volresize`	Resizes an ASM volume	volresize -G DG_FLASH –s 2G advm_vg
`volstat`	Reports volume I/O statistics	volstat -G DG_FLASHASM

Creating an ASM volume with the ALTER DISKGROUP SQL statement

Another technique for creating and managing the ASM volume is using the SQL statement: `ALTER DISKGROUP`. As the volume is created within a disk group, ensure that the required ASM disk group is created and mounted with the compatible parameters, such as `COMPATIBLE.ASM` and `COMPATIBLE.ADVM` set to `11.2`.

The following SQL statements cover a few examples that illustrate how to manage ASM volumes. Before you successfully execute any statement, connect to an ASM instance through the `sqlplus` command on the local node:

```
SQL> ALTER DISKGROUP dg_flash ADD VOLUME advm_vg SIZE 1G;
```

The preceding command will create a new ASM volume with `1G` size under `dg_flash` disk group.

```
SQL> ALTER DISKGROUP dg_flash RESIZE VOLUME advm_vg SIZE 2G;
```

The preceding command will resize the existing volume `advm_vg` to `2G`.

```
SQL> ALTER DISKGROUP dg_flash DISABLE VOLUME advm_vg;
```

The preceding command will disable the volume advm_vg and remove the volume device on the operating system.

```
SQL> ALTER DISKGROUP dg_flash ENABLE VOLUME advm_vg;
```

The preceding command will enable volume.

```
SQL> ALTER DISKGROUP ALL DISABLE VOLUME ALL;
```

The preceding command will disable all volumes in all disk groups.

```
SQL> ALTER DISKGROUP dg_flash DROP VOLUME advm_vg;
```

The preceding command will drop a volume.

Querying V$ASM views to obtain information about ASM volumes

ASM volume information can be obtained by querying the following new dynamic V$ASM views, added in 11g R2:

View	Description
V$ASM_VOLUME	Displays information about all volumes that are part of the instance.
V$ASM_VOLUME_STAT	Displays statistical information about each volume.

Using the following example, you can view the useful information for volume groups, their size, status, and the device attached to the volumes:

```
SQL> SELECT volume_name,size_mb,state,usage,volume_device,mountpath

      FROM v$asm_volume;
```

The following image shows how the output will look when you run the preceding query:

```
VOLUME_NAME            SIZE_MB STATE    USAGE      VOLUME_DEVICE        MOUNTPATH
-------------------- ---------- -------- ---------- -------------------- ------------------------------
ADVM_VG                    1024 ENABLED  ACFS       /dev/asm/advm_vg-86  /u01/app/oracle/acfsmounts/dg_
                                                                         flash_advm_vg

ADVM_VG2                   1024 ENABLED  ACFS       /dev/asm/advm_vg2-86 /u01/app/oracle/acfsmounts/db_
                                                                         home
```

Using the following example, you can display the volume group statistical information, which includes the number of reads, writes, and bytes written to the volume.

```
SQL> SELECT volume_name,reads,writes,read_errs,bytes_read,bytes_written
      FROM v$asm_volume_stat;
```

The following image shows how the output will look when you run the preceding query:

```
VOLUME_NAME                READS     WRITES  READ_ERRS BYTES_READ BYTES_WRITTEN
-------------------- ---------- ---------- ---------- ---------- -------------
ADVM_VG                       0          0          0          0             0
ADVM_VG2                    114          5          0      65536          6144
```

Automatic Storage Management Cluster File System (ACFS)

When ASM was first introduced in Oracle 10g, it was strictly intended for managing Oracle database-related files only. However, an ASM Cluster File System (ACFS), a new feature in Oracle 11g R2 Grid Infrastructure, extends ASM's capabilities significantly to manage all types of data.

Oracle ACFS is designed as a general purpose, standalone, and cluster-wide filesystem solution, which now supports the data that is maintained outside the Oracle database. Apart from Oracle database datafiles, ACFS can also be used to store Oracle binaries, application files, executables, database trace and log files, BFILEs, video, audio, and other configuration files. The following diagram illustrates the Oracle ASM storage layers:

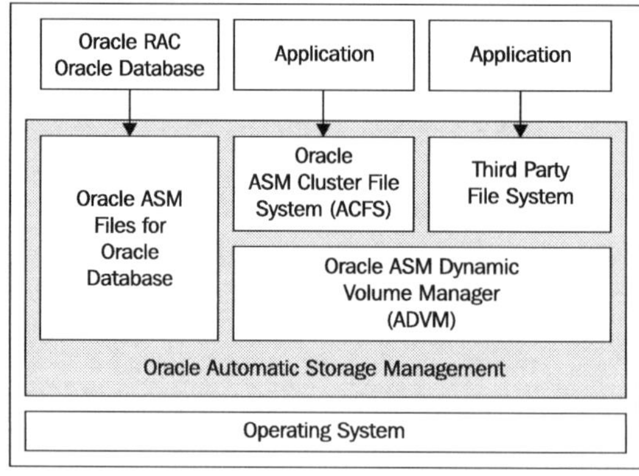

ACFS also supports larger files with 64-bit file and filesystem data structure sizes, leading to the capability of Exabyte files and filesystems on 64-bit platforms. Filesystem integrity and fast recovery is achieved through Oracle ACFS metadata checksums and journaling.

Oracle ACFS filesystem provides the following key advantages, which leverage ASM core functionality:

- An Oracle ACFS filesystem can be dynamically resized, which minimizes the downtime needed to manage the filesystem
- Oracle ACFS filesystem evenly distributes the extents of the ACFS filesystem across all disks of an ASM disk group
- Oracle ACFS filesystem maximizes performance through direct access to Oracle ASM disk group storage
- Oracle ACFS filesystem leverages data reliability through the ASM mirroring protection mechanism

Using ACFS as Oracle database home

An ACFS filesystem can be used for a shared or non-shared Oracle database home (binaries) in an RAC environment. The Oracle homes configured on ACFS should be stored directly under the `$ORACLE_BASE/acfsmounts` location. After the clusterware is successfully configured and if you intend to use ACFS filesystem to configure Oracle homes, you need to first create the ACFS filesystem using ASMCA and then configure Oracle database software using OUI.

Oracle ACFS drivers

The following mandatory drivers are installed as part of the Grid Infrastructure installation and are dynamically loaded to support ACFS and ADVM functionality:

- `oracleacfs` (oracleacfs.ko): The ACFS filesystem module manages all ACFS filesystem operations
- `oracleavdm` (oracleavdm.ko): The AVDM module provides capabilities to directly interface with the filesystem
- `oracleoks` (oracleoks.ko): The kernel services module provides memory management, and lock and cluster synchronization

On Linux, these modules are stored under `/lib/modules/2.6.18-8.el5/extra/usm` and for Windows system, it can be found under `$GRID_HOME/bin folder`. As the root user, you can view the status of these modules by using the `lsmod |grep oracle` command:

```
lsmod |grep oracle


oracleacfs          787460  0

oracleadvm          177792  0

oracleoks           226656  2 oracleacfs,oracleadvm
```

ACFS filesystem-related drivers can also be loaded manually using the following command, which should be executed as the root user:

```
$GRID_HOME/bin/acfsload start -s
```

Prerequisites for creating ACFS

Prior to creating the ACFS filesystem, ensure that the ASM instance is running and the required volumes are created and active.

ACFS creation methods

There are various methods that exist to configure and manage ACFS, such as Enterprise Manager (Grid Control), ASCMA, and ASMCMD. However, our primary focus will be on ASMCA and ASMCMD methods.

Creating an ACFS filesystem using ASMCA

In this example, we will have a close look at how to create a general purpose ACFS filesystem using the ASMCA tool.

1. Run `$GRID_HOME/bin/asmca` at a command prompt from the console. When ASMCA is initiated, it will take you to the main screen where you need to click on the **ASM Cluster File Systems** tab and then click on the **Create** button, as shown in the following screenshot:

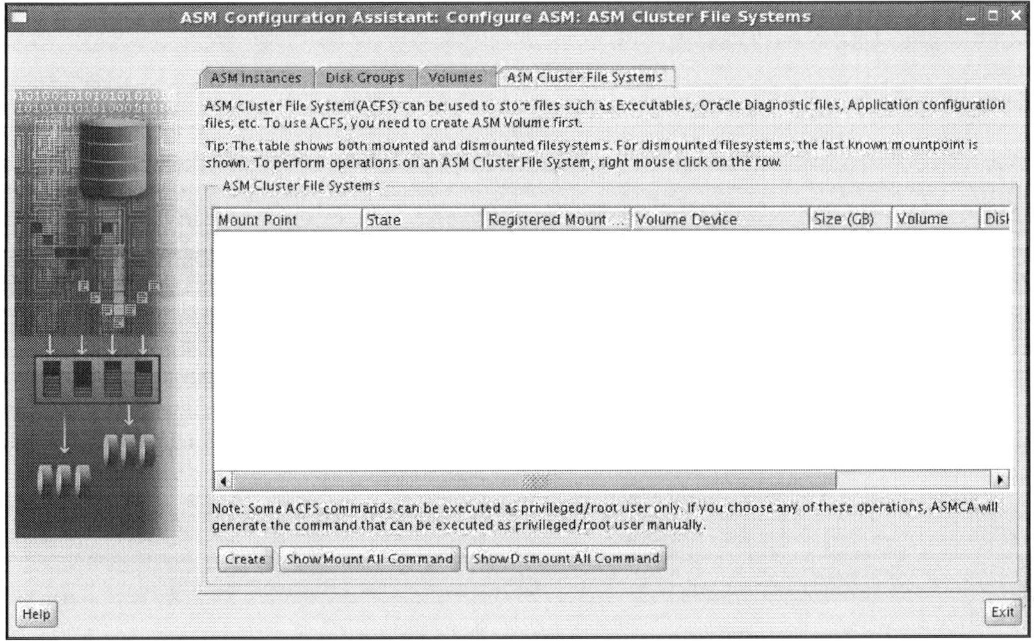

2. On the **Create ASM Cluster File System** screen, select any existing volume from the drop-down list on which you need to configure the ACFS filesystem. In addition, there is also an option available in the drop-down list to create a new volume.
3. You have the option to create a filesystem to use either for Oracle Binaries (shared Oracle Home) or a **General Purpose File System** (GPFS). When you choose a filesystem type for GPFS, the filesystem is created under `$ORACLE_BASE/acfsmounts` (non-CRS ORACLE_BASE).

Don't forget to select the **YES** option to register the mount point; otherwise, you need to manually mount the ACFS filesystem across reboots.

4. After selecting the **YES** option, this filesystem will now be managed as a cluster resource, mounting, and dismounting automatically at Oracle cluster restarts.
5. When you click on the **Show Command** button, you are shown all the commands that would be executed during the filesystem creation.

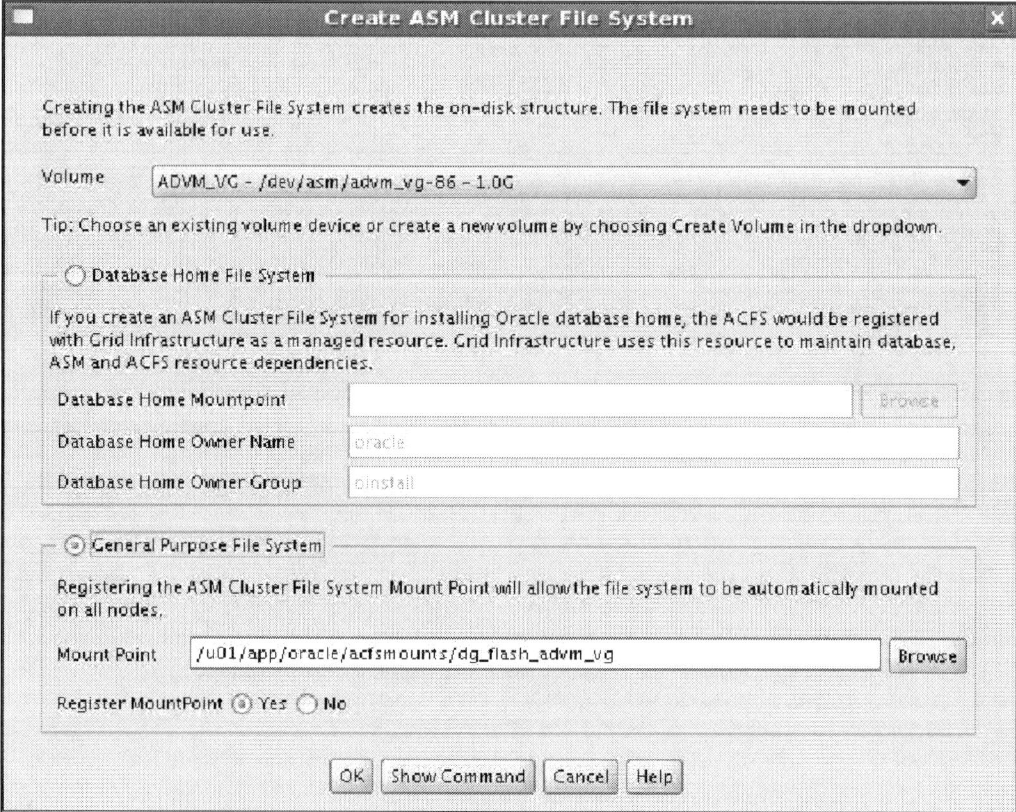

6. Click on **OK** to begin the ACFS filesystem creation process. The ACFS creation window will appear, and the following **Creation** window will be displayed upon the successful filesystem creation.

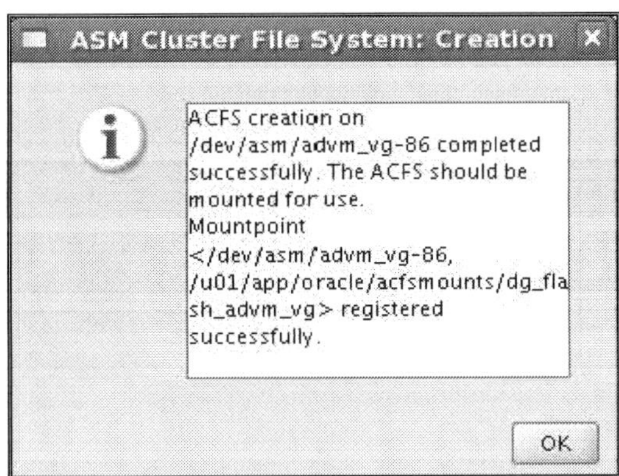

7. Click on **OK** to return to the ASMCA main screen.
8. Now you can see that the filesystem is created and mounted across nodes. Click on the **EXIT** button to quit.
9. The newly created ACFS mount directory can be found under `$ORACL_BASE/acfsmounts`. By default, the mount point is owned by the root. Change the ownership and permissions accordingly for other users to utilize. For example, on UNIX OS, use the `chown` and `chmod` commands to achieve the same.

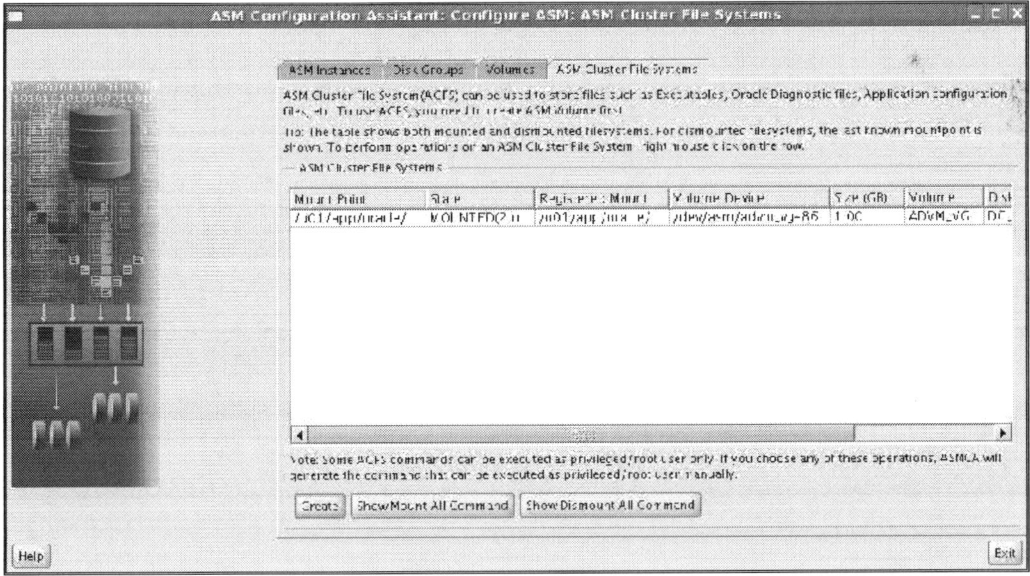

Creating ACFS for Oracle Binaries with ASMCA

When you choose to use the ACFS filesystem for Oracle binaries, you can simply run `./asmca` at a command prompt from the `$GRID_HOME/bin` location and on the ASMCA main screen, click on the **Disk Groups** tab and select one of the existing disk groups, click the right mouse button, and choose the option to create ACFS for Database Home, as shown in the following screenshot:

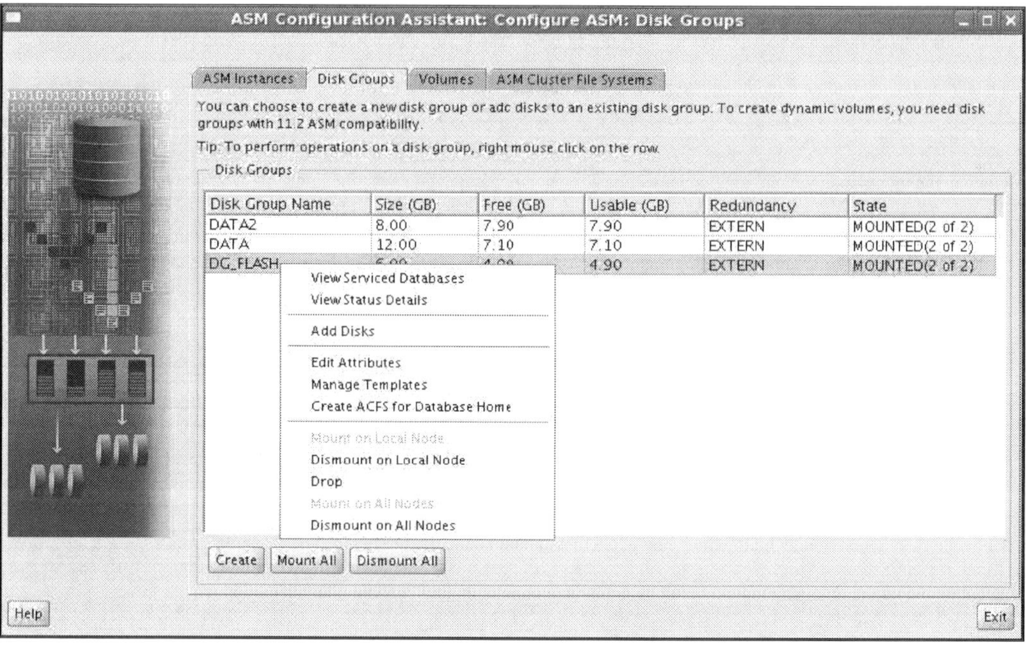

On the **Create ACFS Hosted Database Home** screen, fill in the required columns (shown in the following screenshot) and then click on **OK** to begin the ACFS creation process.

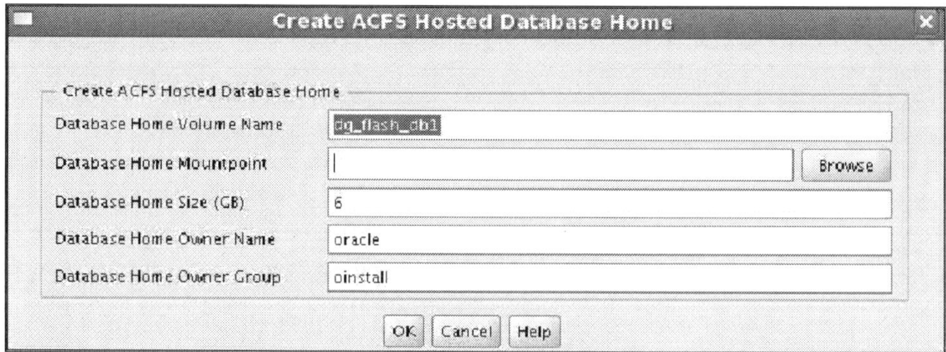

Creating an ACFS filesystem with ASMCMD

ASMCMD is a command-line utility and another way to create and manage an Oracle ACFS filesystem. When you decide to create the ACFS filesystem using ASMCMD, you need to complete the following steps:

1. Before we start creating the ACFS with ASMCMD, ensure the ADVM is already configured. If no ADVM was configured before, then create one using the method explained previously.
2. Create a filesystem using the operating system-specific filesystem creation command.
3. Map the mount point through the Oracle ACFS mount registry.
4. Mount the specific mount point using the operating system-specific command, for example, the `mount` command.

To create the ACFS filesystem using ASMCMD (in non-interactive mode), consider the following sequence of steps:

The following non-interactive example from the command prompt creates a new volume named `advm_vg2` with 1 GB size on the `DG_FLASH` disk group:

```
$GRID_HOME/bin/asmcmd volcreate -G DG_FLASH -s 1g advm_vg2
```

The following example from the command prompt creates a new ACFS filesystem using the previously created volume device:

```
mkfs -t acfs -b 4k /dev/asm/advm_vg2-86
```

When this step is executed, the following details are shown:

```
mkfs.acfs: version                    = 11.2.0.1.0.0
mkfs.acfs: on-disk version            = 39.0
mkfs.acfs: volume                     = /dev/asm/advm_vg2-86
mkfs.acfs: volume size                = 1073741824
mkfs.acfs: Format complete.
```

Before registering the filesystem with the ACFS mount registry option, create the required OS directory using the following example, under `$ORACLE_BASE/acfsmounts` and set appropriate permissions to the directory. To execute the following, you need to be the root user on the system:

```
mkdir -p $ORACLE_BASE/acfsmounts/db_home
chmod 775 -R $ORACLE_BASE/acfsmounts/db_home
chown -R oracle:oinstall $ORACLE_BASE/acfsmounts/db_home
```

Now it's time to register the filesystem as a cluster resource on the required raclinux1 and raclinux2 using the following example:

```
/sbin/acfsutil registry -a -f -n raclinux1,raclinux2 /dev/
  asm/advm_vg-86 /u01/app/oracle/acfsmounts/db_home


acfsutil registry: mount point /u01/app/oracle/acfsmounts/

  db_home successfully added to Oracle Registry
```

After all commands are executed, $ORACLE_BASE/acfsmounts/db_home is successfully added to the Oracle registry, which will enable auto mount of the file-system on the nodes.

Use the following mount command to mount the filesystem:

```
/bin/mount -t acfs /dev/asm/advm_vg2-86 /u01/app/oracle/acfsmounts/db_
home
```

After the filesystem is successfully mounted, you can check the /etc/mtab operating system file to confirm the filesystem is registered and use the df -h command to list the filesystem:

```
more /etc/mtab


/dev/asm/advm_vg-86 /u01/app/oracle/acfsmounts/dg_flash_advm_vg acfs rw 0
0

/dev/asm/advm_vg2-86 /u01/app/oracle/acfsmounts/db_home acfs rw 0 0


df -h


/dev/asm/advm_vg-86    1048576     73964    974612   8% /u01/app/oracle/
acfsmounts/dg_flash_advm_vg

/dev/asm/advm_vg2-86   1048576     39192   1009384   4% /
  u01/app/oracle/acfsmounts/db_home
```

This confirms that the filesystems have been successfully added and are visible on the server.

ACFS mount registry

Generally, whenever a filesystem is created and mounted manually on the operating system, an entry pertaining to the filesystem will be added to the OS-specific file (`/etc/fstab` on most of UNIX OS; `/etc/filesystems` on AIX) for auto mount across reboots. Similarly, when an Oracle ACFS general file system needs to be mounted persistently across cluster or system reboots, it can be registered with the ACFS mount registry using the `acfsutil` registry command. However, automatic mounting of registered Oracle ACFS filesystems are not supported for Oracle restart configurations. Moreover, in a cluster configuration, registered ACFS filesystems are automatically mounted by the mount registry.

Managing ACFS

Although various methods exist to manage ACFS, the ASMCMD command-line tool simplifies the ACFS management.

Acfsutil utility

The Acfsutil utility is installed under the `/sbin` directory and is used to obtain various Oracle ACFS filesystem information.

The following example fetches the existing filesystem information:

```
/sbin/acfsutil registry


Mount Object:
  Device: /dev/asm/advm_vg-86
  Mount Point: /u01/app/oracle/acfsmounts/dg_flash_advm_vg
  Disk Group: DG_FLASH
  Volume: ADVM_VG
  Options: none
  Nodes: all
```

The following example displays information about existing volume devices:

```
/sbin/acfsutil info fs
  -- to list all existing file system configuration
    information in the cluster


/sbin/acfsutil info fs /u01/app/oracle/acfsmounts/dg_flash_advm_vg
-- to list a particular file system configuration
  information in the cluster
```

```
/u01/app/oracle/acfsmounts/dg_flash_advm_vg
    ACFS Version: 11.2.0.1.0.0
    flags:        MountPoint,Available
    mount time:   Thu Nov 12 23:24:38 2009
    volumes:      1
    total size:   1073741824
    total free:   998002688
    primary volume: /dev/asm/advm_vg-86
        label:
        flags:                    Primary,Available,ADVM
        on-disk version:          39.0
        allocation unit:          4096
        major, minor:             252, 44033
        size:                     1073741824
        free:                     998002688
        ADVM diskgroup            DG_FLASH
        ADVM resize increment:    268435456
        ADVM redundancy:          unprotected
        ADVM stripe columns:      4
        ADVM stripe width:        131072
    number of snapshots:  0
    snapshot space usage: 0
```

The following set of examples demonstrates how to de-register, dismount, and disable volumes and ACFS.

This example shows how to de-register a filesystem. When you de-register a file-system, it won't mount automatically.

```
/sbin/acfsutil registry -d /u01/app/oracle/acfsmounts/db_home
```

The following example shows how to dismount a filesystem. The ACFS filesystem can be mounted without de-registering the filesystem:

```
/bin/umount /u01/app/app/acfsmounts/db_home
```

Finally, to disable a volume, you need to first dismount the filesystem on which the volume is mounted. The following example shows how to dismount a filesystem and then disable the volume:

```
/bin/umount /u01/app/oracle/acfsmounts/db_home


asmcmd voldisable -G dg_flash advm_vg2-86
```

ASM new background processes to support ACFS

Whenever a new feature is added, it is important for us to understand how it works and which background process plays a significant role in handling the process management. The following new background processes have been added in Oracle 11g R2 to attain the support of the ACFS-related functionality.

The `ps -ef |grep asm` command at a command prompt exhibits the following information about the background processes that are supporting ASM functionality:

```
oracle   13604     1  0 Nov12 ?        00:00:04 asm_vdbg_+ASM1
oracle   13613     1  0 Nov12 ?        00:00:00 asm_vmb0_+ASM1
oracle   13623     1  0 Nov12 ?        00:00:00 asm_vbg0_+ASM1
oracle   12491     1  1 Nov12 ?        00:00:43 asm_acfs_+ASM1
```

Volume Driver Background (VDBG)

The **Volume Driver Background** (**VDBG**) is an important background process that forwards ASM requests to the ADVM driver. More importantly, it is a fatal background process; thus, any unplanned death of this process will bring down the ASM instance. `+ASM_vdbg_<pid>.trc` contains the information related to the VDBG process.

Volume Background process (VBGn)

The **Volume Background process** (**VBGn**) is a pool of worker processes, which determines the processes that will wait in the ADVM driver for requests (for example, opening and closing an ADVM dynamic file). Unlike the VDBG process, any unplanned death of this process will not bring down the ASM instance. `+ASM_vbg0_<pid>.trc` contains the information related to the VBGn process.

ACFS Background process (ACFS)

The ACFS Background process (ACFS) manages all of the clusterware membership and state transitions within ASM. `+ASM_acfs_<pid>.trc` contains the information related to the ACFS process.

Volume Membership Background processes (VMB0)

The **Volume Membership Background processes** (**VMB0**) plays the role of an I/O barrier and I/O fencing function. Interestingly, during an ASM instance failure, this process continues to exist until the ADVM driver has had a chance to write out pending I/O. `+ASM_vmb_<pid>.trc` contains the information related to the VMB0 processes.

Querying V$ASM views to obtain information about ACFS

You can query the following `V$ASM` dynamic views to obtain information about Oracle ACFS filesystems:

`V$ASM_FILESYSTEM`	Displays information about every mounted ACFS filesystem.
`V$ASM_ACFSVOLUMES`	Displays information about volumes that are correlated with ACFS filesystems.

The following examples demonstrate the usage of the `V$ASM` views:

```
SELECT fs_name,available_time,block_size,state FROM v$asm_filesystem;


FS_NAME                                   AVAILABLE  BLOCK_SIZE  STATE
---------------------------------------------------------------------
/u01/app/oracle/acfsmounts/db_home         14-NOV-09  4        AVAILABLE
/u01/app/oracle/acfsmounts/dg_flash_advm_vg 14-NOV-09  4        AVAILABLE
```

ACFS snapshots

In a typical computing term, a snapshot technology signifies the ability to record the state of a current storage device at any given point and in the event of a failure, use the preserved snapshot as a guide for restoring the storage device. In other words, a snapshot primarily creates a point-in-time copy of the data, which provides an excellent means of data protection. The snapshot technology uses a **Copy-On-Write (COW)** methodology.

Oracle ACFS snapshot technology provides such capability using the **First Copy on Write (FCOW)** methodology. It provides an online read-only point-in-time image of an ACFS filesystem by capturing block/extend updates of a filesystem, which is available for immediate use. It supports a maximum of 64 snapshots per filesystem.

Continuing from our previous examples, we will now demonstrate an example of creating a snapshot and its usage. Before we proceed with the actual example, let's examine the details of an existing filesystem (`db_home`) using the following command:

```
/sbin/acfsutil info fs


/u01/app/oracle/acfsmounts/db_home
    ACFS Version: 11.2.0.1.0.0
    flags:        MountPoint,Available
    mount time:   Sat Nov 14 22:39:17 2009
    volumes:      1
    total size:   1073741824
    total free:   1033609216
    primary volume: /dev/asm/advm_vg2-86
        label:
        flags:                   Primary,Available,ADVM
        on-disk version:         39.0
        allocation unit:         4096
        major, minor:            252, 44034
        size:                    1073741824
        free:                    1033609216
        ADVM diskgroup           DG_FLASH
        ADVM resize increment: 268435456
        ADVM redundancy:         unprotected
        ADVM stripe columns:     4
        ADVM stripe width:       131072
    number of snapshots:  0
    snapshot space usage: 0
```

We will use the `db_home` ACFS filesystem for our demonstration. As you see in the previous output, the filesystem doesn't contain any snapshots, nor is there any space utilized for snapshots. Typically, when an ACFS filesystem is created, it contains a hidden subdirectory named `ACFS` and this subdirectory contains two more subdirectories, `snaps` and `repl`. When a snapshot is taken, a directory with the snapshot name is constructed under the snaps subdirectory. Use the `ls -la` command at the command prompt at the `db_home` location to view the hidden files and directories under this directory.

Snapshots should be managed either through the Acfsutil utility or through Enterprise Manager (Grid Control). Here, we will cover the examples using the Acfsutil utility.

For test purposes, create a small text file using the following example under `db_home`:

```
echo "This is my file" > ashfaq.txt


ls -ltr /u01/app/oracle/acfsmounts/db_home


drwx------ 2 root   root     65536 Nov 13 00:06 lost+found
-rw-r--r-- 1 oracle oinstall    16 Nov 14 22:57 ashfaq.txt.


more ashfaq.txt
This is my file
```

Now, let's create a snapshot.

Creating a snapshot

Using the following `acfsutil snap create` command, we will create a snapshot of `db_home` filesystem:

```
/sbin/acfsutil snap create acfs_snap1 /u01/app/oracle/acfsmounts/db_home


acfsutil snap create: Snapshot operation is complete.
```

After the command is successfully executed, a snapshot directory named `acfs_snap1` of `db_home` ACFS filesystem is created under the `.ACFS/snap` location as shown in the following output.

```
ls -la /u01/app/oracle/acfsmounts/db_home/.ACFS/snaps


drwxr-xr-x 4 oracle oinstall 4096 Nov 14 23:01 acfs_snap1
```

We will now obtain information about the ACFS filesystem to identify the changes after the snapshot has been taken, using the following example:

```
/sbin/acfsutil info fs
```

```
/u01/app/oracle/acfsmounts/db_home
    ACFS Version: 11.2.0.1.0.0
    flags:        MountPoint,Available
    mount time:   Sat Nov 14 22:39:17 2009
    volumes:      1
    total size:   1073741824
    total free:   968667136
    primary volume: /dev/asm/advm_vg2-86
        label:
        flags:                 Primary,Available,ADVM
        on-disk version:       39.0
        allocation unit:       4096
        major, minor:          252, 44034
        size:                  1073741824
        free:                  968667136
        ADVM diskgroup         DG_FLASH
        ADVM resize increment: 268435456
        ADVM redundancy:       unprotected
        ADVM stripe columns:   4
        ADVM stripe width:     131072
    number of snapshots:  1
    snapshot space usage: 32768
```

Now the filesystem contains a snapshot and it utilizes a few bytes of size as well. Our next step is to modify the contents of the file. When the contents of a file are changed for the first time, a copy of the file will be immediately generated under the `acfs_snap1` subdirectory in a read-only mode. If at any time you want to revert back to the original version of the file, then you can copy the file from the subdirectory to the original location. Let's demonstrate here what we have discussed:

```
echo "updating the file" >> ashfaq.txt
```

We are modifying the file named `ashfaq.txt` with some additional content.

`more ashfaq.txt` displays the contents of the file, as follows:

```
   --- file contents
This is my file
updating the file
/sbin/acfsutil info fs


    number of snapshots:  1
    snapshot space usage: 36864
```

As can be seen, the used size has slightly increased by adding more content to the file.

Connect to an ASM instance on the local node through SQLPLUS and use the `v$asm_acfssnapshots` dynamic view to obtain information about the newly created snapshot. Use the following SQL statement:

```
select substr(fs_name,1,20) FS,vol_device device,substr
  (snap_name,1,30) SNAP_NAME,create_time from v$asm_acfssnapshots
```

```
FS                   DEVICE               SNAP_NAME                      CREATE_TI
-------------------- -------------------- ------------------------------ ---------
/u01/app/oracle/acfs /dev/asm/advm_vg2-86 acfs_snap1                     14-NOV-09
```

Removing a snapshot

To remove an existing snapshot created on an ACFS filesystem, use the following command:

```
/sbin/acfsutil snap delete acfs_snap1 /u01/app/oracle/acfsmounts/db_home



acfsutil snap delete: Snapshot operation is complete.
```

ASM Intelligent Data Placement (IDP)

Oracle 11g R2 offers another new exciting ASM feature, **Intelligent Data Placement (IDP)**, which enables you to denote disk regions on a bunch of ASM disks for improved performance. When the disk region settings are in place, you can improve I/O performance by placing the more frequently accessed files (data) on the outermost (HOT) tracks, which will have greater speed and higher bandwidth. In addition, files that have similar access patterns are located closely to each other to reduce the latency. Moreover, IDP allows the placement of primary and mirror extents into different HOT or COLD regions. The IDP settings can be specified for a file or in disk group templates, which can be modified after the disk group is created, provided that the `COMPATIBLE.ASM` and `COMPATIBLE.RDBMS` disk group attributes are set to `11.2` or higher.

IDP works best in the following circumstances:

- When disk groups are more than 25% full
- When database data files are accessed at different rates

Managing IDP settings

IDP settings could be managed through Enterprise Manager (Grid Control), ASMCA, and the `ALTER DISKGROUP` SQL statement. Here, we are going to demonstrate the examples using SQL statements.

```
ALTER DISKGROUP dg_data ADD TEMPLATE dbfile_hot ATTRIBUTES
  (hot mirrorhot);
```

The preceding statement creates a template to use the feature.

```
ALTER DISKGROUP dg_data MODIFY FILE '+dg_data/RACDB/datafile/
  users.2.58864'ATTRIBUTE (hot mirrorhot) /(cold mirrorcold);
```

The preceding statement alters file attributes of the feature.

When you modify an existing file disk region setting, the changes will only apply to the subsequent extensions; exiting file contents are not affected until a rebalance operation is performed.

Finding IDP setting information

Disk region setting information can be obtained using `V$ASM_DISK`, `V$ASM_FILE`, `V$ASM_DISK_IOSTAT`, and `V$ASM_TEMPLATE` views.

ASMCMD enhancements

ASMCMD is a command-line utility located under the $GRID_HOME/bin location, which can be used in either interactive or non-interactive mode to manage ASM instance operations. In Oracle 11g R2, ASMCMD supports most of the ASM operations that are performed through a set of SQL statements. The newly added functionality includes an Oracle ASM instance startup/shutdown, disk group operations (create, mount, drop), template operations, Oracle ASM file access control user and group operations, **ASM Dynamic Volumes (ADVM)** operations, and so on.

Before you execute the asmcmd at a command prompt on the host, ensure that you have properly set ORACLE_SID and ORACLE_HOME environmental variables. For interactive mode, use asmcmd -p at a command prompt and for non-interactive mode, use the asmcmd command.

The following examples demonstrate the usage of asmcmd commands to stop/start the ASM instance.

At the command prompt, type the following command:

```
asmcmd -p
```

Once the command is successfully executed, you will need to connect the ASMCMD prompt and use the following examples:

```
ASMCMD [+] > shutdown

ASMCMD [+] > shutdown --immediate

ASMCMD [+] > shutdown --abort

ASMCMD> startup
```

The following example backs up the ASM spfile from the disk to the ASM disk group:

```
ASMCMD> spbackup /u01/app/oracle/product/11.2.0/dbs/
  spfile+ASM.ora +DG_DATA/bakspfileASM.ora
```

The following example drops the dg_data ASM disk group:

```
ASMCMD [+] > dropdg -r dg_data
```

The following example obtains disk I/O statistics for all the disks of the ASM disk group dg_data:

```
ASMCMD [+] > iostat -G dg_data
```

For example:

```
Group_Name      Dsk_Name          Reads         Writes
DATA            DATA_01           7788463616    6805613568
DATA            DATA_02           7828541440    6894161920
DATA            DATA_03           7865860096    7135420416
```

The following example shows how to mount a disk group dg_data in different modes—force, restricted, and with all options:

```
ASMCMD [+] > mount -f dg_data
ASMCMD [+] > mount --restrict dg_data
ASMCMD [+] > mount -a
```

The following example shows how to perform a rebalancing operation on a dg_data disk group with a rebalance power of four:

```
ASMCMD [+] > rebal --power 4 dg_data
```

ASM backup strategies

You may have been surprised when you first heard of backup strategies for ASM because ASM doesn't have any physical structure (no physical datafiles); it is just a special kind of instance, and there is actually no need to back it up. Having said so, it is strongly advised to back up all the important information in case of a disaster.

Pre-Oracle ASM 11g, there was no direct option to back up the ASM configuration and its metadata information. However, the recommended option in pre-11g was to gather the important information by spooling it in a text or HTML file through querying the ASM specific dynamic views, such as VASM_DISK, VASM_FILES, V$ASM_DISKGROUP, V$ASM_CLIENT, and so on.

md_backup and md_restore commands

With 11g R2, Oracle provides two new commands: md_backup and md_restore, which can be used within the ASMCMD utility to backup and restore the disk group metadata.

The purpose of the md_backup command is to back up the metadata for one or more disk groups, which include disk name, failure groups, attributes, directory structure, and so on. The following example demonstrates various options available with the md_backup command:

```
ASMCMD [+] > md_backup /tmp/asmbackups/datapbkps -G DATA
Disk group metadata to be backed up: DATA
Current alias directory path: RACDB
Current alias directory path: RACDB/TEMPFILE
Current alias directory path: RACDB/PARAMETERFILE
Current alias directory path: RACDB/ONLINELOG
Current alias directory path: RACDB/CONTROLFILE
Current alias directory path: RACDB/DATAFILE
```

The preceding example backs up the metadata for DATA disk group in a backup file, named datapbkps, under the pre-existing /tmp/asmbackups directory. Navigate through the /tmp/asmbackups directory and run the ls -ltr command on the local node to determine the file existence. You should get the identical output as shown below:

```
-rw-r--r--   1 oracle    oinstall    20420 Oct 19 09:12 emrepbkps
```

The following syntax demonstrates a procedure to back up the metadata for all disk groups using the md_backup command within the ASMCMD utility:

```
ASMCMD [+] > md_backup /tmp/asmbackups/alldgbkps
```

Note: Ensure the disk groups are in MOUNT state on the local ASM instance before you run the backup command. The name of the backup file must be unique.

When an ASM disk group is lost in ASM Version 11g R1 or 11g R2 with the md_restore command, you are able to reconstruct the disk group to its previous state, which includes the disk group and its metadata, using the previously taken backup file. The md_restore command supports various options, such as restoring the entire disk group, restoring only metadata for a disk group, restoring the disk group with a new disk group name, and so on. The following restore examples explain the various options available to use in different scenarios:

```
ASMCMD [+] > md_restore --full -G data /tmp/asmbackups/databkps
```

This example re-creates the DATA disk group and its metadata.

```
ASMCMD [+] > md_restore --nodg -G data /tmp/asmbackups/databkps
```

This example re-creates only metadata for the DATA disk group.

```
ASMCMD [+] > md_restore --newdg -o 'data:data2' /tmp/asmbackups/databkps
```

This example helps you to re-create the full DATA disk group into a new disk group, named `data2`.

Summary

In this chapter, we have thoroughly discussed how the Oracle Automatic Storage Management (ASM) feature simplifies database datafile management, and the benefits provided by using it. We have also covered the 11g R1 and 11g R2 feature enhancements in great detail. We have discussed how to manage an ASM instance using ASMCA and the functionality and usage of ASM Dynamic Volume Manager (ADVM), ASM Cluster File System (ACFS), and ASM Snapshot technology. Additionally, we discussed how to place the data that is accessed more frequently on the edge of disk spindles to gain increased performance. Towards the end of this chapter, we also covered the topic of ASM backup and restore strategies.

In the next chapter, we will look at managing and troubleshooting clusterware and cluster administration.

5

Managing and Troubleshooting Oracle 11g Clusterware

One of the biggest challenges for both the experienced and junior Oracle RAC DBA in terms of supporting the Oracle 11g Real Application Cluster environment lies in the tasks involved to keep the Oracle 11g Clusterware at a high level of operation without failures. Clusterware is the heart and soul of the Oracle 11g RAC environment. In this chapter, we will provide you with key tips and techniques on how to manage the complex 11g Clusterware in the best possible way. We will also provide troubleshooting methods to quickly resolve and prevent errors and critical failures. In summary, we will discuss the following topics:

- Oracle 11g RAC Clusterware administration
- Managing Oracle 11g Clusterware utilities
- Troubleshooting Oracle 11g Clusterware
- New Features in Oracle 11g R2 Clusterware

Oracle 11g RAC Clusterware administration

Before we investigate the nature of Oracle 11g RAC issues, we first need to provide an introduction to how the Oracle 11g Clusterware functions. We will begin with a quick overview of the key 11g Clusterware processes that compose the architecture of the Oracle 11g RAC environment. We will also discuss the primary role of the Oracle 11g Clusterware within an Oracle 11g RAC environment.

About Oracle Clusterware

Oracle 11g Clusterware is Oracle's implementation of cluster management software, which was introduced in the 10g release of Oracle RAC software. It was originally called **Cluster Ready Services** (**CRS**) and is the complex software that exists under the hood of all Oracle 11g RAC environments. Oracle Clusterware provides several key services essential to an Oracle 11g RAC configuration, including the following:

- Group Services to manage cluster services within 11g RAC
- Node Monitor or the "heartbeat" to monitor the status of nodes in 11g RAC cluster
- Locking services performed by the LMS database process to manage concurrency activities for 11g RAC cluster
- HA Resource management for failover or load-balancing activities in 11g RAC

Oracle Clusterware is a different piece of software compared to other RAC components or the RAC database. One key point is not to confuse the Clusterware operations and architecture with 11g RAC! They are both crucial for a complete clustering solution and interact with each other, but are not the same thing. Clusterware consists of the Oracle clustering software as well as background processes that are unique and required for an Oracle RAC environment. In contrast, the Oracle RAC architecture contains Clusterware as well as additional hardware, network, storage, and database components required for Oracle 11g RAC. Many DBAs confuse Clusterware with RAC and think that they are same, which is indeed not the case.

Oracle 11g Clusterware concepts

In order to manage a large 11g RAC environment, one must first understand the key processes that make up the Oracle 11g Clusterware architecture. Oracle Clusterware consists of the following items:

- Oracle Cluster Registry
- Voting disk
- Control files (`SCLS_SRC`) for Clusterware
- Initialization and shutdown scripts for Clusterware
- Oracle 11g Clusterware background processes
- Additional background processes for Oracle 11g Clusterware

Oracle Cluster Registry

The Oracle Cluster Registry's purpose is to hold cluster and database configuration information for RAC and Cluster Ready Services (CRS) such as the cluster node list, cluster database instance to node mapping, and CRS application resource profiles. As such, the OCR contains all configuration information for Oracle 11g Clusterware, including network communication settings where the Clusterware daemons or background processes listen, along with the cluster interconnect information for 11g RAC network configuration and the location of the 11g voting disk.

The OCR must be stored on shared raw devices, **OCFS/OCFS2 (Oracle Cluster Filesystem or an approved NFS or supported cluster filesystem)** within an Oracle 11g RAC environment. After you have set the `$PATH` value for your Oracle 11g RAC environment, you can verify the status of the OCR configuration by issuing the `OCRCHECK` command as shown below:

```
[oracle@raclinux1 ~]$ ocrcheck
Status of Oracle Cluster Registry is as follows :
        Version                  :          2
        Total space (kbytes)     :     297084
        Used space (kbytes)      :       3852
        Available space (kbytes) :     293232
        ID                       : 2007457116
        Device/File Name         : /dev/raw/raw5
                                   Device/File integrity check succeeded
        Device/File Name         : /dev/raw/raw6
                                   Device/File integrity check succeeded

        Cluster registry integrity check succeeded
```

Voting disk

The **Voting disk** manages cluster node membership and must be stored on either a shared raw disk or **OCFS/OCFS2** cluster filesystem. As such, the Voting disk is the key communication mechanism within the Oracle Clusterware where all nodes in the cluster read and write heartbeat information. In addition, the Voting disk is also used to shut down, fence, or reboot either single or multiple nodes whenever network communication is lost between any node within the cluster, in order to prevent the dreaded split-brain condition and thus protect the database information. You can check the status of the vote disk as well as view detail configuration information, by using the `crsctl` command as shown next:

```
[oracle@raclinux1 ~]$ crsctl query css votedisk
 0.     0    /dev/raw/raw7
```

```
1.     0     /dev/raw/raw8
2.     0     /dev/raw/raw9

located 3 votedisk(s).
```

This output from `crsctl` tells us that we have three vote disks for the 11g Clusterware environment and that they are available and free of errors. The Control Files (SCLS_SRC) for Clusterware are the following:

- `crsdboot`
- `crsstart`
- `cssrun`
- `noclsmon`
- `nooprocd`

Within Oracle 11g Clusterware, key control files called `SCLS_SRC` that control some important cluster functions exist since release 10g for Oracle RAC.

These control files enable and disable processes, such as allowing the Oracle 11g Clusterware processes **Oprocd** and **Oslsvmon** to be either enabled or disabled, stopping key daemons for the Clusterware for `crsd.bin` and `ocssd.bin`, and preventing the Oracle Clusterware from being started up when the machine reboots occur, within the CSSD family of Clusterware background processes.

For the Linux operating system, these control files are located under the following directories: `/etc/oracle/scls_scr/raclinux1` and `/etc/oracle/scls_scr/raclinux1/root`.

The first directory structure under `/etc/oracle/scls_scr` contains the control file `cssfatal`, whereas the second directory structure located under the `/etc/oracle/scls_scr/{nodename}/root` contains the other configuration file required for the CSSD process.

These control files must never be manipulated manually or corruption may occur within the Oracle 11g Clusterware. To note, some of these control files have been changed via the `init.cssd` startup processes or by the `crsctl` utility during the Clusterware management and operations. In addition, the actual filesystem location may vary based on your specific operating system implementation. Throughout this book, we will focus on the Linux operating system (such as Red Hat Linux, Oracle Enterprise Linux) as the core platform for our examples.

Initialization and shutdown scripts for Clusterware

Oracle Clusterware makes use of many system-level background scripts to shut down and start the cluster environment. For UNIX and LINUX platforms, these scripts originate from the `inittab` entries located under the `/etc/init.d` directory location.

These initialization scripts must run before the Oracle Clusterware daemons can start in the 11g Clusterware environment. Within UNIX and LINUX, these initialization scripts are started and stopped by the `init daemon`. In order for the `init daemon` to perform these tasks, entries are written to the `/etc/inittab` configuration file as shown next:

```
[root@raclinux1 init.d]# cat /etc/inittab
# Run xdm in runlevel 5
x:5:respawn:/etc/X11/prefdm -nodaemon
h1:35:respawn:/etc/init.d/init.evmd run >/dev/null 2>&1 </dev/null
h2:35:respawn:/etc/init.d/init.cssd fatal >/dev/null 2>&1 </dev/nul l
h3:35:respawn:/etc/init.d/init.crsd run >/dev/null 2>&1 </dev/null
```

These processes are spawned on boot and reboot times by the root superuser account. As for the `init daemon` process, scripts that are referenced in the `/etc/inittab` configuration file, there are several of these init scripts that are executed by root within UNIX and LINUX to start and stop the Clusterware environment. These scripts are located under the `/etc/init.d` directory for LINUX and most UNIX implementations as shown here:

```
[root@raclinux1 init.d]# pwd
/etc/init.d
[root@raclinux1 init.d]# ls -l ini*
-r-xr-xr-x  1 root root  1951 Jun 27  2005 init.crs
-r-xr-xr-x  1 root root  4735 Jun 27  2005 init.crsd
-r-xr-xr-x  1 root root 35401 Jun 27  2005 init.cssd
-r-xr-xr-x  1 root root  3197 Jun 27  2005 init.evmd
```

Several key points need to be kept in mind regarding these initialization scripts for 11g Clusterware. First, whenever the Clusterware is stopped, the daemons for the Clusterware will be shut down within the 11g RAC cluster. However, these `init` scripts will continue to run in the background. As of Oracle 10.1.0.4 release of the Oracle Clusterware, these initialization scripts are required for manual Clusterware startup procedures. Finally, if the `init` scripts are not running within the operating system, the Clusterware daemons such as **Oracle Cluster Synchronization Services Daemon** (CRSD) will not be started.

Oracle 11g Clusterware background processes

Oracle 11g Clusterware contains many special background processes that perform the maintenance and operational tasks for Oracle 11g RAC environments. The following daemons or background processes exist in a standard 11g Clusterware environment:

- Cluster Ready Services Daemon
- Oracle Cluster Synchronization Services Daemon
- Cluster Synchronization Services Daemon
- Event Monitor Daemon

Cluster Ready Services Daemon

The **Cluster Ready Services Daemon** (**CRSD**) performs many critical functions within the Oracle 11g Clusterware environment. As a daemon process, it is the engine that drives High Availability-related operations. CRSD manages the Clusterware resources for applications and handles the process for starting, stopping, and failing over application resources within the Clusterware. It also spawns different actions as required to start, stop, or verify the status of application resources during these HA activities. Another critical task performed by CRSD is to maintain all configuration profiles within the Oracle Configuration Repository. For example, CRSD records the currently known state of the cluster within the OCR on a regular basis. The CRSD daemon process runs as the root superuser within the LINUX and UNIX operating system. It is restarted automatically in the event of failure.

Oracle Cluster Synchronization Services Daemon

The **Oracle Cluster Synchronization Services Daemon** (**OCSSD**) is a unique daemon that fulfills a dual role within Oracle 11g. The first purpose of the OCSSD background process is that it performs tasks for single-instance, non-RAC environments in terms of the Oracle 11g Automatic Storage Management instance functionality. In addition, OCSSD is a mandatory process for the 11g Clusterware with RAC and performs several key functions for Clusterware operations. First of all, the OCSSD provides the mechanism that grants access to node membership on a clusterwide basis. As such, it provides group services as well as basic cluster locking and concurrency operations. Secondly, OCSSD integrates the Oracle 11g RAC environment with third-party vendor Clusterware if used within an 11g RAC configuration. For example, if Sun Cluster HA software is used for the Clusterware software with 11g RAC, the OCSSD process would allow this configuration to coexist with 11g RAC, instead of using the Oracle 11g Clusterware. One key difference between OCSSD and CRSD is that the OCSSD runs as Oracle user within the 11g Clusterware environment.

In the event that OCSSD experiences a failure or abnormal termination, it will cause a machine reboot. This helps prevent data corruption in the event of a dreaded "split-brain" condition.

Cluster Synchronization Services Daemon

The **Cluster Synchonization Services Daemon** (**CSSD**) manages cluster configuration by controlling which nodes are members of the cluster and by notifying members whenever a node joins or leaves the cluster. The `cssdagent` process monitors the cluster and provides I/O fencing. Prior to Oracle 11g R2, the service was provided by Oracle Process Monitor Daemon OPROCD, also known as OraFenceService on Windows. A `cssdagent` failure results in a node restart by the Clusterware.

Event Monitor Daemon

The **Event Monitor Daemon** (**EVMD**) performs essential management of event-and message-based activities within the Oracle 11g Clusterware environment for 11g RAC. As such, the EVMD process generates events whenever different conditions occur that impact or affect the Clusterware operations. EVMD spawns a permanent child process called `evmlogger`. The `evmlogger` process thereby generates additional child processes as needed. As `evmlogger` creates various logfiles located under `$ORA_CRS_HOME/evm/admin/conf/evmlogger.conf`, you can edit the size of these logfiles by editing the `maxsize` parameter of the `evmlogger.conf` file. Another task performed by EVMD is the handling of callout functions within 11g Clusterware. For instance, EVMD scans the callout directory and is also responsible for invocation of callout scripts. Like OCSSD, the EVMD process runs as the Oracle user in the background of the LINUX and UNIX operating system. Upon failure, EVMD is restarted automatically.

Additional background processes for Oracle 11g Clusterware

In addition to the mandatory core background processes required for Oracle 11g Clusterware, you may have several additional background processes running as part of your Oracle 11g RAC and Clusterware environment, which include the following:

- Oracle Clusterware Process Monitor Daemon
- OCLSVMON
- OCLSOMON

- DISKMON
- OCLSKD
- RACG

Oracle Clusterware Process Monitor Daemon OPROCD

The **Oracle Clusterware Process Monitor Daemon** (**OPROCD**) runs on Oracle Clusterware for releases as of 10.2.0.4 for Linux platforms. It functions to monitor the cluster system state and Clusterware health for each cluster node within an Oracle 11g RAC configuration.

OPROCD is the tag team partner process that runs along with the `hangcheck-timer` module on Linux platforms. OPROCD is spawned by `init.cssd` and runs as the root superuser. Oracle locks the OPROCD process into memory so that it can monitor every local cluster node where it executes. Another key task that OPROCD performs is to detect hardware and driver hang conditions on a server as part of the Clusterware health checks. OPROCD also provides I/O fencing functions; however, the manner in which OPROCD performs I/O fencing differs from the method performed by SCSI fencing operations. For instance, in the event that a server within the cluster is frozen for a long period of time so that it is evicted from the database cluster, it must be forcefully rebooted by itself to prevent any queued-up I/O operations from being issued and executed to the shared cluster disk where the Oracle data files live after the remainder of the cluster has performed the remastering process for the failed node locks. OPROCD provides these functions by running a status check and then waits in sleep mode, and once the wake-up time is reached beyond the threshold set within the cluster, OPROCD will reboot the local node in the cluster.

> The OPROCD process is usually found to exist for platforms that do not use the vendor Clusterware with Oracle Clusterware. As such, OPROCD will always be present with Oracle Clusterware 11g R1 and for releases 10.2.0.4 and above in Linux environments.

OPROCD has the following two key parameters at startup time:

- `-t` : This is the timeout value (`OPROCD_DEFAULT_TIMEOUT=1000`). This value is the length of time between executions (in milliseconds). It defaults to 1000 ms.
- `-m` : This is the margin value (`OPROCD_DEFAULT_MARGIN=500`). This is the permitted margin of time to wait (in milliseconds) before the reboot of the server node is affected (milliseconds). The normal default value is set to 500 ms.

One key point that needs to be mentioned is that OPROCD has no relationship or dependency whatsoever on the hangcheck-timer module. This is important to understand because they fulfill different functions—hangcheck-timer is module dependent and built into the Linux kernel for the Linux operating system and OPROCD is an Oracle Clusterware process.

Based on tests conducted by Oracle referenced in My Oracle Support (formerly Metalink) Note 567730.1, which is available to the reader with an active Oracle CSI Support account from the My Oracle Support (formerly Metalink) website at `http://support.oracle.com`, Oracle Corporation has discovered a large discrepancy for latencies between operating system platforms and OS versions. As a result, the default settings for OPROCD parameter values may be affected by intense loads on systems, which may cause false restarts by affected nodes in the cluster. It is recommended that scheduling latencies are configured, based on support provided by the operating system vendor so that issues can be eliminated in terms of reboot conditions caused by OPROCD.

The general recommendation from Oracle support is to set the Oracle Clusterware parameter `DIAGWAIT` to a value of 13. This will increase timings for any failed nodes to flush out currently open trace files, which will provide critical assistance in debugging the root cause of node failure.

You must shut down the cluster in order to change the `DIAGWAIT` setting, which will bring down all database services on the node. Another option is to use the default timing threshold for `DIAGWAIT`. Best practices dictate setting `DIAGWAIT` either after the initial 11g Clusterware installation or during the maintenance period. My Oracle (formerly Metalink) Support Note 559365.1 provides further information on this parameter.

OCLSVMON

The `oclsvmon.bin` is an optional daemon process that runs in conjunction when third-party Clusterware is used. Root owns these processes, which perform Clusterware monitoring tasks.

OCLSOMON

The `oclsomon.bin` process performs verification for the `ocssd.bin process.`

DISKMON

The `diskmon.bin` background process is a new optional daemon that appears in Oracle 11g R1 (11.1.0.7) RAC environments that use the Oracle Exadata machine. It functions as the "master" disk monitor process within Oracle 11g Clusterware for managing resources within an Oracle Exadata and 11g RAC environment.

OCLSKD

The `oclskd.bin` daemon process is a new Oracle 11g R1 (11.1.0.6) process that fulfills the task of rebooting nodes whenever an Oracle 11g instance in the 11g RAC cluster experiences a hang condition.

RACG

RACG runs as the **racgmain** and **racgimon** background daemon processes under LINUX and UNIX, and as `racgmain.exe` and `racgimon.exe` on Windows platforms. The purpose of RACG is to extend Clusterware support for server callout scripts that occur whenever **Fast Active Notification** events occur within the Oracle 11g RAC environment.

Fatal Clusterware processes and Oracle 11g RAC

Within the Oracle 11g Clusterware software for Oracle RAC environments, there are three different fatal processes. Fatal processes in the 11g Clusterware are unique processes. This is because in the event that an abnormal termination of kill condition causes these fatal processes to end, a node reboot will occur. Three of the fatal Clusterware processes are as follows:

- OCSSD
- OPROCD
- OCLSOMON

As for the non-fatal Clusterware daemon processes (that is EVMD), they will restart automatically if they are terminated or if they die over a period of time.

Managing Oracle 11g Clusterware utilities

Oracle provides a suite of utilities and scripts that are to be used by the database administrator in charge of an Oracle 11g RAC environment. It is imperative to master these tools so that the 11g Clusterware can be monitored on a proactive basis to avoid any failures or downtimes in the clustered environment for Oracle 11g RAC. The key Clusterware administration utilities that we will discuss in this chapter include the following:

- CRSCTL (Clusterware Control utility)
- CRS_STAT (Cluster Ready Services Statistics)
- OCRCHECK (Oracle Cluster Registry Check Utility)
- OCRCONFIG (Oracle Cluster Registry Config Utility)
- CLSCFG (Clusterware Config Tool)
- CLUVFY (Clusterware Verification Utility)

CRSCTL

The CRSCTL command utility is an essential tool to master in the DBA toolbox for Clusterware maintenance and administration. It provides Clusterware monitoring functions as well as the ability to add and remove key components of the Oracle 11g Clusterware such as adding or removing vote disks and management of Clusterware processes and resources. Furthermore, as we will present in the troubleshooting examples, CRSCTL is a critical tool for debugging Clusterware problems to isolate and find the root cause for quick resolution. In a nutshell, CRSCTL is a powerful tool in your arsenal for the management and administration of 11g Clusterware with Oracle RAC environments.

The complete syntax for the `crsctl` command is available by entering it at the command line:

```
$ crsctl
Usage: crsctl check  crs  - checks the viability of the CRS stack
       crsctl check  cssd - checks the viability of CSS
       crsctl check  crsd - checks the viability of CRS
       crsctl check  evmd - checks the viability of EVM
       crsctl set    css <parameter> <value> - sets a parameter override
       crsctl get    css <parameter> - gets the value of a CSS parameter
       crsctl unset  css <parameter> - sets CSS parameter to its default
       crsctl query  css votedisk    - lists the voting disks used by CSS
```

```
crsctl add    css votedisk <path> - adds a new voting disk
crsctl delete css votedisk <path> - removes a voting disk
crsctl enable  crs    - enables startup for all CRS daemons
crsctl disable crs    - disables startup for all CRS daemons
crsctl start crs  - starts all CRS daemons.
crsctl stop  crs  - stops all CRS daemons. Stops CRS resources in
  case of cluster.
crsctl start resources  - starts CRS resources.
crsctl stop resources  - stops  CRS resources.
crsctl debug statedump evm  - dumps state info for evm objects
crsctl debug statedump crs  - dumps state info for crs objects
crsctl debug statedump css  - dumps state info for css objects
crsctl debug log css [module:level]{,module:level} ...
                      - Turns on debugging for CSS
crsctl debug trace css - dumps CSS in-memory tracing cache
crsctl debug log crs [module:level]{,module:level} ...
                      - Turns on debugging for CRS
crsctl debug trace crs - dumps CRS in-memory tracing cache
crsctl debug log evm [module:level]{,module:level} ...
                      - Turns on debugging for EVM
crsctl debug trace evm - dumps EVM in-memory tracing cache
crsctl debug log res <resname:level> turns on debugging for
  resources
crsctl query crs softwareversion [<nodename>] - lists the version
  of CRS software installed
crsctl query crs activeversion - lists the CRS software operating
  version
crsctl lsmodules css - lists the CSS modules that can be used for
  debugging
crsctl lsmodules crs - lists the CRS modules that can be used for
  debugging
crsctl lsmodules evm - lists the EVM modules that can be used for
  debugging
```

If necessary, any of these commands can be run with additional tracing by adding a "trace" argument at the very front—for example, `crsctl trace check css`.

One important task that Oracle RAC DBAs are tasked with is to add new voting disks. The Oracle user can be used to add the voting disks or the root account can be used as shown in the example listed next.

You can use `crsctl` command to add a new vote disk to a raw device as shown in the following example:

```
[root@raclinux1 ~]# mkdir -p /11g/votedisk
 [root@raclinux1 ~]# chmod 777 //11g/votedisk
[root@raclinux1 ~]# /u01/app/oracle/product/11.1.0/db_1/bin/crsctl add
css votedisk /11g/votedisk/vdisk4
Cluster is not in a ready state for online disk addition
[root@raclinux1 ~]# /u01/app/oracle/product/11.1.0/db_1/bin/crsctl stop
crs Stopping resources.

Successfully stopped CRS resources
Stopping CSSD.
Shutting down CSS daemon.
Shutdown request successfully issued.
[root@raclinux1 ~]#
[root@raclinux1 ~]# /u01/app/oracle/product/11.1.0/db_1/bin/crsctl add
css votedisk /11g/votedisk/vdisk4 -force
Now formatting voting disk: /11g/votedisk/vdisk4
successful addition of votedisk /11g/votedisk/vdisk4.
[root@raclinux1 ~]# /u01/app/oracle/product/11.1.0/db_1/bin/crsctl add
css votedisk /11g/votedisk/vdisk5 -force
Now formatting voting disk: /11g/votedisk/vdisk5
successful addition of votedisk /11g/votedisk/vdisk5.
[root@raclinux1 ~]# /u01/app/oracle/product/11.1.0/db_1/bin/crsctl start
crs Attempting to start CRS stack
The CRS stack will be started shortly
```

Now, we need to verify that both the Oracle Clusterware and vote disks are created and have now come back online after we have added the new disks and restarted the Cluster Ready Services. We can verify that these Clusterware processes have come back online with the commands shown in the following example:

```
[oracle@raclinux1 ~]$ crsctl query css votedisk
 0.     0     /dev/raw/raw7
 1.     0     /dev/raw/raw8
 2.     0     /dev/raw/raw9
 3.     0     /11g/votedisk/vdisk4
 4.     0     /11g/votedisk/vdisk5

located 5 votedisk(s).
$ crsctl check crs
```

```
CSS appears healthy
CRS appears healthy
EVM appears healthy
```

According to My Oracle Support (formerly Metalink) Note **329734.1,** we first need to shut down the Clusterware to add new vote disks to the configuration, due to how it functions within Oracle 11g RAC Clusterware. This explains the initial error message, **Cluster is not in a ready state for online disk addition**, when we first attempted to add the new vote disks online while the 11g Clusterware was running. Should the user see this error, it is due to not having shut down the Clusterware. This issue is most likely to exist only with older versions of the Oracle Clusterware and may not be an issue with 11g R1 and 11g R2 Clusterware. The `crsctl set <parameter>` command can be used to modify Clusterware parameter settings as required. For example, to change the miscount parameter for the Clusterware, you will need to input the following command:

```
# crsctl set css misscount 90
Configuration parameter misscount is now set to 90.
```

Exercise great caution when changing 11g Clusterware parameters! It is recommended to do so only after installation based on testing in non-production support or under the guidance of Oracle support.

CRS_STAT

Another useful tool for 11g Clusterware administration is that of the `CRS__STAT` utility. `CRS_STAT` is of paramount importance to monitor the status of Clusterware resources in Oracle 11g RAC environments. The complete syntax for the `CRS_STAT` command is provided next:

```
$ crs_stat -h
Usage:  crs_stat [resource_name [...]] [-v] [-l] [-q] [-c cluster_member]
        crs_stat [resource_name [...]] -t [-v] [-q] [-c cluster_member]
        crs_stat -p [resource_name [...]] [-q]
        crs_stat [-a] application -g
        crs_stat [-a] application -r [-c cluster_member]
        crs_stat -f [resource_name [...]] [-q] [-c cluster_member]
        crs_stat -ls [resource_name [...]] [-q]
```

Considering that we want to examine the general status for Clusterware resources and applications, the `crs_stat -t` command can be issued as shown next to display the status of these resources in a tabular format:

```
$ crs_stat -t
Name           Type           Target    State     Host
------------------------------------------------------------
ora....B1.inst application    ONLINE    OFFLINE
ora....B2.inst application    ONLINE    OFFLINE
ora.RACDB.db   application    ONLINE    OFFLINE
ora....SM1.asm application    ONLINE    OFFLINE
ora....X1.lsnr application    ONLINE    OFFLINE
ora....X1.lsnr application    ONLINE    OFFLINE
ora....ux1.gsd application    ONLINE    ONLINE    raclinux1
ora....ux1.ons application    ONLINE    ONLINE    raclinux1
ora....ux1.vip application    ONLINE    OFFLINE
ora.target.db  application    ONLINE    OFFLINE
ora....t1.inst application    ONLINE    OFFLINE
ora.test.db    application    ONLINE    OFFLINE
ora....t1.inst application    ONLINE    OFFLINE
```

Another useful feature with `crs_stat` is to examine the Clusterware parameter settings by using the `crs_stat -p` option as shown here:

```
$ crs_stat -p
NAME=ora.RACDB.RACDB1.inst
TYPE=application
ACTION_SCRIPT=/u01/app/oracle/product/11.1.0/db_1/bin/racgwrap
ACTIVE_PLACEMENT=0
AUTO_START=1     dictates whether resource will restart on crs restart
CHECK_INTERVAL=600  how often crs checks this resource
DESCRIPTION=CRS application for Instance
FAILOVER_DELAY=0
FAILURE_INTERVAL=0
FAILURE_THRESHOLD=0
HOSTING_MEMBERS=raclinux1
OPTIONAL_RESOURCES=
PLACEMENT=restricted
```

```
REQUIRED_RESOURCES=ora.raclinux1.vip ora.raclinux1.ASM1.asm
RESTART_ATTEMPTS=5
SCRIPT_TIMEOUT=600 è timeout for script which checks resource
START_TIMEOUT=0
STOP_TIMEOUT=0
UPTIME_THRESHOLD=7d
USR_ORA_ALERT_NAME=
USR_ORA_CHECK_TIMEOUT=0
USR_ORA_CONNECT_STR=/ as sysdba
USR_ORA_DEBUG=0
USR_ORA_DISCONNECT=false
```

Sometimes there will be a problem that causes the Oracle Clusterware to fail or resources to become unavailable due to permission and ownership settings for the Oracle Clusterware. If you wish to examine the Clusterware permissions and ownership, you can use the `crs_stat -ls` option as shown here:

```
]$ crs_stat -ls
Name           Owner          Primary PrivGrp          Permission
-----------------------------------------------------------------
ora....B1.inst oracle         oinstall                 rwxrwxr--
ora....B2.inst oracle         oinstall                 rwxrwxr--
ora.RACDB.db   oracle         oinstall                 rwxrwxr--
ora....SM1.asm oracle         oinstall                 rwxrwxr--
ora....X1.lsnr oracle         oinstall                 rwxrwxr--
ora....X1.lsnr oracle         oinstall                 rwxrwxr--
ora....ux1.gsd oracle         oinstall                 rwxr-xr--
ora....ux1.ons oracle         oinstall                 rwxr-xr--
```

OCRCHECK

In order to monitor the status of the Oracle Cluster Registry for the Oracle 11g RAC Clusterware, you can run the OCRCHECK command-line utility. The `ocrcheck -help` command gives you a brief description of the tool:

```
$ ocrcheck -help
Name:
        ocrcheck - Displays health of Oracle Cluster Registry.
```

```
Synopsis:
        ocrcheck

Description:
        prompt> ocrcheck
        Displays current usage, location and health of the cluster
registry

Notes:
        A log file will be created in
        $ORACLE_HOME/log/<hostname>/client/ocrcheck_<pid>.log. Please
          ensure you have file creation privileges in the above directory
          before running this tool.
```

As part of the RAC DBA management tasks, the OCR should be monitored on a regular basis to ensure that the 11g Clusterware is error free and available. For normal configurations with normal redundancy, the loss of a single OCR will not cause the entire cluster to fail. Nonetheless, monitoring of the cluster should still be performed by the DBA as part of normal operations. An example of using this utility is shown next:

```
$ ocrcheck
Status of Oracle Cluster Registry is as follows :
         Version                     :          2
         Total space (kbytes)        :     297084
         Used space (kbytes)         :       3860
         Available space (kbytes) :     293224
         ID                          : 2007457116
         Device/File Name            : /dev/raw/raw5
                                       Device/File integrity check succeeded
         Device/File Name            : /dev/raw/raw6
                                       Device/File integrity check succeeded

         Cluster registry integrity check succeeded
```

You can then verify the details from the output logfile from OCRCHECK as shown in the following sample log file:

```
Oracle Database 11g CRS Release 11.1.0.6.0 Production Copyright 1996,
2007 Oracle.  All rights reserved.
2009-06-21 18:26:04.049: [OCRCHECK][3086935744]ocrcheck starts...
```

```
2009-06-21 18:26:05.649: [OCRCHECK][3086935744]protchcheck: OCR status
: total = [297084], used = [3860], avail = [293224]

2009-06-21 18:26:05.664: [OCRCHECK][3086935744]Exiting
[status=success]...
```

OCRCONFIG

The OCRCONFIG utility provides you with the ability to manage the Oracle 11g Cluster Registry. As such, it provides you with the following functionalities to administer the OCR:

- Exporting and importing OCR contents to a file
- Restoring a corrupted OCR from a physical backup
- Adding or replacing an OCR copy with another OCR file
- Repairing a damaged OCR with a new OCR version

The syntax and functions provided by OCRCONFIG are provided by issuing the `ocrconfig -help` command line as shown here:

```
$ ocrconfig -help
Name:
ocrconfig - Configuration tool for Oracle Cluster Registry.

Synopsis:
 ocrconfig [option]
 option:
 -export <filename> [-s online]
              - Export cluster register contents to a file
 -import <filename>
              - Import cluster registry contents from a file
 -upgrade [<user> [<group>]]
              - Upgrade cluster registry from previous version
 -downgrade [-version <version string>]
        - Downgrade cluster registry to the specified version
 -backuploc <dirname>     - Configure periodic backup location
 -showbackup              - Show backup information
 -restore <filename>      - Restore from physical backup
 -replace ocr|ocrmirror [<filename>]
                    - Add/replace/remove a OCR device/file
```

```
 -overwrite           - Overwrite OCR configuration on disk

-repair ocr|ocrmirror <filename> - Repair local OCR configuration

-help                  - Print out this help information
```

Note: A log file will be created in `$ORACLE_HOME/log/<hostname>/client/ocrconfig_<pid>.log`. Please ensure you have file creation privileges in the above directory before running this tool.

We will further illustrate some of the features of OCRCONFIG later in the chapter, for troubleshooting issues with the OCR.

CLSCFG

Another useful but poorly documented 11g Clusterware tool is the Clusterware configuration tool or CLSCFG. This utility provides a host of features for managing and updating your Oracle 11g RAC Clusterware configurations, allowing you to perform the following administration tasks for the Oracle 11g Clusterware:

- Creating a new 11g Clusterware configuration
- Upgrading existing Clusterware
- Adding or removing nodes from the current 11g Clusterware

In order to display all of the possible options and parameters when using this utility for `clscfg`, you can issue the `-help` parameter to the `clscfg` command utility. The help option to `clscfg` provides the general syntax as shown next:

```
$ clscfg -help
clscfg: EXISTING configuration version 3 detected.
clscfg: version 3 is 11G Release 1.
clscfg -- Oracle cluster configuration tool

  This tool is typically invoked as part of the Oracle Cluster Ready
  Services install process. It configures cluster topology and other
  settings. Use -help for information on any of these modes.
  Use one of the following modes of operation.
  -install     - creates a new configuration
  -upgrade     - upgrades an existing configuration
  -downgrade   - downgrades an existing configuration
```

```
  -add          - adds a node to the configuration
  -delete       - deletes a node from the configuration
  -local        - creates a special single-node configuration for ASM
  -concepts     - brief listing of terminology used in the other modes

  -trace        - may be used in conjunction with any mode above for
tracing
WARNING: Using this tool may corrupt your cluster configuration. Do not
         use unless you positively know what you are doing.
```

Another nifty feature of the CLSCFG utility is to provide basic self documentation and self help on the Oracle 11g Clusterware environment, by using the concepts parameter for the `clscfg` utility as shown here:

```
$ clscfg -concepts
clscfg: EXISTING configuration version 3 detected.
clscfg: version 3 is 11G Release 1.
clscfg -- concepts and terminology
```

1. Private Interconnect Name

   On most clusters an interconnect will be supplied that is only accessible within the cluster. It will generally have a non-routable IP sequence such as 10.x.x.x, 172.16.x.x, or 192.168.x.x. (RFC1918)

   Specifying that IP is sufficient for clscfg's purposes, however an alternative practice is to specify a name in the host's file or in the name server which resolves to these IPs, configures the name, and then if the need arises, changes the mappings with all machines down or in maintenance mode. Any such changes must be performed while the Oracle instances and Cluster Ready Service daemons are down on all machines of the cluster. `ifconfig` (or `ipconfig` on Windows) can be used to look up information about or configure interconnects.

   Omitting the private interconnect and using the public network may result in poor performance and instability of the cluster.

2. Host Names

   The hostname will be used to refer to the machine in remote management tools, a few logfiles, and some other places. It should be the same name returned by `/bin/hostname` or on Windows by `echo %COMPUTERNAME%` at the command prompt.

3. Node Names

   If another vendor's clustering software is installed, the nodenames should be obtained from their configuration. Otherwise, it is best to use the hostnames.

4. Voting Disk

   The voting disk specified should be a raw device or file on a cluster filesystem. NFS is generally not acceptable because it may cache reads and writes. It will be used by the CSS daemon to arbitrate with peers that it cannot see over the private interconnect in the event of an outage, allowing it to salvage the largest fully connected subcluster for further operation.

5. OCSSD (Cluster Synchronization Service)

   This monitors node health through any vendor clusterware, or in its absence makes its own determination. Provides notifications to Oracle instances about each other, and notifies CRSD and EVMD of the health of the cluster.

6. EVMD (Cluster Event Manager)

   Provides local and cluster-wide event notification systems for Oracle applications.

7. CRSD (Cluster Ready Service)

   Provides application and Oracle instance failover using OCSSD and EVMD.

8. OCR (Oracle Cluster Repository)

   Stores configuration information for CRS daemons and Oracle managability applications.

This `clscfg -concepts` report is significant as it shows the built-in knowledge transfer, which we like to show new DBAs on Oracle 11g RAC. It's a quick method to introduce the key concepts and best practices for Oracle 11g RAC and Clusterware.

> Be extremely careful when using CLSCFG in a production 11g RAC environment! As Oracle Support cautions, the careless usage of this tool is dangerous and may corrupt your 11g Clusterware. Our advice is to use this with guidance from Oracle support and to test in a non-production environment.

CLUVFY

Last but not least in our tour of essential Oracle 11g RAC Clusterware tools is the **Clusterware Verification Utility** or **CLUVFY**. CLUVFY provides status checks for the before and after conditions of the 11g Clusterware installation. The syntax for the Cluster Verification Utility, `cluvfy`, is complex, so we will provide you with some examples to understand how to use this tool in the best possible manner for installation tasks related to Oracle 11g RAC Clusterware. If you want to see the general syntax of the Cluster Verification Utility, type in `cluvfy` at the command line as shown in this example:

```
$ cluvfy


USAGE:
cluvfy [ -help ]
cluvfy stage { -list | -help }
cluvfy stage {-pre|-post} <stage-name> <stage-specific options>
[-verbose]
cluvfy comp  { -list | -help }
cluvfy comp  <component-name> <component-specific options>  [-verbose]
```

Best practices for cluster installation dictate that you should run the cluster verification utility from the installation media to ensure that all prerequisites are met. Furthermore, we advise you to also run these for each stage of the installation and also post-installation to ensure that the environment has been configured without errors. For instance, use the script `runcluvfy.sh` before installation:

```
cd $ORA_CRS_HOME/bin
./runcluvfy.sh stage -pre crsinst -n <node1>,<node2> -verbose | tee /tmp/
cluvfy_preinstall.log
./cluvfy stage -post crsinst -n all -verbose | tee /tmp/cluvfy_
postinstall.log
```

The help option for `cluvfy` will show further details on how to use the tool:

```
$ cluvfy -help


USAGE:
cluvfy [ -help ]
cluvfy stage { -list | -help }
cluvfy stage {-pre|-post} <stage-name> <stage-specific options>
[-verbose]
cluvfy comp  { -list | -help }
cluvfy comp  <component-name> <component-specific options>  [-verbose]
```

We will provide an example of using the Cluster Verification Utility to diagnose the status for post-installation of the Oracle 11g Clusterware as follows:

```
$ cluvfy stage -post crsinst -n raclinux1 -verbose
Performing post-checks for cluster services setup
Checking node reachability...
Check: Node reachability from node "raclinux1"
  Destination Node                      Reachable?
  ------------------------------------  ------------------------
  raclinux1                             yes
Result: Node reachability check passed from node "raclinux1".

Checking user equivalence...
Check: User equivalence for user "oracle"
  Node Name                             Comment
  ------------------------------------  ------------------------
  raclinux1                             failed
Result: User equivalence check failed for user "oracle".
ERROR:
User equivalence unavailable on all the nodes.
Verification cannot proceed.

Post-check for cluster services setup was unsuccessful on all the
nodes.
```

This tells us that we need to fix the issues with `ssh` equivalency setup before we perform the installation of Oracle 11g Clusterware. In the following section, we will examine in more detail these issues and other common problems with Oracle 11g Clusterware, including resolution methods.

Troubleshooting Oracle 11g Clusterware

In the previous section, we provided details on how to perform basic maintenance and administration tasks for Oracle 11g Clusterware for RAC environments. We will now provide you with the necessary tools to perform troubleshooting and problem solving of difficult Oracle 11g Clusterware issues. As an Oracle RAC database administrator, one of the most challenging things that you will need to account for in terms of database administration with Oracle 11g RAC environments will be the unique situations that occur in Oracle 11g Clusterware and which do not exist in single-instance Oracle database environments. In order to provide the best approach, we will use examples to examine a root-cause methodology to quickly pinpoint the source of Clusterware issues within an Oracle 11g RAC environment. Through our analysis of problems via mini case studies, you will be well equipped to best address and resolve difficult Oracle 11g RAC and Clusterware issues and be equipped with tips and tricks for solving the common issues with the Oracle 11g Clusterware.

Oracle 11g RAC and Clusterware challenges can be summarized as follows:

- Failed, missing, or offline 11g Clusterware resources
- Voting disk issues with 11g Clusterware resources
- OCR problems
- RAC node reboot issues
- Hardware, storage, or network problems with RAC

Next we will take a look at how to resolve these issues for Oracle RAC environments.

Failed, missing, or offline 11g Clusterware resources

Perhaps one of the most frequently experienced problems that one faces as an Oracle RAC DBA is that of failing, missing, or offline Clusterware resources. In Oracle 11g RAC Clusterware parlance, resources are applications, processes, or components of the Oracle 11g Clusterware that are responsible for the proper functioning of the Oracle 11g RAC infrastructure. When managing Oracle 11g RAC Clusterware, resources sometimes fail to start after maintenance activities have been performed on the cluster environment. However, we can use the `crs_stat` command to show us the current state of the Oracle 11g Clusterware resources. In the following example, the output from the `crs_stat` command shows that the VIP resource for the Oracle 11g RAC Clusterware is offline, and trying to start it gives us the dreaded error:

```
CRS-0215: Could not start resource 'ora.dbtest2.vip'
$$ crs_stat -t

Name Type Target State Host
------------------------------------------------------------
ora....st2.gsd application ONLINE ONLINE rac01
ora....st2.ons application ONLINE ONLINE rac01
ora....st2.vip application ONLINE OFFLINE
```

To solve this issue, we need to perform additional debugging and investigation to discover the root cause. The following case study will provide you with a better understanding of how to approach the issue of offline Clusterware resources for problem resolution.

Offline Clusterware resources for Oracle 11g RAC

In the following example, you can either use Oracle or the root user to perform the tasks to resolve the offline Clusterware resources. We will attempt to start the offline Clusterware resources by using the `srvctl` command as shown in the following example, which gives us the `CRS-0215` error message:

```
[root@sdrac01]# ./srvctl start nodeapps -n sdrac01
  sdrac01:ora.sdrac01.vip:Interface eth0 checked failed (host=sdrac01.
  ben.com)
  sdrac01:ora.sdrac01.vip:Invalid parameters, or failed to bring up VIP
  (host=sdrac01.ben.com)
  sdrac01:ora.sdrac01.vip:Interface eth0 checked failed (host=sdrac01.
  ben.com)
  sdrac01:ora.sdrac01.vip:Invalid parameters, or failed to bring up VIP
  (host=sdrac01.ben.com)
CRS-1006: No more members to consider
CRS-0215: Could not start resource 'ora.sdrac01.vip'.
  sdrac01:ora.sdrac01.vip:Interface eth0 checked failed (host=sdrac01.
  ben.com)
  sdrac01:ora.sdrac01.vip:Invalid parameters, or failed to bring up VIP
  (host=sdrac01.ben.com)
  sdrac01:ora.sdrac01.vip:Interface eth0 checked failed (host=sdrac01.
  ben.com)
  sdrac01:ora.sdrac01.vip:Invalid parameters, or failed to bring up VIP
  (host=sdrac01.ben.com)
      CRS-1006: No more members to consider
     CRS-0215: Could not start resource 'ora.sdrac01.LISTENER_SDRAC01.
     lsnr'.
```

You can run `srvctl` as either Oracle or root user account. For the sake of best practices for IT security reasons, we recommend that you use a least privileged-level account to perform these tasks.

The first step in diagnosing the root cause is to debug the errors so that we can pinpoint the failure with the `vip` for the Oracle 11g RAC Clusterware.

We will need to examine the current settings for the `vip`, which we will do by using the `srvctl` utility that takes the two key parameters as shown in the following example:

```
[root@sdrac011 bin]# ./srvctl config nodeapps -n sdrac01 -a -g -s --l
VIP exists.: /sdrac01-vip.ben.com/192.168.203.111/255.255.255.0/eth0
GSD exists.
ONS daemon exists.
Listener exists.
```

More details on the syntax and usage of the `srvctl` utility are available in the Oracle 11g Clusterware reference documentation online at `http://tahiti.oracle.com`. We need to enable the debugging facility for the Oracle 11g Clusterware environment as part of the troubleshooting process. To do so, you need to set the `_USR_ORA_DEBUG` debug flag with the CRSCTL utility. Furthermore, you will need to use the debug parameter in the CRSCTL utility to start a new debugging session.

Now, let's take a look at an example on how to perform some troubleshooting with the CRSCTL utility. In order to do this, you will need to start `debug` for failed resources by using the `crsctl` debug command shown here:

```
# ./crsctl debug log res "ora.sdrac01.vip:5"
Set Resource Debug Module: ora.sdrac01.vip  Level: 5
```

In this example, the problem was that the network adapter configuration for the `vip` was not working correctly. When you enable debugging sessions with the `crsctl` command, the output will provide you with the specific module in the Oracle 11g Clusterware that is being traced and debugged, as shown in this instance.

Problems with the Voting disk and OCR

As key components of the Oracle 11g Clusterware architecture, the vote disk and Oracle Cluster Registry are critical to the health and operations of the Oracle 11g RAC environment. If either of these key resources ever fails, the entire clustered environment for Oracle 11g RAC will be adversely affected and a possible outage may result if either the vote disks and/or OCR are lost. As we mentioned earlier, the `OCRCHECK` utility gives you the ability to monitor the status of the OCR for the Oracle 11g Clusterware. We advocated the usage of the `OCRCHECK` command to perform a regular status check for ongoing monitoring to ensure the availability of the OCR. The purpose of using the `OCRCHECK` command is to verify the status and availability of the OCR during all phases of analysis.

Vote disk issues with 11g Clusterware resources

The vote disks provide a quorum process for access to the Oracle 11g Clusterware resources. If the vote disk fails, the entire cluster is affected. As such, we recommend that you maintain multiple copies of the voting disks on separate disk LUNs so that you eliminate a **Single Point of Failure** (**SPOF**) in your Oracle 11g RAC configuration. Another common problem that causes issues with the Oracle 11g vote disks is that ownership and/or permissions are either changed or set incorrectly, thereby causing errors within the Oracle 11g Clusterware for Oracle 11g RAC. To verify the status and location of the vote disks for Oracle 11g RAC and Clusterware, you can issue the `CRSCTL QUERY CSS VOTEDISK` command as:

```
$ crsctl query css votedisk
 0.     0    /dev/raw/raw7
 1.     0    /dev/raw/raw8
 2.     0    /dev/raw/raw9

located 3 votedisk(s).
```

If any vote disks are missing or unavailable, these will need to be added or updated with the Oracle 11g RAC Clusterware utilities. In addition, we also need to check the operating-system level to ensure that all of the required Oracle 11g Clusterware processes for RAC are online and running for the Clusterware. We can check the status for Oracle 11g RAC and Red Hat Linux using the `ps` command in Unix and Linux, as shown next:

```
[oracle@sdrac01 11.1.0]$ ps -ef|grep crsd
root       2853      1  0 Apr04 ?        00:00:00
/u01/app/oracle/product/11.1.0/crs/bin/crsd.bin reboot
[oracle@sdrac01 11.1.0]$ ps -ef|grep cssd
root       2846      1  0 Apr04 ?        00:03:15 /bin/sh /etc/init.d/init.
cssd fatal
root       3630   2846  0 Apr04 ?        00:00:00 /bin/sh /etc/init.d/init.
cssd daemon
/u01/app/oracle/product/11.1.0/crs/bin/ocssd.bin

[oracle@sdrac01 11.1.0]$ ps -ef|grep evmd
oracle     3644   2845  0 Apr04 ?        00:00:00
/u01/app/oracle/product/11.1.0/crs/bin/evmd.bin
oracle     9595 29413  0 23:59 pts/3     00:00:00 grep evmd
```

Failed or corrupted Vote Disks

Failed or corrupted vote disks will negatively impact your Oracle 11g RAC environment. The following guidelines will ensure best practices for the vote disk component of the Oracle 11g Clusterware:

- Implement multiple copies of the vote disk on different disk volumes to eliminate Single Point of Failure.
- Make sure that you take regular backups for vote disks with the dd utility (Unix/Linux) or copy utility (Windows).

- If you are using the dd utility for backing up the vote disks, there should be 4k block size on a Linux/Unix platform to ensure complete blocks are backed up for the voting disk. For syntax on how to use the `dd` command to back up the vote disks, consult the Oracle Clusterware documentation and the Unix/Linux manual pages for `dd`.

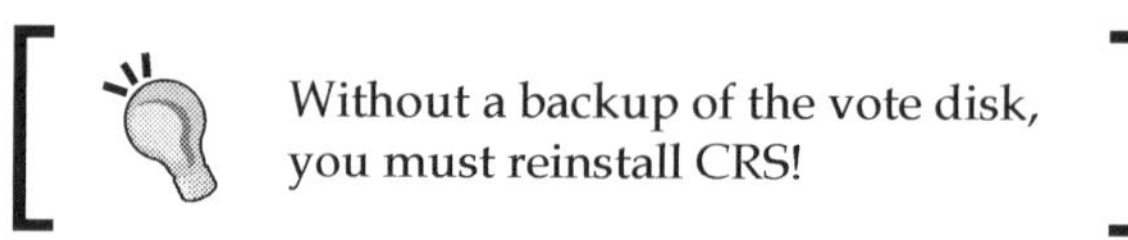

Without a backup of the vote disk, you must reinstall CRS!

Failed or corrupted OCR

Whenever the OCR is damaged or lost due to either a disk failure or other problem, the Oracle 11g Clusterware will cease to function normally. In order to proactively avoid such a disaster, we recommend the following guidelines for the OCR:

- Maintain frequent backups of OCR on separate disk volumes to avoid Single Point of Failure whenever a change is made to the cluster resources
- Use the OCRCONFIG utility to perform recovery
- Find and maintain safe backups for the OCR
- Export the OCR whenever changes are made to cluster resources

We will next discuss the methodology to recover a damaged or corrupted OCR from a recent backup.

How to recover the OCR from backup

One of the potential failures that can plague an Oracle RAC database administrator is when the Oracle Cluster Registry fails or becomes unavailable to the Oracle 11g Clusterware. In order to resolve these failures, you need to perform the repair or recovery operation for the OCR using the Oracle Clusterware tools. As part of the Oracle 11g Clusterware, we have a powerful Clusterware utility called OCRCONFIG that can be used to recover a lost or corrupted OCR from a recent backup. You will need to use the OCRCONFIG utility to recover the OCR, as this is the supported method from Oracle with your Oracle 11g RAC environment.

In order to do this, we will first need to find our backups of the OCR with the OCRCONFIG utility. The following code example will show you how to find the current backup copy of the OCR by using the `ocrconfig -showbackup` command:

```
# ./ocrconfig -showbackup

rac01     2009/04/07 23:01:40     /u01/app/oracle/product/11.1.0/crs/
cdata/crs

rac01     2009/04/07 19:01:39     /u01/app/oracle/product/11.1.0/crs/
cdata/crs

rac01     2009/04/07 01:40:31     /u01/app/oracle/product/11.1.0/crs/
cdata/crs

rac01     2009/04/06 21:40:30     /u01/app/oracle/product/11.1.0/crs/
cdata//crs

rac01     2009/04/03 14:12:46     /u01/app/oracle/product/11.1.0/ crs/
cdata/crs
```

Here, it is clear that we have several available backups for our OCR to use for the recovery operation. Now, we can do our restore to recover the OCR for the Oracle 11g Clusterware environment.

Steps to perform recovery of lost and/or corrupted OCR

The process of recovery for lost or damaged Oracle Cluster Registry files is complex and involves the use of the `ocrconfig` command. You will need to implement the following steps:

The first step is for us to check the status and location of the OCR backup files. We can use the `ls` command for Linux to show the files under the OCR directory structure.

```
$ ls -l
total 24212
-rw-r--r--  1 oracle oinstall 2949120 Aug 29  2008 backup00.ocr
-rw-r--r--  1 oracle oinstall 2949120 Aug 21  2008 backup01.ocr
-rw-r--r--  1 oracle oinstall 2949120 Aug 20  2008 backup02.ocr
-rw-r--r--  1 root   root     2949120 Apr  4 19:26 day_.ocr
-rw-r--r--  1 oracle oinstall 2949120 Aug 29  2008 day.ocr
-rw-r--r--  1 root   root     4116480 Apr  7 23:01 temp.ocr
-rw-r--r--  1 oracle oinstall 2949120 Aug 29  2008 week_.ocr
-rw-r--r--  1 oracle oinstall 2949120 Aug 19  2008 week.ocr
```

Now that we have located our copies of the OCR backup files, which are denoted with the ending `.ocr`, we can perform the recovery and restore operation to bring back our lost or damaged OCR files. To do the recovery, you will need to use the `-restore` parameter for the `ocrconfig` command. The syntax for this process is shown in the following example:

```
$ ocrconfig -restore backup00.ocr
```

Once we have executed the restore operation to recover the OCR files, we need to perform our due diligence steps to bring the Clusterware back online and verify that the OCR is available.

To complete the recovery for the OCR and vote disks, we will use the Oracle 11g Clusterware utilities that we introduced earlier in the chapter.

Check status 11g RAC Clusterware

The `crsctl` command is your friend for Clusterware monitoring and administration. As part of the post-recovery operations for the Oracle Clusterware Registry files, we need to verify the status of the Clusterware and check to ensure that it is in sync with the newly restored OCR files. To check the status of the Clusterware for Oracle 11g, you need to use the `crsctl` command as shown in the example listed here:

```
[oracle@sdrac01 11.1.0]$ crsctl

Usage: crsctl check  crs          - checks the viability of the CRS stack
       crsctl check  cssd         - checks the viability of CSS
       crsctl check  crsd         - checks the viability of CRS
       crsctl check  evmd         - checks the viability of EVM
```

We issue the `CRSCTL CHECK CRS` command to display the status availability of the Oracle Clusterware for our Oracle 11g RAC environment as shown next:

```
[oracle@sdrac01 11.1.0]$ crsctl check crs
CSS appears healthy
CRS appears healthy
EVM appears healthy
```

Now we need to verify that the clusterware resources are back online after the OCR and vote disk recovery process has been completed. To verify the status for all of the Oracle 11g Clusterware resources, you need to execute the `crs_stat` command. In the example below, we use the `crs_stat -t` option to display the current status of the Clusterware resources in a tabular format:

```
$ crs_stat -t
Name           Type         Target    State     Host
------------------------------------------------------------
ora....B1.inst application  ONLINE    ONLINE
ora....B2.inst application  ONLINE    ONLINE
ora....ux1.gsd application  ONLINE    ONLINE    sdrac01
ora....ux1.ons application  ONLINE    ONLINE    sdrac01
ora....ux1.vip application  ONLINE    ONLINE
ora....t1.inst application  ONLINE    ONLINE
ora.test.db    application  OFFLINE   ONLINE
ora....t1.inst application  ONLINE    ONLINE
```

Now that we have verified that all of our Oracle Clusterware resources are back online and available, we have completed the recovery operation for the Oracle Clusterware Registry. In the following sections, we will teach you a core methodology to use for the root cause analysis that will provide you with a sound approach to resolve Oracle 11g Clusterware issues.

Root cause analysis 11g RAC

The purpose of using root cause analysis is to provide you with a valid approach based on a scientific method to solve difficult problems with your Oracle 11g RAC environments. In the following section, we will teach you a basic set of procedures that you can use to isolate and resolve most Oracle 11g Clusterware failures. The focus of our problem-solving skills for your Oracle 11g Clusterware issues lies in the holistic method of examining all of the key components of the Oracle 11g Clusterware stack and how they relate to the entire Oracle 11g RAC architecture. By using a cross-disciplinary approach, you will be equipped with the best method to quickly and painlessly resolve your Oracle 11g RAC problems with the Clusterware stack.

Oracle 11g Clusterware log file analysis

First, we want to have a look at the current status of your Clusterware by locating and reviewing the logfiles that are generated by the Oracle 11g Clusterware and operating system. Logfiles are the clues to the current health and status of your entire Oracle 11g RAC and Grid ecosystem. You will need to do the following:

- First, we need to locate and examine our Oracle 11g Clusterware logfiles.
- The Oracle 11g Clusterware logfiles exist under several directory structures for both the Oracle and root operating system user accounts within the platform operating system. In our examples, these will be for the Linux and Unix operating systems. The following locations contain these logfiles:

 - `$CRS_HOME` contains the logfiles for the Clusterware base directory
 - `$CRS_HOME\log\nodename\racg` contains logfiles for the VIP and ONS resources

* For the Oracle 11g RAC cluster database logfiles, these exist and can be found under the `$RDBMS_HOME` directory structure filesystem. For instance, these log files exist under the `$ORACLE_HOME/log/nodename/racg`. For example:

  ```
  cd /u01/app/oracle/product/11.1.0/db_1/log/sdrac01/racg
  ```

Errors are reported to `imon<DB_NAME>.log` files. The following entry from the `imon.log` file shows the errors that have occurred:

```
$ view imon.log
2009-03-15 21:39:38.497: [    RACG][3002129328]  [13876][3002129328]
[ora.RACDB.RACDB2.inst]: clsrfdbe_enqueue: POST_ALERT() failed:
evttypname='down' type='1' resource='ora.RACDB.RACDB2.inst'
node='sdrac01' time='2009-03-15 21:39:36.0 -05:00' card=0
2009-03-15 21:40:08.521: [    RACG][3002129328]  [13876][3002129328]
[ora.RACDB.RACDB2.inst]: CLSR-0002: Oracle error encountered while
executing DISCONNECT

2009-03-15 21:40:08.521: [    RACG][3002129328]  [13876][3002129328]
[ora.RACDB.RACDB2.inst]: ORA-03114: not connected to ORACLE
```

The logfile review and analysis is the integral first step to problem resolution for all of your Oracle 11g Clusterware issues within the Oracle RAC environment. It holds the key to solving the vast majority of issues with the Clusterware.

Oracle 11g RAC node reboot issues

Another common problem that plagues the Oracle RAC database administrator is the question of node reboots within Oracle RAC environments. The root cause of node reboots is difficult to diagnose, thereby making these problems complex to resolve. Node reboots also cause outages in the RAC environment, especially with smaller cluster environments with less than three-node configurations.

The key to the resolution of node reboots for clustered Oracle RAC environments is to first take a holistic approach to the issue. All of the primary architecture components need to be reviewed for possible sources of the failure. This means you should first look at your network and storage configuration and then perform a health check of the shared storage and network interfaces for the Oracle 11g RAC environment.

In addition, you should examine the status for all of the primary Oracle 11g RAC and Clusterware daemon processes, along with their associated logfiles, to pinpoint where and when these processes may have failed. One point to keep in mind is when the Oracle Cluster Synchronization Daemon process fails within the Oracle 11g Clusterware. If, at any time, there is a `ocssd.bin problem/failure` or in the event that the oprocd daemon detects a scheduling problem or some other fatal problem, a node will reboot in an RAC cluster. The reason this occurs is by design. This functionality is used for I/O fencing to ensure that writes from I/O-capable clients can be cleared, avoiding potential corruption scenarios in the event of a network split, node hang, or some other fatal event.

Oracle 11g RAC Clusterware processes—node reboot issues

Whenever the `ocssd.bin` process dies, it sends out a notification to the OPROCD process to "shoot the node in the head" and causes the node to reboot (STONITH). The OCSSD or CSS daemon is spawned under the `init.cssd` initialization script for UNIX and LINUX platforms. It runs in both vendor Clusterware and non-vendor Clusterware environments, and is armed with a node kill via the `init` script. OCSSD's primary job is internode health monitoring and RDBMS instance endpoint discovery. It runs as the Oracle user. The `INIT.CSSD` initialization script provides the task of spawning the `init.cssd` initialization process, which in turn spawns OCSSD as a child process within Unix and Linux. If, for any reason, the OCSSD process dies or is killed, as a consequence, the node kill functionality of the `init` script will kill the node. Again, this is by design within the Oracle 11g Clusterware kernel operations.

Oracle Process Daemon

The **Oracle Process Daemon** (**OPROCD**) is spawned in any non-vendor Clusterware environment except on the Windows platform. The Windows platform differs for OPROCD in terms of where Oracle uses a kernel driver to perform actions similar to those found with Unix and Linux operating systems. If OPROCD detects a problem within the Oracle 11g Clusterware, it will kill the node. As we mentioned earlier, OPROCD is spawned by `init.cssd` and runs as root superuser at the operating system level on Unix and Linux. This daemon is used to detect hardware and driver freezes on the machine. If a machine is frozen for a long period past the default threshold so that the other nodes evict it from the cluster, it will need to kill itself to prevent any I/O from being reissued to the disk after the rest of the cluster has remastered locks.

OCLSOMON

The OCLSOMON process monitors the status of the CSS daemon for hang and scheduling issues. In the event that OCLSOMON is unable to contact the CSS daemon, it will reboot a node if there is a perceived hang. So, you are now wondering how we can prevent and avoid such node reboot issues within the Oracle 11g Clusterware? The primary solution is to be proactive in your monitoring of these key Clusterware background processes. As such, data collection is crucial to your efforts to diagnose the root cause of the node reboot in your Oracle 11g RAC configuration. Fortunately, Oracle provides us with a powerful and free tool called **OSWatcher** that can be used to collect the vitals for the Oracle 11g Clusterware stack. The OSWatcher tool is available for download on the My Oracle Support (formerly known as Metalink) site: `http://support.oracle.com`.

For reference, you need to review the My Oracle Support (formerly Metalink) Notes 301137.1 and 433472.1, which provide the details on how to set up this diagnosis tool for Linux/Unix and Windows platforms. The OS watcher tool is different from RDA in that it provides additional features that are not available with RDA for operating system-level details.

Root cause analysis for solving node reboots with 11g RAC

The first step that you need to undertake is to locate the process or processes that are the guilty culprits behind the node reboot for the Oracle 11g Clusterware. We advise that you examine all log files generated by the Clusterware background processes that we mentioned earlier. In addition, you would be wise to also review any and all trace files which have been generated by the operating system and Clusterware to determine the failed process for your Oracle 11g RAC and Clusterware. To aid you in your quest, we will summarize the location and names of key log and trace files.

Oracle 11g RAC log files for troubleshooting

The Oracle 11g Clusterware generates logfiles as part of daily operations. In order to be successful as an Oracle RAC DBA, you should review these logfiles on a regular basis to be proactive to resolve issues before they become a disaster. Oracle also creates trace files when failures or errors occur within the Clusterware. Both the Clusterware log and trace files are the best place to start when troubleshooting a node reboot condition for Oracle 11g RAC. In addition to these files, the operating system will spawn logfiles called message files. For Unix and Linux platforms, these message files are located under the following directories:

- Sun: `/var/adm/messages`
- HP-UX: `/var/adm/syslog/syslog.log`

- Tru64: /var/adm/messages
- Linux: /var/log/messages
- IBM: /bin/errpt -a > messages.out

Message files are the operating system logfiles that are generated on a regular basis as part of the operating system functions. These can be viewed with your favorite editor such as the **vi** or **Emacs** editor in Linux and/or Unix.

Next, we need to view the Clusterware log and trace files for the Clusterware. The following example provides the location for these files. For the CSS logfiles, we have the following locations:

- 11.1 and 10.2: <CRS_HOME>/log/<node name>/cssd
- 10.1: <CRS_HOME>/css/log

For the Linux platform, you would be wise to review the OPROCD logfiles as well. These files are located under /etc/oracle/oprocd or /var/opt/oracle/oprocd, depending on your particular implementation version and platform.

The Clusterware log and trace files are located under the following directory and filesystems for Linux and most Unix implementations. For 10.2 and above, all are files under <CRS_HOME>/log. For earlier releases of the Oracle Clusterware such as version 10.1, the logfiles are located in the following directory and filesystem locations:

```
<CRS_HOME>/crs/log
<CRS_HOME>/crs/init
<CRS_HOME>/css/log
<CRS_HOME>/css/init
<CRS_HOME>/evm/log
<CRS_HOME>/evm/init
<CRS_HOME>/srvm/log
```

Another useful tool is the **RAC DDT,** which provides you with a one-stop method to collect and gather all of the Oracle 11g RAC log and trace files for analysis and to send off to Oracle support engineers. In addition to collecting all of the relevant trace and logfiles for your Oracle 11g RAC environment, you should also collect OS and network information by using system-level tools such as the Unix/Linux commands for **netstat, iostat, vmstat** and **ping** on behalf of all of your Oracle 11g RAC cluster nodes. RAC DDT is available for download on the Oracle Technology Network at: http://otn.oracle.com or **My Oracle Support Website (MOS)** at http://support.oracle.com. Detailed instructions on how to run the tool for RAC DDT are available with the file download.

OCSSD Reboots and 11g RAC

The main cause of node reboots in the case of the **Oracle Cluster Synchronization Daemon (OCSSD)** is due to network failures or latency issues between the cluster nodes for an Oracle 11g RAC configuration. This problem usually manifests itself with the OCSSD process in terms of what is called a missed checkin condition. For instance, it may take at least 30 consecutive missed checkins to cause a node reboot within the cluster where heartbeats are issued once per second within the Oracle 11g RAC environment. How do we find out whether or not we have these missed checkin conditions? Easy, the solution lies in the logs for the CSS processing. Whenever missed checkins occur with OCSSD within the Oracle 11g Clusterware, they will appear in the `log` files. Next is an example of this condition from the CSS logfile with Oracle 11g RAC and LINUX:

```
WARNING: clssnmPollingThread: node <node> (1) at 50% heartbeat fatal,
eviction in 29.100 seconds
```

In addition, you should also review the LINUX or UNIX system `messages` file to determine the root cause for these OCSSD failures with your Oracle RAC configuration. We provide the following guidelines to help you understand why node reboots occur in terms of missed checkins and OCSSD operations for the Oracle 11g Clusterware:

- If the `messages` file reboot time is less than the missed checkin time, then the node eviction was likely not due to these missed checkins
- If the `messages` file reboot time is greater than the missed checkin time, then the node eviction was likely a result of the missed checkins

The previous formula will help you to understand why node evictions occur with missed checkins and the OCSSD failure conditions for the Oracle 11g Clusterware stack. Another reason why node reboots occur lies in problems when the Clusterware daemon OCSSD cannot read or write to or from the voting disk. We can find out whether or not this is indeed the case by a quick review of the CSS logfiles. The following example from the Oracle 11g CSS log file shows the problem of failed access to the voting disks:

```
ERROR: clssnmDiskPingMonitorThread: voting device access hanging (160008
miliseconds)
```

Now that we have presented these initial causes of node reboot conditions with the Oracle 11g Clusterware, let's examine failures with the OPROCD process and how these are related to node reboot conditions within the Oracle 11g Clusterware.

OPROCD failure and node reboots

The following are four primary conditions that will cause the **Oracle Process Daemon** (**OPROCD**) to fail within the Oracle 11g RAC environment:

- An OS scheduler problem
- The OS is getting locked up in a driver or hardware issue
- Excessive amounts of load on the machine, thus preventing the scheduler from behaving reasonably
- An Oracle bug such as Bug 5015469

An OS scheduler issue is solved by correctly setting the operating system scheduler so that the ntpd daemon is in sync with the Oracle 11g Clusterware, in particular with the OPROCD process on LINUX. To verify that ntpd is synchronized with Clusterware, you can check the logs for ntpd and the Clusterware logs. The ntp logfiles live under the `/var/log` directory structure for Linux and most UNIX platforms. Configuration for ntp is carried out by editing the `ntpd.conf` file located under the `/etc` directory for Linux and most UNIX platforms.

If the OS is getting locked up in a driver or there is a hardware issue which is dependent on the operating system, storage device, and hardware configuration, by working with the vendor and Oracle support this issue can be resolved when OS conditions cause a node reboot.

If there is an excessive amount of load on the machine, this issue could be caused by improper system design for the Oracle 11g RAC environment. Adequate memory, shared storage, and network capacity are required to prevent and avoid scheduler failures with the Oracle 11g Clusterware.

An Oracle software bug might be the root cause of the OPROCD failure that results in a node reboot condition for the cluster, which will occur depending on the environment. Now let's review some node reboot conditions that are linked directly to the operation of the OCLSOMON daemon process within the Oracle 11g Clusterware.

OCLSOMON-RAC node reboot

There are several root causes that will cause a node reboot to occur if the OCLSOMON daemon process fails within the Unix and Linux environments for the Oracle 11g Clusterware. These can be summarized as follows:

- Hung threads within the CSS daemon
- OS scheduler problems

- Excessive amounts of load on the machine
- Oracle software bugs with Clusterware and database

When the OCLSOMON process fails, it results in a node reboot condition with Oracle 11g RAC environments. Unix and Linux operating systems are multithreaded operating system platforms that use shared memory. Whenever threads are unable to be accessed by the Clusterware to allocate resources for the operating system scheduler, node reboots occur.

The next condition that may cause a node reboot is related to architecture and system implementation for the hardware, shared storage, and network configuration in terms of placing excessive load on the systems within the Oracle 11g RAC ecosystem. Proper planning will prevent this issue.

The last condition is due to software bugs that may exist within the Oracle 11g Clusterware software. By consulting with Oracle support and opening a support escalation ticket—for example, iTar or service request—a patch can be generated to provide resolution on account of a bug that may be the root cause of the node reboot with the OCLSOMON process within the Oracle 11g Clusterware. Now that we have discussed the primary causes and solutions to node reboots within the Oracle 11g Clusterware, we will discuss how to address issues that arise with the Clusterware as a result of system and network conditions.

Hardware, storage, and network problems with RAC

On many occasions, the root cause of failures with the Oracle 11g Clusterware lies with the hardware, network, and storage devices that build the infrastructure required to support the clustered environments for Oracle 11g RAC. While a complete discussion of hardware, network, and storage technologies is beyond the scope of this chapter and the book as a whole, we will provide a few essential guidelines for you to be able to efficiently manage these components, in conjunction with the Oracle 11g Clusterware operations for Oracle RAC environments.

The first recommendation is for you to review all of the supported and validated configurations for Oracle 11g RAC and the Oracle 11g Clusterware on the My Oracle Support site (formerly Oracle Metalink) located online at `http://support.oracle.com`. As such, you will need a valid Oracle support contract and CSI to access the certification matrix.

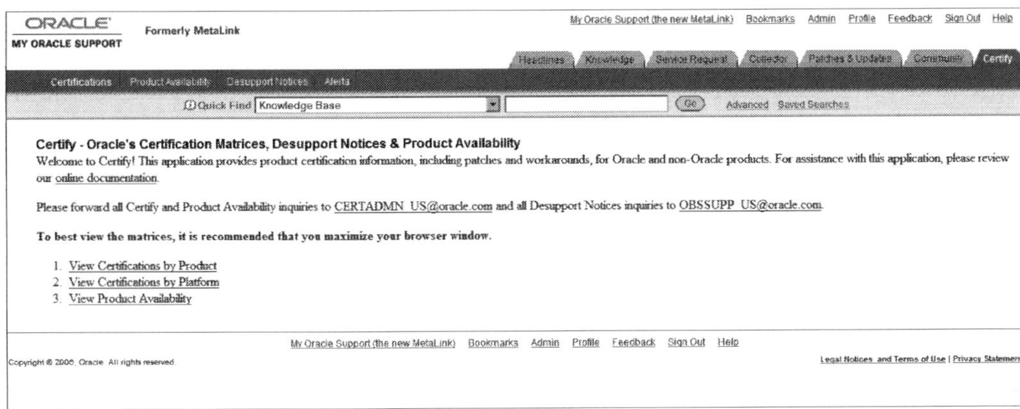

The previous certification matrix can be used to validate your Oracle 11g RAC environment so that storage, network, and hardware configurations are supported, thereby minimizing issues with your particular Oracle 11g RAC architecture. For example, we have the following validated configuration for Oracle 11g RAC with Linux platforms:

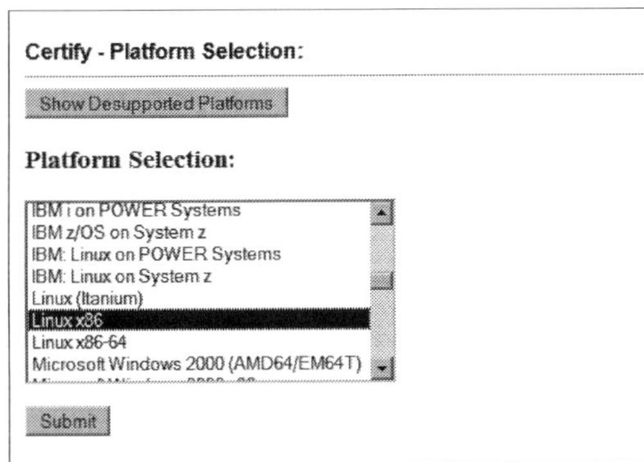

In our case, we want to validate all supported configurations with the Linux x86 platform for a general database server configuration as shown in the following example:

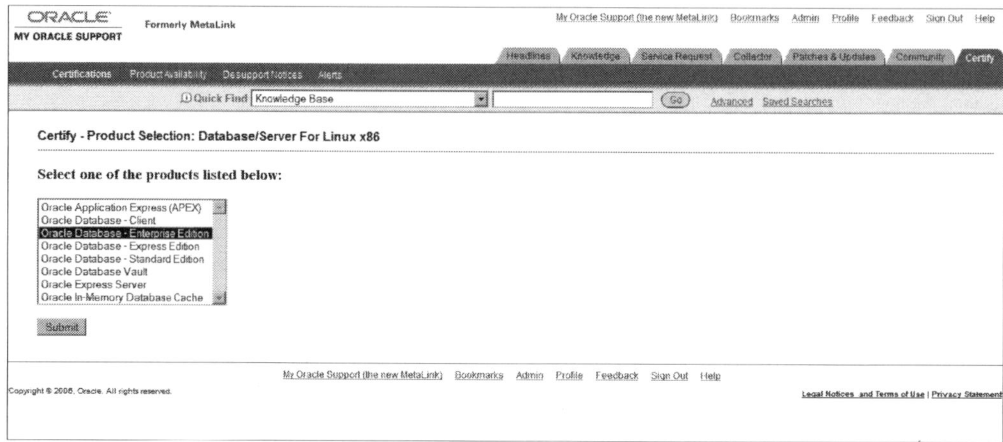

Once you have entered all of your configuration details for the database version and platform, the certification matrix results will be generated with the supported configurations as shown in the listing example in the next screenshot:

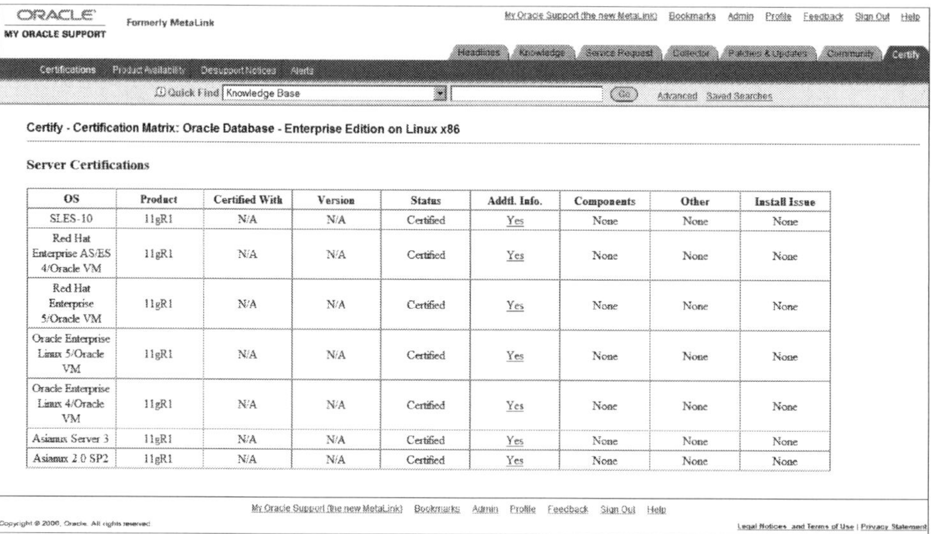

Certify - Certification Matrix: Oracle Database - Enterprise Edition on Linux x86

Server Certifications

OS	Product	Certified With	Version	Status	Addtl. Info.	Components	Other	Install Issue
SLES-10	11gR1	N/A	N/A	Certified	Yes	None	None	None
Red Hat Enterprise AS/ES 4/Oracle VM	11gR1	N/A	N/A	Certified	Yes	None	None	None
Red Hat Enterprise 5/Oracle VM	11gR1	N/A	N/A	Certified	Yes	None	None	None
Oracle Enterprise Linux 5/Oracle VM	11gR1	N/A	N/A	Certified	Yes	None	None	None
Oracle Enterprise Linux 4/Oracle VM	11gR1	N/A	N/A	Certified	Yes	None	None	None
Asianux Server 3	11gR1	N/A	N/A	Certified	Yes	None	None	None
Asianux 2.0 SP2	11gR1	N/A	N/A	Certified	Yes	None	None	None

By using the certification matrix tools available online from My Oracle Support, you can minimize the possible likelihood of problems with your Oracle system architecture for your Oracle 11g RAC implementation.

Hardware, storage, and network resolutions

The next item to address with respect to Oracle 11g Clusterware issues that arise from hardware, network, and storage issues is to understand how to work closely with your system and network administration team members to monitor and resolve outages to the Oracle 11g RAC environment caused by failure of any of these components. In addition, we advise that you monitor the health and condition of the entire system and network environment by using the system-level tools available to you for storage, network, and server-level environments. Most **Storage Area Networks** (**SANs**) and **Network Attached Storag**e (**NAS**) disk array vendors provide monitoring and diagnostic tools to track the status of shared disks within these environments. For example, IBM provides a set of graphical user interface monitoring and configuration tools for their XIV SAN disk arrays. In addition to these tools supplied with disk arrays, we also recommend that you use the core operating system utilities for Unix, Windows, and Linux platforms such as **ifconfig, netstat, ping**, and **traceroute**. These system tools are essential for the proper care and feeding of your entire Oracle 11g RAC ecosystem. We have discussed these topics for the Oracle 11g R1 version of RAC. *Chapter 2, Oracle 11g RAC Architecture*, provides more in-depth information for the 11g R2 release of RAC and ASM.

New features in Oracle 11g R2 Clusterware

Oracle 11g R2 introduces a multitude of new features and enhancements to the tech stack for the Oracle Clusterware. These include:

- Oracle RAC one node
- Clusterware resource modeling
- Policy-based cluster and capacity management
- Cluster time synchronization service
- OCR and voting disks storage within Oracle ASM
- Oracle Clusterware out-of-place upgrade
- Enhanced **Cluster Verification Utility** (**CVU**)
- Zero downtime for patching Oracle Clusterware

Oracle Real Application Clusters one node (Oracle RAC one node)

Oracle database 11g R2 provides a new feature called **Oracle Real Application Clusters One Node (Oracle RAC One Node)**. Oracle RAC One Node is a single instance of Oracle Real Application Clusters (Oracle RAC) that runs on the node in a cluster. The benefit of the RAC One Node option is that it allows you to consolidate many databases into one cluster without a lot of overhead, while also providing high availability benefits of failover protection, as well as for online rolling patch application and rolling upgrades for the Oracle Clusterware. Another aspect of RAC One Node allows you to limit the CPU utilization of individual database instances within the cluster through a feature called **Resource Manager Instance Caging**, which gives you the ability to dynamically change the limit as required. Furthermore, with RAC One Node there is no limitation for server scalability, so that if applications outgrow the current resources that a single node can supply, you can then upgrade the applications online to Oracle RAC. In the event that the node that is running Oracle RAC One Node becomes saturated and out of resources, you can migrate the instance to another node in the cluster using Oracle RAC One Node and another new utility called Omotion without a downtime. The OMotion feature for Oracle 11g R2 RAC allows you to migrate a running instance to another server without downtime or disruption in service for your environment. In addition, Omotion provides you with load-balancing benefits by allowing a migration of an Oracle 11g database from a busy server to another server with spare capacity. Thus, Omotion leverages the ability of Oracle Real Application Clusters to simultaneously run multiple instances servicing a single database. Oracle support is provided for Oracle RAC One Node with all platforms for which Oracle RAC is certified by Oracle.

Improved Oracle Clusterware resource modeling

With 11g R2, the Oracle Clusterware can manage different types of applications and processes including third-party vendor applications. With 11g R2, you have the ability to create dependencies among applications and processes, and to manage them as a single entity. Oracle Clusterware uses different entities to manage applications and processes such as resources and server pools. Furthermore, with 11g R2, Oracle has delivered a new set of APIs to manage these Clusterware entities.

Policy-based cluster and capacity management

With 11g R2, Oracle Clusterware allows you to improve the manner in which server capacity management is performed through the logical separation of an 11g R2 RAC cluster into server pools. These server pools allow you to determine where and how resources run in the cluster by using a cardinality-based approach. By using server pools, cluster nodes become anonymous, thereby eliminating the need to identify each cluster node when allocating resources to them. Server pools are assigned different levels of importance. Whenever a failure occurs, the clusterware will automatically reallocate and assign the available capacity for applications to another server pool within the cluster, based on the user-defined policies in place. This benefit enables a much faster resource failover and dynamic capacity assignment.

Cluster time synchronization service

With 11g R2, Oracle provides a new background process called the Cluster time synchronization service. This service synchronizes the system time on all of the cluster nodes in a cluster whenever the vendor time synchronization software (such as NTP on Unix) is not installed. One of the requirements to install and run an RAC cluster is to use a synchronized system time process across the cluster. Rather than depending on an outside time synchronization service, this allows Oracle to improve the reliability of the entire Oracle cluster environment.

Oracle Cluster Registry and voting disks within Oracle ASM

Prior to 11g R2, Oracle required that the Oracle Cluster Registry and vote disks be stored either on raw devices or within a clustered filesystem such as **OCFS (Oracle Cluster Filesystem)**. Now, with the release of 11g R2, you can store and manage both the OCR and voting disks within the Oracle Automatic Storage Management environment. The new mechanism that makes this possible is the function between Oracle ASM and the Oracle status table (PST), which is replicated on multiple disks and extended to store OCR. This allows the OCR to tolerate the loss of the same number of disks as are in the underlying diskgroup and be relocated in response to any disk failures. In addition, Oracle ASM reserves several blocks at a fixed location for every Oracle ASM disk used for storing the voting disk. In the event that the disk containing the voting disk fails, Oracle ASM will choose another disk on which to store this data. The key benefit to storing the OCR and voting disk on Oracle ASM is that it eliminates the need for using a third-party cluster volume manager. Furthermore, by using ASM to store the OCR and vote disks, you can reduce the complexity of managing disk partitions for OCR and voting disks during Oracle Clusterware installations.

New features for upgrading to Oracle 11g Clusterware

With 11g R2, you have the option to install a new version of the Oracle Clusterware into a separate home before an upgrade. By installing Oracle Clusterware into a separate home directory before the upgrade, you can reduce the planned outage time required, thereby meeting business availability service-level agreements. Then, after you have installed the new Oracle Clusterware software, the upgrade can be performed for the cluster by stopping the previous version of the Oracle Clusterware software and starting the new version node-by-node in a rolling upgrade fashion without downtime.

Oracle 11g R2 Cluster Verification Utility new features

Oracle 11g R2 has added new enhancements to the Cluster Verification Utility to include the following new checks:

- Before and after node addition
- Before and after node deletion
- Before and after storage addition
- Before and after storage deletion
- After network modification
- Oracle ASM integrity

Zero downtime patching for Oracle Clusterware

With 11g R2, you can now perform patching of the Oracle Clusterware and Oracle RAC environment without shutting the entire cluster down. This allows for upgrades to the cluster software and Oracle RAC database with the important benefit of a reduced maintenance downtime window. For instance, you can use rolling upgrades with the Clusterware and ASM to reduce the downtime as well as Data Guard standby database to minimize the outage window for these patch downtimes.

Summary

In this chapter, we discussed the key tips and techniques on how best to manage complex Oracle 11g Clusterware, including the various components and concepts that allow an Oracle RAC environment to function. We also discussed the utilities and tools that an Oracle database administrator must be competent with to administer and maintain Oracle Clusterware.

In addition, we looked at the various troubleshooting methods to quickly resolve and prevent errors and critical failures by providing a set of tips and techniques via the root cause analysis method to diagnose and resolve failures within the Oracle 11g Clusterware stack. In the next chapter, we will explain how to leverage the power of Oracle workload management via the Oracle 11g RAC services. This will provide you with the skills to optimize the performance and availability of Oracle 11g RAC environments by distributing application and network load within your Oracle clustered systems.

6

RAC Database Administration and Workload Management

Typically, when you have completed the Clusterware setup and it is operational, the next big thing on your priority list is creating the RAC databases, administering and managing the application workload.

To present a better understanding of various database creation methods, managing the RAC database, and handling application workload effectively in your cluster environment, we have split this chapter into two sections. In the first section, we will discuss the key points and various methods of RAC database configuration and creation. In the second section, we will discuss how to manage the application workload in the RAC database by taking the advantages of Oracle RAC database prime features such as scalability and high availability. We shall discuss the following topics:

- RAC database configuration and creation
- What's new in Oracle 11g R1 and R2 database
- RAC database administration
- Automatic workload management

RAC database configuration and creation

A RAC database can be created either using the **Database Configuration Assistant (DBCA)** (an interactive GUI tool) or the manual approach, which is comprised of the `CREATE DATABASE` SQL statement and running a couple of predefined Oracle post-database creation scripts.

Creating a RAC database using the `CREATE DATABASE` SQL statement, and running the additional post-database creation RAC-related scripts, may not guarantee a fully operational RAC database functionality and may lead to problems with support. Therefore, creating a RAC database using DBCA is the most convenient and preferred method as DBCA lets you configure and create the database through interactive slides that are very easy to comply.

Creating a database using DBCA

Before you actually start creating a RAC database, it is highly recommended that you verify the readiness of selected nodes in the cluster on which you want to place the instances of the database. The following `cluvfy` command verifies whether your system meets all criteria for creating a database or for making a database configuration change:

```
$ORA_CRS_HOME/bin/cluvfy stage -pre dbcfg -n node_list -d DB_HOME
```

```
Example:
$ORA_CRS_HOME/bin/cluvfy stage -pre dbcfg -n raclinux1,raclinux2 -d /u01/
app/oracle/product/11.1.0/db_1
```

Using DBCA to create a RAC database is similar to creating a standalone database, except that an additional node selection screen exists while creating the RAC database.

Before we proceed further with the database creation, we presume that the ASM instance and required ASM disk groups (DATA & FLASH) are already configured and `MOUNTED` across the ASM instance in the cluster.

Upon launching the DBCA (`./dbca`) from the `$ORA_DB_HOME/bin` location, the following welcome screen will appear. This screen accompany both RAC and standalone database creation selections.

Select the **Oracle Real Application Clusters database** option and click on **Next** to proceed further, as shown in the following screenshot:

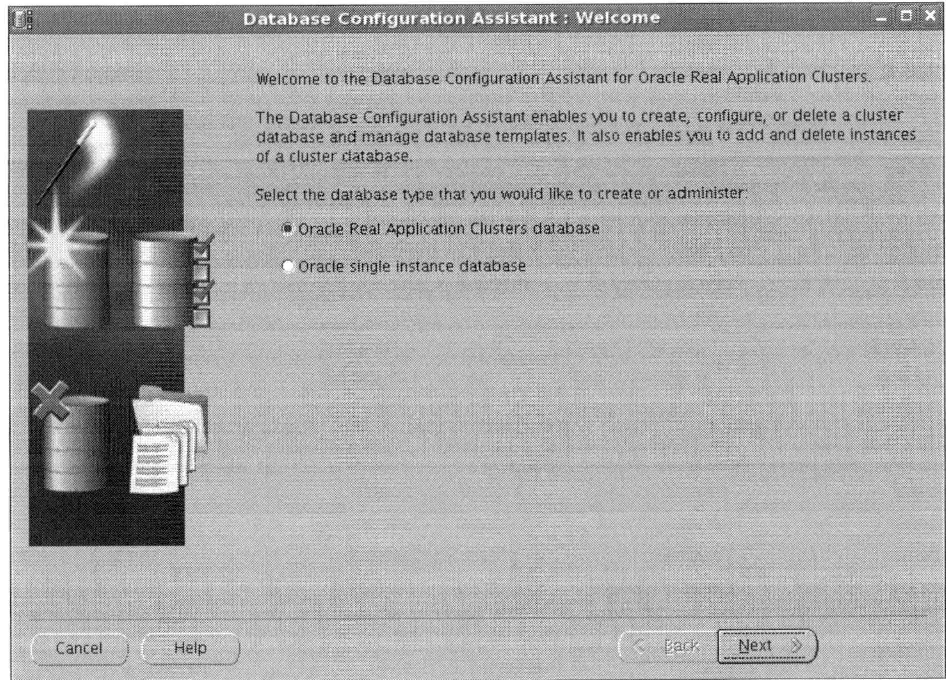

The RAC database creation choice will appear only when the Clusterware is configured and is running properly on the selected nodes.

There are various options such as creating a database, deleting a database, managing database templates, instance management, and ASM configuration available with the Oracle Real Application Clusters Database.

Since this is the very first database to be created on the node, you can see a few options are not available for selection. Select the **Create a Database** option and click on **Next** to proceed further, as shown in the following screenshot:

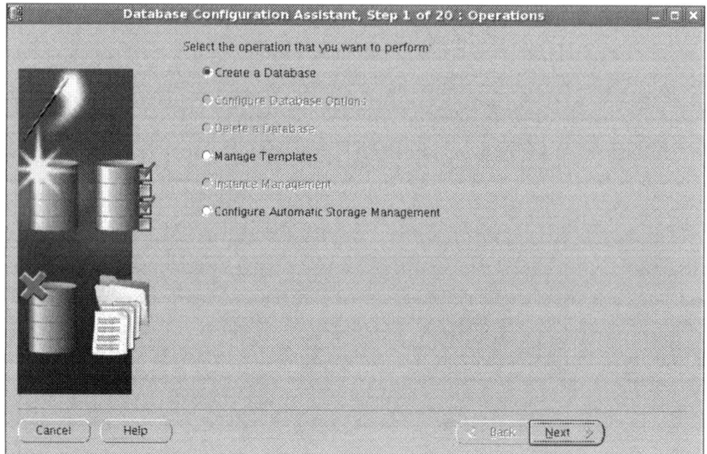

If you have experience with Oracle 10g DBCA, you will have probably noticed that the **Service Management** option is missing here.

More details on managing services will be discussed in the Workload management section later in this chapter.

However, in Oracle 11g R2 or above, the **Operations** screen shows that the ASM configuration option is no longer available as ASM is completely managed through a new tool named **Automatic Storage Management Configuration Assistant (ASMCA)**, which is as shown in the following screenshot:

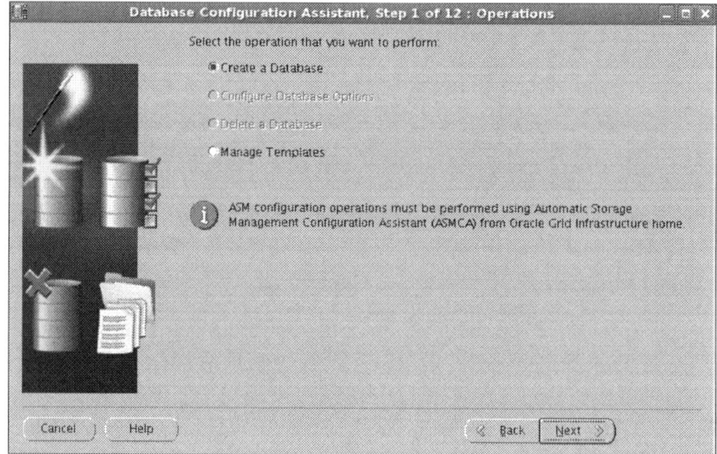

While the RAC database is being created, there is an additional **Node Selection** screen that appears here. You have the choice either to select all nodes or a subset of nodes where the RAC database instance will be configured and run. The default selection is always the local node from where you executed the DBCA. After the node selection, you will then need to click on **Next**.

If all of the nodes in the cluster are not listed here, you may need to pause the database creation process for a while and have a look at the cluster configuration on the nodes that have not appeared.

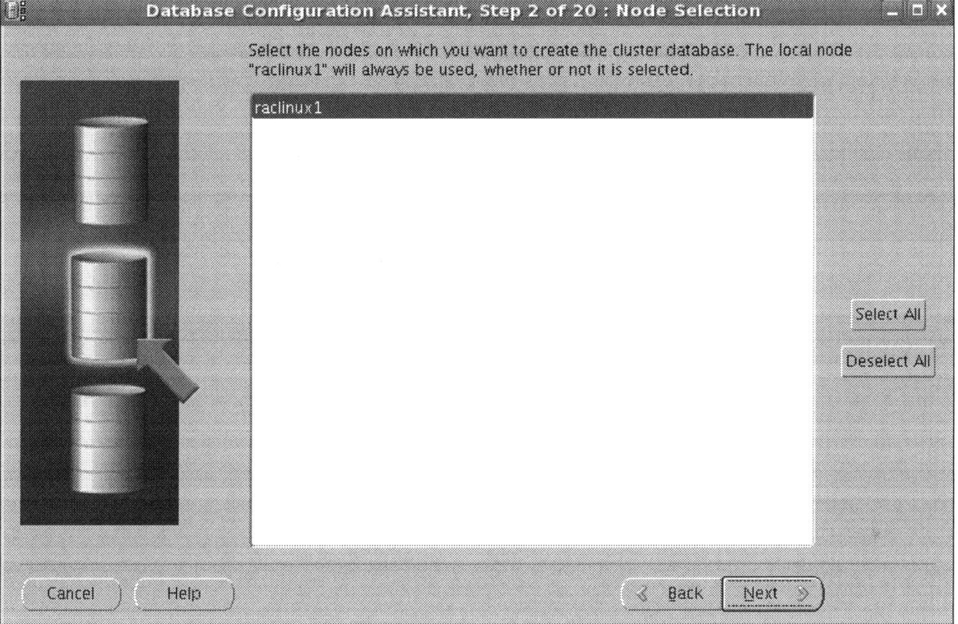

The **Database Templates** screen displays all predefined database configuration templates. The default **General Purpose or Transaction Processing** option is an easy and quick way of creating a database with a handful of interactive screens. The **Custom Database** option allows you to modify the options best suited to your requirements while creating the database. For any OLTP applications, you can choose either option. The **Data Warehouse** option is best suited to data warehouse applications with options such as a bigger block size and higher values for some initialization parameters that are most suited to data warehouse databases.

After you choose the right option to create the database, click on **Next** to proceed further.

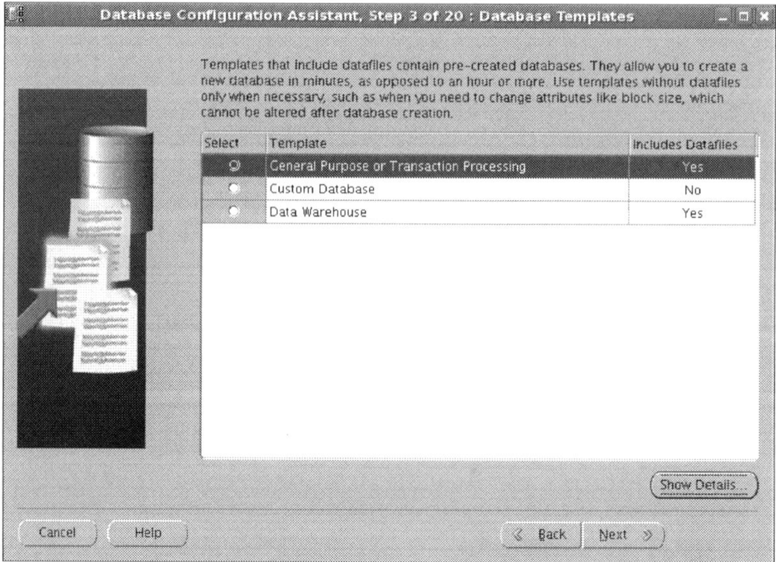

The **Database Identification** screen allows you to enter the global and database name (**SID**) for this database.

Typically, a global database name is formed from a database name and a domain name. For example, the global name for this database would be `RACDB.mydomain.com`. Moreover, this information will be stored in the Data Dictionary and can be changed at any given time using the `ALTER DATABASE` SQL statement, if required. When you click on **Next** to proceed further, DBCA automatically creates an instance with a number suffix such as SIDnn—RACDB1 in our example.

The `nn` indicates the number of selected nodes.

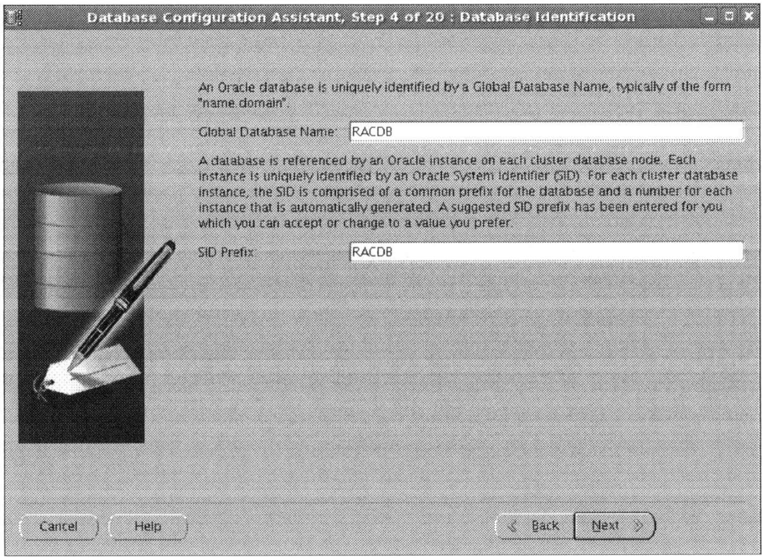

With Oracle 11g R2 or above, the **Database Identification** screen provides multiple cluster database configuration types such as **Admin-Managed** and **Policy-Managed** databases.

The **Admin-Managed** database type is similar to previous RAC databases for an admin-managed RAC database; you must provide a **Global Database Name** and an **SID Prefix**. You will also need to specify the appropriate nodes on which the RAC database instance will run.

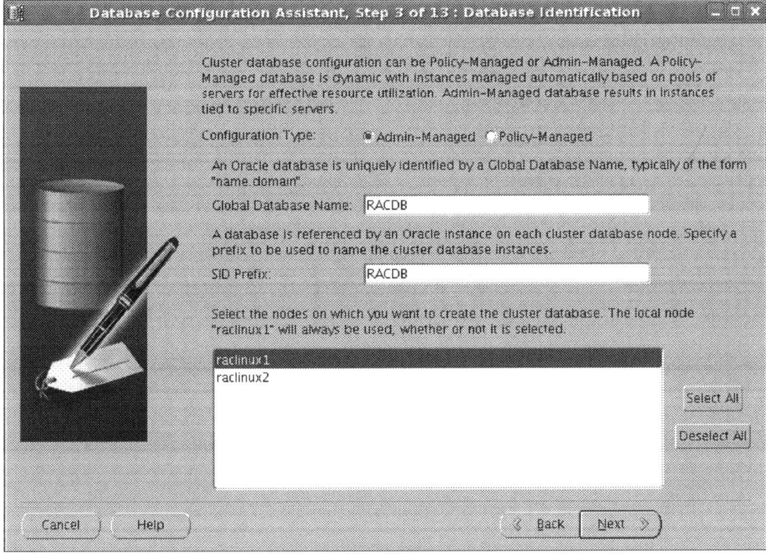

Policy-Managed databases introduce the new server pool concept. You must set the Global Database Name and specify the list of nodes on which the database will run. It is the Oracle cluster that is responsible for choosing the nodes on which to place the resources. When there is no server pool defined, you must create a new sever pool with the maximum number of nodes that are assigned to the server pool. To do this, select the **Create New Server Pool for this database** option and enter the name and cardinality (number of servers), as shown in the following screenshot:.

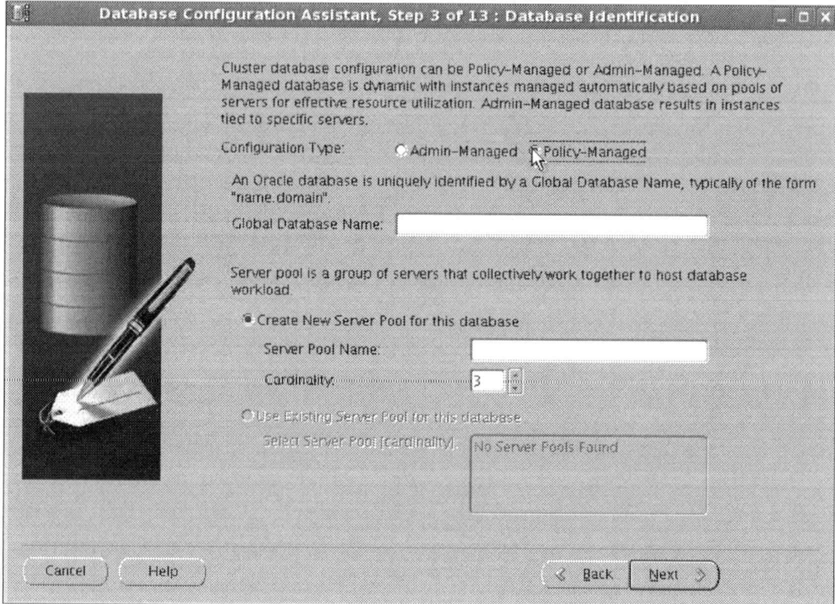

To create a new server pool using the command-line prompt, log in as the root user on Node1 and use the following example:

```
crsctl add serverpool mynewpool -attr "MAX_SIZE=2"
```

Use the following command as the root user to find the server pools created in the cluster:

```
crsctl status serverpool
```

You will then be presented with options to either **Configure Enterprise Manager** or register this database with an existing Grid Control in your environment, presuming that an enterprise manager agent is deployed and active on the nodes.

The **Enterprise Manager** console, either **Database Control** or **Grid Control** provides the easiest way to manage and administer a database and all its associated objects. The prime difference between the Database Control and the Grid Control is that the Database Control will be assosiated with one database and will allow you to manage this database and its objects, whereas the Grid Control provides a centralized integrated framework to manage multiple databases and a variety of Oracle products and third-party products from a single user interface.

If the Enterprise Manager is configured, you can also manage alerts via e-mail or through SMS. **Simple Mail Transport Protocol (SMTP)** must be configured on the nodes. Optionally, disk-based daily backups can also be scheduled. Click on **Next** to proceed further, as shown in the following screenshot:

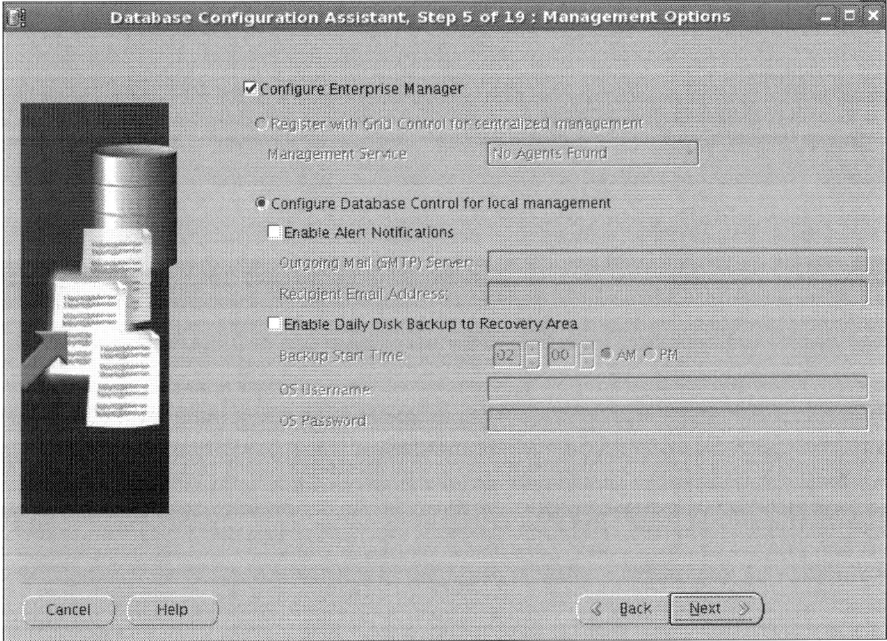

The **Database Credentials** screen lets you decide the password management for the important database default users such as SYS, SYSTEM, and so on. You have an option to choose either an identical password for all the database default users or a unique password for each database default user. Select the appropriate option and click on **Next** to proceed further.

Typically, for production databases, it is highly recommended that you set a very strong, complex, and unique password for each of the default database users for security reasons.

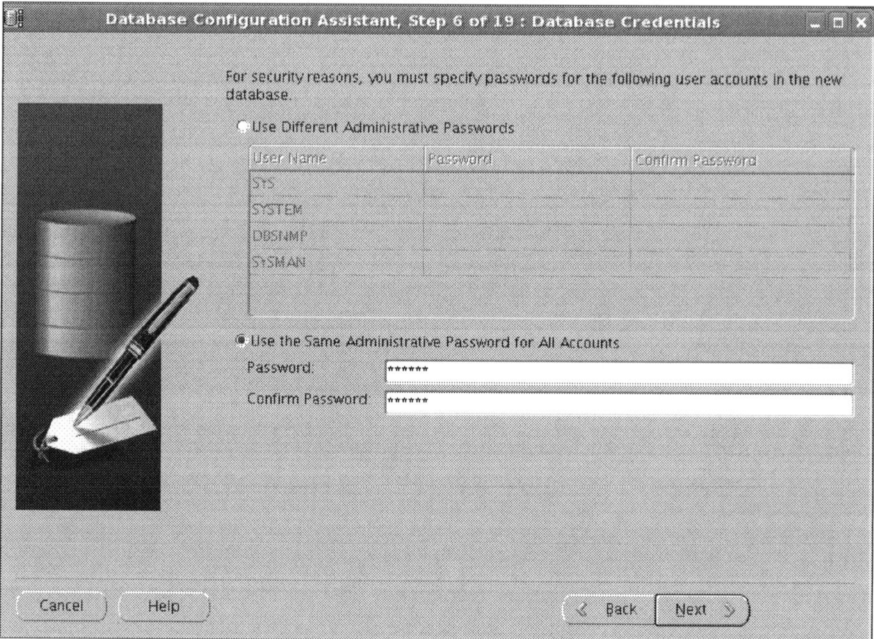

As of Oracle 11g R2, if the given password for the database default users does not satisfy Oracle's recommended password complexity policy, a warning pop-up window will appear. If you have given a strong password, then you can safely ignore this warning message and click on **Yes** to proceed further.

On the **Network Configuration** screen, DBCA detects any pre-existing listeners that are running on the node, lists their names, and will allow you to select one or more listeners to register with this database. Then click on **Next** to proceed further.

If you need to add a new listener to your database, you have to first create the required listener using the Network Configuration Assistant (`./netca`) tool, which can be found under the `$ORA_DB_HOME/bin` location.

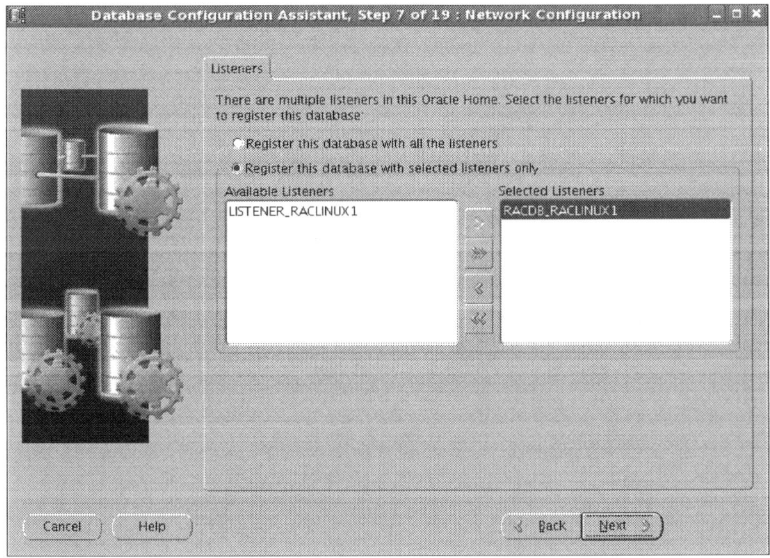

Choosing database storage options

Now it is time to make a decision about the database storage option. The **Storage Options** screen provides multiple storage choices such as the **Cluster File System, Automatic Storage Management (ASM)**, and **Raw Devices**.

Choose the storage option that is appropriate or configured in your environment. As we have decided to use the ASM for our examples, select the **ASM** storage option. Click on **Next** to proceed further, as shown in the following screenshot:

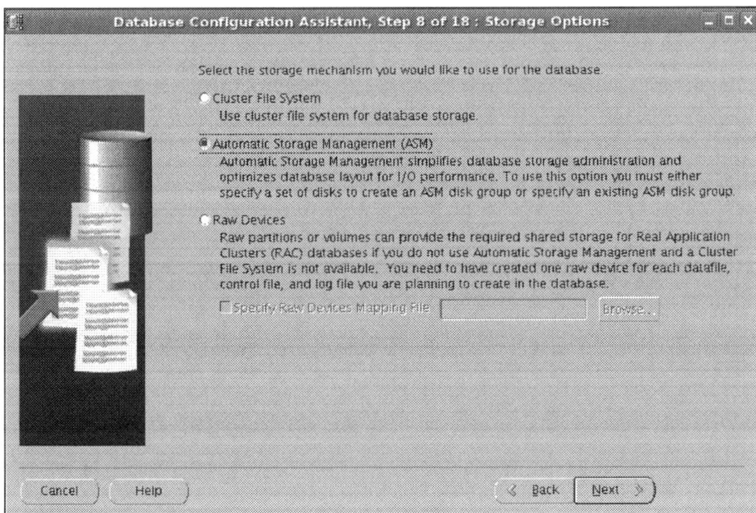

When there is no ASM instance configured on the selected nodes, the Database Configuration Assistant will automatically initiate new ASM instance configuration and creation procedures on all selected nodes. You will then be able to create ASM instances by following the instructions through the interactive slides.

You could be asked, before the following screen, to enter the system user password credentials for an ASM instance to connect to an existing ASM instance of the selected nodes.

As we mentioned earlier, concerning the existence of an ASM instance with DATA and FLASH diskgroups in our testing environment, the **ASM Disk Groups** screen fetches and lists all existing ASM disk group information. Select the **DATA** disk group for storing database datafiles and click on **Next** to proceed further, as shown in the following screenshot:

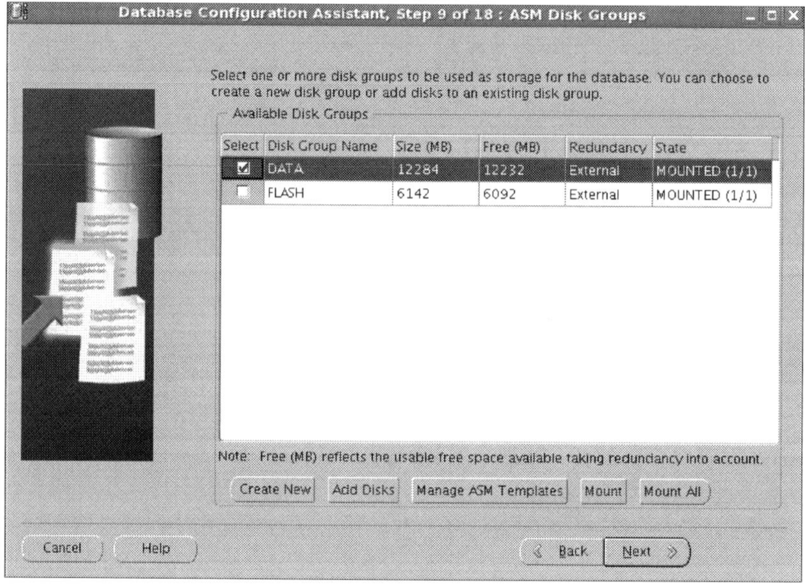

The **Database File Locations** screen displays the information about the disk group selected in the previous screen where the database datafiles will be created.

When no ASM is used as a storage option, you may choose **Use Common Location for All Database Files**. After making the storage decision, click on **Next** to proceed further, as shown in the following screenshot:

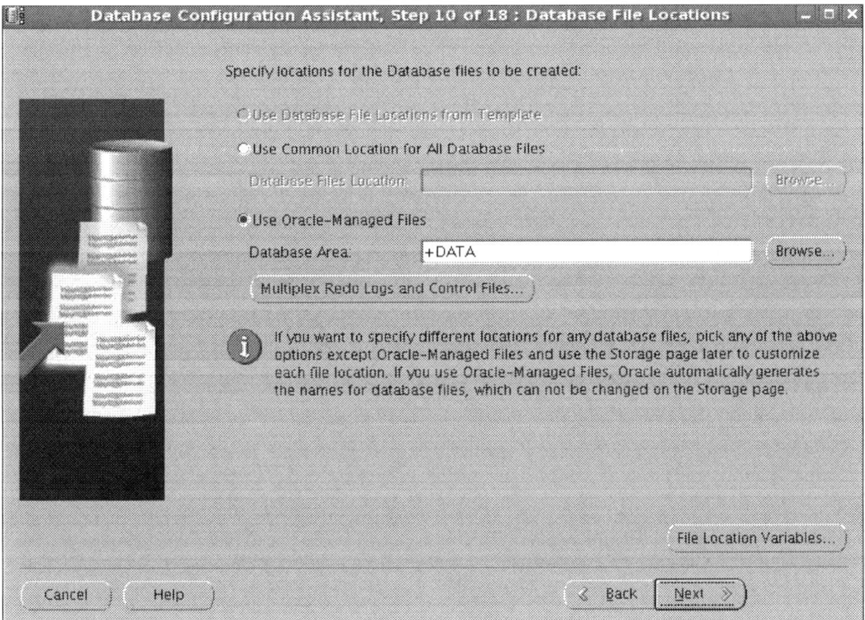

As of Oracle 11g R2, the **Database File Locations** screen is slightly different in contrast to previous Oracle versions, as follows:

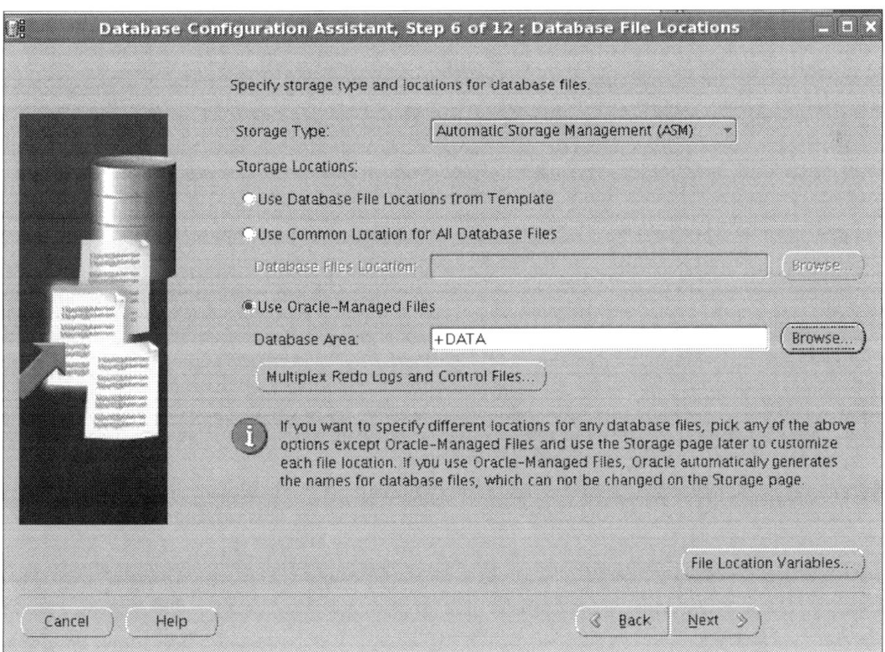

On the **Recovery Configuration** screen, you will then be able to put the database in **Archiving mode** (which is recommended for a production database) and decide the location and size for the **Flash Recovery Area (FRA)**, where the database archive logs will be stored. Set the FRA size to an appropriate size or accept the default settings as the FRA size can increase or decrease dynamically.

Click on the **Browse...** button to select a disk group for the FRA. Check the **Enabling Archiving** option to operate your database in `Archivelog` mode and click on **Next** to proceed further. The **Enabling Archiving** option will put the database in `Archivelog` mode and generate `Archivelogs` while running post-database creation scripts, thereby increasing the database creation time. To speed up the database creation process, we advise you to leave the **Enabling Archiving** option unchecked as you can easily put the database in Archivelog mode after the database creation.

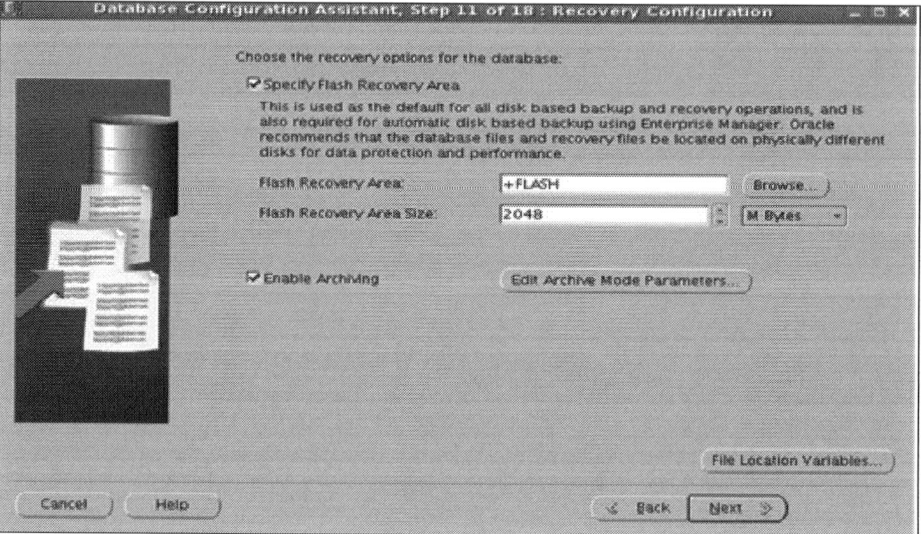

The **Database Content** screen provides an option to configure a few predefined sample schemas in the database. Leave it unchecked if you do not want to install sample schemas and click on **Next.**

[This screen may or may not appear depending on the database creation template you selected earlier.]

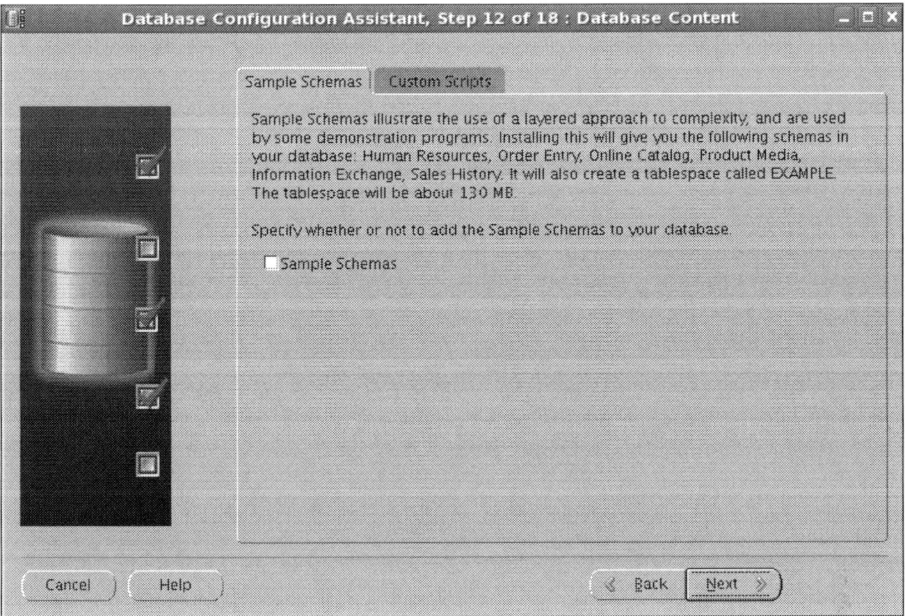

The **Initialization Parameters** screen is considered to be a vital screen when configuring the RAC database, with key settings such as **Memory sizes**, **Character Set**, and **Connection Mode** settings. The DBA needs to pay attention here in order to define optimal memory sizes for the instances, to choose the right database block size, pick up the correct character set, and so on for the database.

Starting with Oracle 11g, you can manage Oracle memory components (SGA and PGA) with a single parameter, **Automatic Memory Management** (**AMM**), which is the default selection while creating a database through DBCA. You can also use customized memory sizes for Oracle 11g memory components, where you can define the custom values for SGA and PGA respectively.

If you are looking for any sort of rule of thumb to define the Oracle memory components, you will be disappointed to know that there is none. There could be a huge impact on the overall database performance if the memory components (SGA) are set to a huge size or if they are under sized. Although these settings are closely related to the application behavior, we recommend that you start with a reasonable memory size value for these components, considering the physical memory available on the nodes. It is also feasible for each instance of a RAC database to have a different SGA and PGA size.

You will need to click on the **All Initialization Parameters...** button to define any non-default initialization parameters suited to your application's behavior. Consider twice before you plan to leave them at their default or while adjusting to custom values.

The **Sizing** tab provides options to choose the DB block size and maximum number of sessions for the database. The default maximum sessions is 150. The 8 Kb default block size is best suited for most OLTP environments.

The **Character Sets** tab provides you with the choices to set the **Character** and **National Character** sets for this database. Here, you need to make a decision about what sort of character set is required to support your data.

The **Connection Mode** tab provides you with the choices to operate the database connection in either **Dedicated** or **Shared** mode. Select the default choice, **Dedicated**, which is favored for most applications. Click **Next** to continue with your Oracle 11g RAC Database creation setup.

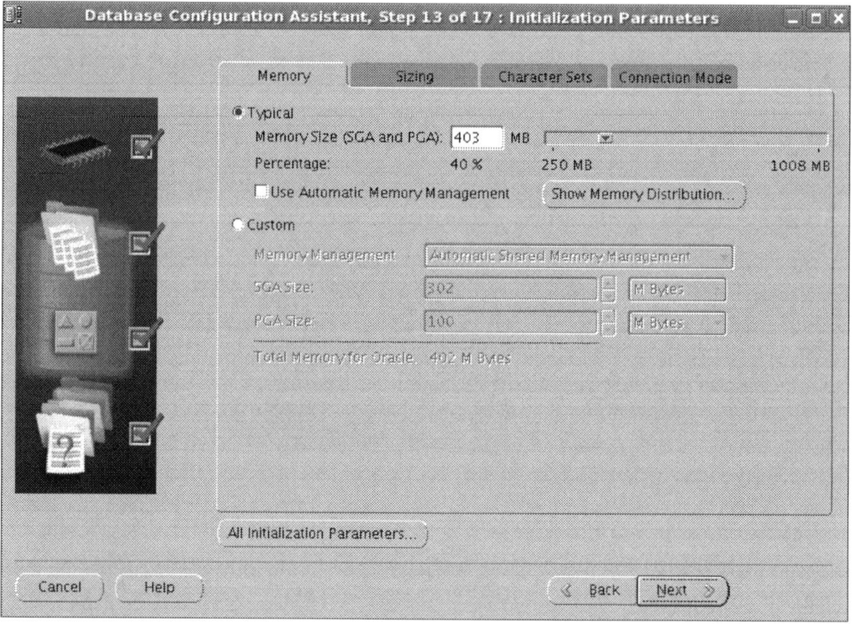

The **Security Settings** screen appears with Oracle 11g DBCA, with the option to either keep the enhanced 11g default setting, the recommended one, or revert to pre-11g default settings. The enhanced 11g default security settings enable auditing and new default password profile parameter values. Choose the default option and click on **Next**, as shown in the following screenshot:

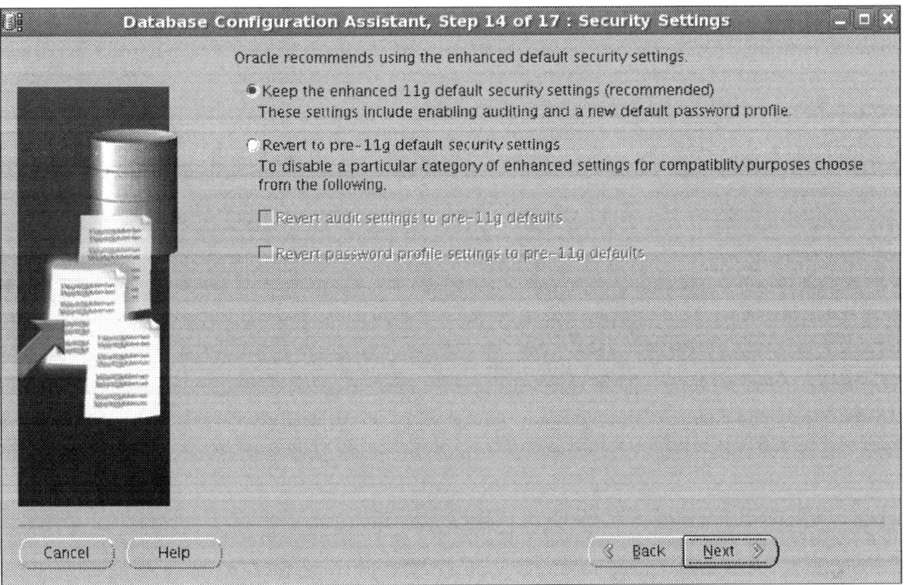

The **Automatic Maintenance Tasks** screen is also new in Oracle 11g DBCA, providing the enhanced functionality of optimizer statistics collection, proactive advisor report, and so on. However, these settings can be changed later using the Database/Grid Control. As of now, choose the default option and click on **Next** to continue the setup process.

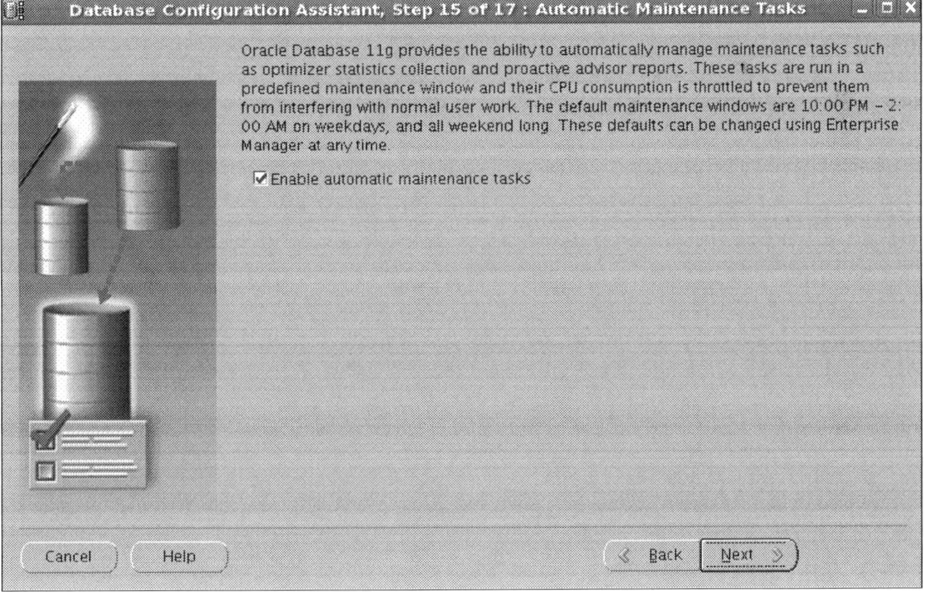

Optionally, you can adjust the redo group sizes, and add more redo groups and members as per your requirements. The typical recommendation is to have two or more redo groups per instance with multiplexing redo members.

You have to be careful while deciding on the number of redo groups along with the number of redo members and sizes as these settings may impact the database performance. When you run a highly OLTP application on a database with small-sized redo members or with a few redo groups, you are likely to encounter performance-related issues and may also notice redo related wait events.

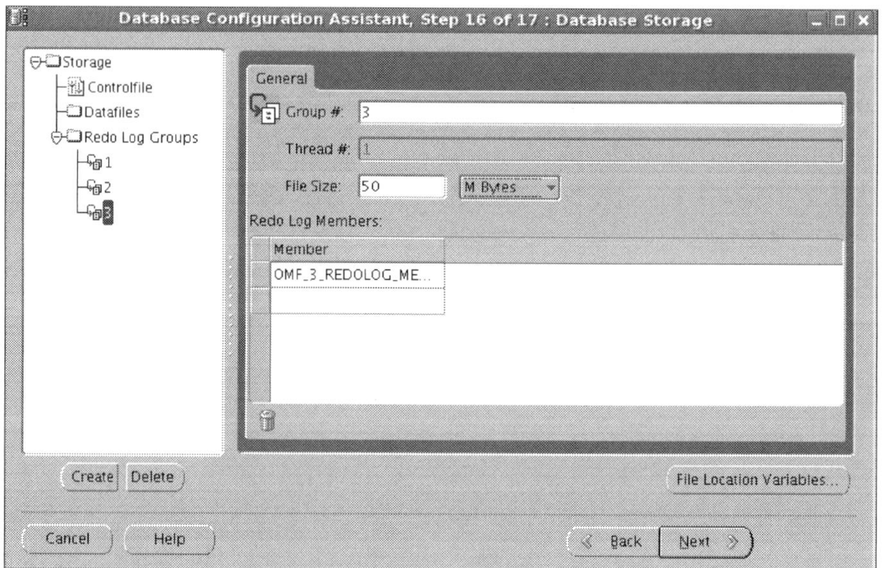

Click on **Next** to proceed further.

Click on **Finish** to commence the database creation process. If selecting the **Generate Database Creation Scripts** option along with the **Create Database** option, the database scripts will be generated and stored in the destination directory. When you select only the **Generate Database Creation Scripts** option, the OUI generates a script under the specified location, which can be later used to create the database.

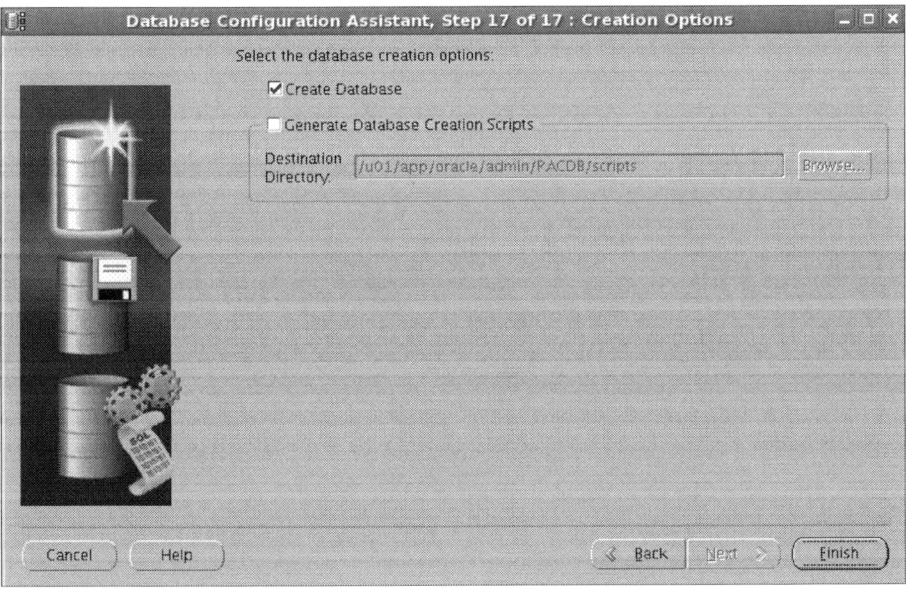

The next screen shows the common options selected for this database. Click on **OK** to close this screen and the database creation screen will follow. At this point, the DBCA program will create the database as shown in the following screenshot. It will take some time for DBCA to perform these tasks, so this is a good moment to grab a cup of coffee!

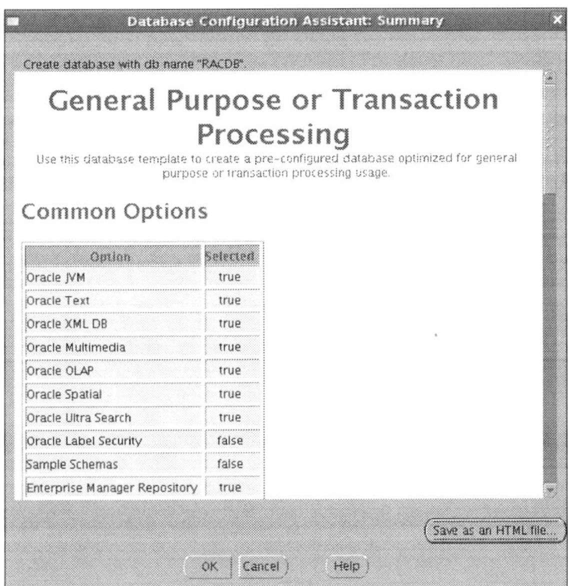

Don't panic if the database creation process screen doesn't appear immediately. Sometimes it might take a couple of minutes before it starts.

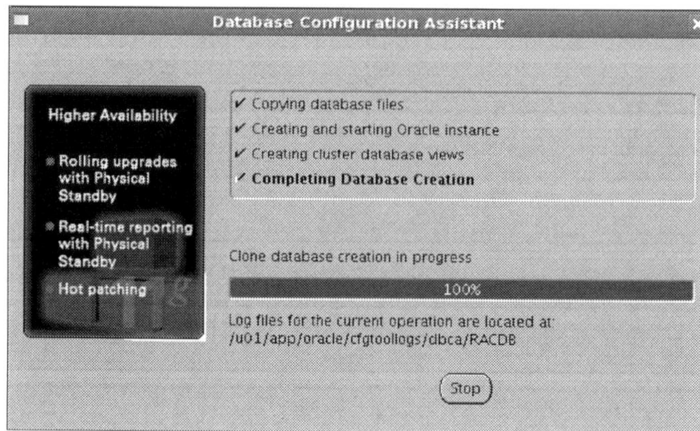

Upon reaching 100%, the DBCA subsequently displays information such as the global database name, database name, the location of the SPfile (parameter) file, and an option for password management.

After DBCA has completed the database creation process successfully, a window to manage the password for the database default users will appear. This lets you either lock or unlock the default database users. Most of the default users will be in a locked state by default. The screen also lets you change the passwords for these database default users. The screen also lists the database information, SPfile location, and list location for the installation logs.

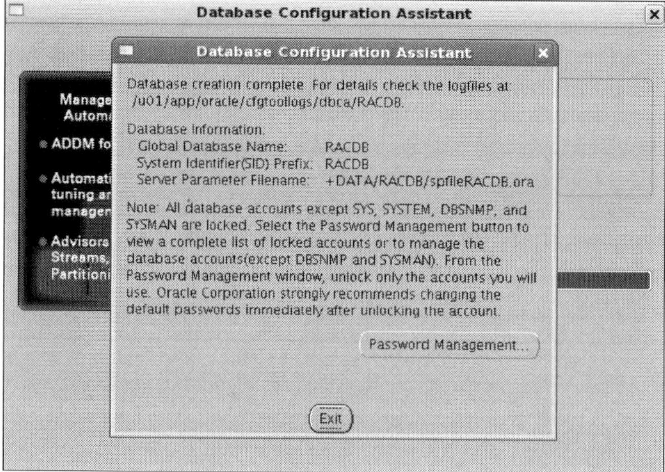

Click on **Exit** to quit from the screen and an Instance Service adding screen will appear subsequently. If the screen doesn't appear, it means you have some issues in the cluster. You will need to look at the errors reported and try to resolve them, or once the database is created, you can use the cluster command `crsctl add database/instance` to add the database and its instance manually to the cluster.

We have created a database using DBCA—now what?

Before we move on further and discuss what we are required to do post database creation, you will need to understand the architectural differences between a standalone database and a RAC database, especially if you are migrating from a standalone environment to the RAC environment.

In contrast to a standalone database, every instance of a RAC database consists of its own set of redo groups, a separate UNDO tablespace, and a few additional RAC-related parameters. Moreover, if the location of Redo Logs and Archive Logs is defined locally for each instance, make sure the other instances of this RAC database have read permission to that location and vice versa, as it is crucial during the instance recovery phase and so forth. The typical recommendation is to have a shared location—FRA is the best option. You also need to understand the initialization parameters, as some must have identical values and others must have unique values across all the instances of a RAC database.

The following are important initialization parameters that must have the same values across all the instances of an RAC database:

- `CLUSTER_DATABASE`
- `CONTROL_FILES`
- `DB_BLOCK_SIZE`
- `COMPATIBLE`
- `DB_NAME`
- `ACTIVE_INSTANCE_COUNT`
- `UNDO_MANAGEMENT`
- `RESULT_CACHE_MAX_SIZE`
- `DB_UNIQUE_NAME`
- `CLUSTER_DATABASE_INSTANCES`
- `INSTANCE_TYPE`
- `REMOTE_LOGIN_PASSWORDFILE`
- `DB_RECOVERY_FILE_DEST`
- `DB_RECOVERY_FILE_DEST_SIZE`

The following are important initialization parameters that must have a unique value across all instances of an RAC database:

- INSTANCE_NAME
- INSTANCE_NUMBER
- UNDO_TABLESPACE
- THREAD

After the database is successfully created, use the cluster commands such as `$ORA_CRS_HOME/bin/crs_stat` and `$ORA_CRS_HOME/bin/srvctl` to administer and manage the RAC database. The `./crs_stat.sh` (or `crs_stat`) command shows output similar to the following sample:

```
[oracle@raclinux1 ~]$ ./crs_stat.sh
HA Resourrce                              Target    Stage
------------                              ------    -----
ora.RACDB.RACDB1.inst                     ONLINE    ONLINE on raclinux1
ora.RACDB.db                              ONLINE    ONLINE on raclinux1
ora.raclinux1.ASM1.asm                    ONLINE    ONLINE on raclinux1
ora.raclinux1.LISTENER_RACLINUX1.lsnr     ONLINE    ONLINE on raclinux1
ora.raclinux1.RACDB_RACLINUX1.lsnr        ONLINE    ONLINE on raclinux1
ora.raclinux1.gsd                         ONLINE    ONLINE on raclinux1
ora.raclinux1.ons                         ONLINE    ONLINE on raclinux1
ora.raclinux1.vip                         ONLINE    ONLINE on raclinux1
```

`crs_stat.sh` is an external script to display long names correctly.

Use the server control utility (`srvctl`) to query the database configuration and status with the following example:

```
[oracle@raclinux1 ~]$ srvctl config database -d RACDB
raclinux1 RACDB1 /u01/app/oracle/product/11.1.0/db_1
[oracle@raclinux1 ~]$ srvctl status database -d RACDB
Instance RACDB1 is running on node raclinux1
[oracle@raclinux1 ~]$ srvctl status instance -d RACDB -i RACDB1
Instance RACDB1 is running on node raclinux1
```

As of Oracle 11g R2, the `srvctl config` command produces more useful information about the database such as database name, domain, SPfile location, and Disk Group used in this database. Use the following sample command:

```
srvctl config database -d RACDB

Database unique name: RACDB
Database name: RACDB
```

```
Oracle home: /u01/app/oracle/product/11.2.0/dbhome_1
Oracle user: oracle
Spfile: +DATA/RACDB/spfileRACDB.ora
Domain:
Start options: open
Stop options: immediate
Database role: PRIMARY
Management policy: AUTOMATIC
Server pools: RACDB
Database instances: RACDB1
Disk Groups: DATA
Services:
Database is administrator managed
```

What's new in Oracle 11g R1 and R2 databases?

Oracle technologies emerge stronger with every new release, and with every new release, come significant new features and key enhancements. Oracle 11g is no exception to this trend.

Before you begin managing the database of a new release, it is essential that you thoroughly understand the concepts, usage, and overall impact of those new features.

Although there are many exciting new features such as **Database Replay**, **Automatic Memory Management (AMM)**, **Interval Partitioning**, **SQL Performance Analyzer (SPA)**, **Total Recall**, **Instance caging**, **Database Smart Flash Cache**, and so on introduced in the Oracle 11g Database R1 and R2, we will focus on the key new features of Oracle 11g R1 and R2 that can be commonly implemented in most environments. For the complete list of new features, we encourage you to refer to the Oracle 11g database new features document at `http://download.oracle.com/docs/cd/E11882_01/server.112/e17120/whatsnew.htm#i969790`.

Automatic Memory Management

Previously in Oracle 10g, the instance memory structures were managed for **System Global Area (SGA)** and **Program Global Area (PGA)** by two initialization parameters. However, with Oracle 11g R1 or higher, Oracle database instance memory structures such as SGA and PGA can be managed using the **Automatic Memory Management (AMM)** feature, setting a single initialization parameter. To enable this feature, you need to set adequate values to the two new initialization parameters named `MEMORY_TARGET` and `MEMORY_MAX_TARGET`. When the total memory size is defined for an Oracle instance, Oracle automatically redistributes or transfers memory sizes dynamically between SGA and PGA as needed to satisfy process demands or according to the current workload in the instance. It also tunes the sizes of SGA and individual PGAs automatically. The two initialization parameters are described next:

- `MEMORY_MAX_TARGET`: Defines the maximum limit of SGA and PGA size for this Oracle instance. You cannot change the value to this parameter dynamically.
- `MEMORY_TARGET`: Specifies the amount of shared memory allocated at instance startup. Oracle dynamically manages the SGA plus PGA values. Unlike the `MEMORY_MAX_TARGET` parameter, it is a dynamic parameter and it can be increased or decreased provided that its value doesn't exceed the value of the `MEMORY_MAX_TARGET` parameter.

Use the following SQL command to find out the current values of AMM parameters on this instance:

```
SELECT name,value/1024/1024 size_in_mb FROM v$parameter where NAME in
('memory_max_target','memory_target');
NAME                                    SIZE_IN_MB
--------------------------------------- -----------------------------
memory_max_target                              404
memory_target                                  404
```

When the `MEMORY_MAX_TARGET` initialization parameter is unset, the database automatically sets its value equal to `MEMORY_TARGET` value. You can easily disable this feature by setting the `MEMORY_TARGET` initialization parameter value to 0.

You can use the following command to disable the AMM feature dynamically:

```
alter system set MEMORY_TARGET=0 scope=both sid='*';
```

The value `sid='*'` indicates that the change should apply to all the instances of this database.

New AMM dynamic performance V$ views

To administer, manage, and tune the AMM size in the instance, Oracle 11g has introduced new V$ views. The following are the new AMM V$ views, which will help you to manage and tune the AMM size in the instance.

```
SQL> select table_name from dict where table_name like 'V$MEMORY%';

TABLE_NAME
------------------------------
V$MEMORY_CURRENT_RESIZE_OPS
V$MEMORY_DYNAMIC_COMPONENTS
V$MEMORY_RESIZE_OPS
V$MEMORY_TARGET_ADVICE
```

The following table describes the functionality of the new AMM V$ views:

View	Description
V$MEMORY_CURRENT_RESIZE_OPS	Database ongoing memory resize operation details are recorded and displayed in dynamic view.
V$MEMORY_DYNAMIC_COMPONENTS	Records the historical (since the database startup) details about all dynamic SGA components and resizes that took place.
V$MEMORY_RESIZE_OPS	Records about 800 historical dynamic memory resize operation details. A very useful view to analyze the impact of frequently resizing memory components.
V$MEMRY_TARGET_ADVICE	Helps you to analyze and tune the AMM value for this instance, based on satisfaction metric details in the view.

The automatic memory size allocated for each dynamic component can be viewed using the dynamic view `V$MEMORY_DYNAMIC_COMPONENTS`. The following output shows the current, minimum, and maximum dynamically allocated sizes for all the memory components. The sizes are expressed in bytes:

```
SQL> SELECT component,current_size,min_size,max_size
  2  FROM v$memory_dynamic_components
  3  WHERE current_size > 0
  4  ORDER BY component;

COMPONENT                        CURRENT_SIZE   MIN_SIZE   MAX_SIZE
------------------------------ ------------ ---------- ----------
DEFAULT buffer cache               54525952   54525952   54525952
PGA Target                        167772160  167772160  167772160
SGA Target                        255852544  255852544  255852544
java pool                          12582912   12582912   12582912
large pool                          4194304    4194304    4194304
shared pool                       176160768  176160768  176160768
```

For the current and historical (last 800) status of all memory dynamic components, resize requests can be analyzed and queried using the dynamic views—`V$MEMORY_CURRENT_RESIZE_OPS` and `V$MEMORY_RESIZE_OPS`.

Tuning AMM

To ensure that you have adequately set the **AMM** size on your RAC database instance, the `V$MEMORY_TARGET_ADVICE` view can be used to tune the AMM size. It consists of the current and estimated factors based on current workload in the instance. This information may help you tune AMM and allows you to set a reliable value for the `MEMORY_TARGET` initialization parameter. The following sample output shows the memory advisory of AMM:

```
SQL> SELECT * FROM V$MEMORY_TARGET_ADVICE;

MEMORY_SIZE MEMORY_SIZE_FACTOR ESTD_DB_TIME ESTD_DB_TIME_FACTOR    VERSION
----------- ------------------ ------------ ------------------- ----------
        404                  1          167                   1          0
        303                .75          194              1.1616          0
        505               1.25          167                   1          0
        606                1.5          167                   1          0
        707               1.75          167                   1          0
        808                  2          167                   1          0
```

Special considerations on Linux

You must be cautious when deciding to use the AMM feature on the Linux operating system, as it has a different behavior compared to other OS platforms. When the AMM feature is enabled on the database on the Linux OS, Oracle maintains the SGA and PGA memory allocation and deallocation by files in the `/dev/shm` directory on the OS. The size of the file depends upon your AMM settings. For example, if the `MEMORY_MAX_TARGET <= 1024M`, the file will be of size 4 MB, otherwise it will be a 16 MB file. The following sample output shows all the allocated files at `/dev/shm` for the RACDB database:

```
[oracle@raclinux1 shm]$ pwd
/dev/shm
[oracle@raclinux1 shm]$ ls -ltr |more |grep 'RACDB1'
-rw-rw---- 1 oracle oinstall 4194304 Jun 26 18:30 ora_RACDB1_458762_1
-rw-rw---- 1 oracle oinstall 4194304 Jun 26 18:30 ora_RACDB1_458762_0
-rw-rw---- 1 oracle oinstall 4194304 Jun 26 18:30 ora_RACDB1_458762_61
-rw-rw---- 1 oracle oinstall 4194304 Jun 26 18:30 ora_RACDB1_458762_19
-rw-rw---- 1 oracle oinstall 4194304 Jun 26 18:30 ora_RACDB1_458762_20
-rw-rw---- 1 oracle oinstall 4194304 Jun 26 18:30 ora_RACDB1_458762_21
-rw-rw---- 1 oracle oinstall 4194304 Jun 26 18:30 ora_RACDB1_458762_22
-rw-rw---- 1 oracle oinstall 4194304 Jun 26 18:30 ora_RACDB1_458762_23
-rw-rw---- 1 oracle oinstall 4194304 Jun 26 18:30 ora_RACDB1_458762_24
-rw-rw---- 1 oracle oinstall 4194304 Jun 26 18:30 ora_RACDB1_458762_25
-rw-rw---- 1 oracle oinstall 4194304 Jun 26 18:30 ora_RACDB1_458762_26
```

The management of these files is dynamically handled, as these files will be created immediately upon instance startup and will be removed automatically when the instance shuts down. It was observed that Oracle uses these files to manage the memory sizes dynamically between SGA and PGA, as you may see file sizes reducing to zero size sometimes.

/dev/shm sizing issues

While trying to configure the AMM feature without a properly sized `/dev/shm` filesystem on the node, you are likely to receive an **ORA-00845: MEMORY_TARGET not supported on this system** error. To avoid such errors, ensure that you configure the `/dev/shm` filesystem on the nodes large enough to support the AMM feature.

It is also advised that you have the `/dev/shm` filesystem configured with the `tmpfs` option instead of `ramfs` while working with the AMM feature, as `ramfs` is not supported with AMM on Linux. The following examples demonstrate how to modify and set a large size for `/dev/shm` on Linux OS as the root user:

```
mount -t tmpfs shmfs -o size=4g /dev/shm
```

To make the changes persistent when the system reboots, add the following code in /etc/fstab:

```
shmfs /dev/shm tmpfs size=4g 0
```

As you can see in the following sample output, the /dev/shm is configured with the tmpfs option and 4 G size option:

```
[oracle@raclinux1 shm]$ df
Filesystem           1K-blocks      Used Available Use% Mounted on
/dev/mapper/VolGroup00-LogVol00
                       1015704    232316    730960  25% /
/dev/sda10              101086      6692     89175   7% /opt
/dev/sda8               396623     60248    315894  17% /var
/dev/sda7              1019208     34788    931812   4% /home
/dev/sda6              1019208     36344    930256   4% /tmp
/dev/sda5              2972236   2481156    337664  89% /usr
/dev/sda11              101086      5713     90154   6% /usr/local
/dev/sda3              4956316   2007816   2692668  43% /stage
/dev/sda2             19840924   9539332   9277452  51% /u01
/dev/sda1               147764     11791    128344   9% /boot
tmpfs                   517624    408912    108712  79% /dev/shm
```

Database Smart Flash Cache

In Oracle 11g R2, a new memory component **Database Smart Flash Cache** has been added as an extension of the SGA-resident buffer cache, which provides a second-level cache provision for the database blocks. For read-intensive OLTP application workloads, it may greatly improve response time and overall throughput.

The Flash Cache typically resides on one or more flash disk devices, which are solid state devices using flash drives.

Configuring Smart Flash Cache

The following are situations where you may consider configuring and taking advantage of Smart Flash Cache:

- In the process of tuning SGA, if the Buffer Pool Advisory section of the AWR report or STATSPACK report advice doubles the current size of buffer cache
- When you consistently observe that db sequential reads is a top event on the database
- When you have spare CPUs

As of now, this feature is supported only when you run the database on Sun Solaris or Oracle Enterprise Linux OS, because the Flash Cache is only supported on these operating systems.

To configure Smart Flash Cache, you need to set two new initialization parameters named `db_flash_cache_file` and `db_flash_cache_size`.

- `db_flash_cache_file`: Specify the path and filename for the file to contain the flash cache—for example, `/dev/fioa`. This file will be automatically created during the database creation if the file doesn't already exist.
- `db_flash_cache_size`: Specify the size of the flash cache. The value can be defined in GB as long as the value is less than or equal to the physical memory of the flash disk device.

You can use the `ALTER SYSTEM` command to disable and re-enable the flash cache size.

On a RAC database, either you enable the flash cache on all instances or none of the instances.

Instance caging

In Oracle 11g R2, **Instance Caging** is introduced to manage the amount of CPU consumed by an Oracle instance on a multi-CPU server, running multiple database instances. When Instance Caging is set through an Oracle resource manager and `cpu_count` initialization parameter, it limits the maximum number of CPUs that any one database can use. (Please note that the `cpu_count` value has no influence on the number of CPU licenses.)

A new attribute named `MAX_UTILIZATION_LIMIT` is used to impose an upper limit on CPU utilization for a resource consumer group. To implement this feature, you need to enable a resource manager and set the `cpu_count` initialization parameter.

New background processes in Oracle 11g

In addition to previous database background processes, Oracle 11g has added more new background processes to support some of its new features effectively. The following is the description of some of the background processes along with their roles and responsibilities:

- **Diagnosability process (DIA0)**: This is responsible for hang detection and deadlock resolution.
- **Database Resource Management (DBRM)**: This is responsible for resource plans and other resource manager-related tasks.
- **Space Management Coordinator (SMCO)**: This coordinates the execution of various space-related tasks. It dynamically spawns slave processes (Wnn) to implement the task.

- **Global Transaction (GTX0-j)**: This provides transparent support for XA global transactions in an Oracle RAC environment. The database autotunes the number of these processes based on the workload of XA global transactions, which can be seen only in an Oracle RAC environment.
- **Virtual Keeper of time (VKTM)**: This is responsible for providing a wall-clock time, updates every second, and reference-time counter every 20 ms, and is available only when running at elevated priority.

Finding the alert.log file location in Oracle 11g

While working with Oracle 11g database for the first time, with pre-Oracle 11g experience, you may find it difficult to locate the database alert log (`alert_SID.log`) file and its background along with users and other log and trace files in contrast to previous Oracle releases.

Beginning with Oracle 11g R1, the `alert.log` file is written as both an XML formatted (`log.xml`) and as a text file (`alert_INSTANCE_ID.log`), and these files are then stored under the **Automatic Diagnostic Repository** (**ADR**) home (yet another new home in Oracle). It is the root directory for all diagnostic data, including trace files and `listener.log` and `alert.log` files (equal to all dump directories in previous releases), and is controlled by the `DIAGNOSTIC_DEST` initialization parameter. The directory structure is stored outside the database.

When the parameter is unset or omitted, then the database automatically sets this parameter as follows during startup:

- When the `ORACLE_BASE` environment variable is set on the node, then `DIAGNOSTIC_DEST` is set to the directory designed by `ORACLE_BASE`.
- If no `ORACLE_BASE` environment variable is set, then `DIAGNOSTIC_DEST` is set to `ORACLE_HOME/log` directory.

The following sample output shows the `ORACLE_BASE` directory settings on the node and in the database:

```
[oracle@raclinux1 ~]$ echo $ORACLE_BASE
/u01/app/oracle
```

```
SQL> show parameter DIAGNOST

NAME                                 TYPE        VALUE
------------------------------------ ----------- ------------------
diagnostic_dest                      string      /u01/app/oracle
```

Automatic Diagnostic Repository

The **Automatic Diagnostic Repository** (**ADR**) is the centralized repository for the database diagnostic-related data such as the `altert.log` file, trace files, incident dumps, and health monitoring reports.

With Oracle 11g, all Clusterware, ASM, and other Oracle components' diagnostic data is stored under this home. When a critical database error occurs, an incident number is assigned and diagnostic data trace for this error is immediately captured and tagged with this number and then the data is stored under the ADR, outside the database.

All `_dump_dest` initialization parameters are ignored with Oracle 11g and the `DIAGNOSTI_DEST` is not equal to `_dump_dest` initialization parameters.

The following diagram shows the structure of the ADR home, which will assist when locating the XML `alert.log`, text-based `alert.log` file, and other files and their locations:

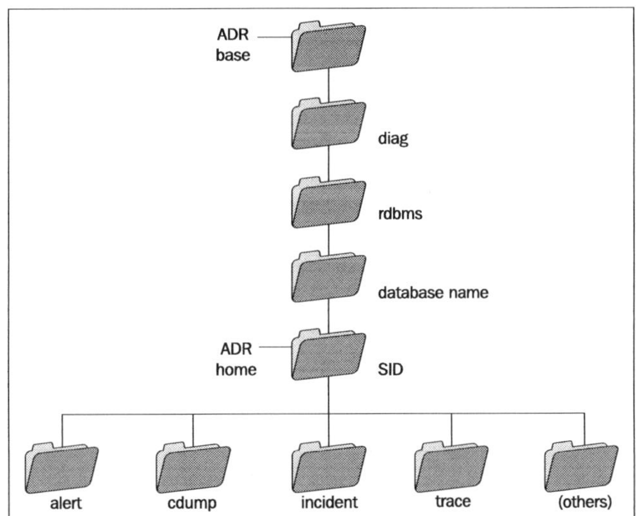

In an RAC environment, each instance will have its own ADR home on its own local storage.

Managing ADR using the Automatic Diagnostic Repository Command Interface tool

The **Automatic Diagnostic Repository Command Interface tool** (**ADRCI**) is another new utility in Oracle 11g, which can be found under the `$ORACLE_HOME/bin` directory. It allows you to investigate database problems, view health-check reports, and upload first-failure diagnostic data to Oracle Support, all within a command-line environment. The ADRCI is also used to find all trace files, `listener.log`, and view incidents associated with the instance. The following examples demonstrate how to use the ADRCI, and list the commands using the `help` command:

```
[oracle@raclinux1 bin]$ adrci

ADRCI: Release 11.1.0.6.0 - Beta on Sat Jul 7 21:54:46 2009

Copyright (c) 1982, 2007, Oracle.  All rights reserved.

ADR base = "/u01/app/oracle"

adrci> help
```

This utility is much more helpful than what we have discussed here. It can also be used to find incidents in the database instance, via view alert log and trace files information. For the complete list of ADRCI utility usage, we recommend the *Oracle Utilities Document* available at `http://download.oracle.com/docs/cd/B28359_01/server.111/b28319/adrci.htm#SUTIL700`.

V$DIAG_INFO view

The easiest way to find the locations of alert log, trace files, core dump, and all database diagnostic-related files in Oracle 11g is to query the new dynamic `v$diag_info` view. It lists all important ADR locations for the current Oracle instance.

The following sample query on `v$diag_info` view shows the location of all trace, alert, and incident log file locations set up for this instance:

```
SQL> select * from v$diag_info;

   INST_ID NAME                           VALUE
---------- ------------------------------ ----------------------------------------------------------------
         1 Diag Enabled                   TRUE
         1 ADR Base                       /u01/app/oracle
         1 ADR Home                       /u01/app/oracle/diag/rdbms/racdb/RACDB1
         1 Diag Trace                     /u01/app/oracle/diag/rdbms/racdb/RACDB1/trace
         1 Diag Alert                     /u01/app/oracle/diag/rdbms/racdb/RACDB1/alert
         1 Diag Incident                  /u01/app/oracle/diag/rdbms/racdb/RACDB1/incident
         1 Diag Cdump                     /u01/app/oracle/diag/rdbms/racdb/RACDB1/cdump
         1 Health Monitor                 /u01/app/oracle/diag/rdbms/racdb/RACDB1/hm
         1 Default Trace File             /u01/app/oracle/diag/rdbms/racdb/RACDB1/trace/RACDB1_ora_18981.trc
         1 Active Problem Count           0
         1 Active Incident Count          0
```

RAC database administration

Managing a RAC database is nearly identical to managing a standalone database, in terms of creating and administering tablespaces, datafiles, users, and other database operations. Like a standalone database, the RAC database and its instances can be started up and shut down using the startup and shutdown SQL commands. However, the recommended way to administer an Oracle RAC database is to use the **Server Control Utility**.

Using the Server Control Utility

The **Server Control Utility** (**SRVCTL**), `srvctl`, is a cluster command-line utility that is installed by default on all nodes and is used to administer and manage the RAC database and its associated instances for operations such as start and stop, enable and disable, moving a database and instances across nodes, and adding and removing instances/database. When `srvctl` is used for some of the operations such as add, remove, enable, disable, and move a database and its instances, the information is stored in the Oracle Cluster Registry.

However, the start and stop operations of a database and instances are done with the cooperation of the **Cluster Ready Service Daemon process (CRSD)** in the cluster environment.

The following sample code demonstrates the usage and parameters associated with the `SRVCTL` utility:

```
[oracle@raclinux1 bin]$ srvctl
Usage: srvctl <command> <object> [<options>]
    command: enable|disable|start|stop|relocate|status|add|remove|modify|getenv|setenv|unsetenv|config
    objects: database|instance|service|nodeapps|asm|listener
For detailed help on each command and object and its options use:
    srvctl <command> <object> -h
[oracle@raclinux1 bin]$
```

Any time you need to list the parameters supported by the utility, use the `srvctl -h` command to get help for the complete list of `srvctl`-supported parameters and their usage. The following sample code can be used to find which nodes the RAC database instances are configured on and where the instances are running:

```
[oracle@raclinux1 bin]$ srvctl status database -d RACDB
Instance RACDB1 is running on node raclinux1
```

The following sample code demonstrates how to stop and start an RAC database or individual RAC database instances using the SRVCTL utility:

```
srvctl stop database -d RACDB
srvctl start database -d RACDB
srvctl stop instance -d RACDB -i RACDB1
srvctl start instance -d RACDB -i RACDB1
```

The following sample code demonstrates how to stop and start a RAC database or individual RAC database instances through the SQLPLUS prompt.

Before you run the following SQL statement, make sure you set the correct ORACLE_SID of the relevant instance and connect as a sysdba:

```
export ORACLE_SID=RACDB1
sqlplus / as sysdba
```

```
SQL> shutdown immediate
Database closed.
Database dismounted.
ORACLE instance shut down.
```

```
SQL> startup
ORACLE instance started.

Total System Global Area  255291392 bytes
Fixed Size                  1299172 bytes
Variable Size             184552732 bytes
Database Buffers           62914560 bytes
Redo Buffers                6524928 bytes
Database mounted.
Database opened.
```

It is highly recommended that you use the srvctl utility to manage the RAC database and its associated instances rather than manual startup and shutdown SQL commands. When you stop an instance or an RAC database manually, it is possible that the status of this database in the cluster still looks ONLINE and the subsequent startup with the srvctl command would result in an error. In such a case, you need to make sure the resource is set to OFFLINE and you can do that using the crs_stop command.

Automatic Workload Management

In this section, we are going to discuss **Automatic Workload Management** concepts and the advantages offered to the applications that run on the RAC database. We will also take a closer look at how to fully utilize the RAC database prime features such as **Load Balancing (Scalability)** and **Failover (High Availability)** to improve a connection management and optimize the application workload.

By using the RAC features, the application can take complete advantage of scaling workload among available active RAC database instances and can also re-establish the lost user connection to surviving active RAC database instances.

In its simplest terms, Automatic Workload Management allows you to manage the workload distribution among available active instances of a RAC database, to provide optimal performance benefits for users and applications.

Automatic Workload Management comprises:

- Services
- Connection Load Balancing
- Fast Application Notification
- Load Balancing Advisory
- Fast Connection Failover
- Run Time Connection Load Balancing
- Single Client Access Name (SCAN, in 11g R2)

Overview of services

The concept of services was first introduced in Oracle 8i, and since then the service usage has been significantly expanded.

A **service** feature is the grouping of related tasks within the database, with common functionality that provides a single system image to the users working within the cluster environment. In an RAC environment, the High Availability configuration for each service is stored in Oracle Cluster Registry. Several database features support services, wherein performance-related events and statistics are traced by services. **Automatic Workload Repository** (**AWR**) records the services' performance, including SQL execution time with the wait class and the resources consumed by the services. Starting with Oracle 10g R2, services can be effectively used with Database Resource Manager to prioritize application workload within the RAC database instances. Services are can also be used within the Oracle Scheduler.

Creating and managing services

A service can be created and managed using one of the following standard interfaces in an RAC environment:

- Database Configuration Assistant (in pre-Oracle 11g)
- Enterprise Manager
- Server Control Utility
- DBMS_SERVICE PL/SQL package

Although there are multiple options available to create and manage the services in the database, we will have a close look at `SRVCTL` and the `DBMS_SERVICE` PL/SQL package options in our subsequent sample demos.

As discussed earlier in this chapter, with Oracle 11g, the DBCA no longer supports the **Service Management option**. Therefore, the Oracle 11g DBCA cannot be used to create and manage the services and so you need to use one of the other three available methods.

Creating services with the SRVCTL utility

Apart from administering the Clusterware, ASM, and the RAC databases, the `SRVCTL` cluster utility can also be used to create and manage the services. The utility allows you to add, remove, modify, enable, disable, start, and stop the services in a RAC environment. Most of the operations done through the `SRVCTL` utility are stored in the OCR file.

For a complete list of `SRVCTL ADD SERVICE` supported parameters, use the `-h` option as demonstrated in the following example:

```
[oracle@raclinux1 ~]$ srvctl add service -h
Usage: srvctl add service -d <name> -s <service_name> -r "<preferred_list>" [-a "<available_list>"] [-P <TAF_policy>]
    -d <name>           Unique name for the database
    -s <service>        Service name
    -r "<pref_list>"    List of preferred instances
    -a "<avail_list>"   List of available instances
    -P <TAF_policy>     TAF policy (NONE, BASIC, or PRECONNECT)
Usage: srvctl add service -d <name> -s <service_name> -u {-r "<new_pref_inst>" | -a "<new_avail_inst>"}
    -d <name>           Unique name for the database
    -s <service>        Service name
    -u                  Add a new instance to service configuration
    -r <new_pref_inst>  Name of new preferred instance
    -a <new_avail_inst> Name of new available instance
    -h                  Print usage
```

SRVCTL ADD SERVICE syntax and options

The following syntax displays the complete usage of adding a service using `srvctl`:

```
] srvctl add service -d db_unique_name -s service_name
   -r  preferred_list [-a available_list] [-P TAF_policy
```

The following examples demonstrate how to create a service named RACDB_MAIN with preferred_instance as RACDB1 and available_instance as RACDB2 with the default TAF policy:

```
srvctl add service -d RACDB -s RACDB_MAIN -r RACDB1 -a RACDB2
```

When a RAC database consists of two or more instances, you can specify a set of instances in the preferred instances list or in the available instances list. An available instance doesn't initially support a service, it rather accepts connections when a preferred list of instances can't support the service; for example, when the instance or the node is no longer accessible. Once a service is defined, details for this service are recorded in the Oracle Cluster Register file. You can use the cluster command crs_stat to list the details and current status of the service as demonstrated in the following example:

```
[oracle@raclinux1 ~]$ ./crs_stat.sh
HA Resourrce                              Target     Stage
------------                              ------     -----
ora.RACDB.RACDB1.inst                     ONLINE     ONLINE on raclinux1
ora.RACDB.RACDB_MAIN.RACDB1.srv           OFFLINE    OFFLINE
ora.RACDB.RACDB_MAIN.cs                   OFFLINE    OFFLINE
```

As you can see in this output, the service Target and Stage appear OFFLINE because the newly created service will not start automatically; it must be started manually for the first time using the srvctl start service command.

The following command will attempt to start the RACDB_MAIN service of RACDB database across all its instances:

```
srvctl start service -d RACDB -s RACDB_MAIN
```

After startup, the service automatically registers with the associated listener and the status will become ONLINE:

```
[oracle@raclinux1 ~]$ ./crs_stat.sh
HA Resourrce                              Target     Stage
------------                              ------     -----
ora.RACDB.RACDB1.inst                     ONLINE     ONLINE on raclinux1
ora.RACDB.RACDB_MAIN.RACDB1.srv           ONLINE     ONLINE on raclinux1
ora.RACDB.RACDB_MAIN.cs                   ONLINE     ONLINE on raclinux1
```

The following listener status shows the service registration in the `LISTENER`:

`c:>lsnrctl status`

```
LSNRCTL for Linux: Version 11.1.0.6.0 - Production on 09-JUL-2009 14:41:38

Copyright (c) 1991, 2007, Oracle.  All rights reserved.

Connecting to (DESCRIPTION=(ADDRESS=(PROTOCOL=TCP)(HOST=raclinux1-vip.localdomain)(PORT=1522)(IP=FIRST)))
STATUS of the LISTENER
------------------------
Alias                     RACDB_RACLINUX1
Version                   TNSLSNR for Linux: Version 11.1.0.6.0 - Production
Start Date                09-JUL-2009 13:26:18
Uptime                    0 days 1 hr. 15 min. 20 sec
Trace Level               off
Security                  ON: Local OS Authentication
SNMP                      OFF
Listener Parameter File   /u01/app/oracle/product/11.1.0/db_1/network/admin/listener.ora
Listener Log File         /u01/app/oracle/diag/tnslsnr/raclinux1/racdb_raclinux1/alert/log.xml
Listening Endpoints Summary...
  (DESCRIPTION=(ADDRESS=(PROTOCOL=tcp)(HOST=192.168.2.111)(PORT=1522)))
  (DESCRIPTION=(ADDRESS=(PROTOCOL=tcp)(HOST=192.168.2.101)(PORT=1522)))
Services Summary...
Service "RACDB" has 1 instance(s).
  Instance "RACDB1", status READY, has 2 handler(s) for this service...
Service "RACDBXDB" has 1 instance(s).
  Instance "RACDB1", status READY, has 1 handler(s) for this service...
Service "RACDB_MAIN" has 1 instance(s).
  Instance "RACDB1", status READY, has 2 handler(s) for this service...
```

The following sample command is used to stop all the services that are part of RACDB database:

```
srvctl stop service -d RACDB
```

Using the following commands, a particular service can be started and stopped on a particular instance:

```
srvctl stop service -d RACDB -s RACDB_MAIN -i RACDB1
```

```
srvctl start service -d RACDB -s RACDB_MAIN -i RACDB1
```

Configuring a TNS entry with a service

The following **TNS** entry in the `$ORA_DB_HOME/network/admin/tnsnames.ora` file allows client connections to use the `RACDB_MAIN` service to connect to the RACDB database:

```
RACDB_MAIN =
  (DESCRIPTION =
    (ADDRESS_LIST =
      (ADDRESS = (PROTOCOL = TCP)(HOST = raclinux1-vip.localdomain)(PORT = 1522))
    )
    (CONNECT_DATA =
      (SERVICE_NAME = RACDB_MAIN)
    )
  )
```

The following sample SQL query displays information about session connection credentials:

```
sqlplus system/syssys@RACDB_MAIN
```

```
  1* select username,failover_type,failover_method,failed_over,service_name from v$session
where service_name = 'RACDB_MAIN'
SQL> /

USERNAME        FAILOVER_TYPE FAILOVER_M FAI SERVICE_NAME
--------------- ------------- ---------- --- --------------------
SYSTEM          NONE          NONE       NO  RACDB_MAIN
```

DBMS_SERVICE PL/SQL package

Another way of creating and managing the service in an RAC environment is by using the `DBMS_SERVICE` PL/SQL package. However, the negative aspect of this package is that it only allows you to manage the services on the local instance rather than on all instances of an RAC database. In other words, this method is more suitable for a single-instance environment than a RAC environment.

The following is the complete list of options available with the `DBMS_SERVICE` PL/SQL package, which may assist you to create the service in the instance:

```
DBMS_SERVICE.CREATE_SERVICE(
   service_name        IN VARCHAR2,
   network_name        IN VARCHAR2,
   goal                IN NUMBER DEFAULT NULL,
   dtp                 IN BOOLEAN DEFAULT NULL,
   aq_ha_notifications IN BOOLEAN DEFAULT NULL,
   failover_method     IN VARCHAR2 DEFAULT NULL,
   failover_type       IN VARCHAR2 DEFAULT NULL,
   failover_retries    IN NUMBER DEFAULT NULL,
   failover_delay      IN NUMBER DEFAULT NULL,
   clb_goal            IN NUMBER DEFAULT NULL);
```

The simplest way to create the RACDB_MAIN2 service is by using the DBMS_SERVICE PL/SQL package as follows:

```
SQL>  exec dbms_service.create_service(-
> service_name=>'RACDB_MAIN2',-
> network_name=>'RACDB_MAIN2');

PL/SQL procedure successfully completed.

SQL> select service_id,name,network_name,creation_date from dba_services;

SERVICE_ID NAME                           NETWORK_NAME         CREATION_
---------- ------------------------------ -------------------- ---------
         1 SYS$BACKGROUND                                      03-AUG-07
         2 SYS$USERS                                           03-AUG-07
         3 seeddataXDB                    seeddataXDB          03-AUG-07
         4 seeddata                       seeddata             03-AUG-07
         5 RACDBXDB                       RACDBXDB             24-JUN-09
         6 RACDB                          RACDB                24-JUN-09
         7 RACDB_MAIN                     RACDB_MAIN           09-JUL-09
         8 RACDB_MAIN2                    RACDB_MAIN2          10-JUL-09
```

Once a service is created, use the following commands to start, stop, or delete the service:

```
exec dbms_service.start_service('RACDB_MAIN2');
```

```
exec dbms_service.stop_service('RACDB_MAIN2');
```

```
exec dbms_service.delete_service('RACDB_MAIN2');
```

Although there are various methods available to add and manage the services, we advise you to use the SRVCTL utility instead of the DBMS_SERVICE package to manage services in a RAC environment. The advantage of using the SRVCTL utility over DBMS_SERVICE is that it gives you the flexibility to manage the service on all instances from any active node of the cluster. However, this is not possible with the DBMS_SERVICE PL/SQL package, as this package is not integrated with the Oracle Clusterware to define the preferred and available options. When you start a service using the DBMS_SERVICE package, the service is started on the node, although the status in the OCR will still be set to OFFLINE.

You can also manage and administer the services using GUI tools such as Database Control or Grid Control.

Database internal default services

There are two internal services named SYS$BACKGROUND and SYS$USER, which exist by default upon creating the database, and these services are always available on all instances. Both services support all workload management features and you cannot modify or disable these services; in other words, they are not controllable by DBAs.

- SYS$BACKGROUND is used by the background processes only
- SYS$USERS is the default service for all sessions that are not part of any application service

All defined and active services in an RAC database can be monitored using dba_services and gv$active_services views. The **Memory Monitor Lite** (**MMNL**) background process measures the average service time and service throughput, and these values can be viewed using the GV$SERVICEMETRIC and GV$SERVICEMETRIC_HISTORY global views.

Service performance views

You can query the following dynamic performance views, specific to the services, for call-time performance statistics:

Name	Description
V$SERVICE_EVENT	Displays aggregated wait counts and wait times for all services, each wait statistic.
V$SERVICE_WAIT_CLASS	Displays aggregated wait count and wait time for all services, each wait class.
V$SERVICEMETRIC	Displays the information about services' values measured on the most recent time interval period in the database.
V$SERVICEMETRIC_HISTORY	Displays recent history of the metric values measured in predefined time interval for the services executing in the database.

Services' characteristics

Typically, when a node restarts, all the cluster components and its services such as database, instance, services, ASM Instance, LISTENERS, and node applications (gsd, ons, vip), and so on will start automatically.

When an Oracle 10g RAC database or an instance is stopped using `SRVCTL` or using the SQL `shutdown` command, associated services are left `OFFLINE` in the cluster. Upon a subsequent database or instance startup, the associated services do not start automatically. Thus, services must be started manually using the `srvctl start service` command, which can be a problem when dealing with multiple services on multiple databases.

A workaround for this problem is to write a small Perl script, FAN callout, and place it under the `$ORA_CRS_HOME/racg/usrco` directory. Cluster callouts are small scripts or programs that will run whenever cluster events, such as an instance start or instance stop, occur.

A script **Start Service on Instance up** has been written by the Oracle Cluster team to resolve this issue, which can be found at `http://www.oracle.com/technology/sample_code/products/rac/index.html`.

The ZIP file contains a couple of Perl scripts—`startMatchedSRVonUp.pl` and `startSRVonUp.pl`.

As we mentioned earlier, you need to place a copy of these scripts under the `$ORA_CRS_HOME/racg/usrco` location. Ensure you set the permission to these files to 710. You also need to edit these scripts to change the `CRS_HOME` and `ORACLE_HOME` parameters to match those suitable to your environment and then to copy these files across all nodes of your RAC cluster. You may refer to the logfile named `SRV_co.log` created under the `/tmp` location.

What's new in Oracle 11g services' behavior?

In contrast to previous Oracle releases, Oracle 11g has slightly enhanced its service behavior when a RAC database or an instance is stopped using either `SRVCTL` or the SQL shutdown command. In a similar situation, when the services are started on some remote nodes, the instance startup on the local node will autostart the service on it.

Now, let's have a closer look at the following cluster prime features:

- **Scalability (Load Balancing)**
- **High Availability (Failover)**

Scalability (Load Balancing)

The Oracle Load Balancing feature provides the facility to scale the application workload across available instances of an RAC database. It supports two types of load balancing features—Client Side Connect Time Load Balance and Server Side Listener Connection Load Balance.

Client Side Connect Time Load Balance

The **Client Side Connect Time Load Balance** feature is enabled by specifying the `LOAD_BALANCE=YES|ON|TRUE` clause, in the connection configuration file (`tnsnames.ora`), within the `ADDRESS_LIST` parameter. It enables clients to randomize connection requests across all available listeners. When `LOAD_BALANCE` is set to `OFF`, the addresses are tried sequentially until one succeeds.

Configuring Client Side Connect Time Load Balancing

The following is an example of a simple TNS connection with the Load Balancing feature enabled:

```
RACDB =
(DESCRIPTION =
(LOAD_BALANCE = yes)
(ADDRESS = (PROTOCOL = TCP)(HOST = raclinux1-vip.localdomain)
(PORT = 1522))
(ADDRESS = (PROTOCOL = TCP)(HOST = raclinux2-vip.localdomain)
(PORT = 1522))
(CONNECT_DATA =
(SERVICE_NAME = RACDB_MAIN)))
```

An Example of a `jdbc` connection string using the load balancing feature can be seen here:

```
url="jdbc:oracle:thin:@(DESCRIPTION=(LOAD_BALANCE=on)
(ADDRESS=(PROTOCOL=TCP)(HOST=raclinux1-vip.localdomain)(PORT=1522))
(ADDRESS=(PROTOCOL=TCP)(HOST=raclinux2-vip.localdomain)(PORT=1522))
 (CONNECT_DATA=(SERVICE_NAME=RACDB_MAIN)))"
```

The flip side of this feature is that regardless of the current load on the database instances, it always allows clients to randomize the user connection across available database instances. This scenario may lead to an unbalanced user connection situation across instances, where a single instance may have many user connections and other instances may have a lesser user connection load.

Server Side Listener Connection Load Balance

The **Server Side Listener Connection Load Balance** feature allows the listener to route the incoming user connections to the least-loaded node and then to the least loaded instance using the information from the Load Balance Advisory. This feature balances the number of active connections among multiple instances, which improves the connection performance. To enable this feature, the `remote_listener` parameter must be configured in the RAC instances.

In a dedicated server configuration, the listener selects an instance in the following manner:

- Least Loaded Node
- Least Loaded Instance

In a shared server configuration, the listener selects a dispatcher in the following manner:

- Least Loaded Node
- Least Loaded Instance
- Least Loaded dispatcher for the listener

In Oracle 11g R2, when the server-side load balancing is set, it is the SCAN listener that uses the load balancing advisory and directs a connection to the best instance currently providing the service.

Configuring Server Side Listener Connection Load Balancing

While configuring the **Server Side Listener Connection Load Balancing** feature, the following TNS entry must exist in all instances in the `$ORA_DB_HOME/network/admin/tnsnames.ora` file:

```
LISTENER_RACDB = (DESCRIPTION =
(ADDRESS = (PROTOCOL = TCP)(HOST = raclinux1-vip.localdomain)
(PORT = 1522))
(ADDRESS = (PROTOCOL = TCP)(HOST = raclinux2-vip.localdomain)
(PORT = 1522))
(CONNECT_DATA =
(SERVICE_NAME = RACDB_MAIN)))
```

Once the TNS name is configured on all instances, we will need to set the `remote_listener` parameter value equal to the TNS name as follows:

```
    alter system set remote_listener='LISTENERS_RACDB'
scope=both sid='*';
```

Make sure the values are correctly set in this parameter; otherwise the subsequent instance startup will fail, resolving the name defined with this parameter.

Transparent Application Failover

When a RAC database instance crashes due to a technical or non-technical reason and the **Transparent Application Failover TAF** policy is set, the TAF policy will re-establish lost user connections to any of the surviving RAC database instances.

In the event of TAF being configured, active transactions are rolled back and the client connection re-establishes to another surviving node, allowing the user to continue their work with minimal interruption.

As of now, the TAF policy supports two types of failover methods—`BASIC` and `PRECONNECT`. The `BASIC` method configuration re-establishes the connection at failover time. With the `PRECONNECT` method configuration, a shadow connection will be created on another available instance anticipating the failover. It also supports two failover types—**SESSION** and **SELECT**.

The SESSION configuration re-establishes the lost connection and all previously running queries will be cancelled. When SELECT is configured, in addition to re-establishing the lost user connection on a surviving instance, it also replays the queries that were in progress. In any failover type configuration, the uncommitted transactions will be rolled back.

The TAF can be used only with applications and interfaces that have OCI support. The TAF policy doesn't go well with JDBC connections. To configure TAF with JDBC connections, you need to implement **Fast Connection Fallover (FCF)**.

Configuring Transparent Application Failover

The TAF policy can be configured either in the client-side TNS connection entry, defining the `FAILOVER_MODE` parameter within the `CONNECT_DATA` section, or at the server-side service attributes. When both methods are defined, the server-side service attributes take precedence. A simple client-side TAF TNS connection entry is as follows:

```
RACDB_TAF =
(DESCRIPTION =
(ADDRESS_LIST =
(LOAD_BALANCE = YES)
(FAILOVER = ON)
(ADDRESS = (PROTOCOL = TCP)(HOST = raclinux1-vip.lcoaldomain)
(PORT = 1522))
(ADDRESS = (PROTOCOL = TCP)(HOST = raclinux2-vip.localdomain)
(PORT = 1522))
 )
  (CONNECT_DATA =
    (SERVICE_NAME = RACDB_MAIN)
    (failover_mode=(type=select)(method=basic)(retries=5)(delay= 15)
     ))
```

FAILOVER_MODE parameters

The following table describes the parameters that are associated with the `FAILOVER_MODE`:

Parameter	Values	Description
TYPE	Session	When a user connection is lost due to an instance crash, a new session is automatically established on a surviving instance. This type of failover does not support replay of the queries that were in progress.
	Select	Re-establishes the lost user connection on a surviving instance, and replays the queries that were in progress.
	None	Is the default mode without failover functionality.
METHOD	Basic	Re-establishes the lost user connections at failover time. Doesn't require much work on the backup server until failover time.
	Preconnect	Pre-establishes the connection on another instance to provide rapid failover facility.
DELAY		Specifies the amount of time (in seconds) to wait between connect attempts.
RETRIES		Specifies the number of re-attempts to connect after a failover.

Once the TAF policies are set and connections are established in the instance using these policies, you can obtain the TAF policy details of the connections querying the `v$session` view in the database using the following SQL statement:

```
SELECT  machine,failover_type,failover_method,failed_over
FROM v$session
```

Before implementing the TAF policies, make sure the `remote_listener` parameter is set to an appropriate TNS name for all instances in the RAC database.

Fast Connection Failover

Starting with Oracle 10g, the TAF policy for JDBC thin and JDBC OCI drivers is supported by setting up a new **Fast Connection Failover** (**FCF**) feature. However, you need to modify the application code in order to implement this functionality; in other words, the TAF isn't truly transparent with JDBC connections. The prime advantage of setting FCF is that a SQL exception is thrown instantly to the application's code once **Oracle Notification Server (ONS)** detects an RAC database instance failure. The application should then catch the error such as **17008, Closed Connection** along with other related errors, call the connection `close()` method, and release the connection back to cache.

Configuring Fast Connection Failover

In order to enable the FCF feature for the JDBC connection failover, you should do the following:

- Create a service name
- Configure ONS for FCF
- In the application code, define the `FastConnectionFailoverEnabled` property before calling the first `getConnection` request
- Use the service name instead of Instance SID while setting the `OracleDataSource url` property

Configuring Fast Connection Failover in the client environment

The FCF can also be configured on the client side. In such cases, make sure you are using a JDBC driver of version equal to or greater than the Oracle 10.2.0.3 JDBC drivers. You also need to copy the `ons.jar` file, which can be obtained from the database server under the `$ORACLE_HOME/opmn/lib` location. Set the `ons.jar` and `ojdbc14.jar` files in your classpath.

For the complete usage of FCF and ONS configuration, you can refer to Oracle documentation at `http://download.oracle.com/docs/cd/E11882_01/server.112/e17120/restart002.htm#ADMIN13193`.

Summary

In this chapter, we discussed the key aspects of RAC database configuration, creation, and options to manage an Oracle RAC database such as using the Server Cluster Utility (`SRVCTL`) and `sqlplus` commands. We then looked at Automatic Workload Management, which provides High Availability and Scalability solutions to your application while working in an RAC environment.

By the end of this chapter, you should understand how to configure and manage the RAC database in your environment and be able to use the RAC features such as distributing the workload across all instances in the RAC database and re-routing lost connections to surviving instances. In the next chapter, we are going to deal with backup and recovery scenarios for different types of database and cluster components such as OCR and Voting Disk.

7
Backup and Recovery

Data and its continuous availability indeed play a vital role in building up an organization's reputation and helps in its growth. Therefore, protecting the precious data against any type of data loss is one of the critical responsibilities of a database administrator.

Unfortunately, some people believe that Oracle RAC not only provides high availability, but also guards against media failures. Perhaps, it is important to understand the individual roles played by Oracle RAC and Oracle Recovery Manager (RMAN) utilities. Although Oracle RAC provides defense against an instance or node failure, it cannot be used to guard against data loss events. However, the Oracle RMAN utility supports numerous backup and recovery solutions to protect the database.

In this chapter, we are going to help you understand the importance and role of Oracle RMAN. At the same time, we will describe and demonstrate the best backup and recovery solutions and strategies for a RAC environment. The following topics will be discussed:

- An overview of backup and recovery
- An overview of Recovery Manager (RMAN)
- Backup types and methods
- RMAN new features in 11g R1 and 11g R2
- RMAN best practices for RAC
- OCR and Voting disk backup and recovery strategies

An overview of backup and recovery

A backup is a method adopted by an organization to copy its business-critical data to a particular location (disk or tape), guarding it against any natural or unanticipated data failure events. These backup copies could be used later to recover the data after any data loss event. There are various options and technologies available across different vendors to fulfill these requirements.

A data loss or corruption event could occur in a number of ways:

- Data being deleted
- Hardware failure
- Server crashing

Recovery is a process to repair data loss events using the pre-existing copies of the data.

An overview of Recovery Manager (RMAN)

Recovery Manager (RMAN) is an Oracle database command-line utility that was first commercially introduced with Oracle version 8 to assist DBAs in performing different types of Oracle database physical backups (online or offline) and several recovery operations effectively. This utility is installed by default with the Oracle software and comes with no extra cost. RMAN is initiated by executing the `./rman` path, executable from the `$ORACLE_HOME/bin` location. You can also call the GUI interface RMAN in Enterprise Manager (EM) or Database Grid Control. RMAN can be used in interactive and non-interactive mode.

The following example demonstrates how to connect to the database using the RMAN utility as sysdba (super user):

```
[oracle@raclinux1 bin]$ ./rman target /

Recovery Manager: Release 11.2.0.1.0 - Production on Wed Dec 1 06:40:38 2010

Copyright (c) 1982, 2009, Oracle and/or its affiliates.  All rights reserved.

connected to target database: RACDB (DBID=730923912)

RMAN>
```

Execute the following command at the RMAN prompt to list the default RMAN configuration settings:

```
RMAN> show all;


using target database control file instead of recovery catalog
RMAN configuration parameters for database with db_unique_name RVCATDB
are:
CONFIGURE RETENTION POLICY TO REDUNDANCY 1; # default
CONFIGURE BACKUP OPTIMIZATION OFF; # default
CONFIGURE DEFAULT DEVICE TYPE TO DISK; # default
CONFIGURE CONTROLFILE AUTOBACKUP OFF; # default
CONFIGURE CONTROLFILE AUTOBACKUP FORMAT FOR DEVICE TYPE DISK TO '%F'; #
default
CONFIGURE DEVICE TYPE DISK PARALLELISM 1 BACKUP TYPE TO BACKUPSET; #
default
CONFIGURE DATAFILE BACKUP COPIES FOR DEVICE TYPE DISK TO 1; # default
CONFIGURE ARCHIVELOG BACKUP COPIES FOR DEVICE TYPE DISK TO 1; # default
CONFIGURE MAXSETSIZE TO UNLIMITED; # default
CONFIGURE ENCRYPTION FOR DATABASE OFF; # default
CONFIGURE ENCRYPTION ALGORITHM 'AES128'; # default
CONFIGURE COMPRESSION ALGORITHM 'BASIC' AS OF RELEASE 'DEFAULT' OPTIMIZE
FOR LOAD TRUE ; # default
CONFIGURE ARCHIVELOG DELETION POLICY TO BACKED UP 2 TIMES TO DISK;
```

RMAN functionality has been significantly strengthened in Oracle releases (9i, 10g, and 11g) to support various backup and recovery operations since its introduction. RMAN supports a wide range of backup and recovery operations, such as individual or multiple datafiles, single or multiple tablespaces, an entire database, and much more. Whenever a backup and recovery operation has been performed, it keeps the details (history) in the controlfile for 7 days by default.

In order to maintain more than 7 days of backup and recovery operation historical information, you need to modify the `control_file_record_keep_time` parameter from the default value to a desired value (specified in days). Additionally, you can also configure a recovery catalog that will allow you to store the information much longer.

The following are a few advantages of RMAN:

- RMAN can be used to back up the database physically either in `OFFLINE` or `ONLINE` mode.
- RMAN supports different `INCREMENTAL` levels, `COMPRESSION`, or Encrypted type backups.
- RMAN provides the ability to back up the database and archive logs with a single command and can be configured to delete archive logs after they are backed up.
- When RMAN is used to back up the database, you do not need to remember details such as location and name for the database-related files. RMAN uses the controlfile to retrieve such information during the backup.
- RMAN is the only option available to back up and restore the database related files when they are configured on ASM storage.
- RMAN is required to convert non-ASM databases to ASM.
- RMAN has the ability to perform different levels of recovery operations, such as datafile, block, tablespace, point-in-time, incomplete, and complete recovery.
- RMAN effectively supports the backup and recovery of both non-RAC and RAC databases.
- RMAN provides an option to back up either to disk or tape.
- RMAN provides the ability to identify and recover corrupted data blocks.
- RMAN provides one of the easiest ways to duplicate a database for standby or cloning operations.
- RMAN provides the ability to check the corrupted blocks and missing files from the existing backup and determine where the backup can be restored.

RMAN architecture

The following diagram illustrates the architecture when RMAN connects to the target database and optionally to a recovery catalog. This diagram also represents the fact that you can back up the database either to disk or to a tape. However, if you are using a third-party vendor backup solution, the tape backups are accomplished in association with a third-party vendor **Media Manager Layer** (**MML**).

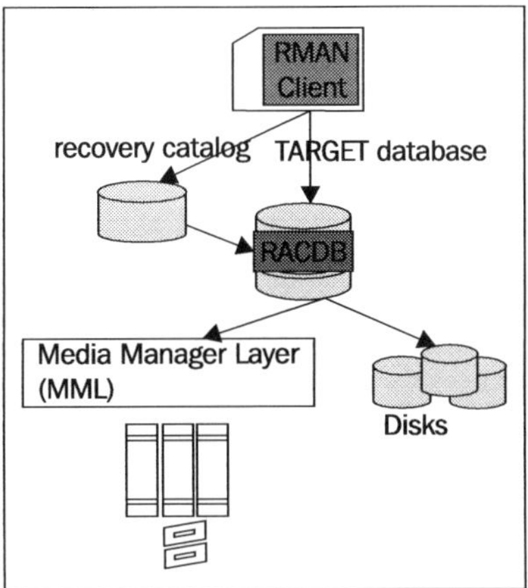

RMAN performance tuning tips

The following guidelines are helpful to improve the performance of RMAN for backup and recovery operations:

- Turn on the BACKUP OPTIMIZATION settings in the RMAN configuration by using the following example:

  ```
  RMAN> CONFIGURE BACKUP OPTIMIZATION ON;

  new RMAN configuration parameters:
  CONFIGURE BACKUP OPTIMIZATION ON;
  new RMAN configuration parameters are successfully stored
  ```

- Use multiple RMAN channels to improve the backup and recovery durations.
- Consider using I/O slaves, setting the `DBWR_IO_SLAVE` parameters to a non zero value, if your OS doesn't support asynchronous I/O.
- When backing up to tape, set the appropriate value for the `LARGE_POOL_SIZE` initialization parameter, as RMAN uses this memory area. The following Oracle recommended formula should also be used to set the value:

  ```
  LARGE_POOL_SIZE =  number_of_allocated_channels *
                      (16 MB + ( 4 *  size_of_tape_buffer ) )
  ```

- Tuning the `ioo -o maxpgahead` and `wmo -o minfree` parameters on the AIX 5L operating system enables around 15% performance improvement in RMAN.

- You may also consider using RMAN's **Block Change Tracking** (**BCT**) feature to ensure your incremental backups are faster.
- While backing up to tape, adjust the tape I/O buffer and configure `PARMS` and `BLKSIZE` parameters.

Backup types and methods

Oracle Enterprise Server supports a wide range of backup solutions. This section will focus on and illustrate those methods. Oracle backup solutions are mainly categorized into two types:

- Logical backup
- Physical backup

Logical backup

A Logical backup is initiated by either running the traditional export (`exp`) or data pump (`expdp`) utilities from the `$ORACLE_HOME/bin` location. The restoral of these backups is initiated by either running the traditional import (`imp`) or data pump (`impdb`) utilities. These utilities are typically used to move database structures and data between Oracle databases, between different Oracle versions, and between databases running across operating systems. The following are the usage and benefits of Logical backup:

- A Logical backup is the process for unloading the data into a binary file (dump file) from the database using a set of SQL statements.
- Using Logical backup, you can perform object-level, schema-level, tablespace-level, or entire database-level backups.
- The dump file is later used by the import utility for restoring the data to an Oracle database.
- The dump file is compatible with different Oracle versions and portable across different operating systems.
- Logical backup (export and import) is one of the methods used for database upgrades from a lower version to a higher version or for database migrations over different operating systems.
- Backup and restoration must be performed while the database is online.

Physical backup

A Physical backup involves backing up the database's physical structure that includes datafiles, controlfiles, archive logs, and so on. RMAN lets you put these backup copies either on disk or on tape. You can back up the databases as per your organizational backup policies, either in `ONLINE` or `OFFLINE` mode with RMAN.

ONLINE RMAN backups

An `ONLINE` RMAN physical database backup is performed when the database is `OPEN` and available to the end users. This type of backup is best suited for the databases whose availability is critical. As a general rule, the database must be configured in `ARCHIVELOG` mode to perform online physical backups. The following are the characteristics of `ONLINE` backups performed via the RMAN utility, though are not limited to what has been outlined here:

- The database is available while the backup is being performed.
- The user does not need to explicitly put the tablespace or database into backup mode while performing the backup.
- Backups can be performed at different levels in the database, an individual data file, a single tablespace, or the full database or just archived logs.

OFFLINE RMAN backups

An `OFFLINE` RMAN physical database backup is performed on those databases that can afford the database downtime or that operate in no archivelog mode. To perform an `OFFLINE` backup, the database must first be shut down with either `NORMAL` or `IMMEDIATE` option. You will then need to start up the database in `MOUNT` state subsequently. However, during the course of an `OFFLINE` backup, the database will not be available for the users. In other words, this type of backup is best suited to those databases whose data is not modified frequently, where downtime is acceptable. This type of backup is not acceptable for databases that are required to be available all the time.

RMAN new features in 11g R1 and 11g R2

Although there have been quite a large number of new features and significant enhancements incorporated in RMAN 11g R1 and 11g R2, this section primarily focuses on the core new features and enhancements of RMAN that are valuable to apply into your respective databases. These are:

- Database Recovery Advisor
- Multisection backups for very large datafiles

- Undo tablespace optimization
- Faster backup compression
- Active database duplication
- Archivelog deletion policy enhancements
- Automatic Block Recovery
- Tablespace point-in-time recovery enhancements

Database Recovery Advisor

The **Database Recovery Advisor** (**DRA**) is a new database built-in tool in 11g R1. The DRA enables DBAs to automatically detect, analyze, and diagnose potential data block corruptions or data failures due to a lost or inaccessible data file. This helps reduce the mean time to recover a database.

Whenever a data error or a failure is detected in the database, the DRA recommends an automatic repair option, such as repairing an individual data block or restoring and recovering a data file. Therefore, you can either repair the error manually or allow the DRA to automatically diagnose and repair the failure for you. The DRA can be accessed in multiple ways, through the RMAN command-line or through Database Grid Control or **Enterprise Manager** (EM).

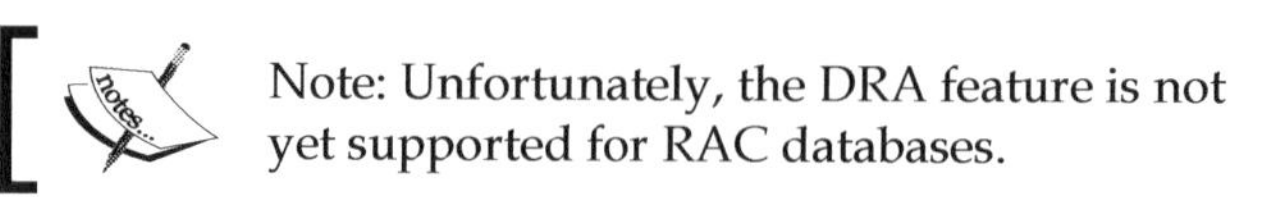

Note: Unfortunately, the DRA feature is not yet supported for RAC databases.

Multisection backups for very large datafiles

Typically, when you issue a backup command in RMAN to back up an entire database, or datafile in the database, RMAN considers the overall size of the input files and the number of allocated channels. These are deciding factors as to whether to put them in a single backup set or multiple back up sets. However, until 11g R1, there was no option available in RMAN to backup a large datafile in parallel. With the Multisection backup feature in 11g R1, you can now back up a large sized datafiles in parallel to improve the backup duration and split the file size into multiple backup sets with uniform sizes. For example, if datafile one in the database is currently 1GB in size, you can use the following to backup the datafile into multiple sections/pieces, limiting the size of each backup piece to 250 MB:

```
RMAN> BACKUP SECTION SIZE 250M DATAFILE 1;
```

The `SECTION SIZE` clause with the backup command in the RMAN, splits the datafile size to 250MB backup pieces and uses multiple channels, if configured.

Note: RMAN does not use the Multisection backup feature if the `SECTION SIZE` specified is above the actual datafile size.

Undo tablespace backup optimization

With the undo tablespace backup optimization feature, whenever a backup is executed, RMAN will exclude the `UNDO` tablespace information that is not required for recovery operations. In general, when a transaction is triggered either by the `UPDATE` or `DELETE` statement committed in the database, the changes are reflected in its associated tablespace accordingly and the before (old) image copy (data block) of the changed data block is stored in the `UNDO` tablespace. With the undo tablespace backup optimization feature, the subsequent RMAN backup operations bypass the undo information of the committed transactions in the `UNDO` tablespace, as this information is no longer required for the recovery operations. Therefore, bypassing the `UNDO` information that is no longer required would not only significantly reduce the `UNDO` tablespace backup size, but also reduce the time required for the recovery operations. You must set the `COMPATIBLE` initialization parameter to 11.0 or higher to enable the undo optimization feature.

Faster backup compression

As part of the Oracle Advanced Compression Option (ACO) option, RMAN now offers a new ZLIB algorithm for faster binary compression backups in addition to the previously existing BZIP2 (default) algorithm. The ZLIB compression algorithm uses less CPU resources in comparison to the previous algorithm. On the flipside, ZLIB algorithm produces larger files. You can switch between the default and non-default algorithms, using `CONFIGURE COMPRESSION ALGORITHM TO BZIP2/ZLIB` in the RMAN settings. However, this feature is part of the **Advanced Compression Option** (**ACO**) and usually comes with an additional licensing cost. To enable this feature, the `COMPATIBLE` initialization parameter must be set to 11.0 or higher.

In RMAN 11g R2, the ACO offers more compression levels: `LOW`, `MEDIUM`, `HIGH`, in addition to the existing compression options to achieve a greater compression ratio and better speed. The `MEDIUM` compression level provides a good combination of compression ratio and speed and is the most suitable compression level in many environments. To enable the `MEDIUM` compression level, connect to RMAN and issue the following command:

```
RMAN> CONFIGURE COMPRESSION ALGORITHM 'MEDIUM';
```

Note: We strongly advise you to test the various compression options and levels before you implement them to your production databases.

Active database duplication

It is common practice in many organizations to duplicate the database for various business and application needs. For example, to test a new application feature, the development team might request that the DBA clones the production database. To protect a business-critical database, you need to clone the production database in order to configure a standby database. Oracle provides a method to clone databases easily from RMAN. One of the easiest ways to duplicate (clone) or configure a physical standby database for the production database is to use the `DUPLICATE DATABASE` command in the RMAN.

Pre-11g, in order to execute the command, you must ensure that you have a pre-existing and valid database backup. The following section will explain the basic procedure that is involved in duplicating (cloning) an active database.

In 11g R1, RMAN now supports active database duplication in addition to the backup-based duplication procedure. When the following new active duplicate database command is run through the RMAN command prompt, it copies all required datafiles, SPfiles, and archived logs over the network to the destination host before it duplicates the databases. The following example illustrates how to use this new feature:

```
RMAN> DUPLICATE TARGET DATABASE
            TO dupracdb
        FROM ACTIVE DATABASE
        SPFILE
            NOFILENAMECHECK;
```

This example assumes that you are duplicating the active database on to a new host where the datafile location remains the same across the source and target servers. When the example is run, RMAN performs the below outlined procedure:

1. RMAN copies the SPfile (initialization parameter) to the destination server.
2. RMAN copies the required datafiles and archived logs over the network to the destination server.
3. RMAN performs the media recovery, if required.
4. RMAN opens the database with the `RESETLOGS` option.

Note: If you are executing the DUPLICATE command on 11g R1, you must connect to the active database, auxiliary instance, and also connect to the recovery catalog.

Active database duplication enhancements

In 11g R2, RMAN leverages the active database duplication functionality further by eliminating the need to connect to the target database and recovery catalog. With this key enhancement, the user no longer needs to connect to the source database and doesn't have to worry about not having the recovery catalog to use the active database duplication feature. The only additional requirement for this feature is to specify the location for the valid backup for this database. The following command should be used in RMAN when connected to the auxiliary instance. However, there is no need to connect the target (source) database and recovery catalog:

```
RMAN> DUPLICATE DATABASE to dupracdb
--UNTIL TIME "TO_DATE('specify the date and required timehere')"
--UNTIL TIME "TO_DATE('01-MAR-2011','DD/MON/YYYY')"
SPFILE
BACKUP LOCATION 'existing backup location'
NOFILENAMECHECK;
```

The above example is used to duplicate a database without actually connecting to the target (source) database and recovery catalog. It assumes that the path for the database files on the target and remote host are the same.

The following diagram illustrates the mechanism used for the active database duplication without connecting to the target (source) database and recovery catalog:

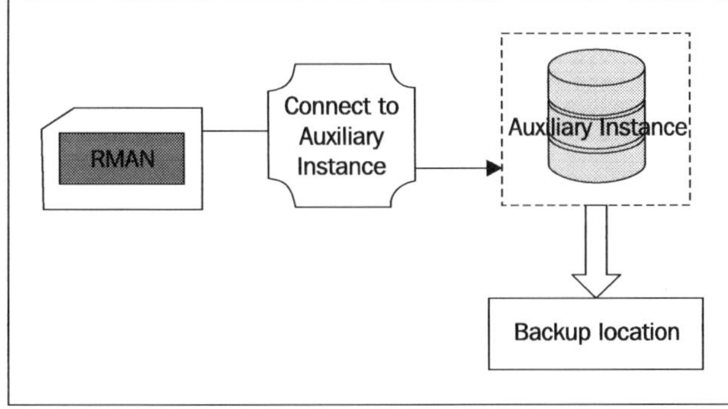

Archivelog deletion policy enhancements

The database archive logs play a very important role during the course of a complete or incomplete database recovery. Therefore, you need to be very vigilant before you delete them. For instance, assuming that there is a standby database in place, you will need to make sure the required archive logs from the primary databases are not deleted from the disk before they are shipped to the standby destination and are applied to the standby database.

In context, you can define a deletion policy for archived logs to become eligible for the delete operation once they are applied to the necessary standby database(s), or when they are successfully backed up. To configure the deletion policy, you need to execute the following command in the RMAN settings. The policy applies to the flash recovery and also the archivelog destinations:

```
RMAN> CONFIGURE ARCHIVELOG DELETION POLICY TO BACKED UP 2 TIMES TO DISK;
```

Up on successfully executing the command, you are like to see the following message at the RMAN prompt:

```
using target database control file instead of recovery catalog
new RMAN configuration parameters:
CONFIGURE ARCHIVELOG DELETION POLICY TO BACKED UP 2 TIMES TO DISK;
new RMAN configuration parameters are successfully stored
```

The above policy makes the archive logs eligible for deletion once they are backed up twice to the disk.

The following policy makes archive logs eligible for deletion once they are applied to the standby database.

```
RMAN> CONFIGURE ARCHIVELOG DELETION POLICY
          TO APPLIED ON STANDBY;
```

Automatic Block Recovery (ABR)

In general, when data blocks become physically or logically corrupted, user queries via SQLPLUS that touch the bad blocks will encounter `ORA-01578` and `ORA-01110` errors. When the corrupted blocks are reported via the SQL queries, RMAN, DBV, or ANALYZE utilities, the corrupted block details are automatically listed in the `V$DATABASE_BLOCK_CORRUPTON` view.

For databases configured with Oracle Data Guard: primary and standby databases, the Block Recovery mechanism has been strengthened and simplified in previous Oracle releases. In 11g R2, when an SQL query encounters corrupted blocks in a primary database, ABR will automatically repair the blocks by copying good data blocks from the physical standby database, if available. This operation is transparent to the user. The query result will be displayed to the user instead of throwing an `ORA-01578` error. During the course of this internal operation, the user will experience a pause before the query result is displayed. In the event that a good copy of the corrupted blocks is not available from a physical standby database, the standard error is raised as normal.

Tablespace point-in-time recovery enhancements

The purpose of the Tablespace point-in-time recovery (TSPITR) operation in RMAN is to recover one or more user-managed tablespaces in the database effectively without affecting the rest of the tablespaces' ongoing operations in the database. One of the constraints pre-11g R2 was that this method could not be used to recover a dropped tablespace. Fortunately, with 11g R2, you can use the TSPITR feature to recover a dropped tablespace to the point in time before the tablespace was dropped. The procedure to recover a tablespace to a point in time remains the same.

RMAN best practices for RAC

Managing backup and recovery for RAC databases is no different from managing those for single-instance databases. You do not need to expend additional efforts to work with RAC databases. The prime goal of this section is to discuss the essential configuration settings that are required for RAC databases. The following will be covered in detail:

- Configuring the Flash Recovery Area for a RAC database
- Instance recovery versus Crash recovery in RAC
- Configuring multiple channels
- Parallelism for backup and recovery in RAC
- Backing up a RAC database via RMAN

Configuring the Flash Recovery Area for a RAC database

The significant architectural dissimilarity between a single-instance and an RAC database is that multiple instances access a single database with RAC, in contrast to one instance per database configuration in a single-instance database.

Each instance of a RAC database has its own set of redo groups, which generate archive logs, and an UNDO tablespace. Although each instance has its own set of redo groups and generates archive logs, other instances of the RAC database must have READ access to those redo and archive logs as they are essential during instance or media recovery operations. Considering the above fact, Oracle strongly advises that you configure the Flash Recovery Area (FRA) on an ASM, Cluster File System (CFS), or Network File System (NFS) mount point with local instance read-write permission and remote instance READ access. The FRA is set by the `DB_RECOVERY_FILE_DEST` initialization parameter. The FRA can then be used as the centralized location for all backup and recovery-related files such as, backupsets, archived logs, online redoe multiplexing copies, flashback logs, and so on. You will need to ensure the parameter is configured to the same value across all the instances and the database is operating in archive log mode. Connect to the local instance via SQLPLUS as SYSDBA privilege and use the following example to set the FRA:

```
SQL> ALTER DATABASE SET DB_RECOVERY_FILE_DEST_SIZE=10G scope=both;


SQL> ALTER DATABASE SET DB_RECOVERY_FILE_DEST = 'DG_FRA' scope=both;
```

The first command sets the upper size limit for the recovery area and the second command configures the `DG_FRA` diskgroup as the location for FRA.

The following diagram illustrates a RAC database named RACDB with multiple instances. RACDB1 and RACDB2 share a centralized Flash Recovery Area and the FRA could be configured on ASM diskgroup, Network File System, or Cluster File System.

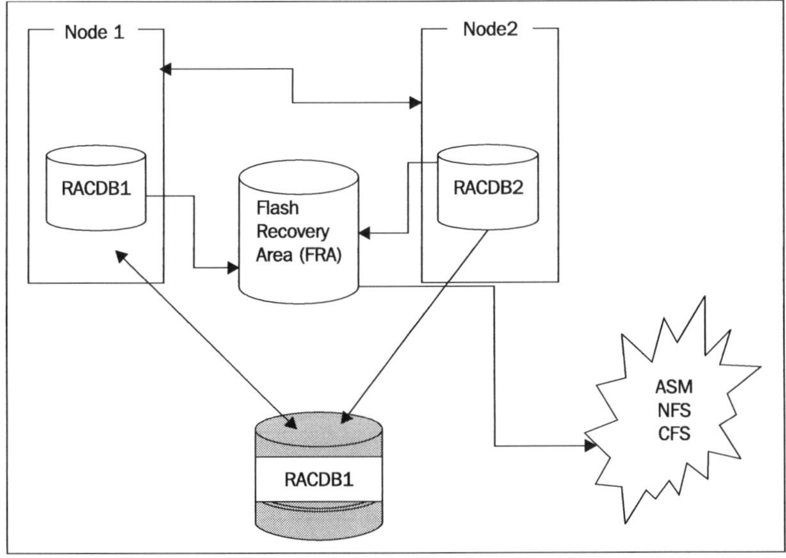

Instance recovery versus Crash recovery in RAC

Fundamentally, an Instance recovery operation is managed by Oracle automatically whenever an instance subsequently starts up after it has terminated or crashed. There are several scenarios that would cause an instance to go down abruptly (crash). For example, when a DBA issues the `SHUTDOWN ABORT` command, when the server where the instance is running has failed due to hardware or software problems, or power failures in the data center. Oracle does not require DBA intervention to perform the instance recovery as it will be performed by Oracle automatically using the roll back (transaction recovery) and roll forward (cache recovery) phases of the recovery procedure. Although the instance recovery procedure is the same in both single-instance and RAC databases, there is a notable difference as to which instance would perform the instance recovery in the RAC database, when multiple instances exist.

As mentioned before, in a RAC environment, two or more instances access a single database. Each instance contains its own set of redo groups that are identified by a redo thread number. As explained previously, you will need to ensure that you either configure the path for the redo and archive logs in a shared location, or where the local instance has read-write permissions and the other remote instances have read permission.

When an instance failure is detected by the surviving instance(s) in a RAC database, the surviving instance(s) take the responsibility to perform the instance recovery for the crashed instance using the redo information (online redo logs) generated by the crashed instance. It is the SMON background process of the instance that performs the recovery operations by reading the online redo logs. This behavior is called instance recovery in RAC.

In the event that all the instances belonging to a RAC database fail, the Oracle database will perform a crash recovery on behalf of all the failed instances when the database is restarted. This behavior is called crash recovery in RAC.

You can estimate the recovery duration for the instance/crash recovery by querying the useful `TARGET_MTTR`, `ESTIMATED_MTTR` columns in the `V$INSTANCE_RECOVERY` dynamic view. However, during the course of instance recovery operations, the following steps will need to be completed by Oracle before it brings up the database in normal conditions:

1. The Global Enqueue Services remasters enqueue resources in the first phase.
2. The Global Enqueue Services remasters cache resources only for those caches that lost their masters.
3. The surviving node of a RAC database places the instance recovery enqueue after enqueues that are reconfigured. SMON determines the list of data blocks that require recovery at the same time as the cache resources are remastered.
4. Almost 50 percent of the default buffer cache memory area is allocated for the recovery cache and the data blocks identified in the earlier step are claimed as recovery resources.
5. At this point, the data blocks that are not part of the recovery operations can be accessed and the system is partially available now.
6. The SMON background process then performs recovery on data blocks identified previously and releases the locks immediately to make them available.
7. The system will be fully available after all the data blocks have been recovered.

We have simulated a crash recovery scenario to demonstrate the action that Oracle takes to manage and complete the recovery operations. In our simulation, we terminate the mandatory PMON background process with an OS-level kill `-9 <ospidforPMON> command>`. We strongly recommend you not to simulate the same with your production databases of all instances of the RACDB database. The following is a walkthrough of an `alert_RACDB1.log` file of the first instance of a RACDB database:

```
RBAL (ospid: 4693): terminating the instance due to error 472
System state dump is made for local instance
System State dumped to trace file /u01/app/oracle/diag/rdbms/racdb/
RACDB1/trace/RACDB1_diag_4622.trc
Instance terminated by RBAL, pid = 4693
Mon Nov 29 09:41:34 2010
Starting ORACLE instance (normal)
Reconfiguration started (old inc 0, new inc 2)
List of instances:
 1 (myinst: 1)
 Global Resource Directory frozen
* allocate domain 0, invalid = TRUE
 Communication channels reestablished
 Master broadcasted resource hash value bitmaps
 Non-local Process blocks cleaned out
Mon Nov 29 09:43:23 2010
 LMS 0: 0 GCS shadows cancelled, 0 closed, 0 Xw survived
 Set master node info
 Submitted all remote-enqueue requests
 Dwn-cvts replayed, VALBLKs dubious
 All grantable enqueues granted
 Post SMON to start 1st pass IR
 Submitted all GCS remote-cache requests
 Post SMON to start 1st pass IR
 Fix write in gcs resources
Reconfiguration complete
Mon Nov 29 09:43:27 2010
ALTER DATABASE MOUNT
Database mounted in Shared Mode (CLUSTER_DATABASE=TRUE)
Lost write protection disabled
Mon Nov 29 09:43:38 2010
Completed: ALTER DATABASE MOUNT
ALTER DATABASE OPEN
This instance was first to open
Beginning crash recovery of 1 threads
Started redo scan
```

```
Completed redo scan
 read 57 KB redo, 67 data blocks need recovery
Started redo application at
 Thread 1: logseq 3, block 51479
Recovery of Online Redo Log: Thread 1 Group 3 Seq 3 Reading mem 0
  Mem# 0: +DATA/racdb/onlinelog/group_3.263.733307163
Completed redo application of 0.02MB
Completed crash recovery at
 Thread 1: logseq 3, block 51593, scn 870757
 67 data blocks read, 67 data blocks written, 57 redo k-bytes read
Picked broadcast on commit scheme to generate SCNs
Thread 1 advanced to log sequence 4 (thread open)
Thread 1 opened at log sequence 4
  Current log# 1 seq# 4 mem# 0: +DATA/racdb/onlinelog/
group_1.261.733307153
Successful open of redo thread 1
Completed: ALTER DATABASE OPEN
```

As you can see, the RBAL background process has been terminated upon terminating the mandatory PMON background process. After a small pause, the instance has been restarted automatically. Subsequently the Global Resource Directory (GRD) becomes frozen and sets the master node information before bringing the database into `MOUNT` state. Just before bringing the database into `OPEN` mode, SMON has initiated the crash recovery, applied the online redo information, and finished the crash recovery successfully.

We strongly recommend that you do not imitate the scenario on your production databases as our goal was to brief you about the action that Oracle takes during the crash recovery operations.

Even though the database becomes available after a successful instance/crash recovery, it is always essential to tune the recovery time to bring the system online as quickly as possible. The guidelines outlined below will help to optimize the instance recovery duration to bring back the system online faster:

- Ensure the `RECOVERY_PARALLELISM` parameter value is set.
- Configure the degree of parallelism by setting the `PARALLEL_MIN_SERVER` initialization parameter. As a recommendation, set the parameter value using the formula `CPU_COUNT value -1`.
- Configure asynchronous I/O.

- Set the `FAST_START_MTTR_TARGET` initialization parameter to reduce the recovery time. The value is specified in seconds. The maximum duration one could set for this parameter is 3600 seconds (1 hour). However, you need to carefully test the impact of setting this parameter in the database. Once this parameter is configured, it manages the incremental checkpoints to meet the target criteria.

Parallelism for backup and recovery in RAC

An Oracle database recovery is mainly classified into two categories:

- Instance/Crash
- Media Recovery

As discussed earlier, Instance/Crash recovery is managed by Oracle automatically applying online redo information. However, Media Recovery is initiated by a DBA running the `RESTORE` and `RECOVER` commands via RMAN. To speed up the recovery operations, you can configure parallelism by setting up the parallel parameters in the database. When parallelism is configured, Oracle automatically applies the optimal degree of parallelism during the course of Instance/Crash recovery and also uses parallelism during media recovery operations, such as restoring datafiles, applying incremental backups, and applying archived logs.

You can also disable the Instance /Crash recovery parallelism on the node with multiple CPU resources by setting the `RECOVERY_PARALLELLISM` parameter value to 0. Additionally, use the `NOPARALLEL` clause with the `RECOVER` command in RMAN to disable the Media Recovery parallelism.

Backing up a RAC database with RMAN

Depending upon your organizational backup policy standards, you need to ensure that all business-critical databases are fully protected to safeguard against any type of data failure scenarios. Therefore, RMAN is the best utility to perform all database-related backups. In this section we will provide a couple of online RMAN backup scripts to back up the database with level 0, followed by the incremental level 1.

The following script is intended to perform a level-0 online backup with one channel with RMAN and the backup files stored in the disk location. To be able to back up the database `ONLINE`, you must ensure that the database is configured in `ARCHIVELOG` mode, if not, you need to configure the database in `ARCHIVELOG` mode first and then proceed with the backup. Connect to the RMAN command-line prompt to run the following script.

The incremental level-0 backup script is as follows:

```
RMAN> RUN
  {
    ALLOCATE CHANNEL ch01 DEVICE TYPE DISK FORMAT
      'racdb_level0_%U.bak';
    BACKUP INCREMENTAL LEVEL 0 DATABASE PLUS ARCHIVELOG;
    RELEASE CHANNEL ch01;
  }
```

After the above command is successfully executed, you can run the following command in the RMAN to confirm the backup's success:

```
RMAN> list backup of database;


List of Backup Sets
===================


BS Key  Type LV Size       Device Type Elapsed Time Completion Time
------- ---- -- ---------- ----------- ------------ ---------------
2       Full    925.68M    DISK        00:02:10     01-DEC-10
        BP Key: 2   Status: AVAILABLE  Compressed: NO  Tag: TAG20101201T064812
        Piece Name: /u01/app/oracle/backup/RACDB/backupset/2010_12_01/o1_mf_nnndf_TAG201
01201T064812_6hckd197_.bkp
  List of Datafiles in backup set 2
  File LV Type Ckp SCN    Ckp Time  Name
  ---- -- ---- ---------- --------- ----
  1       Full 892407     01-DEC-10 +DATA/racdb/datafile/system.256.733306679
  2       Full 892407     01-DEC-10 +DATA/racdb/datafile/sysaux.257.733306687
  3       Full 892407     01-DEC-10 +DATA/racdb/datafile/undotbs1.258.733306691
  4       Full 892407     01-DEC-10 +DATA/racdb/datafile/users.259.733306691

RMAN>
```

Upon having a level-0 backup, you can run the subsequent incremental level-1 cumulative backup script as follows:

```
RMAN> RUN
  {
    ALLOCATE CHANNEL ch01 DEVICE TYPE DISK FORMAT
      'racdb_level0_%U.bak';
    BACKUP INCREMENTAL LEVEL 1 CUMULATIVE DATABASE;
    RELEASE CHANNEL ch01;
  }
```

As part of the database-backup strategy, you can run the level-0 backup script on the weekend and the level-1 cumulative backup script during the week.

Note: The scripts provided here are for educational use only. You may need to develop your own backup scripts and strategies that best suit your organization's needs.

Configuring multiple channels

An RMAN channel, either to disk or tape, must be allocated or preconfigured just before you back up the database through RMAN. However, in a RAC environment, you are able to either allocate multiple channels on one instance or configure one channel on each instance to load-balance a backup operation across the instances.

The following example shows the commands to configure the settings for two channels, one at each instance, using the TNS names needed to connect to the instances via RMAN:

```
RMAN> CONFIGURE DEVICE TYPE disk/sbt PARALLELISM 2;
RMAN> CONFIGURE CHANNEL ch1 CONNECT 'user/password@racdb1';
RMAN> CONFIGURE CHANNEL ch2 CONNECT 'user/password@racdb2';
```

If you have a TNS service name defined with the load-balancing feature on, you can use the following command:

```
RMAN> CONFIGURE CHANNEL DEVICE TYPE disk/sbt CONNECT
 'user/password@service_tns';
```

The following example is used to allocate channels manually during the backup run time. The channel must be allocated within the `RUN` block of RMAN:

```
RMAN> RUN {
ALLOCATE CHANNEL ch1 CONNECT 'user/password@racdb1';
ALLOCATE CHANNEL ch2 CONNECT 'user/password@racdb2';
....
}
```

This example assumes that you have already configured the `DEVICE TYPE` either to DISK or SBT (tape) and the `RACDB1`,`RACDB2` TNS entries are pre-defined in the local node's `tnsnames.ora` file. The following diagram illustrates the channels' configuration on multiple instances:

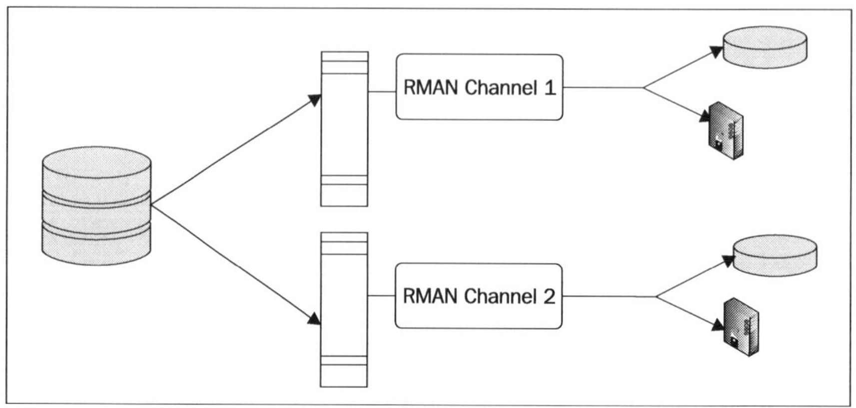

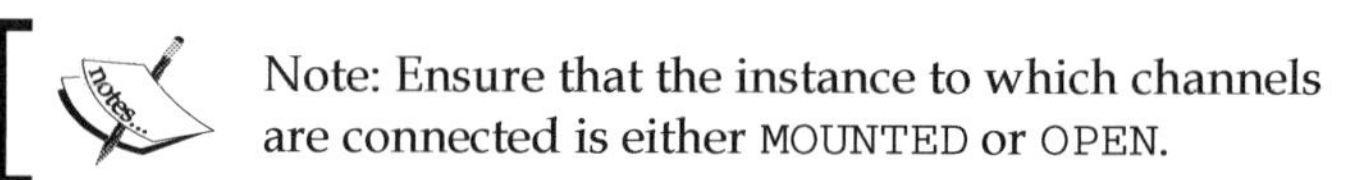

Note: Ensure that the instance to which channels are connected is either `MOUNTED` or `OPEN`.

OCR and Voting disk backup and recovery strategies

This section mainly focuses on the essential concepts and various approaches available to safeguard the Clusterware critical components OCR and Voting disk file from a single point of failure. We will also illustrate the various methods available to back up and recover the OCR and voting disk files.

Adding a Mirror location for the OCR and Voting disk

Considering the vital information held by the OCR and Voting disk, and the pivotal role played by these two critical cluster components for smooth cluster functionality, Oracle strongly recommends that you keep redundant copies of these components to avoid a single point of failure. If you have not selected the redundant option during the clusterware configuration, or you have just upgraded clusterware that consists of a single OCR and Voting disk, you can use the following procedure to add redundant copies to these components either on a shared storage device or on ASM diskgroups.

With 11g R1, you can add the redundant copies of OCR and the Voting disk while the Clusterware is running across the nodes. The following set of examples demonstrates this procedure. You need to log in as `root` to run the commands.

To add a redundant copy for OCR on a shared storage location, run the following command:

```
./$ORA_GRID_HOME/bin/ocrconfig -add /dev/sdf1 --new_location_path
```

To place a redundant copy for OCR on an ASM diskgroup, use the following command. Ensure the diskgroup is created with the `COMPATIBLE.ASM` attribute and that the value is set to `11.2` and mounted on all ASM instances of the cluster.

```
./ocrconfig -add +OCRVOTE
```

To add a redundant copy of a Voting disk file on a shared storage location, use the following command as root user. However, you cannot add a redundant copy of a Voting disk when it is placed on the ASM storage.

```
./$ORA_GRID_HOME/bin/crsctl add css votedisk /dev/sdg1 --
  new_location_path
```

OCR automatic backups

The Oracle Clusterware (on the master node of a cluster) is responsible for performing automatic OCR backups at these predefined scheduled intervals: every four hours, end of the day, and end of the week. These backup copies are kept under the `$ORA_GRID_HOME/cdata/CLUSTERNAME` location on the local node.

In the event of a master node reboot, the other node that subsequently takes over as the master node will be responsible for performing the automatic OCR backups on its local file system. At a given time, Oracle Clusterware retains three backup copies of the OCR file. As a DBA, you have no control over the frequency and number of backup copies that the Oracle Clusterware retains.

Run the following command as Oracle user on a node to list the details for automatically-generated OCR backups:

```
./$ORA_GRID_HOME/bin/ocrconfig -showbackup
raclinux1     2010/11/08 12:15:04     /u00/grid/oracle/product/11.2.0/
grid/cdata/crsgrid-scan/backup00.ocr
raclinux1     2010/11/08 08:15:03     /u00/grid/oracle/product/11.2.0/
grid/cdata/crsgrid-scan/backup01.ocr
raclinux1     2010/11/08 04:15:03     /u00/grid/oracle/product/11.2.0/
grid/cdata/crsgrid-scan/backup02.ocr
raclinux1     2010/11/07 04:15:00     /u00/grid/oracle/product/11.2.0/
grid/cdata/crsgrid-scan/day.ocr
raclinux1     2010/10/27 04:14:30     /u00/grid/oracle/product/11.2.0/
grid/cdata/crsgrid-scan/week.ocr
```

To view the OCR backup default path details and verify the OCR integrity, the following commands can be used:

```
./ocrcheck
Status of Oracle Cluster Registry is as follows :
         Version                  :          3
         Total space (kbytes)     :     262120
         Used space (kbytes)      :       2832
         Available space (kbytes) :     259288
         ID                       : 1803794662
         Device/File Name         : +DATA      <<>>
                                    Device/File integrity check succeeded
./cluvfy comp ocr -n all -verbose
Verifying OCR integrity
Checking OCR integrity...
Checking the absence of a non-clustered configuration...
All nodes free of non-clustered, local-only configurations
ASM Running check passed. ASM is running on all cluster nodes
Checking OCR config file "/etc/oracle/ocr.loc"...
OCR config file "/etc/oracle/ocr.loc" check successful
```

```
Disk group for ocr location "+DATA" available on all the nodes
Checking OCR device "+DATA" for sharedness...
Checking size of the OCR location "+DATA " ...
raclinux1:Size check for OCR location "+DATA" successful...
raclinux2:Size check for OCR location "+DATA" successful...
```

You can also navigate to the `ocr.loc` file to determine the path defined for the OCR and its mirror location. Use the following command:

```
more /etc/oracle/ocr.loc
ocrconfig_loc=+DATA
ocrmirrorconfig_loc=+VOTEOCR
```

The path for the default automatic and manual OCR backups can be customized using the `ocrconfig` command. The following example demonstrates how to modify the default path. However, you need to be the `root` user to successfully run the command:

```
./$ORA_GRID_HOME/bin/ocrconfig -backuploc <new_location_details>
```

After changing the default path, all the subsequent OCR automatic and manual backups will be generated in the new location.

Performing OCR manual backups

The content of the OCR file is essential to the cluster functionality; hence you need to ensure it is protected after a significant amount of changes happen to the OCR. Pre-Oracle 11g, there was no option to perform an on-demand binary backup for OCR. Although you could perform a logical backup, you had to wait for a pre-defined automatic backup schedule, that is, at every four hours interval.

The on-demand OCR binary backup option is available with 11g R1; therefore, you are allowed to perform a manual on-demand binary backup of the OCR file using the `ocrconfig` utility with the `-manual` option.

Run the following command as root user to perform the on-demand OCR binary backup:

```
./ocrconfig -manualbackup <directory_name>
```

When the directory name is not specified with the command, the backup copy will be created in the default OCR backup location on the local node.

Voting disk manual backups

Although the Voting disk contents are not changed frequently, you will need to back up the Voting disk file every time you add or remove a node from the cluster or immediately after you configure or upgrade a cluster. Oracle Clusterware doesn't back up the Voting disk as it does for OCR, so you will need to manually back up the Voting disk.

To back up the Voting disk, you need to use the operating system-specific copy command: `dd` for UNIX and `ocopy` for Windows. The following example demonstrates how to back up the Voting disk file on the UNIX operating system using the `dd` command:

```
dd if=voting_disk_name of=backup_file_name
```

Fortunately, in 11g R2 the Voting disk contents are now backed up automatically in OCR; therefore, you are no longer required to back up the Voting disk manually.

Restoring OCR

Imagine if your OCR files were to be corrupted, removed from the storage type, or the ASM diskgroup that holds the OCR were corrupted; to be able to resolve the issue, you would need to restore the OCR from the previous valid backup copy. In this section we are going to demonstrate the different approaches that there are to restore the OCR when it is placed either on the ASM diskgroup or on a shared storage disk.

The following steps demonstrate the procedure to restore the OCR using the latest binary backup copy on a shared storage device, applicable for 11g R1 and 11g R2.

1. Firstly, you will need to locate the latest binary backup copy of the OCR. As root user on any node of a cluster, execute the following command to find out the latest backup copy details:

   ```
   ./ocrconfig -showbackup
   ```

2. After identifying and determining the backup file to be restored, ensure you are logged in as root user and stop the cluster stack across the nodes of the cluster by using the following command:

   ```
   ./crsctl stop crs (repeat the command on all nodes in 11g R1)
   ```

3. In 11g R2:

   ```
   ./crsctl stop cluster -all (just from the first node)
   ./crsctl stop crs (repeat the command on all nodes in 11g R2)
   ```

4. After the cluster stack is successfully stopped on all the nodes, proceed to restore the backup file identified previously using the following command:

   ```
   ./ocrconfig -restore <backup_copy_location_filename>
   ```

5. Once you have successfully restored the backup file, bring up the cluster stack on all the nodes of a cluster using the following command:

   ```
   ./crsctl start crs
   ```

6. Perform the OCR integrity checks using the following commands to ensure the restoration is successful:

   ```
   ./ocrcheck
   ./cluvfy comp ocr -n all -verbose
   ```

Now, we will look at the procedure to restore an OCR and Voting disk file that are stored together in the same ASM diskgroup. The steps demonstrate how to reconstruct the corrupted or lost diskgroup followed by restoring/recovering the OCR and Voting disk file:

1. Firstly, you will need to locate the latest binary backup copy of the OCR. As root user on any node of a cluster, run the following command to find out the latest backup file details:

   ```
   ./ocrconfig -showbackup
   ```

2. After identifying and determining the backup file to be restored, stop the cluster stack across the nodes of a cluster and run the following command as `root` user:

   ```
   ./crsctl stop crs (use -f flag if you have any issues
     stopping the cluster stack)
   ```

3. Start up the cluster stack in exclusive mode on a node that holds the latest binary backup file for OCR. Run the following command as `root` user:

   ```
   ./crsctl start crs -excl
   ```

4. Connect to the local ASM instance on the node to recreate the diskgroup first, ensure the diskgroup `COMPATIBLE.ASM` attribute is set to `11.2`, and run the following commands as GRID software owner:

   ```
   export ORACLE_SID=+ASM1 - assuming it is on the first node
   export ORACLE_HOME=$ORA_GRID_HOME - set gird home


   sqlplus / as sysasm
   SQL> CREATE DISKGROUP data EXTERNAL REDUNDANCY
     DISK '/dev/diskname1'
     ATTRIBUTE 'COMPATIBLE.ASM'='11.2';
   ```

   Exit from the SQLPLUS prompt upon creating the diskgroup successfully.

5. As root user, run the following command to restore the OCR from a backup copy:

   ```
   ./ocrconfig -restore /u00/grid/oracle/product/11.2.0/cdata/
   crsgrid-scan/backup00.ocr
   ```

6. Upon restoring the OCR file successfully, you then need to run the following command as root user to recreate the Voting disk file on the newly-recreated diskgroup:

   ```
   ./crsctl start res ora.crsd -init
   ./crsctl replace votedisk +DATA
   ```

7. After restoring the Voting disk file successfully on to the diskgroup, stop the cluster stack on the local node and start the cluster stack subsequently across all the nodes of the cluster using the following command:

   ```
   ./crsctl stop crs
   ./crsctl start crs (repeat this command on all nodes)
   ```

8. Perform the OCR integrity checks after starting up the cluster stack successfully on all the nodes, using the following command:

   ```
   ./ocrcheck
   ./cluvfy comp ocr -n all -verbose
   ```

Restoring the Voting disk

Consider a scenario where the entire Voting disk files of the Clusterware are removed or corrupted and you need to restore the Voting disk from the previous valid backup copies in order to avoid node evictions problems. We will now explain how to restore the Voting disk on a shared storage device, when all Voting disk copies are lost, using the UNIX operating system-specific command (`dd`).

To be able to run the following command, ensure you have a recent backup copy of the Voting disk file available. Log on as `root` user on a node that has the most recent backup Voting disk copy and execute the following command:

```
dd if=<backup_file_path_name> of=<voting_disk_path>
```

For instance, if the Voting disk file was placed alongside the OCR file on an ASM diskgroup, you will need to follow the procedure specified above, applicable only in 11g R2.

Now let's extend the above scenario further. Assuming that the Voting disk was initially configured on a separate ASM diskgroup of the OCR, and the Voting disk is lost due to ASM diskgroup corruption or any other valid reasons, you will need to restore the Voting disk either in an ASM diskgroup or on the shared storage disk. The following procedure describes the steps required to restore the Voting disk from the above scenario. Ensure you are logged in as root user while executing the commands:

1. Start up the Clusterware stack on the first node of the cluster in exclusive mode, using the following command:

   ```
   ./crsctl start crs -excl
   ```

2. Use the following command to restore the Voting disk to a diskgroup irrespective of where it was stored earlier either on a diskgroup or on shared storage:

   ```
   ./crsctl replace voting disk +DISKGROP_NAME
   ```

3. If the Voting disk was previously stored on shared storage and you want to restore it on shared storage, use the following command, applicable only in 11g R2:

   ```
   ./crsctl query css votedisk
   Note down the File Universal Id (FUID) of the voting disk


   ./crsctl delete css votedisk <FUID>
   ./crsctl add css votedisk <destination_for_votedisk>
   ```

4. Bring down the cluster on the local node and start up the cluster stack subsequently, by using the following set of commands as root user:

```
./crsctl stop crs -f
./crsctl start crs
```

Summary

In this chapter, we discussed the different roles played by the RAC and RMAN and how the RMAN utility can help businesses safeguard against data failures. We also discussed RMAN and its advantages and architecture. However, the core focus of this chapter was towards configuring RMAN for the RAC environment to achieve the best results. It also provided example backup scripts and suggested a good backup strategy.

Towards the end of this chapter, we also discussed the various methods to overcome a Single Point of Failure and the best backup and recovery strategies for the cluster critical components: OCR and Voting disks.

In the next chapter we will discuss the Performance Tuning options for RAC databases and clusterware.

8
Performance Tuning

Performance tuning is as much an art as a science when it comes to Oracle database systems. In the past, different performance tuning methodologies were used in a random fashion without a valid scientific method. For example, Oracle DBAs would use methods for tuning the buffer cache hit ratios based on experience rather than tested formulae. Using so called silver bullets produced a haphazard solution at best, without a true understanding of the root cause of a performance issue. With the advent of the **Oracle Wait Interface** (**OWI**), many of these old and inaccurate techniques have finally been laid to the dustbins of false myths. The first step in the performance tuning of Oracle RAC environments is to tune the database itself, as you would for a non-clustered Oracle database environment. By assessing basics such as database instance tuning, as well as efficient SQL query tuning, most of your performance issues can be addressed before moving on to the more challenging aspects unique to Oracle RAC performance.

We discussed earlier in the book that with an Oracle RAC environment, multiple Oracle instances share a common RAC database on shared storage. Typically, the RAC database is housed in a **Storage Area Network** (**SAN**) or **Network Attached Storage** (**NAS**), such as an EMC DMX high performance SAN.

Due to the fact that performance tuning is a massive discipline, it would be impossible to adequately address every aspect of how to tune an Oracle database. As such, we will examine key topics unique to Oracle RAC implementations that will benefit the RAC DBA, including the following:

- Single instance database versus parallel database tuning considerations
- How to leverage new Oracle performance optimization features
- Understanding how Cache Fusion affects RAC performance
- Tuning Oracle RAC Cluster Interconnect Performance
- Wait events and RAC Performance

Tuning differences: single instance versus RAC

Many DBAs are confused about how to approach performance tuning for Oracle RAC environments in contrast to single instance databases. By understanding the system architecture differences, as well as how Cache Fusion affects an RAC environment, you will be prepared to tune Oracle RAC. Cache Fusion brings new challenges and performance optimizations unique to RAC as opposed to single instance Oracle database environments, which we will examine later in this chapter.

Oracle 11g single instance database

Single instance database environments for Oracle are simpler to tune than RAC environments for the simple reason that you do not have to worry about tuning issues with respect to interconnect cluster communication. We believe that an holistic view is paramount when tuning RAC environments for Oracle. After you have tuned SQL, as well as sized the database correctly, you should address the unique characteristics for an RAC environment.

Oracle RAC 11g database

RAC has multiple database instances in comparison to a single instance Oracle database, with each cluster instance in the environment functioning separately, yet in unison with the entire cluster. At the central point of performance, bottlenecks may arise in an RAC database because all of the cluster instances must share access to the RAC database. As such, tuning the pathways to the RAC database is important to ensure a high level of performance. RAC uses a parallel processing-based architecture that shares the resources among all of the cluster nodes. Cache Fusion is the mechanism that provides throughput for the RAC database by using an algorithm to send data between cluster nodes without the previous issues caused by block disk pinging in older versions of the Oracle cluster technology, which was called **Oracle Parallel Clusters** (**OPS**).

New Oracle 11g performance tuning features

With Oracle 11g Release 2, a plethora of new performance features provide you with the instrumentation framework to manage and tune complex environments.

Database Replay

Database Replay is part of the Oracle 11g Enterprise Edition **Real Application Testing (RAT)** suite that provides the ability to capture and simulate workloads. It is a powerful tool in tuning arsenal for load testing and provides benchmarking tools for serious performance analysis. The beauty of this feature is that you can capture a real workload on a production system and then replay it in another environment. By using database replay for impact analysis, you can preview the effects of parameter changes, application patches, and storage changes to an RAC environment with Oracle. Database Replay uses a four-phase approach:

1. First, you record the workload from a database. It is similar to when you record a television show using a digital video recorder (DVR).
2. Workload pre-processing performs the conversion of the workload into replay files.
3. Workload replay plays back the captured workload in the test database environment.
4. Analysis and reporting generates a report that gives you the list of errors and consequences of the changes to be made.

There is some initial setup required to use the Database Replay feature with Oracle 11g. You will need to configure the **Workload Replay Client (WRC)** first, before capturing a new workload.

Database Replay will only capture DML, DDL, system, and session calls for a database environment. It will not capture flashback queries, scheduled jobs, or non PL/SQL advanced queue statements (AQ). Furthermore, the following changes are not captured by Database Replay:

- Direct path loads from external files using SQL*Loader
- Database links
- External tables
- Oracle streams objects
- Distributed transactions

SQL Performance Analyzer

The **SQL Performance Analyzer** (**SPA**) allows you to test the impact of applying changes against the database in terms of SQL application performance. If performance deficiencies are found within the SQL code, the SPA will generate a set of recommendations to improve SQL performance. This is beneficial to the DBA because he/she can analyze the impact of key changes to the Oracle database environment in terms of application performance for SQL statements, for example, if you want to upgrade an Oracle 11g R1 RAC database to Oracle 11g R2 RAC. With the SPA tool, you can find out the performance implications of a database upgrade. There are two methods to run the SPA. The first method is through the Oracle Enterprise Manager (OEM) graphical interface. Please keep in mind that usage of the SPA requires the purchase of an Oracle Enterprise Edition (EE) license and option for this tool, as it is not included with standard Oracle licenses. For old school DBAs, you can also call the SPA with the `DBMS_SQLPA` package. In order to use SPA, you need to execute the following steps:

1. Capture the workload for SQL statements within the database.
2. Measure the workload performance before changes are made.
3. Perform changes to the database environment.
4. Measure the workload performance after changes have been made.
5. Analyze and compare performance differences.

We recommend that you perform a database clone of the source database to generate a target database, apply changes to the target database, and then run SPA against the target database, to measure the impact of these changes. For performance testing and analysis, we recommend that you maintain the test environment as close as possible to the source database. You can use Data Guard snapshot standby database or the RMAN `duplicate` command to create a target clone database environment for this purpose.

Database Health Monitor

With the release of Oracle 11g, a new monitoring framework named **Database Health Monitor** came onto the scene. The Database Health Monitor provides automated diagnostic operational checks to assess potential database failures and anomalies. By running the Database Health Monitor on a regular basis, you can catch potential failures before they cause outages and serious problems to data integrity and operational availability. The Database Health Monitor provides the following checks for database errors:

- Database structure check

- Data block integrity check
- Redo integrity check
- Undo segment integrity check
- Transaction integrity check
- Dictionary integrity check

The following query will display a complete listing of database health checks that are available:

```
SELECT  NAME,  DESCRIPTION,  OFFLINE_CAPABLE  FROM  V$HM_CHECK;
```

The `OFFLINE_CAPABLE` column defines whether or not you can perform the check when the database is offline.

PL/SQL Native Compilation

PL/SQL Native Compilation arrived with Oracle 9i. Now, with Oracle 11g, the PL/SQL compiler has the functionality to generate native code directly from PL/SQL source code without the need to use a third-party compiler. When a PL/SQL program unit is required, the Oracle executable loads the necessary code directly from the database catalog into system memory without the need to first stage it as a `.DLL` (in Windows) or `.so` (Linux/UNIX) file. This provides the following advantages:

- No requirement for a third-party C compiler
- Enhanced compilation speed
- Reduced execution time

This feature is not available with all releases for Oracle 11g R1 with certain platforms. With Oracle 11g R2, PL/SQL Native Compilation can be performed without additional setup steps. We advise that you check the Oracle system documentation for your platform, to verify whether or not additional configurations are advised for this.

Server Result Cache

Oracle 11g provides an additional performance tool named **Server Result Cache**, which provides you with the ability to cache SQL and PL/SQL query results in SGA memory. Instead of reparsing the query, the Server Result Cache generates the results of the query from memory, which results in a dramatic boost in the database performance. The initial query execution will run at a normal computation level of performance, until the result cache has taken note of the execution, due to the fact that it must be computed to calibrate the environment. Subsequent query executions will then appear from memory with immediate results, thus reducing execution times. However, there is a caveat: cached results will be invalid if any dependent database objects are modified. The following restrictions exist with respect to using SQL result cache:

- Data dictionary objects and temporary tables are not supported
- SQL functions, including `CURRENT_DATE`, `CURRENT_TIMESTAMP`, `LOCAL_TIMESTAMP`, `USERENV/SYS_CONTEXT`, `SYS_GUID`, `SYSDATE`, and `SYS_TIMESTAMP` are not supported
- Bind variables can only reuse cached results for identical variable values
- Query results that retrieve non-current versions of data will not be cached
- Flashback queries are not cached

The following restrictions for PL/SQL function result cache exist:

- Functions cannot be defined in modules that use invoker's rights.
- You cannot use it with functions within an anonymous PL/SQL block.
- Functions cannot have an `OUT` or `IN OUT` parameter.
- Functions cannot have `IN` parameters such as `BLOB`, `CLOB`, `NCLOB`, `REF CURSOR`, `collections`, `objects`, or `records`.
- Functions cannot return any `BLOB`, `CLOB`, `NCLOB`, `REF CURSOR`, `objects`, or `records`. However, you can return collections given that a collection does not contain one of the unsupported types listed in this section. If you do not have these requirements met, then you will not be able to take advantage of the PL/SQL result cache functionality available in Oracle 11g.

Client Side Result Cache

Oracle 11g also allows you to configure client processes to cache query results into client side memory. This new feature allows Oracle database clients to cache SQL query results locally apart from on the database server.

By using the Client Result Cache, you can free up system resources by caching SQL queries on the client side memory. This boosts the overall database performance by the elimination of round trips to the server. It is recommended that you take the following points into consideration when using Client Result Cache:

You must use Oracle 11g client libraries and connect to Oracle 11g databases.

Applications can use Client Result Cache for any database application that uses Oracle Database 11g OCI clients, including ODBC and PHP.

The following parameters must be set to use Client Side Result Cache with Oracle 11g:

Parameter	Description
`CLIENT_RESULT_CACHE_SIZE`	It's a database initialization parameter that specifies the maximum size of client per-process result set cache (in bytes). Provides the combined cache size for all clients. Note: if set to `zero` (default), client cache will be disabled.
`CLIENT_RESULT_CACHE_LAG`	It's a database initialization parameter that provides the maximum time (in milliseconds) for when the last round trip to the server occurred. In other words, by setting this database initialization parameter, you can reduce the latency for application network performance.

Optional client configurations can be made to the `sqlnet.ora` file for the database client.

Note: Client settings will override the default client cache settings on the database server.

Parameter	Description
OCI_RESULT_CACHE_MAX_SIZE	Provides the client maximum size on a process basis for result set cache (in bytes).
OCI_RESULT_CACHECACHE_MAX_RSET_SIZE	Provides the maximum size of a single query result set in client cache for a process (in bytes).
OCI_RESULT_CACHECACHE_MAX_RSET_ROWS	Provides the maximum number of rows that a single query results set in the client cache for a process.

After implementing client side server result set, you need to use the `/*+ result_cache */` hint in your query. When you execute the query, OCI performs a look up in the result cache memory to check if the result for the query already exists in the OCI client cache. If it exists, then the result is retrieved from the cache. Otherwise, results will be returned as immediate output and then stored within the client result cache memory. This caches the query results at the client side, thereby reducing overhead on network and system resources. Statistics can be viewed for the client result cache by using the following query:

```
SELECT * FROM  V$CLIENT_RESULT_CACHE_STATS;
```

Additional details are available in Oracle 11g in `V$SYSTEM_EVENT` to examine further details about client side process operations.

SQL Tuning Advisor

The **SQL Tuning Advisor (STA)** now executes automatically on a nightly basis with Oracle 11g. This is a change from how the STA behaved in Oracle 10g, where it had to be run on a manual basis. The beauty of the STA utility is that it will capture any SQL statements from the AWR that are prime candidates for tuning exercises during several unique time periods. The results are then generated into a new SQL tuning profile for deficient SQL statements.

SQL Access Advisor provides the following enhancements with Oracle 11g:

- The STA now generates tuning recommendations for partitioning strategies
- Performance optimization benefits gain estimations
- Generates publish points or intermediate results
- STA can be called from within Oracle Enterprise Manager (OEM) or through the `DBMS_SQLTUNE` package

New performance features in Oracle 11gR2

Now, let's take a look at the new performance tuning features in Oracle 11g R2.

In-Memory Parallel Execution

In-Memory Parallel Execution utilizes aggregated memory in a system to optimize database query performance by reducing or eliminating physical I/O required for parallel operations. Oracle will automatically make a decision as to whether or not an accessed database object, which is using parallel execution, will benefit from being placed into the SGA buffer cache. For Oracle RAC, fragments of the object are mapped into each of the buffer caches on the active instances. These mappings allow Oracle to determine which buffer cache to access specific parts or partitions of the object to respond a granted SQL query. As a result of this new functionality, large parallel operations for RAC are optimized and physical I/O utilization is greatly reduced, as the parallel operation can now be performed in memory.

To use the In-Memory Parallel Execution, you must set the initialization parameter `PARALLEL_DEGREE_POLICY` to `AUTO` (default `MANUAL`).

Analyzing the Cache Fusion impact on RAC performance

In order to optimize the performance of Oracle RAC environments, you need to understand how Cache Fusion operates in terms of inter-instance messaging and block transfers. It is essential to gain mastery of the key performance views, wait events, and statistics generated within AWR and ADDM to successfully tune Oracle RAC. By understanding these key RAC wait events, you can identify bottlenecks with RAC processing and find the root cause and the solution to resolve performance issues. To help you with gaining this knowledge for tuning wait events, we will take a look into some of these core factors that are the capstone of tuning Oracle RAC.

Cache Fusion

Cache Fusion is the engine behind the robust level of performance that is Oracle RAC. In the past incarnation of RAC, called Oracle Parallel Server (OPS), disk performance issues arose from a condition called block pinging due to latency for disk and network I/O contention. Cache Fusion is the new algorithm that was devised to avoid and remediate this issue that plagued OPS. With Cache Fusion, disk reads only occur if the block is not available within the buffer caches of the other instances. We can determine Cache Fusion performance by analyzing RAC wait events and statistics. How do we assess the cost of block access and cache coherency with RAC? This is represented by **Global Cache Services** (**GCS**) statistics and Global cache services wait events. Let's examine the overhead in response time for cache fusion transfers. These can be understood by the following:

- **Physical private interconnects**: Multiple interconnects are required with RAC, and with additional interconnects, redundancy and increased bandwidth are available for messages and cache fusion block transfers. You should aim for low latency as the goal with interconnect performance for RAC. Watch out for collisions with the network interconnects as these will kill performance for your RAC cluster. Interconnect performance is dependent upon the network interface speed that is set, as well as the redundancy of the network interface for the interconnects.
- **IPC protocol**: Oracle RAC prefers using IPC-based inter-process communications for sending data from one node to another, as it does not require expensive context switches or using kernel mode. You will need to check with the network hardware vendor for IPC protocol details.

GCS protocol: GCS protocol is dependent upon the IPC protocol and private interconnect. Disk I/O does not affect the GCS performance unless there are performance problems with the operation of the **Oracle Log Writer Process** (**LGWR**). As such, disk I/O is either performed by LGWR or used to replace aged out blocks from the buffer cache. LGWR may impact Cache Fusion performance. An LGWR I/O operation occurs whenever dirty blocks in the buffer cache are sent across the RAC interconnect to another instance.

Latency statistics

Some latency statistics for RAC from the Oracle documentation and support notes are shown next.

The CR block and current block request times are considered as follows:

- CR block request time is the time necessary to build the CR block in an instance that contains the image along with the necessary amount of time to dispose of it. This requires a write to disk, and the duration of time required to send the data across interconnect. The following rule of thumb can be taken into consideration when calculating CR block time: CR block request time = time to build CR block + time to flush it by writing the redo data to disk + time to send the block across the interconnect.
- **Current block** request time is the time necessary to send the block owning instance image in the RAC cluster, as well as the time required to flush it out of buffers and send it across the interconnect. This means that the image needs to be pinned in memory, as we cannot send it while the instance is changing the block simultaneously. This explains why we need to pin the block in exclusive mode, then flush the block from buffers and send it over the interconnect. The following rule of thumb from Oracle documentation shows us that the Current block request time = pin time + time to flush the block by writing to disk the redo data + time to send the block across the interconnect.

You are probably wondering how to find these details for Oracle RAC and Cache Fusion performance. You can query the detailed statistics through the `GV$sysstat` Oracle performance views. The `V$` and `GV$` dynamic performance views provide core details for database instance wide operations to the Oracle DBA, which are essential for performance monitoring. In contrast to `V$` dynamic performance views, which show the behavior for a single instance Oracle database, the `GV$` dynamic views are for a global database-wide cluster RAC environment. For RAC analysis, we recommend that you query the `gv$$sysstat` dynamic performance view to obtain performance statistics for Oracle RAC. You can find additional network latency issues by querying the `v$$ges_statistics` and `GV$ges_statistics` views.

The thing we want to understand and assess is the average time to process CR block and the current block. You need to run AWR and ADDM reports either from OEM or through SQL*PLUS to obtain these statistics.

RAC wait events

As you may recall from your performance tuning experience with single instance databases, wait events provide you with a treasure trove of performance details that are critical to examine for such issues as why sessions are stuck in wait mode and have performance problems. RAC wait events build on this concept to look at Cache Fusion performance.

Let's review the `v$session_wait` view. Oracle includes some common columns in `v$session` and `v$session_wait` views. The interesting columns are `wait_time` and `event`, containing respectively the time waited and name of the event in both views.

If an Oracle session is currently waiting, when you query `v$session_wait`, the `event` column will show the name of the event on which a session is waiting. The `event` column value may contain a value for the wait event, such as `db sequential read`.

When Cache Fusion executes within RAC, the server process associated with the user session makes a request to the LMS background process handling Cache Fusion. Once the LMS process is invoked, several events take place. Block access requests require anywhere between one and three instances within an RAC cluster.

So, lets say that we have a requesting instance where the initial request is made for a block image by the server process corresponding to the user session connected to the instance. We have an instance that functions as the image named the owning or serving instance, and we have an instance that owns the metadata in GRD for the particular block number and file number which is referred to as the mastering instance.

The worst situation is when the owning, master, and requesting instances are separate instances. The best situation is when they are in the same instance. We will see how this affects wait events. All wait events related to the global cache are then collected in the cluster wait class in `V$` or `GV$` performance views, and can be viewed querying the `V$` and `GV$` views or using EM Database Control or EM Grid Control. Wait events for RAC help you analyze the sessions for which you are waiting. Wait times are attributed to events that reflect the outcome of a request. Global cache waits are summarized in a broader category named cluster wait class. These events are used in ADDM or (G)V$ views to enable cache fusion diagnostics.

Let's look at the wait event `V$` views and their descriptions:

View	Description
`(G)V$SYSTEM_EVENT`	Total waits for an event
`(G)V$SESSION_WAIT_CLASS`	Waits for a wait event class by a session
`(G)V$SESSION_EVENT`	Waits for an event by a session

View	Description
(G)V$ACTIVE_SESSION_HISTORY	Activity of recent active sessions
(G)V$SESSION_WAIT_HISTORY	Last 10 wait events for each active session
(G)V$SESSION_WAIT	Events for which active sessions are waiting
(G)V$SQLSTATS	Identify SQL statements impacted by interconnect latencies

In a single instance, we have only actual wait events. In RAC, there are two major categories of events—placeholder events and actual events. It is important to note that there are separate wait events for the placeholder and, when the event is over, this event is replaced in `(G)V$session_wait` with the actual event depending on the number of hops.

The preceding points cover the most common scenarios and the respective actual wait events. Looking at (G)V$ views or AWR reports, we need to see if we observe congestion, contention, concurrency, buffer busy, failures, or retries. If any are discovered, further investigation is required. Additionally, performance tuning becomes necessary if we observe high wait time or undesirable events. If the events that we have just seen are in the top five events in the AWR report, we can investigate the potential performance problems further.

Issuing the `desc (g)v$sysstat` SQL statement at SQL*Plus prompt will show the description of the view. The `(g)v$sysstat` view can also be used to obtain information for cluster events.

```
SQL> select distinct(name) from v$sysstat where name like 'gc%';


NAME
----------------------------------------------------------------
gc local grants
gc remote grants
gc claim blocks lost
gc cr blocks received
gc cr block receive time
gc current blocks received
gc blocks lost
gcs messages sent
gc current block receive time
gc CPU used by this session
gc cr block build time
gc cr blocks served
```

```
gc current blocks served
gc current block flush time
gc blocks corrupt
gc cr block flush time
gc current block pin time
gc current block send time
gc cr block send time
```

The following are undesirable statistics, or statistics for which the values should always be as near to zero as possible:

- **global cache blocks lost**: This statistic shows block losses during transfers. High values indicate network problems. The use of an unreliable IPC protocol, such as UDP, may result in the value for global cache blocks lost being non-zero. When this occurs, take the ratio of global cache blocks lost, divided by global cache current blocks served, plus global cache cr blocks served. This ratio should be as small as possible. Many times, a non-zero value for global cache blocks lost does not indicate a problem because Oracle will retry the block transfer operation until it is successful.
- **global cache blocks corrupt**: This statistic shows if any blocks were corrupted during transfers. If high values are returned for this statistic, there is probably an IPC, network, or hardware problem.

For example, the `SELECT` command can be used to determine if further examination is needed and would look like the following:

```
SELECT
      A.VALUE "GC BLOCKS LOST 1",
      B.VALUE "GC BLOCKS CORRUPT 1",
      C.VALUE "GC BLOCKS LOST 2",
      D.VALUE "GC BLOCKS CORRUPT 2"
FROM GV$SYSSTAT A, GV$SYSSTAT B, GV$SYSSTAT C, GV$SYSSTAT D
WHERE A.INST_ID=1 AND A.NAME='gc blocks lost'
  AND B.INST_ID=1 AND B.NAME='gc blocks corrupt'
  AND C.INST_ID=2 AND C.NAME='gc blocks lost'
  AND D.INST_ID=2 AND D.NAME='gc blocks corrupt';
```

Active Session History (ASH) can also be used for identifying potential problems.

```
select wait_class_id, wait_class, count(*) cnt
from dba_hist_active_sess_history
where snap_id between 12831 and 12838
group by wait_class_id, wait_class
order by 3;
```

```
WAIT_CLASS_ID WAIT_CLASS                            CNT
------------- ------------------------------ ----------
   3290255840 Configuration                         169
   2000153315 Network                               934
   4108307767 System I/O                           7199
   3386400367 Commit                               7809
   4217450380 Application                         12248
   3875070507 Concurrency                         14754
   1893977003 Other                               35499
                                                  97762
   3871361733 Cluster                            104810
   1740759767 User I/O                           121999
```

You can see that there are a very large number of cluster events recorded in the ASH. Let's look a little closer.

```
select event_id, event, count(*) cnt from dba_hist_active_sess_history
where snap_id between 12831 and 12838 and wait_class_id=3871361733
group by event_id, event
order by 3;

EVENT_ID   EVENT                                           CNT
---------- ---------------------------------------- ----------
3905407295 gc current request                                4
3785617759 gc current block congested                       10
2705335821 gc cr block congested                            15
512320954  gc cr request                                    16
3794703642 gc cr grant congested                            17
3897775868 gc current multi block request                   17
1742950045 gc current retry                                 18
1445598276 gc cr disk read                                 148
1457266432 gc current split                                229
2685450749 gc current grant 2-way                          290
957917679  gc current block lost                           579
737661873  gc cr block 2-way                               699
2277737081 gc current grant busy                           991
3570184881 gc current block 3-way                         1190
3151901526 gc cr block lost                               1951
111015833  gc current block 2-way                         2078
3046984244 gc cr block 3-way                              2107
661121159  gc cr multi block request                      4092
3201690383 gc cr grant 2-way                              4129
1520064534 gc cr block busy                               4576
2701629120 gc current block busy                         14379
1478861578 gc buffer busy                                67275
```

The waits may constitute serious serialization points because enqueues are frequent events in a single instance and in RAC. In addition to serialization that occurs due to enqueues, waits are exacerbated due to the private interconnect latency. If something does not scale well in a single instance, it will not scale well in RAC due to contention problems and additional overhead contributed by the private interconnect latencies. We have various dynamic views to look at in order to determine if we have performance problems with RAC environments:

- `(G)V$SYSSTAT` to characterize the workload.
- `(G)V$SESSSTAT` to monitor important sessions.
- `(G)V$SEGMENT_STATISTICS` includes RAC statistics on per-segment statistics, identifying which segments are hot in regards to GES and GCS. It helps to identify segments that are contended over the interconnect.
- `(G)V$ENQUEUE_STATISTICS` determines the enqueues with the highest impact.
- `(G)V$INSTANCE_CACHE_TRANSFER` breaks down GCS statistics into block classes. The kind of blocks—data blocks, index blocks, or any other block—which are giving the most contention can be determined by querying `(G)V$INSTANCE_CACHE_TRANSFER`.

Global locking poses a threat to performance within RAC in the sense that it produces increased wait times. There are some ways to reduce these issues caused by global locking. Due to the fact that the majority of global locking issues are based on parsing activity, you should avoid unnecessary parsing of SQL and PL/SQL applications as much as possible. For OLTP transactional environments, you should replace literals in the application code with bind variables. You will need to work with the development team to modify the source code to achieve this result. In the event that this is not possible, another option is to enable cursor sharing. `CURSOR_SHARING` dictates the types of SQL statements that are able to share the same cursors within the application code. The default value for cursor sharing within Oracle is `EXACT`, which only allows SQL statements with the same text to share the same cursor. Oracle recommends that you set cursor sharing to `SIMILAR`, so that SQL statements can share a cursor in situations where the `EXACT` parameter is not valid.

Monitoring RAC cluster interconnect performance

In order to allow Cache Fusion to work its magic in the best way possible, you should take the RAC cluster interconnect design into serious consideration for optimum performance. For cluster interconnect performance to function at optimum levels, you need to ensure low latency and high throughput of the public and private interfaces for the interconnect. These connections affect the overall performance of Cache Fusion with RAC.

By tuning the private interconnect to ensure high bandwidth and low latency between cluster nodes, you can ensure timely delivery of clusterware messages and block image copies.

Oracle provides a useful tool to monitor the entire RAC cluster. The tool is called the **Oracle Cluster Health Monitor (IPD/OS)**. Information about this tool is available at the following URL: `http://www.oracle.com/technology/products/database/clustering/ipd_download_homepage.html`.

This is now called Cluster Health Monitor or CHMOS.

Oracle cluster interconnects

To verify the interconnect settings, query the `(G)V$CLUSTER_INTERCONNECTS` and the `(G)V$CONFIGURED_INTERCONNECTS`. For example, in order to verify interconnect settings with `V$CLUSTER_INTERCONNECTS`, issue the following SQL statement:

```
SQL> SELECT * FROM V$CLUSTER_INTERCONNECTS;

NAME     IP_ADDRESS       IS_ _     SOURCE

--------------- ---------------- --- -------------------------------

Eth0     10.10.10.34      NO        Oracle Cluster Repository
```

To verify the interconnect settings with `V$CONFIGURED_INTERCONNECTS`, issue the SQL statement, as specified in the following example:

```
SQL> SELECT * FROM V$CONFIGURED_INTERCONNECTS;

NAME     IP_ADDRESS       IS_        SOURCE

--------------- ---------------- --- -------------------------------

eth1     10.10.10.34      NO         Oracle Cluster Repository

eth0     10.10.10.144     YES        Oracle Cluster Repository
```

```
SQL> DESC V$CONFIGURED_INTERCONNECTS

Name    Null?           Type

--------------------------------------- -------- -----------------

NAME                    VARCHAR2(15)

IP_ADDRESS              VARCHAR2(16)

IS_PUBLIC               VARCHAR2(3)

SOURCE                  VARCHAR2(31)
```

Latency in the context of RAC Cache Fusion is defined as roundtrip time. Latency variation (and CPU cost) correlates with the following:

- Processing time in Oracle and OS kernel
- `db_block_size`
- Interconnect saturation
- Load on node (CPU starvation)

The active session wait history in AWR for Oracle 11g will show the actual performance metrics. These include optimal values for both 2-way and 3-way block transfers.

Monitoring RAC wait events

As the RAC DBA, it is critical to monitor wait events on a regular basis before users complain about performance problems. When you execute AWR and ADDM reports, you should further analyze any wait event that occurs in the top of the AWR report listing.

By taking an holistic approach to monitoring wait events for RAC, you will avoid tunnel vision and discover the root cause of the performance issue. We recommend that you use the ADDM, AWR, and ASH reports as a starting point for RAC performance analysis, as these tools are highly instrumented and provide a bird's eye view into the entire RAC cluster performance. Furthermore, using queries against the `V$` views are also very useful in providing thorough information for troubleshooting and performance tuning.

Each RAC instance takes its own AWR snapshot at approximately the same time. Each instance has its own `MMON` background process writing into AWR repository in the `SYSAUX` tablespace. The main change in AWR reporting between Oracle 10g and Oracle 11g is that each instance takes an AWR report.

Prior to Oracle 11g, you did not receive a summary total for the entire RAC cluster database. In Oracle 11g, we now obtain a detailed summary report for the entire cluster database that produces AWR and ADDM reports on a cluster-wide basis versus a per instance basis. You can execute an ADDM or AWR report either by using the `addmrpt.sql` or `awrrpt.sql` scripts for Oracle 11gR1 and `awrgrpt.sql` for Oracle 11gR2 in the `$ORACLE_HOME/rdbms/admin` directory. Additionally, you can also use the EM Database Control or EM Grid Control. The process of gathering the AWR snapshot data into the AWR repository from the RAC instance's SGA by the MMON process is illustrated as follows.

We can benefit from the following RAC-specific ADDM findings:

- Interconnect latencies
- LMS congestions
- Top SQL
- Instance contention
- Hot blocks
- Hot objects

Using a top-down approach for performance analysis can be helpful. We can start with ADDM analysis and then continue with AWR detail statistics and historical data. Active Session History will provide you with session-specific data that can also be very useful for the performance tuning of Oracle RAC databases due to the following:

- I/O issues at log switch time imply either checkpoint occurrence or log archiver being slow
- Process stuck waiting for I/O
- Connection storm

Active Session History (ASH) information is available through the following:

- Dumping to trace file:

  ```
  SQL>oradebug setmypid
  Statement Processed.
  SQL>oradebug dump ashdump 10
  Statement Processed.
  ```

  Or

  ```
  SQL>alter session set events 'immediate trace name ashdump level
  10';

  Session altered.
  ```

- Querying the `V$ACTIVE_SESSION_HISTORY` view
- Querying the `DBA_HIST_ACTIVE_SESS_HISTORY` data dictionary table
- Running the `ashrpt.sql` from the `$ORACLE_HOME/rdbms/admin` directory
- Using Oracle Enterprise Manager

Information obtained from AWR may also be obtained from the `V$` and `GV$` dynamic performance views as well. The DBA will be interested in some of the common waits and statistics representing known performance problems. Let's look at some of these wait events, which are worth further investigation, as they represent a potential performance problem if the wait time is excessive or the event wait time is among the top five listed in the AWR report:

- `global cache blocks lost`: This statistic shows block losses during transfers. High values indicate network problems. The use of an unreliable IPC protocol, such as UDP, may result in the value for lost global cache blocks being non-zero. When this occurs, take the ratio of lost global cache blocks, divided by global cache current blocks served, plus global cache cr blocks served. This ratio should be as small as possible. If high values are returned for this statistic, there is probably an IPC, network, or hardware problem.
- `global cache blocks corrupt`: This statistic shows if any blocks are corrupted during transfers. If high values are returned for this statistic, there is probably an IPC, network, or hardware problem.
- `global cache open s` and `global cache open x`: The initial access of a particular data block by an instance generates these events. The duration of the wait should be short, and the completion of the wait is most likely followed by a read from disk. This wait is a result of the blocks that are being requested and not being cached in any instance in the cluster database. This necessitates a disk read. When these events are associated with high totals or high per-transaction wait times, it is likely that data blocks are not cached in the local instance and that the blocks cannot be obtained from another instance, which results in a disk read. At the same time, suboptimal buffer cache hit ratios may also be observed. Unfortunately, other than preloading heavily used tables into the buffer caches, there is little that can be done about this type of wait event.

- `global cache null to s` and `global cache null to x`: These events are generated by inter-instance block ping across the network. Inter-instance block ping is said to occur when two instances exchange the same block back and forth. Processes waiting for global cache null to `s` events are waiting for a block to be transferred from the instance that last changed it. When one instance repeatedly requests cached data blocks from the other RAC instances, these events consume a greater proportion of the total wait time. The only method for reducing these events is to reduce the number of rows per block to eliminate the need for block swapping between two instances in the RAC cluster.
- `global cache cr request`: This event is generated when an instance has requested a consistent read data block and the block to be transferred has not arrived at the requesting instance. Other than examining the cluster interconnects for possible problems, there is nothing that can be done about this event, except to modify objects to reduce the possibility of contention.
- `gc cr block lost`: This event almost always represents a severe performance problem and can reveal network congestion involving discarded packets and fragments, packet reassembly or timeouts, buffer overflows, and flow control. Checksum errors or corrupted headers are also often the reason for the wait event. It is worth investigating the IPC configuration and possible downstream network problems (NIC, switch, and so on). Operating system data needs to be gathered with `ifconfig`, `netstat`, and `sar` to name a few. The `.cr` request retry event is likely to be seen when `gc cr` blocks lost show up, and as in the case of a lost packet, there is always a retry.
- `gc buffer busy`: This event can be associated with a disk I/O contention, for example, slow disk I/O due to a rogue query. Slow concurrent scans can cause buffer cache contention. However, note that there can be multiple symptoms for the same cause. It can be seen together with the db file scattered reads event, which is caused by global cache access and serialization. Serialization is likely to be due to log flush time on another node or immediate block transfers.
- `congested`: The events that contain "congested" suggest CPU saturation (runaway or spinning processes), long running queues, and network configuration issues. It indicates performance problems. While investigating, you need to maintain a global view and keep in mind that symptom and cause can be on different instances. This event can also happen if LMS cannot dequeue messages fast enough. The `gcs_server_processes init` parameter controls a number of LMS processes, although in most cases the default value is sufficient. Excessive memory consumption leading to memory swapping can be another reason.

- `busy`: The events that contain "busy" indicate contention. This needs investigating by drilling down into either SQL with highest cluster wait time or segment statistics with highest block transfers. Also, one needs to look at objects with the highest number of block transfers and global serialization.
- `Gc [current/cr][failure/retry]`: This event is not received because of failure, checksum error, usually in the protocol of the private interconnects due to network errors, or hardware problems. This is worth investigating, as a failure means that the block image cannot be received. Retry means that due to problems, the sending instance needs to retry sending the block image. In most cases, the block is eventually received and the problem is resolved.
- Gc `[current/cr] [2/3]-way`: If we have a two-node cluster, only a 2-way cluster is possible, as we can have at most two hops. If we have three or more RAC instances, then 2-way or 3-way cluster is possible. Events are received immediately after two or three network hops. The event is not subject to any tuning, except increasing private interconnects bandwidth and decreasing the private interconnects latency.
- `Gc [current/cr] grant 2-way`: A grant occurs when a request is made for a block image and no instance in the cluster has the image in its local buffer cache. The requesting instance performs an I/O from a data file to get the block. A grant can be either `cr` or `current`. A `current` grant reads the block from the database files. A `cr` grant reads the block from disk and builds a read consistent block, as of a certain time in the past. This event is not subject to any tuning, except increasing private interconnects bandwidth and decreasing the private interconnects latency.
- `Gc [current/cr][block/grant] congested`: This event has been received eventually, but with a delay because of intensive CPU consumption, lack of memory, LMS overload, paging, and swapping. This is worth investigating, as it provides room for improvement.
- `Gc [current/cr] block busy`: This event has been received but not sent immediately due to high concurrency or contention, indicating that the block is busy—for example, someone has issued a block recover command from RMAN. There are a variety of reasons why the block may be busy. This event means that the block image cannot be sent immediately. This may be because it is Oracle-oriented and not because of memory, LMS, or operating system-oriented reasons. This is worth investigating.
- `Gc current grant busy`: A grant is received, but there is a delay due to shared block images or load. For example, we are extending the high watermark of a segment and we are formatting the block images or blocks with block headers, requesting for a block image from the requesting instance at the same time.

- `Gc [current/cr][failure/retry]`: This event is not received because of failure, checksum errors, usually in the protocol of the private interconnect due to network errors, or hardware problems. This is worth investigating. Failure means that the block image cannot be received. Retry indicates that, due to problems, the sending instance needs to retry sending the block image, but eventually the block is received as the problem recovers.
- `Gc buffer busy`: This event occurs when the time between block accesses is less than the buffer pin time. Buffers are pinned in exclusive mode if the buffers are allowed to be modified and they are pinned in shared mode if the buffers are read-only. Obviously, if there is a lot of contention for the same block by different processes belonging to different instances, this event can manifest itself in a greater magnitude. Buffer busy is a global cache event. A request is made from one instance and the block is available in another instance. During the request, a block is busy due to contention from many concurrent requests for the same block.

Summary

In this chapter, we examined tips and tricks for Oracle RAC performance optimization. We also discussed Cache Fusion concepts and methods for tuning Cache Fusion. Furthermore, we surveyed new Oracle 11g performance tuning features with a focus on tuning Oracle 11g RAC environments. Oracle 11g performance features highlight the instrumentation approach that Oracle has taken to enhance optimization techniques for the developer and Oracle DBA.

In the next chapter, we will discuss upgrade techniques for legacy RAC environments to Oracle 11g R1 and Oracle 11g R2 with the mindset to ensure a high level of availability, performance, and with minimal downtime.

9
Oracle 11g Clusterware Upgrade

The first thing that probably comes into your mind whenever Oracle launches a new version of Clusterware is whether or not to upgrade the existing environment. In this chapter, we will look at some of the key factors that should be taken into account when considering an upgrade or when deciding against an upgrade.

In summary, we will discuss the following topics:

- Overview of an upgrade
- Upgrading Oracle 10g R2 Clusterware to Oracle 11g R1
- Upgrading to Oracle 11g R2 Clusterware
- Downgrading Oracle Clusterware after an upgrade

Overview of an upgrade

If we decide to welcome an upgrade, then we can potentially have many exciting new features that may be useful for our applications. At the same time, if we decide against an upgrade, it is very important that we are aware of the negative aspects of not upgrading.

It is not mandatory to upgrade an existing environment whenever a new version is released; however, there are many circumstances that may prompt you to consider an upgrade. The following presents a few possible situations and scenarios where you may opt for an upgrade:

- You may not be able to resist the temptation of an upgrade, with the possibility of the new release/version's features being more advanced than the previous version.
- Your organization may have a set policy or standards to stay updated with the latest technologies.
- You may need to upgrade a version that is being de-supported by Oracle. In this case, Oracle does offer the option of an extended support period.

It is strongly recommended that you back up your current environment prior to commencing an upgrade in order for you to be able to revert to the previous state in case of upgrade failures. It is also recommended that you first upgrade development, test, or UAT environments, and test all your application functionality thoroughly before proceeding to the production environment.

Upgrade sequence

As part of the Clusterware upgrade procedure, there is an upgrade sequence that should be followed:

1. Upgrade existing Clusterware.
2. Install new version binaries for RDBMS and ASM, preferably in new HOMES.
3. Upgrade Automatic Storage Management instance, if it exists.
4. Upgrade previous version databases, if it exists.
5. Remove the older version HOMES and files.

Upgrading Oracle 10g R2 Clusterware to Oracle 11g R1

Let's assume that currently you have an Oracle 10g R2 Clusterware running in your environment and you have planned to upgrade the Clusterware to Oracle 11g R1. In this section, we will demonstrate how to upgrade an existing Oracle 10g R2 Clusterware to Oracle 11g R1 on the same servers.

The following tables illustrate the environmental settings that have been used in this chapter to simulate an upgrade procedure on Oracle Enterprise Linux V5:

Oracle 10g R2 environment settings:

Host name	Clusterware version	Clusterware home	ASM and RDBMS homes
raclinux1 raclinux2	10.2.0.4	/u01/app/oracle/product/10.2.0/crs	/u01/app/oracle/product/10.2.0/asm /u01/app/oracle/product/10.2.0/db_1

Oracle 11g R1 environment settings:

Host name	Clusterware version	Clusterware home	ASM and RDBMS home
raclinux1 raclinux2	11.1.0.6	/u01/app/oracle/product/10.2.0/crs	/u01/app/oracle/product/11.1.0/asm /u01/app/oracle/product/11.1.0/db_1

Kernel parameter values

While installing or upgrading any Oracle software on any UNIX or Linux Operating System, it is highly recommended to check whether the system kernel parameter settings match the Oracle recommendation, in order to complete the task smoothly. The following are the minimal kernel parameter values that are required for an Oracle 11g R1 upgrade on Linux OS V5:

Parameter	Value
kernel.shmall	2097152
kernel.shmmax	2147483648
kernel.shmmni	4096
kernel.sem	250 32000 100 128
fs.file-max	65536
net.ipv4.ip_local_port_range	1024 65000
net.core.rmem_default	4194304
net.core.rmem_max	4194304
net.core.wmem_default	262144
net.core.wmem_max	262144

Packages required on Linux 5

Prior to performing an installation or upgrade procedure of Oracle software on any Unix or Linux OS, it is essential to verify whether or not the Oracle-recommended packages are installed on the OS. If you are on Linux V5 OS, you will need to ensure that the following package versions or later versions are installed across all nodes of the cluster:

- `libaio-devel-0.3.106`
- `elfutils-libelf-devel-0.125`
- `unixODBC-2.2.11`
- `unixODBC-devel-2.2.11`

Oracle 11g R1 Clusterware upgrade steps

Before commencing the upgrade procedure, let's verify the active and software versions of an existing Clusterware using the following examples from Node1 of the cluster:

```
crsctl query crs activeversion
Oracle Clusterware active version on the cluster is [10.2.0.4.0]
crsctl query crs softwareversion
Oracle Clusterware version on node [raclinux1] is [10.2.0.4.0]
```

This output confirms that the active and software versions are the same and that the cluster is ready for upgrade. If, for any reason, you see different active and software versions, it is an indication that your last upgrade was unsuccessful or incomplete.

If you are performing an upgrade procedure from 10g R2 (10.2.0.4) to 11g R1, you can skip the following guidelines as they are intended for environments that focus on either 10g R1 or 10g R2 with 10.2.0.1 or 10.2.0.2 patch sets.

Subsequently, after verifying the required packages along with kernel parameters and their values, you will need to ensure that the following criteria are met at your end, prior to commencing an Oracle 11g Clusterware upgrade:

- Any existing Oracle 10g R1 should be first patched to 10.1.0.3 (referenced to unpublished bug 5860479). This also applies when you are running pre-Oracle 10g R1 (10.1.0.3) Clusterware.
- Upgrade the Clusterware 10.1.0.3 to Oracle 11g R1 Clusterware. This applies when you are running an Oracle 10g R1 Clusterware.

- Any existing Oracle 10g R2 (either 10.2.0.1 or 10.2.0.2) should be first patched to a minimum of 10.2.0.3 or 10.2.0.2, with CRS Bundle patch# 2 (referenced to unpublished bug 5256865).
- Finally, upgrade the Clusterware 10g R2 to Oracle 11g R1 Clusterware.

Performing preinstallation checks with cluvfy

When an existing clusterware is ready for an upgrade process, you will need to perform various preinstallation checks using the cluster verification utility (cluvfy).

To start with, unzip or extract the 11g R1 Clusterware software into a staging area, on Node 1 of the cluster, and use the `runcluvfy.sh` script with the following example from the `/stagingarea/clusterware` location to verify the system readiness:

```
/stagingarea/clusterware/.runcluvfy.sh stage -pre crsinst -n
raclinux1,raclinux2 -verbose
```

Any errors reported during the verification phase must be fixed prior to commencing the upgrade procedure.

Executing runInstaller.sh script

Now it's time to start the actual upgrade procedure. To start this, you need to extract or unzip the Oracle 11g R1 Clusterware software from the DVD or from any resource into a staging location on Node 1 of the cluster. Once you have extracted the software into a staging area, execute the `runInstaller.sh` script from the `/stageingarea/Clusterware` location.

During the upgrade process, the **Oracle Universal Installer** (**OUI**) automatically detects any pre-existing cluster running on the nodes and automatically selects all the nodes for an upgrade procedure. If, for any reason, all the nodes are not listed as part of an upgrade, you need to halt the upgrade process and check the status of those nodes that are not selected as part of the upgrade. Resolve any problems in order to make those nodes available for an upgrade process. As part of the upgrade process, you may also choose a subset of nodes, though it is not recommended.

On the **Welcome** screen, click on **Next** to proceed further. Existing Clusterware details such as cluster home name and location are automatically extracted and displayed on the **Specify Home Details** screen. Then click on **Next**.

Existing cluster node names are extracted automatically and selected by default for an upgrade on the **Specify Hardware Cluster Installation Mode** screen. Click on **Next**.

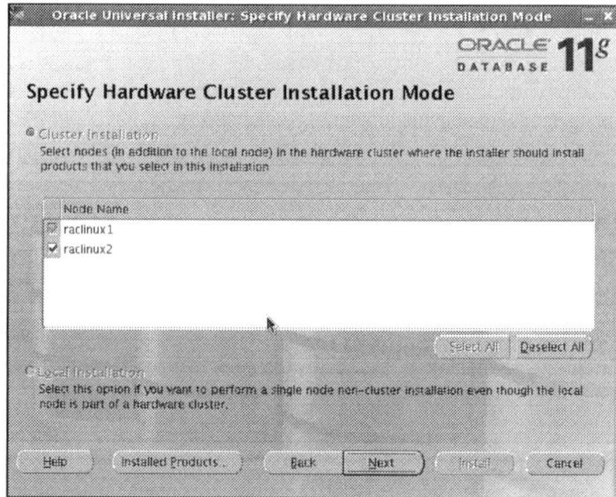

The OUI then performs prerequisite checks on the **Product-Specific Prerequisite checks** screen. You will notice that the **Checking Cluster Synchronization Services (CSS)** verification status fails as it detects that the Clusterware stack is currently active across all nodes.

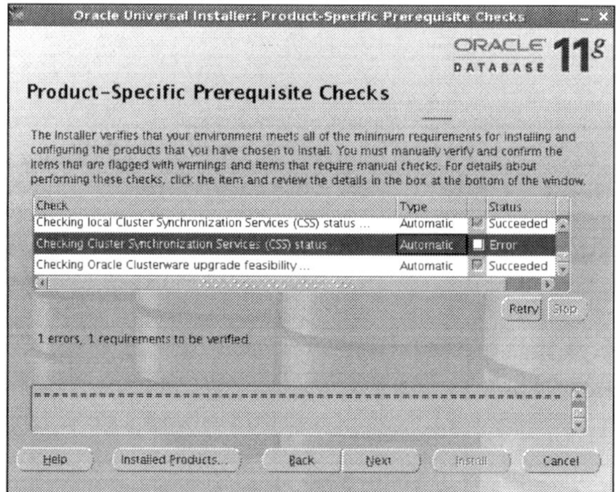

To address the CSS verification failure, Oracle provides the `preupdate.sh` script under the `/stagingarea/clusterware/upgrade` location as part of Oracle 11g software. As root from a new window on the local node, you will need to execute the following example where this script stops the clusterware stack and set the appropriate permissions to the Clusterware home. You also need to execute the following script across all nodes in sequence:

```
./preupdate.sh -crshome /u01/app/oracle/product/10.2.0/crs -crsuser
oracle
```

After the script is executed, you will then see the following message on the respective nodes:

```
Shutting down Oracle Cluster Ready Services (CRS):
Sep 22 07:23:37.455 | INF | daemon shutting down
Stopping resources. This could take several minutes.
Successfully stopped CRS resources. Stopping CSSD.
Shutting down CSS daemon.
Shutdown request successfully issued.
Shutdown has begun. The daemons should exit soon.
Checking to see if Oracle CRS stack is down...
Oracle CRS stack is down now.
```

After the script is successfully run across all nodes of the cluster, click on **Retry** to perform the prerequisite checks on the failed checks. Click on **Next** to proceed to the **Summary** page.

Review the summary page to see if there are any recommendations on this page and click on **Next** to proceed to the installation process where OUI performs Clusterware 11.1.0.6 installation on the **Install** screen.

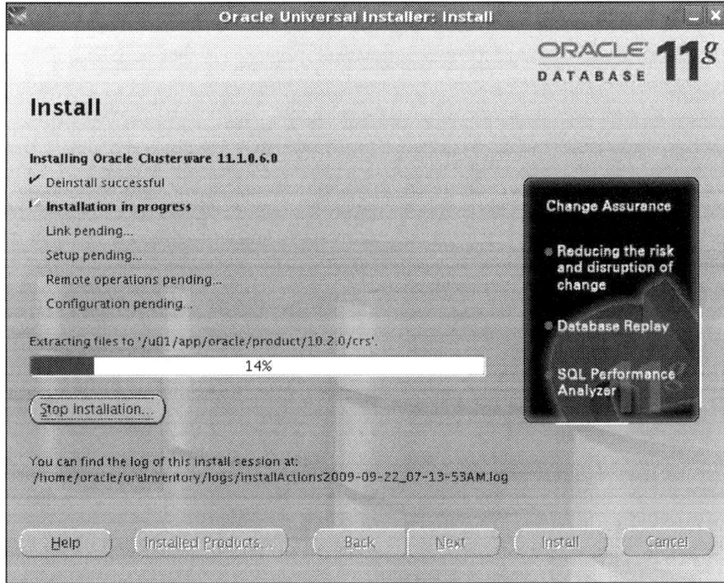

After the installation process comes to an end, you will then be prompted to execute the `rootupgrade.sh` script across all nodes of the cluster:

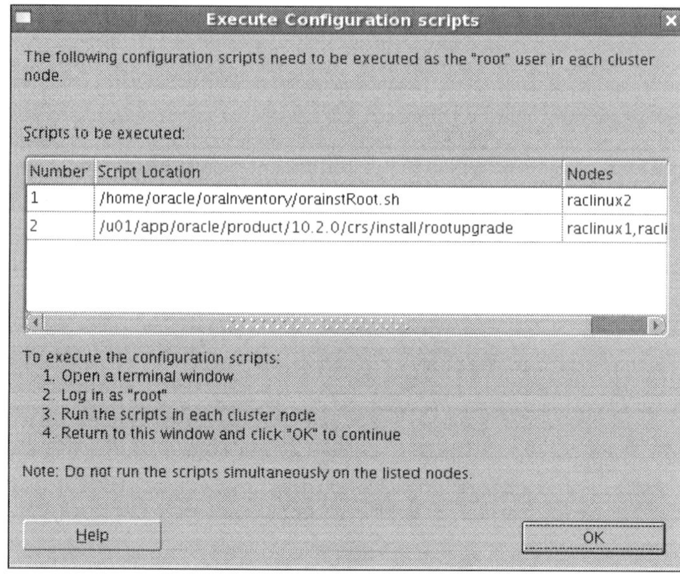

As root, execute the `orainstRoot.sh` script on all the nodes listed under the **Nodes** heading against this script. Once this script is executed, you will then need to run the `rootupgrade` script on all the nodes participating in an upgrade process, starting from Node 1 of your cluster.

When you run the `rootupgrade` script, you are likely to come across the following output on your screen:

```
/u01/app/oracle/product/10.2.0/crs/install/rootupgrade
Checking to see if Oracle CRS stack is already up...
copying ONS config file to 11.1 CRS home
/bin/cp: `/u01/app/oracle/product/10.2.0/crs/opmn/conf/ons.config' and `/u01/app/oracle/product/10.2.0/crs/opmn/conf/ons.config' are the same file
/u01/app/oracle/product/10.2.0/crs/opmn/conf/ons.config was copied successfully to /u01/app/oracle/product/10.2.0/crs/opmn/conf/ons.config
WARNING: directory '/u01/app/oracle/product/10.2.0' is not owned by root
WARNING: directory '/u01/app/oracle/product' is not owned by root
WARNING: directory '/u01/app/oracle' is not owned by root
WARNING: directory '/u01/app' is not owned by root
WARNING: directory '/u01' is not owned by root
Oracle Cluster Registry configuration upgraded successfully
```

```
Adding daemons to inittab
Attempting to start Oracle Clusterware stack
Waiting for Cluster Synchronization Services daemon to start
Waiting for Cluster Synchronization Services daemon to start
Waiting for Cluster Synchronization Services daemon to start
Cluster Synchronization Services daemon has started
Waiting for Event Manager daemon to start
Event Manager daemon has started
Cluster Ready Services daemon has started
Oracle CRS stack is running under init(1M)
clscfg: EXISTING configuration version 3 detected.
clscfg: version 3 is 10G Release 2.
Successfully accumulated necessary OCR keys.
Using ports: CSS=49895 CRS=49896 EVMC=49898 and EVMR=49897.
node <nodenumber>: <nodename> <private interconnect name> <hostname>
node 1: raclinux1 raclinux1-priv raclinux1
```

As the script finishes, it will automatically bring up the Clusterware stack of the new version and also brings up all existing resources on the node (such as database, listener, ASM, nodeapps, and services) online.

After this script is successfully executed across all nodes, click on **OK** on the **Execute Configuration Scripts** screen. Subsequently, OUI will perform post-CRS installation checks with **Oracle Clusterware Verification Utility** on the **Configuraion Assistants** screen, such as CRS health checks and other integrity checks.

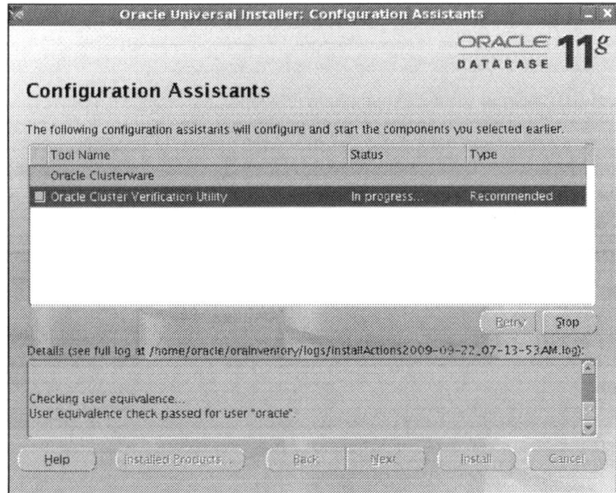

After the checks are performed, OUI will automatically take you to the **Exit** page where you will be able to click on **Exit** to quit from the OUI screen.

After executing all the above scripts successfully across all nodes of the cluster, at this stage, we should have successfully upgraded our existing Oracle 10g R2 (with 10.2.0.4 patch set) Clusterware to Oracle 11g R1. Let's verify the upgrade achievement by querying the active and software versions of the new Clusterware stack:

```
crsctl query crs activeversion
Oracle Clusterware active version on the cluster is [11.1.0.6.0]
crsctl query crs softwareversion
Oracle Clusterware version on node [raclinux1] is [11.1.0.6.0]
```

Both active and software versions reflect the new release, that is, 11.1.0.6, indicating that the upgrade process is a success. You will also need to run the `crs_stat -t` cluster command to ensure that all the resources are online.

If there are any new patches available for your operating system. such as for 11.1.0.7, you may proceed with applying those patches at this point.

Post-upgrade steps for 11g R1 Clusterware

Though you can still manage the previous version of ASM instance and Oracle databases with the new Clusterware, it is highly advised that, as part of the Oracle Real Application Cluster upgrade, you upgrade the Clusterware first, followed by ASM, DB homes, ASM instance upgrade, and existing database upgrades. Hence, after a successful Clusterware upgrade, the following post-upgrade steps will have to be completed:

1. Extract or unzip the Oracle 11g R1 Database software into a staging area on Node1 of the cluster. Install Oracle 11g R1 Oracle binaries for ASM and RDBMS into new homes, respectively across all nodes.
2. After the Oracle 11g binaries are installed in ASM and DB homes respectively, you will then need to upgrade an ASM instance across all nodes using one of the upgrading methods.
3. After the ASM instance upgrade, modify existing diskgroup parameters to support new version databases.
4. Upgrade any existing databases either using the **Database Upgrade Configuration Assistant** (**DBUA**) from the new Oracle home or using the manual upgrade method.
5. Back up new Clusterware, Oracle Homes, and Databases.

6. Back up the OCR file and voting disk.
7. Finally, delete the previous version ASM and DB homes to reclaim the space from all the nodes.

Upgrading to Oracle 11g R2 Clusterware

Oracle 11g R2 comes with many exciting new features. The look and feel of OUI has also totally changed in contrast to its previous versions. When you experience the new features, you may plan an upgrade to your TEST, DEVELOPMENT, or UAT environments to test the functionality of this new version.

When you plan to upgrade your existing Oracle 11g R1 Clusterware environment, skip the following recommendations. If you plan to upgrade your 10g clusterware directly to 11g R2, you will need to ensure that the following criteria are met at your end, prior to commencing the upgrade process:

If you are performing an upgrade from Oracle 10.1.0.2 to 11g R2:

1. Upgrade Oracle Clusterware (cluster home) to Oracle 10.1.0.3.
2. Then, upgrade Oracle 10.1.0.3 Clusterware (cluster home) to Oracle 11g R2.

If you are performing an upgrade from Oracle 10.2.0.1 or 10.2.0.2 to 11g R2:

1. Upgrade Oracle Clusterware (cluster home) to Oracle 10.2.0.2 or 10.2.0.3 with CRS Bundle Patch#2.
2. Then upgrade Oracle 10.2.0.3 Clusterware (cluster home) to Oracle 11g R2.

Overview of our environment

The following are the environmental settings that are used to simulate an upgrade from Oracle 11g R1 to Oracle 11g R2 on Oracle Enterprise Linux V5, on the same servers.

Oracle 11g R1 Environment settings:

Host name	Clusterware version	Clusterware home	ASM and RDBMS homes
`raclinux1` `raclinux2`	11.1.0.6	`/u01/app/oracle/product/11.1.0/crs`	`/u01/app/oracle/product/11.1.0/asm` `/u01/app/oracle/product/11.1.0/db_1`

Oracle 11g R2 Environment settings:

Host name	Clusterware version	Clusterware and ASM home	RDBMS home
raclinux1 raclinux2	11.2.0.1	/u01/app/11.2.0/grid	/u01/app/oracle/product/11.2.0/db_1

Upgrading nodes

Starting with Oracle 11g R2, Oracle supports in-place and out-of-place upgrades, and both strategies support rolling upgrades. When an upgrade is planned for a rolling fashion, the other nodes of a cluster remain active and available ensuring the High Availability (HA) of Oracle Clusterware, while one node is going through the upgrade phase. However, starting with Oracle 11g R2, in-place upgrades are only supported for applying patches, such as patch bundles and one-off patches. The major releases are supported for out-of-place upgrades only.

It is highly recommended that before you make any structural changes to the Clusterware, you ensure you have the latest valid backups for Cluster and other homes along with OCR and Voting disk backups.

11g R2 upgrade changes and restrictions

It is essential to realize the changes and restrictions of the Oracle 11g R2 prior to commencing the actual upgrade process. The following are a few changes and restrictions that will apply while upgrading to 11g R2:

- The new grid infrastructure, referred to as `$GRID_HOME` starting with 11g R2, consists of Oracle Clusterware and Automatic Storage Management (ASM) together in a single home. Now, although they both run from `GRID_HOME`, their usage is totally different.
- Unlike the previous versions, as of 11g R2, the Clusterware and ASM upgrade is a supported out-of-place upgrade. An in-place upgrade of Oracle Clusterware is not supported in 11g R2.
- Unlike the in-place upgrades, the out-of-place upgrade method will have a new Clusterware home, `$GRID_HOME`, where the newer version Clusterware and ASM-related binaries are installed together in a GRID directory. Therefore, after doing the out-of-place upgrade, you will end up having the older and newer version Clusterware software in different directories. However, at any given time, only one version of Clusterware must be running.
- After an 11g R2 upgrade, you may need to change the `CRS_HOME` environment parameter pointing to the new `$GRID_HOME`.

Kernel parameter values

If you are performing an upgrade from 11g R1 to 11g R2 on Linux OS V5, ensure that the following kernel parameter values are met and defined in the `sysctl.conf` file across all nodes of a cluster for a smooth upgrade.

```
fs.file-max = 6815744
net.ipv4.ip_local_port_range = 9000 65500
net.core.wmem_max = 1048576
fs.aio-max-nr = 1048576
```

Packages required on Linux 5

If you are on Linux V5 OS, ensure that the following package versions or later versions are installed across all nodes of the cluster:

- `binutils-2.17.50.b0.6`
- `compat-libstdc++-33-3.2.3`
- `elfutils-libelf-0.125`
- `elfutils-libelf-devel-0.125`
- `elfutils-libelf-devel-static-0.125`
- `gcc-4.1.2`
- `gcc-c++-4.1.2`
- `glibc-2.5-24`
- `glibc-common-2.5`
- `glibc-devel-2.5`
- `glibc-headers-2.5`
- `kernel-headers-2.6.18`
- `ksh-20060214`
- `libaio-0.3.106`
- `libaio-devel-0.3.106`
- `libgcc-4.1.2`
- `libgomp-4.1.2`
- `libstdc++-4.1.2`
- `libstdc++-devel-4.1.2`
- `make-3.81`
- `sysstat-7.0.2`
- `unixODBC-2.2.11`
- `unixODBC-devel-2.2.11`

Performing preinstallation checks with cluvfy

After installing all the required packages and kernel parameter's right value settings, you will need to perform various preinstallation checks with the cluster verification utility (cluvfy). Use the cluvfy from the grid directory of the 11g R2 DVD/CD, or from the staging area of the software, to perform the prechecks on the nodes to recognize the new requirements. Optionally, use the `fixup` flag to have the fixes in a script file, which can be used to fix the errors that are reported during the prechecks phase. You may use the following example:

```
/stage/grid/.runcluvfy.sh stage -pre crsinst -n raclinux1,raclinux2
-fixup -
    fixupdir <dirname> -verbose
```

Any errors reported during the precluster install checks phase must be fixed first and then you can proceed with the upgrade procedure.

Oracle 11g R2 Clusterware upgrade steps

As we did earlier, let's begin this procedure by verifying the active and software versions of an existing Clusterware, using the following examples, on Node1 of your cluster:

```
crsctl query crs activeversion
Oracle Clusterware active version on the cluster is [11.1.0.6.0]
crsctl query crs softwareversion
Oracle Clusterware version on node [raclinux1] is [11.1.0.6.0]
```

As we have decided to go for a rolling upgrade method in our example, ensure that the current Clusterware stack and other resources are left running across all the nodes; in other words, don't stop the cluster. Moreover, during an upgrade process, when you prompt to run the `rootupgrade.sh` script, the existing Clusterware stack will automatically be brought down and the new version Clusterware stack will start automatically at the end of the script.

You have to shut down any database or its associated instances that are running on the local node before you run the `rootupgrade.sh` script. Use the `crs_stat` command as shown here to verify the resources that are running on the nodes:

```
[oracle@raclinux1 ~]$ ./crs_stat.sh

HA Resource                                   Target   Stage
-----------                                   ------   -----
ora.raclinux1.ASM1.asm                        ONLINE   ONLINE on raclinux1
ora.raclinux1.LISTENER_RACLINUX1.lsnr         ONLINE   ONLINE on raclinux1
```

```
ora.raclinux1.LISTENER_RCONFIG_RACLINUX1.lsnr ONLINE   ONLINE on raclinux1
ora.raclinux1.RACDB_RACLINUX1.lsnr            ONLINE   ONLINE on raclinux1
ora.raclinux1.gsd                             ONLINE   ONLINE on raclinux1
ora.raclinux1.ons                             ONLINE   ONLINE on raclinux1
ora.raclinux1.vip                             ONLINE   ONLINE on raclinux1
ora.raclinux2.ASM2.asm                        ONLINE   ONLINE on raclinux2
ora.raclinux2.LISTENER_RACLINUX2.lsnr         ONLINE   ONLINE on raclinux2
ora.raclinux2.RACDB_RACLINUX2.lsnr            ONLINE   ONLINE on raclinux2
ora.raclinux2.gsd                             ONLINE   ONLINE on raclinux2
ora.raclinux2.ons                             ONLINE   ONLINE on raclinux2
ora.raclinux2.vip                             ONLINE   ONLINE on raclinux2
```

As you can observe in the output provided here, the Clusterware stack is up and running on both nodes of the cluster.

Executing the runInstaller.sh script

Now it's time to start the actual upgrade process. For this, you first need to extract (unzip) the Oracle 11g R2 (grid software) from the DVD, or from any resource, into a staging area on Node 1 of the cluster, and execute `runInstaller.sh` script from the grid directory.

During the upgrade process, the Oracle Universal Installer automatically detects any pre-existing Clusterware on the node and automatically selects the **Upgrade Grid Infrastructure** option on the **Select Installation Option** screen.

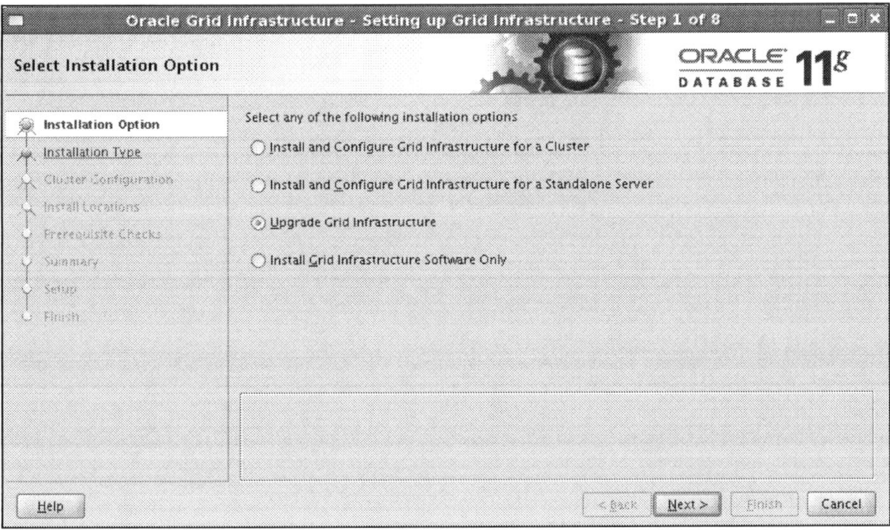

As part of an upgrade, any existing `ASM_HOME` on the selected nodes will be automatically upgraded as well. If any existing ASM instance is detected, the following message pop-up window is displayed upon clicking on **Next**. Ensure that the ASM instance and any database instances on this node are stopped before you start the upgrade operation.

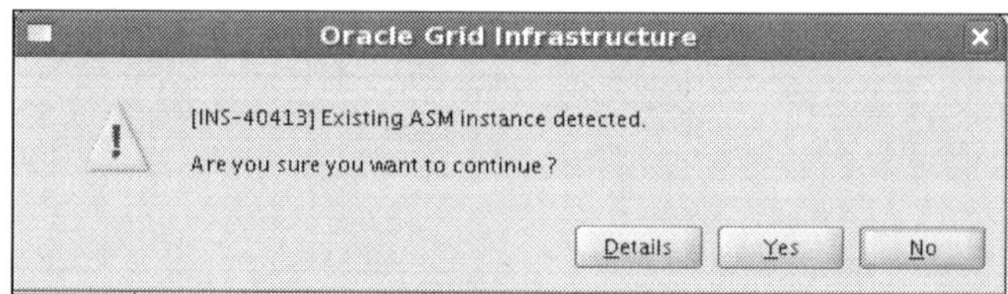

Click on **Yes** to proceed further and review the language settings on the **Product Language** option tab. Then click on **Next**.

On the **Node Selection** screen, all the participating nodes of an existing cluster are fetched and, by default, all nodes are selected for the upgrade operation, which is highly recommended during an upgrade. You may use the **Select All** or **Deselect All** options as per your requirements.

SSH Connectivity verification can be performed between the nodes by clicking the **SSH Connectivity** button.

Check the **Upgrade Current Automatic Storage Management (ASM)** option to upgrade an existing ASM instance as part of an upgrade process. You can choose to upgrade the ASM instance at this time or upgrade it later. However, it is strongly recommended that you upgrade the ASM during the Clusterware upgrade. When the upgrade option is checked, ASM Configuration Assistant will be started to upgrade the current ASM instance to Oracle 11g R2.

When you click on **Next**, a pop-up window is displayed testing the password-less SSH connectivity between the selected nodes, which is a recommended configuration. It might take a few minutes depending on the number of nodes participating in the upgrade.

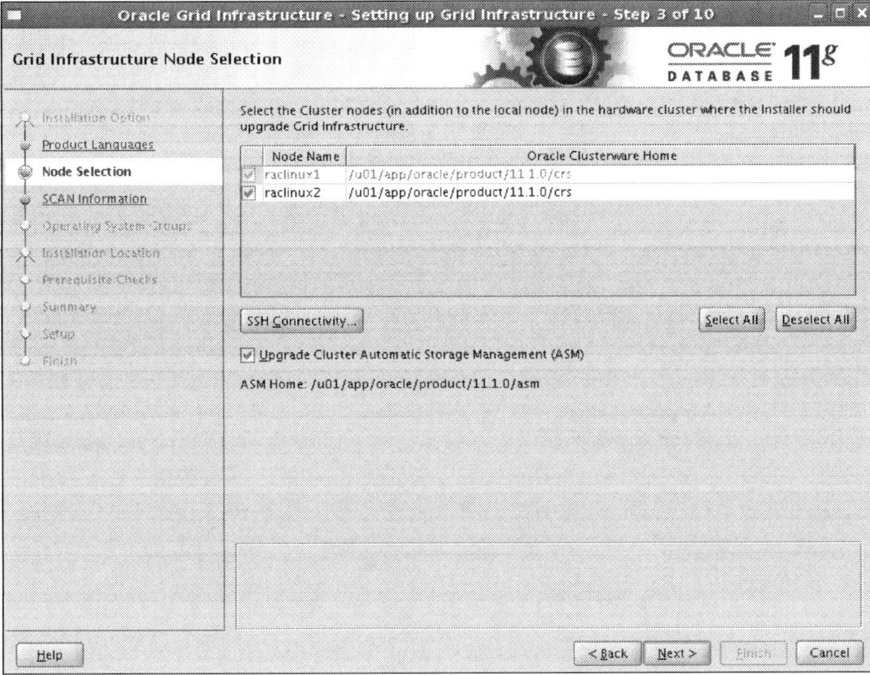

You will then be prompted to enter the **Single Client Access Name (SCAN)** and its port number here. The default SCAN port is 1521 or, if this port is in use or not available for any reason, you can change it to any available port.

SCAN, which is new in Oracle 11g R2, is the hostname that enables all clients to connect to the cluster, eliminating the need to modify clients when nodes are added or removed from the cluster. Typically, the SCAN name is the same as the cluster name. Make sure the SCAN name has three IP addresses specified either in the DNS or in the **Grid Naming Service (GNS)**.

Click on **Next** and the SCAN information will be validated before proceeding to the next screen.

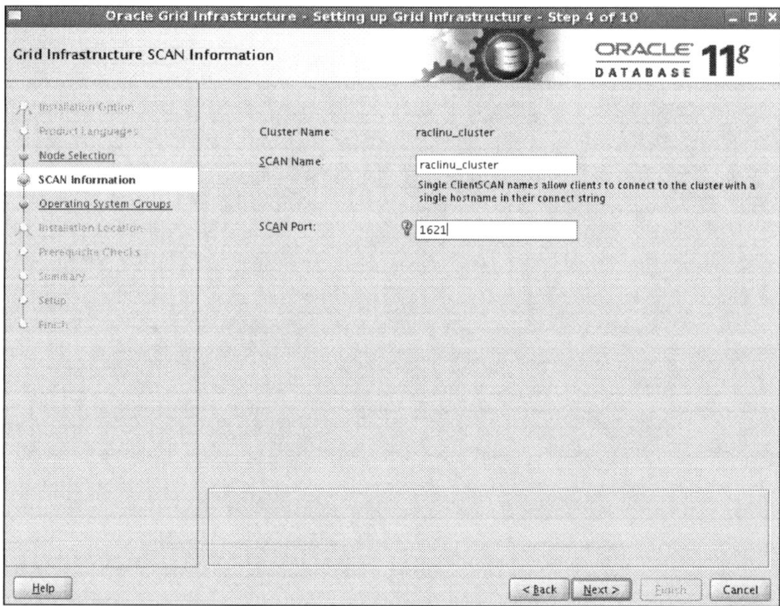

On the **ASM Monitor Password** screen, enter a password for the ASMSNMP user, which is required for the ASM upgrade. Make sure you enter a strong password or else an error message about a non-Oracle standard password window will appear. Then click on **Next**:

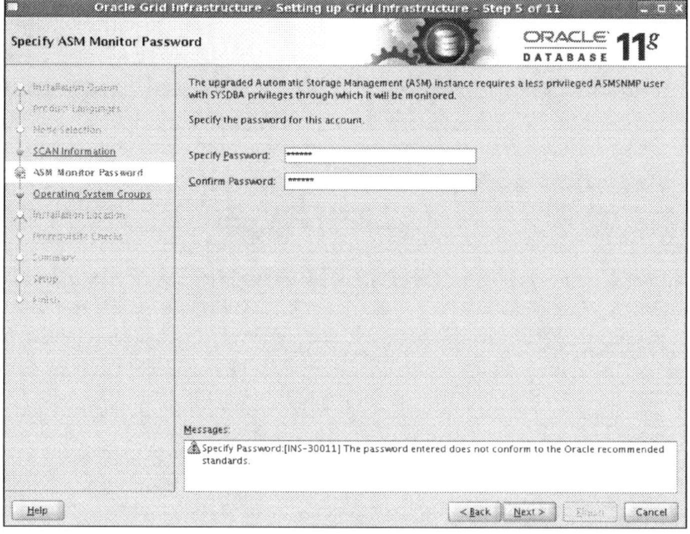

Subsequently, select the **OS...** groups from the drop-down list on the **Operating System Groups** screen and click on **Next**.

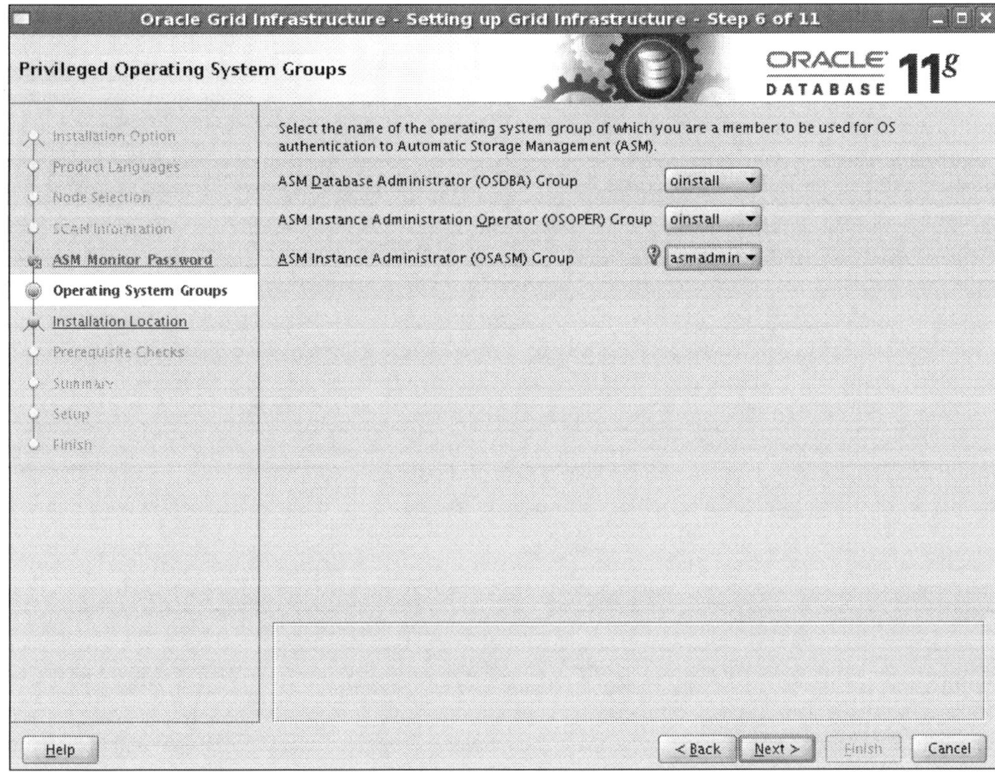

On the **Specify Installation Location** screen, enter the grid infrastructure home location details, where 11g R2 Clusterware and ASM binaries will be installed together, typically in the `/u01/app/11.2.0/grid` directory.

Upon clicking on **Next,** the prerequisite checks are subsequently performed. Any missing patches, inadequate space in the `/tmp filesystem`, or any missing kernel parameters along with their recommended values and errors (if any) will be reported.

The YES value under the fixable column header for any failed verifications indicates that you can fix this error without quitting from the current installation page. For example, you can open a new window and repair the error reported. Once the errors are fixed, you can click on the **Check Again** button on the top to perform the checks again.

The **Fix & Check Again** option can be used to dynamically adjust the errors reported here. The **Show Failed option** will produce the error details.

If you feel that the reported errors are not going to cause any damage to your upgrade/installation process, you will need to check **Ignore All** to ignore all the check errors reported here and proceed further with the upgrade procedure. However, it is strongly recommended that you resolve any serious errors before proceeding further and clicking on **Next**.

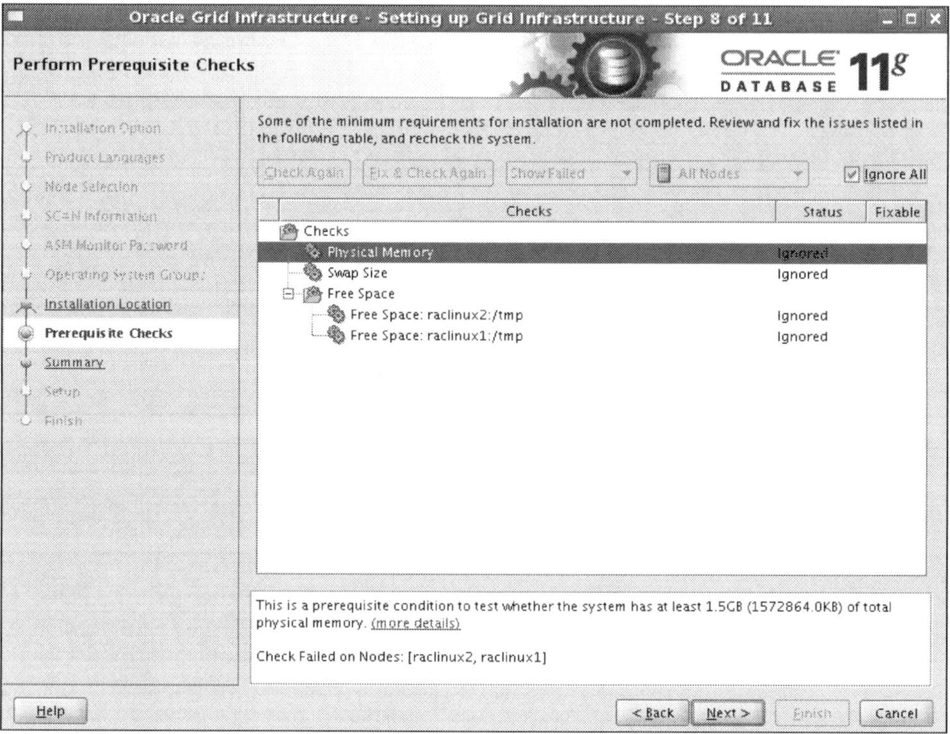

Review the summary on the **Summary** screen and click on **Finish** to start the upgrade operation.

As root, execute the `rootupgrade.sh` script on all nodes when prompted. This script will shut down the existing Oracle Clusterware stack and replace it with the new version of Clusterware and start the new Clusterware stack.

After the script is executed on a node, the Oracle Clusterware Stack and AUTOSTART resources on the node are started immediately:

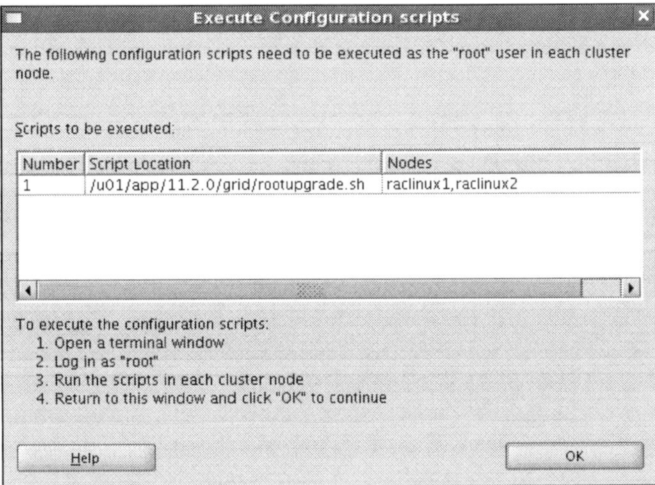

When the `rootupgrade.sh` script is executed on a node, the following output will be displayed on your screen:

```
[root@raclinux1 ~]# /u01/app/11.2.0/grid1/rootupgrade.sh
Running Oracle 11g root.sh script...

The following environment variables are set as:
    ORACLE_OWNER= oracle
    ORACLE_HOME=  /u01/app/11.2.0/grid1

Enter the full pathname of the local bin directory: [/usr/local/bin]:
The file "dbhome" already exists in /usr/local/bin.  Overwrite it? (y/n)
[n]:
The file "oraenv" already exists in /usr/local/bin.  Overwrite it? (y/n)
[n]:
The file "coraenv" already exists in /usr/local/bin.  Overwrite it? (y/n)
[n]:

Entries will be added to the /etc/oratab file as needed by
Database Configuration Assistant when a database is created
Finished running generic part of root.sh script.
Now product-specific root actions will be performed.
2009-09-07 23:52:12: Parsing the host name
2009-09-07 23:52:12: Checking for super user privileges
2009-09-07 23:52:12: User has super user privileges
```

```
Using configuration parameter file: /u01/app/11.2.0/grid1/crs/install/
crsconfig_params
Creating trace directory
Cluster Synchronization Services appears healthy
Event Manager appears healthy
Cluster Ready Services appears healthy
Shutting down Oracle Cluster Ready Services (CRS):
Sep 07 23:52:47.651 | INF | daemon shutting down
Stopping resources.
This could take several minutes.
Successfully stopped Oracle Clusterware resources
Stopping Cluster Synchronization Services.
Shutting down the Cluster Synchronization Services daemon.
Shutdown request successfully issued.
Shutdown has begun. The daemons should exit soon.
LOCAL ADD MODE
Creating OCR keys for user 'root', privgrp 'root'..
Operation successful.
Adding daemon to inittab
CRS-4123: Oracle High Availability Services has been started.
ohasd is starting
CRS-2672: Attempting to start 'ora.mdnsd' on 'raclinux1'
CRS-2676: Start of 'ora.mdnsd' on 'raclinux1' succeeded
CRS-2672: Attempting to start 'ora.gipcd' on 'raclinux1'
CRS-2676: Start of 'ora.gipcd' on 'raclinux1' succeeded
CRS-2672: Attempting to start 'ora.gpnpd' on 'raclinux1'
CRS-2676: Start of 'ora.gpnpd' on 'raclinux1' succeeded
CRS-2672: Attempting to start 'ora.cssdmonitor' on 'raclinux1'
CRS-2676: Start of 'ora.cssdmonitor' on 'raclinux1' succeeded
CRS-2672: Attempting to start 'ora.cssd' on 'raclinux1'
CRS-2672: Attempting to start 'ora.diskmon' on 'raclinux1'
CRS-2676: Start of 'ora.diskmon' on 'raclinux1' succeeded
CRS-2676: Start of 'ora.cssd' on 'raclinux1' succeeded
CRS-2672: Attempting to start 'ora.ctssd' on 'raclinux1'
CRS-2676: Start of 'ora.ctssd' on 'raclinux1' succeeded
CRS-2672: Attempting to start 'ora.crsd' on 'raclinux1'
```

```
CRS-2676: Start of 'ora.crsd' on 'raclinux1' succeeded
CRS-2672: Attempting to start 'ora.evmd' on 'raclinux1'
CRS-2676: Start of 'ora.evmd' on 'raclinux1' succeeded
clscfg: EXISTING configuration version 4 detected.
clscfg: version 4 is 11 Release 1.
Successfully accumulated necessary OCR keys.
Creating OCR keys for user 'root', privgrp 'root'..
Operation successful.

raclinux1     2009/09/07 23:58:08     /u01/app/11.2.0/grid1/cdata/
raclinux1/backup_20090907_235808.olr
Preparing packages for installation...
cvuqdisk-1.0.7-1
Configure Oracle Grid Infrastructure for a Cluster ... succeeded
Updating inventory properties for clusterware
Starting Oracle Universal Installer...

Checking swap space: must be greater than 500 MB.   Actual 2579 MB
Passed
The inventory pointer is located at /etc/oraInst.loc
The inventory is located at /u01/app/oraInventory
'UpdateNodeList' was successful.
Starting Oracle Universal Installer...

Checking swap space: must be greater than 500 MB.   Actual 2161 MB
Passed
The inventory pointer is located at /etc/oraInst.loc
The inventory is located at /u01/app/oraInventory
'UpdateNodeList' was successful.
```

After the script is executed on the first node, let's query the active and software versions of the Clusterware using the following commands from `$GRID_HOME/bin` location:

```
./crsctl query crs activeversion
Oracle Clusterware active version on the cluster is [11.1.0.6.0]

./crsctl query crs softwareversion
Oracle Clusterware version on node [raclinux1] is [11.2.0.1.0]
```

The Clusterware software version now displays 11.2.0.1.0, reflecting the newer version, whereas the active version is still showing the previous version. This is due to the fact that the active version doesn't show the new version until the script is successfully run on all the nodes.

The following output is expected when you execute the `rootupgrade.sh` script on the last node of the cluster:

```
[root@raclinux2 ~]# /u01/app/11.2.0/grid1/rootupgrade.sh
Running Oracle 11g root.sh script...

The following environment variables are set as:
    ORACLE_OWNER= oracle
    ORACLE_HOME=  /u01/app/11.2.0/grid1

Enter the full pathname of the local bin directory: [/usr/local/bin]:
The file "dbhome" already exists in /usr/local/bin.  Overwrite it? (y/n)
[n]:
The file "oraenv" already exists in /usr/local/bin.  Overwrite it? (y/n)
[n]:
The file "coraenv" already exists in /usr/local/bin.  Overwrite it? (y/n)
[n]:

Entries will be added to the /etc/oratab file as needed by
Database Configuration Assistant when a database is created
Finished running generic part of root.sh script.
Now product-specific root actions will be performed.
2009-09-08 00:03:19: Parsing the host name
2009-09-08 00:03:19: Checking for super user privileges
2009-09-08 00:03:19: User has super user privileges
Using configuration parameter file: /u01/app/11.2.0/grid1/crs/install/
crsconfig_params
Creating trace directory
Cluster Synchronization Services appears healthy
Event Manager appears healthy
Cluster Ready Services appears healthy
Shutting down Oracle Cluster Ready Services (CRS):
Sep 08 00:05:14.458 | INF | daemon shutting down
Stopping resources.
This could take several minutes.
```

```
Successfully stopped Oracle Clusterware resources
Stopping Cluster Synchronization Services.
Shutting down the Cluster Synchronization Services daemon.
Shutdown request successfully issued.
Shutdown has begun. The daemons should exit soon.
LOCAL ADD MODE
Creating OCR keys for user 'root', privgrp 'root'..
Operation successful.
Adding daemon to inittab
CRS-4123: Oracle High Availability Services has been started.
ohasd is starting
CRS-2672: Attempting to start 'ora.mdnsd' on 'raclinux2'
CRS-2676: Start of 'ora.mdnsd' on 'raclinux2' succeeded
CRS-2672: Attempting to start 'ora.gipcd' on 'raclinux2'
CRS-2676: Start of 'ora.gipcd' on 'raclinux2' succeeded
CRS-2672: Attempting to start 'ora.gpnpd' on 'raclinux2'
CRS-2676: Start of 'ora.gpnpd' on 'raclinux2' succeeded
CRS-2672: Attempting to start 'ora.cssdmonitor' on 'raclinux2'
CRS-2676: Start of 'ora.cssdmonitor' on 'raclinux2' succeeded
CRS-2672: Attempting to start 'ora.cssd' on 'raclinux2'
CRS-2672: Attempting to start 'ora.diskmon' on 'raclinux2'
CRS-2676: Start of 'ora.diskmon' on 'raclinux2' succeeded
CRS-2676: Start of 'ora.cssd' on 'raclinux2' succeeded
CRS-2672: Attempting to start 'ora.ctssd' on 'raclinux2'
CRS-2676: Start of 'ora.ctssd' on 'raclinux2' succeeded
CRS-2672: Attempting to start 'ora.crsd' on 'raclinux2'
CRS-2676: Start of 'ora.crsd' on 'raclinux2' succeeded
CRS-2672: Attempting to start 'ora.evmd' on 'raclinux2'
CRS-2676: Start of 'ora.evmd' on 'raclinux2' succeeded
clscfg: EXISTING configuration version 5 detected.
clscfg: version 5 is 11g Release 2.
Successfully accumulated necessary OCR keys.
Creating OCR keys for user 'root', privgrp 'root'..
Operation successful.

raclinux1     2009/09/08 00:14:03     /u01/app/11.2.0/grid1/cdata/
raclinu_cluster/backup_20090908_001403.ocr
```

```
raclinux1     2009/08/23 20:12:17     /u01/app/oracle/product/11.1.0/crs/
cdata/raclinu_cluster/backup_20090823_201217.ocr

raclinux2     2009/08/17 22:38:40     /u01/app/oracle/product/11.1.0/crs/
cdata/raclinu_cluster/backup_20090817_223840.ocr
Start upgrade invoked..
Started to upgrade the Oracle Clusterware. This operation may take a few
minutes.
Started to upgrade the CSS.
The CSS was successfully upgraded.
Started to upgrade the OCR.
Started to upgrade the CRS.
The CRS was successfully upgraded.
Successfully upgraded the Oracle Clusterware.
Oracle Clusterware operating version was successfully set to 11.2.0.1.0

raclinux2     2009/09/08 01:00:28     /u01/app/11.2.0/grid1/cdata/
raclinux2/backup_20090908_010028.olr
Preparing packages for installation...
cvuqdisk-1.0.7-1
Configure Oracle Grid Infrastructure for a Cluster ... succeeded
Updating inventory properties for clusterware
Starting Oracle Universal Installer...

Checking swap space: must be greater than 500 MB.   Actual 2081 MB
Passed
The inventory pointer is located at /etc/oraInst.loc
The inventory is located at /u01/app/oraInventory
'UpdateNodeList' was successful.
Starting Oracle Universal Installer...

Checking swap space: must be greater than 500 MB.   Actual 2071 MB
Passed
The inventory pointer is located at /etc/oraInst.loc
The inventory is located at /u01/app/oraInventory
'UpdateNodeList' was successful.
```

Click on **OK** to exit from the script screen and to proceed further:

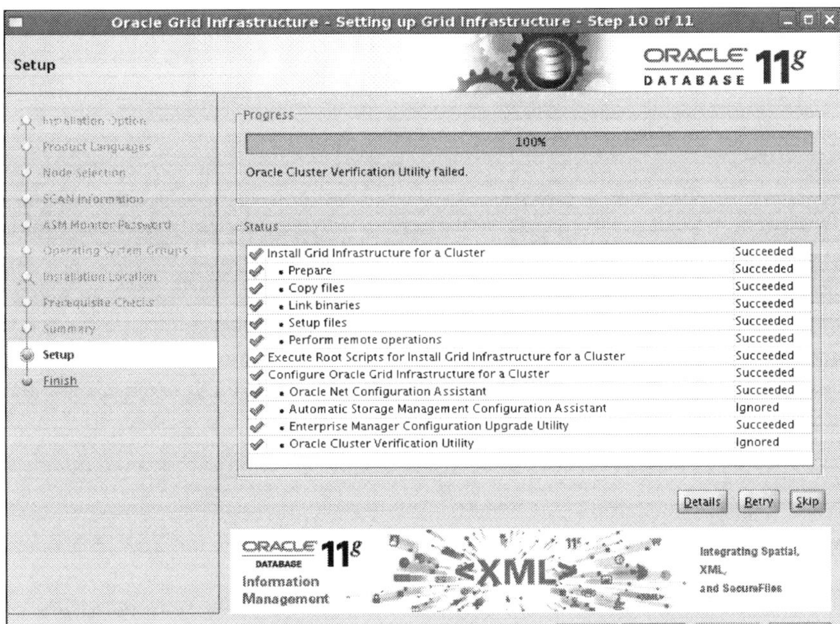

After executing the script successfully across all nodes of a cluster, ASMCA automatically starts upgrading an existing ASM instance to the newer version. Subsequently, Enterprise Manager (Database EM), if it exists, is upgraded along with the Cluster Verification Utilities, and the Clusterware upgrade is completed. For any failed upgrades, you can click on **Skip** to ignore this feature and proceed to the next feature.

At this stage, we have successfully completed an upgrade. Click on **Finish** to exit from the OUI.

Post-upgrade checks for 11g R2 Clusterware

After a successful 11g R2 Clusterware upgrade, let's verify the Clusterware active and software versions. Unlike before, both should now provide the newer version status. Use the following sample command on any node of the cluster:

```
crsctl query crs activeversion
Oracle Clusterware active version on the cluster is [11.2.0.1.0]

 crsctl query crs softwareversion
Oracle Clusterware version on node [raclinux2] is [11.2.0.1.0]
```

As we said earlier, the active version of the clusterware won't show you the upgraded version state unless all the nodes of the cluster are successfully upgraded. As we can see that the active version and software version of the clusterware are showing the new version state, we can determine that the clusterware upgrade is a success and can continue further with the post-upgrade tasks.

Use the following familiar cluster command to list the cluster stack and resources involved with this cluster. Execute `crsctl check cluster/crs` from the `$GRID_HOME/bin` location on any node in the cluster to check the status of the Clusterware stack:

```
crsctl check crs(provides current clusterware stack status
                   on the local node)
```

The following is what this command produces:

```
CRS-4638: Oracle High Availability Services is online << a new service in
11gR2 Clusterware>>
CRS-4537: Cluster Ready Services is online
CRS-4529: Cluster Synchronization Services is online
CRS-4533: Event Manager is online
```

`crsctl check cluster  is new in 11gR2`, provides current clusterware stack status across all nodes of a cluster. Therefore, this is one of the useful commands to check cluster status across all nodes from any node.

The Oracle High Availability service stack, new in 11g R2, comprises the following important processes:

- **Grid Plug and Play (GPNDP)**: This process provides access to the Grid Plug and Play profile and ensures that all of the nodes have the most recent profile.
- **Oracle Grid Naming Service (GNS):** This is a gateway between the cluster DNS and external DNS servers. This is responsible for name resolution within the cluster.

After the successful clusterware upgrade, all the cluster resources must be online. To verify the status, execute `crs_stat` from any node.

```
[oracle@raclinux2 ~]$ ./crs_stat.sh
HA Resourrce                                   Target     Stage
------------                                   ------     -----
ora.DATA.dg                                    ONLINE     ONLINE on raclinux1
ora.DATA2.dg                                   ONLINE     ONLINE on raclinux1
ora.FLASH.dg                                   ONLINE     ONLINE on raclinux1
ora.LISTENER_RCONFIG.lsnr                      ONLINE     ONLINE on raclinux1
ora.LISTENER_SCAN1.lsnr                        ONLINE     ONLINE on raclinux1
ora.asm                                        ONLINE     ONLINE on raclinux1
ora.eons                                       ONLINE     ONLINE on raclinux1
ora.gsd                                        ONLINE     OFFLINE
ora.net1.network                               ONLINE     ONLINE on raclinux1
ora.oc4j                                       OFFLINE    OFFLINE
ora.ons                                        ONLINE     ONLINE on raclinux1
ora.raclinux1.ASM1.asm                         ONLINE     ONLINE on raclinux1
ora.raclinux1.LISTENER_RCONFIG_RACLINUX1.lsnr ONLINE     ONLINE on raclinux1
ora.raclinux1.gsd                              ONLINE     OFFLINE
ora.raclinux1.ons                              ONLINE     ONLINE on raclinux1
ora.raclinux1.vip                              ONLINE     ONLINE on raclinux1
ora.raclinux2.ASM2.asm                         ONLINE     ONLINE on raclinux2
ora.raclinux2.LISTENER_RCONFIG_RACLINUX2.lsnr ONLINE     ONLINE on raclinux2
ora.raclinux2.gsd                              OFFLINE    OFFLINE
ora.raclinux2.ons                              ONLINE     ONLINE on raclinux2
ora.raclinux2.vip                              ONLINE     ONLINE on raclinux2
ora.registry.acfs                              ONLINE     ONLINE on raclinux1
ora.scan1.vip                                  ONLINE     ONLINE on raclinux1
```

In contrast to the previous Oracle version, you will find the extra clusterware resources such as ASM Cluster File System (ACFS), SCAN VIP, SCAN Listener, oc4j, and so on. Additionally, all the diskgroups created, or diskgroups that exist in the ASM instance, are now registered as a resource in the OCR.

Post-upgrade steps for 11g R2 Clusterware

An Oracle RAC upgrade consists of upgrading Clusterware first and then subsequently upgrading DB homes and databases respectively. After the successful Clusterware upgrade, the following post-clusterware 11g R2-upgrade steps will have to be completed:

- If the ASM upgrade option was not selected during the Clusterware upgrade process, run the ASM Configuration Assistant (`./asmca`) from `$GRID_HOME/bin` location to upgrade the ASM in a rolling upgrade fashion.
- Make sure you set the following environment values on the node on which you are upgrading ASM:

  ```
  export ASMCA_ROLLING_UPGRADE=true
  ```
- After an ASM upgrade, install Oracle 11g R2 RDBMS software binaries in a different location. Please refer to *Chapter 3, Clusterware Installation*, for a step-by-step installation procedure.

- After the database software is installed on all nodes in the cluster, move on to upgrading databases to Oracle 11g R2 using any one of the convenient methods such as the **Database Upgrade Assistant** (**DBUA**) utility from the new Oracle 11g R2 bin location or the manual method of upgrading the database.
- Back up new `$GRID_HOME` and Oracle Homes and databases.
- Back up the OCR file.
- After successfully upgrading and thoroughly testing the application functionality, you may then remove the previous version CRS, ASM, and RDBMS homes (directories) to reclaim the space on the nodes.

Downgrading Oracle Clusterware after an upgrade

For any technical or non-technical reason, you may want to downgrade a successful or failed upgrade of Oracle Clusterware 11g R2 to the previous version as it was before 11g R2. In order to do so, you will need to complete the following downgrade procedure:

1. As root, navigate through the `$GRID_HOME/crs/install` directory and execute the `rootcrs.pl -downgrade` script on all nodes in a cluster. This script will stop the resources and shut down the cluster stack on the node.

   ```
   /u01/app/11.2.0/grid/crs/install/rootcrs.pl -downgrade [-force]
   ```

2. Use the `-force` flag to stop partial or failed 11g R2 upgrades. However, this command neither resets the OCR nor deletes `ocr.loc`.
3. After the `rootcrs.pl -downgrade` script is successfully executed on all nodes, as the root user on the local Node 1 of the cluster, you will need to navigate through the `GRID_HOME/crs/install` directory and execute the following sample command:

   ```
   /u01/app/11.2.0/grid/crs/install/rootcrs.pl -downgrade -lastnode
   -oldcrshome /u01/app/oracle/product/11.1.0/crs -version 11.1.0.6.0
   [-force]
   ```

The following table explains the flags used in this command:

Flag	Description
`-lastnode`	Indicates the last node of the cluster
`-oldcrshome`	Pre-11g R2 upgrade Clusterware home
`-version`	Pre-11g R2 upgrade Clusterware version
`-force`	Used for any partial or failed upgrades

This script downgrades the OCR and clean-up binaries from the newly created `$GRID_HOME`.

Once you execute the script successfully across all nodes, you are then prompted to execute the `root.sh` script from the previous version of Oracle Clusterware home in sequence on each node of the cluster. This script brings up the Clusterware stack from the previous version and automatically starts all the resources registered with the old Clusterware, and also configures the old initialization scripts (`/init.d/init.*`) to run the previous version Clusterware stack.

All the configuration changes that you have made during or after an 11g R2 upgrade are removed permanently and cannot be recovered.

Summary

In this chapter, we discussed the possibilities of an upgrade scenario such as why an upgrade is necessary and also the prerequisites that are needed before commencing an upgrade process. We have demonstrated upgrade scenarios of Oracle Clusterware from Oracle 10g R2 to 11g R1 and then from 11g R1 to the latest Oracle 11g R2.

At the end of this chapter, we also briefly explained the process of how to downgrade an Oracle Clusterware after an 11g R2 upgrade to the previous version. You should now feel you have sufficient information and feel confident to plan your upgrade efficiently. Moreover, we strongly recommend that you take the current environment backups prior to performing any upgrade process. In the next chapter, we are going to discuss some of the best real-world scenarios, such as extending cluster capabilities by adding more nodes and converting a non-RAC database to RAC.

10
Real-world Scenarios

In this chapter, we will consider some real-world business scenarios that are very essential for any RAC database administrator. Let's begin this chapter by considering some important questions regarding situations you may possibly find yourself in, while handling Oracle Clusterware and dealing with business-critical RAC databases:

- First, how will you manage if the database server has reached the maximum resource capacity and you are unable to add any additional resources, in terms of CPU and memory?
- How will you handle the workload pressure of your application if the number of business users increases drastically?
- How will you provide users the uninterrupted service of your business-critical applications during a prolonged planned or unplanned downtime or prevent any single-point of failure situations?

When facing real-world business scenarios similar to the ones in this bullet list, an Oracle Real Application Cluster (RAC) could be the answer to all of your concerns. It has the ability to provide rich flexibility by adding more new nodes on demand to extend your existing cluster environment and allows you to add more instances to existing RAC databases and move databases or instances between nodes.

In summary, we will discuss the following topics:

- Adding a new node to an existing cluster
- Removing a node from the cluster
- Adding an RAC database instance
- Deleting an RAC database instance
- Converting a single-instance database to an RAC database
- Relocating an RAC database and instances across nodes

Adding a new node to an existing cluster

The prime objective of this scenario is to describe and demonstrate the tools and methods to add a new node to an existing cluster environment to verticality scale up the environment. Although there are various methods that exist to add a new node, we consider the procedure using the `addNode.sh` shell script to perform this task among other methods. Just before we initiate the procedure, we assume that there is an existing cluster environment to which a new node, `raclinux2`, will be added on non-shared Oracle homes.

Please note that until pre 11g R2, we maintained a separate Oracle home for ASM and RDBMS binaries.

Before adding a new node to an existing cluster, the following prerequisites must be met:

- You should have successfully installed Oracle Clusterware on at least one of the nodes in an existing cluster environment.
- All existing nodes in the cluster must be up and running. For any reason, if a node is having problems, you must solve the problems first or remove the node from the cluster, if required.
- Prepare the OS with recommended kernel parameters and apply latest patches/packages on the new nodes.
- Create OS groups, typically oinstall, dba, and an Oracle software user on the new nodes. Ensure that group name and ID, and usenames and ID remain the same across the nodes.
- Configure the required three IPs for the new servers—public, private, and VIP, and include these details in the `/etc/hosts` file across all nodes, including new nodes, or in the DNS (if it exists).
- If you are on Oracle 11g R2, make sure you have the new Single Client Access Name (SCAN) with three IPs defined in the DNS. Set up the user `ssh` equivalence (rsa and dsa keys) on all existing nodes, including new nodes.
- Prepare the shared disks, as new nodes must have read and write permissions on those shared disks.

Don't forget to synchronize the time on new nodes. If you are on Oracle 11g R2, Oracle uses **Cluster Time Synchronize Service** (**CTSS**) functionality.

Once these mandatory prerequisites are met, the following stages must be completed while adding a new node to an existing cluster:

- Verify pre-requisites with the `cluvfy` utility
- Install (clone) Oracle Clusterware
- Install (clone) ASM software in a separate home—in Oracle 11g R2, Cluster and ASM exist in a single home, for example, `$GRID_HOME`
- Install (clone) RDBMS software

Performing prechecks with the cluvfy utility

It is mandatory to verify the prerequisites on the new nodes before actually starting the node addition process. To verify the hardware and OS prerequisites on the new nodes such as packages, kernel parameters, network interfaces, or shared storage, use the cluvfy (cluster verification) utility. Do this by running the following sample command from the `$ORA_CRS_HOME/bin` location, preferably on Node 1 of your cluster.

```
$ ./cluvfy stage -post hwos -n raclinux2 [-verbose]
```

This command is likely to produce the following sample output, which will verify and confirm the readiness of hardware and OS on the new nodes:

```
Performing post-checks for hardware and operating system setup

Checking node reachability...
Node reachability check passed from node "raclinux1".


Checking user equivalence...
User equivalence check passed for user "oracle".

Checking node connectivity...

Node connectivity check passed for subnet "192.168.2.0" with node(s)
raclinux2.
Node connectivity check passed for subnet "192.168.0.0" with node(s)
raclinux2.

Interfaces found on subnet "192.168.2.0" that are likely candidates for a
private interconnect:
raclinux2 eth0:192.168.2.102 eth0:192.168.2.112

Interfaces found on subnet "192.168.0.0" that are likely candidates for a
private interconnect:
raclinux2 eth1:192.168.0.102
```

```
WARNING:
Could not find a suitable set of interfaces for VIPs.

Node connectivity check passed.

Checking shared storage accessibility...

WARNING:
Package cvuqdisk not installed.
        raclinux2

Shared storage check failed on nodes "raclinux2".

Post-check for hardware and operating system setup was unsuccessful on
all the nodes.
```

The VIP warning message in this output is expected and it can be safely ignored as the VIP will be configured at a later stage. However, you will need to examine the other errors reported here as it is necessary to repair all the errors before proceeding further. Therefore, after successfully performing the storage and OS prechecks, you will need to verify the user equivalence and node connectivity, and the interconnect interfaces and system requirements.

Use the following example from the `$ORA_CRS_HOME/bin` location as part of the pre-cluster installation:

```
./cluvfy stage -pre crsinst -n raclinux2 -verbose
```

This command produces the following sample output:

```
Performing pre-checks for cluster services setup

Checking node reachability...
Node reachability check passed from node "raclinux1".


Checking user equivalence...
User equivalence check passed for user "oracle".

Checking administrative privileges...
User existence check passed for "oracle".
Group existence check passed for "oinstall".
Membership check for user "oracle" in group "oinstall" [as Primary]
passed.
```

```
Administrative privileges check passed.

Checking node connectivity...

Node connectivity check passed for subnet "192.168.2.0" with node(s)
raclinux2.
Node connectivity check passed for subnet "192.168.0.0" with node(s)
raclinux2.

Interfaces found on subnet "192.168.2.0" that are likely candidates for a
private interconnect:
raclinux2 eth0:192.168.2.102 eth0:192.168.2.112

Interfaces found on subnet "192.168.0.0" that are likely candidates for a
private interconnect:
raclinux2 eth1:192.168.0.102

WARNING:
Could not find a suitable set of interfaces for VIPs.

Node connectivity check passed.


Checking system requirements for 'crs'...
Total memory check failed.
Check failed on nodes:
        raclinux2
Free disk space check passed.
Swap space check passed.
System architecture check passed.
Kernel version check passed.
Package existence check passed for "make-3.81".
Package existence check passed for "binutils-2.17.50.0.6".
Package existence check passed for "gcc-4.1.1".
Package existence check passed for "libaio-0.3.106".
Package existence check passed for "libaio-devel-0.3.106".
Package existence check passed for "libstdc++-4.1.1".
Package existence check passed for "elfutils-libelf-devel-0.125".
Package existence check passed for "sysstat-7.0.0".
Package existence check passed for "compat-libstdc++-33-3.2.3".
Package existence check passed for "libgcc-4.1.1".
```

```
Package existence check passed for "libstdc++-devel-4.1.1".
Package existence check passed for "unixODBC-2.2.11".
Package existence check passed for "unixODBC-devel-2.2.11".
Package existence check passed for "glibc-2.5-12".
Group existence check passed for "dba".
Group existence check passed for "oinstall".
User existence check passed for "nobody".

System requirement failed for 'crs'

Pre-check for cluster services setup was unsuccessful on all the nodes.
```

If there are any errors reported during the prechecks, such as missing packages or a lack of sufficient kernel parameters, you are required to resolve them to ensure a successful node addition operation.

However, in Oracle 11g R2, you can simply use the following cluster preinstall `cluvfy` command from `$GRID_HOME/bin`, to verify the integrity of the cluster and the new nodes, before adding to an existing cluster:

```
./cluvfy stage -pre nodeadd -n node_list [-fixup [-fixupdir fixup_dir_
location] ] [-verbose]
```

When the fixup argument is used and its directory location is specified, the `cluvfy` utility will print instructions to fix the cluster and the node verification failures. This will help you resolve any issues before proceeding further, by executing the given script on the respective nodes.

addNode.sh

The `addNode.sh` shell script makes the process of adding a new node very simple and straightforward. First, when the addNode.sh script is executed from `$ORA_CRS_HOME/oui/bin`, preferably on Node 1 in the cluster, it invokes Oracle Universal Installer (OUI) and displays a **Welcome** screen as in the following screenshot:

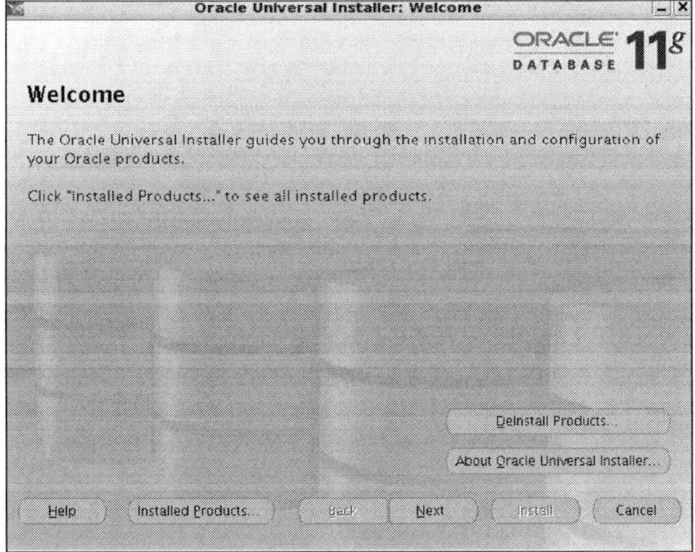

You will then need to click click on **Next** to continue.

On the **Specify Cluster Nodes to Add to Installation** screen, it lists details about all existing nodes that are part of the existing cluster and allows you to enter new node details that are required. Enter **public, private,** and **VIP** host names (alias) in the **Specify New Nodes** tab, as specified in the `/etc/host` file on the nodes. Then click on **Next**.

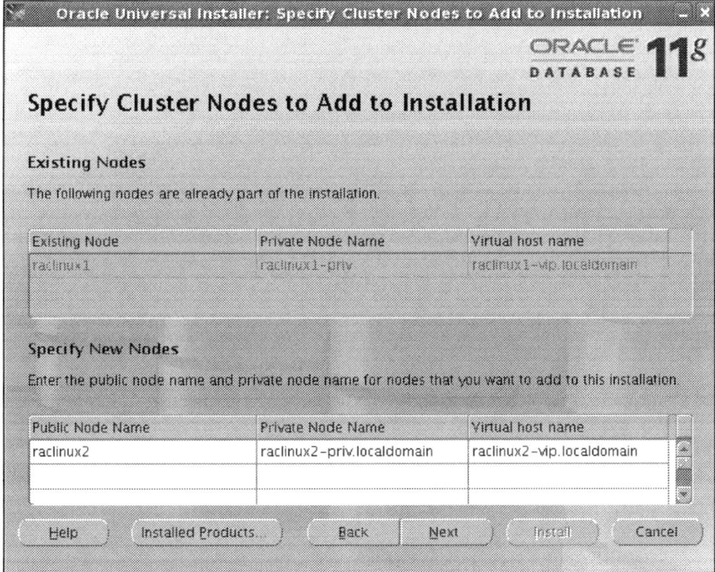

Review the **Summary** screen and click on **Install** to begin the process of adding the node.

Subsequently, the **Cluster Node Addition Progress** screen appears.

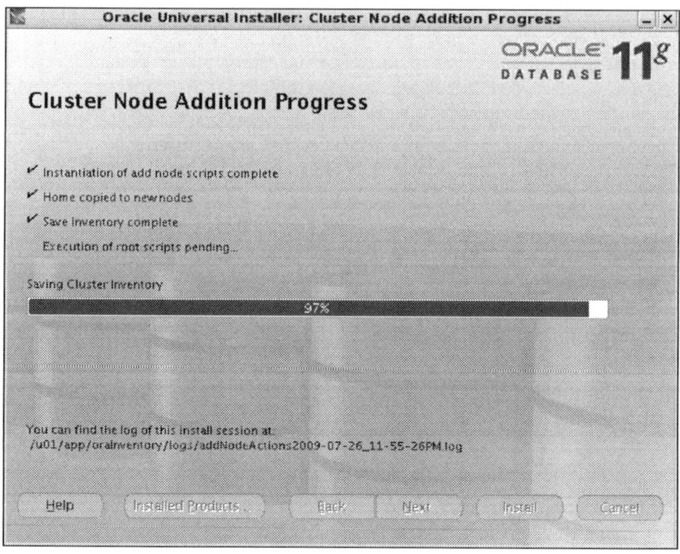

When the **Cluster Node Addition Progress** reaches 97%, a pop-up box appears with the instructions to run the `oraInstRoot.sh`, `rootaddnode.sh`, and `root.sh` scripts as root user on Node 1 (from where you executed the add-node process) and subsequently on the new node.

After the required scripts have been executed successfully on all the nodes, click on **OK** to finish the process of adding a node and click on **YES** on the **EXIT** pop-up window to quit from the **Oracle Universal Installer** (**OUI**).

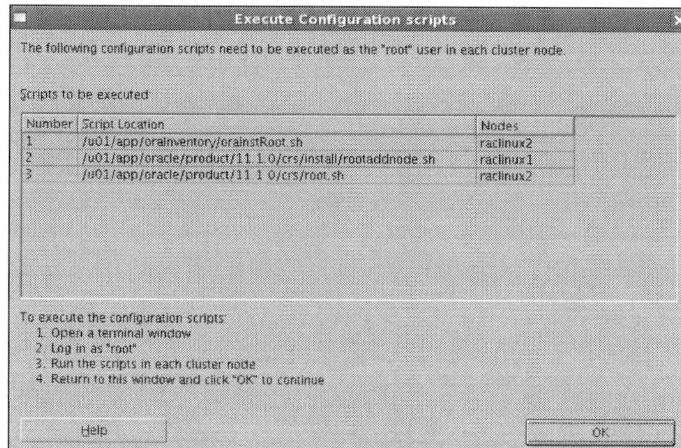

When you execute these scripts on respective nodes, the following sample output is expected:

```
[root@raclinux2 ~]# id
uid=0(root) gid=0(root) groups=0(root),1(bin),2(daemon),3(sys),4(adm),6(disk),10
(wheel)
[root@raclinux2 ~]# /u01/app/oraInventory/orainstRoot.sh
Changing permissions of /u01/app/oraInventory to 770.
Changing groupname of /u01/app/oraInventory to oinstall.
The execution of the script is complete
[root@raclinux2 ~]#
```

After the `rootaddnode.sh` script is run, it will add new-node OCR keys to the OCR file and will automatically run the nodeapps operations as shown in the following sample output:

```
[root@raclinux1 ~]# id
uid=0(root) gid=0(root) groups=0(root),1(bin),2(daemon),3(sys),4(adm),6(disk),10(wheel
)
[root@raclinux1 ~]#
[root@raclinux1 ~]# /u01/app/oracle/product/11.1.0/crs/install/rootaddnode.sh
clscfg: EXISTING configuration version 4 detected.
clscfg: version 4 is 11 Release 1.
Attempting to add 1 new nodes to the configuration
Using ports: CSS=49895 CRS=49896 EVMC=49898 and EVMR=49897.
node <nodenumber>: <nodename> <private interconnect name> <hostname>
node 2: raclinux2 raclinux2-priv raclinux2
Creating OCR keys for user 'root', privgrp 'root'..
Operation successful.
/u01/app/oracle/product/11.1.0/crs/bin/srvctl add nodeapps -n raclinux2 -A raclinux2-v
ip.localdomain/255.255.255.0/eth0
[root@raclinux1 ~]#
```

The `root.sh` sets the permission, creates `/etc/oracle` directory, sets the OCR location, and creates an OCR backup location:

```
[root@raclinux2 ~]# /u01/app/oracle/product/11.1.0/crs/root.sh
WARNING: directory '/u01/app/oracle/product/11.1.0' is not owned by root
WARNING: directory '/u01/app/oracle/product' is not owned by root
WARNING: directory '/u01/app/oracle' is not owned by root
WARNING: directory '/u01/app' is not owned by root
WARNING: directory '/u01' is not owned by root
Checking to see if Oracle CRS stack is already configured
/etc/oracle does not exist. Creating it now.
OCR LOCATIONS =  /dev/sdb1
OCR backup directory '/u01/app/oracle/product/11.1.0/crs/cdata/raclinu_cluster' does not exist. Creating now
Setting the permissions on OCR backup directory
Setting up Network socket directories
Failed to upgrade Oracle Cluster Registry configuration
[root@raclinux2 ~]#
```

Adding a node in silent mode in Oracle 11g R2

In Oracle 11g R2, you can also use the –silent option with the `addNode.sh` script to perform the precedure of adding a node silently. Use the following set of commands:

- If you are using the **Grid Naming Server** (**GNS**), which is new in 11g R2, use the following command from the `$GRID_HOME/oui/bin` location:

```
./addNode.sh -silent "CLUSTER_NEW_NODES={raclinux2}"
```

- If you are not using the Grid Naming Service, use the following command from the `$GRID_HOME/oui/bin` location:

```
./addNode.sh -silent "CLUSTER_NEW_NODES={raclinux2}" "CLUSTER_NEW_
VIRTUAL_HOSTNAMES={raclinux2_vip}"
```

You must add the host name and IP address of new nodes to DNS, if you are not using Oracle Grid Naming Service.

Post-installation status checks for Clusterware

At this stage, we should have successfully added a new node to our existing cluster—now what next? The next stage would be to verify the node addition by considering the following steps:

1. Upon successful node addition, run the familiar cluster commands—`crs_stat` and `olsnodes`—from the `CLUSTER_HOME/bin` location to verify the new node addition:

```
[oracle@raclinux1 ~]$ ./crs_stat.sh
HA Resourrce                                  Target     Stage
------------                                  ------     -----
ora.RACDB.RACDB1.inst                         ONLINE     ONLINE on raclinux1
ora.RACDB.RACDB_MAIN.RACDB1.srv               ONLINE     ONLINE on raclinux1
ora.RACDB.RACDB_MAIN.cs                       ONLINE     ONLINE on raclinux1
ora.RACDB.db                                  ONLINE     ONLINE on raclinux1
ora.raclinux1.ASM1.asm                        ONLINE     ONLINE on raclinux1
ora.raclinux1.LISTENER_RACLINUX1.lsnr         ONLINE     ONLINE on raclinux1
ora.raclinux1.RACDB_RACLINUX1.lsnr            ONLINE     ONLINE on raclinux1
ora.raclinux1.gsd                             ONLINE     ONLINE on raclinux1
ora.raclinux1.ons                             ONLINE     ONLINE on raclinux1
ora.raclinux1.vip                             ONLINE     ONLINE on raclinux1
ora.raclinux2.gsd                             ONLINE     ONLINE on raclinux2
ora.raclinux2.ons                             ONLINE     ONLINE on raclinux2
ora.raclinux2.vip                             ONLINE     ONLINE on raclinux2
```

2. As you can see in the output, the new node named `raclinux2` has been successfully added to the cluster and all its components are up and running. In Oracle 11g R2, you may see different screenshots with a few more additional cluster components. The `olsnodes` command will list all the participating nodes of an existing cluster:

```
$ORA_CRS_HOME/bin/olsnodes -n
raclinux1       1
raclinux2       2
```

3. Verify whether the cluster stack is started on the new nodes, by executing the following command on the new nodes:

   `$ORA_CRS_HOME/bin/crsctl check crs`

4. In Oracle 11g R2, you can use the following command to check the entire cluster stack on all nodes from any node. This command is not available pre-Oracle 11g R2:

   `$GRID_HOME/bin/crsctl check cluster`

5. Ensure that the clusterware stack—CRSD, CSSD, and EVM—along with possible **Oracle High Availability Services (OHASD)** (in Oracle 11g R2) are up and running on all the new nodes added just a while ago, as shown here:

```
[oracle@raclinux2 bin]$ ./crsctl check crs
CRS-4638: Oracle High Availability Services is online
CRS-4537: Cluster Ready Services is online
CRS-4529: Cluster Synchronization Services is online
CRS-4533: Event Manager is online
```

6. The following command shows the cluster OS daemon process in Oracle 11g R1:

   `ps -ef |grep init.d`

```
root      6493     1  0 19:37 ?        00:00:00 /bin/sh /etc/init.d/init.evmd run
root      6494     1  0 19:37 ?        00:00:11 /bin/sh /etc/init.d/init.cssd fatal
root      6508     1  0 19:37 ?        00:00:00 /bin/sh /etc/init.d/init.crsd run
root     12108  6494  0 19:48 ?        00:00:00 /bin/sh /etc/init.d/init.cssd oprocd
root     12121  6494  0 19:48 ?        00:00:00 /bin/sh /etc/init.d/init.cssd oclsomon
root     12145  6494  0 19:48 ?        00:00:00 /bin/sh /etc/init.d/init.cssd daemon
```

7. On Oracle 11g R2, only the **Oracle High Availability Service Daemon (OHASD)** will appear:

```
root      6539     1  0 16:16 ?        00:00:00 /bin/sh /etc/init.d/init.ohasd run
```

8. The following command shows the following cluster OS background process in Oracle 11g R1 and Oracle 11g R2:

   `ps -ef |grep d.bin`

9. On Oracle 11g R1, you will see the following cluster daemons running on the nodes:

```
root      6493     1  0 19:37 ?        00:00:00 /bin/sh /etc/init.d/init.evmd run
root      6494     1  0 19:37 ?        00:00:11 /bin/sh /etc/init.d/init.cssd fatal
root      6508     1  0 19:37 ?        00:00:00 /bin/sh /etc/init.d/init.crsd run
root     12108  6494  0 19:48 ?        00:00:00 /bin/sh /etc/init.d/init.cssd oprocd
root     12121  6494  0 19:48 ?        00:00:00 /bin/sh /etc/init.d/init.cssd oclsomon
root     12145  6494  0 19:48 ?        00:00:00 /bin/sh /etc/init.d/init.cssd daemon
```

10. On the other hand, on Oracle 11g R2, you will see the following cluster daemons running on the nodes:

```
[oracle@raclinux1 bin]$ ps -ef |grep d.bin
root      6371     1  4 20:02 ?        00:00:21 /u01/app/11.2.0/grid1/bin/ohasd.bin reboot
oracle    6787     1  0 20:03 ?        00:00:00 /u01/app/11.2.0/grid1/bin/gipcd.bin
oracle    6792     1  0 20:03 ?        00:00:00 /u01/app/11.2.0/grid1/bin/mdnsd.bin
oracle    6807     1  1 20:03 ?        00:00:05 /u01/app/11.2.0/grid1/bin/gpnpd.bin
oracle    6887     1  4 20:03 ?        00:00:16 /u01/app/11.2.0/grid1/bin/ocssd.bin
root      7228     1  0 20:04 ?        00:00:01 /u01/app/11.2.0/grid1/bin/octssd.bin reboot
oracle    7735     1  1 20:04 ?        00:00:04 /u01/app/11.2.0/grid1/bin/evmd.bin
root      7737     1  3 20:04 ?        00:00:11 /u01/app/11.2.0/grid1/bin/crsd.bin reboot
root      7816     1  0 20:05 ?        00:00:01 /u01/app/11.2.0/grid1/bin/oclskd.bin
oracle    8625     1  0 20:08 ?        00:00:00 /u01/app/11.2.0/grid1/bin/oclskd.bin
```

11. You must then verify the post-clusterware installation by running the following command:

```
./cluvfy stage -post crsinst -n raclinux2
```

12. When this command is used, the following post-cluster addition sample output is expected that shows the extent of success of the new node addition:

```
Performing post-checks for cluster services setup

Checking node reachability...
Node reachability check passed from node "raclinux2".
Checking user equivalence...
User equivalence check passed for user "oracle".

Checking Cluster manager integrity...
Checking CSS daemon...
Daemon status check passed for "CSS daemon".

Cluster manager integrity check passed.
Checking cluster integrity...
Cluster integrity check passed
Checking OCR integrity...
```

```
Checking the absence of a non-clustered configuration...
All nodes free of non-clustered, local-only configurations.

Uniqueness check for OCR device passed.

Checking the version of OCR...
OCR of correct Version "2" exists.
Checking data integrity of OCR...
Data integrity check for OCR passed.

OCR integrity check passed.

Checking CRS integrity...
Checking daemon liveness...
Liveness check passed for "CRS daemon".
Checking daemon liveness...
Liveness check passed for "CSS daemon".
Checking daemon liveness...
Liveness check passed for "EVM daemon".
Checking CRS health...
CRS health check passed.

CRS integrity check passed.

Checking node application existence...
Checking existence of VIP node application (required)
Check passed.
Checking existence of ONS node application (optional)
Check passed.
Checking existence of GSD node application (optional)
Check passed.
Post-check for cluster services setup was successful.
```

We will then need to back up the OCR file and Voting Disk (as of 11g R2, the OCR backs up the voting disk contents so the voting disk backup is not required anymore).

Starting with Oracle 11g R1, `ocrconfig -manualbackup` can be used to perform a manual OCR physical backup on demand. When the `manualbackup` option is used, an OCR backup file named `backup_<sysdate>_<nnnnn>.ocr` will be created under the `/u01/app/oracle/product/11.1.0/crs/cdata/locaton`.

OCR file manual backup syntax

As root, preferably on Node 1 of your cluster, use the following command to perform an OCR file manual backup:

```
ocrconfig -manualbackup
```

Voting Disk backup syntax

As root user, use the following command to back up the voting disk (this is not supported in 11g R2):

```
dd if=voting_disk_name of=backup_file_name
```

In Oracle 11g R2, you can use the `post nodeadd` option with the `cluvfy` utility to verify whether or not the specified new nodes have been successfully added:

```
cluvfy stage -post nodeadd -n raclinux2 [-verbose]
```

This command verifies the network, shared storage, and cluster levels in the specified nodes.

In Oracle 11g R2, Voting disks are automatically backed up in OCR after any changes are made to the cluster.

Installing ASM and RDBMS software using addNode.sh script

Once the Clusterware is installed or cloned successfully, the subsequent step is to add Automatic Storage Management (ASM) and Oracle RDBMS software binaries in Oracle 11g R1.

Make a note that starting with Oracle 11g R2, the Clusterware and ASM homes are stored in a single home called `$GRID_HOME`. If you are on Oracle 11g R1 and have been maintaining ASM and RDBMS homes separately, it is strongly recommended that you install ASM and RDBMS software.

Cloning ASM software using addNode.sh script on Oracle 11g R1

In order to install or clone ASM software on the new node, we will first have to execute the `addNode.sh` script from the `$ORA_ASM_HOME/oui/bin` location, preferably from Node 1 in the cluster. This in turn invokes an Oracle Universal Installer (OUI) automatically. We will then need to click on **Next** on the **Welcome** screen.

We will then be presented with the **Specify Cluster Nodes to Add to Installation** screen, which fetches all participating node names from an existing cluster and displays the node names (as specified in the `/etc/hosts` file) that you want to add to an existing cluster under the **Specify New Nodes** section. Once we select the required new nodes from the list, click on **Next** to proceed further.

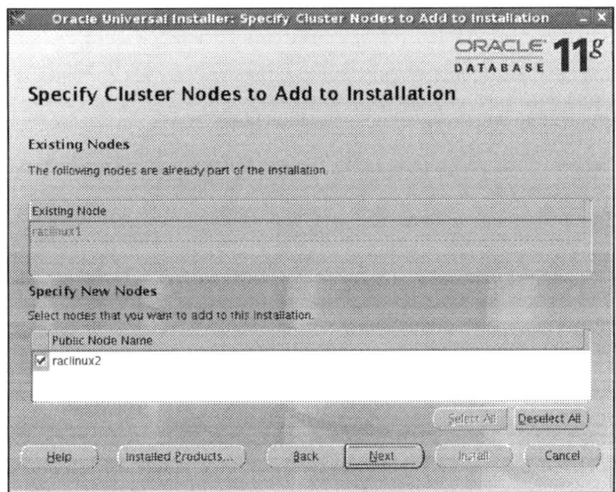

Next, review the **Node Addition Summary** screen and click on **Install** to proceed with the installation. When the Node Addition progress bar reaches 97%, a pop-up, **Execute configuration scripts** window appears on the screen. As root user, run the script (`root.sh`) on the new node as shown in the following example:

```
[root@raclinux2 ~]# /u01/app/oracle/product/11.1.0/asm/root.sh
Running Oracle 11g root.sh script...

The following environment variables are set as:
    ORACLE_OWNER= oracle
    ORACLE_HOME=  /u01/app/oracle/product/11.1.0/asm

Enter the full pathname of the local bin directory: [/usr/local/bin]:
   Copying dbhome to /usr/local/bin ...
   Copying oraenv to /usr/local/bin ...
   Copying coraenv to /usr/local/bin ...


Creating /etc/oratab file...
Entries will be added to the /etc/oratab file as needed by
Database Configuration Assistant when a database is created
Finished running generic part of root.sh script.
Now product-specific root actions will be performed.
Finished product-specific root actions.
```

Click on **OK** upon successfully running the script and click on **Exit** to quit the OUI.

After the scripts have been successfully executed, it indicates the completion of the ASM software addition or cloning process on the new node. We will then need to install RDBMS software by executing the `$ORA_DB_HOME/oui/bin/addNode.sh` from Node 1 of the cluster and repeat the above steps.

Post-node addition steps

After successfully adding the new node, you will need to perform the following steps:

1. Back up the OCR file and voting disk. Backing up the voting is not required in 11g R2 as it is done automatically.
2. Add ASM instances and RAC database instances (if required) as shown in the subsequent RAC database instance examples.
3. Create cluster listeners on the new nodes.

Removing a node from the cluster

Oracle RAC provides a rich flexibility to scale up the cluster environment by adding new nodes, along with the ability to remove a node from an existing cluster when it is no longer required.

The most important steps involved in removing a node from the cluster are as follows:

1. Performing the OCR and voting disk backup (in Oracle 11g R1).
2. Identifying all instances running on the node to be removed and removing the instances using the DBCA tool.
3. Stopping active ASM instances on the node.
4. Removing an ASM instance using the DBAC tool and ASMCA utility in Oracle 11g R2 or above.

Once these steps are complete, you need to stop the nodeapps services (such as gsd, vip, and ons) on the node which is going to be removed from the cluster. As the Oracle user from any node, execute the following command:

```
srvctl stop nodeapps -n <deleting_node_name>
```

From the deleted node, remove all the existing listeners using the **Network Configuration Assistant** (**./netca**) tool as explained here:

5. Choose the **Cluster Configuration** and select the node from the given list, which we are deleting. Then choose **Listener Configuration** and click on **Next**.
6. Select the **Delete** option and delete all the listeners that are running on the node to be removed.

After the listeners are successfully removed ensure that there are no databases, ASM instances, or nodeapps services running on this node. If any database is registered on this node, you must relocate the service using the `crs_relocate` cluster command.

Now, run the following command to detach the Oracle homes command from the node which you want to delete:

```
$ORA_DB_HOME/runInstaller -updateNodeList ORACLE_HOME=$ORA_DB_HOME
CLUSTER_NODES="" -local
```

To remove the `nodeapps` as the root user, use the following command:

```
srvctl remove nodeapps -n deleting_node_name
```

As Oracle user, from any remaining node such as Node 1 of the cluster, start `runInstaller` with the `updateNodeList` argument and other options as shown in the following example:

```
$ORA_DB_HOME/oui/bin/runInstaller -updateNodeList
ORACLE_HOME=$ORA_DB_HOME CLUSTER_NODES=<remaing_node_list>
```

As root user, stop the cluster (using `crsctl stop cluster`) on the node which you want to delete and execute the following `root delete` command, which will disable the clusterware on this node:

```
$ORA_CRS_HOME/install/rootdelete.sh local nosharedvar nosharedhome
```

From any remaining node, such as Node 1 of the cluster, identify the node number which you want to delete, using the `olsnodes -n` command.

Execute the `./rootdeletenode.sh` script from `$ORA_CRS_HOME/install`. This script in turn calls the `clscfg -delete` script and deletes the node from the cluster and updates the OCR file. If you omit this step, the `olsnodes` command will continue to display the deleted node number as part of the existing cluster.

The following is the `deletenode` example:

```
./rootdeletenode.sh raclinux2,2
```

Confirm the node deletion using the `olsnodes -n` cluster command, as at this time, the deleted node should not be listed. Next, define the cluster home in the Oracle inventory on the nodes that exist in the cluster using the following example:

```
$ORA_CRS_HOME/oui/bin/runInstaller -updateNodeList ORACLE_HOME=$ORA
_CRS_HOME
CLUSTER_NODES=remaining_node_names CRS=TRUE
```

Finally, delete the CRS, Oracle homes (ASM and RDBMS) using the following command on the deleted node:

```
$ORA_DB_HOME: rm -rf *
$ORA_ASM_HOME: rm -rf *
$ORA_CRS_HOME: rm -rf *
```

Ensure that the initialization scripts, `init.d`, and soft links are removed from the deleted node as root, using the following example on a Linux system:

```
rm -f /etc/init.d/init.cssd
rm -f /etc/init.d/init.crs
rm -f /etc/init.d/init.crsd
rm -f /etc/init.d/init.evmd
rm -f /etc/rc2.d/K96init.crs
rm -f /etc/rc2.d/S96init.crs
rm -f /etc/rc3.d/K96init.crs
rm -f /etc/rc3.d/S96init.crs
rm -f /etc/rc5.d/K96init.crs
rm -f /etc/rc5.d/S96init.crs
rm -Rf /etc/oracle/scls_scr
```

Optionally, remove the `/etc/oracle` and `/etc/oratab` file and Oracle inventory from the deleted node, when no other Oracle homes exist.

In Oracle 11g R2, the delete node procedure can be done using the following two steps if you are running a Dynamic Grid Plug and Play Cluster using DHCP and GNS:

1. On the node to be deleted, disable the Clusterware applications and daemons running on the node and run the following command from the `$GRID_HOME/crs/install` directory as root user:

   ```
   ./rootcrs.pl -delete -force
   ```

   Repeat the same command on all the nodes to be deleted.

2. Update the Oracle inventory on the remaining nodes using the following command from the `$GRID_HOME/oui/bin` directory at any existing node:

```
./runInstaller -updateNodeList ORACLE_HOME=$GRID_HOME "CLUSTER_
NODES={remaining_node_list}" CRS=TRUE
```

If dynamic Grid Plug and Play using DHCP and GNS is not enabled, follow the procedure mentioned next to remove a node from the cluster on Oracle 11g R2:

1. On the node to be deleted, disable the cluster applications and daemons, and run the following as root user:

   ```
   ./rootcrs.pl -delete -force
   ```

2. From any node that is not going to be deleted, run the following command as root user from the `$GRID_HOME/bin` directory:

   ```
   ./crsctl delete node -n node_to_be_deleted
   ```

3. On the deleted node, as clusterware owner user, run the following command for a non-shared home from the `$GRID_HOME/deinstall` directory:

   ```
   ./deinstall -local
   ```

4. Update Oracle inventory on the remaining nodes using the following command from any existing node from the `$GRID_HOME/oui/bin` directory:

   ```
   ./runInstaller -updateNodeList ORACLE_HOME=$GRID_HOME "CLUSTER_
   NODES={remaining_node_list}" CRS=TRUE
   ```

Adding an RAC database instance

Assuming that you have created an RAC database with a single instance named RACDB, later on you may want to add a new instance to the RAC database to avoid a single point of failure, or to scaleup your application workload over multiple instances. One of the primary advantages of an RAC database, in contrast to a standalone database, is that an RAC database can consist of two or more instances accessing a single database. Having two or more instances enables you to achieve scalability by balancing the application workload across available instances to achieve better performance. It also provides a high availability solution by rapidly reestablishing the lost user connections from a failed instance to the other surviving instance in the RAC database.

Adding more instances to an RAC database is a very simple task and Oracle provides the following ways to achieve this:

- DBCA
- Enterprise Manager (grid control)
- Manual method

Adding a new instance using DBCA

Although various methods exists to add new instances, we are going to demonstrate adding new instance procedure using the DBCA utility. DBCA automates most of the steps that are required for adding an instance, such as undo tablespace creation, adding Redo logs, and configuring all the initialization parameters required for this operation. However, before we proceed, the following will need to be ready on all the nodes where you require new instances to be added:

- Oracle Clusterware must be configured and running across the nodes
- ASM instance must be configured and running across the nodes
- An RAC database named RACDB (in our example) will need to be created and running at least with a single instance

First, we will need to execute `$ORA_DB_HOME/bin/dbca` on the command prompt of a node where the RAC database instance is configured and running. On the **Welcome** screen, we need to select the **Oracle Real Application Clusters Database** option and click on **Next**:

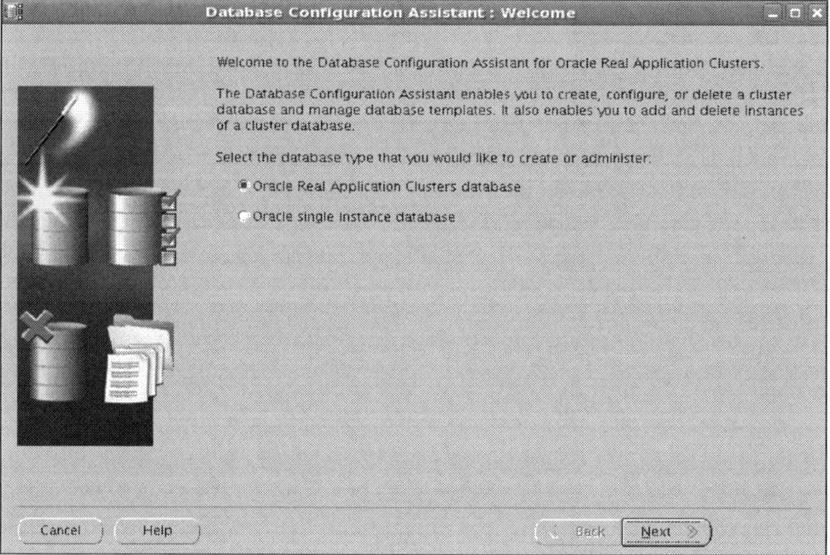

Unlike the previous database creation example that was featured in *Chapter 6, RAC Database Administration and Workload Management*, we can see that the **Operations** screen comes with all the options visible. Select the **Instance Management** option and click on **Next:**

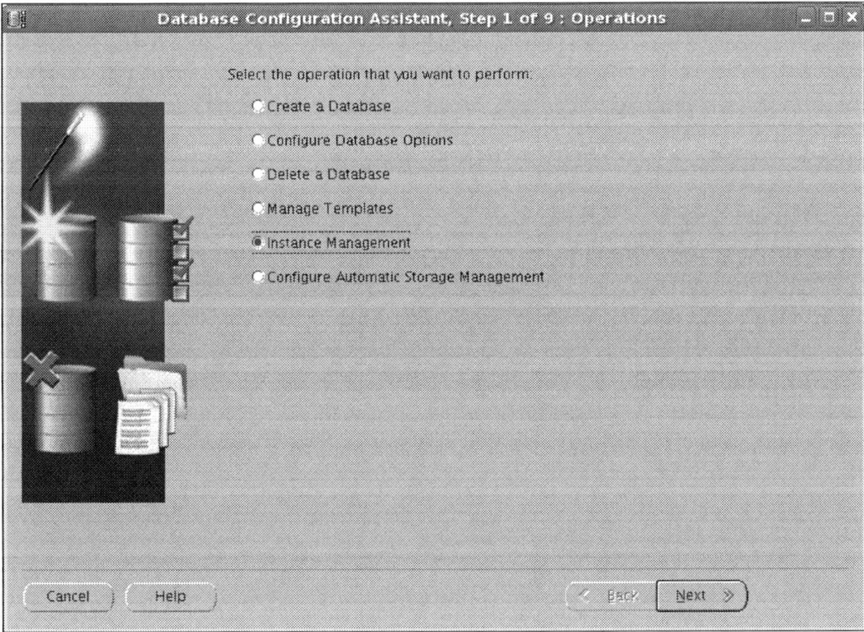

The following is the slightly amended screenshot of Oracle 11g R2 where the ASM option is no longer available with DBCA. For any sort of ASM operations, you explicitly need to run the `asmca` from the `$GRID_HOME/bin` directory.

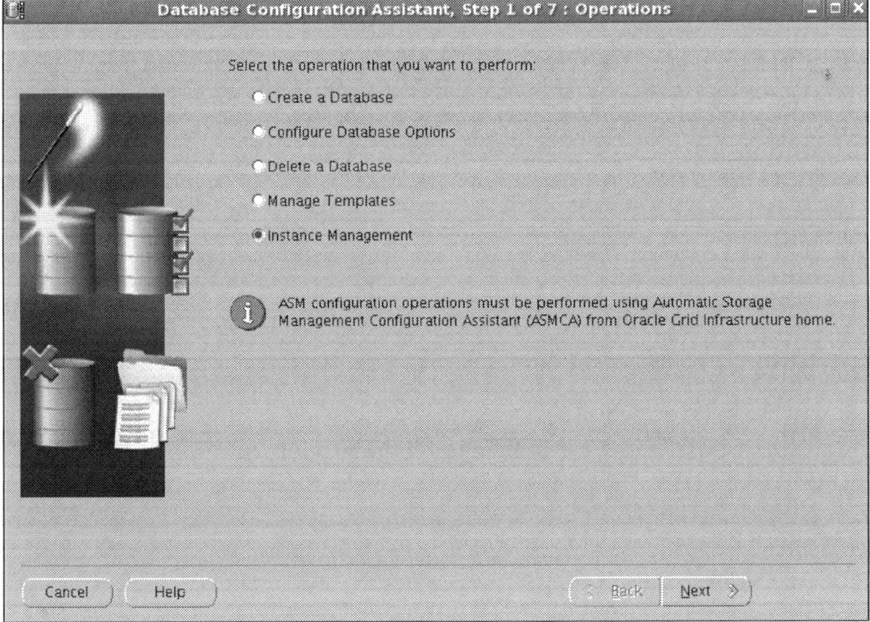

The **Instance Management** screen comes with two choices—**Add an instance** and **Delete an instance**. Select the **Add an instance** option and click on **Next**:

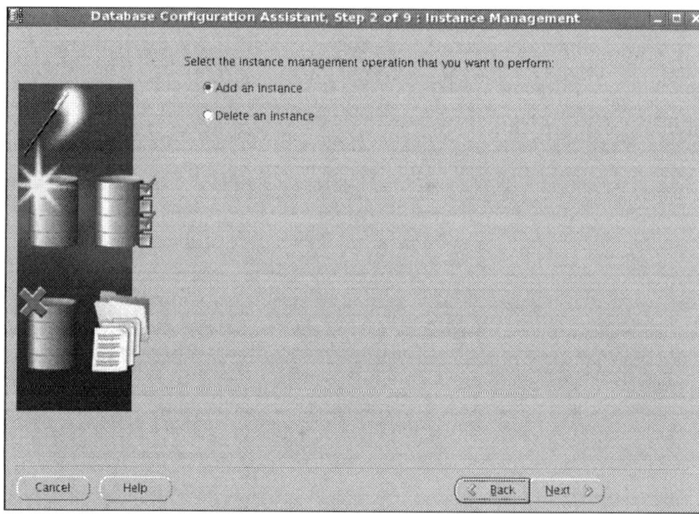

The **List of cluster databases** screen extracts all the RAC databases created under your cluster environment. Select the target database for your instance. For our example, select the `RACDB` database. Make sure the status is active and that the database is up and running. Specify the SYSDBA credentials—username as **sys** and password of your choice. Click on **Next**:

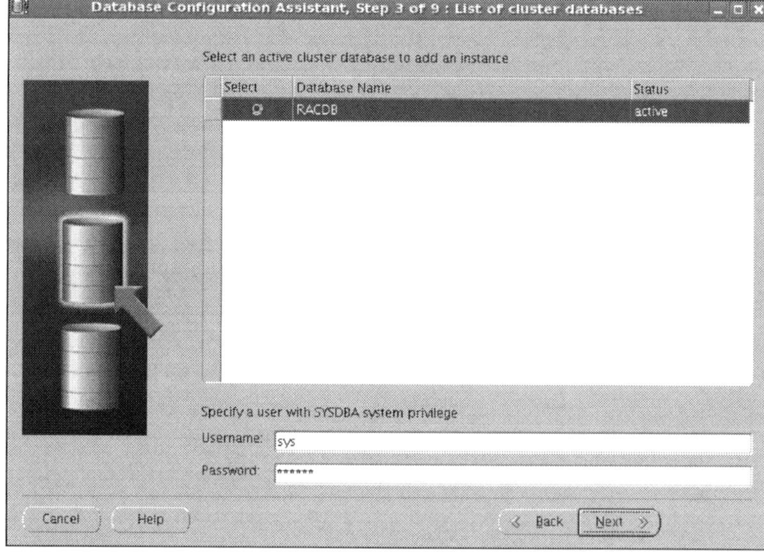

The following is the slightly amended screenshot of Oracle 11g R2 where you can see the database configuration type:

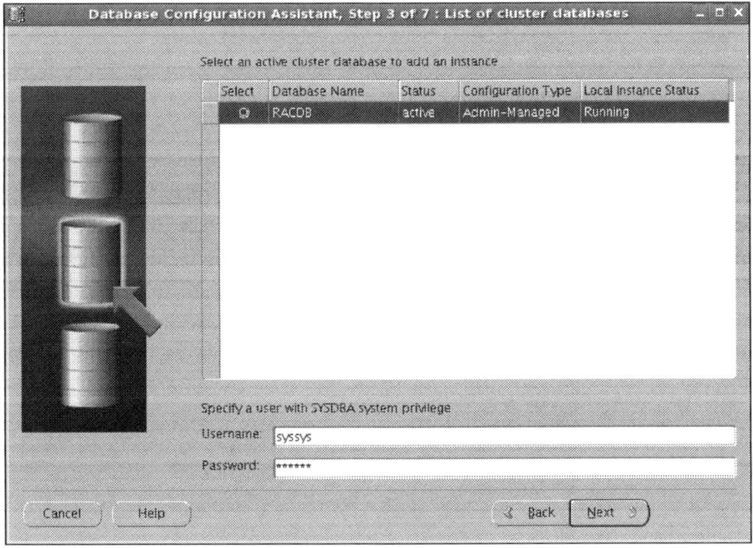

On the **List of cluster instances** screen, it shows the names of existing instances against the selected cluster database. Click on **Next**.

The **Instance naming and node selection** screen is one of the most important screens when adding an instance. It shows all the node names that exist in the cluster and allows you to select the nodes on which you want to add an instance. It also provides an option to set an instance name. However, the default naming convention is the preferred one—SID<nodenumber>. Once you select the node as raclinux2, click on **Next**:

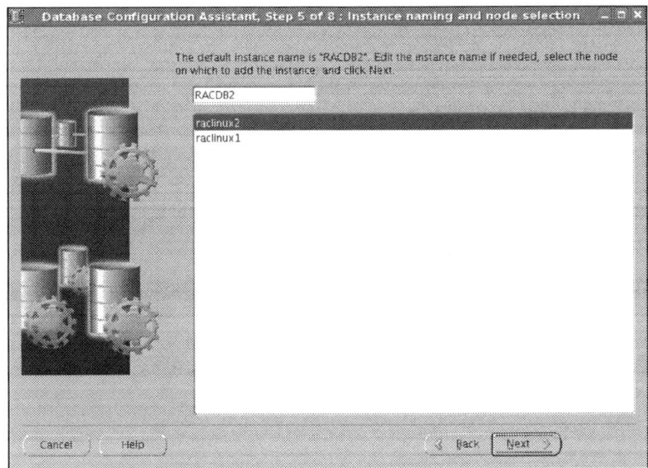

On the **Instance Storage** screen you have the flexibility to resize the Redo groups optimally for the instance. Once you are done with resizing, click on **Finish**.

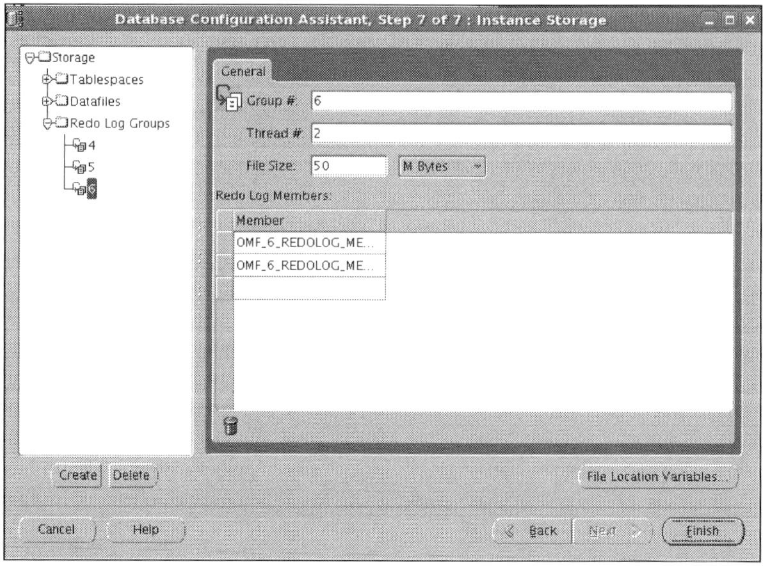

Review the **Summary** screen and click on **OK** to proceed towards adding an instance. Once the DBCA progresses to 100%, a small window with an option to perform any other operation will pop up. Click on **No** to finish the operation and to return to the command prompt, as shown on the following screen:

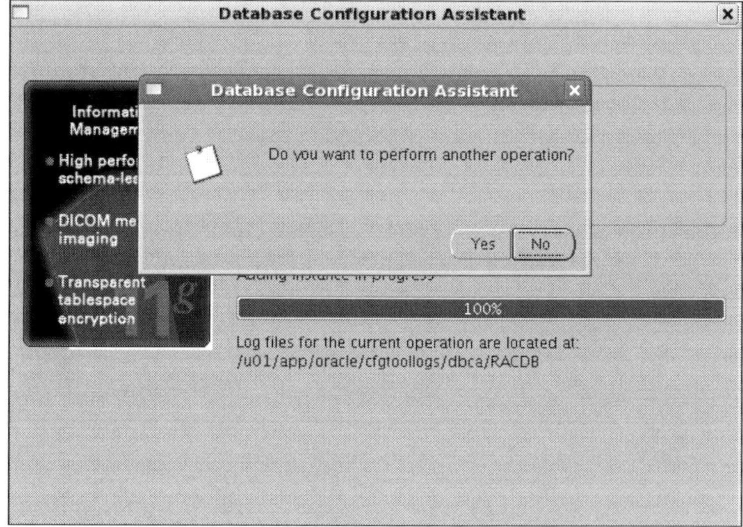

We have added an instance—what next?

We should have now successfully added the RACDB2 instance of an RACDB database on the `raclinux2` node. Next, let's verify the existence of the new instance using the familiar cluster command—`crs_stat` and `srvctl`.

As you can see in the following example, the RACDB2 instance has been successfully added on the `raclinux2` node and its `Target` and `Stage` is set `ONLINE`:

```
[oracle@raclinux1 ~]$ ./crs_stat.sh
HA Resourrce                              Target     Stage
------------                              ------     -----
ora.RACDB.RACDB1.inst                     ONLINE     ONLINE on raclinux1
ora.RACDB.RACDB2.inst                     ONLINE     ONLINE on raclinux2
ora.RACDB.RACDB_MAIN.RACDB1.srv           ONLINE     ONLINE on raclinux1
ora.RACDB.RACDB_MAIN.cs                   ONLINE     ONLINE on raclinux1
ora.RACDB.db                              ONLINE     ONLINE on raclinux1
```

Verifying new instance status

You can use the following command to find on how many nodes a particular cluster database is configured:

```
srvctl config database -d RACDB
raclinux1 RACDB1 /u01/app/oracle/product/11.1.0/db_1
raclinux2 RACDB2 /u01/app/oracle/product/11.1.0/db_1
```

Use the following code example to find on how many nodes the cluster database instances are running or not running:

```
srvctl status database -d RACDB
Instance RACDB1 is running on node raclinux1
Instance RACDB2 is running on node raclinux2
```

To check the same from the database level, connect to any instance using `SQLPLUS` and run the following command:

```
SELECT * FROM v$active_instances;

   INST_ID INSTANCE_NAME
---------- ---------------
         1 RACDB1
         2 RACDB2
```

Using DBCA in silent mode to add an instance

If your environment doesn't support GUI mode, or you have no Xwindows terminal to support the GUI, you may also use DBCA in silent mode to add an instance to an RAC database using the following example:

```
dbca -silent -addInstance -nodeList raclinux2 -gdbName RACDB
[-instanceName RACDB2] -sysDBAUserName sys -sysDBAPassword mypassword
```

Make sure the `$ORACLE_HOME` environment variable is set properly on all existing nodes before you execute this command.

Post-add instance steps

After adding a new instance using DBCA, there are no mandatory post-add instance steps involved; however, you may be interested to perform a few housekeeping steps as specified here:

1. Back up the OCR file.
2. In case you want this instance to be attached with a separate listener on to a specific port, create a clustered listener using the `netca` tool and assign this instance to the LISTENER.
3. Add or modify services as explained in *Chapter 6, RAC Database Administration and Workload Management* to have the newly added instance as a preferred or available option.
4. Modify your connection string (`tns` names) entry by adding the new instance details to configure load balancing and the failover options in the `$ORA_DB_HOME/network/admin/tnsnames.ora` file.

Deleting an RAC database instance

When you find that an RAC database in your environment is overdone in terms of the number of active instances, or due to the non-criticality of the application, you can delete an instance.

Relax readers, we are not going to demonstrate this through several screenshots; rather, we will explain this process through a few simple steps that can be easily followed.

Like adding an instance, deleting an instance can also be done using DBCA, Enterprise Manager, and manual methods. However, as we mentioned earlier, the DBCA is one of the simplest ways to perform these operations, so we recommend that you use the DBCA.

You will need to perform the following steps before you start deleting the instance:

- If there is no recent OCR file backup, perform the OCR file backup
- Modify or remove services that are associated with the deleted instance

In order to perform the delete instance operation, the following procedure will need to be completed:

1. From the command prompt of Node 1, execute `$ORACLE_HOME/bin/dbca`. Choose the **Oracle Real Application Clusters database** option on the **Welcome** screen and click on **Next**.
2. On the **Operations** screen, choose the **Instance Management** option and click on **Next**.
3. Select **Delete an Instance** option on the **Instance Management** screen and click on **Next**.
4. Select the database whose instance needs to be removed from the given list of databases in the **List of Cluster database** screen. Enter **SYSDBA** user and password credentials and click on **Next**.
5. Select the instance that needs to be deleted from the **List of cluster instances** screen and click on **Finish**. A small reconfirmation pop-up window to delete an instance will appear here. Click on **OK**. Another subsequent DBCA pop-up window appears here saying that the DBCA will delete an instance and its associated OFA directory structure. Click on **OK** to begin the delete instance operation.
6 The DBCA immediately starts the delete instance operation. Once you see that it is fully completed, a small pop-up window will be displayed asking whether you want to perform another operation; click on **No** to finish the operation and it will return to the command prompt.

Using DBCA in silent mode to delete an instance

If your environment doesn't have Xwindows, or doesn't support any GUI tools facility, you can also use DBCA in silent mode to delete an instance of an RAC database using the following example:

```
dbca -silent -deleteInstance -nodeList raclinux2 -gdbName RACDB
[-instanceName RACDB2] -sysDBAUserName sys -sysDBAPassword mypassword
```

Once you have successfully deleted an instance, you can confirm this using the following command examples:

```
srvctl config database -d RACDB
raclinux1 RACDB1 /u01/app/oracle/product/11.1.0/db_1

srvctl status database -d RACDB
Instance RACDB1 is running on node raclinux1
```

As you can see in the examples, the RACDB2 instance has been successfully deleted and there is no information about this instance in the cluster.

Converting a single-instance database to an RAC database

When migrating from a non-RAC environment to an RAC environment, one of the most challenging aspects for an Oracle Database Administrator is converting a single-instance database to an RAC database. As of now, Oracle supports the following methods to convert a single-instance database to an RAC database as long as the RAC and the standalone environments are running on the same operating system and using the same Oracle release:

- DBCA
- Oracle Enterprise Manager (grid control)
- RCONFIG
- Manual method

Although there are several ways to perform the conversion process, we are going to focus and demonstrate this using the `rconfig` command-line tool, which is a very easy and convenient method.

The following screenshot illustrates a conversion process where a `RACNVT` single instance database is being converted to an RAC database with one instance.

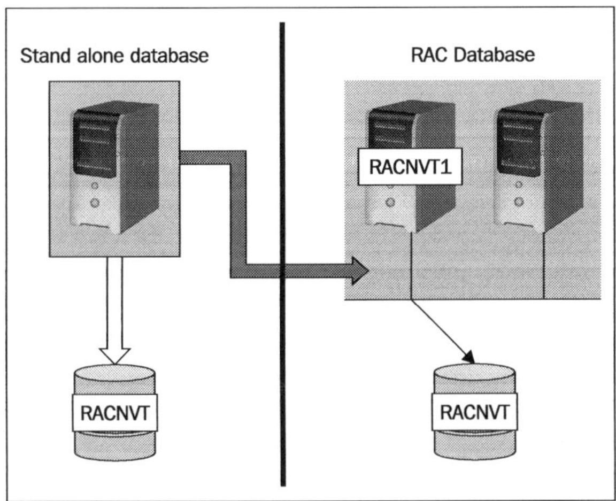

Overview of RCONFIG command-line tool

Converting a single-instance database to an RAC database was made a lot easier starting with Oracle 10g R2. The `rconfig` command-line tool was introduced for automating the process of converting a single-instance database to an RAC database. The executable rconfig can be found at `$ORA_DB_HOME/bin` directory.

When you navigate through the `$ORACLE_HOME/assistants/rconfig/sampleXMLS` directory, you will find two sample XML input files—`ConvertToClusteredASM.xml` and `ConvertToRAC.xml`—that are used for the conversion purpose. The following is a brief summary of those input files:

- `ConvertToClusteredASM.xml`: Introduced in Oracle 11g to convert ASM, configured for single instance to ASM for RAC
- `ConvertToRAC.xml`: The input file used for converting a single-instance database to an RAC database

During the conversion, rconfig performs the following steps automatically:

- Migrating the database to ASM, if specified
- Creating RAC database instances on all specified nodes in the cluster
- Configuring the Listener and NetService entries
- Registering services with CRS
- Starting up the instances and listener on all nodes

`rconfig` provides the ability to test the conversion without it actually being performed. In this regard, the `ConvertToRAC.xml` input file provides an option to Convert Verify with the following choices:

- `YES`: Checks to ensure all the prerequisites for converting a single-instance database to an RAC database have been met before the conversion process starts
- `NO`: Bypasses the prerequisite checks and starts the conversion straightaway
- `ONLY`: Only prerequisite checks are performed; no actual conversion will take place

Before you modify the contents of any of these files, first back them up and then do the necessary changes.

In Oracle 11g R2, a single-instance database can either be converted to an administrator-managed cluster database or a policy-managed cluster database modifying the parameters in either `ConvertToRAC_AdminManaged.xml` or `ConvertToRAC_PolicyManaged.xml` files.

What you need to accomplish the conversion task

Before you plan to test the examples, make sure the following setup is ready in your environment:

- Oracle Clusterware is configured and the cluster is up and running
- Single-instance database, `RACNVT`, is running
- An ASM instance with DATA and FLASH diskgroups is configured

Sample of a modified ConvertToRAC.xml input file

The following is a sample of a `ConvertToRAC.xml` input file used with the `rconfig` tool for conversion purposes. Please note that we have highlighted the changes in the input file and you need to amend the changes that suit your environmental settings. Ensure you have backed up this file before making any changes to the original file.

From the command prompt, issue the following command to edit the XML file and make necessary changes:

```
vi $ORACLE_HOME/assistants/rconfig/sampleXMLS/ConvertToRAC.xml
```

```
<?xml version="1.0" encoding="UTF-8"?>
<n:RConfig xmlns:n="http://www.oracle.com/rconfig"
           xmlns:xsi="http://www.w3.org/2001/XMLSchema-instance"
```

```
            xsi:schemaLocation="http://www.oracle.com/rconfig">
    <n:ConvertToRAC>
<!-- Verify does a precheck to ensure all pre-requisites are met, before
the conversion is attempted. Allowable values are: YES|NO|ONLY -->
        <n:Convert verify="YES">
<!--Specify current OracleHome of non-rac database for SourceDBHome -->
<n:SourceDBHome>/u01/app/oracle/product/11.1.0/db_1</n:SourceDBHome>
<!--Specify OracleHome where the rac database should be configured. It
can be same as SourceDBHome -->
<n:TargetDBHome>/u01/app/oracle/product/11.1.0/db_1</n:TargetDBHome>
<!--Specify SID of non-rac database and credential. User with sysdba role
is required to perform conversion -->
              <n:SourceDBInfo SID="RACNVT">
                <n:Credentials>
                  <n:User>sys</n:User>
                  <n:Password>syssys</n:Password>
                  <n:Role>sysdba</n:Role>
                </n:Credentials>
              </n:SourceDBInfo>
<!--ASMInfo element is required only if the current non-rac database uses
ASM Storage -->
              <n:ASMInfo SID="+ASM1">
                <n:Credentials>
                  <n:User>sys</n:User>
                  <n:Password>syssys</n:Password>
                  <n:Role>sysasm</n:Role>
                </n:Credentials>
              </n:ASMInfo>
<!--Specify the list of nodes that should have rac instances running.
LocalNode should be the first node in this nodelist. -->
              <n:NodeList>
                <n:Node name="raclinux1"/>
              </n:NodeList>
<!--Specify prefix for rac instances. It can be same as the instance name
for non-rac database or different. The instance number will be attached
to this prefix. -->
              <n:InstancePrefix>RACNVT</n:InstancePrefix>
<!--Specify port for the listener to be configured for rac database.If
port="", alistener existing on localhost will be used for rac database.
The listener will be extended to all nodes in the nodelist -->
```

```
              <n:Listener port="1551"/>
<!--Specify the type of storage to be used by rac database. Allowable
values are CFS|ASM. The non-rac database should have same storage type.->
              <n:SharedStorage type="ASM">
<!--Specify Database Area Location to be configured for rac database.If
this field is left empty, current storage will be used for rac database.
For CFS, this field will have directory path. -->
                <n:TargetDatabaseArea>+DATA</n:TargetDatabaseArea>
<!--Specify Flash Recovery Area to be configured for rac database. If
this field is left empty, current recovery area of non-rac database will
be configured for rac database. If current database is not using recovery
Area, the resulting rac database will not have a recovery area. -->
<n:TargetFlashRecoveryArea>+FLASH</n:TargetFlashRecoveryArea>
              </n:SharedStorage>
        </n:Convert>
    </n:ConvertToRAC>
</n:RConfig>
```

How to test a conversion without actually performing the conversion

Well, it would be a wise decision to check all the prerequisites on the server that are required for a smooth conversion. To test the conversion operation without it actually being performed, you first need to modify the Convert Verify = "ONLY" option in the `ConvertToRAC.xml` input file and use the following example:

```
$ORA_DB_HOME/bin/rconfig $ORA_DB_HOME/assistants/rconfig/sampleXMLS/
ConvertToRAC.xml
```

When this command is executed on the local server, Oracle automatically performs the checks for all the prerequisites and the following output will be displayed:

```
<?xml version="1.0" ?>
<RConfig version="1.1" >
<ConvertToRAC>
       <Convert>
       <Response>
               <Result code="0" >
               Operation Succeeded
              </Result>
       </Response>
```

```
    <ReturnValue type="object">
There is no return value for this step     </ReturnValue>
   </Convert>
  </ConvertToRAC></RConfig>
```

`Result code 0` indicates that all the prerequisites are met and you can go ahead with the conversion operation. However, if the process ends with `Result code 1`, which is the indication of failure, it subsequently shows the reason for the failure. Correct the reported errors and go ahead and retest it.

Converting a single-instance database to an RAC database

As we have already completed the conversion testing in the previous example, it is now time to move on to the actual conversion. To do this, we first need to modify the `Convert Verify = "NO"` option that bypasses the verification steps. In the `ConvertToRAC.xml` input file, use the following example to perform the conversion:

```
$ORA_DB_HOME/bin/rconfig $ORA_DB_HOME/assistants/rconfig/sampleXMLS/
ConvertToRAC.xml
```

Once this command is executed from the local server, Oracle skips the verification steps and immediately starts the conversion operation as follows:

```
Converting Database RACNVT to Cluster Database. Target Oracle Home : /
u01/app/oracle/product/11.1.0/db_1.
Setting Data Files and Control Files
Adding Database Instances
Adding Redo Logs
Enabling threads for all Database Instances
Setting TEMP tablespace
Adding UNDO tablespaces
Adding Trace files
Setting Flash Recovery Area
Updating Oratab
Creating Password file(s)
Configuring Listeners
Configuring related CRS resources
Adding NetService entries
Starting Cluster Database
```

```
Starting Listeners
<?xml version="1.0" ?>
<RConfig version="1.1" >
<ConvertToRAC>
    <Convert>
      <Response>
        <Result code="0" >
          Operation Succeeded
        </Result>
      </Response>
      <ReturnValue type="object">
<Oracle_Home>
         /u01/app/oracle/product/11.1.0/db_1
       </Oracle_Home>
        <SIDList>
          <SID>RACNVT1<\SID>
        <\SIDList>     </ReturnValue>
    </Convert>
  </ConvertToRAC></RConfig>
```

As you can see in the output, the conversion process successfully ended with code `0`, indicating that the operation succeeded. Now let's use the following examples to check how it is going:

```
srvctl config database -d RACNVT
raclinux1 RACNVT1 /u01/app/oracle/product/11.1.0/db_1

srvctl status database -d RACNVT
Instance RACNVT1 is running on node raclinux1
./crs_stat.sh
HA Resource                                     Target  Stage
-----------                                     ------  -----
ora.RACNVT.RACNVT1.inst                         ONLINE  ONLINE on raclinux1
ora.RACNVT.db                                   ONLINE  ONLINE on raclinux2
ora.raclinux1.ASM1.asm                          ONLINE  ONLINE on raclinux1
ora.raclinux1.LISTENER_RACLINUX1.lsnr           ONLINE  ONLINE on raclinux1
ora.raclinux1.LISTENER_RCONFIG_RACLINUX1.lsnr ONLINE  ONLINE on raclinux1
ora.raclinux1.RACDB_RACLINUX1.lsnr              ONLINE  ONLINE on raclinux1
```

It is clear that the single-instance database RACNVT has been successfully converted to an RAC database. The RACNVT1 instance is running on raclinux1 node with ONLINE status.

How to resume a failed rconfig operation

While running the conversion procedure, if you come across any fatal errors, such as a lack of adequate disk space, shared storage issues, or problems with initialization parameters, the conversion can be safely resumed using the rconfig command with the XML input file. This will first perform the clean-up operation such as deleting files created by the earlier run and starting the conversion process again.

Checking log files

rconfig log file, for example, rconfig_07_31_09_15_06_50.log, can be found under the $ORACLE_BASE/cfgtoollogs/rconfig directory. While the conversion is taking place, you may refer to the database alert.log files as well to monitor the proceedings.

How to optimize rconfig to run faster

You are probably wondering how to optimize rconfig operation to run faster while planning to convert a fairly large-sized or very huge-sized database, say around 5 to 10 TB size. Well, despite the fact that currently there is no direct option available to do so, you may try an out-of-the-box workaround solution by applying a degree of parallelism in an RMAN on the local server.

While converting a single-instance database, with filesystem storage, to an RAC database with Automatic Storage Management (ASM), rconfig invokes RMAN internally to back up the database to proceed with converting non-ASM to ASM. Therefore, configuring parallel options to use multiple RMAN channels in the RMAN on the local node may make backup run faster, which eventually reduces the conversion duration.

For example, you may configure the following in the RMAN settings of RACNVT database on the local node.

```
RMAN> CONFIGURE DEVICE TYPE DISK PARALLELISM 6;
```

Post-conversion steps

Once you have successfully converted the single-instance database to an RAC database and tested your application functionality thoroughly on the RAC, you may need to consider the following points as post-conversion steps:

1. Drop the single-instance database to release the resources used as this database is no longer needed.
2. Increase the buffer cache and shared pool sizes by 15% as Oracle RAC database requirements are slightly greater in contrast to a single-instance database.
3. Back up the RAC database.
4. Depending on your application requirements, configure Load Balancing and TAF policies as specified in *Chapter 6, RAC Database Administration and Workload Management*.
5. Back up the OCR file.

Relocating an RAC database and instances across nodes

Presuming you have an RAC database named `RACNVT` with an instance `RACNVT1` running on `raclinux1` node and you wish to relocate the instance permanently or temporally to `raclinux2` node due to a prolonged maintenance scheduled on the raclunux1 node, or maybe the node resources are heavily consumed and you want to reduce the usage by relocating the instance. We are going to demonstrate here how to relocate an instance from one node to another.

The following output demonstrates where the RAC database and its instances are running:

```
[oracle@raclinux1 ~]$ ./crs_stat.sh
HA Resource                                   Target  State
------------                                  ------  -----
ora.RACNVT.RACNVT1.inst                       ONLINE  ONLINE on raclinux1
ora.RACNVT.db                                 ONLINE  ONLINE on raclinux2
ora.raclinux1.ASM1.asm                        ONLINE  ONLINE on raclinux1
ora.raclinux1.LISTENER_RACLINUX1.lsnr         ONLINE  ONLINE on raclinux1
ora.raclinux1.LISTENER_RCONFIG_RACLINUX1.lsnr ONLINE  ONLINE on raclinux1
ora.raclinux1.RACDB_RACLINUX1.lsnr            ONLINE  ONLINE on raclinux1
ora.raclinux1.gsd                             ONLINE  ONLINE on raclinux1
```

```
ora.raclinux1.ons                           ONLINE   ONLINE on raclinux1
ora.raclinux1.vip                           ONLINE   ONLINE on raclinux1
ora.raclinux2.ASM2.asm                      ONLINE   ONLINE on raclinux2
ora.raclinux2.LISTENER_RACLINUX2.lsnr       ONLINE   ONLINE on raclinux2
ora.raclinux2.RACDB_RACLINUX2.lsnr          ONLINE   ONLINE on raclinux2
ora.raclinux2.gsd                           ONLINE   ONLINE on raclinux2
ora.raclinux2.ons                           ONLINE   ONLINE on raclinux2
ora.raclinux2.vip                           ONLINE   ONLINE on raclinux2
```

This output confirms that the RAC database `RACNVT` is registered on the `raclinux2` node and its instance `RACNVT1` is running on the `raclinux1` node, which is the expected behavior in an RAC environment. Assuming for any valid reasons you wish to relocate the instance from `raclinux1` node to `raclinux2` node, you will need to complete the following sequence on the `raclinux2` node:

1. Prepare an spfile on `raclinux2` for the `RACNVT2` instance, and make any necessary changes. (We will change the instance name to match the node number.)
2. Create a password file for the `RACNVT2` instance on `raclinux2` node.
3. Ensure that the disk groups used for `RACNVT` database are mounted on `raclinux2` node, via an ASM instance.
4. Create a Listener on `raclinux2` node with the required port.

Relocating the instance

Once we have performed the above steps, let's move on to relocating the instance using the examples mentioned below.

First, stop the instance on `raclinux1` node using the following command:

```
srvctl stop instance -d RACNVT -i RACNVT1
```

When the RAC database contains only one instance, it is advised to stop the database instead of stopping the instance.

After the instance is stopped successfully, remove it from the `raclinux1` node using the following command:

```
srvctl remove instance -d RACNVT -i RACNVT1
Remove instance RACNVT1 from the database RACNVT? (y/[n]) y
```

If the RACNVT1 instance is not stopped properly when you attempt to remove it from the node, the following cluster error will be shown:

```
PRKP-1023 : The instance {0} is still running.RACNVT
```

Adding the instance example

After successfully removing the instance from the node, use the following example to add the instance on the raclinux2 node:

```
srvctl add instance -d RACNVT -i RACNVT2 -n raclinux2
```

As we mentioned earlier, while adding the instance, you have the flexibility to change its name according to the standards that you follow in your environment. We changed the instance name from RACNVT1 to RACNVT2. However, ensure that you have made the changes accordingly to your passwordfile and instance_name parameter in the spfile to reflect the new name.

Once the instance is added successfully, bring up the instance using the following cluster command:

```
srvctl start instance -d RACNVT -I RACNVT2
```

Using the following cluster command, you can verify that the database/instance has been successfully moved to raclinux2 node:

```
[oracle@raclinux2 ~]$ ./crs_stat.sh
HA Resource                          Target     State
------------                          ------     -----
ora.RACNVT.RACNVT2.inst               ONLINE     ONLINE on raclinux2
```

Workaround when a database and instance are configured on the same node

In a situation where an RAC database and its instances are configured on the same node, though the possibilities are very remote when there are many nodes in the cluster, you need to either relocate the database logical entry using the crs_relocate command from the node or remove the database logical entry from this node, which automatically removes all its associated instances using the srvctl remove database command. The following example demonstrates the situation using the srvctl remove command.

First, stop the database from the node using the following example:

```
srvctl stop database -d RACNVT
```

After the database is successfully stopped, use the following command to remove it from the node:

```
srvctl remove database -d RACNVT
```

```
Remove the database RACNVT? (y/[n]) y
```

Make sure the database is stopped before it is removed, otherwise the following cluster error will be displayed:

```
PRKP-1022 : The database RACNVT is still running.
```

Upon successful database removal, you simply need to add the database first, then add the instance on the new node.

The following is the `add database` syntax with supported parameters:

```
srvctl add database -h
```

```
Usage: srvctl add database -d <name> -o <oracle_home> [-m <domain_name>]
[-p <spfile>] [-A <name|ip>/netmask] [-r {PRIMARY | PHYSICAL_STANDBY |
LOGICAL_STANDBY | SNAPSHOT_STANDBY}] [-s <start_options>] [-n <db_name>]
[-y {AUTOMATIC | MANUAL}]

    -d <name>           Unique name for the database

    -o <oracle_home>    ORACLE_HOME path

    -m <domain>         Domain for cluster database

    -p <spfile>         Server parameter file path

    -A <addr_str>       Database cluster alias

    -n <db_name>        Database name (DB_NAME), if different from the
unique name given by the -d option

    -r <role>           Role of the database (primary, physical_standby,
logical_standby, snapshot_standby)

    -s <start_options>  Startup options for the database

    -y <dbpolicy>       Management policy for the database (automatic,
manual)

    -h                  Print usage
```

Adding the database example

Use the following example on the new node to add the `RACNVT` database. This command also registers the entry in the OCR file as a resource.

```
srvctl add database -d RACNVT -o /u01/app/oracle/product/11.1.0/
db_1 -y AUTOMATIC
```

Upon adding the database successfully, use the add instance example, explained in the earlier section, to add an instance.

Post-relocation steps

After relocating a database or instances across nodes, there are two post-relocation steps that you will need to complete, as follows:

1. After the database or instances are moved across nodes, any existing services that belong to the database/instance need to be modified using the `srvctl` utility (refer to *Chapter 6, RAC Database Administration and Workload Management* for more details) to point to a new node to avoid any connection problems.
2. After the database or instances are moved across nodes, you need to modify connection strings (tns names) in the `$ORA_DB_HOME/network/admin/tnsnames.ora` file to point to a new node so that the user connects to the correct node without running into any kind of connection trouble.

Summary

In this chapter, we discussed various real-world business scenarios covering Oracle 11g R1 and R2 such as scaling an existing cluster vertically by adding new nodes, removing nodes, adding instances to an existing RAC database to optimize the workload, and preventing any single point of failure situations. We also looked at converting a standalone database to an RAC database using the rconfig tool and also demonstrated how to move resources such as databases and instances from one node to another. This chapter should have provided you with useful scenarios in which to incorporate an RAC database.

In the next chapter, we will discuss how to manage the E-Business Suite (EBS) on an RAC environment.

11
Enabling RAC for EBS

Oracle E-Business Suite (EBS) is one of the key players in the **Enterprise Resource Product (ERP)** market along with SAP, JD Edwards, and PeopleSoft. Corporate ERP systems provide the engine that powers the operations of large corporate global financial and manufacturing systems. As availability, performance, and data protection are even more critical in today's world of 24x7x365 ERP systems, the requirements for disaster recovery solutions such as Oracle Data Guard and Oracle RAC are even more critical for the Oracle E-Business Suite. Fortunately, Oracle EBS can be implemented with RAC and Data Guard, so that these systems remain online without costly downtime in the event of disasters such as earthquakes, power outages, and terrorist attacks.

The massive volumes of data processing performed by Oracle EBS environments pose a unique challenge in terms of overall performance requirements to satisfy business and operational Service Level Agreements (SLAs). With the large number of invoices, payments, and financial payroll data that flow through Oracle EBS systems, there is a need to scale out for current and future growth to fulfill these data processing requirements. Oracle RAC provides one of the best solutions in the marketplace to satisfy these high performance and availability requirements. To meet the need for future scalability, additional RAC cluster nodes can be added by using inexpensive blade servers.

In this chapter, we will show you how to implement RAC with Oracle EBS. This will include a detailed discussion of the required procedures to implement RAC with Oracle EBS. While there are still hundreds of Oracle 11i EBS production environments still in operation, we will focus on how to implement RAC with Oracle R12 EBS. The most current version for Oracle EBS is 12.1.3 with Oracle Fusion Applications in beta release used by a few key Oracle customers. Based on Larry Ellison's announcements at the 2010 OpenWorld conference, Fusion Apps may be available for general acceptance (GA) release by the end of 2011. While there is no point base installation release for Oracle 12.1.3 with Oracle EBS, you will need to install an Oracle EBS 12.1.1 system first and then apply a large maintenance pack to bring it current up to the 12.1.3 release.

In summary, we will discuss the following topics:

- Oracle R12 EBS architecture
- Implementing Oracle 11g RAC with Oracle EBS
- Configuring RAC with Oracle R12 EBS

Each section will emphasize the importance of leveraging the application architecture, enabling us to achieve the scalability and high availability demanded by the constantly increasing workload and number of users.

EBS architecture

The Oracle EBS is the most comprehensive suite ever produced for enterprise global business applications. Oracle EBS contains hundreds of applications with dozens of individual financial, manufacturing, and customer sales (CRM) modules and products. Some of the product modules are Oracle Financials, Oracle Projects and Grants, CRM, and Oracle Human Resources (HR) Payroll and Benefits Compensation. Oracle EBS uses an "n-tier" based client server web-enabled architecture.

The architecture for Oracle EBS includes the following:

- Client tier: The client tier consists of Internet web browsers for accessing the Oracle R12 EBS web-based interface. As of the latest version, Oracle EBS supports web browsers including Microsoft Internet Explorer 7 and 8, Mozilla Firefox 3.5, and Safari 3. Jinitiator was de-supported at the end of July 2009. For Oracle R12 EBS, you must now use the native Sun J2SE 1.5 (5.0) and 1.6 (6.0) with the native Sun Java plugin.
- Application tier: The middle tier includes the Apache-based **Oracle HTTP Server (OHS)**, web server, forms server, and concurrent processing server. The forms server previously used in 11i for EBS has now been replaced with Oracle BI publisher. In addition, the middle tier also includes the admin server and also allows the Oracle Discoverer server to be installed and configured as an optional component.

  For EBS 12.1.3, we have the following:

    - Oracle Application Server 10g 10.1.2 contains the Oracle Forms and Reports Services. These replace the old 8.0.6-based Oracle_Home used by Oracle Internet Application Server (9iAS) 1.0.2.2 in Oracle EBS 11i.
    - Oracle Application Server 10g 10.1.3 for Oracle Containers for Java (OC4J) replacing the 8.1.7-based Oracle_Home provided by iAS 1.0.2.2 in EBS 11i.

    - Oracle JDeveloper 10.1.3

- Database tier: By default for Oracle R12 (12.0.1-12.0.4), the database server is an Oracle 10g R2 instance. However, with Oracle R12 EBS 12.1.1 and later including 12.1.13, the default database server for a fresh install now includes an Oracle 11g (11.1.0.7) database server, which is either a single stand-alone database (default) or a clustered Oracle 11g RAC. As we shall see, additional configurations are required to migrate from the default single instance database tier to an Oracle RAC database.

With Oracle EBS version 12.1.1 release and later, it is now possible to implement all of the 11g database new features, such as Oracle Advanced Compression, Oracle 11g Database Replay, and Oracle 11g Real Application Test Suite (RAT). The following summary highlights important major tech-stack components that have been implemented with the Rapid Install process for Oracle EBS 12.

	EBS Release 12 12.0.0	**Rapid Install 12.0.4**	**Version 12.1.1**
Database	10.2.0.2	10.2.0.4	11.1.0.7
OracleAS 10.1.2 Forms & Reports	10.1.2.0.2	10.1.2.2	10.1.2.3
OracleAS 10.1.3 OC4J	10.1.3.0.0	10.1.3.0.0	10.1.3.4
App Tier Java (JDK)	1.5.0_10	1.5.0_13	1.6.0_10
Desktop Client Java (JRE)1.5.0_10-erdist1.5.0_131.6.0_u10	1.5.0_10-erdist	1.5.0_13	1.6.0_u10

The database tier within Oracle R12 EBS plays a central role in the transactional operations for the entire environment. The database provides this role by storing data and is accessed constantly by all modules within the Oracle EBS. Due to the massive demands placed on the application suite for running these business operations, leveraging additional technologies, such as RAC is critical to provide the Oracle R12 EBS ecosystem with a sufficient level of performance for handling these increased workloads.

As we have discussed earlier, you need to have the database up and running without downtime or performance degradation for Oracle EBS. With the huge amount of batch processing, especially in the concurrent server node, you need a powerful way to allow for load balancing and optimization of key database services with the Oracle EBS. It is here that RAC plays a useful role that the database tier cannot handle by itself. Response time can be greatly enhanced by implementing RAC nodes along with application server load balancers, such as Cisco ACE hardware to resolve performance bottlenecks within the Oracle EBS.

In addition to performance considerations, you also need to worry about availability and disaster recovery issues for the Oracle EBS. It is here that the Oracle **Maximum Availability Architecture** (**MAA**) can be deployed for Oracle EBS, which provides data protection and maintains availability against disasters. Oracle Data Guard along with Oracle GoldenGate can be used for data protection, disaster recovery, and reporting needs with Oracle EBS.

Now, let's take a look into how we can implement Oracle Data Guard and Oracle GoldenGate to accommodate these requirements for availability and reporting. Let's take an example where we have a primary site running an Oracle R12 EBS Financials environment along with Oracle 11g RAC for scalability and Oracle Data Guard for high availability purposes. We can use Oracle GoldenGate to provide for replication and reporting needs to a third reporting database to capture all committed transactions for Accounts Payable (AP) and Accounts Receivable (AR). We also have a physical and logical Data Guard implementation with a secondary remote site in Arizona, for example, that can deploy an RAC database for business continuity if the primary site fails. While Oracle RAC provides us with load balancing and performance resources, it does not address potential site failures. By using Oracle Data Guard, GoldenGate, and RAC together, we can achieve a sweet spot in terms of providing the most elegant solution for reporting, disaster recovery (DR), performance, and high availability.

As we mentioned earlier, the default out-of-box standard installation for Oracle EBS poses a risk in terms of being a **Single Point of Failure** (**SPOF**) at the database and application-tier layers of the EBS architecture, as it contains a single database shared by the application. We need to deploy Oracle RAC with ASM along with Oracle Data Guard at the database tier to satisfy the requirement for high availability and performance. If we choose to also offload reporting and replication tasks, then we need to additionally install and configure Oracle GoldenGate.

Now, let's take a look at the application tier in terms of how we can implement the Oracle MAA architecture. As, by default, the application middle tier contains the Concurrent Processing Node (CP), admin server, BI forms, and a web server (Apache OHS) along with a few Oracle Containers for Java (OC4J) instances, we have limited choices on how to configure availability for this tier as follows:

- OC4J clustering
- Load balancing with web cache for Oracle R12 EBS
- **Parallel Concurrent Processing** (**PCP**) for Concurrent Management Servers

Clustering and load balancing of the OC4J instances can be performed at the software layer through configurations provided by Oracle. Hardware load balancers such as Cisco ACE and Big IP provide a more robust hardware solution. Load balancers distribute client requests over multiple application-tier nodes, as well as functionality to scale out for future growth requirements along with fault tolerance against failures. To implement these tasks, you must add and configure the application-tier nodes and load-balancer hardware. My Oracle Support (formerly Metalink) Note 380489.1 *Using Load-Balancers with Oracle EBS Release 12* describes the application configuration options in detail. Remember that load-balancer configuration is vendor specific. For instance, you will need to consult the Cisco ACE documentation if you choose to use Cisco ACE load balancers for Oracle R12 EBS.

Oracle 11g RAC suitability

Oracle EBS places additional demands for resources and performance in terms of application server and database requirements. As we discussed earlier, Oracle RAC provides benefits for scalability and availability. With ever larger demands for resources, RAC can expand the capabilities by adding additional nodes to the Oracle EBS architecture, thus allowing larger numbers of users to use the system. As a result, greater computing power is available on demand when needed.

Oracle RAC provides that robust scale out, or horizontal functionality, by adding new nodes to Oracle EBS. By expanding the cluster for EBS and RAC, you will also be able to support larger numbers of concurrent users. In addition, new instances introduced into the RAC system for EBS will also free up additional memory buffers, along with more CPUs, and permit many new user connections without affecting the performance of the other instances.

Transparent Application Failure (**TAF**) provides EBS with additional capabilities with RAC. You can perform database-level load balancing and failover to take advantage of the performance and availability features included with RAC for EBS.

In addition, you can also assign instances to different service groups with RAC for EBS. This is particularly useful if you want to offload the performance and operations of different EBS modules, such as AP and AR at different times of the day to minimize contention for database resources.

Installing EBS 12.1.1

Before you install the Oracle EBS, we highly recommend that you first review the online documentation from Oracle (`http://otn.oracle.com`) to learn about the many prerequisites and concepts for an Oracle R12 EBS 12.1.1 installation. You have a few different options to install and configure EBS. The default installation uses what is called a fresh install that installs the application and technology stack along with the Oracle database server with no sample data. For demo and training purposes, there is also a Vision instance that may be installed that contains sample data for a fictitious company. For a new installation, you have the choice between using the Express install, which creates only a single node that combines the database tier and application middle tier on one server along with a single user account, or a complex multi-node installation that will set up one or more application-tier servers and a separate database-tier server. In most cases, you will most likely install a multi-node environment with the Oracle EBS. The key thing to take into consideration here is that every Oracle EBS installation requires you to run the Rapid Install program through the `rapidwiz` utility.

For our demo and case study, we will use a regular fresh install process. The selected approach requires that you set up an Oracle Linux systems-level account for the database tier (for example, Oracle) and an application-tier Linux OS account (for example, `applmgr`) for the application tier.

Please refer to the earlier chapters for Oracle 11g RAC Installation and Oracle 11g Clusterware Upgrade, to understand the Oracle 11g prerequisites for the Oracle CRS and RDBMS installation. Please also refer to My Oracle Support (formerly Metalink) note 761564.1 *Oracle® E-Business Suite Installation and Upgrade Notes* for the EBS 12.1.1 installation prerequisites on Linux.

We are not going to cover the Linux and TCP/IP configuration in this section. An operating system-level patch for Linux, patch number 6078836, needs to be installed, so that the EBS installation completes successfully. Otherwise, errors will occur when the Oracle HTTP server is started for the Oracle EBS. It is best that this patch is applied before starting the EBS installation. There is a workaround to complete the installation after applying the patch. The EBS 12.1.1 documentation is available at the following URL:

`http://download.oracle.com/docs/cd/B53825_03/current/html/docset.html`

The Oracle document E12842-03 *Installation Guide: Using Rapid Install Release 12.1 (12.1.1)* from this site provides detailed installation and upgrade instructions.

In this section, we assume that you have used a staged environment with all of the Oracle R12 EBS software available. Oracle provides a Perl script named `adautostg.pl` that can be used to create the staging directories and place the EBS software in the correct format for installation. You will need to make sure to have performed the required planning for the installation or upgrade to Oracle R12 EBS.

For our test Oracle R12 EBS environment, we will use a single node, non-express install using a root Linux account. The installation process assumes that an Oracle and `applmgr` Linux account are created. We get to the directory in the stage area where the `rapidwiz` is and execute it as follows:

```
# cd /u01/StageEBS/startCD/Disk1/rapidwiz
# ./rapidwiz
```

The following window appears and provides information about the components included in EBS 12.1.1:

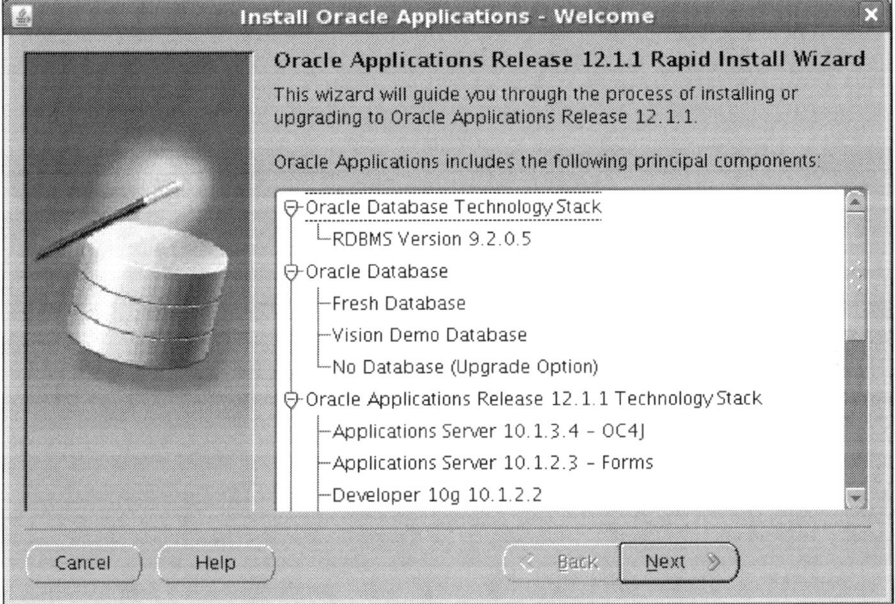

If you click on **Next**, you will be directed to the next screen. Here, we select the option to perform a fresh install of the EBS. We ignore the **Use Express Install** option, as we are going to install EBS using the following two precreated Linux user accounts:

- Oracle for the database tier
- `applmgr` for the application tier

The upgrade option is for an upgrade to EBS 12.1.1 and we will not discuss it. The express account uses only one Linux account for both application and database tiers. We will then need to click on **Next**, as shown in the following screenshot:

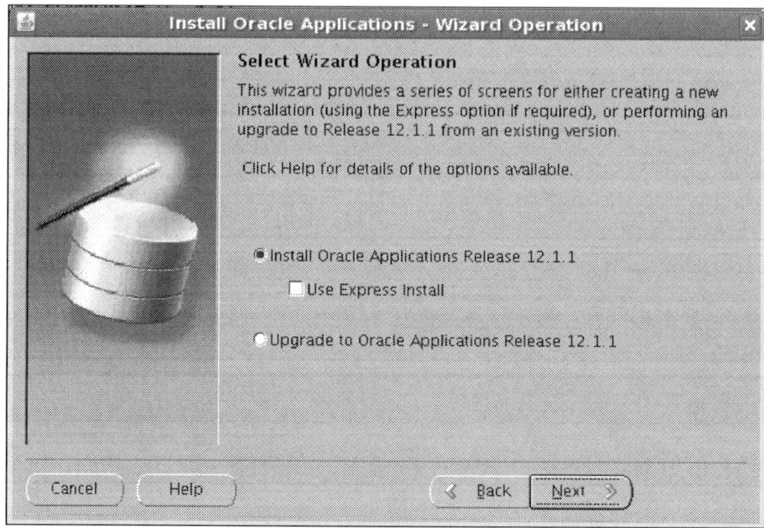

Here, we can create either a new configuration or use an existing one. We are going to create a new configuration, as we are installing a fresh EBS. The option of using a saved configuration is useful for restarting a failed installation or for a complex multi-node install. After making the selection, we then need to click on **Next**, as shown in the following screenshot:

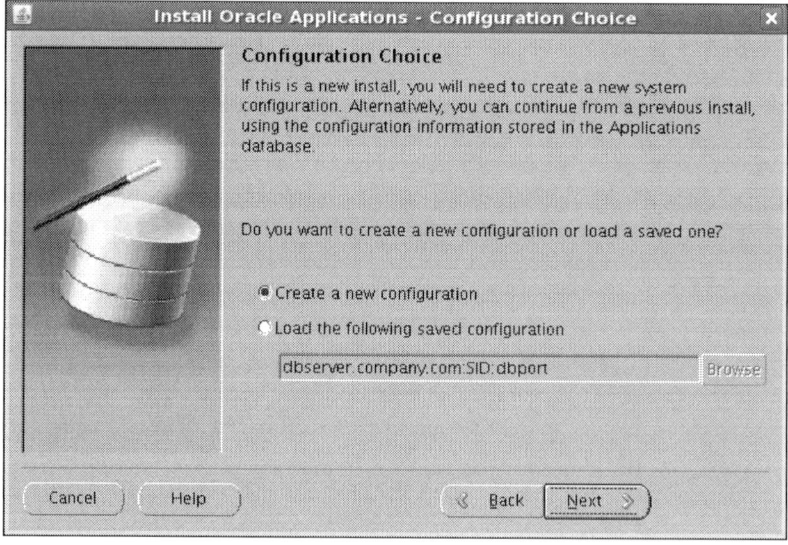

We are now prompted to select a port pool and values for each of the ports. This is to enable the user to have EBS on a single server. Although we are able to select an individual value for each port by clicking on **Edit Ports**, we select **3** as the value for **Port Pool** and keep the defaults as they are. We then click on **Next**, as shown in the following screenshot:

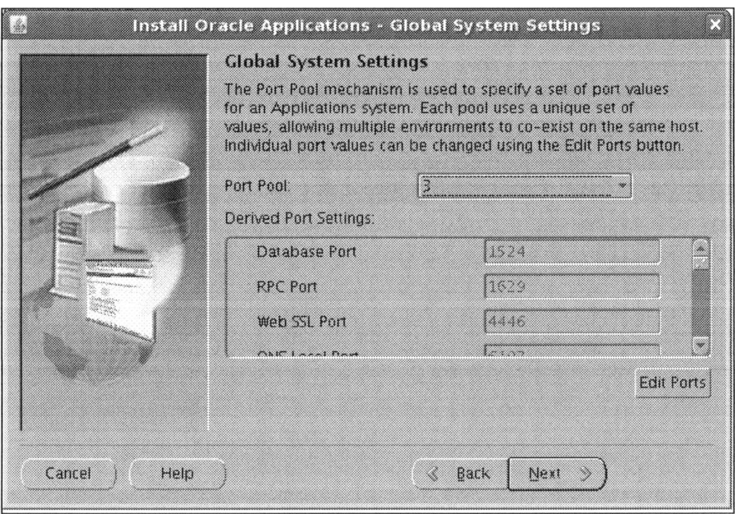

For the database node, we select the **VIS** database, which is a pre-seeded database, and then specify the database name, hostname, domain, OS type, base directory, OS username, and group for the database tier. Then we click on **Next** to continue, as shown in the following screenshot:

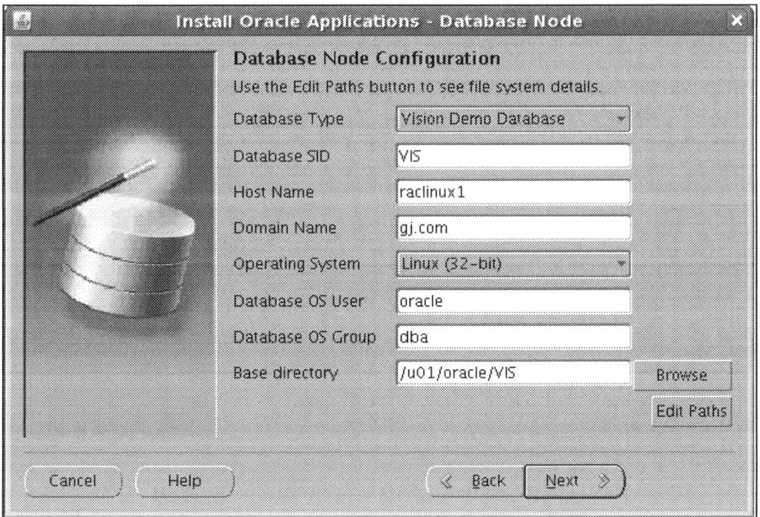

As the application node, we again select the VIS database, which is pre-seeded, and then specify the database name, hostname, domain, OS type, base directory, instance directory, OS username, and group for the application tier. Then click on **Next** to continue.

Here we make our selection for single-node EBS install, although we can have a complex multi-node EBS install. We can add more servers until we ensure compliance with the architecture we need. Then click on **Next** to continue, as shown in the following screenshot:

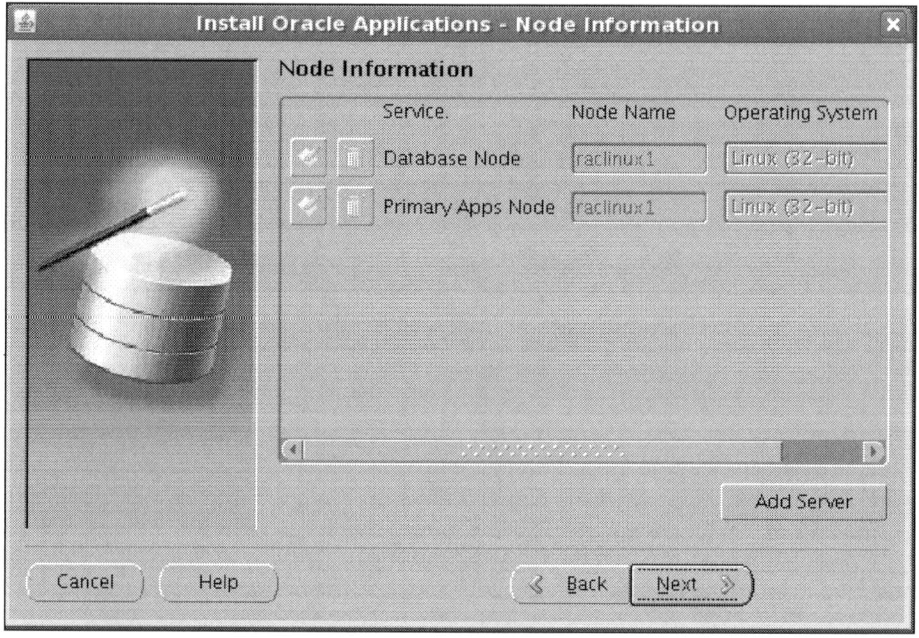

The installation process should now begin and we will need to wait until all verifications are made and are eventually complete. Usually, the installation takes four to six hours depending on hardware resources and platform.

As mentioned earlier, the operating system-level patch `6078836` needs to be installed, so that the EBS installation completes successfully. Earlier, we mentioned that it solves a bug at the shared library and linking level for the Oracle HTTP (OHS) server to function correctly with Oracle EBS. It is best if the patch is applied before starting the EBS installation. There is a workaround to complete the installation after applying the patch. If the installation shows an error, we will need to exit `rapidwiz`, apply the patch, and restart the `rapidwiz`. Here we cancel the `rapidwiz` utility and verify the status of the HTTP server. As we can see in the following screenshot, it is down. Issuing `adapcctl.sh status` confirms it. We apply `6078836` patch as root:

```
% cd 6078836
% mv /usr/lib/libdb.so.2 /usr/lib/libdb.so.2.6078836 (if libdb.so.2
exist already in /usr/lib)
% cp libdb.so.2 /usr/lib
```

Then, we will need to restart the HTTP server by issuing the `adapcctl.sh` start command, as shown in the following screenshot:

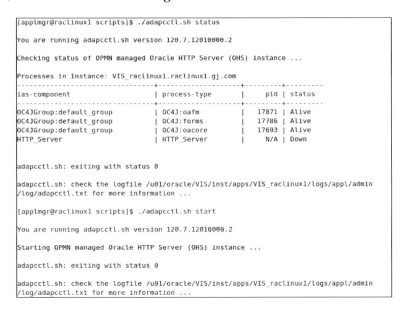

```
[applmgr@raclinux1 scripts]$ ./adapcctl.sh status

You are running adapcctl.sh version 120.7.12010000.2

Checking status of OPMN managed Oracle HTTP Server (OHS) instance ...

Processes in Instance: VIS_raclinux1.raclinux1.gj.com
---------------------------------+--------------------+---------+---------
ias-component                    | process-type       |     pid | status
---------------------------------+--------------------+---------+---------
OC4JGroup:default_group          | OC4J:oafm          |   17871 | Alive
OC4JGroup:default_group          | OC4J:forms         |   17786 | Alive
OC4JGroup:default_group          | OC4J:oacore        |   17693 | Alive
HTTP_Server                      | HTTP_Server        |     N/A | Down


adapcctl.sh: exiting with status 0

adapcctl.sh: check the logfile /u01/oracle/VIS/inst/apps/VIS_raclinux1/logs/appl/admin
/log/adapcctl.txt for more information ...

[applmgr@raclinux1 scripts]$ ./adapcctl.sh start

You are running adapcctl.sh version 120.7.12010000.2

Starting OPMN managed Oracle HTTP Server (OHS) instance ...

adapcctl.sh: exiting with status 0

adapcctl.sh: check the logfile /u01/oracle/VIS/inst/apps/VIS_raclinux1/logs/appl/admin
/log/adapcctl.txt for more information ...
```

We can restart the `rapidwiz` utility by issuing the `./rapidwiz -restart` command. After a while, we will see a screen confirming that the installation is now successfully complete, as shown in the following screenshot:

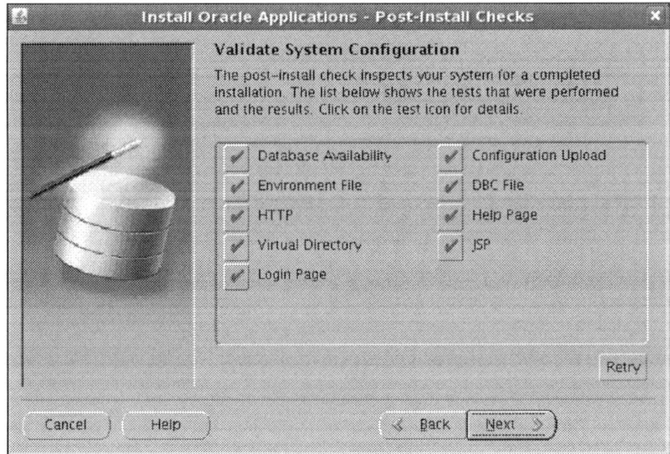

We can also double-check the status of the HTTP server, as shown in the following screenshot, by issuing the `adapcctl.sh status` command:

```
[applmgr@raclinux1 scripts]$ ./adapcctl.sh status

You are running adapcctl.sh version 120.7.12010000.2

Checking status of OPMN managed Oracle HTTP Server (OHS) instance ...

Processes in Instance: VIS_raclinux1.raclinux1.gj.com
--------------------------------+--------------------+---------+--------
ias-component                   | process-type       |     pid | status
--------------------------------+--------------------+---------+--------
OC4JGroup:default_group         | OC4J:oafm          |   17871 | Alive
OC4JGroup:default_group         | OC4J:forms         |   17786 | Alive
OC4JGroup:default_group         | OC4J:oacore        |   17693 | Alive
HTTP_Server                     | HTTP_Server        |   13461 | Alive


adapcctl.sh: exiting with status 0

adapcctl.sh: check the logfile /u01/oracle/VIS/inst/apps/VIS_raclinux1/logs/appl/admin
/log/adapcctl.txt for more information ...
```

A screen is displayed confirming that the EBS 12.1.1 installation is successful. We need to click on **Finish** to exit the installer and log in to the EBS, as shown in the following screenshot:

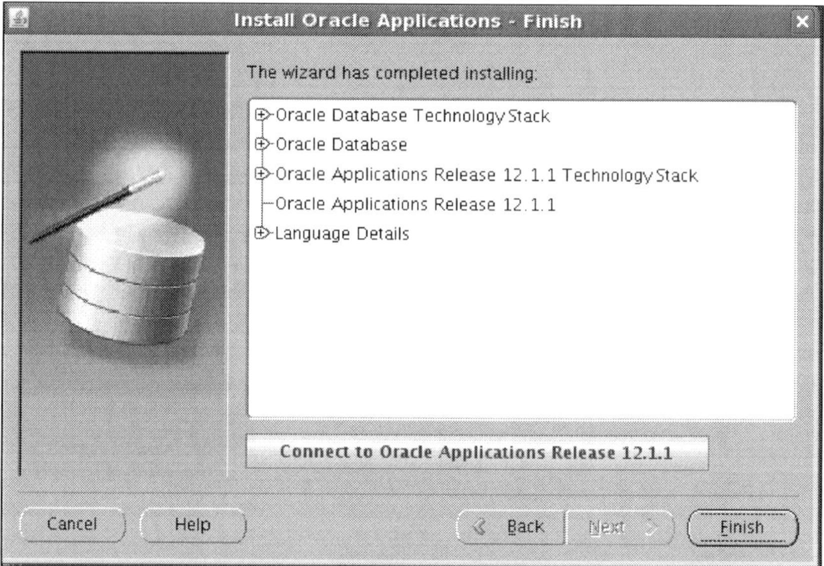

Now, we have a fully functional EBS at our disposal.

Now that we have Oracle R12 EBS installed, we will walk through the process to implement high availability and scalability for the database tier.

EBS implementation on Oracle 11g RAC

Oracle software has evolved over time along with dozens of recent acquisitions of major software and hardware vendors, including Sun Microsystems, BEA, and GoldenGate. To manage the complex integrations of these technologies with Oracle, there is a useful certification matrix from Oracle available online at the My Oracle Support website `http://support.oracle.com`.

As mentioned in the earlier part of the book, we advise that you consult the matrix to verify that the version of EBS you implement is supported with Oracle 11g RAC.

While most versions for Oracle RAC are supported with respect to both Oracle EBS 11i and R12, you need to be sure that this is the case for your particular platform and software release. My Oracle Support (formerly Metalink) Note 986673.1 *General Notes For E-Business Suite Release 12* contains the latest certifications for EBS with Oracle 11g RAC. In this chapter, we will focus on Release 12 for EBS with RAC.

In the context of this chapter, we will show you the steps to create the context file with the new Oracle 11g (11.1.0.7) Oracle home and to make EBS aware of these changes. You will also need to change the context file on the application tier, so that the application tier is able to communicate with the database tier. While we will not show all the steps required to upgrade the database to 11g, we refer you to My Oracle Support (formerly Metalink) note 466649.1 Using *Oracle 11g Release 1 (11.1.0.7) Real Application Clusters and Automatic Storage Management with Oracle E-Business Suite Release 12* for additional information. In any case, let's make the following assumptions for the installation with EBS and RAC:

- The Oracle home for the Oracle 11g R1 RDBMS has already been upgraded to the latest Oracle RDBMS and for RAC enabling the EBS `/u01/app/oracle/product/11.1.0/db_2`.
- The Oracle home for the Oracle 11g R1 ASM has been upgraded to the latest Oracle RDBMS and/or for RAC enabling the EBS `/u01/app/oracle/product/11.1.0/db_1`.
- The Oracle home for the Oracle 11g R1 CRS for RAC enabling the EBS `/u01/crs/oracle/product/11.1.0/crs_1`.
- `/u01/oracle/VIS` has been created as a result of EBS R12 12.1.1 installation.

Upgrading an EBS 12 with the latest release of Oracle involves the following steps:

1. Create the new Oracle home for Oracle 11g and install the Oracle 11g software. Do not create a starter database! If you have a sandbox or test environment, you may optionally install the sample schemas. However, we do not recommend this for a production environment due to security risk with the sample schemas, as hackers have the known default passwords for the sample schemas. Be sure to also apply the latest Oracle 11g database patch. Be sure to also apply the interoperability patches for both the EBS application middle tier and database tier.
2. Shut down application-tier nodes and listeners. Next, perform the database upgrade to 11g R1 or 11g R2, as well as to update the database initialization parameters, and post installation tasks.
3. Start the new listener after the database upgrade has completed. Be sure to run the `adgrants.sql` script from SQLPLUS as SYSDBA.
4. Execute the following command:

```
$ sqlplus apps/<APPS password> @ adctxprv.sql <SYSTEM password>
  CTXSYS
where adctxprv.sql is from $AD_TOP/patch/115/sql/adctxprv.sql.
```

```
Execute:
```

```
sqlplus <APPS user>/<APPS password> @wfaqupfix.sql
  <APPLSYS user> <APPS user>
where wfaqupfix.sql is from $FND_TOP/patch/115/sql/wfaqupfix.sql
```

5. Run the AutoConfig utility (`adautocfg.sh`) on the new Oracle database home (`ORACLE_HOME`) from the database server node. AutoConfig is an Oracle EBS database utility, which is used to perform configuration changes to the Oracle R12 EBS environment.

Note: If the database listener of the new Oracle home has been configured in a way that differs from the old Oracle home, then you must also run AutoConfig on each application-tier server node, in order to update the system with the new listener. Please see My Oracle Support (formerly Metalink) note 387859.1 *Using AutoConfig to Manage System Configurations in Oracle E-Business Suite Release 12* for how to use AutoConfig with EBS.

AutoConfig has been used to manage system configurations in the Oracle EBS since Version 11i. Before you run AutoConfig, you must first shut down all processes, including the database and the listener, and restart them to load the new environment settings.

6. Gather statistics for the sys schema. As SYSDBA using SQL*PLUS, execute the `$APPL_TOP/admin/adstats.sql` script in restricted mode as follows:

   ```
   $ sqlplus "/ as sysdba"
   SQL> shutdown normal;
   SQL> startup restrict;
   SQL> @adstats.sql
   SQL> shutdown normal; SQL> startup;
   SQL> exit;
   ```

7. If required, recreate the Demantra privileges.
8. Update and recreate any custom database links.
9. Update and recreate grants and synonyms. On the application tier server, as the applications owner of the application filesystem, run the `AD` administration utility (`adadmin`) and select the option to recreate grants and synonyms for the APPS schema located in the **Maintain Applications Database Objects** menu.
10. Restart all of the middle-tier application server processes. You will also need to restart the database-tier server process, including the Oracle Net listener for the database instance, as well as the database instance itself from the Oracle 11.1 or 11.2 Oracle home. You may be able to use the database scripts located on the database-tier server as part of the EBS process management scripts. Consult the Oracle EBS documentation for details.
11. Synchronize views for Oracle Workflow. To do so, you will need to log into to the Oracle Applications Manager (OAM) welcome page with the System Administrator responsibility.

    As SYSADMIN, navigate to **Requests** | **Run** | **Single Request** and click on the **OK** button. Then enter the following parameters:

    - `Request Name = Workflow Directory Services User/Role Validation`
    - `p_BatchSize = 10000`
    - `p_Check_Dangling = Yes`
    - `Add missing user/role assignments = Yes`
    - `Update WHO columns in WF tables = No`

12. Click on **OK** and submit.

RAC-enabling EBS 12.1.1

By deploying Oracle 11g RAC with Oracle EBS, you will have the ability to scale out the database as it grows. As we discussed earlier, mission-critical business operations around the globe require that core Oracle Financial EBS systems provide resilience and high availability to support 24X7x365 processing requirements to meet business service-level agreements (SLAs).

Next, we will describe how to migrate a single instance non-RAC Oracle R12 EBS Release environment to an Oracle 11g Real Application Clusters (Oracle RAC) environment with Automatic Storage Management (ASM). The most current version of the document describing this can be obtained from My Oracle Support (formerly Oracle Metalink) Knowledge Document 466649.1.

Configuration prerequisites

Before we move on to enabling RAC for EBS, we need to perform some checks and legwork. Carry out the following steps:

1. Install a stand-alone Oracle R12 (12.1.1 or later) EBS environment if you have not already done so. Apply the Oracle R12 E-Business Suite Release 12.1.3 Maintenance Pack (patch 7303030).
2. Install and configure the cluster hardware and interconnects. Also be sure to install the Oracle 11g CRS, ASM, and RDBMS as described in previous chapters along with the required interoperability patches from My Oracle Support (formerly Metalink) note 802875.1. If you decide to implement Oracle 11g R2 RAC with Oracle EBS 12.1.1 or later, consult My Oracle Support (formerly Metalink) note 823587.1 for details.

> Please note that the Oracle homes for CRS, ASM, and RDBMS must be installed with Oracle 11g and patched to the current 11g release.

3. For the ASM and RDBMS Oracle homes, install the Oracle Database 11g from the 11g Examples CD after the Oracle 11g installation but prior to applying the patch for 11g.

4. After the successful installation of the Oracle 11g R1 CRS and ASM, the output of `./crs_stat -t -v` should display the following:

```
Name              Type           Target     State       Host
------------------------------------------------------------
ora..SM1.asm      application    ONLINE     ONLINE      raclinux1
ora..X1.lsnr      application    ONLINE     ONLINE      raclinux1
ora..ux1.gsd      application    ONLINE     ONLINE      raclinux1
ora..ux1.ons      application    ONLINE     ONLINE      raclinux1
ora..ux1.vip      application    ONLINE     ONLINE      raclinux1
ora..SM2.asm      application    ONLINE     ONLINE      raclinux2
ora..X2.lsnr      application    ONLINE     ONLINE      raclinux2
ora..ux2.gsd      application    ONLINE     ONLINE      raclinux2
ora..ux2.ons      application    ONLINE     ONLINE      raclinux2
ora..ux2.vip      application    ONLINE     ONLINE      raclinux2
```

   Also, `./crsctl check crs` should look like the following screenshot:

```
[root@raclinux2 bin]# ./crsctl check crs
Cluster Synchronization Services appears healthy
Cluster Ready Services appears healthy
Event Manager appears healthy
[root@raclinux2 bin]#
```

5. For the sample configuration for RAC and EBS, you need to verify that both CRS and ASM are installed and running on the raclinux1 and raclinux2 nodes of the cluster. As you can see, there are two instances belonging to ASM and two listeners for ASM, one on each node:
   - `ora.raclinux1.+ASM1.asm` on node raclinux1
   - `ora.raclinux2.+ASM2.asm` on node raclinux2
   - `ora.raclinux1.LISTENER_RACLINUX1.lsnr` on node raclinux1
   - `ora.raclinux2.LISTENER_RACLINUX2.lsnr` on node raclinux2

6. There are two disk groups created and mounted in ASM—DATA with 400 GB and FLASH with 200 GB. Now, we can start with RAC-enabling the EBS, as described in the following section.

ASM and RAC-enabling the EBS database with the rconfig utility

So far, we have a single-instance database that was created on a Linux filesystem upon EBS 12.1.1 install. We will use `rconfig` to move the database to ASM and RAC, and enable the VIS EBS database. We will set a **Flash Recovery Area** (**FRA**) for the EBS database VIS using the parameters and commands described next:

```
SQL> alter system set db_recovery_file_dest_size=200g;

System altered.

SQL> alter system set db_recovery_file_dest='+FLASH';

System altered.

SQL> archive log list;
Database log mode              No Archive Mode
Automatic archival             Disabled
Archive destination            USE_DB_RECOVERY_FILE_DEST
Oldest online log sequence     5
Current log sequence           7
SQL>
```

After logging into the server using an Oracle Linux user account, you will need to do the following:

1. Go to the `$ORACLE_HOME/assistants/rconfig/sampleXMLs` directory.
2. Make a copy of the template file `ConvertToRAC.xml` to `convert.xml` and `convert1.xml`.
3. Modify the content of `convert.xml` and `convert1.xml` identically with the exception of `<n:Convert verify="ONLY">`.
4. Place `<n:Convert verify="ONLY">` in the `convert.xml` file, and `<n:Convert verify="YES">` in `convert1.xml`.
5. The possible values for convert verify are `ONLY`, `YES`, and `NO`.
6. A utility named `rconfig` is used along with the XML file to perform the following activities:
    - To migrate the database to ASM storage (only if ASM is specified as a storage option in the configuration XML file)
    - To create database instances on all nodes in the cluster
    - To configure listener and Net Service entries

- To configure and register CRS resources
- To start the instances on all nodes in the clusters

Please note that the value `ONLY` performs a validation of the parameters and will identify any problems that need to be corrected prior to the actual conversion, but does not perform a conversion after completing the prerequisite checks. Setting the parameter `Convertverify="YES"`, `rconfig` performs checks to ensure that the prerequisites for single-instance to Oracle RAC conversion have been met before it starts the conversion. On the other hand, setting `Convertverify="NO"`, `rconfig` does not perform prerequisite checks and starts conversion. The content of the `convert.xml` file is displayed next.

Place `<n:Convert verify="ONLY">` in the `convert.xml` file, and place `<n:Convert verify="YES">` in the `convert1.xml` file. In both files—`convert.xml` and `convert1.xml`—we will need specify the following information:

- Source of pre-conversion EBS RDBMS Oracle home of non-RAC database— `/u01/oracle/VIS/db/tech_st/11.1.0`
- Destination of post-conversion EBS RDBMS Oracle home of the RAC database–`/u01/app/oracle/product/11.1.0/db_2`
- SID for non-RAC database and credentials—VIS
- List of nodes that should have RAC instances running—raclinux1, raclinux2
- Instance prefix—VIS
- Storage type—please note that the storage type is ASM
- ASM disk groups for Oracle data file and FRA—DATA and FLASH

The exact content of the `convert.xml` file is as follows:

```
<?xml version="1.0" encoding="UTF-8" ?>
- <n:RConfigxmlns:n="http://www.oracle.com/rconfig"
xmlns:xsi="http://www.w3.org/2001/XMLSchema-instance"
xsi:schemaLocation="http://www.oracle.com/rconfig">
- <n:ConvertToRAC>
- <!--
Verify does a precheck to ensure all pre-requisites are met,
before the conversion is attempted. Allowable values are:
YES|NO|ONLY
-->
- <n:Convert verify="ONLY">
- <!--
```

```
Specify current OracleHome of non-rac database for SourceDBHome
-->
<n:SourceDBHome>/u01/oracle/VIS/db/tech_st/11.1.0</n:SourceDBHome>
- <!--
Specify OracleHome where the rac database should be configured. It
can be same as SourceDBHome
-->
<n:TargetDBHome>/u01/app/oracle/product/11.1.0/db_2</
n:TargetDBHome>
- <!--
Specify SID of non-rac database and credential. User with sysdba
role is required to perform conversion
-->
- <n:SourceDBInfo SID="VIS">
- <n:Credentials>
<n:User>sys</n:User>
<n:Password>sys1</n:Password>
<n:Role>sysdba</n:Role>
</n:Credentials>
</n:SourceDBInfo>
- <!--
ASMInfo element is required only if the current non-rac database
uses
ASM Storage
-->
- <n:ASMInfo SID="+ASM1">
- <n:Credentials>
<n:User>sys</n:User>
<n:Password>sys1</n:Password>
<n:Role>sysasm</n:Role>

</n:Credentials>
</n:ASMInfo>
- <!--
Specify the list of nodes that should have rac instances running.
LocalNode should be the first node in this nodelist.
-->
- <n:NodeList>
<n:Node name="raclinux1.gj.com" />
<n:Node name="raclinux2.gj.com" />
</n:NodeList>
- <!--
Specify prefix for rac instances. It can be same as the instance
name for non-rac database or different. The instance number will
be attached to this prefix.
-->
<n:InstancePrefix>VIS</n:InstancePrefix>
- <!--
```

```
Specify port for the listener to be configured for rac database.
If port="", alistener existing on localhost will be used for
rac database.The listener will be extended to all nodes in the
nodelist
-->
<n:Listener port="" />
- <!--
Specify the type of storage to be used by rac database. Allowable
values are CFS|ASM. The non-rac database should have same storage
type.
-->
- <n:SharedStorage type="ASM">
- <!--
Specify Database Area Location to be configured for rac database.
If this field is left empty, current storage will be used for rac
database. For CFS, this field will have directory path.
-->
<n:TargetDatabaseArea>+DATA</n:TargetDatabaseArea>
- <!--
Specify Flash Recovery Area to be configured for rac database.
If this field is left empty, current recovery area of non-rac
database will be configured for rac database. If current database
is not using recovery Area, the resulting rac database will not
have a recovery area.
-->
<n:TargetFlashRecoveryArea>+FLASH</n:TargetFlashRecoveryArea>
</n:SharedStorage>
</n:Convert>
</n:ConvertToRAC>
</n:RConfig>
```

7. We can use the `rconfig` utility to verify the conversion process using the `convert.xml` file. The output of the verification is shown in the following screenshot:

```
[oracle@raclinux1 sampleXMLs]$ rconfig convert.xml
<?xml version="1.0" ?>
<RConfig version="1.1" >
<ConvertToRAC>
    <Convert>
      <Response>
        <Result code="0" >
          Operation Succeeded
        </Result>
      </Response>
      <ReturnValue type="object">
There is no return value for this step     </ReturnValue>
    </Convert>
  </ConvertToRAC></RConfig>
[oracle@raclinux1 sampleXMLs]$
```

8. If you wish to specify a NEW_ORACLE_HOME as is the case for the Oracle home of the freshly installed Oracle 11g release 11.1.0.7, start the database from the new Oracle home using the following command:

   ```
   SQL>startup pfile=<OLD_ORACLE_HOME>/dbs/init<ORACLE_SID>.ora;
   ```

9. Shut down the database. Create a spfile from the pfile using the following command:

   ```
   SQL>create spfile from pfile
   ```

10. Move the $ORACLE_HOME/dbs/spfile<ORACLE_SID>.ora for this instance to the shared location. Take a backup of the existing $ORACLE_HOME/dbs/init<ORACLE_SID>. ora and create a new $ORACLE_HOME/dbs/init<ORACLE_SID>.ora, with the following parameter spfile=<Path of spfile on shared disk>/spfile<ORACLE_SID>.ora.
11. Start up the instance. Using netca, create local and remote listener tnsnames.ora aliases for database instances. Use listener_VIS1 and listener_VIS2 as the alias name for the local listener, and listeners_VIS for the remote listener alias. Execute netca from $ORACLE_HOME/bin.

    You will then need to do the following:

    - Choose the Cluster Configuration option in the netca assistant.
    - Choose the current node name from the node list.
    - Choose the **Local Net Service Name Configuration** option and click on **Next**.
    - Select **Add** and on the next screen, enter the service name and click on **Next**.
    - Enter the current node as the server name and the port **1521** defined during the ASM listener creation.
    - Select **Do not perform Test** and click on **Next**.
    - Enter the listener TNS alias name such as LISTENER_VIS1 for local listener.
    - Repeat the previous steps for the remote listener, with the server name as the secondary node and the listener name as LISTENERS_VIS.

> Ensure that local and remote aliases are created on all nodes in the cluster.

12. After making sure that the parameters are valid and that no errors were identified that could cause a problem, we can start the real conversion using the `rconfig` and `convert.xml` file. The output of the execution is shown in the following screenshot:

```
[oracle@raclinux1 sampleXMLs]$ rconfig convert1.xml
Converting Database VIS to Cluster Database. Target Oracle Home : /u01/app/oracl
e/product/11.1.0/db_2.
Setting Data Files and Control Files


Adding Database Instances
Adding Redo Logs
Enabling threads for all Database Instances
Setting TEMP tablespace
Adding UNDO tablespaces
Adding Trace files
Setting Flash Recovery Area
Updating Oratab
Creating Password file(s)
Configuring Listeners
Configuring related CRS resources
Adding NetService entries
Starting Listeners
Starting Cluster Database
```

[root@raclinux1:/u01/crs/oracle/product/11.1.0/crs_1/bin]

13. After the completion of the VIS database conversion from a single-instance database residing on a filesystem to an RAC database on the `raclinux1` and `raclinux2` server cluster residing on ASM, we can validate the conversion by looking at the running services produced by the `./crs_stat -t -v` command output, as shown in the following screenshot:

```
[root@raclinux2 bin]# ./crs_stat -t -v
Name           Type         R/RA   F/FT   Target    State     Host
----------------------------------------------------------------------
ora....S1.inst application  0/5    0/0    ONLINE    ONLINE    raclinux1
ora....S2.inst application  0/5    0/0    ONLINE    ONLINE    raclinux2
ora.VIS.db     application  0/0    0/1    ONLINE    ONLINE    raclinux1
ora....SM1.asm application  0/5    0/0    ONLINE    ONLINE    raclinux1
ora....X1.lsnr application  0/5    0/0    ONLINE    ONLINE    raclinux1
ora....X1.lsnr application  0/5    0/0    ONLINE    ONLINE    raclinux1
ora....X1.lsnr application  0/5    0/0    ONLINE    ONLINE    raclinux1
ora....ux1.gsd application  0/5    0/0    ONLINE    ONLINE    raclinux1
ora....ux1.ons application  0/3    0/0    ONLINE    ONLINE    raclinux1
ora....ux1.vip application  0/0    0/0    ONLINE    ONLINE    raclinux1
ora....SM2.asm application  0/5    0/0    ONLINE    ONLINE    raclinux2
ora....X2.lsnr application  0/5    0/0    ONLINE    ONLINE    raclinux2
ora....X2.lsnr application  0/5    0/0    ONLINE    ONLINE    raclinux2
ora....X2.lsnr application  0/5    0/0    ONLINE    ONLINE    raclinux2
ora....X2.lsnr application  0/5    0/0    ONLINE    ONLINE    raclinux2
ora....ux2.gsd application  0/5    0/0    ONLINE    ONLINE    raclinux2
ora....ux2.ons application  0/3    0/0    ONLINE    ONLINE    raclinux2
ora....ux2.vip application  0/0    0/0    ONLINE    ONLINE    raclinux2
```

Running AutoConfig

Oracle R12 EBS is complex software that uses an XML-based file named the context file to store and manage system configurations for the Oracle EBS.

To change the context file parameter, we need to reconfigure the EBS environment. Note that EBS 12.1.1/12.1.13 Oracle Application Manager (OAM) is the only approved method for changing the context file. You also can run the AutoConfig (`adautocfg.sh`) utility, so that changes to the parameters are stored in the context file. The context file is the data dictionary for Oracle EBS much like the initialization parameter file (`pfile` or `spfile`) is the bible for the Oracle database server. You must use AutoConfig for changing the EBS environment. There is a context file for both the application middle-tier server and also for the database-tier server.

As we have installed the new Oracle 11g homes for ASM and RDBMS, we need to make EBS aware of them. AutoConfig needs to be run on the database tier to make EBS aware of the changes made. This is achieved by running the AutoConfig utility (`adautocfg.sh`) on the database tier in the following scenarios:

- After applying a patch to the database tier, when the `check config` utility reports any potential changes to the templates
- After customizations are made on the database tier
- After a database or application tier is upgraded
- After restoration of the database or Oracle home from a backup tape
- After a JDK upgrade is performed on the database tier
- After the Net Services Topology Information is manually cleaned using one of the supported procedures (such as `fnd_conc_clone.setup_clean`); subsequently, AutoConfig must be run on the application-tier nodes
- After registration of a new RAC node
- After setting up the `APPL_TOP` on a shared filesystem
- All other cases where documentation explicitly says that AutoConfig should be run on the database tier

Now, we are going to enable AutoConfig on the new Oracle 11g 11.1.0.7 home database tier, so you will need to complete certain steps (in the order listed) to migrate to AutoConfig on the database tier:

1. Copy AutoConfig to the new `RDBMS ORACLE_HOME` for Oracle 11g R1.
2. Generate your database context file.
3. Prepare for AutoConfig.
4. Generate and apply AutoConfig configuration files.

5. Execute AutoConfig on all database nodes in the cluster.
6. Perform activities related to `Init` file, `tnsnames`, and `listener` files.

Now, let's see an explanation of each of these steps

Copying AutoConfig to the new RDBMS ORACLE_HOME for Oracle 11g R1 11.1.0.7

Ensure that you have applied any patches listed in the prerequisites section discussed earlier. Update the `RDBMS ORACLE_HOME` filesystem with the AutoConfig files by performing the following steps:

1. On the application tier (as the `applmgr` user), log in to the `APPL_TOP` environment (source the environment file), and create an `appsutil.zip` file:

   ```
   perl <AD_TOP>/bin/admkappsutil.pl
   ```

2. This will create a `appsutil.zip` file in the `$INST_TOP/admin/out` directory:

```
[applmgr@raclinux1 bin]$ cd $AD_TOP/bin
[applmgr@raclinux1 bin]$
[applmgr@raclinux1 bin]$  ls admk*.pl
admkappsutil.pl
[applmgr@raclinux1 bin]$ perl $AD_TOP/bin/admkappsutil.pl
Starting the generation of appsutil.zip
Log file located at /u01/oracle/VIS/inst/apps/VIS_raclinux1/admin/log/MakeAppsUtil_11261058.log
output located at /u01/oracle/VIS/inst/apps/VIS_raclinux1/admin/out/appsutil.zip
MakeAppsUtil completed successfully.
[applmgr@raclinux1 bin]$ echo $INST_TOP
/u01/oracle/VIS/inst/apps/VIS_raclinux1
```

3. On the database tier (as the Oracle user), copy the `appsutil.zip` file to the <`RDBMS ORACLE_HOME`>. You can also upload it using FTP. The following screenshot shows how to copy the file and how to make the file owned by the Oracle user:

```
[root@raclinux1 ~]#  cp /u01/oracle/VIS/inst/apps/VIS_raclinux1/admin/out/appsut
il.zip /u01/app/oracle/product/11.1.0/db_2/appsutil.zip
cp: overwrite `/u01/app/oracle/product/11.1.0/db_2/appsutil.zip'? y
[root@raclinux1 ~]# chmod  777 /u01/app/oracle/product/11.1.0/db_2/appsutil.zip
[root@raclinux1 ~]# chown oracle:oinstall /u01/app/oracle/product/11.1.0/db_2/ap
psutil.zip
[root@raclinux1 ~]#
```

4. Unzip the `appsutil.zip` file to create the `appsutil` directory in the 11g <`RDBMS NEW ORACLE_HOME` after the copy, as follows:

   ```
   cd <RDBMS ORACLE_HOME>
   unzip -o appsutil.zip
   ```

5. Copy the `jre` directory from `<OLD_ORACLE_HOME>/appsutil` to 11g `NEW_ORACLE_HOME>/appsutil`.

```
[oracle@raclinux1 jre]$ pwd
/u01/app/oracle/product/11.1.0/db_2/appsutil/jre
[oracle@raclinux1 jre]$ cp -R /u01/oracle/VIS/db/tech_st/11.1.0/appsutil/jre .
[oracle@raclinux1 jre]$ ls -lastr
total 12
4 drwxr-xr-x 10 oracle oinstall 4096 Nov 26 11:24 ..
4 drwxr-xr-x  3 oracle oinstall 4096 Nov 26 11:26 .
4 drwxr-xr-x  8 oracle oinstall 4096 Nov 26 11:27 jre
[oracle@raclinux1 jre]$ cd ..
[oracle@raclinux1 appsutil]$ cp -R /u01/oracle/VIS/db/tech_st/11.1.0/appsutil/jre .
[oracle@raclinux1 appsutil]$ ls -lastr /u01/oracle/VIS/db/tech_st/11.1.0/appsutil/jre
total 268
  4 drwxr-xr-x  2 oracle oinstall   4096 Apr  6  2009 bin
  4 -r--r--r--  1 oracle oinstall    968 Apr  6  2009 Welcome.html
192 -r--r--r--  1 oracle oinstall 190102 Apr  6  2009 THIRDPARTYLICENSEREADME.txt
  4 drwxr-xr-x  2 oracle oinstall   4096 Apr  6  2009 .systemPrefs
 16 -r--r--r--  1 oracle oinstall  15362 Apr  6  2009 README
  4 drwxr-xr-x  4 oracle oinstall   4096 Apr  6  2009 plugin
  4 drwxr-xr-x  4 oracle oinstall   4096 Apr  6  2009 man
 16 -r--r--r--  1 oracle oinstall  12345 Apr  6  2009 LICENSE
  4 drwxr-xr-x  2 oracle oinstall   4096 Apr  6  2009 javaws
  8 -r--r--r--  1 oracle oinstall   4137 Apr  6  2009 COPYRIGHT
  4 drwxr-xr-x  8 oracle oinstall   4096 Oct 31 10:27 .
  4 drwxr-xr-x 18 oracle oinstall   4096 Oct 31 10:31 lib
  4 drwxr-xr-x 18 oracle oinstall   4096 Nov 19 12:47 ..
[oracle@raclinux1 appsutil]$ cd jre
[oracle@raclinux1 jre]$ ls -lastr
total 272
  4 drwxr-xr-x 10 oracle oinstall   4096 Nov 26 11:24 ..
  4 drwxr-xr-x  8 oracle oinstall   4096 Nov 26 11:27 jre
192 -r--r--r--  1 oracle oinstall 190102 Nov 26 11:33 THIRDPARTYLICENSEREADME.txt
 16 -r--r--r--  1 oracle oinstall  15362 Nov 26 11:33 README
  4 drwxr-xr-x  4 oracle oinstall   4096 Nov 26 11:33 plugin
  4 drwxr-xr-x  4 oracle oinstall   4096 Nov 26 11:33 man
 16 -r--r--r--  1 oracle oinstall  12345 Nov 26 11:33 LICENSE
  4 drwxr-xr-x  2 oracle oinstall   4096 Nov 26 11:33 javaws
  8 -r--r--r--  1 oracle oinstall   4137 Nov 26 11:33 COPYRIGHT
  4 drwxr-xr-x  2 oracle oinstall   4096 Nov 26 11:33 bin
  4 -r--r--r--  1 oracle oinstall    968 Nov 26 11:34 Welcome.html
  4 drwxr-xr-x  2 oracle oinstall   4096 Nov 26 11:34 .systemPrefs
  4 drwxr-xr-x 18 oracle oinstall   4096 Nov 26 11:34 lib
  4 drwxr-xr-x  9 oracle oinstall   4096 Nov 26 11:34 .
[oracle@raclinux1 jre]$ pwd
/u01/app/oracle/product/11.1.0/db_2/appsutil/jre
[oracle@raclinux1 jre]$
```

6. Create a `<CONTEXT_NAME>` directory under `$ORACLE_HOME/network/admin`. Use the new instance name while creating the context directory. Append the instance number to the instance prefix that you put in the `rconfig` XML file. For example, if your database name is `VIS` and you want to use `VIS` as the instance prefix, create the `CONTEXT_NAME` directory as `VIS1_<hostname>` or `VIS2_<hostname>` where the hostname can be either raclinux1 or raclinux2.

7. Set the following environment variables in the `.bash_profile`, as follows:

```
# .bash_profile

# Get the aliases and functions
if [ -f ~/.bashrc ]; then
        . ~/.bashrc
fi

# User specific environment and startup programs

TMP=/tmp; export TMP
TMPDIR=$TMP; export TMPDIR
ORACLE_HOSTNAME=raclinux1.gj.com; export ORACLE_HOSTNAME
ORACLE_BASE=/u01/app/oracle; export ORACLE_BASE
ORACLE_HOME=$ORACLE_BASE/product/11.1.0/db_2; export ORACLE_HOME
ORACLE_SID=VIS1; export ORACLE_SID
ORACLE_TERM=xterm; export ORACLE_TERM
PATH=/usr/sbin:$PATH; export PATH
PATH=$ORACLE_HOME/bin:$PATH; export PATH

ORA_NLS10=/u01/app/oracle/product/11.1.0/db_2/nls/data/9idata; export ORA_NLS10

LD_LIBRARY_PATH=$ORACLE_HOME/lib:$ORACLE_HOME/ctx/lib:/lib:/usr/lib; export LD_LIBRARY_PATH
CLASSPATH=$ORACLE_HOME/JRE:$ORACLE_HOME/jlib:$ORACLE_HOME/rdbms/jlib; export CLASSPATH


TNS_ADMIN=$ORACLE_HOME/network/admin/VIS1_raclinux1; export TNS_ADMIN

if [ $USER = "oracle" ]; then
  if [ $SHELL = "/bin/ksh" ]; then
        ulimit -p 16384
        ulimit -n 65536
  else
    ulimit -u 16384 -n 65536
  fi
fi

DB_HOME=/u01/oracle/VIS/db/tech_st/11.1.0; export DB_HOME
APPL_TOP=/u01/oracle/VIS/apps/apps_st/appl; export APPL_TOP
COMMON_TOP=/u01/oracle/VIS/inst/apps/VIS_raclinux1; export COMMON_TOP


PATH=$PATH:$HOME/bin

export PATH
[oracle@raclinux1 VIS1_raclinux1]$
```

8. De-register the current configuration using the `Apps` schema package, `FND_CONC_CLONE.SETUP_CLEAN`, by executing the command `SQL>exec fnd_conc_clone.setup_clean;` while logged into the database as `apps` user.

9. Copy the `tnsnames.ora` file from `$ORACLE_HOME/network/admin` to `$TNS_ADMIN/tnsnames.ora` and edit it to change the aliases for `SID=<new Oracle RAC instance name>`.

10. To preserve the TNS aliases (`LISTENERS_<service>` and `LISTENER_<asminstance>`) of ASM, create a file named `<context_name>_ifile.ora` under `$TNS_ADMIN`, and copy those entries to that file.
11. Create the `listener.ora` file as per the sample file in the appendix. Change the instance name and Oracle home to match this environment.
12. Start the listener.

Generating your database context file

From the 11g `ORACLE_HOME/appsutil/bin` directory, create an instance-specific XML context file by executing the following command on Linux:

```
cd <RDBMS ORACLE_HOME>
. <CONTEXT_NAME>.env
cd <RDBMS 11g ORACLE_HOME>/appsutil/bin
perl adbldxml.pl tier=db appsuser=<APPSuser>
```

Note that `adbldxml.pl` uses your current environment settings to generate the context file. Therefore, ensure that your environment is correctly sourced. Also note, if you build the context file for an EBS instance that runs on RAC, all your RAC instances have to be up and running while executing the `adbldxml` utility. This utility connects to all RAC instances to gather information about the configuration.

Preparing for AutoConfig by completing the following AutoConfig steps

The context file acting as a centralized repository for the configuration needs to be updated, so that after running AutoConfig, all of the configuration parameter files of the various components of EBS are aware of the implemented changes.

1. Set the value of `s_virtual host_name` to point to the virtual hostname (VIP alias) for the database host, by editing the database context file `$ORACLE_HOME/appsutil/<sid>_hostname.xml`.
2. Rename `$ORACLE_HOME/dbs/init<Oracle RAC instance>.ora` to a new name—`init<racinstance>.ora.old`—in order to allow AutoConfig to regenerate the file using the Oracle RAC-specific parameters.

3. Ensure that the following context variable parameters are correctly specified:
   - `s_jdktop=<11g ORACLE_HOME_PATH>/appsutil/jre`
   - `s_jretop=<11g ORACLE_HOME_PATH>/appsutil/jre`
   - `s_adjvaprg=<11g ORACLE_HOME_PATH>/appsutil/jre/bin/java`
4. Review prior manual configuration changes. The database context file may not include manual post-install configuration changes made after the Rapid Install is completed. Before running the AutoConfig portion of this patch, review any modifications to specific configuration files and reconcile them with the database context file.

Prior modifications include any changes made to configuration files as instructed in patch "readme" or other accompanying documents.

Generating and applying AutoConfig configuration files

Now it is time to generate the AutoConfig configuration files, so that all the changes get propagated to the configuration files of the EBS components.

This step performs the conversion to the new context files by using the AutoConfig utility. Once completed, the previous configuration will not be available.

The database server and the database listener must remain available during the AutoConfig run. All the other database-tier services should be shut down.

Execute the following commands on Linux/UNIX:

```
cd <RDBMS ORACLE_HOME>
/appsutil/bin/perl adconfig.pl
```

> Running AutoConfig on the database node will update the RDBMS network listener file. Be sure to review the configuration changes from the previous section. The new AutoConfig network listener file supports the use of IFILE to allow for values to be customized or added as needed.
>
> Running AutoConfig on the database tier will not overwrite any existing `init.ora` file in the `<ORACLE_HOME>/dbs` directory. If no `init.ora` file exists for your instance, AutoConfig will generate an `init.ora` file in the `<ORACLE_HOME>/dbs` directory for you.
>
> Running AutoConfig might change your existing environment files. After running AutoConfig, you should always set the environment before you run any application utilities, in order to apply the changed environment variables.

Check the AutoConfig logfile to find where the control file is located in 11g:

```
$ view ORACLE_HOME/appsutil/log/<CONTEXT_NAME>/<MMDDhhmm.
```

If ASM/OCFS is being used, make note of the new location of the control file:

```
sqlplus / as sysdba;
SQL> show parameters control_files
```

Perform all of the preceding steps on all other database nodes in the cluster.

Executing AutoConfig on all database nodes in the cluster

Execute AutoConfig on all database nodes in the cluster, by running the `$ORACLE_HOME/appsutil/scripts/adautocfg.sh` command. Then, shut down the instances and listeners.

Performing Init file, tnsnames, and listener file activities

Carry out the following steps:

1. Edit the `$ORACLE_HOME/dbs/<SID>_APPS_BASE.ora` file on all nodes. If ASM is being used, change the `control_files = <new location` parameter from the *Generating and applying AutoConfig configuration files* section. Use the location of the control file in the previous step:

   ```
   sqlplus / as sysdba;
   SQL> show parameters control_files
   ```

2. Create an `spfile` from the `pfile` on all nodes. Create an `spfile` from the `pfile` and then create a `pfile` in a temporary location from the new `spfile`, with the help of the following commands:

```
SQL>create spfile=<temp location> from pfile.
SQL>create pfile=/tmp/init<ins1>.ora from spfile=<temp location>.
```

3. Repeat this step on all nodes.
4. Combine the initialization parameter files for all instances into one `init<SID>.ora` file by copying all existing shared contents. All shared parameters defined in your `init<SID>.ora` file must be global, with the format `*.parameter=value`.
5. Modify all instance-specific parameter definitions in `init<SID>.ora` files using the `<SID>.parameter=value` syntax, where the `<SID>` variable is the system identifier of the instance.

   The previous two points refer to the init parameters from the old init EBS file to be modified in the parameter file or the RAC-enabled EBS. It is necessary to modify the old EBS init parameters into a new parameter file for the RAC-enabled EBS.

Ensure that the parameters `LOCAL_LISTENER`, `diagnostic_dest`, `undo_tablespace`, `thread`, `instance_number`, and `instance_name` are in the `<SID>.parameter` format. For example, `<SID>. LOCAL_LISTENER=<local_listener_name>`. These parameters must have one entry for an instance.

6. Create the `spfile` in the shared location where `rconfig` created the `spfile` from the `init<SID>.ora` `pfile`, as follows:

```
SQL>create spfile=<shared location> from pfile;
```

7. As AutoConfig creates the `listener.ora` and `tnsnames.ora` files in a context directory and not in the `$ORACLE_HOME/network/admin` directory, the `TNS_ADMIN` path must be updated in CRS. Run the following command as the root user:

```
# srvctl setenv nodeapps -n <node> \
-t TNS_ADMIN=<Full Path of ORACLE HOME>/network/admin/<context_
directory>
```

8. Start up the database instances and listeners on all nodes.
9. Run AutoConfig on all nodes to ensure each instance registers with all remote listeners.
10. Shut down and restart the database instances and listeners on all nodes.

11. De-register any old listeners and register the new listeners with CRS using the commands:

```
# srvctl remove listener -n <nodename> -l <listener_name>
# srvctl add listener -n <nodename> -o <oracle_home> -l
<listener_name>
```

Establishing applications environment for Oracle RAC

It is relevant to ensure that EBS is aware of the new database tier and that load balancing is implemented and operational. We address this in the following sections.

The following steps are important, as they ensure that the application tier is aware of the new database tier. You will need to carry out the following steps on all application-tier nodes:

1. Source the Oracle applications environment.
2. Edit `SID=<Instance 1>` and `PORT=<New listener port>` in `$TNS_ADMIN/tnsnames.ora` file, to set up a connection with one of the instances in the Oracle RAC environment.
3. Confirm that you are able to connect to one of the instances in the Oracle RAC environment.
4. Edit the context variable `jdbc_url`, adding the instance name to the `connect_data` parameter.
5. Run AutoConfig using the following command:

```
$AD_TOP/bin/adconfig.sh contextfile=$INST_TOP/appl/
admin/<context_file>
```

> For more information on AutoConfig, see My Oracle Support Knowledge Document (formerly Metalink) note 387859.1, *Using AutoConfig to Manage System Configurations with Oracle E-Business Suite Release 12.*

6. Check the `$INST_TOP/admin/log/<MMDDhhmm>` AutoConfig logfile for errors.
7. Source the environment by using the latest environment file generated.

8. Verify the `tnsnames.ora` and `listener.ora` files. Copies of both are located in the `$INST_TOP/ora/10.1.2/network/admin` directory and `$INST_TOP/ora/10.1.3/network/admin` directory. In these files, ensure that the correct TNS aliases have been generated for load balancing and failover, and that all the aliases are defined using the virtual hostnames.
9. Verify the `dbc` file located at `$FND_SECURE`. Ensure that the `APPS_JDBC_URL` parameter is configured with all instances in the environment and that the `load_balance` parameter is set to `YES`.

Setting up load balancing

Load balancing is important, as it enables you to distribute the load of the various EBS components to the less-active instances. Implementing load balancing for the Oracle Applications database connections is achieved by following the steps outlined here:

1. Run the Context Editor (through the Oracle Applications Manager interface) and set the value of **Tools OH TWO_TASK** (s_tools_two_task), **iAS OH TWO_TASK** (s_weboh_twotask), and **Apps JDBC Connect Alias** (s_apps_jdbc_connect_alias).
2. To load-balance the forms-based applications database connections, set the value of **Tools OH TWO_TASK** to point to the `<database_name>_balance` alias generated in the `tnsnames.ora` file.
3. To load-balance the self-service applications database connections, set the value of **iAS OH TWO_TASK** and **Apps JDBC Connect Alias** to point to the `<database_name>_balance` alias generated in the `tnsnames.ora` file:

   Execute AutoConfig by running the command:

   ```
   $AD_TOP/bin/adconfig.sh contextfile=$INST_TOP/appl/admin/<context_
   file>
   ```

4. Restart the applications process, using the new scripts generated by AutoConfig.
5. Ensure that the value of the profile option **Application Database ID** is set to the `dbc` filename generated in `$FND_SECURE`.

[If you are adding a new node to the application tier, repeat steps 1 to 6 for setting up load balancing on the new application-tier node.]

Configuring Parallel Concurrent Processing

Parallel Concurrent Processing (PCP) is an extension of the Concurrent Processing architecture. PCP allows concurrent processing activities to be distributed across multiple nodes in an Oracle RAC environment, maximizing throughput, and providing resilience and high availability user interactions. With EBS, data can be conducted through HTML-based applications or the more traditional forms-based applications. However, there are also reporting programs and data update programs that need to run either periodically or on an ad hoc basis. These programs, which are running in the background while users continue to work on other tasks, may require a large number of data-intensive computations and can utilize the Concurrent Processing architecture.

Concurrent Processing is an Oracle EBS feature that allows these non-interactive and potentially long-running functions to be executed efficiently alongside interactive operations. It uses the operating system resources to facilitate background scheduling of data or resource-intensive jobs through a set of programs and forms. To ensure that resource-intensive concurrent processing operations do not interfere with the interactive operations, they are run on a specialized server—the Concurrent Processing Server. It is worth evaluating whether to place the Concurrent Processing tier on either the application or database tier. In some cases, running the Concurrent Processing Server on the database tier improves performance.

Prerequisites for setting up Parallel Concurrent Processing

To set up Parallel Concurrent Processing, you must have more than one Concurrent Processing node in your environment. If you have not done this, then follow the appropriate instructions in My Oracle Support Knowledge Document 406982.1, *Cloning Oracle Applications Release 12 with Rapid Clone*.

> If you are planning to implement a shared application tier filesystem, refer to My Oracle Support Knowledge Document 384248.1, *Sharing the Application Tier File System in Oracle E-Business Suite Release 12*, for configuration steps. If you are adding a new Concurrent Processing node to the application tier, you will need to set up load balancing on the new application by repeating the steps mentioned in the *Setting up load balancing* section.

Cloning EBS concepts in brief

Cloning in EBS is a method that allows you to move components of an existing EBS system to a different location, either on the same server or a different server without reinstalling the EBS. Cloning is the process used to create a copy of an existing EBS system. There are various scenarios for cloning an EBS system, which are as follows:

- Standard cloning: Making a copy of an existing Oracle Applications system, for example, a copy of a production system to test updates
- System scale up: Adding new machines to an Oracle Applications system to provide the capacity for processing an increased workload
- System transformations: Altering system data or filesystems, including actions such as platform migration, data scrambling, and provisioning of high availability architectures
- Patching and upgrading: Delivering new versions of Applications components, and providing a mechanism for creating rolling environments to minimize downtime

An important principle in EBS cloning is that the system is cloned, rather than the topology. Producing an exact copy of the patch level and data is much more important than creating an exact copy of the topology, as a cloned system must be able to provide the same output to the end user as the source system. While a cloned system need not have the full topology of its source, it must have all the topology components that are available to the source. Cloning in EBS basically involves the following four steps:

1. First, we prepare the source system.
2. We then copy the source system to the target system.
3. Now, we configure the target system.
4. The cloning method also enables us to add a new node to an existing EBS system or to clone RAC-enabled EBS.

Preparing the source system

Execute the following commands to prepare the source system for cloning, while the database and applications are running. The following steps describe the commands that must be executed, in order to prepare the source system for cloning both at database and application tiers respectively:

1. Prepare the source system database tier for cloning, by logging on to the source system as the Oracle user and running the following commands:

   ```
   $ cd <RDBMS ORACLE_HOME>/appsutil/scripts/<CONTEXT_NAME>
   $ perl adpreclone.pl dbTier
   ```

2. Prepare the source system application tier for cloning, by logging on to the source system as the `applmgr` user and running the following commands on each node that contains an `APPL_TOP`:

   ```
   $ cd <INST_TOP>/admin/scripts
   $ perl adpreclone.pl appsTier
   ```

If new Rapid Clone or AutoConfig updates are applied to the system, `adpreclone.pl` must be executed again on the `dbTier` and on the `appsTier` in order to apply the new files into the clone directory structures that will be used during the cloning configuration stage.

Copying the source system

You now need to copy the application-tier filesystem from the source EBS system to the target node, by executing the following steps in the order listed. Ensure that the application-tier files copied to the target system are owned by the target `applmgr` user, and that the database node files are owned by the target Oracle user.

The `tar` command can be used to compress the directories into a temporary staging area. If you use this command, you may require the `-h` option to follow symbolic links, as following symbolic links is not the default behavior on all platforms. Consult the Unix man page for the `tar` command.

1. Copy the application-tier filesystem by logging on to the source system application-tier nodes as the `applmgr` user and shutting down the application-tier server processes. Copy the following application-tier directories from the source node to the target application-tier node:
   - `<APPL_TOP>`
   - `<COMMON_TOP>`

- Applications Technology Stack: `<OracleAS Tools ORACLE_HOME>`
- Applications Technology Stack: `<OracleAS Web IAS_ORACLE_HOME>`

2. Copy the database-node filesystem by logging on to the source system database node as the Oracle user and then performing the following:
   - Perform a normal shutdown of the source system database.
   - Copy the database (`.dbf`) files from the source system to the target system.
   - Copy the source database `ORACLE_HOME` to the target system.
   - Start the source Applications system database and application-tier processes.

Configuring the target system

Configure the target system by running the following commands. You will be prompted for specific target-system values such as SID, paths, and ports to name a few.

1. Configure the target-system database server by logging on to the target system as the Oracle user and then entering the following commands:
   ```
   $ cd <RDBMS ORACLE_HOME>/appsutil/clone/bin
   $ perl adcfgclone.pl dbTier
   ```
2. Configure the target-system application-tier server nodes by logging on to the target system as the `applmgr` user and then entering the following commands:
   ```
   $ cd <COMMON_TOP>/clone/bin
   $ perl adcfgclone.pl appsTier
   ```

Adding a new node to an existing EBS system

You can use Rapid Clone to clone a node and add it to the existing EBS system—a process also known as scale up or scale out. The new node can run the same services as the source node or different services. Follow the instructions in the Application tier part of Cloning Tasks in My Oracle Support (formerly Metalink) note 406982.1.

As per the instructions discussed in this My Oracle Support Note (406982.1), after the `adcfgclone.pl` script completes execution, you need to source the EBS environment and run the following commands on the target system:

```
$ cd <COMMON_TOP>/clone/bin
$ perl adaddnode.pl
```

After adding new nodes, refer to My Oracle Support Knowledge Document Metalink note 380489.1 for details of how to set up load balancing. If SQL*Net Access security is enabled in the existing system, you first need to authorize the new node to access the database through SQL*Net. See the Oracle Applications Manager online help for instructions on how to accomplish this.

As downtime is costly to business operations running mission-critical ERP systems, Oracle also provides a hot-cloning method to allow you to clone the database tier without shutting down the database environment. Hot cloning requires that you perform an online "hot" backup with RMAN. Details on hot cloning with Oracle R12 EBS are provided by My Oracle Support Note 362473.1, *Cloning E-Business Suite Using Hot Backup for Minimal Downtime of Source Environment*. You can also perform a hot-cloning operation for Oracle EBS by using the Oracle **Applications Management Pack (AMP)**. Additional cloning strategies for Oracle R12 EBS are available in the white paper *Oracle EBS DBA Techniques: Install and Cloning Best Practices* at the following URL:

`http://www.oracle.com/technetwork/oem/app-mgmt/s318133-ebs-install-cloning-184671.pdf`

One pitfall of cloning Oracle R12 EBS is the downtime that is required to complete the operation for both the application middle tier and database tier. EMC provides storage software named **EMC Replication Manager** that can be used in conjunction with Oracle EBS to perform a hot clone of Oracle EBS environments without costly downtime. Further details on how to perform online cloning operations with Oracle R12 EBS, RAC and, EMC Replication Manager software are available online in the white paper *Rapid Deployment and Scale Out for Oracle EBS Enabled by EMC RecoverPoint, EMC Replication Manager, and VMware vSphere* at the following URL:

`http://www.emc.com/collateral/software/white-papers/h7270-rapid-deployment-scale-out-oracle-wp.pdf`

Setting up Parallel Concurrent Processing

Parallel Concurrent Processing allows concurrent processing activities to be distributed across multiple nodes in an Oracle Real Application Clusters (Oracle RAC) environment. By distributing concurrent processing in this way, hardware resources can be fully utilized, maximizing throughput, and providing resilience to node failure, while retaining a central point of control. The steps to set up PCP are outlined as follows:

1. Edit the applications context file through Oracle Applications Manager and set the value of the `APPLDCP` variable to `ON`.
2. Execute AutoConfig by running the following command on all concurrent processing nodes:

   ```
   $INST_TOP/admin/scripts/adautocfg.sh
   ```

3. Source the applications environment.
4. Check the `tnsnames.ora` and `listener.ora` configuration files, located in `$INST_TOP/ora/10.1.2/network/admin`. Ensure that the required `FNDSM` and `FNDFS` entries are present for all other concurrent nodes.
5. Restart the applications listener processes on each application-tier node.
6. Log on to Oracle EBS Release 12 using the `SYSADMIN` account, and choose the System Administrator Responsibility. Navigate to **Install | Nodes screen**, and ensure that each node in the cluster is registered.
7. Verify that the Internal Monitor for each node is defined properly, with correct primary and secondary node specification, and work shift details. For example, Internal Monitor: Host2 must have a primary node as Host2 and a secondary node as Host3. Also, ensure that the Internal Monitor manager is activated.

   This can be done from **Concurrent | Manager | Administrator** after logging into the EBS as SYSADM and choosing **System Administrator Responsibility**.

8. Set the `$APPLCSF` environment variable on all the Concurrent Processing nodes to point to a log directory on a shared filesystem.
9. Set the `$APPLPTMP` environment variable on all the CP nodes to the value of the `UTL_FILE_DIR` entry in `init.ora` on the database nodes. (This value should be pointing to a directory on a shared filesystem.)
10. Set the Concurrent: PCP Instance Check profile option to `OFF` if the database instance-sensitive failover is not required. By setting it to `ON`, a concurrent manager will fail over to a secondary application-tier node if the database instance to which it is connected becomes unavailable for some reason.

Setting up Transaction Managers

Transaction Managers support synchronous request processing, whereby a pool of server processes respond to requests from client programs. Instead of polling the concurrent requests table to obtain instructions, a Transaction Manager waits to be signaled by a client. An example is an approval of an order, where execution of the request must take place quickly. The relevant Transaction Manager program runs on the server, transparent to the client. All transaction programs for a given manager process run in the same database session. Communication between the client and server is conducted synchronously through pipes, using the `FND_TRANSACTION.SYNCHRONOUS` function. At the end of program execution, the client program receives a completion message and a return value, for example, denoting approval of the order. This strategy of using non-persistent connections between the client and Transaction Manager processes enables a small pool of server processes to service a large number of clients with near real-time response. You will need to accomplish the following steps to set up/configure the Transactions Manager:

1. Shut down the application services (servers) on all nodes.
2. Shut down all the database instances cleanly in the Oracle RAC environment, using the following command:

   ```
   SQL>shutdown immediate
   ```

3. Edit `$ORACLE_HOME/dbs/<context_name>_ifile.ora`. Add the parameters `lm_global_posts=TRUE` and `_immediate_commit_ propagation=TRUE`.
4. Start the instances on all database nodes, one by one.
5. Start up the application services (servers) on all nodes.
6. Log on to Oracle E-Business Suite Release 12 using the SYSADMIN account, and choose the System Administrator responsibility. Navigate to **Profile | System**, change the profile option **Concurrent**: **TM Transport Type** to **QUEUE**, and verify that the Transaction Manager works across the Oracle RAC instance.
7. Navigate to the **Concurrent | Manager | Define screen**, and set up the primary and secondary node names for Transaction Managers.
8. Restart the concurrent managers.
9. If any of the Transaction Managers are in deactivated state, activate them from **Concurrent | Manager | Administrator**.

Setting up load balancing on concurrent processing nodes

Setting up the load balancing at the concurrent processing tier is the only possible load balancing option at the concurrent processing tier. If the concurrent managers are deployed on many nodes, load balancing can be achieved across the nodes among the managers. Each node operates independently of other nodes, except when sharing a resource, such as a disk. Specialization rules can be written in Oracle to execute particular managers on a node. For example, PO Document manager can be deployed on a certain node by carrying out the following steps:

1. Edit the applications context file through the Oracle Applications Manager interface and set the value of Concurrent Manager TWO_TASK (s_cp_twotask) to the load balancing alias (<service_name>_balance>).
2. Execute AutoConfig by running the following command:

   $INST_TOP/admin/scripts/adautocfg.sh on all concurrent nodes.

Summary

In this chapter, we covered the EBS architecture and saw how it can achieve maximum availability. We looked at why Oracle RAC is suitable for addressing the needs of EBS for a scalable and resilient database solution in near-zero downtime environments. We also looked at the steps and utilities to enable Oracle 11g RAC with EBS environments. First we explained how to use the Oracle R12 EBS utility AutoConfig to update the configuration for EBS and then we discussed the Oracle R12 EBS installation process. Lastly we discussed how to use the Rapid Clone utility provided with Oracle R12 EBS to configure EBS for RAC.

12
Maximum Availability

Oracle has provided technologists and businesses with a suite of technologies, to ensure high availability as a protection against data loss caused by natural disasters and unplanned events. The suite of these technologies is known as the Maximum Availability Architecture (MAA). In this chapter, we will discuss how to implement best practices for the Oracle 11g MAA using Oracle 11g Streams and Data Guard with Oracle 11g RAC environments. In a nutshell, these comprise the following core technologies within Oracle 11g:

- Oracle 11g Streams Replication
- Oracle GoldenGate Replication
- Oracle 11g Standby Databases (Data Guard)

GoldenGate is a third-party solution for replication that will not be discussed as Streams provides a similar functionality. It is now part of the Oracle product family after a recent purchase by Oracle.

We will illustrate and enable you to understand, through concepts and examples, the detailed process comprising the best practices related to implementing MAA for Oracle 11g RAC environments, using Oracle 11g Streams and Data Guard with Oracle 11g.

Specifically, we will look at the following topics:

- Oracle 11g Streams for RAC
- Best practices for Streams in an RAC environment
- New features for Streams in Oracle 11g R2
- Oracle 11g Data Guard and RAC
- New features for Data Guard in Oracle 11g R2

Oracle 11g Streams for RAC

Oracle 11g Streams is a robust data replication technology built into the Oracle database engine. It has existed in various incarnations since Oracle 9i database release. However, with each major release of Oracle, enhancements and new features have been added to make Streams one of the premier data replication tools, to complement the high availability features in addition to other maximum availability technologies such as Data Guard and RAC. Streams uses **Advanced Queuing (AQ)** in the form of a message queuing system similar to that found in other queuing technologies such as Tuxedo and IBM M/Q series queuing packages. The advantage of Streams over other replication technologies, including Oracle advanced replication, is the presence of certain features that don't exist within these other applications. Streams is also able to extract data from the redo logs within the Oracle database. Advanced replication uses triggers, which causes performance delays compared to the performance of mining the redo logs directly. Furthermore, Streams allows the DBA to replicate either an entire database (replica) or subset of the data, and provides heterogeneous support between platforms.

These Capture and Apply processes are critical to how Streams operates within an RAC or single-instance Oracle environment. As Streams uses advanced queuing technology, we have multiple queue tables as part of the source to target mappings for replication, which will be seen in more detail later in the chapter. In a nutshell, the **Streams Capture** process mines data from the online redo logs in the source database and the **Apply** process on the target database server is responsible for propagating these changes to the target database.

Oracle 11g Streams architecture for RAC

Oracle Streams requires processes to be configured on the source database environment to perform capturing of data from online redo logs of the source RAC database server. These logs are then staged into the queue areas before they are applied to the target database as part of the consumption process.

Capture

The **Capture** function in Oracle Streams captures all the database changes and application-generated messages into the staging area (Queue). For Streams, changes are captured in two ways—implicit and explicit capture methods.

With **implicit capture**, the Oracle database server captures DML and DDL events at the source database. **Explicit capture** allows applications to explicitly generate events and place them in the staging area. Implicit capture mines the redo log, either by hot mining the online redo log or, if necessary, by mining archived logfiles.

After retrieving the data, the Capture process formats it into a **Logical Change Record** (**LCR**) and places it into the staging area for further processing. The capture process has the ability to filter LCRs based on defined rules. This allows for changes only to desired objects to be captured.

User applications can explicitly enqueue user messages representing events into the staging area. These messages can be formatted as LCRs, which will allow them to be consumed by the apply engine, or they can be formatted for consumption by another user application.

Staging

Staging references the location where these events are placed into the staging area before processing. The staging area is a queue that provides a service to store and manage captured events. Subscribers examine the contents of the staging area and determine whether or not they have an interest in an event. A subscriber can be a user application, another staging area (usually on another system), or the default Apply process.

Propagation

If the subscriber is another staging area, the event is propagated to the other staging area, either within the same database or in a remote database. To simplify network routing and reduce WAN traffic, events do not need to be sent to all databases and applications. Rather, they can be directed through staging areas on one or more systems until they reach the subscribing system. For example, an event may propagate via a hub database that does not actually apply the event. A single staging area can stage events from multiple databases, simplifying setup and configuration.

Consumption

Events in a staging area are consumed by the apply engine, where the changes they represent are applied to a database or are consumed by an application. Oracle Streams includes a flexible apply engine that allows use of a standard or custom apply function. This enables data to be transformed when necessary. Support for explicit de-queue allows application developers to use Oracle Streams in order to notify applications of changes to data, while still leveraging the change capture and propagation features of Oracle Streams.

Default apply

The **default apply** engine applies DML changes and DDL changes represented by implicitly or explicitly captured LCRs. The default apply engine will detect conflicts where the destination row has been changed and does not contain the expected values. If a conflict is detected, then a resolution routine may be invoked.

User-defined function apply

The apply engine can pass the LCR or a user message to a user-defined function. This provides the greatest amount of flexibility in processing an event. A typical application of a user-defined function would be to reformat the data represented by the LCR before applying it to a local table, for example, field format, object name, and column name mapping transformations. A user-defined function could also be used to perform column subsetting or to update other objects that may not be present in the source database.

Explicit de-queue

User applications can explicitly de-queue LCRs or user messages from the receiving staging area. This allows a user application to efficiently access the data in a Streams staging area. Streams can send notifications to registered PL/SQL or OCI functions, giving the applications an alternative to poll for new messages. Of course, applications can still poll, or even wait for new subscribed messages in the staging area to become available.

Understanding Oracle Streams rules

Streams lets users control which information to share and where to send it by specifying rules. At the highest level, users can indicate if they want to capture, propagate, or apply changes at the table, schema, or global (database) level. For more complex requirements, for example, to apply these changes only to a particular subset of data at a given location, users can specify a rule condition similar to the condition in the `WHERE` clause of a SQL query. If necessary, related rules can be grouped into rulesets.

Transformations and Streams

A **transformation** is a change in the form of an object participating in capture and apply, or a change in the data the object holds. Transformations can include changing the data type representation of a particular column in a table at a particular site, adding a column to a table at one site only, or including a subset of the data in a table at a particular site.

A transformation can be specified during en-queue, to transform the message to the correct type before inserting it into the staging area. It can also be specified for propagation, which may be useful for subsetting data before it is sent to a remote site. Finally, it can be specified at de-queue or local apply, which can be useful for formatting a message in a manner appropriate for a specific destination.

Capture and Apply processes in an RAC instance

Because there are multiple instances within an RAC environment, database changes can occur from any instance in the cluster. These database changes are recorded in the associated redo logs of the instance and corresponding archive logfiles. A Capture process configured within any instance of the RAC cluster database can extract transactions from all of the participating instances' redo logfiles and then transform them into LCR events. Even though the Capture process is running only on one instance, it is aware of all the redo logs of all the RAC instances and no transactions are missed during the Capture process.

Each Capture process is started on the owning instance in the RAC cluster database for its `SYS.AnyData` queue, even if the start capture is executed on a different instance. The `dba_queue_tables` data dictionary view contains information about the owning instance for the queue table. Parallel execution servers used by a single Capture process run on one instance in an RAC environment.

Streams in the RAC environment

In order to improve the performance of Streams for RAC databases, a Capture process can now capture changes from archived redo logs or from the online redo logfiles. This feature allows changes to be captured closer to the time they were executed, thereby reducing the capture latency. In other words, the moment that database changes are affected and committed, the transactions are available for the Capture process to extract.

When the owner instance for a queue table containing a queue used by a Capture process or Apply process fails, queue ownership is automatically transferred to another instance in the cluster. Then the Capture process or Apply process is restarted automatically, if it has been running. In previous releases, the Capture process or Apply process used to be `ABORTED` under these circumstances, which would warrant a manual restart. This is an important improvement from the administrative point of view. Without the intervention of the DBA, the Streams process will be restarted.

Additional details on how to set up and configure Oracle 11g Streams are provided in the Oracle Streams Concepts and Administration 11g R2 (11.2) documentation available online at the OTN website `http://www.oracle.com/technology/documentation/index.html`.

New features in Oracle 11g Streams

Oracle 11g introduced many new features for Streams. The following are a few of the new features of Streams in Oracle Database 11g:

- Synchronous Capture
- Splitting and merging of a Stream Destination
- Tracking LCRs through a Stream
- Oracle Streams Topology and Oracle Streams Performance Advisor
- Combined Capture and Apply

Synchronous Capture

Synchronous Capture is a new Streams client that captures Data Manipulation Language (DML) changes made to tables immediately after the changes are committed. Synchronous Capture uses an internal mechanism to capture DML changes to specified tables.

Splitting and merging of a Stream Destination

When a destination in a Streams replication environment becomes unavailable, it can cause performance problems. Changes that cannot be sent to the unavailable destination build up in buffered queues at other databases. In time, these changes can spill to disk and cause performance problems.

Splitting and merging of a Stream Destination enables you to split an unavailable destination off from a Stream. After the problem is solved at the destination and it becomes available again, you can merge the split Stream back to the original Stream. This feature uses two new procedures in the `DBMS_STREAMS_ADM` package: `SPLIT_STREAMS` and `MERGE_STREAMS`. Additional details are provided in My Oracle Support (formerly Metalink) note 732642.1, available online at `http://support.oracle.com`.

Tracking LCRs through a Stream

The new `SET_MESSAGE_TRACKING` procedure in the `DBMS_STREAMS_ADM` package lets you specify a tracking label for Logical Change Records (LCRs) generated by a database session. You can query the new `V$STREAMS_MESSAGE_TRACKING` view to track the LCRs through the stream and see how they were processed by each Streams client.

LCR tracking is useful if LCRs are not being applied as expected by one or more Apply processes. When this happens, you can use LCR tracking to determine where the LCRs are stopping in the stream and address the problem at that location. More details are provided in My Oracle Support (formerly Metalink) note 563774.1.

Streams Message Tracking in 11g information is available online, with a valid Oracle CSI account for My Oracle Support (MOS), at `http://support.oracle.com`.

Streams Topology and Performance Advisor

The Streams Topology identifies individual streams of messages and the Streams components configured in each stream. A Streams environment typically covers multiple databases, and the Streams topology provides a comprehensive view of the entire Streams environment. My Oracle Support (formerly Metalink) note 732643.1 has details on this new feature and its usage is available online at `http://support.oracle.com` with a valid Oracle CSI account.

The Streams Performance Advisor reports performance measurements for a Streams Topology, including throughput and latency measurements. The Streams Performance Advisor also identifies bottlenecks in a Streams topology so that they can be corrected. In addition, the Streams Performance Advisor examines the Streams components in a Streams topology and recommends ways to improve their performance. My Oracle Support (formerly Metalink) note 732644.1 provides additional information on this new advisor. You can use Oracle Enterprise Manager 10g Grid Control to configure and set up the Streams Advisor to monitor and troubleshoot your Oracle Streams configuration for 11g and RAC.

Combined Capture and Apply

A Capture process can send Logical Change Records (LCRs) directly to an apply process under specific conditions. This configuration is called Combined Capture and Apply. My Oracle Support (formerly Metalink) note 463820.1 provides details on the steps required to implement this new feature with Streams in 11g.

Here is how it works in a nutshell. First, the publisher and subscriber need to be set up on both source and target. These are set up in the form of a Capture process and capture queue on the source, and the target requires both Apply process and apply queue. Once you have set up the source and target processes, you need to verify that all is functioning correctly. The following SQL query will tell you whether or not your Oracle Streams capture and apply are working:

```
SQL> select capture_name,apply_name,apply_dblink,apply_messages_
sent,apply_bytes_sent from v$streams_capture;

CAPTURE_NAME    APPLY_NAME    APPLY_DBLINK          APPLY_MESSAGES_SENT
OE_CAPTURE          OE_APPLY          RAC1.LINUX.COM                     22

SQL> select apply_name,proxy_sid,proxy_serial,proxy_spid,capture_bytes_
received from v$streams_apply_reader;

APPLY_NAME  PROXY_SID PROXY_SERIAL PROXY_SPID  CAPTURE_BYTES_RECEIVED
OE_APPLY                  201                         5              63
9                                      3701
```

This query uses the `V$STREAMS_CAPTURE dynamic V$` view to return the status on source and target for the Capture and Apply processes with your Oracle 11g Streams configuration.

Best practices for Streams in an RAC environment

While the installation and configuration of Oracle 11g Streams is outside the scope of this chapter, we will provide you with some best practices and design considerations for Oracle Streams with RAC environments. To ensure a successful Streams implementation in an Oracle RAC environment, use the following recommendations when constructing a Streams environment.

Additional configuration of RAC environments for a Source Database

The archive log threads from all instances must be available to any instance running a Capture process. This is true for both local and downstream capture.

It is recommended not to have Flash Recovery Area (FRA) as the location of the archived logs because logfiles can be removed from the FRA, even if capture needs them to restart. In the event that you decide not to use the FRA to store your archived logfiles, another option is to back these logs up to another disk volume on your SAN or NAS filesystem. For added protection, you can also take a backup from disk to tape.

Queue ownership

When Streams is configured in an RAC environment, each queue table has an "owning" instance. All queues within an individual queue table are owned by the same instance. The Streams components (capture/propagation/apply) all use that same owning instance to perform their work. This means:

- A Capture process is run at the owning instance of the source queue
- A propagation job must run at the owning instance of the queue
- A propagation job must connect to the owning instance of the target queue

Ownership of the queue can be configured to remain on a specific instance, as long as that instance is available, by setting the `PRIMARY _INSTANCE` and/or `SECONDARY_INSTANCE` parameters of `DBMS_AQADM.ALTER_QUEUE_TABLE`. If the `primary_instance` is set to a specific instance (not 0), the queue ownership will return to the specified instance whenever the instance is up.

Capture will automatically follow the ownership of the queue. If the ownership changes while Capture is running, Capture will stop on the current instance and restart at the new owner instance.

For queues created with Oracle Database 11g Release 2, a service will be created with the `name = schema.queue` service and the network name as `SYS$schema.queue.global_name` for that queue. If the `global_name` of the database does not match the `db_name.db_domain name` of the database, be sure to include the `global_name` as a service name in the `init.ora`.

For propagations created with the Oracle Database 11g Release 2 code with the `queue_to_queue` parameter set to `TRUE`, the propagation job will deliver only to the specific queue identified. Also, the source `dblink` for the target database connect descriptor must specify the correct service (global name of the target database) to connect to the target database. For example, the `tnsnames.ora` entry for the target database should include the `CONNECT_DATA` clause in the connect descriptor for the target database. This clause should specify `CONNECT_DATA=(SERVICE_NAME='global_name of target database'`. Do not include a specific instance in the `CONNECT_DATA` clause.

For example, consider the `tnsnames.ora` file for a database with the global name `racdb.mycompany.com`. Assume that the alias name for the first instance is raclinux1 and that the alias for the second instance is raclinux2. The `tnsnames.ora` file for this database might include the following entries:

```
racdb.mycompany.com=
(description=
(load_balance=on)
(address=(protocol=tcp)(host=raclinux1-vip)(port=1521))
(address=(protocol=tcp)(host=raclinux2-vip)(port=1521))
(connect_data=
(service_name=racdb.mycompany.com)))

racdb1.mycompany.com=
(description=(address=(protocol=tcp)(host=raclinux1-vip)(port=1521))
(connect_data=
(service_name=racdb.mycompany.com)
(instance_name=raclinux1)))

racdb2.mycompany.com=
(description=(address=(protocol=tcp)(host=raclinux2-vip)(port=1521))
(connect_data=(service_name=racdb.mycompany.com)
(instance_name=raclinux2)))
```

`DBA_SERVICES` lists all services for the database. `GV$ACTIVE_SERVICES` identifies all active services for the database. In non-RAC configurations, the service name will typically be the `global_name`. However, it is possible for users to manually create alternative services and use them in the TNS `connect_data` specification.
For RAC configurations, the service will appear in these views as `SYS$schema.queue.global_name`.

Propagation restart

Use the procedures `START_PROPAGATION` and `STOP_PROPAGATION` from `DBMS_PROPAGATION_ADM` to enable and disable the propagation schedule. These procedures automatically handle `queue_to_queue` propagation.

Consider the following example:

```
exec DBMS_PROPAGATION_ADM.stop_propagation('name_of_propagation'); or

exec DBMS_PROPAGATION_ADM.stop_propagation('name_of_
propagation',force=>true);

exec DBMS_PROPAGATION_ADM.start_propagation('name_of_propagation');
```

If you use the lower-level `DBMS_AQADM` procedures to manage the propagation schedule, be sure to explicitly specify the `destination_queue` name when the `queue_to_queue` propagation has been configured.

Consider the following example:

```
DBMS_AQADM.UNSCHEDULE_PROPAGATION('source_queue_
name','destination',destination_queue=>'specific_queue');

DBMS_AQADM.SCHEDULE_PROPAGATION('source_queue_
name','destination',destination_queue=>'specific_queue');

DBMS_AQADM.ENABLE_PROPAGATION_SCHEDULE('source_queue_
name','destination',destination_queue=>'specific_queue');

DBMS_AQADM.DISABLE_PROPAGATION_SCHEDULE('source_queue_
name','destination',destination_queue=>'specific_queue');

DBMS_AQADM.ALTER_PROPAGATION_SCHEDULE('source_queue_
name','destination',destination_queue=>'specific_queue');
```

Changing the GLOBAL_NAME of the source database

The following are some additional considerations when running in an RAC environment:

- If the `GLOBAL_NAME` parameter of the database is changed, ensure that any propagations are dropped and recreated with the `queue_to_queue` parameter set to `TRUE`
- In addition, if the `GLOBAL_NAME` does not match the `db_name.db_domain` of the database, include the `GLOBAL_NAME` for the queue (`NETWORK_NAME` in `DBA_QUEUES`) in the list of services for the database in the database parameter initialization file

Additional configuration for RAC environments for the Apply Database

When Streams is configured in an RAC environment, each queue table has an "owning" instance. All queues within an individual queue table are owned by the same instance. The Streams components (capture/propagation/apply) all use the same owning instance to perform their work. This means:

- The database link specified in the propagation must connect to the owning instance of the target queue
- The Apply process is run at the owning instance of the target queue

Ownership of the queue can be configured to remain on a specific instance, as long as that instance is available, by setting the `PRIMARY _INSTANCE` and `SECONDARY_INSTANCE` parameters of `DBMS_AQADM.ALTER_QUEUE_TABLE`. If the `PRIMARY _INSTANCE` is set to a specific instance (not 0), the queue ownership will return to the specified instance whenever the instance is up.

Apply will automatically follow the ownership of the queue. If the ownership changes while Apply is running, Apply will stop on the current instance and restart at the new owner instance.

Changing the GLOBAL_NAME of the Target Database

If the `GLOBAL_NAME` of the database is changed, ensure that the queue is empty before changing the name and that the Apply process is dropped and recreated with the `apply_captured` parameter set to `TRUE`.

In addition, if the `GLOBAL_NAME` does not match the `db_name.db_domain` of the database, include the `GLOBAL_NAME` in the list of services for the database in the database parameter initialization file.

New features for Streams in Oracle 11g R2

There are a variety of new features for Streams in Oracle Database 11g R2 (11.2):

- XStream
- Statement DML Handlers
- Ability to record table changes with Oracle Streams

- SQL generation
- Support for compressed tables
- Support for SecureFile LOBS
- Automatic split and merge
- New Apply process parameters
- Monitoring jobs
- New Streams Views

XStream

XStream provides you with a set of Application Programming Interfaces (APIs) for information sharing between Oracle databases and other systems. For example, developers can use the XStream API to develop interfaces in their programs to access third-party databases, filesystems, and applications.

Statement DML Handlers

Oracle 11g R2 Streams now comes with a new type of apply handler called a **Statement DML Handler** that will process row LCRs in customizable ways by using a collection of SQL statements. These Statement DML Handlers usually provide you with better performance over procedure DML Handlers because they do not require any PL/SQL processing overhead.

Ability to record table changes

The new `MAINTAIN_CHANGE_TABLE` procedure in the `DBMS_STREAMS_ADM` package gives you an easy way to record changes made to a table in an Oracle 11g R2 Streams environment.

SQL generation

SQL generation gives you the ability to generate SQL statements required to perform changes encapsulated in a row Logical Change Record (LCR).

Support for compressed tables

Before 11g R2, Oracle Streams did not provide support for capturing changes made to Oracle compressed tables. Oracle 11g R2 Streams now supports the capturing of changes made to compressed tables, which are compressed using either basic table compression or OLTP table compression. Furthermore, apply processes can apply changes to compressed tables.

Support for SecureFile LOBs

Previous releases of Oracle Streams did not support SecureFile LOBs. SecureFiles allow you to store various types of Oracle data outside of the database. Now with Oracle 11g R2 , Oracle Streams supports the capturing and applying of changes made to SecureFile `CLOB`, `NCLOB`, and `BLOB` columns.

Automatic splitting and merging

Oracle 11g R2 Streams introduces two new Capture process parameters that provide the new automatic split and merge feature: `split_threshold` and `merge_theshold`.

When you set the parameters for 11g R2 Streams to specify automatic split and merge, the Oracle Scheduler jobs will monitor streams flowing from a capture process. If Oracle Scheduler job identifies a problem with the stream, the job submits a new Oracle Scheduler job to split the problem stream off from the other streams flowing from the capture process. While this occurs, the other Oracle Scheduler jobs will continue to monitor the stream process and, as soon as the problem has been corrected, another Oracle Scheduler job will then merge the stream back with the other streams.

New Apply process parameter

Oracle 11g R2 provides a new Streams Apply process parameter named `txn_age_spill_threshold` . This parameter allows you to set the amount of time allowed to wait before a Streams apply process flushes messages from memory to disk for a transaction, whenever the amount of time that any message in the transaction has been in memory exceeds the specified number of seconds set in this database initialization parameter.

Monitoring jobs

Oracle 11g R2 Streams has a new procedure called START_MONITORING that allows you to create a monitoring job for tracking Oracle Streams' performance continually at specified intervals. The procedure is available in the UTL_SPADV package. Other new procedures in this package enable you to manage monitoring jobs.

New 11g R2 Oracle Streams view

Oracle 11g R2 Streams introduces a new view called DBA_RECOVERABLE_SCRIPT_HIST that stores the results of recovery operations that were performed by the RECOVER_OPERATION procedure in the DBMS_STREAMS_ADM package.

Oracle 11g Data Guard and RAC

Data Guard is Oracle's true Disaster Recovery (DR) solution and answer to customers who require uptime and zero data loss for their mission-critical data center environments.

Oracle Data Guard has been around for a long time--since version 8 of the Oracle database server when it was first called Oracle Physical Standby database. It evolved into Data Guard in Oracle 9i release. Since 9i and 10g, many new enhancements have been incorporated into the Data Guard solution to optimize performance and availability as well as to ease maintenance of the Data Guard operations. In a nutshell, Data Guard implements a physical or logical copy of the primary database at a remote standby site that can be used to failover or switchover to the standby database server on the remote site in the event of a disaster or planned maintenance operation. Data Guard ships redo logs from the primary database to the standby database and applies the redo to the standby site.

New features for Oracle 11g Data Guard

Oracle Data Guard has been enhanced with new features including Active Data Guard and Snapshot Standby options to improve availability and performance for high availability implementations.

Active Data Guard

Oracle Active Data Guard 11g extends basic Data Guard functionality. **Active Data Guard** enables read-only access to a physical standby database while continuously applying changes received from the production database. This enables an active standby database to deliver a high return on investment by supporting ad-hoc queries, web-based access, reporting, backups, or test activity, while it provides disaster protection. Using the standby for queries and reports also validates the production readiness of a standby database, without impacting on data protection or the ability to immediately transition it to the primary role. One caveat to mention about the Active Data Guard option for Oracle 11g R2 is that it requires an additional license from Oracle. As this requires additional cost to deploy with your Oracle environments, you really should first have a valid business need to justify the added cost of this feature before deploying it within your data center infrastructure for RAC and Data Guard.

Snapshot Standby

A Snapshot Standby database is a fully updatable standby database. Like a physical or logical standby database, a snapshot standby database receives and archives redo data from a primary database. Unlike a physical or logical standby database, a snapshot standby database does not apply the redo data that it receives. The redo data received by a snapshot standby database is not applied until the snapshot standby is converted into a physical standby database, after first discarding any local updates made to the snapshot standby database.

A snapshot standby database is best used in scenarios that require a temporary, updatable snapshot of a physical standby database. Note that because redo data received by a snapshot standby database is not applied until it is converted into a physical standby, the time needed to recover from a primary database failure is directly proportional to the amount of redo data that needs to be applied.

Configuring Data Guard Physical Standby for 11g RAC

The setup and configuration of the Data Guard Physical Standby poses unique changes with Oracle 11g RAC environments.

You will need to perform the following steps to configure an Oracle RAC standby database to receive redo data from a primary database:

1. Create standby redo logs on the standby database. The redo log files on the standby database must reside in a location that can be accessed by all of the standby database instances, such as on a cluster filesystem or ASM instance.

2. Configure standby redo log archival on each standby database instance. The standby redo logs must be archived to a location that can be accessed by all of the standby database instances, and every standby database instance must be configured to archive the standby redo log to the same location.

Configuring Oracle RAC primary database to send redo data

You will need to configure each instance of the RAC primary database to send its redo data to the RAC standby database.

Oracle recommends the following best practices when configuring an Oracle RAC primary database to send redo data to an Oracle RAC standby database:

1. Use the same `LOG_ARCHIVE_DEST_n` parameter on each primary database instance to send redo data to a given standby database.
2. Set the `SERVICE` attribute of each `LOG_ARCHIVE_DEST_n` parameter that corresponds to a given standby database to the same net service name.
3. The net service name should resolve to an Oracle Net connect descriptor that contains an address list, and that address list should contain connection data for each standby database instance.

Design considerations in an Oracle RAC environment

This section contains the Data Guard configuration information that is specific to Oracle RAC environments as follows:

- Format for archived redo logs
- Data protection modes
- Role transitions

Format for archived redo log filenames

The format for archived redo log filenames is in the form of `log_%parameter`, where `%` parameter can include one or more of the parameters in the following table:

Directives	Description
`%a`	Database activation ID
`%A`	Database activation ID, zero filled

Directives	Description
%d	Database ID
%D	Database ID, zero filled
%t	Instance thread number
%T	Instance thread number, zero filled
%s	Log file sequence number
%S	Log file sequence number, zero filled
%r	Reset logs ID
%R	Reset logs ID, zero filled

Consider the following example:

```
LOG_ARCHIVE_FORMAT = log%d_%t_%s_%r.arc
```

The thread parameters `%t` or `%T` are mandatory for Oracle RAC to uniquely identify the archived redo logfiles with the `LOG_ARCHIVE_FORMAT` parameter.

Switchover considerations for 11g RAC and Data Guard

For an Oracle RAC database, only one primary instance can be active during a switchover when the target database is a physical standby. Therefore, before a switchover to a physical standby database, shut down all but one primary instance. After the switchover completes, restart the instances that were shut down during the switchover. This limitation does not exist when performing a switchover to a logical standby database.

> The `SQL ALTER DATABASE` statement used to perform the switchover automatically creates redo logfiles if they do not already exist. Because this can significantly increase the time required to complete the `COMMIT` operation, Oracle recommends that you manually add redo logfiles when creating physical standby databases.

Troubleshooting Oracle 11g Data Guard and RAC

The following section will provide you with tips for troubleshooting problems with Oracle 11g RAC and Data Guard.

Switchover fails in an Oracle 11g RAC configuration

When your database is using Oracle RAC, active instances prevent a switchover from being performed. When other instances are active, an attempt to switch over fails with the following error message:

```
SQL> ALTER DATABASE COMMIT TO SWITCHOVER TO STANDBY;


ALTER DATABASE COMMIT TO SWITCHOVER TO STANDBY *

ORA-01105: mount is incompatible with mounts by other instances
```

In this instance, you will need to query the GV$INSTANCE view as follows to determine which instances are causing the problem:

```
SQL> SELECT INSTANCE_NAME, HOST_NAME FROM GV$INSTANCE WHERE INST_ID <>
(SELECT INSTANCE_NUMBER FROM V$INSTANCE);


INSTANCE_NAME HOST_NAME

-----------------------

RACLINUX2      racstdby
```

In the previous example, the identified instance must be manually shut down before the switchover can proceed. You can connect to the identified instance from your instance and issue the SHUTDOWN statement remotely as follows:

```
SQL> CONNECT SYS@racstdby AS SYSDBA

Enter Password:

SQL> SHUTDOWN;

SQL> EXIT
```

How to recover from corrupt datafile on standby

One issue that may occur within Data Guard environments for Oracle 11g RAC is that you may receive a disk failure or operating system failure that corrupts one or more datafiles on your standby environment. In this case, Oracle will generate an error message advising that it cannot read or access the datafile in question. By using the Oracle Recovery Manager (RMAN) utility, you can recover the corrupt datafile on your standby environment.

Having a central administration area for backup and recovery is a good thing. As such, we recommend that you take advantage of using an RMAN catalog as part of your backup and recovery strategy with Oracle RAC environments. In certain recovery scenarios, you may face limitations. For instance, if you choose not to configure and use a RMAN catalog, the backups are configured to use the database control file for backup and recovery information. If you lose the control file, then your history of backups are lost as well. Hence, we advise you to use an RMAN catalog database. To resolve the issue of a corrupted datafile on the standby database, you first need to locate archive logfiles and backup pieces for the most recent backup of the primary database. Of course, as a smart DBA, you already realize that archivelog mode is a requirement for a solid backup and recovery process; so, it's just a matter of tracking down a backup of the most recent archivelogs.

Next, connect to the RMAN catalog and perform the RMAN recovery of the corrupted datafile as shown in the example:

```
$ export ORACLE_SID=rac_stdby1
$> export ORACLE_HOME=/u01/app/oracle/product/11.1.0/racdb
$> rman target / catalog rcat/rcat@rcatdb

Recovery Manager: Release 11.1.0.7.0 - Production on Fri Jun 11 10:12:46 2009

Copyright (c) 1982, 2007, Oracle.  All rights reserved.

connected to target database: RACDB (DBID=1210121736, not open)
connected to recovery catalog database

RMAN>RUN {
    SQL "alter tablespace users offline";
    RESTORE TABLESPACE users;
}
RMAN> exit;

$> sqlplus / as sysdba


SQL> ALTER TABLESPACE users ONLINE;
SQL> ALTER DATABASE RECOVER MANAGED STANDBY DATABASE
   >USING CURRENT LOGFILE DISCONNECT;
```

How to recover from a corrupt block on standby

During the operation of your standby system, if there is a failure with the disk or filesystem when redo is shipped from the primary to the standby system, data blocks may be corrupted as a result. When you have data blocks that are corrupted on the standby database, Oracle will generate an error message advising that it cannot access or read the data blocks in question.

In this scenario, based on how you have configured your Data Guard environment with 11g RAC, you have a choice of two options to repair the block corruption in your standby RAC environment. The first method involves automatic block repair using the built-in recovery mechanisms for Data Guard. The second method is manual block recovery with RMAN.

Automatic repairing of corrupt data blocks

A physical standby database operating in real-time query mode can also be used to repair corrupt data blocks in a primary database. If possible, any corrupt data block encountered, when a primary database is accessed, is automatically replaced with an uncorrupted copy of that block from a physical standby database operating in real-time query mode. For this to work, the standby database must be synchronized with the primary database.

If a corrupt data block is discovered on a physical standby database, the server attempts to automatically repair the corruption by obtaining a copy of the block from the primary database if the following database initialization parameters are configured on the standby database.

The `LOG_ARCHIVE_CONFIG` parameter is configured with a `DG_CONFIG` list and a `LOG_ARCHIVE_DEST_n` parameter is configured for the primary database, or you can use the `FAL_SERVER` parameter if it is configured and its value contains an Oracle Net service name for the primary database.

If you receive an **ORA-1578** error, this indicates that you cannot perform an automatic repair of corrupt blocks on the standby and you must use a manual process to repair the block corruption.

In this case, when automatic block repair is not possible, you can use the `RMAN RECOVER BLOCK` command to manually repair a corrupted data block on the standby. This command searches several locations for an uncorrupted copy of the data block. By default, one of the locations is any available physical standby database operating in real-time query mode. The `EXCLUDE STANDBY` option of the `RMAN RECOVER BLOCK` command can be used to exclude physical standby databases as a source for replacement blocks.

New features for Data Guard in Oracle 11g R2

With the Oracle 11g R2 database, the following new features are provided for Oracle Data Guard:

- Oracle Data Guard configurations now consist of a primary database and up to a maximum of 30 standby databases.
- The `FAL_CLIENT` database parameter is optional and no longer required.
- The default archive destination used by Oracle Automatic Storage Management (Oracle ASM) and the Fast Recovery Area (FRA) feature has been changed from `LOG_ARCHIVE_DEST_10` to `LOG_ARCHIVE_DEST_1`.
- Redo transport compression is no longer limited to compressing redo data only when redo gaps are resolved; whenever compression has been enabled for a destination, all of the redo data sent to that destination is compressed.
- The new `ALTER SYSTEM FLUSH REDO` SQL statement can be used during failover time to flush all unsent redo from a mounted primary database to a standby database, thus allowing for zero data loss failover to be performed even if the primary database is not running in a zero data loss data protection mode. This is a significant enhancement over previous limitations before 11g R2 for Data Guard failover operations.

New Oracle Data Guard 11g R2 features for Redo Apply

With the Oracle 11g R2 database, the following new Oracle Data Guard features for Redo Apply are provided:

- You can now configure the apply lag tolerance in a real-time query environment by using the new database parameter `STANDBY_MAX_DATA_DELAY`.
- You can use the new SQL statement `ALTER SESSION SYNC WITH PRIMARY` to ensure that a properly configured physical standby database is synchronized with the primary database at the time the statement is issued.
- The `V$DATAGUARD_STATS` view has been enhanced to be more accurate in terms of the column definitions such as those for including apply lag and transport lag.

- You can view histograms for apply lag values on the physical standby. To do so, you need to query the new `V$STANDBY_EVENT_HISTOGRAM` view.
- Corrupted data blocks on a primary database can be automatically replaced with an uncorrupted copy of that block from a physical standby database that is operating in real-time query mode. Furthermore, corrupted blocks in a physical standby database may also be automatically replaced with an uncorrupted copy of the block from the primary database.

New Oracle 11g R2 Data Guard features for SQL Apply

With the Oracle 11g R2 database, the following new Oracle 11g R2 Data Guard features for SQL Apply are provided:

- Logical Standby Databases and LogMiner are now able to provide support for tables with basic table compression and OLTP table compression. LogMiner is an audit tool that allows you to view changes made to the database as well as giving you the ability to roll back changes made in the database. Previous releases of Data Guard Logical Standby before 11g R2 did not support table compression operations with SQL Apply. However, hybrid columnar compression is not supported.
- Logical Standby and the LogMiner now support tables with SecureFile LOB columns. In addition, compression and encryption-based operations on SecureFile LOB columns are now supported in 11g R2. However, de-duplication operations and fragment-based operations are not supported.
- You can now capture changes made in the context of XA global transactions on an Oracle RAC primary database, which will then be replicated to a Logical Standby Database.
- Logical Standby Databases now support Oracle Streams Capture operations. This allows you to offload data processing from the primary database in one-way propagation configuration and to turn the logical standby into a main data hub that propagates information to multiple databases.

Summary

In this chapter, we discussed the high available solutions offered for Oracle 11g that complement Oracle RAC clustered environments. We provided a conceptual overview of the following Maximum Available Architecture (MAA) solutions:

- Streams replication
- Standby databases (Data Guard)
- New features in Oracle 11g R2 for Streams and Data Guard

In addition, we provided a discussion of how to best leverage Streams and Data Guard with the help of new and existing RAC clustered environments, along with tips and best practices to enhance performance and scalability for RAC with Data Guard and Streams. Furthermore, we provided an overview on the latest features available in 11g R2 for Data Guard and Streams.

Additional Resources and Tools for the Oracle RAC Professional

Now that you have finished reading the book, we felt a need to provide you with a suite of tools and tips for managing Oracle RAC environments. Many of these utilities are hidden in the Oracle documentation—undocumented or poorly documented at best. As such, we will provide a detailed listing and tips on the following topics:

- Sample configurations
- Oracle RAC commands and tips
- Operating system-level commands for tuning and diagnosis
- Additional references and tips
- Clusterware startup sequence for 11g R2 RAC
- Logfile locations for Oracle RAC and ASM

Sample configurations

The sample `LISTENER.ORA` file for the database node (without virtual host name) looks as follows:

```
<SID> =
|     (ADDRESS_LIST =
          (ADDRESS= (PROTOCOL= IPC) (KEY= EXTPROC<SID>))
          (ADDRESS= (PROTOCOL= TCP) (Host= host2)
             (Port= db_port)
          )
      )
```

```
SID_LIST_<SID> =
      (SID_LIST =
        (SID_DESC =
            (ORACLE_HOME= <11g ORACLE_HOME>)
            (SID_NAME = <SID>)
         )
         (SID_DESC =
             (SID_NAME = PLSExtProc)
             (ORACLE_HOME = <11g ORACLE_HOME>)
             (PROGRAM = extproc)
          )
      )

STARTUP_WAIT_TIME_<SID> = 0
CONNECT_TIMEOUT_<SID> = 10
TRACE_LEVEL_<SID> = OFF
```

The following settings for Oracle 11g now exist in the Automatic Diagnostic Repository (ADR) and can be viewed from the `adrci` utility:

```
LOG_DIRECTORY_<SID> = <11g ORACLE_HOME>/network/admin
LOG_FILE_<SID> =<SID>
TRACE_DIRECTORY_<SID> = <11g ORACLE_HOME>/network/admin
TRACE_FILE_<SID> = <SID>
ADMIN_RESTRICTIONS_<SID> = OFF
```

The sample `LISTENER.ORA` file for database nodes (with virtual host name) looks similar to the following:

```
LISTENER_<host_name> =
       (DESCRIPTION_LIST =
          (DESCRIPTION =
              (ADDRESS_LIST =
                  (ADDRESS = (PROTOCOL = TCP)
                    (HOST = <Virtual IP Address>)
                    (PORT = <db_port>)(IP = FIRST)
                  )
              )
              (ADDRESS_LIST =
                  (ADDRESS = (PROTOCOL = TCP)
                     (HOST = <host_name>)
                     (PORT = <db_port>)(IP = FIRST)
                  )
              )
              (ADDRESS_LIST =
                  (ADDRESS = (PROTOCOL = IPC)
                    (KEY = EXTPROC<SID>)
                  )
              )
```

```
            )
        )

SID_LIST_LISTENER_<host_name> =
            (SID_LIST =
                (SID_DESC = (ORACLE_HOME = <11g ORACLE_HOME>)
                             (SID_NAME = <SID>)
                )
                (SID_DESC = (SID_NAME = PLSExtProc)
                            (ORACLE_HOME = <11g ORACLE_HOME>)
                            (PROGRAM = extproc)
                )
            )

STARTUP_WAIT_TIME_LISTENER_<host_name> = 0
CONNECT_TIMEOUT_LISTENER_<host_name> = 10
TRACE_LEVEL_LISTENER_<host_name> = OFF
```

The following settings for Oracle 11g now exist in the Automatic Diagnostic Repository (ADR) and can be viewed from the `adrci` utility:

```
LOG_DIRECTORY_LISTENER_<host_name> = <11g ORACLE_HOME>/network/admin
LOG_FILE_LISTENER_<host_name> = <SID>
TRACE_DIRECTORY_LISTENER_<host_name> = <11g ORACLE_HOME>/network/admin
TRACE_FILE_LISTENER_<host_name> = <SID>
ADMIN_RESTRICTIONS_LISTENER_<host_name> = OFF
IFILE=<11g
ORACLE_HOME>/network/admin/<CONTEXT_NAME>/listener_ifile.ora
```

The sample `TNSNAMES.ORA` file for database nodes (with virtual host name) is as follows:

```
<CONNECT_STRING>=
      (DESCRIPTION=
            (ADDRESS=(PROTOCOL=tcp)
               (HOST=<Virtual IP Address>)
               (PORT=<db_port>)
            )
            (CONNECT_DATA=
               (SERVICE_NAME=<Service_name>)
               (INSTANCE_NAME=<SID>)
               )
      )
```

Reviewing and resolving manual configuration changes

In the Oracle R12 E-Business Suite (EBS), the `adchkcfg` utility verifies the context file.

The Oracle EBS uses the context file to store the configuration settings for the Oracle EBS environment. You would want to use the `adchkcfg` utility to check for errors in the context file to avoid problems with the operation of the Oracle EBS.

adchkcfg utility

The `adchkcfg` utility has a lot of functionality associated with it.

The CheckConfig utility (`adchkcfg`) is located as specified below.

Tier	Location
Application	`<AD_TOP>/bin`
Database	`<RDBMS ORACLE_HOME>/appsutil/bin`

Check the AutoConfig configuration files by executing the following commands:

- On Unix: `adchkcfg.sh contextfile=<CONTEXT>`
- On Windows: `adchkcfg.cmd contextfile=<CONTEXT>`

The `adchkcfg.sh` script will generate both web-based HTML formatted and text reports that provide information about all of the changes made to the Oracle R12 EBS environment. These changes made to the Oracle R12 EBS Context file include file changes, profile option changes, and other important database updates performed by the AutoConfig utility. The report consists of the following two tabs:

1. **File System Changes**:
   This report provides information about all the files that will be changed during the next normal execution of AutoConfig. The report is divided into the following sections:
   - **AutoConfig Context File Changes**: It displays information about the location of the context file, the content of the currently active context file, and the content of the context file that will be generated in the next AutoConfig run. In addition, it also displays an HTML report highlighting the differences between the current and the new context file.

- **Changed Configuration Files**: It displays a list of all the files that will be changed during an AutoConfig execution. For each file, information is displayed about the location of the runtime file, the content of the currently active file, the content of the file that will be generated in the next AutoConfig run, an HTML report highlighting the differences between the current and the new configuration file, and the location of the AutoConfig template file.
- **New Configuration Files**: It displays a list of all the new files that will be created during an AutoConfig execution. For each file, information is displayed about the location of the runtime file, the content of the new file, and the location of the AutoConfig template file.

2. **Database Changes**:
   This report provides information about all the profile options that get changed during the normal execution of AutoConfig. This report is divided into the following three sections:
   - **Profile Value Changes**: It displays the details for profiles whose value would be changed in the next AutoConfig run. For each profile, the current value in the database, the new AutoConfig value that would be set for it, the profile level, and the name of the AutoConfig script that changes the profile value that is displayed.
   - **Profile Values**: It displays the details as in the previous section for all Apps Database profiles managed by AutoConfig.
   - **Other Database updates**: It displays the details for important database updates that will be carried out in the next run of AutoConfig. The table name, column name, the current column value in the database, and the new AutoConfig value is displayed along with the name of the updating AutoConfig script.

You will need to resolve any reported differences between your existing files and the files that AutoConfig will create.

The script will also create a ZIP file report, `ADXcfgcheck.zip`, that contains all the files and reports mentioned earlier, so that `ADXcfgcheck.zip` can be copied to a local desktop PC and the HTML report can be viewed there without breaking the hyperlinks in the report. The following is a worked example of how to use the `adchkcfg` utility and sample output for an Oracle R12 EBS environment on the Linux platform.

```
[applmgr@tusebs ~]$ adchkcfg.sh
Enter the full path to the Applications Context file:
/appstier12/CLONE/inst/apps/CLONE_tusebs/appl/admin/CLONE_tusebs.xml
Enter the APPS password:
```

```
The log file for this session is located at: /appstier12/CLONE/inst/apps/
CLONE_tusebs/admin/log/02271723/adconfig.log

AutoConfig is running in test mode and building diffs...

AutoConfig will consider the custom templates if present.
        Using CONFIG_HOME location     : /appstier12/CLONE/inst/apps/
CLONE_tusebs
        Classpath                   : /appstier12/CLONE/comn/java/lib/
appsborg2.zip:/appstier12/CLONE/comn/java/classes

        Using Context file          : /appstier12/CLONE/inst/apps/CLONE_
tusebs/admin/out/02271723/CLONE_tusebs.xml

Context Value Management will now update the test Context file

        Updating test Context file...COMPLETED

        [ Test mode ]
        No uploading of Context File and its templates to database.

Testing templates from all of the product tops...
        Testing AD_TOP........COMPLETED
        Testing FND_TOP.......COMPLETED
        Testing ICX_TOP.......COMPLETED
        Testing IEO_TOP.......COMPLETED
        Testing BIS_TOP.......COMPLETED
        Testing AMS_TOP.......COMPLETED
        Testing CCT_TOP.......COMPLETED
        Testing WSH_TOP.......COMPLETED
        Testing CLN_TOP.......COMPLETED
        Testing OKE_TOP.......COMPLETED
        Testing OKL_TOP.......COMPLETED
        Testing OKS_TOP.......COMPLETED
        Testing CSF_TOP.......COMPLETED
        Testing IGS_TOP.......COMPLETED
        Testing IBY_TOP.......COMPLETED
        Testing JTF_TOP.......COMPLETED
        Testing MWA_TOP.......COMPLETED
        Testing CN_TOP........COMPLETED
        Testing CSI_TOP.......COMPLETED
```

```
        Testing WIP_TOP.......COMPLETED
        Testing CSE_TOP.......COMPLETED
        Testing EAM_TOP.......COMPLETED
        Testing FTE_TOP.......COMPLETED
        Testing ONT_TOP.......COMPLETED
        Testing AR_TOP........COMPLETED
        Testing AHL_TOP.......COMPLETED
        Testing OZF_TOP.......COMPLETED
        Testing IES_TOP.......COMPLETED
        Testing CSD_TOP.......COMPLETED
        Testing IGC_TOP.......COMPLETED

Differences text report is located at: /appstier12/CLONE/inst/apps/CLONE_
tusebs/admin/out/02271723/cfgcheck.txt

        Generating Profile Option differences report...COMPLETED
        Generating File System differences report......COMPLETED
Differences html report is located at: /appstier12/CLONE/inst/apps/CLONE_
tusebs/admin/out/02271723/cfgcheck.html

Differences Zip report is located at: /appstier12/CLONE/inst/apps/CLONE_
tusebs/admin/out/02271723/ADXcfgcheck.zip

AutoConfig completed successfully.

[applmgr@tusebs 02271723]$ ls
adadmat.pl                                  httpd.conf
adadmprf.sh                                 ias.properties
adadmprf.sql                                iasschema.xml
adadmrat.sql                                ibywebprf.sql
adalldefaults.txt                           icxwebprf.sql
ADXcfgcheck.zip                             jtfsvfm.sh
```

Oracle RAC commands and tips

We will now discuss tools and scripts that will benefit you in the administration of Oracle 11g RAC environments. First, we will discuss clusterware configuration tools such as the cluster deconfig tool, which can be used to remove the Oracle clusterware software from your Oracle RAC environment.

Cluster deconfig tool for Oracle RAC

As referenced in the Oracle Database De-installation Tool for Oracle Clusterware and Oracle Real Application 10g Release 2 (10.2) for Unix and Windows documentation, the cluster deconfig tool allows you to uninstall RAC cluster configurations.

The tool was released after 10.2.0.2 and is available on the OTN website from Oracle (`http://otn.oracle.com`). It provides you with the following benefits:

- The cluster deconfig tool removes and deconfigures all of the software and shared files that are associated with an Oracle Clusterware or Oracle RAC database installation.
- The cluster deconfig tool removes software, clusterware, and database files, along with the global configuration across all of the nodes in a cluster environment.
- On Windows-based systems, the cluster deconfig tool removes Windows Registry entries.

It is advised to use the cluster deconfig tool to prepare a cluster, to reinstall Oracle Clusterware and Oracle database software after a successful or failed installation.

The cluster deconfig tool restores your cluster to its state prior to the installation, enabling you to perform a new installation. You can also use the **Oracle Cluster Verification Utility** (**CVU**) to determine the cause of any problems that may have occurred during an installation, so that you can correct the errors.

The cluster deconfig tool will not remove third-party software that depends on Oracle Clusterware. In addition, the cluster deconfig tool provides no warnings about any third-party software dependencies that may exist with the Oracle Clusterware or Oracle database homes prior to removing the respective homes.

To download the cluster deconfig tool, go to the following website: `http://download.oracle.com/otndocs/products/clustering/deinstall/clusterdeconfig.zip`.

The cluster deconfig tool needs to be run as the root OS user and provides a built-in help feature to display available options and details for command syntax:

```
clusterdeconfig  -help or -h
```

On Unix-based systems and Windows-based systems, the logfile for the `clusterdeconfig` utility output is located on the cluster node where you ran the tool in the cluster `deconfig path/logs` directory.

Depending on the software that you want to uninstall, plan the uninstallation so that the components are removed in the correct order.

As such, due to the dependencies among the Oracle Clusterware and the Oracle database software components, you must uninstall the components in a specific order as follows:

1. Uninstall all Oracle database homes that do not include ASM software.
2. Uninstall the Oracle database home that includes ASM software, if you have one.
3. Uninstall the Oracle Clusterware home.

Using the cluster deconfig tool

You would want to use the cluster deconfig tool to clean failed installation operations for Oracle 11g RAC setups. For example, you would need to use this tool in the event that the installation halts due to a hardware or operating system failure, and you need to clean up the failed installation as a result. Another reason that you may want to use this tool would be to remove existing databases along with their associated database home and cluster home directories.

Use this tool with caution on production clusters and databases. Always test in a sandbox environment first, if possible.

The cluster deconfig tool can only remove Oracle database components from cluster nodes that are active. For cluster nodes that are inactive, one must rerun the tool when those nodes are active to complete the deconfiguration.

Use the cluster deconfig tool to remove installed components in the following situations:

- When you have encountered errors during or after installing Oracle database software on a cluster and you want to reattempt an installation.
- When you have stopped an installation and do not know how to restart it. In such cases, use the cluster deconfig tool to remove the partially-installed product and restart your installation.
- When you have researched all of the problems with your existing installation using the CVU, or by examining the installation logfiles, and cannot determine the cause of a problem.

Limitations of the cluster deconfig tool

If you attempt to run the cluster deconfig tool to uninstall Oracle Clusterware without first removing the related Oracle Database homes, then the cluster deconfig tool reports an error instead of a warning. The following example shows how to use the cluster deconfig tool for Oracle 11g R1 and Oracle 11g R2 environments:

```
[oracle@raclinux1]$ ./clusterdeconfig -checkonly -home /u01/app/oracle/
product/crs
ORACLE_HOME = /u01/app/oracle/product/11gR1/crs
############ CLUSTERWARE/RAC DEINSTALL DECONFIG TOOL START ############
######################## CHECK OPERATION START ########################
Install check configuration START
Make sure that all Real Application Cluster (RAC) database homes are de-
installed, before you choose to de-install the Oracle Clusterware home.
Exited from Program
```

Problems and limitations of the cluster deconfig tool

We can examine a few of the limitations for the cluster deconfig tool. Be sure to check the latest bug list available online at My Oracle Support (`http://support.oracle.com`) to remain up to date on the latest issues with Oracle. The following bugs mention some key problems that may arise while using the cluster deconfig tool.

BUG 5181492: Listener is not downgraded to 10.1 if 10.2 home missing: The cluster deconfig tool fails to downgrade listener configurations to its original home during de-installation and downgrade of Oracle 10.2 RAC home. This happens only if the Oracle 10.2 RAC home that is being deconfigured does not have Oracle software present and listener configurations do not exist in Oracle's `home/network/admin` directory.

Workaround: Run Oracle `home/bin/netca` from the original home to recreate listener configurations.

BUG 5364797: DC Tool not deleting home completely when home is shared: The cluster deconfig tool fails to delete Oracle software completely from a shared Oracle RAC database home or Oracle Clusterware home. It completely removes Oracle configuration that exists on all nodes of the cluster.

Workaround: Run the `rm -rf <Oracle home path>` command on any one node in the cluster to completely remove the software.

Starting the cluster deconfig tool

There are two ways to start the cluster deconfig tool depending on the platform in which you have Oracle 11g RAC. For Unix and Linux-based systems, you would start the utility by logging in as the Oracle user account that performed the installation for the Oracle Clusterware and Oracle database home that is being uninstalled. For Windows, you would need to log in to the host as the user who is a member of the local administrators group.

To start the tool, you will need to issue the `clusterdeconfig` command.

Before you perform the uninstallation with the `clusterdeconfig` utility, you must first confirm that the connected user has user equivalence on all of the nodes in the cluster. This means users can automatically establish an ssh or rsh session between host nodes without a password. This can be verified by using the `ssh` command in Unix or Linux to verify that access is permitted without a password between all cluster nodes.

To begin the de-installation tool, connect to one of the nodes in your cluster that contains the installation that you want to remove. You can connect to the node directly or you can connect from a client.

Open a command-line interface and enter the following command:

```
$ clusterdeconfig
```

The output from this command displays the required and optional parameters.

You can also use the `-help` or `-h` option to obtain more information about the `clusterdeconfig` tool commands and their use.

Silent mode operations using cluster deconfig

The deconfiguration tool also supports the silent (`-silent`) option.

It is mandatory to have the `<Deconfiguration tool home>/ templates /rac.properties` file to de-install or downgrade an RAC database.

It is strongly advised that you run the cluster deconfiguration tool using the `checkonly` option to generate the properties file such as `<Deconfiguration tool home>/templates/rac.properties` before running the tool to remove the configuration or downgrading the Oracle RAC database configuration.

The deconfiguration tool supports the silent (`-silent`) option to operate without prompting you for information. In this mode, the deconfiguration tool will try to discover the Oracle network listener, the Oracle database, the Oracle ASM instance, and Oracle Enterprise Manager Database Control information. The successful discovery of these components depends on the configuration of the Oracle listener, Oracle RAC database, Oracle ASM instance, Oracle EM database control, and the availability of the Oracle RAC database software.

An example of using the cluster deconfig tool in non-silent mode for Oracle 11g R1 RAC is as follows:

```
[oracle@raclinux1 clusterdeconfig]$ ./clusterdeconfig -home /home/oracle/
product/11.1.0/db -checkonly

ORACLE_HOME = /home/oracle/product/11.1.0/db

#### CLUSTERWARE/RAC DEINSTALL DECONFIG TOOL START ############

################### CHECK OPERATION START ########################

Install check configuration START

The cluster node(s) on which the Oracle home exists are: raclinux1,
raclinux2


Checking for existance of the Oracle home location /home/oracle/
product/11.1.0/db

Checking for existance of central inventory location /home/oracle/
raclinux

Checking for existance of the Oracle clusterware home   /home/oracle/
product/11.1.0/crs_raclinux

The following nodes are part of this cluster: raclinux1,raclinux2

Install check configuration END

Network Configuration check config START

Network de-configuration trace file location: /home/oracle/
clusterdeconfig/logs/netdc_check.log.

Location /home/oracle/product/11.1.0/db/network/tools does not exist!

Specify the list of listener prefixes that are configured in this Oracle
home. For example, MYLISTENER would be the prefix for listeners named
MYLISTENER_node1 and MYLISTENER_node2 []:LISTENER_RACLINUX1,LISTENER_
RACLINUX2

Specify prefixes for all listeners to be migrated to another database
or ASM home. The target Oracle Database home version should be 10g
or above. This ensures that clients can continue to connect to other
Oracle instances after the migration. Specify "." if you do not want to
migrate any listeners. Listeners that you do not specify here will be de-
configured. []:
```

```
Network Configuration check config END

Database Check Configuration START

Database de-configuration trace file location '/home/oracle/
clusterdeconfig/logs/assistantsdc_check3731.log'

Specify the list of database names that are configured in this Oracle
home []: racdb

Specify if Automatic Storage Management (ASM) instance is running from
this Oracle home y|n [n]: y

###### For Database 'racdb' ######

Specify the nodes on which this database has instances [raclinux1,
raclinux2]:

Specify the instance names [raclinux1, raclinux2]:

Specify the local instance name on node raclinux1  [raclinux1]:

Specify whether this was an upgraded database. The de-configuration tool
will attempt to downgrade the database to the lower version if it is an
upgraded database y|n [n]:

Specify the storage type used by the Database ASM|CFS|RAW []: ASM

Specify the list of directories if any database files exist on a shared
file system. If 'racdb' subdirectory is found, then it will be deleted.
Otherwise, the specified directory will be deleted. Alternatively, you
can specify list of database files with full path [ ]: /oradata/racdb

Specify the flash recovery area location, if it is configured on the file
system. If 'racdb' subdirectory is found, then it will be deleted. []:

Specify the database spfile location [ ]:

Specify the database dump destination directories. If multiple
directories are configured, specify comma separated list []:

Specify the archive log destination directories []:

Database Check Configuration END

Enterprise Manager Configuration Assistant START

Checking configuration for database racdb

Enterprise Manager Configuration Assistant END

##################### CHECK OPERATION END #########################


########################### SUMMARY ###############################

Oracle Home selected for de-install is: /home/oracle/oracle/
product/11.1.0/db

Inventory Location where the Oracle home registered is: /home/oracle/
racdb

Oracle Clusterware Home is: /home/oracle/product/11.1.0/crs_racdb
```

```
The cluster node(s) on which the Oracle home exists are:
raclinux1,raclinux2

The following databases were selected for de-configuration : racdb

Database unique name : racdb

Storage used : ASM
A log of this session will be written to: '/home/oracle/clusterdeconfig/
logs/deinstall_deconfig.out2'

Any error messages from this session will be written to: '/home/oracle/
clusterdeconfig/logs/deinstall_deconfig.err2'

################## ADDITIONAL INFORMATION ########################

The clusterdeconfig tool has detected that the Oracle home, /home/oracle/
product/11.1.0/db, was removed without properly deconfiguring all of the
Oracle database components related to that Oracle home.  Because of this,
processes such as tnslsnr, dbcontrol and so on that depend on this Oracle
home might still be running on the cluster nodes, raclinux1,raclinux2.

Oracle recommends that you kill these processes on these cluster nodes
before attempting to re-install the Oracle database software.  You can
use the command ps -efw to see the full paths of the processes that
were started that have an absolute pathname of the Oracle home.  Or you
can also use lsof +D <Oracle home> to show all the open files in that
directory and which user owns them.  The -t option to the lsof command
displays the process identifiers.

###### CLUSTERWARE/RAC DEINSTALL DECONFIG TOOL END #############
```

Manual cleanup for RAC

In the event that you cannot use the clusterware deconfig tool, you will need to manually clean up the RAC environment by using OS commands as shown next.

On the Linux platform, you will need to use the Linux `ps` (process status) and `kill` commands to shut down the Oracle RAC and clusterware background processes:

- Kill EVM, CRS, and CSS processes if they are currently running:

  ```
  ps -efl | grep crs
  kill <crs pid> <evm pid> <css pid>
  ```

Now, you will need to log in as root user at the Linux OS prompt and execute the `rm` command to delete the clusterware files from the `/etc/oracle`, `/etc/init.d`, and additional directory structures as follows.

- As root user, remove the following files:

  ```
  rm /etc/oracle/*
  rm -f /etc/init.d/init.cssd
  rm -f /etc/init.d/init.crs
  ```

```
rm -f /etc/init.d/init.crsd
rm -f /etc/init.d/init.evmd
rm -f /etc/rc2.d/K96init.crs
rm -f /etc/rc2.d/S96init.crs
rm -f /etc/rc3.d/K96init.crs
rm -f /etc/rc3.d/S96init.crs
rm -f /etc/rc5.d/K96init.crs
rm -f /etc/rc5.d/S96init.crs
rm -Rf /etc/oracle/scls_scr
rm -f /etc/inittab.crs
cp /etc/inittab.orig /etc/inittab
```

- If you are using `oraInventory` that has other Oracle software installed, then uninstall the CRS home using the **Oracle Universal Installer (OUI)**
- If `oraInventory` has only `CRS_HOME` that you plan to remove, then as root user, remove `CRS_HOME`:

```
# rm -Rf CRS_HOME/*
```

For RDBMS installation, if you are using `oraInventory` that has other Oracle software installed, then uninstall the CRS home using the Oracle Universal Installer.

To know about the required steps for other platforms, refer to My Oracle Support (formerly Metalink) note 239998.1.

If `oraInventory` has only the `RDBMS_HOME` that you plan to remove, then as oracle user, remove the `RDBMS_HOME`:

```
rm -Rf  $ORACLE_ HOME/*
```

For ASM, clean up any ASM disks if they have already been used.

If there is no other Oracle software running, you can remove the files in `/var/tmp/.oracle or /tmp/.oracle`:

```
# rm -f /var/tmp/.oracle or rm -f /tmp/.oracle
```

Now that we have cleaned up the environment, let's review how to repair the RAC environment, using the `rootdelete.sh` and `rootdeinstall.sh` commands, which doesn't require reinstallation.

Repairing the RAC environment without reinstalling

Under some circumstances, you may need to clean up an existing failed RAC install and run `root.sh` without reinstalling CRS. To do so, you can execute the following scripts:

```
$ORA_CRS_HOME/install/rootdelete.sh
$ORA_CRS_HOME/install/rootdeinstall.sh
```

You can also run these scripts if you want to reinitialize the OCR and Voting Disk without reinstalling CRS.

Reinitializing OCR and Voting Disks without reinstalling RAC

To perform the reinitialization of the OCR and Voting Disks without an RAC reinstallation, perform the following tasks:

1. Obtain approval for a maintenance window for downtime, to reinitialize OCR. All resources and CRS must be stopped.
2. Run the `rootdelete.sh` script and then the `rootdeinstall.sh` script from the `$ORA_CRS_HOME/install` directory.
3. These scripts will stop CRS and clean up SCR settings in `/etc/oracle/scls_scr` or `/var/opt/oracle/scls_scr` (depending on your platform) directory and remove contents from OCR and OCR mirror using `dd` command.
4. If this succeeds, then reinitialize the OCR and Voting Disk. If, for any reason, there is a problem with the script, then you will need to perform a manual clean up as mentioned earlier.
5. Stop all resources on all nodes in the RAC cluster using the following commands:

   ```
   srvctl stop database -d <dbname>
   srvctl stop asm -n <node name>
   srvctl stop nodeapps -n <node name>
   ```

6. Stop CRS on all nodes while logged in as root user:

   Oracle 10.1: `/etc/init.d/init.crs stop`

   Oracle 10.2 and later: `$ORA_CRS_HOME/bin/crsctl stop crs`

7. Format the OCR and Voting Disk while logged in as root user using the following:

```
# dd if=/dev/zero of=<OCR disk> bs=125829120 count=1
# dd if=/dev/zero of=<Voting disk> bs=20971520 count=1
```

If OCR or the Voting Disk is on a shared filesystem, delete them from OS level.

8. Remove the `scls_scr` directory on all nodes in order to allow `root.sh` to re-execute using the following:

```
# rm -r /etc/oracle/scls_scr
```

9. In a new shell window, execute the following `root.sh` script as the root OS user:

```
# $ORA_CRS_HOME/root.sh
```

This needs to be executed on all nodes one after the other (similar to the CRS installation time running `root.sh`). It cannot be executed at the same time on all nodes.

The `root.sh` script must be the original file from the original installation. If there is a node added or deleted from the first installation and current environment, then this `root.sh` cannot be used. In this case, a clean reinstall of CRS would be required.

10. Once `root.sh` successfully completes execution on all nodes, CRS should start automatically.
11. If VIPCA errors at the `root.sh` for the last node in the cluster due to an IP address issue, run the VIPCA manually from an X-Window session with the display set up correctly to create the VIP/ONS/GSD resources.

```
# cd $ORA_CRS_HOME/bin
# vipca
```

12. Run `oifcfg` to configure the private interface.
13. As the Oracle user, issue the following `oifcfg` command to set the network interfaces for the cluster nodes:

```
oifcfg setif -global <if_name>/<subnet>:public
oifcfg setif -global <if_name>/<subnet>:cluster_interconnect
```

14. Run the NETCA utility to create a listener. Rename the `$ORACLE_HOME/network/admin/listener.ora` (under RDBMS `ORACLE_HOME`) to `# $ORACLE_HOME/bin/netca` on all cluster nodes. Enter the correct information as prompted. Now, the `crs_stat -t` output should display the listener resource for all cluster nodes.

The `asm_inst_name` can only be +ASM1, +ASM2, and so on. Failure to provide the correct name may cause OCR corruption.

15. Once all resources are registered, start them using the `srvctl` command as the Oracle user:

```
$ srvctl start asm -n <node_name>
$ srvctl start instance -d <db_name> -i <inst_name>
```

16. Check the `crs_stat -t` output. It should now display all cluster resources with an ONLINE status on ALL nodes.

Now that we have verified the status for the Clusterware services, we are ready to show you how to use the `rootdelete.sh` script to remove a node from the Oracle 11g RAC environment.

Using ROOTDELETE.SH in debug mode

Oracle 11g provides you with `the rootdelete.sh` script to remove one or more nodes from the Oracle RAC configuration. To issue the script, you need to run it as the root OS user account by entering the `rootdelete.sh` command from the Oracle 11g `CRS_HOME` directory on the master cluster node. The following example shows the option to debug is the removal process while executing the `rootdelete.sh` script:

```
[root@raclinux1 install]# ./rootdelete.sh
+ ORA_CRS_HOME=/home/oracle/product/11.1.0/crs_raclinux
+ ORACLE_OWNER=oracle
Start of script
+ DBA_GROUP=oinstall
+ USER_ARGS=
+ LOCALNODE=local
+ SHAREDVAR=nosharedvar
+ SHAREDHOME=sharedhome
+ DOWNGRADE=false
+ VERSION=11.1
```

```
+ CH=/home/oracle/product/11.1.0/crs_raclinux
+ ORACLE_HOME=/home/oracle/product/11.1.0/crs_raclinux
+ export ORA_CRS_HOME
+ export ORACLE_HOME
.
+ verifyCRSResources
+ VIP_SUFFIX=.vip
+ GSD_SUFFIX=.gsd
+ ONS_SUFFIX=.ons
+ LSNR_SUFFIX=.lsnr
+ DB_SUFFIX=.db
+ /home/oracle/product/11.1.0/crs_raclinux/bin/crs_stat
+ return 0
+ /bin/echo 'Checking to see if Oracle CRS stack is down...'
Checking to see if Oracle CRS stack is down...

+ /home/oracle/product/11.1.0/crs_raclinux/bin/crs_stat
+ /bin/echo 'Oracle CRS stack is not running.'
Oracle CRS stack is not running.
.
+ /bin/echo 'Oracle CRS stack is down now.'
Oracle CRS stack is down now.
.
+ /sbin/init q
+ /bin/echo 'Removing script for Oracle Cluster Ready services'
Removing script for Oracle Cluster Ready services
+ /bin/rm /etc/init.d/init.crs /etc/init.d/init.crsd /etc/init.d/init.
cssd
.
+ '[' local = remote ']'
+ /bin/echo 'Cleaning up SCR settings in '\''/etc/oracle/scls_scr'\'''
Cleaning up SCR settings in '/etc/oracle/scls_scr'
+ /bin/rm -rf /etc/oracle/scls_scr
root@raclinux1 install]# ./rootdeinstall.sh
+ ORACLE_OWNER=oracle
+ DBA_GROUP=oinstall
+ ORA_CRS_HOME=/home/oracle/product/11.1.0/crs_raclinux
```

```
.
+ /bin/echo 'Removing contents from OCR device'
Removing contents from OCR device
+ /bin/dd if=/dev/zero skip=25 bs=4k count=2560 of=/ocfs21/oradata/test2/
ocrtest2
2560+0 records in
2560+0 records out
+ /bin/rm /etc/oracle/ocr.loc
.
+ /bin/chown oracle /oradata/raclinux/ocrtest2
+ /bin/chgrp oinstall /ocfs21/oradata/raclinux/ocrtest2
+ /bin/chmod 644 /ocfs21/oradata/raclinux/ocrtest2
```

Using rootdeinstall.sh

The `rootdeinstall.sh` script allows you to format the **Oracle Cluster Registry (OCR)** by using the Unix/Linux `dd` command. In addition, it allows you to change the OCR device owner back to the Oracle user and dba group. All you will still need to manually remove the `/var/oracle or /tmp/oracle` directory to clean up the failed installation.

Reinstalling CRS on the same cluster in another CRS_HOME

Now let's illustrate how to reinstall the **Cluster Ready Services (CRS)** on the same cluster into another CRS_HOME directory. The following example will use the `SRVCTL` and `CRSCTL` commands to shutdown and disable the Oracle 11g Clusterware services. This is mandatory before we can re-install the Cluster Ready Services.

Stopping CRS processes

1. Stop Nodeapps:

   ```
   ./srvctl stop nodeapps -n prrrac1
   ./srvctl stop nodeapps -n prrrac2
   ```

2. Stop CRS:

   ```
   ./crsctl stop crs
   ```

3. Disable CRS:

   ```
   ./crsctl disable crs
   ```

4. Check the CRS process:

```
ps -ef | grep crs css evm
```

Reinstalling CRS on same cluster in another CRS_HOME

Now let's explain how to perform the reinstallation for the CRS software to the same cluster with a different `CRS_HOME` directory. To do so, you must log into the server as the root user.

1. Restore original `inittab`:

```
# cp /etc/inittab /etc/inittab_pretest1
# mv /etc/inittab.orig /etc/inittab
```

2. Reboot the node:

```
# /sbin/shutdown -r now
```

3. Move the CRS files to a backup location under the `/etc/init.d` directory as shown here:

```
# mv /etc/init.d/init.cssd /etc/init.d/init.cssd_pretest
# mv /etc/init.d/init.evmd /etc/init.d/init.evmd_pretest
# mv /etc/init.d/init.crsd /etc/init.d/init.crsd_pretest
# mv /etc/init.d/init.crs /etc/init.d/init.crs_pretest
# mv /etc/oracle /etc/oracle_pretest
# mv /etc/oraInst.loc /etc/oraInst.loc_pretest
```

For Oracle 11g R2, we recommend that you use the new utility named `rootcrs.pl` or `roothas.pl` as mentioned in My Oracle Support (formerly Metalink) note 942166.1, *How to Proceed from Failed 11g R2 Grid Infrastructure (CRS) Installation.*

Oracle 11g R2 cluster removal tools for RAC

Oracle 11g R2 has a new tool named `roothas.pl` for standalone grid instances and `rootcrs.pl` for RAC configurations. To execute the script for an Oracle 11g R2 RAC environment, you will need to run the script as follows:

1. Execute the following script as root:

```
$GRID_HOME/crs/install/rootcrs.pl -verbose -deconfig -force
```

2. Execute the script on all nodes except for the last node in the cluster where `$GRID_HOME` is the environment variable for your 11g R2 RAC grid infrastructure directory.
3. As root user, execute the script:

   `$GRID_HOME/crs/install/rootcrs.pl -verbose -deconfig -force -lastnode` on the last node in the cluster. This command will also format the OCR and Vote Disks.
4. As the Oracle Grid user account, execute the following script:

   `$GRID_HOME/deinstall/deinstall`

Tracing RAC issues with Oradebug

Oradebug is an excellent, but poorly understood, utility for diagnosing database issues. It has features to trace and monitor all of the critical items for Oracle RAC environments, including the ability to monitor and trace the Oracle RAC Clusterware (CRS) stack and Oracle 11g RAC interconnect operations for the Interprocess Communications usage. You must be logged into SQL*PLUS as SYSDBA to use Oradebug. The Oradebug help command will display its functions and general commands in the window within SQL*Plus, in Oracle 11g Release 1 (11.1) on the Red Hat Enterprise Linux platform, as shown next:

```
SQL> oradebug help
HELP            [command]                  Describe one or all commands
SETMYPID                                   Debug current process
SETOSPID        <ospid>                    Set OS pid of process to debug
SETORAPID       <orapid> ['force']         Set Oracle pid of process to
debug
SETORAPNAME     <orapname>                 Set Oracle process name to debug
SHORT_STACK                                Get abridged OS stack
CURRENT_SQL                                Get current SQL
DUMP            <dump_name> <lvl> [addr]   Invoke named dump
DUMPSGA         [bytes]                    Dump fixed SGA
DUMPLIST                                   Print a list of available dumps
EVENT           <text>                     Set trace event in process
SESSION_EVENT   <text>                     Set trace event in session
DUMPVAR         <p|s|uga> <name> [level]   Print/dump a fixed PGA/SGA/UGA
variableDUMPTYPE        <address> <type> <count>  Print/dump an address
with type info
SETVAR          <p|s|uga> <name> <value>   Modify a fixed PGA/SGA/UGA
variable
```

```
PEEK            <addr> <len> [level]       Print/Dump memory
POKE            <addr> <len> <value>       Modify memory
WAKEUP          <orapid>                   Wake up Oracle process
SUSPEND                                    Suspend execution
RESUME                                     Resume execution
FLUSH                                      Flush pending writes to trace
file
CLOSE_TRACE                                Close trace file
TRACEFILE_NAME                             Get name of trace file
LKDEBUG                                    Invoke global enqueue service
debugger
NSDBX                                      Invoke CGS name-service debugger
-G              <Inst-List | def | all>    Parallel oradebug command prefix
-R              <Inst-List | def | all>    Parallel oradebug prefix (return
outputSETINST        <instance# .. | all>       Set instance list in
double quotes
SGATOFILE       <SGA dump dir>          Dump SGA to file; dirname in double
quotesDMPCOWSGA      <SGA dump dir> Dump & map SGA as COW; dirname in
double quotes
MAPCOWSGA       <SGA dump dir>          Map SGA as COW; dirname in double
quotes
HANGANALYZE     [level] [syslevel]         Analyze system hang
FFBEGIN                                    Flash Freeze the Instance
FFDEREGISTER                               FF deregister instance from
cluster
FFTERMINST                                 Call exit and terminate instance
FFRESUMEINST                               Resume the flash frozen instance
FFSTATUS                                   Flash freeze status of instance
SKDSTTPCS       <ifname>  <ofname>         Helps translate PCs to names
WATCH           <address> <len> <self|exist|all|target>  Watch a region of
memoryDELETE         <local|global|target> watchpoint <id>    Delete a
watchpoint
SHOW            <local|global|target> watchpoints        Show  watchpoints
DIRECT_ACCESS   <set/enable/disable command | select query> Fixed table
access
CORE                                       Dump core without crashing
process
IPC                                        Dump ipc information
UNLIMIT                                    Unlimit the size of the trace
file
```

```
PROCSTAT                                  Dump process statistics
CALL          [-t count] <func> [arg1]...[argn]  Invoke function with
argumentsSQL>
```

In order to trace the interconnect events with Oracle RAC, you will need to issue the `oradebug ipc` command.

The following example will show you how to use Oradebug to trace the interconnect and IPC activities.

```
[oracle@raclinux1 ~]$ sqlplus "/as sysdba"
SQL*Plus: Release 11.1.0.7.0 - Production on Fri Aug 15 21:43:46 2008
Connected to:
Oracle Database 11g Enterprise Edition Release 11.1.0.7.0 - Production
With the Partitioning, Real Application Clusters, Oracle Label Security,
OLAP
and Data Mining Scoring Engine options
SQL> oradebug setmypid                              First we need to
set the process id to trace
Statement processed.
SQL> oradebug unlimit
Statement processed.
SQL> oradebug ipc
Then we set trace option for IPC memory
Information written to trace file.
SQL> oradebug tracefile_name Give the trace a name to identify the file
/u01/app/oracle/admin/RACDB/udump/racdb1_ora_6391.trc
SQL>

[oracle@raclinux1 ~]$ cd /u01/app/oracle/admin/RACDB/udump   change to
the user dump directory
[oracle@raclinux1 udump]$ view racdb1_ora_6391.trc  open the file to look
at contents of the trace
/u01/app/oracle/admin/RACDB/udump/racdb1_ora_6391.trc
Oracle Database 11g Enterprise Edition Release 11.1.0.7.0 - Production
With the Partitioning, Real Application Clusters, Oracle Label Security,
OLAP
and Data Mining Scoring Engine options
ORACLE_HOME = /u01/app/oracle/product/11.1.0/db_1
System name:    Linux
Node name:      raclinux1.us.oracle.com
```

```
Release:        2.6.9-5.EL
Version:        #1 Sun Jun 12 12:31:23 IDT 2005
Machine:        i686
Instance name: RACDB1
Redo thread mounted by this instance: 1
Oracle process number: 20
Unix process pid: 6391, image: oracle@raclinux1.us.oracle.com (TNS V1-V3)
shows us the process id for the trace
system cpu time since last wait 0 sec 0 ticks    gives us the amount of
CPU time that has occurred
locked 1
blocked 0
timed wait receives 0
admno 0x769fcb68 admport:
SSKGXPT 0xcc75e9c flags SSKGXPT_READPENDING     info for network 0
        socket no 7     IP 10.10.10.11  UDP 2247          Here we can
find the network configuration details
        sflags SSKGXPT_UP
        info for network 1
        socket no 0     IP 0.0.0.0      UDP 0
        sflags SSKGXPT_DOWN
        active 0        actcnt 1
context timestamp 0
        no ports
    sconno      accono   ertt  state   seq#   sent  async   sync rtrans
acks
```

The above output from the oradebug utility represents the network configuration details for the Oracle 11g RAC cluster obtained by the dump trace file

Using Oradebug to trace Oracle 11g Clusterware

We can use Oradebug to trace events for Oracle RAC Clusterware (CRS) by using the following command:

```
SQL> oradebug dump crs 3
```

We can also trace the behavior of the Oracle RAC Cluster Synchronization (CSS) operations with the following Oradebug command:

```
SQL> oradebug dump css 3
```

Traces can also be performed for the Oracle Cluster Registry (OCR), with Oracle RAC, with the help of the Oradebug command:

```
SQL> oradebug dump ocr 3
```

The output for oradebug is generated to a trace file under the trace file directory specified by the `USER_DUMP_DEST` database initialization parameter. You can use the oradebug `tracefile_name` command to display the trace file name and location linked to the current oradebug operation.

Server Control Utility

The **Server Control Utility (SRVCTL)** utility gives you the ability to manage RAC and ASM services. The following examples display the options available with this utility. A complete listing is available in Appendix A of the Oracle Real Application Clusters Administration and Deployment Guide 11g Release 2 (11.2) documentation, available online from either `http://tahiti.oracle.com` or `http://otn.oracle.com`.

As there are hundreds of `SRVCTL` commands explained in detail in the Oracle documentation, we will present only a few brief examples for Oracle 11g R2 RAC to illustrate how you can use this utility.

Oracle 11g R2 SRVCTL commands

The following SRVCTL commands are available only with Oracle 11g R2:

- `SRVCTL ADD EONS`: Adds an eONS daemon to the RAC Grid Infrastructure
- `SRVCTL ADD FILESYSTEM`: Adds a volume to Oracle ACFS (ASM Cluster Filesystem)

To manage Oracle ASM with Oracle Database 11g R2 (11.2), you need to use the SRVCTL binary in the Oracle Grid infrastructure home (`$GRID_HOME`) for a cluster. If you have Oracle RAC or Oracle Database installed, then you cannot use the SRVCTL binary in the database home (`$ORACLE_HOME`) to manage the Oracle 11g R2 ASM.

To manage Oracle ACFS on Oracle Database 11g R2 (11.2) installations, use the SRVCTL binary in the Oracle grid infrastructure home for a cluster (Grid home). If you have Oracle RAC or Oracle database installed, then you cannot use the SRVCTL binary in the database home to manage Oracle ACFS.

Managing Oracle Clusterware with the CRSCTL utility

CRSCTL commands function in tandem with the Oracle 11g RAC environment to provide tools to manage the operation of the Oracle 11g Clusterware.

While SRVCTL provides a more comprehensive suite of tools for managing all aspects of the Oracle RAC environment, the CRSCTL utility pertains only to the behavior of the Oracle Clusterware. A complete discussion of every `CRSCTL` command is beyond the scope of this book. We will instead highlight key usages of the tool. For a complete listing of the syntax and commands for `CRSCTL`, we recommend reading Appendix E of the Oracle Clusterware Administration and Deployment Guide 11g Release 2 (11.2) that provides a complete discussion of the CRSCTL utility.

If you wish to receive help when using `CRSTCTL`, you can issue the following command:

```
$ crsctl -help
```

If you want help for a specific command such as `start`, then enter the command and append `-help` at the end, as shown in the following example:

```
$ crsctl start -help
```

You can also use the abbreviations `-h` or `-?` instead of `-help`— this option functions in Linux, Unix, and Windows environments.

Differences between 11g R1 and 11g R2 syntax for CRSCTL

Oracle 11g R2 introduces clusterized commands that are operating system independent. They rely on the **Oracle High Availability Service Daemon** (OHASD). If the OHASD daemon is running, then you can perform remote operations such as starting, stopping, and checking the status of remote nodes.

In addition, the following CRSCTL commands are left over from earlier releases, and as such are deprecated and no longer used in 11g R2:

- `crs_stat`
- `crs_register`
- `crs_unregister`
- `crs_start`
- `crs_stop`
- `crs_getperm`

- `crs_profile`
- `crs_relocate`
- `crs_setperm`
- `crsctl check crsd`
- `crsctl check cssd`
- `crsctl check evmd`
- `crsctl debug log`
- `crsctl set css votedisk`
- `crsctl start resources`
- `crsctl stop resources`

You can use the `crsctl add resource` command to register a resource to be managed by Oracle Clusterware. A resource can be an application process, a database, a service, a Listener, and so on. We will look at an example of how to use the `crsctl` command:

```
$ crsctl check css
```

Use the `crsctl check css` command to check the status of Cluster Synchronization Services. This command is most often used when Oracle Automatic Storage Management (Oracle ASM) is installed on the local server.

CRS_STAT

For Oracle 11g R1 and earlier versions of Oracle RAC, the `CRS_STAT` utility provides you with the ability to monitor the condition of your Oracle RAC environment.

The utility is based on the script named `crs_stat.sh`.

For Oracle 11g R2:

- The `crs_stat` utility has been deprecated in 11g R2, so do not use it anymore. To find out all user resource state, use `$GRID_HOME/bin/crsctl stat res -t` script.
- By default, `ora.gsd` is offline if there is no 9i database in the cluster. `ora.oc4j` is OFFLINE in 11.2.0.1 as Database Workload Management (DBWLM) is unavailable.

In 11g R2, you can use the following command to find out the clusterware process state:

```
$GRID_HOME/bin/crsctl stat res -t -init
```

The kernel file OSM discovery tool

Oracle provides an undocumented command named the **kernel file OSM discovery (KFOD)** tool to monitor Oracle ASM (Automatic Storage Management) environments. To obtain a listing of the available options for this utility, at a Unix or Linux shell prompt, enter `kfod help=y` as follows:

```
[oracle@raclinux1 ~]$ kfod help=y
_asm_a/llow_only_raw_disks              KFOD allow only raw devices [_
asm_allow_only_raw_disks=TRUE/(FALSE)]
_asm_l/ibraries         ASM Libraries[_asm_libraries=lib1,lib2,...]
_asms/id                ASM Instance[_asmsid=sid]
a/sm_diskstring         ASM Diskstring [asm_diskstring=discoverystring,
discoverystring ...]
c/luster                KFOD cluster [cluster=TRUE/(FALSE)]
db/_unique_name         db_unique_name for ASM instance[db_unique_
name=dbname]
di/sks          Disks to discover [disks=raw,asm,all]
ds/cvgroup              Include group name [dscvgroup=TRUE/(FALSE)]
g/roup          Disks in diskgroup [group=diskgroup]
h/ostlist               hostlist[hostlist=host1,host2,...]
metadata_a/usize                AU Size for Metadata Size Calculation
metadata_c/lients               Client Count for Metadata Size
Calculation
metadata_d/isks         Disk Count for Metadata Size Calculation
metadata_n/odes         Node Count for Metadata Size Calculation
metadata_r/edundancy            Redundancy for Metadata Size Calculation
n/ohdr          KFOD header suppression [nohdr=TRUE/(FALSE)]
o/p             KFOD options type [OP=DISKS/CANDIDATES/MISSING/GROUPS/
INSTS/VERSION/CLIENTS/RM/RMVERS/DFLTDSTR/GPNPDSTR/METADATA/ALL]
p/file          ASM parameter file [pfile=parameterfile]
s/tatus         Include disk header status [status=TRUE/(FALSE)]
v/erbose                KFOD verbose errors [verbose=TRUE/(FALSE)]
KFOD-01000: USAGE: kfod op=<op> asm_diskstring=... | pfile=...
```

The KFOD utility also allows you to view the current Oracle ASM configuration by using the `kfod disk=all` command as shown in the following example:

```
oracle@raclinux1 ~]$ kfod disk=all
--------------------------------------------------------------------------
-------
 Disk          Size Path                                  User     Group
==========================================================================
=======
   1:       15358 Mb /dev/sdb1                          oracle   oinstall
   2:       15358 Mb /dev/sdc1                          oracle   oinstall
   3:       15358 Mb /dev/sdd1                          oracle   oinstall
   4:       40954 Mb /dev/sde1                          oracle   oinstall
--------------------------------------------------------------------------
-------
ORACLE_SID ORACLE_HOME
==========================================================================
=======
     +ASM1 /u01/app/11.2.0/grid
```

To view the disk groups in your Oracle 11g ASM configuration, you can issue the `kfod op=groups` command as shown here:

```
[oracle@raclinux1 ~]$ kfod op=groups
--------------------------------------------------------------------------
-------
Group          Size
==========================================================================
=======
   1:       40954 Mb       30440 Mb      EXTERN FLASH
   2:       46074 Mb       42080 Mb      NORMAL DATA
[oracle@raclinux1 ~]$
```

In case of Oracle 11g, you can examine the instance configuration for Oracle RAC and ASM by using the `kfod op=inst` command.

```
[oracle@raclinux1 ~]$ kfod op=insts
--------------------------------------------------------------------------
-------
ORACLE_SID ORACLE_HOME
==========================================================================
=======
```

```
     +ASM1 /u01/app/11.2.0/grid
[oracle@raclinux1 ~]$
[oracle@raclinux1 ~]$ kfod op=version
---------------------------------------------------------------------------
-------
ORACLE_SID RAC VERSION
===========================================================================
=======
     +ASM1 YES 11.2.0.1.0
```

The KFOD command may also be used to display a list of current Oracle RAC and ASM instances by using the `kfod op=clients` command.

```
[oracle@raclinux1 ~]$ kfod op=clients
---------------------------------------------------------------------------
-------
ORACLE_SID VERSION
===========================================================================
=======
   RACDB_1 11.2.0.1.0
     +ASM1 11.2.0.1.0
     +ASM1 11.2.0.1.0
   RACDB_1 11.2.0.1.0
```

Another useful function with the KFOD utility is to monitor the Oracle RAC configuration, during a rolling migration procedure, with the help of the `kfod op=rm` command.

```
[oracle@raclinux1 ~]$ kfod op=rm
---------------------------------------------------------------------------
-------
Rolling Migration State
===========================================================================
=======
Inactive
```

Once the rolling migration and upgrade is complete, you can use the `kfod op=rmvers` command to verify that it has completed successfully and that the versions have been upgraded to the new release.

```
[oracle@raclinux1 ~]$ kfod op=rmvers
----------------------------------------------------------------------
-------
Rolling Migration Compatible Versions
======================================================================
=======
11.1.0.6.0
11.1.0.7.0
[oracle@raclinux1 ~]$
```

As you can see, the `kfod` utility is a powerful tool to keep in your suite of Oracle RAC and ASM toolkit!

Operating system-level commands for tuning and diagnosis

While the previous Oracle database commands prove useful for managing and troubleshooting Oracle RAC and Oracle Clusterware issues, there is a critical need to use operating system commands with the Linux and Unix environment to diagnose and tune difficult issues that may arise in the Oracle RAC ecosystem. We will now provide you with some useful details on tools that can benefit you in these situations.

Strace

Linux provides a useful tracing tool for system calls that can be used for diagnosis and debugging issues with Oracle 11g RAC environments. As DBAs, we often have problems with our database environments when a runaway Oracle database process causes a performance problem in consuming excessive memory from the operating system. By understanding how to use a trace tool, such as strace for your Linux environment, you can pinpoint the root cause of such a problem and find a solution to the failure more effectively.

To display the options for strace, enter the strace at a Linux or Unix shell prompt session as follows:

```
[oracle@raclinux1 ~]$ strace
usage: strace [-dffhiqrtttTvVxx] [-a column] [-e expr] ... [-o file]
              [-p pid] ... [-s strsize] [-u username] [-E var=val] ...
              [command [arg ...]]
   or: strace -c [-e expr] ... [-O overhead] [-S sortby] [-E var=val] ...
              [command [arg ...]]
-c -- count time, calls, and errors for each syscall and report summary
-f -- follow forks, -ff -- with output into separate files
-F -- attempt to follow vforks, -h -- print help message
-i -- print instruction pointer at time of syscall
-q -- suppress messages about attaching, detaching, etc.
-r -- print relative timestamp, -t -- absolute timestamp, -tt -- with
usecs
-T -- print time spent in each syscall, -V -- print version
-v -- verbose mode: print unabbreviated argv, stat, termio[s], etc. args
-x -- print non-ascii strings in hex, -xx -- print all strings in hex
-a column -- alignment COLUMN for printing syscall results (default 40)
-e expr -- a qualifying expression: option=[!]all or option=[!]
val1[,val2]...
   options: trace, abbrev, verbose, raw, signal, read, or write
-o file -- send trace output to FILE instead of stderr
-O overhead -- set overhead for tracing syscalls to OVERHEAD usecs
-p pid -- trace process with process id PID, may be repeated
-s strsize -- limit length of print strings to STRSIZE chars (default 32)
-S sortby -- sort syscall counts by: time, calls, name, nothing (default
time)
-u username -- run command as username handling setuid and/or setgid
-E var=val -- put var=val in the environment for command
-E var -- remove var from the environment for command
[oracle@raclinux1 ~]$
```

Now, let's take a look at how to use STRACE to trace an Oracle 11g RAC process:

```
[oracle@raclinux1 ~]$ strace oracle
execve("/u01/app/oracle/product/11.1.0/11g/bin/oracle", ["oracle"], [/*
41 vars */]) = 0
uname({sys="Linux", node="raclinux1.us.oracle.com", ...}) = 0
brk(0)                                  = 0xf56b000
```

```
access("/etc/ld.so.preload", R_OK)      = -1 ENOENT (No such file or
directory)
open("/u01/app/oracle/product/11.1.0/11g/lib/tls/i686/sse2/libskg
```

We can also use STRACE to examine system calls for an Oracle 11g database instance, in an Oracle 11g RAC environment, using the following example:

```
[oracle@raclinux1 bin]$ strace -c oracle
% time     seconds  usecs/call     calls    errors syscall
------ ----------- ----------- --------- --------- ----------------
  4.19    0.865232       41202        21           write
  4.02    0.831352      207838         4           lstat64
  4.02    0.831329      207832         4           _llseek
  4.02    0.831327      207832         4           times
  3.42    0.707903      707903         1           io_setup
  3.42    0.707867      707867         1           _sysctl
  3.42    0.707864      707864         1           socket
  3.42    0.707843      707843         1           bind
  3.42    0.707839      707839         1           set_thread_area
  3.42    0.707837      707837         1           futex
  3.42    0.707836      707836         1           dup
  3.42    0.707836      707836         1           set_tid_address
  3.42    0.707835      707835         1           gettid
  3.42    0.707833      707833         1           fcntl64
  3.42    0.707831      707831         1           getuid32
  3.42    0.707831      707831         1           geteuid32
  3.21    0.662962       82870         8           mprotect
  3.21    0.662671       82834         8           gettimeofday
  2.77    0.572299       26014        22           fstat64
  2.71    0.560835       12192        46           old_mmap
  2.66    0.549201      109840         5           shmdt
  2.61    0.539206      107841         5           shmat
  2.61    0.539194      107839         5         5 access
  2.61    0.539158      107832         5           rt_sigprocmask
  2.46    0.509131        2204       231           close
  2.39    0.494136       41178        12         9 shmget
  2.01    0.415677      207839         2           uname
  1.57    0.325381       20336        16        16 mkdir
```

```
  1.30    0.268287        5708         47        17 stat64
  1.27    0.263489         909        290        61 open
  1.19    0.246993       41166          6           getrlimit
  1.19    0.246990       41165          6           rt_sigaction
  0.87    0.179247        2938         61           read
  0.60    0.123500       41167          3           brk
  0.60    0.123500       41167          3           setrlimit
  0.60    0.123494       41165          3           lseek
  2.70   -1.1557161       2786        200            mmap2
  1.52   -1.1313491       2986        105            munmap
------ ----------- ----------- --------- --------- ---------------
100.00   20.669398                   1134       108 total
```

Truss

Truss is a useful utility available for the Sun Solaris Unix operating system that can be used for tracing Oracle 11g background processes.

Truss provides the ability to walk through trace, step by step, for Oracle 11g internal processes, by using the `-p` parameter to the `truss` command, followed by the Solaris process id (PID). You can also trace child processes for Oracle background processes by using the `truss` command with the `-f` parameter. The parameters available for the truss command are listed next:

```
truss [-fcaeil] [-[tvx] [!]syscall...] [-s [!]signal...] [-m [!]fault...]
[-[rw] [!]fd...] [-o outfile] command | -p pid
```

Some typical options for truss are as follows:

- `-o`: output to file
- `-f`: trace child processes
- `-c`: count system calls
- `-p`: trace calls based on Unix PID

Now, let's take a look at how to trace the Oracle 11g database instance process by using the truss utility with Solaris:

```
solaris06$ truss -cp 7612
^C
Syscall           seconds           calls           errors
read                 .900              55
```

```
Write               .500              1
times               .100             93
yield               .500            426
```

GDB

GDB is a system debugger available for the Linux platform that can be used to discover problems with Oracle system processes. The man page available in Unix and Linux platforms for GDB will provide you with all of the command-line syntax options. To display the syntax for GDB, enter the `man GDB` command at a Unix or Linux shell prompt. Further details on GDB are also available online at `http://linux.die.net/man/1/gdb`.

GDB provides you with the ability to trace system memory usage for background processes, as well as the ability to dump memory values for these background processes. This is useful in troubleshooting difficult problems, such as when a memory leak occurs with an Oracle 11g database process. Before you can use the GDB utility to trace the Oracle 11g database instance process, you will first need to determine the specific Process ID (PID) in Linux by using the `ps` and `grep` Linux/Unix operating system commands. In the following example, we will use GDB to trace an open SQL*PLUS session within the Linux operating system.

After finding the process id (4107) for the SQL*PLUS session, we can begin the debug session with GDB:

```
[oracle@raclinux1 ~]$ gdb $ORACLE_HOME/bin/oracle 4107 start the new
session for GDB

GNU gdb Red Hat Linux (6.1post-1.20040607.62rh)

Copyright 2004 Free Software Foundation, Inc.

GDB is free software, covered by the GNU General Public License, and you
are

welcome to change it and/or distribute copies of it under certain
conditions.

Type "show copying" to see the conditions.

There is absolutely no warranty for GDB.  Type "show warranty" for
details.

This GDB was configured as "i386-redhat-linux-gnu"...(no debugging
symbols found)...Using host libthread_db library "/lib/tls/libthread_
db.so.1".


Attaching to program:   /u01/app/oracle/product/11.1.0/11g/bin/oracle,
process 4107   The GDB dump starts by attaching to the PID we gave it
earlier
```

```
Reading symbols from /u01/app/oracle/product/11.1.0/11g/lib/libskgxp11.
so...(no debugging symbols found)...done.
Loaded symbols for /u01/app/oracle/product/11.1.0/11g/lib/libskgxp11.so
Reading symbols from /lib/tls/librt.so.1...(no debugging symbols
found)...done.
Loaded symbols for /lib/tls/librt.so.1  GDB loads the shared libraries
for Oracle to perform the memory dump trace
Reading symbols from /u01/app/oracle/product/11.1.0/11g/lib/libnnz11.
so...(no debugging symbols found)...done.
Loaded symbols for /u01/app/oracle/product/11.1.0/11g/lib/libnnz11.so
Reading symbols from /u01/app/oracle/product/11.1.0/11g/lib/libclsra11.
so...done.
Loaded symbols for /u01/app/oracle/product/11.1.0/11g/lib/libclsra11.so
Reading symbols from /u01/app/oracle/product/11.1.0/11g/lib/libdbcfg11.
so...done.
Loaded symbols for /u01/app/oracle/product/11.1.0/11g/lib/libdbcfg11.so
Reading symbols from /u01/app/oracle/product/11.1.0/11g/lib/libhasgen11.
so...done.
Loaded symbols for /u01/app/oracle/product/11.1.0/11g/lib/libhasgen11.so
Reading symbols from /u01/app/oracle/product/11.1.0/11g/lib/libskgxn2.
so...done.Loaded symbols for /u01/app/oracle/product/11.1.0/11g/lib/
libskgxn2.so
Reading symbols from /u01/app/oracle/product/11.1.0/11g/lib/libocr11.
so...done.
Loaded symbols for /u01/app/oracle/product/11.1.0/11g/lib/libocr11.so
Reading symbols from /u01/app/oracle/product/11.1.0/11g/lib/libocrb11.
so...done.Loaded symbols for /u01/app/oracle/product/11.1.0/11g/lib/
libocrb11.so
Reading symbols from /u01/app/oracle/product/11.1.0/11g/lib/libocrutl11.
so...done.
Loaded symbols for /u01/app/oracle/product/11.1.0/11g/lib/libocrutl11.so
Reading symbols from /usr/lib/libaio.so.1...done.
Loaded symbols for /usr/lib/libaio.so.1
Reading symbols from /lib/libdl.so.2...done.
Loaded symbols for /lib/libdl.so.2
Reading symbols from /lib/tls/libm.so.6...done.
Loaded symbols for /lib/tls/libm.so.6
Reading symbols from /lib/tls/libpthread.so.0...done.

(gdb) stepi we use the STEPI command for GDB to walk the dump through the
memory
[Switching to Thread -1208035648 (LWP 4107)]
0x0090a7a2 in _dl_sysinfo_int80 () from /lib/ld-linux.so.2
```

```
(gdb) call ksudss(10)   We issue the CALL command to move through the
memory stack

$1 = 0

(gdb) detach   we use the detach command for GDB to end our memory
tracing session

Detaching from program: /u01/app/oracle/product/11.1.0/11g/bin/oracle,
process 4107
```

The next step is to attach the Oracle process id (PID) 4107 found earlier to the GDB debugger. Before we can make use of the GDB functions, we must first use the GDB attach command to link the debugger to the Oracle process that will be traced. This will enable us to drill down further into the tracing for Oracle 11g by using the attach command with GDB, as well as show the memory dump information:

```
(gdb) attach 4107  we start a new memory dump trace by using the attach
command for GDB

Attaching to program: /u01/app/oracle/product/11.1.0/11g/bin/oracle,
process 4107

[New Thread -1208035648 (LWP 4107)]

Symbols already loaded for /u01/app/oracle/product/11.1.0/11g/lib/
libskgxp11.so

Symbols already loaded for /lib/tls/librt.so.1

Symbols already loaded for /u01/app/oracle/product/11.1.0/11g/lib/
libnnz11.so

Symbols already loaded for /u01/app/oracle/product/11.1.0/11g/lib/
libclsra11.so

Symbols already loaded for /u01/app/oracle/product/11.1.0/11g/lib/
libdbcfg11.so

Symbols already loaded for /u01/app/oracle/product/11.1.0/11g/
lib/libhasgen11.soSymbols already loaded for /u01/app/oracle/
product/11.1.0/11g/lib/libskgxn2.so

Symbols already loaded for /u01/app/oracle/product/11.1.0/11g/lib/
libocr11.so

Symbols already loaded for /u01/app/oracle/product/11.1.0/11g/lib/
libocrb11.so

Symbols already loaded for /u01/app/oracle/product/11.1.0/11g/lib/
libocrutl11.soSymbols already loaded for /usr/lib/libaio.so.1

Symbols already loaded for /lib/libdl.so.2

Symbols already loaded for /lib/tls/libm.so.6

Symbols already loaded for /lib/tls/libpthread.so.0

Symbols already loaded for /lib/libnsl.so.1
```

```
Symbols already loaded for /lib/tls/libc.so.6
Symbols already loaded for /lib/ld-linux.so.2
Symbols already loaded for /usr/lib/libnuma.so
Symbols already loaded for /lib/libnss_files.so.2
Symbols already loaded for /u01/app/oracle/product/11.1.0/11g/lib/
libnque11.so
[Switching to Thread -1208035648 (LWP 3107)]
0x0090a7a2 in _dl_sysinfo_int80 () from /lib/ld-linux.so.2
```

Now, to get the stack dump, we will need to issue the `bt` command for our GDB session:

```
(gdb) bt We issue the BT command for GDB to obtain a listing of the
memory stack dump
#0  0x0090a7a2 in _dl_sysinfo_int80 () from /lib/ld-linux.so.2
#1  0x003d14c3 in __read_nocancel () from /lib/tls/libpthread.so.0
#2  0x0e5b652e in sntpread ()
#3  0x0e5b64cf in ntpfprd ()
#4  0x0e59b3c7 in nsbasic_brc ()
#5  0x0e59e20e in nsbrecv ()
#6  0x0e5a2d20 in nioqrc ()
#7  0x0e39da65 in __PGOSF20_opikndf2 ()
```

Additional references and tips

To aid you in your quest to master the challenges of supporting the Oracle RAC ecosystem, the following My Oracle Support Notes will benefit you:

Topic	Oracle notes to refer to
What you need to know	My Oracle Support (formerly Metalink) note 1053147.1
How to troubleshoot grid infrastructure startup issues	My Oracle Support (formerly Metalink) note 1050908.1
Troubleshooting 11.2 grid infrastructure installation Root.sh issues	My Oracle Support (formerly Metalink) note 1053970.1
Troubleshooting 11.2 Clusterware node evictions (reboots)	My Oracle Support (formerly Metalink) note 1050693.1

Clusterware startup sequence for Oracle 11g R2

Understanding how the clusterware startup occurs is critical to the diagnosis and resolution of Oracle RAC problems.

In Unix and Linux operating systems, there is a master daemon process named `INIT` that functions to start up additional system background processes. The `INIT` process first spawns the `init.ohasd` process, which in turn starts up the **Oracle High Availability Services Daemon** (**OHASD**). In turn, the OHASD daemon then spawns additional Clusterware processes at each startup level as shown next:

- **Level 1—OHASD spawns**:
    - `Cssdagent`: Agent responsible for spawning CSSD
    - `Orarootagent`: Agent responsible for managing all root-owned ohasd resources
    - `Oraagent`: Agent responsible for managing all Oracle-owned ohasd resources
    - `cssdmonitor`: Monitors CSSD and node health (along wth the cssdagent)
- **Level 2—OHASD rootagent spawns**:
    - Cluster Ready Services Daemon (CRSD)—primary daemon responsible for managing cluster resources
    - Cluster Time Synchronization Services Daemon (CTSSD)
    - Diskmon—provides disk monitoring services
    - ASM Cluster File System (ACFS) Drivers

During the second level of startup for Clusterware, the oraagent spawns the following Clusterware processes for 11g R2:

- **MDNSD**: Used for DNS lookup
- **GIPCD**: Used for inter-process and inter-node communication
- **GPNPD**: Grid Plug and Play Profile Daemon
- **EVMD**: Event Monitor Daemon
- **ASM**: Resource for monitoring ASM instances

- **Level 3—CRSD spawns**:
    - `orarootagent`: Agent responsible for managing all root-owned CRSD resources
    - `oraagent`: Agent responsible for managing all Oracle-owned CRSD resources
- **Level 4—CRSD rootagent spawns**:
    - Network resource: To monitor the public network
    - SCAN VIP(s): Single Client Access Name Virtual IPs
    - Node VIPs: One per node
    - ACFS Registery: For mounting ASM Cluster File system
    - GNS VIP (optional): VIP for GNS

During this phase for Clusterware startup with 11g R2, the `oraagent` spawns the following processes:

- **ASM Resouce**: ASM Instance(s) resource
- **Diskgroup**: Used for managing/monitoring ASM diskgroups
- **DB Resource**: Used for monitoring and managing the DB and instances
- **SCAN Listener**: Listener for single client access name, listening on SCAN VIP
- **Listener**: Node listener listening on the Node VIP
- **Services**: Used for monitoring and managing services
- **ONS**: Oracle Notification Service
- **eONS**: Enhanced Oracle Notification Service
- **GSD**: For 9i backward compatibility
- **GNS (optional)**: It is a grid naming service that performs name resolution

Log file locations for Oracle 11g RAC and ASM

The important Clusterware daemon logs are located under the `<GRID_HOME>/log/<nodename>` directory. There are additional logfiles located under the `<GRID_HOME>/log/<nodename>`directory as listed next:

```
alert<NODENAME>.log - look here first for most clusterware issues
./admin:
./agent:
```

```
./agent/crsd:
./agent/crsd/oraagent_oracle:
./agent/crsd/ora_oc4j_type_oracle:
./agent/crsd/orarootagent_root:
./agent/ohasd:
./agent/ohasd/oraagent_oracle:
./agent/ohasd/oracssdagent_root:
./agent/ohasd/oracssdmonitor_root:
./agent/ohasd/orarootagent_root:
./client:
./crsd:
./cssd:
./ctssd:
./diskmon:
./evmd:
./gipcd:
./gnsd:
./gpnpd:
./mdnsd:
./ohasd:
./racg:
./racg/racgeut:
./racg/racgevtf:
./racg/racgmain:
./srvm:
```

The cleanup of these logfiles can be automated with a shell script that can be scheduled to run from the cron facility. The `cfgtoollogs` directory located under the `$GRID_HOME` and `$ORACLE_BASE` directories contains other important logfiles such as the `rootcrs.pl script` and configuration assistants, such as the **ASM Configuration Assistant (ASMCA)**.

ASM logs are located under `$ORACLE_BASE/diag/asm/+asm/<ASM Instance Name>/trace`.

Oracle provides a useful script named `diagcollection.pl`, which can be found under the `<GRID_HOME>/bin` directory. This script, when executed, will automatically collect important Oracle 11g Clusterware files that can be sent to Oracle support engineers for analysis. You must be logged into Linux as the root user in order to run this script.

Index

Symbols

$ORACLE_HOME/appsutil/scripts/adautocfg.sh command
about 424
init file activities, performing 424, 426
listener activities, performing 424, 426
tnsnames file activities, performing 424, 426
$ORACLE_HOME/bin location
data pump (expdp) utility 274
export (exp) utility 274
-9 <ospidforPMON> command> 284
-deconfig option 111
-fixup flag 71
-force flag 353
-help parameter 193
-h option 430
-lastnode flag 111, 353
-manual option 293
-oldcrshome flag 353
-version flag 353
11g RAC interconnect
choices, selecting 33
ethernet choices 32
(G)V$CLUSTER_INTERCONNECTS
querying 315, 316
(g)v$sysstat view 311
parameter
apply_captured 448
GLOBAL_NAME 447
queue_to_queue 445
% parameter 453
/proc/cpuinfo command 30
./asmca command 138
./crs_stat -t -v command output 417
./runInstaller command 89, 92

A

ACFS
about 152
advantages 153
creating, prerequisites 154
Oracle ACFS drivers 153
shutdown 126
snapshots 164
using, as Oracle database home 153
ACFS, creating
ASMCMD, using 159, 160
filesystem, ASMCA used 154-157
for Oracle Binaries, ASMCA used 158
ACFS mount registry
about 161
Acfsutil utility 161
background processes, for ACFS 163
managing 161
V$ASM views, querying 164
Acfsutil utility 161
ACMS 54
Active Session History. *See* **ASH**
adapcctl.sh start command 405
adapcctl.sh status command 406
adbldxml utility 422
adchkcfg utility
Check Config utility 502
additional configuration for Apply database
GLOBAL_NAME of target database, changing 448
additional configuration for source database
GLOBAL_NAME parameter, changing 447
propagation restart 446, 447

Queue ownership 445, 446
addNode.sh script 360-363
ADR
about 251
managing, ADRCI used 252
structure 251
adrci utility 462
ADRCI 252
Advanced Compression Option (ACO) 277
Advanced Queuing. *See* **AQ**
ADVM
about 137, 145
ASM volumes, creating 146
characteristics 145, 146
volume trivial 145, 146
ADVM functionality
oracleacfs (oracleacfs.ko) 153
oracleavdm (oracleavdm.ko) 153
oracleoks (oracleoks.ko) 153
Allocation Units (AU) 136
ALTER SYSTEM command 249
AMM
/dev/shm file system 247, 248
about 235, 244
tuning 246
using, on Linux 247
V$ views 245
AMM V$ views
about 245, 246
V$MEMORY_CURRENT_RESIZE_OPS 245
V$MEMORY_DYNAMIC_COMPONENTS 245
V$MEMORY_RESIZE_OPS 245
V$MEMRY_TARGET_ADVICE 245
applications environment, for Oracle RAC
establishing 426, 427
Applications Management Pack (AMP) 432
Application tier, EBS architecture
availability, configuring 398
components 396
EBS Release 12 Rapid Install Version 397
for EBS 12.1.3 396
Oracle HTTP Server (OHS) 396
Oracle MAA architecture, implementing 398
apply_captured parameter 448
appsutil.zip file 419
AQ 18, 438
architecture, EBS
about 396-399
Application tier 396
Client tier 396
Database tier 397
architecture, RMAN
diagram 273
Media Manager Layer (MML) 272
performance tuning, tips 273
ARCHIVELOG mode 287
Archiving mode 234
ASH 312
ASM
about 53, 113
backup strategy 171
disk 116
dynamic views 122
filesystem, versus storage architecture 115
IDP 169
initialization parameters 119
instance configuration 118
log file location 501, 502
overview 114
volumes, creating in ADVM 146
volumes, creating with ALTER DISKGROUP SQL statement 150, 151
volumes, creating with ASMCA 146-148
volumes, creating with ASMCMD 148, 150
ASM 11g R1
features 133
ASM 11g R2
features 137
ASMCA
about 137, 224
ASM disk group, creating 143, 144
ASM disk group, creating in silent mode 144
ASM disk group, managing 142
ASM instance, managing 140
initiating 137
new ASM instance, configuring 138, 139, 140
ASMCMD
enhancements 170
managing 130
overview 130

using 131, 132
asmcmd command 170
asmcmd -p at a command 170
ASM disk group
administration 126-129
altering 128, 129
creating 127, 128
creating, in ASMCA 143, 144
creating, in silent mode 144
dropping 129
managing, in ASMCA 142
asm_diskgroups parameter 119
asm_diskstring parameter 119
ASM cluster File System *See* **ACFS**
ASM features
Oracle 11g R1 ASM 58, 59
Oracle 11g R2 ASM 59
ASM instance
about 118
background processes 122
creating 120
DBCA, initializing 120, 121
managing, in ASMCA 140, 141
shutdown 125
startup 126
asm_power_limit parameter 119
ASM volumes, creating
V$ASM views, querying 151
with ALTER DISKGROUP SQL statement 150
with ASMCA 146-148
with ASMCMD 149
with ASMCMD, options 150
Atomic Controlfile to Memory Service. *See* **ACMS**
AutoConfig, running
completion steps, preparing for 422, 423
configuration files, applying 423, 424
configuration files, generating 423, 424
database context file, generating 422
executing, on database nodes 424
RDBMS ORACLE_HOME filesystem, updating 419-422
AutoConfig utility 408
Automatic Block Recovery (ABR) 280
Automatic Diagnostic Repository. *See* **ADR**
Automatic Diagnostic Repository Command Interface tool. *See* **ADRCI**
Automatic Memory Management. *See* **AMM**
Automatic Storage Management. *See* **ASM**
Automatic Storage Management Configuration. *See* **ASMCA**
Automatic Workload Management
components 255
services 255
Automatic Workload Repository. *See* **AWR**
Auto Port Aggregation. *See* **APA**
AWR 255

B

background processes, ASM instance
about 122
ASMB 122
GMON 122
PZ9n 122
RBAL 122
background processes, for ACFS
ACFS Background process 163
VBGn 163
VDBG 163
VMB0 164
background processes, Oracle 11g Clusterware
CRSD 180
CSSD 181
DISKMON 184
EVMD 181
OCLSKD 184
OCLSOMON 183
OCLSVMON 183
OCSSD 180
OPROCD 182
RACG 184
background process, Oracle 11g
ADR 251
alert.log file location, finding 250
DBRM 249
Diagnosability process (DIA0) 249
GTX0-j 250
SMCO 249
v$diag_info view 252
VKTM 250

backup
overview 270
types 274, 275
types, logical backup 274
types, physical backup 275
backup and recovery strategies, OCR
automatic backups 292
manual backups, performing 293
mirror location, adding 291
restoring 294
backup and recovery strategies, Voting disk
manual backup 294
mirror location, adding to 291
restoring 297
backup command 172
backup strategy, ASM
about 171
md_backup and md_restore commands 171, 172
BCP
about 12
DR 12
DRP 12
guidelines 14
High Availability 11
bonding 39
Business Continuity Planning. *See* **BCP**

C

Cache Fusion, Oracle RAC performance
GCS protocol 308
IPC protocol 308
physical private interconnects 308
check config utility 418
CLIENT_RESULT_CACHE_LAG parameter 305
CLIENT_RESULT_CACHE_SIZE parameter 305
cloning, EBS
load balancing, setting up on concurrent processing nodes 435
new node, adding to existing system 431, 432
patching and upgrading 429
PCP, setting up 433
principle 429
source system, copying 430
source system, preparing 430
standard cloning 429
steps 429
system scale up 429
system transformations 429
target system, configuring 431
Transaction Managers, setting up 434
CLSCFG 193, 195
cluster deconfig tool, Oracle RAC
using, in silent mode 473
cluster installation
Grid Infrastructure configuration, reconfiguring 111
Grid Infrastructure configuration, removing 110
Oracle 11g R1 72
Oracle 11g R2 91
pre-requisites 63
CLUSTER_INTERCONNECTS parameter 35, 36
Cluster Ready Services Daemon. *See* **CRSD**
Cluster Ready Services Statistics. *See* **CRS_STAT**
Cluster Synchonization Services Daemon. *See* **CSSD**
Cluster Time Synchronize Service. *See* **CTSS**
Cluster Verification Utility. *See* **CVU**
Clusterware
about 53
control files 178
Clusterware Config Tool. *See* **CLSCFG**
Clusterware Control utility. *See* **CRSCTL**
Clusterware startup sequence
CRSD rootagent spawns 501
CRSD spawns 501
diagrammatic representation 501
OHASD rootagent spawns 500
OHASD Spawns 500
Clusterware Verification Utility. *See* **CLUVFY**
CLUVFY
about 196, 197
using, for prerequisite verification 71
COMPATIBLE.ASM attribute 135

COMPATIBLE.ASM attribute 291, 296
COMPATIBLE.RDBMS attribute 135
connect_data parameter 426
control_file_record_keep_time parameter 271
Copy-On-Write. *See* COW
COW 164
CPU processors
dual core processors 29, 30
hardware architecture, choosing between 27-29
Itanium 26
Linux x86 26
Linux x86 64 26
Linux x86 64 (continued) 26
multicore processors 29, 30
Create ACFS Hosted Database Home screen 158
CRSCTL
about 185-187
11g R1 and 11g R2 syntax, differences 487-491
CRS_STAT 488
Oracle Clusterware, managing 487
CRSCTL CHECK CRS command 204
crsctl check css command 488
CRSCTL QUERY CSS VOTEDISK command 200
crsctl set <parameter> command 188
CRSD 180, 253, 500
crs_relocate cluster command 371
crs_relocate command 392
CRS_STAT 188, 190
crs_stat command 87
crs_stat -t cluster command 332
CSSD 181
CTSS 356
CVU 215

D

DAPL 32
data availability 11
Database Control 229
Database Replay
four-phase approach 301
Database Resource Management. *See* DBRM
Database Smart Flash Cache
about 248
configuring 248
configuring, db_cache_file_name used 249
configuring, db_cache_file_size used 249
Database Upgrade Configuration Assistant. *See* DBUA
data corruption
occuring, ways 270
Data Guard, new features
Active Data Guard 452
snapshot standby 452
Data Guard, Oracle 11g
basic configuration 451
Data Guard Physical Standby, configuring 452
design considerations, in Oracle RAC environment 453
new features 451
problems, troubleshooting 455
switchover consideration 454
Data Guard, Oracle 11g R2
new features 458
new features, for Redo Apply 458
new features, for SQL Apply 459
Data Guard, troubleshooting
corrupt data block, automatic repairing 457
standby corrupt block, recovering from 457
standby corrupt datafile, recovering from 455, 456
Switchover failure 455
Data Manipulation Language. *See* DML
Data Mirror Replication. *See* DMR
db block size 236
DBCA 222
DBMS_SERVICE PL/SQL package
about 259, 260
internal default services 261
performance views 261
service characteristics 261, 262
DBUA 332, 352
dd command 202
Decision Support Systems. *See* DSS
design considerations, in Oracle RAC environment
archived redo log filenames, format 453, 454

df -h command 160
Dirty Region Logging. *See* **DRL**
Disaster Recovery. *See* **DR**
Disaster Recovery Planning. *See* **DRP**
diskmon.bin 184
DML 442
DMR 16
DR
about 12
guidelines 14
DRL 146
DROP DISKGROUP command 129
DRP 12
DSS 22
DUPLICATE DATABASE command, RMAN 278
dynamic views, ASM
about 122
V$ASM_CLIENT 125
V$ASM_DISK 123
V$ASM_DISKGROUP 124
V$ASM_DISKGROUP_STAT 124
V$ASM_DISK_STAT 124
V$ASM_OPERATION 124
Dynamic Volume Manager. *See* **ADVM**

E

EBS
about 395
architecture 396
cloning 429
implementing, in Oracle 11g RAC 407-409
EBS 12.1.1
installing 400
RAC, enabling 410
upgrading 408
EMC Replication Manager 432
enhancements, ASMCMD 170, 171
Enterprise Manager console 229
Enterprise Manager (EM) 276
Enterprise Resource Product. *See* **ERP**
ERP
about 395
Oracle E-Business Suite (EBS) 395
Event Monitor Daemon. *See* **EVMD**
EVMD 181
evmlogger 181
Execute Configuration scripts window 81

F

FAILOVER_MODE
DELAY parameter 266
METHOD parameter 266
RETRIES parameter 266
TYPE parameter 266
FAL_SERVER parameter 457
Fast Connection Failover. *See* **FCF**
FastConnectionFailoverEnabled property 267
fatal process, Oracle 11g Clusterware
OCSSD 184
OPROCD 184
fault tolerant system
characteristics, redundancy 16
characteristics, replication 16
High Availability 14, 15
implementing, requirements 15
FCF
about 267
configuring 267
configuring, in client environment 268
FCOW 164
features
faster backup compression 277
features, ASM 11g R1
disk group compatibility attributes 135
fast mirror resync 133
fast rebalance 135
performance enhancements 136
preferred mirror read 134
SYSASM role 136
features, ASM 11g R2
about 137
ACFS 152
ACFS mount registry 161
ACFS snapshots 164
ADVM 145
ASMCA 137
ASMCMD enhancements 170
ASM IDP 169
features, Oracle 11g performance tuning
Client Side Result Cache 305

Database Health Monitor 302
Database Replay 301
PL/SQL Native Compilation 303
Server Result Cache 304
SPA 302
SQL Tuning Advisor (STA) 306
features, RMAN 11g R1
active database duplication 278, 279
active database duplication, enhancements 279
Archivelog deletion policy, enhancements 280
Automatic Block Recovery (ABR) 280
Database Recovery Advisor (DRA) 276
multisection backups 276
Tablespace point-in-time recovery (TSPITR) 281
undo tablespace backup optimization 277
features, RMAN 11g R2. *See* **features, RMAN 11g R1**
Fibre Channel
about 47
Arbitrated Loop (AL) 47
generic channel-based ports 49
generic node ports 48
Point to Point topology (P2P) 47
ports 48
Switched Fabric (SW) 48
topology, selecting 48
Fibre Channel switch 47
filesystem, versus ASM storage architecture
diagram explanation 115
First Copy on Write. *See* **FCOW**
fixupdir flag 71
Flash Recovery Area (FRA) 412
FND_TRANSACTION. SYNCHRONOUS function 434

G

GCS 308
GDB command
about 496
debug session 496-499
General Purpose File System. *See* **GPFS**
generic channel-based ports, Fibre Channel
auto or auto-sensing ports 49
L_ports 49
U_ports 49
generic node ports, Fibre Channel
EX_port 49
NL_port 49
N_port 48
genksms command 27
Gigabit Ethernet
about 32
alternatives, Infiniband 32
GIPC 56
Global Cache Service. *See* **GCS**
Global Enqueue Service. *See* **GES**
GLOBAL_NAME parameter 447
Global Resource Directory. *See* **GRD**
Global Transaction Process. *See* **GTX0-j**
GNS 56, 350
GoldenGate 437
GPNDP *See* also **GPnP**
GPNDP 350
GPnP 56
GRD 54
Grid Control 229
Grid Infrastructure configuration
reconfiguring 111
removing 110
Grid Interprocess Communication. *See* **GIPC**
Grid Naming Service. *See* **GNS**
Grid Plug and Play. *See* **GPnP**
GTX0-j 54
GV$ges_statistics views 309

H

hardware architecture, Oracle 11g RAC
about 25
CPU processors 26
server configuration 26
HBA 15
help command 252
High Availability
BCP 11
concepts 7
fault tolerant system 14, 15
interpretations 9, 10

planned downtime 8
recovery time 10, 11
SLAs 8
system design 11
unplanned downtime 8
High Availability solutions, Oracle
about 17
Oracle 11g R1 RAC 19
Oracle 11g R2 RAC 19
Oracle Application Server Clustering 18
Oracle Data Guard 17
Oracle Streams 17
Host Bus Adapter. *See* **HBA**
hugemem kernel 29

I

IBM AIX LPAR disk volume management
about 44
feature 45
IDP, ASM
about 169
information, setting 169
settings, managing 169
ifconfig 215
ifconfig command 38
Ignore All option 107
Infiniband 32
initialization parameters, ASM
asm_diskgroups 119
asm_diskstring 119
asm_power_limit 119
instance_type 119
processes 119
In-Memory Parallel Execution
about 307
using 307
installation, EBS 12.1.1
components, screenshot 401
Configuration choice 403
Database Node Configuration 403
documentation, link 400
Global System setting 403
Node Information 404, 405
Oracle document E12842-03 Installation Guide 400
rapidwiz utility, using 405
Select Wizard Operation 402
steps 400-406
Validate System Configuration 404
instance adding, DBCA used
added RACDB2 instance, verifying 379
DBCA, using in silent mode 380
Instance Management screen 376
Instance Storage screen 378
List of cluster databases screen 376
List of cluster instances screen 377
new instance status, verifying 379
post-add instance steps 380
steps 374-378
Summary screen, reviewing 378
Instance Caging 249
instance_type parameter 119
Intelligent Data Placement. *See* **IDP, ASM**
internet choices, Oracle 11g RAC
Ethernet interconnects, network teaming 39
Ethernet interconnects, redundancy 33-38
Internet Small Computer System Interface. *See* **iSCSI**
iostat command 209
iSCSI 45

K

kernel file OSM discovery. *See* **KFOD**
kernel.shmall parameter 325
KFOD 489
kfod disk=all command 490
kfod op=clients command 491
kfod op=groups command 490
kfod op=inst command 490
kfod op=rm command 491
kfod op=rmvers command 492

L

LANs 50
latency statistics, Oracle RAC performance
about 309
CR block 309
current block 309
LCK0 Instance Enqueue Process 55
LCR 443
LGWR 308
LIP 46

LISTENER.ORA file
without virtual host name 462
with virtual host name 461
LMD Global Enqueue Service Daemon 54
LMON Global Enqueue Service Monitor 54
LMS Global Cache Service Process 54
load_balance parameter 427
load balancing
Client Side Connect Time Load Balance 263
Client Side Connect Time Load Balance, configuring 263
Server Side Listener Connection Load Balance 264
Server Side Listener Connection Load Balance, configuring 264
setting up 427
Local Area Networks. *See* **LANs**
LOG_ARCHIVE_CONFIG parameter 457
LOG_ARCHIVE_DEST_n parameter 453
LOG_ARCHIVE_FORMAT parameter 454
logical backup
about 274
benefits 274
Logical Change Record. *See* **LCR**
Logical Volume Group. *See* **LVG**
Loop Initialization Protocol. *See* **LIP**
LVG 115

M

make command 28
Maximum Availability Architecture. *See* **MAA**
MAA 398
Maximum Transmission Unit. *See* **MTU**
maxsize parameter 181
md_backup command 172
mDNS 56
md_restore command 172
Media Manager Layer (MML) 272
MEMORY_MAX_TARGET parameter 244
Memory Monitory Lite. *See* **MMNL**
MEMORY_TARGET parameter 244
MMNL 261
MOS 23
mount command 159
MTU 38
Multicast Domain Name Service. *See* **mDNS**
My Oracle Support. *See* **MOS**

N

NAS 299
National Institute of Standards and Technology. *See* **NIST**
netstat command 209, 215
network architecture, Oracle 11g RAC
private interconnect 31
private network 30
Network Attached Storage. *See* **NAS**
Network Configuration Assistant (./netca) tool 370
Network teaming 39
new node addition, to existing cluster
-silent option, using 363
about 356
addNode.sh script 360-363
ASM, installing 368
ASM software, cloning 369, 370
post-installation status checks 364-367
post-installation status checks, OCR file manual backup 368
post-installation status checks, voting disk backup 368
post-node addition steps 370
prechecks performing, cluvfy utility used 357-360
prerequisites 356
RDBMS, installing 368
stages, completing 356
NIST 14
node reboot issues, Oracle 11g RAC
about 206, 207
OCLSOMON 208
OPROCD 207
problem, OCLSOMON failure 211
problem, OCSSD failure 210
problem, OPROCD failure 211
root cause analysis, using 208
node, removing from cluster
steps 370-373

O

OCFS 217
OCI_RESULT_CACHE_MAX_SIZE parameter 306
OCI_RESULT_CAHCECACHE_MAX_RSET_ROWS parameter 306
OCI_RESULT_CAHCECACHE_MAX_RSET_SIZE parameter 306
oclskd.bin 184
oclsomon.bin 183
oclsvmon.bin 183
OCR
corrupted OCR 202
failed OCR 202
problems 200
recovering, from backup 202
OCRCHECK 190, 191
ocrcheck command 86, 101
OCRCONFIG 192, 193
ocrconfig command 203, 293
ocrconfig -manualbackup command 90
ocrconfig -showbackup command 202
ocrconfig utility 293
OCR recovery, from backup
about 202
log file, analyzing 205, 206
root cause analysis, using 205
status, checking 204
steps 203, 204
OCSSD 180
OEL 45
OHASD 500
oifcfg setif command 35
olsnodes command 101
olsnodes -n command 371
OLTP 22
OMotion feature, Oracle 11g R2 RAC 216
Online Transaction Processing. *See* **OLTP**
operating system commands
about 492
GDB 496
STRACE 492-495
truss 495
Oprocd 178
OPROCD
about 182, 207
key parameters 182
OPS 300, 308
Oracle
High Availability solutions 17
Oracle 10g R2 Clusterware
upgrading to Oracle 11g R1 324
Oracle 10g R2 Clusterware, upgrading to Oracle 11g R1 327
environment settings 325
kernel parameter values 325
Linux V5, required packages 326
post-upgrade steps 332
pre-installation checks performing, cluvfy used 327
runInstaller.sh script, executing 327-333
steps 326
Oracle 11g
Data Guard 451
background process 249
features 262
Oracle 11g Clusterware
background processes 180
fatal process 184
Oracle Cluster Registry 177
scripts, initializing 179
scripts, shutting down 179
troubleshooting 197
utilities, managing 185
voting disk 177
Oracle 11g Disk Group
compatibility features 60
Oracle 11g, features
FCF 267
Load Balancing 263
TAF 265
Oracle 11g R1
AMM 244
features 243
Oracle 11g R1 ASM
SYSASM privilege 58, 59
Oracle 11g R1 Clusterware installation
Oracle Universal Installer, initiating 73-82
requirements 72
Oracle 11g R1 RAC
about 19
background processes 54

Oracle 11g R1 RAC, background processes
ACMS Atomic Controlfile to Memory Service 54
GTX0-j 54
LCK0 Instance Enqueue Process 55
LMD Global Enqueue Service Daemon 54
LMON Global Enqueue Service Monitor 54
LMS Global Cache Service Process 54
RMSn Oracle RAC Management Processes 55
RSMN Remote Slave Monitor 55
Oracle 11g R1, upgrading to Oracle 11g R2
11g R2 Clusterware, post upgrade checks 349-351
11g R2 Clusterware, post upgrade steps 351
changes 334
environment, settings 333, 334
kernel parameter value 335
Linux 5, required packages 335
nodes 334
pre-installation checks performing, cluvfy used 336
restrictions 334
runInstaller.sh script, executing 337-349
steps 336
Oracle 11g R2
Clusterware startup sequence 500
Data Guard 458
Database Smart Flash Cache 248
Oracle 11g R2Instance Caging 249
performance tuning features 307
Oracle 11g R2 ASM
ASM features 59
OCR 59
Oracle ACFS 59
voting disk 59
Oracle 11g R2 Clusterware
features 215
Oracle 11g R2 Clusterware, features
capacity management 217
Cluster Verification Utility 218
improved resource modeling 216
Oracle Cluster Registry, with Oracle ASM 217
Oracle RAC one node 216
policy-based cluster 217
time synchronization service 217
upgrade option 218
voting disks, with Oracle ASM 217
zero downtime patching 218
Oracle 11g R2 Clusterware installation
about 91
features 109
initiating 92-98
Oracle Universal Installer, initiating 88, 89, 103-108
post installation checks 100, 101
post installation tasks 90, 108
RAC software, installing 102
requirements 91
root.sh is run, executing 99
software, installing 88
Oracle 11g R2 RAC
background processes 56
features 19
Oracle 11g R2 RAC, background processes
Grid Interprocess Communication (GIPC) 56
Grid Plug and Play (GPnP) 56
Oracle 11g R2 Streams, new features
automatic merging 450
automatic splitting 450
compressed tables support 450
jobs monitoring 451
new apply process parameter 450
SecureFile LOBs support 450
SQL generation 449
Statement DML Handlers 449
Streams View 451
table changes recording ability 449
XStream 449
Oracle 11g RAC
availability 399
EBS, implementing 407-409
Clusterware administration 175
components 53
hardware architecture 25
internet choices 33
log file location 501, 502
node reboot issue 206
Oracle Cluster Registry, architecture 56
scalability 399
single instance implementation, differentiating 57, 58

storage architecture 39
Oracle 11g RAC architecture
about 21, 22
certification matrix 23,-25
Oracle 11g RAC cluster
configuration 33
redundant clustered interconnects 34
Oracle 11g RAC, components
Oracle 11g R1 RAC, background processes 54
Oracle 11g R2 RAC, background processes 56
Oracle Cluster Registry 53
voting disk 53
Oracle 11g RAC, deploying with EBS 12.1.1
about 410
AutoConfig, running 418
configuration, prerequisites 410, 411
database migration to ASM and RAC, rconfig utility used 412-417
Oracle 11g single instance database
vs Oracle RAC 11g database 300
Oracle 11g Streams
new features 442
Oracle 11g Streams architecture, RAC
about 438
apply process 441
Capture function 438
capture process 441
consumption 439
default apply engine 440
explicit de-queue 440
Oracle Streams rules 440
propagation 439
staging 439
Streams 441, 442
transformation 440
user-defined function, applying 440
Oracle 11g Streams, new features
Combined Capture and Apply 443, 444
LCRs, tracking through Stream 443
Performance Advisor 443
Stream destination, merging 442
Stream destination, splitting 442
Streams Topology 443
synchronous capture 442
Oracle 11g Streams, RAC
about 438
diagrammatic architecture 438
Oracle ACFS 59
Oracle ADVM 19
Oracle Application Server Clustering
about 18
Application Server environment 18
Oracle ASM Dynamic Volume Manager. *See* **Oracle ADVM**
Oracle Automatic Storage Management Cluster File System. *See* **Oracle ACFS**
Oracle Cluster Filesystem. *See* **OCFS**
Oracle Cluster Health Monitor (IPD/OS)
URL 315
Oracle Cluster Registry
about 177
architecture 56, 57
shared storage subsystem, relationship 57
Oracle Cluster Registry Check Utility. *See* **OCRCHECK**
Oracle Cluster Registry Config Utility. *See* **OCRCONFIG**
Oracle Cluster Synchronization Services Daemon. *See* **OCSSD**
Oracle Clusterware
about 176
downgrading 352
upgrading 323
Oracle Clusterware Process Monitor Daemon. *See* **OPROCD**
Oracle Data Guard
about 7, 17
disaster recovery plan 17
OracleDataSource url property 267
Oracle E-Business Suite. *See* **EBS**
Oracle Enterprise Linux. *See* **OEL**
Oracle Grid Naming Service. *See* **GNS**
Oracle High Availability Services Daemon. *See* **OHASD**
ORACLE_HOME/appsutil/bin directory 422
Oracle Log Writer Process. *See* **LGWR**
Oracle Parallel Clusters. *See* **OPS**
Oracle Parallel Server. *See* **OPS**

Oracle Process Daemon. *See* **OPROCD**
Oracle RAC 11g database
vs Oracle 11g single instance database 300
Oracle RAC, commands
CRSCTL utility 487
CRS reinstallation on same cluster in another CRS_HOME directory 480, 481
issues tracing, Oradebug used 482
Oradebug 482
rootdeinstall.sh 480
roothas.pl tool 481
Server Control Utility 486
Oracle RAC performance
Cache Fusion impact, analyzing 308
latency statistics 309
optimizing 307
RAC wait events 310-314
Oracle Recommended Packages. *See* **RPM**
Oracle Recovery Manager (RMAN) 269
Oracle Streams
about 17, 18
additional configuration for Apply database 448
best practices 444
Oracle Streams, best practices
additional configuration for source database 444
Oracle Universal Installer. *See* **OUI, Oracle 11 g R1 Clusterware**
Oracle Wait Interface. *See* **OWI**
Oradebug
issues, tracing 482, 484
Oracle 11g Clusterware, tracing 485
oradebug ipc command 37, 484
Oslsvmon 178
OUI, Oracle 11g R1 Clusterware
about 327
initiating 73-82
Install screen 329
orainstRoot.sh, executing 82-85
post installation checks 86-88
root.sh is run, executing 82-85
OWI 299

P

PAE 28
Parallel Concurrent Processing. *See* **PCP**
parameter
% parameter 453
FAL_SERVER 457
LOG_ARCHIVE_CONFIG 457
LOG_ARCHIVE_DEST_n 453
LOG_ARCHIVE_FORMAT 454
PCP
configuring 428
PCP configuration
concurrent Processing 428
setting up, prerequisites 428
performance tuning
about 299
Oracle 11g features 300
Oracle 11g single instance database 300
Oracle RAC 11g database 300
performance tuning features, Oracle 11g R2
in-Memory Parallel Execution 307
PGA 244
Physical Addressing Extensions. *See* **PAE**
physical backup
about 275
benefits 275
OFFLINE RMAN backups 275
ONLINE RMAN backups 275
ping 215
planned downtime
about 8
example 8
PL/SQL function result cache
restrictions 304
prerequisites, cluster installation
kernel parameters 65, 66
network requirements 65
network requirements, IP addresses 64
operating system packages 66, 67
OS groups 68
OS user settings 68
Secure Shell (SSH), configuring 69, 70
server requirements 64
users 68

verifying, CLUVFY utility used 71
private interconnect 11gRAC
choices, selecting 33
Ethernet 32
processes parameter 119
Program Global Area. *See* **PGA**
ps -ef | grep asm command 163

Q

queue_to_queue parameter 445

R

RAC
ASM features 58
enabling, for EBS 395
Oracle 11g Streams 438
storage protocols 45
RAC cluster interconnect
performance, monitoring 315
RAC database
instance, adding 373
instance adding, DBCA used 374-378
administering 253
initialization parameters, with same values 241
initialization parameters, with unique values 242
RAC database, administering
SRVCTL, using 253
RAC database, creating
ways 222
RAC database creation, DBCA used
ASM Disk Groups screen 232
Automatic Maintenance Tasks screen 237, 238
creation options 238
Database Configuration Assistant 240
Database Content screen 234
database creation, prerequisites 241
Database Credentials screen 229, 230
Database File Locations screen 232, 233
Database Identification screen 226-228
Database Templates screen 225
Initialization Parameters screen 235, 236
management options screen 229
Network Configuration screen 230
Node Selection screen 225
Recovery Configuration screen 234
Security Settings screen 236
steps 222-226
storage options, choosing 231
RAC database instance
adding 373
RAC database instance, deleting
DBCA, using in silent mode 381, 382
presteps 380
RAC database, relocating
and instance, same node configuration 392, 393
database example, adding 393
instance example, adding 392
location, output 390
post-relocation steps 394
RAC DDT 209
RAC, enabling for EBS
applications environment, establishing 426
EBS 12.1.1, installing 400
EBS architecture 396
EBS, cloning 429
EBS, implementing 407
load balancing, setting up 427
PCP, configuring 428
steps 410
suitability feature 399
RACG 184
racgimon 184
racgmain 184
RAC wait events, Oracle RAC performance
about 310, 314
Active Session History (ASH) 317
busy 320
congested 319
gc buffer busy 319
Gc buffer busy 321
gc cr block lost 319
Gc [current/cr] [2/3]-way 320
Gc [current/cr] block busy 320
Gc [current/cr][block/grant] congested 320
Gc [current/cr][failure/retry 320, 321
Gc [current/cr] grant 2-way 320
Gc current grant busy 320
global cache blocks corrupt 312, 318

global cache blocks lost 312, 318
global cache cr request 319
global cache null to s and global cache null to x 319
global cache open s and global cache open x 318
global locking 314
monitoring 316
performance problems, determining 314
RAC specific ADDM findings, benefits 317
V$ views wait events 310
RAID
about 16, 40
configurations 41
error correction 40
RAID 0 (striping) 42
RAID 1 (mirroring) 42
RAID 5 (parity) 41
RAID 5 (striped with parity) 42, 43
RAID 10 and RAID 0+1, differentiating between 43
RAID 10 (striped mirrors) 43
RAID 10 (striped mirrors)
about 43
diagrammatic configuration 43
RAID-DP 44
rapidwiz utility 405
RAT 301
rconfig utility 415
RDMA 31
Real Application Testing. *See* **RAT**
RECOVER command, RMAN 287
Recovery Manager. *See* **RMAN**
RECOVERY_PARALLELISM parameter 286
recovery time
High Availability 10, 11
Redundant Array of Independent Disks. *See* **RAID**
Redundant Array of Inexpensive Disks. *See* **RAID**
Remote Direct Memory Access. *See* **RDMA**
remote_listener parameter 264
Remote Slave Monitor. *See* **RSMN**
RESETLOGS option 278
Resource Manager Instance Caging 216
Return on Investment. *See* **ROI**
RMAN
11g R1 features 275
11g R2 features 275
about 270, 271
advantages 272
architecture 272
best practices, for RAC 281
configuration settings 271
overview 270
RMAN best practices, for RAC
about 281
Flash Recovery Area, configuring 282, 283
Instance/Crash recovery 287
instance recovery vs. crash recovery 283-286
Media Recovery 287
multiple channel configuration 289, 290
RAC database backup, RMAN used 287, 288
RMAN RECOVER BLOCK command 457
RMSn Oracle RAC Management Processes 55
ROI 25
rootdeinstall.sh command
using 480
root delete command 371
roothas.pl tool 481
RPM 66

S

SAME
about 114
key features 114
sample configuration
LISTENER.ORA file 461, 462
TNSNAMES.ORA file 462
SAN 47
SCAN 65
scp command 70
SCSI 45
SDP 32
SELECT command 312
Server Control Utility. *See* **SRVCTL**
server requirements, cluster installation 64

service creating, SRVCTL
about 256-258
TNS entry, configuring 259
Service Level Agreements. *See* **SLAs**
Service Management option 224
services, Automatic Workload Management
creating 256
creating, SRVCTL used 256
DBMS_SERVICE PL/SQL package 259, 260
managing 256
overview 255
Setting up Grid Infrastructure screen 92
SGA 118, 244
Shared Global Area. *See* **SGA**
SHUTDOWN command 125
Single Client Access Name. *See* **SCAN**
single instance database, converting to RAC database
conversion, testing without actual performance 386, 387
ConvertToRAC.xml input file example 384, 386
failed rconfig operation, resuming 389
log files, checking 389
post-conversion steps 390
rconfig command line tool 383, 384
rconfig operation, optimizing 389
setup 384
steps 387, 388
Single Point of Failure. *See* **SPOF**
SPOF 398
SLAs 8, 9
Small Computer System Interface. *See* **SCSI**
SMCO 249
SMTP 229
snapshots, ACFS
about 164, 166
creating 166-168
removing 168
SPA
about 243, 302
using 302
Space Management Coordinator. *See* **SMCO**
Spanning Tree Protocol. *See* **STP**
Specify Hardware Cluster Installation Mode screen 328
SPFILE 128
SPOF 8, 200
SQL Access Advisor. *See* **STA**
sqlnet.ora file 305
SQL Performance Analyzer. *See* **SPA**
SQL Plan Management. *See* **SPM**
sqlplus command 150
SQL result cache
about 303
restrictions 304
SQL shutdown command 262
SRVCTL
about 486
Oracle 11g R2 commands 486
using 253, 255
SRVCTL ADD SERVICE syntax 256
srvctl config command 242
srvctl -h command 253
srvctl remove database command 392
srvctl start service command 257
STA
about 306
enhancements 306
STARTUP command 125
Statement DML Handler 449
storage architecture, Oracle 11g RAC
about 39
RAID configurations 40, 41
Storage Area Network. *See* **SAN**
storage protocols, RAC
Asynchronous I/O 52
choosing 50
Direct I/O 52
Fibre Channel 47
iSCSI 50
SCSI 46
STP 39
STRACE utility
options, displaying 492, 493
RAC process, tracing 493
using 494
Stripe And Mirror Everything. *See* **SAME**
Switch Spanning 39
System Global Area. *See* **SGA**

T

Tablespace point-in-time recovery (TSPITR) 281
TAF
about 265
configuring 266
FAILOVER_MODE, parameters 266, 267
using 265
tar command 430
third party implementations
EMC Corporation 44
IBM AIX LPAR disk volume management 44
Linux volume management 45
NetAPP Data ONTAP 44
TNS entry
configuring 259
TNSNAMES.ORA file
with virtual host name 463
traceroute 215
Transparent Application Failover. *See* **TAF**
troubleshooting, Oracle 11g Clusterware
challenges 198
hardware problems 212, 214
hardware problems, solutions 215
network problems 212, 214
network problems, solutions 215
node reboot issues 206
OCR, problems 200, 202
offline Clusterware resources 198
offline Clusterware resources, for Oracle 11gRAC 199, 200
storage problems 212, 214
storage problems, solutions 215
voting disk, problems 200, 201
truss command
about 495
options 495
parameters 495

U

UDP 33
unplanned downtime 8
upgrade
Oracle 10g R1 Clusterware, to Oracle 11g R2 333
Oracle 10g R2 Clusterware, to Oracle 11g R1 324
overview 323
sequence 324
Use Express Install option 401
User Datagram. *See* **UDP**
utilities, Oracle 11g Clusterware
CLSCFG 193-195
CLUVFY 196, 197
CRSCTL 185-188
CRS_STAT 188, 189
OCRCHECK 190, 191
OCRCONFIG 192, 193

V

v$$ges_statistics views 309
V$ASM_CLIENT 125
V$ASM_DISK 123
V$ASM_DISKGROUP 124
V$ASM_DISKGROUP_STAT 124
V$ASM_DISK_STAT 124
V$ASM_OPERATION 124
v$session view 310
v$session_wait view 310
V$ wait event views
(G)V$ACTIVE_SESSION_HISTORY 311
(G)V$SESSION_EVENT 310
(G)V$SESSION_WAIT 311
(G)V$SESSION_WAIT_CLASS 310
(G)V$SESSION_WAIT_HISTORY 311
(G)V$SQLSTATS 311
(G)V$SYSTEM_EVENT 310
VBGn 163
VKTM 250
VLDB 33
VMB0 164
vmstat command 209
Volume Background process. *See* **VBGn**
Volume Membership Background processes. *See* **VMB0**
voting disk
11g Clusterware resources issues 200, 201
about 177

best practices 201
corrupted disk 201
failed disk 201
problems 200
vRAID 44

WANs 50
Wide Area Networks. *See* **WANs**
Workload Replay. *See* **Database Replay**
Workload Replay Client. *See* **WRC**
World Wide Name. *See* **WWN**
WRC 301
WWN 45

Thank you for buying

Oracle 11g R1/R2 Real Application Clusters Essentials

About Packt Publishing

Packt, pronounced 'packed', published its first book "Mastering phpMyAdmin for Effective MySQL Management" in April 2004 and subsequently continued to specialize in publishing highly focused books on specific technologies and solutions.

Our books and publications share the experiences of your fellow IT professionals in adapting and customizing today's systems, applications, and frameworks. Our solution based books give you the knowledge and power to customize the software and technologies you're using to get the job done. Packt books are more specific and less general than the IT books you have seen in the past. Our unique business model allows us to bring you more focused information, giving you more of what you need to know, and less of what you don't.

Packt is a modern, yet unique publishing company, which focuses on producing quality, cutting-edge books for communities of developers, administrators, and newbies alike. For more information, please visit our website: `www.packtpub.com`.

About Packt Enterprise

In 2010, Packt launched two new brands, Packt Enterprise and Packt Open Source, in order to continue its focus on specialization. This book is part of the Packt Enterprise brand, home to books published on enterprise software – software created by major vendors, including (but not limited to) IBM, Microsoft and Oracle, often for use in other corporations. Its titles will offer information relevant to a range of users of this software, including administrators, developers, architects, and end users.

Writing for Packt

We welcome all inquiries from people who are interested in authoring. Book proposals should be sent to author@packtpub.com. If your book idea is still at an early stage and you would like to discuss it first before writing a formal book proposal, contact us; one of our commissioning editors will get in touch with you.

We're not just looking for published authors; if you have strong technical skills but no writing experience, our experienced editors can help you develop a writing career, or simply get some additional reward for your expertise.

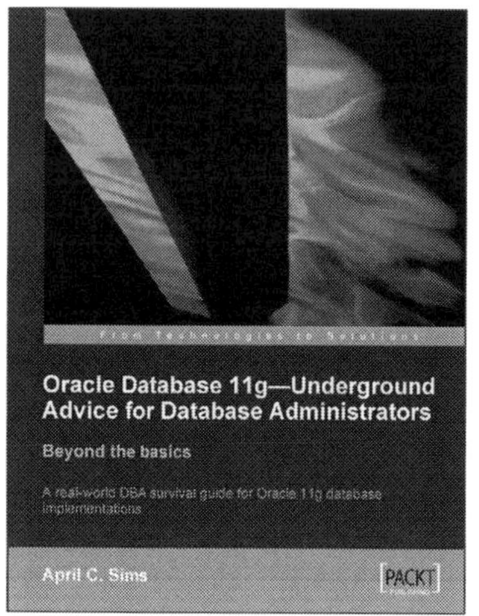

Oracle Database 11g – Underground Advice for Database Administrators

ISBN: 978-1-849680-00-4 Paperback: 348 pages

A real-world DBA survival guide for Oracle 11g database implementations

1. A comprehensive handbook aimed at reducing the day-to-day struggle of Oracle 11g Database newcomers
2. Real-world reflections from an experienced DBA – what novice DBAs should really know
3. Implement Oracle's Maximum Availability Architecture with expert guidance

---

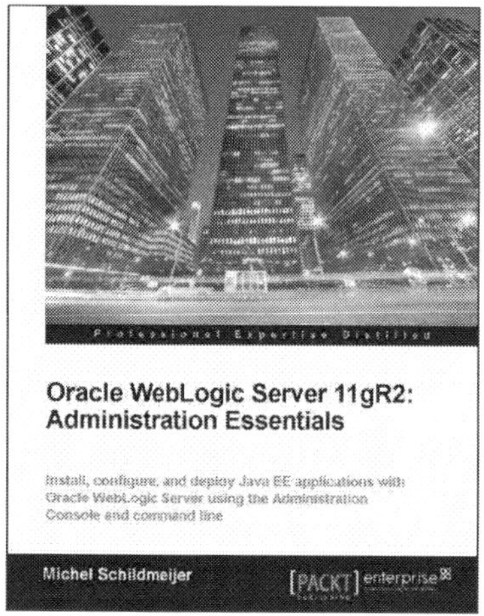

Oracle WebLogic Server 11gR2: Administration Essentials

ISBN: 978-1-849683-02-9 Paperback: 350 pages

Install, configure, and deploy Java EE applications with Oracle WebLogic Server using the Administration Console and command line

1. A practical book with step-by-step instructions for admins in real-time company environments
2. Create, commit, undo, and monitor a change session using the Administration Console
3. Create basic automated tooling with WLST

Please check **www.PacktPub.com** for information on our titles

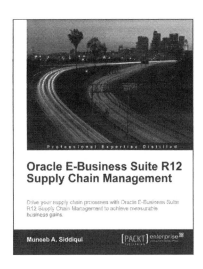

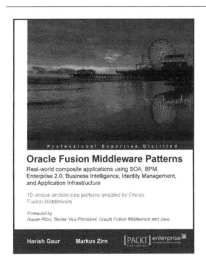

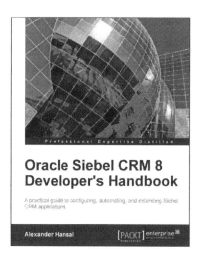

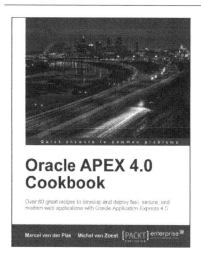

Oracle Application Express 3.2 - The Essentials and More

ISBN: 978-1-847194-52-7 Paperback: 644 pages

Develop Native Oracle database-centric web applications quickly and easily with Oracle APEX

1. Grasp the principles behind APEX to develop efficient and optimized data-centric native web applications, for the Oracle environment
2. Gain a better understanding of the major principles and building blocks of APEX, like the IDE and its modules
3. Review APEX-related technologies like HTML and the DOM, CSS, and JavaScript, which will help you to develop better, richer, and more efficient APEX applications

---

Processing XML documents with Oracle JDeveloper 11g: LITE

ISBN: 978-1-849683-82-1 Paperback: 96 pages

Compare XML documents, convert XML to Excel and PDF formats, and create Oracle XML Publisher Reports

1. Develop applications for processing XML in JDeveloper 11g quickly and easily
2. Create PDF Reports from XML documents
3. Create Excel Spreadsheet reports from XML documents
4. Packed with example code and detailed commentary, the book is fully illustrated with functional step-by-step examples.

Please check **www.PacktPub.com** for information on our titles

Made in the USA
Lexington, KY
24 May 2012